ENVIRONMENTAL ECONOMICS

FIRST CANADIAN EDITION

D1429852

Lauren
823-0910

BARRY C. FIELD
University of Massachusetts at Amherst

NANCY D. OLEWILER
Simon Fraser University

McGraw-Hill Ryerson Limited

Toronto Montreal New York Auckland Bogotá Caracas Lisbon London
Madrid Mexico Milan New Delhi San Juan Singapore Sydney Tokyo

ENVIRONMENTAL ECONOMICS
First Canadian Edition

ISBN: 0-07-551716-7

4 5 6 7 8 9 0 BG 4 3 2 1 0 9

Printed and bound in Canada by Best Gagne.

Care has been taken to trace ownership of copyright material contained in this text. The publishers will gladly take any information that will enable them to rectify any reference or credit in subsequent editions.

Sponsoring Editor: Jennifer Mix
Production Editor: Shirley Corriveau
Cover Design: Dianna Little
Cover Photograph: COMSTOCK

Canadian Cataloguing in Publication Data
Field, Barry C.
Environmental economics

1st Canadian ed.
Includes bibliographical references and index.
ISBN 0-07-551716-7

1. Environmental economics.   2. Environmental policy.
3. Environmental policy—Canada. I. Olewiler, Nancy D., date . II. Title.

HC79.E5F54 1994 333.7 C94-932718-2

ABOUT THE AUTHORS

BARRY C. FIELD is Professor of Resource Economics at the University of Massachusetts in Amherst. Previously he taught at the University of Miami and The George Washington University. He received his B.S. and M.S. degrees from Cornell University, and his Ph.D. from the University of California at Berkeley.

At the University of Massachusetts he has devoted many years to teaching environmental economics to students at all levels, and has worked to develop an undergraduate major in environmental and resource economics.

Professor Field is the author of numerous articles on resource and environmental economics.

NANCY D. OLEWILER is Professor of Economics at Simon Fraser University. She has also taught at Queen's University. Her B.A. is from Columbia University, M.A. from Simon Fraser University, and Ph.D. from the University of British Columbia.

At Simon Fraser University she developed the undergraduate and graduate courses in environmental economics. At Queen's University she initiated undergraduate courses in environmental economics and natural resource economics, as well as a graduate course in natural resource economics.

Professor Olewiler has written a number of articles on environmental and natural resource economics.

CONTENTS

PREFACE

When our descendants look back at the last part of the twentieth century, we want them to be able to say "That's when they began to take the degradation of the natural environment, with its threats to human life and the life of the planet seriously." And we would like them to be able to see that around this time we took serious steps to halt and reverse this process. This book is an introduction to environmental economics, one way of approaching the steps that need to be taken. It's about the way human decisions affect the quality of the environment, how human values and institutions shape our demands for improvement in the quality of that environment, and, most especially, about how to design effective public policies to bring about these improvements.

Problems of environmental quality are not something new; in fact, history is filled with bleak examples of environmental degradation, from deforestation by ancient peoples to mountains of horse manure in urban areas in the days before automobiles. But today's world is different. For one thing, many people in economically developed countries, having reached high levels of material well-being, are beginning to ask questions: What good is great material wealth if it comes at the cost of large-scale disruptions of the ecosystem by which we are nourished? More fundamental, perhaps, is the fact that with contemporary economic, demographic, and technological developments around the world, the associated environmental repercussions are becoming much more widespread and lethal. What once were localized environmental impacts, easily rectified, have now become widespread effects that may very well turn out to be irreversible. Indeed some of our most worrisome concerns today are about global environmental impacts.

It is no wonder, then, that the quality of the natural environment has become a major focus of public concern. As we would expect, people have responded in many ways. Environmental interest groups and advocates have become vocal at every political level, especially in those countries with open political systems. Politicians have taken environmental issues into their agendas; some have sought to become environmental statespersons. Environmental law has burgeoned, becoming a specialty in many law schools. Thousands of environmental agencies have appeared in the public sector, from local conservation commissions to environmental agencies at the United Nations. At the scientific level environmental problems have become a focus for chemists, biologists, engineers, and many others. And within economics a new focus of study has appeared: *environmental economics*, the subject of this book.

Environmental economics focusses on all the different facets of the connection between environmental quality and the economic behaviour of individuals and groups of people. There is the fundamental question of how the economic system shapes economic incentives in ways that lead to environmental degradation as well as improvement. There are major problems in measuring the benefits and costs of environmental quality changes, especially intangible ones. There is a set of complicated macroeconomic questions; for example, the connection between economic growth and environmental impacts and the feedback effects of environmental laws on growth. And there are the critical issues of designing environmental policies that are both effective and equitable.

The strength of environmental economics lies in the fact that it is analytical and deals with concepts like efficiency trade-offs, costs, and benefits. Many believe strongly that the times call for more direct political action, more consciousness-raising, more political organizing, and especially, more representation and influence of environmental interests on the political scene. Nobody can doubt this. We live in a complicated world, however, where human problems abound; domestically we have health care, education, poverty and unemployment, and other critical issues, all competing for attention and public resources. Throughout the world, vast numbers of people struggle to alter their political and economic situations, develop their economies, and raise their material standards of living.

In these settings, just raising the political and public awareness for environmental issues is necessary but not sufficient. We have to get hard scientific results on how people value environmental quality and how they are hurt when this quality is degraded. We also have to put together environmental policy initiatives that get the maximum impact for the economic and political resources spent. This is where environmental economics comes in. It is a way of examining the difficult trade-offs that all environmental issues entail; it is also a valuable means of inquiring why people behave as they do toward the natural environment, and how we might restructure the current system to rectify harmful practices.

The first section of the book is an introduction, beginning with a chapter on what environmental economics is about, followed by one on the basic relationships between the economy and the environment. The next section is devoted to studying the "tools" of analysis, the principles of demand and cost, and the elements of economic efficiency both in market and nonmarket activities. These chapters are not meant to be completely thorough treatments of these theoretical topics. They provide a background for those who have had little previous economics. Even those who have had a course in microeconomic principles might find them valuable for purposes of review. Section 2 also contains a chapter in which these economic principles are applied to a simple model of environmental pollution control. In these chapters, as well as the others, we have tried to leaven the presentation with examples taken from current sources, such as newspapers.

Section 3 is an environmental analysis. Here we look closely at some of the techniques that have been developed by environmental economists to answer some of the fundamental value questions that underlie environmental decision making. We focus especially on the principles of benefit-cost analysis. After this we move to Section 4, on the principles of environmental policy design. It begins with a short chapter dealing with the criteria we might use to evaluate policies, then moves on to chapters on the main approaches to environmental quality management. The focus in these chapters is on the policy instruments that can be used to address environmental problems.

Sections 5 and 6 contain policy chapters, where we examine current developments in environmental policy with the analytical tools developed earlier. Section 5 is devoted to environmental policy in Canada. We begin with a background chapter that illustrates the constitutional framework affecting government policy at the federal and provincial levels. The subsequent chapters cover federal and provincial policy on water, air, toxic materials, and local government issues such as water treatment, waste disposal, and recycling.

Section 6 looks at international issues, such as environmental policy developments in other countries, global environmental issues, and the economics of international environmental agreements.

This book is an introduction to the basic principles of environmental economics as they have been developed in the past and as they continue to evolve. The real world, certainly the real world of environmental policy, is much more complicated than these principles would often seem to imply. The examples discussed represent only a sample of the full range of issues that actually exists. If and when you confront that real world of environmental politics and policy, you will find it necessary to adapt these principles to all the details and nuances of reality. Unfortunately, there is not enough space in one book to look at all the ways that environmental economists have found to make the basic concepts and models more specific and relevant to concrete environmental issues. So we stick to the basic ideas and hope they excite your interest enough to make you want to pursue the refinements and adaptations of these ideas as they relate to a subject of growing relevance and importance.

The book can be used by a variety of different environmental economics courses. For courses where students have had few previous economics courses, more time might be spent on Sections 1, 2, and 3. Chapter 14 in Section 4 can be omitted. If students have had a number of economics courses, Sections 1 and 2 can be covered quickly. Sections 3 and 4 are essential for all courses, as these cover the core of environmental economics. Section 5 covers a broad spectrum of Canadian environmental policy and can be the focus of courses where policy concerns are emphasized. Section 6 can be omitted for courses with limited time, although we encourage everyone to read the material, especially Chapters 21 and 22.

ACKNOWLEDGEMENTS FOR THE U.S. EDITION

This text is the result of teaching the subject for many years in the classroom, so I must first thank all those students through the years who have listened, asked questions, and provided the feedback that shaped the book. Special thanks go to Stephen Fazio for his assistance in tracking down tons of material in the library, to Bill Thompson and the staff of the government documents section of the library at the University of Massachusetts, and to the reference librarians and interlibrary loan staff who helped me locate background material. Sincere thanks also to the following economists who reviewed portions of the manuscript: Roger Bolton, Williams College; John Braden, University of Illinois; Richard Bryant, University of Missouri—Rolla; Dallas Burtraw, Resources for the Future; Donald J. Epp, Pennsylvania State University; Jeffrey Krantkraemer, Washington State University; Henry McCarl, University of Alabama—Birmingham; Lars Olson, University of California—Riverside; J. Barkley Rosser, James Madison University; and John Stranlund, University of Massachussets—Amherst.

Very special thanks go to Darleen Slysz. Without her wizardry and diligence on the word processor, this book would never have seen the light of day. Thanks also to Eileen Keegan for the fine graphics.

I owe a special debt to Scott Stratford, Michael Fried, and Iness Snider at McGraw-Hill, who showed such enthusiasm for the book and so effectively held my hand during its completion.

Finally, enormous gratitude, and love, for Martha, for reading, giving solid advice, and keeping the spirits fresh as the book progressed.

Barry C. Field

ACKNOWLEDGEMENTS FOR THE CANADIAN EDITION

The Canadian material has come from my teaching experience at Simon Fraser and Queen's, and from conversations with a number of my colleagues in the field. A special thanks goes to Tony Scott, who has been a source of inspiration for my entire career. I am most grateful to the following reviewers for their valuable comments and input: Brian Copeland, Associate Professor, Economics, University of British Columbia; Donald N. Dewees, Professor of Economics, Professor of Law, University of Toronto; Peter Kennedy, Assistant Professor, Economics, University of Victoria; Dr. Frank G. Muller, Professor of Economics, Concordia University; A. S. (Tony) Ward, Professor, Department of Economics, Brock University; Ather Akbari, Professor, Department of Economics, St. Mary's University. One reviewer wished to remain anonymous.

Nancy D. Olewiler

INTRODUCTORY

This first section contains two introductory chapters. The first is a brief, nontechnical overview of some of the main topics and ideas within environmental economics. The second is a general view of the interactions between the economy and the environment, and an introduction to the fundamental concepts and definitions we will use throughout the book.

1

WHAT IS ENVIRONMENTAL ECONOMICS?

Environmental economics is the study of environmental problems with the perspective and analytical ideas of economics. You may have thought that economics is mostly about business decisions and how to make profits in a capitalist system. This is not the case. Economics is, rather, the study of how and why "people," whether they are consumers, firms, nonprofit organizations, or government agencies, make decisions about the use of valuable resources. It is divided into microeconomics, the study of the behaviour of individuals or small groups, and macroeconomics, the study of the economic performance of economies as a whole. Environmental economics draws from both sides, but primarily from microeconomics. The study of environmental economics, like all economics courses, is concerned with the fundamental issue of allocating scarce resources among competing uses. The concepts of scarcity, opportunity costs, trade-offs, marginal benefits, and marginal costs are key ingredients to understanding environmental problems and what can be done about them. Environmental economics makes use of many familiar concepts in economics. What is different about environmental economics compared to other economic subjects is the focus on how economic activities affect our natural environment—the atmosphere, water, land, and an enormous variety of living species. Economic decisions of people, firms, and governments can have very deleterious effects on the natural environment. The dumping of waste products into the natural environment creates pollution and degrades ecosystems. It leads to a nonoptimal use of resources. Why does this occur in economic systems? Why don't people take into account the effects of their economic activity on the natural environment? Environmental economics examines these questions. Equally as important, environmental economics investigates and assesses different methods of reaching a socially optimal use of all resources, including environmental ones.

To accomplish these tasks, a simple, but powerful analytical model is developed. As in all aspects of economics, we will focus on marginal valuations which involve trade-offs between marginal costs and marginal benefits. While economic efficiency remains the central criterion for evaluating outcomes and policies, environmental economists also examine other criteria for choosing among alternative policies that attempt to improve the environment. If economic efficiency cannot be obtained, and environmental targets are established using other criteria, an economic approach can greatly assist decision makers in reaching whatever target is set.

One of our first jobs is to get acquainted with some of the basic ideas and analytical tools of microeconomics that are used in environmental economics. But we do not want to jump directly into the study of these principles because that would suggest we are more interested in the tools than in what we can do with them. We are not interested in these ideas for themselves, but for the understanding they can give us about why the natural environment gets degraded, what the consequences are, and what can be done effectively to reduce the degradation. So this first chapter will be devoted to sketching out, in reasonably commonsense terms, the types of questions environmental economists ask and the types of answers they seek. To do this we first consider briefly what we mean by the "economic approach," and then give a series of examples of the types of environmental problems on which economists have worked. Then in the second chapter we will take a look at the broad linkages existing between economy and environment. After that we will be ready to study the economic principles we will need.

THE ECONOMIC APPROACH

Why do people behave in ways that cause environmental destruction? There are several types of answers to this question. One goes like this: Environmental degradation comes about from human behaviour that is unethical or immoral. Thus, for example, the reason people pollute is because they lack the moral and ethical strength to refrain from the type of behaviour that causes environmental degradation. If this is true, then the way to get people to stop polluting is somehow to increase the general level of environmental morality in the society. In fact, the environmental movement has led a great many people to focus on questions of environmental ethics, exploring the moral dimensions of human impacts on the natural environment. These moral questions are obviously of fundamental concern to any civilized society. Certainly one of the main reasons environmental issues have been put on the front burner of social concern is the sense of moral responsibility that has led people to take their concerns into the political arena.

But there are problems with relying on moral reawakening as our main approach to combating pollution. People don't necessarily have readily available moral buttons to push, and environmental problems are too important to wait for a long process of moral rebuilding. Nor does a sense of moral outrage, by itself, help us make decisions about all the other social goals that also have ethical dimensions: housing, health care, education, crime, etc. In a world of competing objectives we have to worry about very practical questions: Are we targeting the right environmental objectives, can we really enforce certain policies, are we getting the most impact for the money, and so on. But the biggest problem with basing our approach to pollution control strictly on the moral argument is the basic assumption that people pollute because they are somehow morally underdeveloped. It is not moral underdevelopment that leads to environmental destruction; rather, it is the way we have arranged the economic system within which people go about the job of making their livings.

So a second way of approaching the question of why people pollute is to look at the way the economy and its institutions are set up, and how they lead people to make decisions that result in environmental destruction. People pollute because it's the cheapest way they have of solving a certain very practical problem. That problem is the disposal of the waste products remaining after consumers have finished using something, or after business firms have finished producing something. People make these decisions on production, consumption, and disposal within a certain set of economic and social institutions;[1] these institutions structure the *incentives* that lead people to make decisions in one direction and not in another. What we have to study is how this incentive process works and, especially, how we might restructure it so that people will be led to make decisions and develop lifestyles that have more benign environmental implications.

One simplistic incentive-type statement that you often hear is that pollution is a result of the profit motive. According to this view, in private enterprise economies like the Western industrialized nations people are rewarded for maximizing profits, the difference between the value of what is produced and the value of what is used up in the production process. Furthermore, the thinking goes, the profits that entrepreneurs try to maximize are strictly monetary profits. In this headlong pursuit of monetary profits, entrepreneurs give no thought to the environmental impacts of their actions because it "doesn't pay." Thus, in this uncontrolled striving for monetary profits, the only way to reduce environmental pollution is to weaken the strength of the profit motive.

But this proposition doesn't stand up to analysis. It is not only "profit-motivated" corporations that cause pollution; individual consumers are also guilty when they do things like pour paint thinner down the drain or let their cars get seriously out of tune. Since individuals don't keep profit-and-loss statements, it can't be profits per se that lead people to pollute. The same can be said of government agencies, which have sometimes been serious polluters even though they are not profit motivated. But the most persuasive argument against the view that the search for profits causes pollution comes from recent political events in Eastern Europe and the former USSR. With the collapse of these ex-communist regimes, we have become aware of the enormous environmental destruction that has occurred in some of these regions—heavily polluted air and water resources in many areas, with major impacts on human health and ecological systems. Many of these problems exceed some of the worst cases of environmental pollution experienced in market-driven countries. But they have happened

---

[1] By "institutions" we mean the fundamental set of public and private organizations, laws, and practices that a society uses to structure its economic activity. Markets are an economic institution, for example, as are corporations, a body of commercial law, public agencies, and so on.

in an economic system where the profit motive has been entirely lacking. Which means, quite simply, that the profit motive, in itself, is not the main cause of environmental destruction.

In the sections and chapters that follow we will place great stress on the importance of incentives in the functioning of an economic system. *Any* system will produce destructive environmental impacts if the incentives within the system are not structured to avoid them. We have to look more deeply into any economic system to understand how its incentive systems work and how they may be changed so that we can have a reasonably progressive economy without disastrous environmental side effects. Two concepts that are important to an understanding of the incentives that exist regarding the environment are "external effects" and "property rights." These concepts are explained in detail in later chapters of the book, but essentially they involve the question of ownership of environmental resources. A key reason why there are few incentives to take environmental consequences of our actions into account is that ownership of many environmental resources is not possible. If no one owns the atmosphere, how can any pricing of its waste disposal services be undertaken? How can anyone who does value clean air prevent others from discharging their waste products freely?

INCENTIVES: A SIMPLE HOUSEHOLD EXAMPLE

An "incentive" is something that attracts or repels people and leads them to modify their behaviour in some way. An "economic incentive" is something in the economic world that leads people to channel their efforts at economic production and consumption in certain directions. We often think of economic incentives as consisting of payoffs in terms of material wealth; people have an incentive to behave in ways that provide them with increased wealth. But there are also nonmaterial incentives that lead people to modify their economic behaviour; for example, self-esteem, the desire to preserve a beautiful visual environment, or the desire to set a good example for others.

For a simple first look at the importance of changing incentives to get improvements in environmental quality, consider the newspaper story shown in Exhibit 1-1. It is about new ways of paying for trash disposal, focussing on the experience of a town in the United States. Before the program, people in the town paid a flat annual fee to have their trash collected. This is also common practice in most communities in Canada. The problem with this approach is that there is simply no incentive for any individual family to limit its trash production, since they will pay the same annual trash-collection fee no matter how much, or little, they produce. This might not be a problem if there were ample landfill space and if there were no danger that the landfill would contaminate the surrounding environment, such as a nearby groundwater system. But for most communities these conditions don't hold any more, if they ever did. The community in the story was in fact paying a stiff price for shipping its solid waste out of town. It faced the problem of how to get a significant reduction in the quantity of solid waste handled by the town.

EXHIBIT 1-1

TOWNS ADOPT PAY-AS-YOU-THROW GARBAGE

By Robert Hanley
Special to The New York Times

CHESTER TOWNSHIP, N.J., July 9—Steve and Cally Frysinger and their four children have almost eliminated the need for the family garbage can.

Wizards at recycling and composting, they have cut the amount of trash they put out for curbside pickup each month to one 30-pound container—a minuscule amount for a household of six.

To cart that off, the Frysingers pay the town's garbage hauler, Waste Management of North Jersey, $1.90 a month.

Mr. Frysinger is an architect and a devotee of a billing system that is slowly taking root in the New York region and other parts of the country and revolutionizing trash disposal.

The new system requires residents to pay a fixed price for each bag or can of garbage they generate, much as they pay on the basis of usage of electricity, water and long-distance telephone service. In most localities, the per-bag or per-container system replaces or reduces flat fees all residents paid garbage haulers directly or through their property taxes.

Proponents say billing by the bag gives a big boost to recycling, thus reducing garbage costs and the expanding need for landfills and multimillion dollar incinerators. And, they argue, the shift of garbage expenses out of the property tax structure promotes fairness. No longer, they say, will small families that produce little garbage underwrite large families that fill several cans a week.

Until Chester Township changed its system in July 1990, each family paid $30 monthly or $360 a year for trash removal. Now residents pay Waste Management $1.90 for each 30-pound can they set out, plus a monthly charge that varies with a home's assessment but averages $9.50, said Mr. Frysinger, who is on the town council. The fee covers the weekly collection of trash and recycling materials.

A resident with the average collection fee and one 30-pound can of garbage a week pays $17.10 a month or $205.20 a year, $154.80 less than the flat $360 fee of two years ago.

Weight limits are enforced informally; Waste Management says its workers can sense when a can is excessively over 30 pounds and will leave it uncollected. Some people weigh their trash themselves on the bathroom scale to make sure they do not exceed the limit.

The Frysinger family's devotion to recycling has meant a saving of $223 a year. Mr. Frysinger said.

"Basically," Mr. Frysinger said, "it's possible for a large family to recycle 80 percent of its garbage.

The family uses no paper towels in the kitchen, only sponges and towels, and buys nothing "excessively packaged," like wrapped fresh fruit or hardware in boxes with plastic or cellophane windows.

Since Chester Township began billing by the container, it has increased the amount of trash it recycles from 540 tons in 1989 to 1,158 tons in 1991, said Sara Noll, the town's recycling coordinator.

The details of the per-container system vary from town to town. Chester Township uses circular stickers that residents buy in sheets of 10 for $19, or $1.90 each. One sticker is attached to the top bag in the 30-pound container each collection day.

Other communities, especially in Columbia County, N.Y., use special bags instead of stickers because stickers are sometimes blown off or stolen and reused by thieves.

Perhaps the largest, oldest and most studied per-container billing system in the country is Seattle's, which started in 1981. Since then, Seattle has increased from 5 to 42 percent the proportion of its trash that is recycled, . . .

The main criticism of billing by the bag or can is that the system encourages illegal dumping. Mr. Pealy said a few Seattle homeowners have probably left garbage in apartment-house Dumpsters. Some companies that use privately owned Dumpsters have started padlocking them, he said. The most flagrant illegal dumping, he said, involves construction debris.

The response in this case was to introduce a system that gives people an incentive to search for ways to reduce the amount of solid waste they produce. This was done by charging people for each bag of trash they put out on the curb. There is also a small monthly fee. What this does is to give families the incentive to reduce the number of bags of trash they set out. They can do this by recycling, by switching to products that have less waste, by putting food scraps in a compost pile, etc. These have led, according to the story, to a large increase in the amount of trash recycled. It proba- bly also induced a reduction in the total amount of trash, although the story does not detail this. The article notes many other communities around the country where this system has been adopted.

In Canada, an increasing number of communities are beginning to charge fees per unit of trash collected. On Vancouver Island, the district of Nanaimo introduced a sys- tem in which each household pays a flat rate in their property taxes for the right to put out one standardized bag of trash per week. Extra bags are collected if the house- holder has purchased a "tag" for $2 per bag. Early indications are that the system is working well. One complaint lodged was from people who put out less than one bag of trash per week. They wanted a discount off the flat rate! Of course, no system is perfect. Increases in illegal dumping and difficulties with applying the plan to apart- ment houses are problems. Nevertheless, the new approach does illustrate in a very clear way the effects of a shift from a system in which there were no incentives for people to reduce their solid waste to one in which there are such incentives.[2]

INCENTIVES: A BUSINESS EXAMPLE

Incentives are also critically important in reducing industrial pollution. All industrial firms work within a given set of incentives: to increase profits if they are firms in mar- ket economies, to fulfill the annual production plan if they are socialist firms. Firms have an incentive to take advantage of whatever factors are available to better their performance in terms of these criteria. One way they have been able to do this his- torically is to use the services of the environment for waste disposal services. The motivation for this is that these services have essentially been free, and by using free inputs as much as possible a firm obviously can increase its profits or better meet its production targets. It's this state of affairs that has contributed to the excessive lev- els of pollution we have today.

One policy approach is to pass and then try to enforce laws making pollution ille- gal. A more effective technique frequently will be to design a system that takes advan- tage of firms' normal monetary incentives in such a way as to lead them to pollute less. The newspaper article in Exhibit 1-2 illustrates a case in the United States where the state of Louisiana seeks to give firms a direct financial incentive to reduce their polluting behaviour. It does this by linking a firm's property taxes to its environmental performance. Specifically, each firm is rated on a scale "according to the number of

---

[2] The technical name for this approach is "unit pricing." See: U.S. Environmental Protection Agency, *Unit Pricing* EPA/530-SW-91-005 (Washington, D.C., February 1991).

EXHIBIT 1-2

USING TAXES TO DISCOURAGE POLLUTION

By Keith Schneider
Special to The New York Times

NEW ORLEANS, Feb. 24—After taking a hard look at the financial and ecological toll from industrial development, Louisiana has enacted a new tax rule that ties the amount of business property taxes a company pays to its environmental record.

Established in December, the new policy was imposed after officials determined that some corporations were benefiting from tax exemptions while being liable for thousands of dollars in pollution fines in a state with some of the worst chemical contamination in the country.

Gov. Buddy Roemer and two state agencies took the action to reduce pollution while trying to collect millions of dollars in industrial property taxes from which the same polluters had been exempted.

The new policy, which has already come under challenge in state court, is considered the most innovative step taken by any state to specifically link its tax policy with the dual goals of reducing pollution and gaining greater compliance with environmental law.

Patterns of Exemptions

For 65 years, an important facet of Louisiana's policy for attracting industry was to exempt from local business property taxes all new equipment and other capital expenditures for 10 years. Exemptions came up for renewal half-way through the 10-year period.

Under the new policy, each company applying for an exemption or seeking renewal is rated on a scale according to the number of environmental violations it has received, the amount of chemicals it releases into the environment and other factors. The worse a company's record, the lower the score and the smaller its tax exemption.

"We weren't trying to be the first state to do this," said Vicki Arroyo, director of policy and planning at the state Department of Environmental Quality. "But in looking to other states for guidance about how to link a company's environmental record to economic incentives, we couldn't find any other program."

Ms. Arroyo added: "We found, on one hand, that we had companies with serious environmental problems liable for hundreds of thousands of dollars in fines, and on the other hand, they were getting millions of dollars of tax exemptions. That is not the message we wanted to send to industry."

In recent years, states have sought to use tax policy to achieve environmental goals. Minnesota exempts some land from property taxes to preserve marshy areas, and New York and New Hampshire reduce property taxes for wetlands that are protected from development. North Carolina charges a fee for personalized license plates to pay for acquiring undeveloped lands and Maryland has a similar program to finance environmental research on Chesapeake Bay.

Missouri designates a portion of its sales tax for environmental programs. Washington State applies part of its cigarette sales tax for curtailing pollution in Puget Sound. And many states exempt pollution control equipment from business property taxes.

environmental violations it has received, the amount of chemicals it releases into the environment and other factors." The worse the firm's rating on the scale, the smaller its property tax exemption and, thus, the higher its tax payments. With this system firms would presumably have a direct incentive to do whatever they could to increase their environmental ratings—provided, of course, that the tax saving was sufficiently large to be attractive. This sort of scheme has not yet been tried in Canada.

There are a lot of questions about how this system might work, especially on what firms have to do to avoid environmental citations, how closely the ranking score reflects actual emissions of polluting substances, and so on. But the important point is that authorities in the United States have apparently recognized the importance of changing the incentive structures of polluting firms in order to motivate them to search for ways of reducing their emissions. In Canada, there is a growing recognition of the importance of incorporating economic incentive approaches into environmental policies at all levels of government. But, as we'll see in later chapters, very little has been done in practice.[3]

The essence of the economic incentives approach is to restructure the incentives facing firms and consumers in such a way that it mobilizes their own energy and ingenuity to find ways of reducing their impacts on the environment.

INCENTIVES IN THE POLLUTION-CONTROL INDUSTRY

Another critical focal point where incentives are vital, and where environmental economics plays an analytically important role, is in the growth and performance of the pollution-control industry. This is the industry that develops waste recycling techniques, new pollution-control equipment, and new pollution-monitoring technology. It sometimes handles and treats waste products, and is often involved in managing waste disposal sites. It also includes firms that develop new environmentally friendly products like low-phosphate detergents and recyclable paper products. A lively and progressive pollution-control industry is obviously needed if we are to come to grips effectively with all of our present and prospective environmental problems. Thus, one of the major things environmental economists must study is the incentives facing this industry—what causes it to grow or decline, how quickly or slowly it responds to new needs, and so on.

A good example of this is illustrated in the news clipping of Exhibit 1-3. It discusses the emergence of a new firm that specializes in finding markets for waste products that used to be dumped into landfills. The company also advises firms on methods of reducing wastes. Environmental policy is becoming increasingly more demanding in Canada. This creates greater incentives for the pollution-control industry to innovate and develop improved means of handling residuals. This incentive effect of environmental laws is often overlooked, but it is a critically important facet of the long-run effort to reduce the environmental impacts of modern economies. Throughout the book we will have much to say about this particular incentive.

EXTERNALITIES AND PROPERTY RIGHTS

Exhibit 1-4 illustrates how environmental problems arise when there are no well-defined property rights to environmental resources. It also shows the difficulties of

---

[3] See Government of Canada, *Economic Instruments for Environmental Protection, Discussion Paper* (Ottawa: Ministry of Supply and Services Canada, 1992), for a discussion of the potential use of economic instruments in Canada.

EXHIBIT 1-3

PROBING GARBAGE FOR GOLD

New breed for consultant analyzes waste for corporate clients

By Bill Knapp
Special to The Globe and Mail

Spiralling costs of waste removal and the growing complexity of environmental legislation have combined to spawn a new breed of industrial consultant: the waste management specialist.

Independent Disposal Group Inc. of Mississauga, a unit of Calgary-based Royaledge Industries Inc., is one such company. Launched in August, 1988, as a one-man shop, IDG now has a staff of 23, supporting clients in industries such as heavy and light manufacturing, food processing and retailing, hospitality, fast food, as well as automotive and truck manufacturers, and financial institutions.

As a waste management consultant, IDG examines how clients generate and dispose of their waste, looking for ways to cut it down, to increase recycling and to streamline disposal and costs.

One important tool IDG uses to reduce disposal costs is finding opportunities to take a company's waste and sell it to another company as raw material. For example, the major waste component generated by Brewers Warehousing Co. Ltd. of Toronto is the cartons that tins of beer are delivered in.

"There weren't local markets available for it, at least on the scale that they generate it. So we went on a worldwide hunt and found some in the United States, some in Italy and some in the Far East," IDG president Alan Jones said in an interview. Some of the material ends up as carrier in composting systems and in animal feed—some becomes cartons again.

Another example is a company that was producing a polystyrene plastic as a waste product and dumping it in landfill. IDG found a manufacturer that could use it as raw material for its plastic products and was willing to pay 50 cents a pound for it. As a result, the company's $300,000 annual cost for waste disposal was replaced with $130,000 in revenue.

Recycling is also a tool in reducing waste disposal costs. During its analysis of a client's waste stream, IDG hunts material that can be recycled instead of dumped. Mr. Jones says his company is constantly evaluating new technologies, such as composting techniques from Europe, wood recycling methods from Switzerland, water and effluent treatments from the United States and techniques from India for recycling plastics and cardboard.

IDG's revenue has grown from $80,000 in its first year to a projected $5-million this year. Its fees are based on a percentage of the money it saves its clients.

Mr. Jones says that the issue of legal liability for pollution is a major concern for many companies. Under most environmental legislation, such as Ontario's Environmental Protection Act, officers and directors are personally liable and face stiff fines and even prison sentences if their companies are found guilty of contaminating the environment.

"Depending on the severity of the circumstances, the courts can fine a company up to $2-million a day for contamination if there has been a spill. And they can strip away all the profits made between the time the problem was identified and the time it was cleaned up," he said.

At the same time, the disposal costs have risen dramatically. According to John Charles, chief executive officer for IDG and Royaledge, the cost of dumping a tonne in a Toronto municipal site has climbed . . . to $150 from $18.50 five years ago. In Kingston, the cost per tonne rose to $120 on Jan. 1 from $20.

So for both legal and economic reasons, the efficient disposal of waste has assumed a much higher priority in corporate thinking.

IDG has recently expanded its operations and is now advising banks and insurance companies on environmental matters as they mobilize to cope with the new set of problems.

According to Mr. Charles, banks are concerned about the impact of pollution on properties used to secure loans. If a property is contaminated and needs to be cleaned up, that reduces its value as a security. And if a bank forecloses on property that

---

EXHIBIT 1-3 *continued*

turns out to be contaminated, as that property's owner it may be liable for the cleanup.

"Basically the thrust of the legislation from the government is whoever's got the deepest pockets is going to be on the hook," Mr. Jones said. "And banks have the deepest pockets. So they're paranoid to a degree."

Insurance companies, too, are concerned about liability because it is not yet clear how liable they are for contamination caused by a company they've insured.

"There's a real shortage of environmental insurance legislation policies in Canada," Mr. Jones said. "They're starting to come in. They're starting to be modelled after the U.S. And companies are going to have to start carrying it.

". . . in the 1990's you have two silent partners in your business. One is your bank and one is your insurance company, relative to environmental issues. Their exposure is so big they are writing in so many clauses and covenants that your ability to get insurance and your ability to carry it, and your ability to get financing and carry it, could be put in jeopardy."

Source: The Globe and Mail, June 4, 1991. Bill Knapp is a Toronto-based, freelance writer specializing in science and technology.

EXHIBIT 1-4

TONNES OF TOXINS POURING INTO RIVER

Ontario Mine Tailings Burst Dam

By Kevin Vincent

TIMMINS, Ont.—Officials in Northern Ontario are warning of an environmental disaster in progress as thousands of tonnes of toxic mine tailings pour into the Montreal River from a broken dam.

"By conservative estimates, there are 10,000 dump-truck loads of old mine tailings that have poured into the river already," said Reeve Terry Fiset of Elk Lake, a town 100 kilometres southeast of Timmins.

"It hasn't stopped and we don't see anyone trying to stop it."

Elk Lake, about half of whose 600 residents are using bottled water for drinking and bathing, is one of several small communities along the Montreal River, a scenic waterway running through the heart of the Temagami wilderness.

The contamination comes from a waste site once owned by Matachewan Consolidated Gold Mines. The mine shut down in 1954.

The waste site, known as a tailings dam, burst last Wednesday after steady rains. Water, silt and heavy metals were swept into the river. By yesterday afternoon, the spill of tailings had travelled 50 kilometres downstream, turning the normally clear river a light grey.

Early tests indicate that lead levels in the river are 13 times the acceptable level. The tailings also contain traces of cyanide, arsenic and mercury. So far, the levels of cyanide and arsenic in the river have been declared to be below ministry guidelines; test results for mercury were not yet available.

Early yesterday, the provincial Ministry of the Environment had agreed to provide emergency financial assistance to help dig new water wells for four displaced families who got their water directly from the Montreal River.

Source: Excerpted from The Globe and Mail, October 24, 1990.

reaching private agreements or designing environmental policy when pollution problems take many years to develop and/or be detected. The source of the pollutants in this case are wastes from a mine that closed down long ago, and have now burst through their containment site. At the time the mine operated, there were no effective regulations against dumping waste products onto the land. This means that the mine had an implicit property right to deposit the wastes at the site. The wastes are an externality. The production of minerals led to the release of toxic chemicals that adversely affected individuals and the ecosystem. The price of minerals extracted from the mine did not reflect these subsequent environmental costs. Nor was there any way that private negotiation could resolve the problem. The mine operators and residents of the area did not know in the 1950s that years later, environmental problems would emerge. Even if they had, would they have done anything about pollution that might occur many years hence? The current residents probably were not around in the 1950s. This makes it virtually impossible to engage in any sort of bargaining between the residents and the mine to reach a mutually agreeable level of waste disposal and compensation for one party or the other. This example illustrates the many difficulties inherent in depending on individuals who act in their own self-interest to reach an efficient allocation of resources. Information about potential problems may be imperfect or nonexistent. People today cannot be counted on to make decisions that maximize the well-being of generations who follow.

As the article indicates, when these conditions exist, some form of government intervention is necessary. In this case, it is in the form of financial assistance to the affected residents. A major focus of environmental economics is to explain why these sorts of problems emerge in market economies and what can be done about them.

THE DESIGN OF ENVIRONMENTAL POLICY

Environmental economics has a major role to play in the design of public policies for environmental quality improvement. There is an enormous range and variety of public programs and policies devoted to environmental matters, at all levels of government: local, provincial, regional, federal, and international. They vary greatly in their efficiency and effectiveness. Some have been well designed and will no doubt have beneficial impacts. Others, perhaps the majority, are not well designed. Not being cost-effective, they will end up costing lots of money and having much smaller impacts on environmental quality than they might have had with better design.

The problem of designing efficient environmental policies is often not given the emphasis it deserves. It is easy to fall into the trap of thinking that any programs or policies that flow out of the rough and tumble of the environmental political process is likely to be of some help, or that they certainly will be better than nothing. But history is full of cases where policymakers and public administrators have pursued policies that don't work; the public is frequently led to believe a policy will be effective even when any reasonable analysis could predict that it will not. All of which means that it is critically important to study how to design environmental policies that accomplish their environmental goals at the lowest possible cost to society.

What does environmental protection cost? Unfortunately, in Canada we have no estimates of the total costs of pollution control and environmental cleanup. In the United States, the U.S. Environmental Protection Agency (EPA) estimated that in 1990 about 2 percent of the total cost of goods and services in the country was devoted to pollution control and environmental cleanup. They expect this percentage to rise to around 2.8 percent by the end of the 1990s. If costs are similar in Canada, these costs would amount to about 13 billion dollars per year for the early 1990s. These are very large sums of money, even though the percentage probably should be higher. But it is important not to get totally fixated on the percentage, whether it is high or low, whether it compares favourably with other countries, etc. Of equal or greater importance is whether we are getting the most improvement possible in environmental quality for the money spent. This means having policies and programs that get the maximum improvement in environmental quality for the resources spent. Everybody has an interest in this: environmentalists, for obvious reasons; public regulators, because they are tapping a limited supply of taxpayer resources and consumer tolerance; and the regulated polluters themselves, because matters of efficiency are critical to business success.

To see what "getting it right" might entail, consider Ontario's water pollution regulation, the Municipal-Industrial Strategy for Abatement (MISA), passed in 1986. MISA is patterned after the 1972 Water Pollution Control Act Amendments in the U.S. The objective of MISA is to eliminate the discharge of toxic contaminants into waterways. Over 200 industrial sources and 400 sewage treatment plants are covered. Regulations for each contaminant are to be established after the industries affected undertake a 12 month study of their effluents. A technical committee for each industrial group (comprised of government and business representatives, as well as some public input) then decides what regulations are economically achievable. This process, still not completed by 1994, has been time-consuming and costly both to the private and the public sector. Some key issues are whether or not zero emissions are an appropriate target, and why no economic incentives for pollution control were considered. The U.S. policy, in place for many more years than that of Ontario, has yet to achieve its objectives. Perhaps an alternative regulatory policy passed in 1986 would have already begun to have an impact on pollution levels, and at lower costs than MISA will entail.

One of the primary jobs for environmental economists is to examine different approaches to pollution control, to cut through all the political hoopla and look carefully at the impacts of different policy approaches. We need to know if these policies are cost-effective, in terms of getting the most pollution reduction possible for the money spent, and whether they are efficient, in terms of appropriately balancing the benefits and the costs of environmental improvements. Thus, policy design and analysis is a major part of environmental economics, and we will spend a great deal of this book on this subject.

ENVIRONMENT, GROWTH, AND SUSTAINABILITY

The incentive issues discussed above are microeconomic problems; they deal with the behaviour of individuals or small groups of consumers, polluting firms, and firms in the pollution-control industry. Environmental economics is based primarily on microeconomic theory. However, economists are increasingly focussing on environmental issues that affect aggregate economies. There are a number of important questions about the relationship between environmental issues and the behaviour of the macroeconomy. One very significant question asks what is the relationship between economic growth and environmental quality. Exhibit 1-5 notes some recent studies trying to look at various aspects of this question. Do higher rates of growth, that is, increases in our traditional measures like GDP, imply greater environmental degradation or might the opposite be true? The answers are not simple. The exhibit cites several recent studies that examined the relationship between growth and the environment. While some types of pollution diminish as a country's income levels grow, others increase. The exhibit also points out that we are still learning about the relationship between international trade and environmental quality. This is an exciting area of research for environmental economists. We come back to these issues in Section 6.

Sustainability

Economists are becoming increasingly aware of the need to link more closely the economy with the natural environment. While the natural environment has always been treated as an essential input into production, few models looked explicitly at the interaction between ecological systems and the economy. A new field called "ecological economics" examines these interactions more fully. An important objective of this field is to search for sustainable paths of economic development—actions that do not destroy ecological systems, but allow for increases in real incomes. This field is quite young, and new insights are occurring all the time. The essential idea is that a sustainable economy is one which has the ability to produce nondecreasing well-being year after year. To accomplish this, a number of economists argue that current generations cannot "use up" so much of the existing stocks of natural and environmental resources that future generations will be impoverished or nonexistent. As economists such as Herman Daly argue, we must examine our economic activities with regard to the carrying capacity of our ecosystem.

All economies use natural and environmental resources to sustain life. Rising world population puts increasing pressure on our natural endowments all the time. Many fear our current path of production and population growth is not sustainable. What can be done? One possible approach put forward by economists such as Robert Solow is to argue that each generation in a sustainable economy has the obligation to replace what it uses with investment in "social capital." This is a very broad definition of "capital." It includes everything the economy can invest in—physical capital to produce goods and services, education, infrastructure, renewable and nonrenewable natural resources, and of course, the environment itself as a stock of capital.

EXHIBIT 1-5

POLLUTION AND PROSPERITY

Do countries with higher levels of national income have more or less pollution per capita than those with low levels? While the picture is far from complete, recent research suggests that a number of pollutants decrease as incomes rise. Recent studies by two Princeton economists, Grossman and Krueger, and economists at the World Bank illustrate the type of results that have been obtained. Grossman and Krueger compared national income figures to air-pollution studies done in a number of cities worldwide over the past 14 years. They found that air pollution was less severe in countries with very low and very high per capita incomes. Pollution was most severe for countries with per capita incomes of $4,000 to 5,000 (U.S. per year). The World Bank study found a similar relationship only for one air pollutant—sulfur dioxide. For other types of pollution, the relationships varied. For example, as incomes rise, urban concentrations of particulates fall, but emissions of carbon dioxide rise. This means that local or regional pollution may tend to get better as a country gets richer, but global pollution problems may worsen. Local environmental quality is greatly influenced by the availability of clean drinking water and adequate sanitation. The World Bank study found that these improve dramatically as incomes rise. Municipal wastes, on the other hand, increase strongly with national income.

Another World Bank study on toxic contaminants found an even more complicated relationship between national income and toxic pollutants. They looked at the pollution intensity of manufacturing industries over time as a function of a country's level of national income and other variables. They find that as national income rises, the pollution intensity of manufacturing does not decline. Rather, what happens is that the composition of output changes to one that has less manufacturing. With less manufacturing, there is less aggregate pollution. This result suggests that aggregate pollution worldwide may or may not fall as countries become more prosperous. What we need to know is how the pollution intensity of production changes. Are developing countries adopting new technologies that are less pollution intensive than the "dirty" industries that typified the developed countries? Or, are these dirty industries simply moving to developing countries that are becoming "pollution havens"? The study on toxic pollutants found that developing countries that were the least open to trade had the highest growth in pollution intensity. Those developing countries with relatively open economies to trade were more likely to import new and cleaner technologies for their industrial growth. What all these results suggest is that there is no simple relationship between economic growth, international trade, and pollution.

Source: Gene Grossman and Alan B. Krueger, "Environmental Impacts of a North American Free Trade Agreement," Discussion Paper No. 158 (Princeton University: Woodrow Wilson School, 1991); R. E. B. Lucas, D. Wheeler, and H. Hettige, "Economic Development, Environmental Regulation and the International Migration of Toxic Industrial Pollution: 1960–1988," in P. Low (ed.), *International Trade and the Environment,* World Bank Discussion Papers (Washington, D.C.: The World Bank, 1992); The World Bank, *World Development Report 1992, Development and the Environment* (Oxford: Oxford University Press, 1992).

When we use up some of our existing capital, the only way the economy can be sustainable over time is to reinvest to keep the social capital stock at least constant. Pollution control and treatment is a means of keeping the environmental capital stock constant. So is recycling to some degree. Whether sustainability is achievable depends on the actions of people, industries, and governments. Will private markets keep the stock of social capital constant? Is government intervention necessary, and if so, in what form? These are the types of questions that are increasingly being asked. Sustainability also depends on the degree of substitutability between natural capital (the environment and natural resources), produced capital, and labour. Technology and technological change is another vital element in the search for sustainable paths. Technology will influence the degree of substitution among factor inputs and affect the amount of inputs needed to produce a unit of output. Some technologies may promote sustainability, others not. Economists play important roles in helping to find answers to all these questions, by building models that explicitly incorporate the role of the natural environment and by examining these issues empirically.

COST-EFFECTIVENESS ANALYSIS

Several types of environmental analysis are common in environmental economics. One is called "cost-effectiveness analysis." This is simply an analysis in which we look for the least expensive way of achieving a given environmental quality target or, to put it in different but equivalent terms, in which we look for the way of achieving the greatest improvement in some environmental target for a given expenditure of resources.

Exhibit 1-6 shows a news clip that illustrates the need for cost-effectiveness studies. B.C. Hydro has engaged in a program called Power Smart to encourage energy conservation. It offers advice on technical alternatives and provides financial incentives to reduce energy consumption. When energy consumption is lowered, energy users save money, the utilities don't have to construct as much new capacity, and the environment wins. With less energy use, there are fewer ecological damages associated with power generation, for example, flooding of river valleys behind dams, release of carbon dioxide from coal-fired plants, problems of storage of nuclear wastes. What is important is to determine which of the possible technical options for improving energy efficiency is most cost-effective. There are many different options—efficiency standards for lights, electric motors, office buildings, and providing incentives for renewable energy, and so on. Power Smart focusses on most of these. What is needed now are calculations of cost-effectiveness of these alternatives. Studies of this sort require close coordination of scientific and engineering analysis to determine realistic technical parameters, and economic analysis to determine the values associated with these parameters.

BENEFIT-COST ANALYSIS

In cost-effective analysis, economists are concerned only with the costs of achieving some stated environmental goal. In benefit-cost analysis, both costs *and* benefits of a policy or program are measured and expressed in comparable terms.

Benefit-cost analysis is the main analytical tool used by economists to evaluate environmental decisions. It was first used in the United States early in the twentieth century to evaluate water-development projects of the U.S. Army Corps of Engineers. In Canada, it is used throughout the public sector, but less so today than in the 1970s when the technique was often misused to justify large "mega" projects involving natural resource use. Benefit-cost analysis can be used as an aid in selecting efficient

EXHIBIT 1-6

B.C. HYDRO TOUTS HIGH-EFFICIENCY ELECTRIC MOTORS

Rebate program attracts increasing number of
energy-conscious buyers

By Patricia Lush
British Columbia Bureau

VANCOUVER—British Columbia Hydro and Power Authority, mindful that it's cheaper to conserve electricity than to produce it, has persuaded about 35 per cent of buyers of new electric motors in the province to choose the high-efficiency models, despite their higher cost.

A year ago, only about 5 per cent of buyers were making that choice. And in the United States, the figure is just 3 per cent, says Arthur Gieke, president of B.C. Hydro's two-year-old Power Smart program.

Electric motors are by far the biggest consumers of energy in Canada—every factory, office and residential building relies on them—and the switch to energy-efficient motors has an especially big impact in a resource-reliant province such as British Columbia with all its pulp mills and mining operations, he said in an interview.

Power Smart achieved the change by offering rebates, on a sliding scale based on horsepower and efficiency rating compared with the base efficiency. It works out to $400 for every kilowatt saved.

"If the purchaser buys the top end, they can get a two-year payback" on the cost difference over a regular motor "and then over the rest of the life of that motor, they enjoy the savings" on their electricity bill, Mr. Gieke said.

B.C. Hydro inaugurated its Power Smart program two years ago, on the basis that energy from conservation is the cheapest and most environmentally benign source of power available today. It began with a 10-year budget of $225-million to finance a variety of educational advertising and financial incentive programs to encourage customers to adopt new energy-efficient products,

such as refrigerators and water heaters, and to encourage manufacturers and distributors to produce and sell them.

But it could be a hard sell, trying to do it in isolation: "Living on this side of the Rockies, the manufacturers aren't here, and national advertising programs for major retailers such as Canadian Tire, the Bay and Sears aren't done in British Columbia."

So to spread the word, to give the name ready recognition like the Good Housekeeping Seal or Participaction, and thus to shorten the time needed to accomplish its goals, Power Smart management took the program across Canada. So far they've signed up 13 utilities, beginning with Nova Scotia.

But a major disappointment is the two most noticeable absentees from the group, Ontario and Quebec. Hydro-Québec is developing conservation programs of its own and there's also a language issue: The name Power Smart doesn't translate readily into French, Mr. Gieke said.

Ontario, too, has already developed a menu of its own programs and has shown little interest in switching to the Power Smart name. Talks continue on things like product labelling "and ways in which we might be able to put together an agreement with Ontario, but I don't expect them to depart from their existing programs," he said.

Meanwhile, in British Columbia, the program is ahead of all of its targets and its budget has been kicked up to $600-million for 20 years. Realistically, though, about $550-million of that will be spent in the next 10 years, Mr. Gieke said.

Source: The Globe and Mail, June 4, 1991.

policies, but it can also be used by agencies to justify what they want to do. As well, officials may use it to try to stop new regulations or weaken old ones. It is such an important and widely used approach that we will devote several chapters to it later in the book (Chapters 6, 7, and 8). In this type of analysis, as the name implies, the benefits of some proposed action are estimated and compared with the total costs that society would bear if that action were undertaken. If it is a proposal for a public park, for example, the benefits in terms of recreational experiences provided by the park are compared with the expected costs of building the park and of using the land in this way rather than some other way. Or a proposal to build a solid-waste incinerator would compare the costs of building and operating the incinerator, including the costs of disposing of the remaining ash and the costs of possible airborne emissions, with benefits, such as reducing the use of landfills for the solid waste.

The benefit-cost approach implies that we need to consider both the benefits and the costs of environmental programs and policies. This often puts benefit-cost studies squarely in the middle of political controversy on many environmental issues. In the political struggles that characterize many environmental problems, groups on one side consist of people whose major concern is with the benefits, while groups on the other side are primarily concerned with costs. Environmental groups typically stress the benefits; business groups usually focus on the costs. Look at the news story excerpted in Exhibit 1-7. It discusses some of the recent efforts to estimate the benefits and costs of CO_2 emission reduction, aimed at forestalling the "greenhouse effect." It describes how many environmental groups, historically somewhat doubtful of the usefulness of benefit-cost analysis, have now accepted the approach, realizing that more careful analysis of environmental programs can be a better way of defending them than an attempt simply to avoid any analysis whatever. The ultimate long-run acceptance of programs to protect the environment depends on people coming to realize that they are worth the cost. The benefit-cost, trade-off type of approach is the best way to accomplish this.[4]

INTERNATIONAL ISSUES

Not all environmental problems are pollution related, and not all are contained within individual countries. In recent years international issues have become increasingly important. The news clipping in Exhibit 1-8 tells about the globally important question of species diversity. Because of disruptions in habitats, such as housing developments in developed countries and deforestation in many developing economies, the rate of extinction among plant and animal species has been increased greatly above its natural level. The clipping tells of some of the manoeuvring leading up to the Earth Summit of 1992, and indicates some of the economic issues involved. These include the question of the most cost-effective ways to reduce the rate of species extinctions, the issue of whether national property rights ought to be exercised over species, the problem of international technology transfers, and the very thorny problem of how the costs of preserving species diversity are to be divided among rich and poor countries. These are all issues of sustainability—how to ensure that economic activities do not unalterably disrupt the ecological health of the planet. Species preservation

---

[4] A brief comment is appropriate about this newspaper article. The writer makes it sound as if benefit-cost analysis has been used historically only by those who have been opposed to environmental programs. This is not true. Environmental economists, most of them passionate advocates of the environment, have been using benefit-cost analysis for decades.

EXHIBIT 1-7

THE NEW ECO-NOMICS

After Years of Pooh-Poohing Cost-Benefit Analyses and Economic Impact Studies, Environmental Activists Have Finally Copied a Page from the Enemy's Playbook. Now They're Fighting Industry's Numbers with Numbers of Their Own.

By Margaret E. Kriz

The way Lester R. Brown, the president of the Worldwatch Institute, sees it, environmental activists are changing the art of economics—and perhaps vice versa.

After years of protesting the government's use of cost-benefit analyses to shape environmental policy, environmentalists are taking a different page out of the same book to argue for tough controls on global warming gases.

Where the cost-benefit analyses of the past measured obvious industrial costs (installing smokestack pollution controls, for example), the new studies are based partly on such less traditional approaches as quantifying the long-term benefits of cleaner air or biological diversity, for example, and predicting quick public adoption of energy-efficient technologies.

"It's not just the cost of manufacturing and income from sales that counts today in public policy making," Brown said. "These externalities are beginning to work their way onto the table, and I see that as an exciting development."

Brown was particularly enthusiastic about a global warming study by William R. Cline, a senior fellow at the Institute for International Economics. Cline's analysis concluded that by taking action to curb global warming, the United States could avoid $350 billion in economic damages over the next 300 years. Among the projected savings totalled up in the report is $4 billion for endangered species protection—a rough number Cline said he developed by figuring out how much it costs to protect the northern spotted owl and multiplying that number by 25.

Cline, in releasing the study, defended his inclusion of such nontraditional calculations. "This issue is a hybrid of science, economics and human behavior," he said. "You can ignore the great bulk of this problem, but you do so at great risk to society."

The environmental community has embraced economics out of necessity, not choice. After years of arguing that environmental protection was morally right at any cost, environmental activists realized that they had to fight economics with economics, particularly during a recession, when industry groups charged that new global warming emission controls would eliminate thousands of jobs.

There's a realization that you cannot afford to cede to the other side the whole economic waterfront," said Alden Meyer, the director of the climate change and energy policy program of the Union of Concerned Scientists. "Policy makers and the public clearly do care what happens to the economy, what happens to job creation. If you don't address the economic issues, you're leaving yourself open to be defeated on the policy front."

Last October, for example, Meyer's group and three other environmental organizations released a study that concluded that the United States could, by cutting its global warming gas emissions, save customers $2.3 trillion by 2030.

Just a decade earlier, however, cost-benefit analyses were fighting words to environmental activists. Rather than issuing their own economic studies, environmental groups were busy criticizing the Reagan Administration's policy of banning pollution controls if it decided that their costs outstripped their likely environmental benefits.

Such strict economic reasoning was anathema to environmentalists. They pointed out that although industry could easily estimate the cost to it of new pollution control equipment, scientists had a far more difficult time calculating the potential long-term health and environmental benefits of regulation.

EXHIBIT 1-8

TALKS SEEK TO PREVENT HUGE LOSS OF SPECIES

Nations Work Toward a Pact, Preserving Biological Diversity

By William K. Stevens

As the world approaches the day of decision on a treaty to deal with the threat of global warming, separate negotiations on another overarching environmental question, maintaining biological diversity, are moving toward their own denouement.

The object of these less prominent but nevertheless high-stakes talks is to forge a binding agreement among the world's nations to slow or halt a steady loss of plant, animal and microbial species that many biologists fear will result in a mass extinction of epic proportions in mere decades.

The basic question involves actions that nations should be required to take in conserving species, habitats and ecosystems. Despite a patchwork of international agreements like the Convention on International Trade in Endangered Species, there is no legally binding treaty that directly and comprehensively addresses the overall problem of preserving biological diversity.

Some countries have developed national action plans to identify, conserve and manage biological resources. But most, including many tropical countries that are richest in species, have not. These are precisely the main countries where economic and development pressures are destroying habitats at a rate that alarms many scientists and conservation biologists.

The negotiators have agreed that such programs should be the primary line of defense, with seed banks, gene banks and zoos secondary.

Issues other than the central question of conservation measures are posing greater difficulty. One of these involves the ownership of genetic materials. Historically, seeds, germ plasm and specimens of individual species have been considered to be in the public domain. Anyone who found them could exploit them without compensating the country of origin. Now developing countries are seeking to claim control over these resources and to share in their economic benefits.

Argument also attends the issue of the terms on which the industrialized countries should transfer conservation technology and know-how to developing countries. But the biggest point of contention is the one between North and South over money.

To many developing countries, conservation is clearly secondary to the day-to-day struggle to support their surging populations. "Seeing it from where you are or I am, the environment might look very important," said Fiona McConnell, the head of the British delegation. "But if your concern is survival, you might need some persuading."

Money is the persuader, and some developing countries are proposing that the North not only bear the costs of putting new conservation measures into effect but also compensate the South for foregoing the economic benefits of cutting down forests to expand commercial agriculture or timbering, for example. But other developing countries believe that if the forests are preserved and properly exploited for medicine and renewable products, they are worth more than if they are cut down.

The United States opened a possible wedge into the financial issue last week when it reversed position and pledged unilaterally to contribute $75 million to developing countries' costs of coping with global warming.

Of that sum, $50 million would be paid into the Global Environmental Facility, a pilot program established last year by the World Bank, the United Nations Environment Program and the United Nations Development program to channel environmental money from North to South. Developing countries welcomed the reversal with reservations. Many fear that the Global Environment Facility, which is controlled by developed countries, will shut them out of a say in administering the funds.

Source: New York Times, March 3, 1992. Copyright © 1992 by the New York Times. Reprinted by permission.

is one part of the sustainability objective. Important questions may include, for example, which species are essential to an ecosystem, and which species can we allow to go extinct, recognizing that extinctions have occurred over time with and without human intervention. This is the subject of a lively debate in the scientific and economic communities.[5]

ECONOMICS AND POLITICS

Finally, we need to discuss briefly the question of how to achieve effective environmental policy in a highly political policy environment. Environmental policies not only affect the natural environment, they also affect people. This means that environmental policy decisions come out of the political process, a process where, at least in democratic systems, people and groups come together and contend for influence and control, where interests collide, coalitions shift, and biases intrude. Policies that come out of a process like this may bear little relationship to what we might think of as efficient approaches to particular environmental problems. Many people have questioned the very idea that a democratic political process could or should strive to produce policies that are efficient in some technical economic sense.

So where does that leave the environmental economist? Why spend so much time and energy on questions of efficiency and cost-effectiveness when the political process most likely is going to override these considerations and go its own way? Why worry about economic incentives and economic efficiency when "everything is political," as the saying goes? The answer is that although we know that the real world is one of compromise and power, the best way for scientists and economists to serve that process is to produce studies that are as clear and as objective as possible. It is the politician's job to compromise or seek advantage; it is the scientist's job to provide the best information he or she can. For economists, in fact, this means studies in which economic efficiency is a central role, but it means more than this. Since the policy process is one where "who gets what" is a dominant theme, environmental economics must also deal with the distribution question, on how environmental problems and policies affect different groups within society. It is also the role of scientists and economists to provide information to policymakers on alternative courses of action. Although we will focus in later chapters on what appear to be "the" most efficient policies or "the" least-cost courses of action, we need to recognize that in the give-and-take of the political world in which policy is actually made, choosing among alternatives is always the order of the day.

But economists have no right these days to bemoan their fate in the environmental policy process. If anything these are the days of the rising influence of economists. Benefit-cost procedures and results have become more widely accepted, in public policy arenas and in law courts hearing environmental cases. New pollution-control initiatives incorporating economic incentive principles are playing an increasingly

---

[5] One area of scientific research is trying to identify "keystone" species. A keystone species is essential to the preservation and ecological health of a particular ecozone.

important role in local, provincial, and federal environmental policies. All the more reason, then, to study and understand the basic economics of environmental analysis and policy.

SUMMARY

The purpose of this brief chapter was to whet your appetite for the subject of environmental economics by indicating some of the main topics that the field encompasses, showing very briefly the approach that economists take in studying them. It's also to give you something to remember. When we get involved in some of the conceptual and theoretical issues that underlie the topic, it is easy to lose sight of what we are trying to accomplish. We are trying to develop these principles so that we can actually use them to address real-world problems like those discussed in this chapter. Although the principles may appear abstract and odd at first, remember the objective: to achieve a cleaner, healthier, and more beautiful natural environment that can be sustained over time.

SELECTED READINGS

Archibugi, F., and P. Nijkamp. *Economy and Ecology. Towards Sustainable Development.* Dordrect, The Netherlands: Kluwer Academic Press, 1989.

Brundtland, G. H., et al. *Our Common Future.* Oxford University Press: Oxford, 1987.

Canadian Council of Resource and Environment Ministers. *Report of the National Task Force of Environment and the Economy.* Downsview, Ontario: CCREM, 1987.

Costanza, Robert (ed.). *Ecological Economics: The Science and Management of Sustainability.* New York: Columbia University Press, 1991.

El-Hinnawi, Essam, and Manzur H. Hashmi. *The State of the Environment.* United Nations Environment Program. London: Butterworth, 1987.

Environment Canada. *The State of Canada's Environment.* Ottawa: Ministry of Supply and Services, 1991.

Miller, Alan S. *Gaia Connections: An Introduction to Ecology, Ecoethics, and Economics.* Lanham, Md.: Rowman and Allenheld, 1991.

Repetto, Robert C. *World Enough and Time: Successful Strategies for Resource Management.* New Haven, Conn.: Yale University Press, 1986.

Yandle, Bruce. *The Political Limits of Environmental Regulation: Tracking the Unicorn.* New York: Quorum Books, 1989.

2

THE ECONOMY AND THE ENVIRONMENT

The economy is a collection of technological, legal, and social arrangements through which a group of people seek to augment their material and spiritual standards of life. In any economic system, the elementary functions of production, distribution, and consumption take place within an all-encompassing natural world. One role the natural world plays is that of provider of raw materials and energy inputs, without which production, consumption, and indeed, life itself would be impossible. Thus, one type of impact that an economic system has on nature is by drawing upon raw materials to keep the system functioning. Production and consumption activities also produce leftover waste products, called "residuals," and sooner or later these must find their way back into the natural world. Depending on how they are handled, these residuals may lead to pollution or the degradation of the natural environment. We can illustrate these fundamental relationships with a simple schematic:

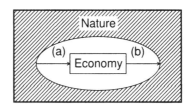

The link marked (a) represents raw materials flowing into production and consumption. The study of nature in its role as provider of raw materials is called *natural resource economics*. The link labelled (b) shows the impact of economic activity on the quality of the natural environment. The study of this residuals flow and its resultant impacts in the natural world comes under the heading of *environmental eco-*

nomics. While pollution control is the major topic within environmental economics, it is not the only one. Human beings impact on the environment in many ways that are not pollution related in the traditional sense. Habitat disruption from housing developments and scenic degradation from any number of human activities are examples of environmental impacts that are not related to the discharge of specific pollutants.

The topic of this book is environmental economics. We will study the management of waste flows and the impacts of human activity on environmental resources. But in a real sense many of these problems originate back in the initial, raw material phase of the nature-economy interaction. So before proceeding we will consider briefly the major dimensions of natural resource economics.

NATURAL RESOURCE ECONOMICS

In modern societies it is sometimes easy to overlook the fact that economic activity makes use of a great variety of natural resource inputs. In recent years events have reminded us of the importance of energy resources, especially the fossil-based ones such as coal, petroleum, and natural gas. The massive petrochemical industry is also based on these resources. The vast number of materials used in industrial societies, and even in the so-called "information society," come from various minerals and forest resources. Water is an essential input in many production processes as well as directly in household consumption. Food production depends on the natural resource base, either for direct harvesting, as in fisheries, or to provide the essential inputs for plant and animal growth. Air is an essential input in virtually all economic production processes.

To sort out this variety of natural resources the most common distinction is between *renewable* and *nonrenewable resources.* The living resources, like fisheries and timber, are renewable; they grow in time according to biological processes. Some nonliving resources are also renewable, the classic example being the sun's energy that reaches the earth. Nonrenewable resources are those for which there are no processes of replenishment—once used, they are gone forever. Classic examples are petroleum reservoirs and nonenergy mineral deposits. Certain resources, such as many groundwater aquifers, have replenishment rates that are so low that they are in effect nonrenewable.

A resource that has only recently impressed itself upon us is one that resides not in any one substance but in a collection of elements: biological diversity. Biologists estimate that there may be as many as 30 million different species of living organisms in the world today. These represent a vast and important source of genetic information, useful for the development of medicines, natural pesticides, resistant varieties of plants and animals, and so on. Human activities have substantially increased the rate of species extinctions, so habitat conservation and species preservation have become important contemporary resource problems.

One of the distinguishing features of most natural resource issues is that they are heavily "time dependent." This means that their use is normally spread out over time, so rates of use in one period affect availabilities and use rates in later periods. In the case of nonrenewable resources this is relatively easy to see. How much petroleum should be pumped from a deposit this year, realizing that the more we pump now the less there will be available in future years? But these trade-offs between present and future also exist for many renewable resources. What should today's salmon harvesting rate be, considering that the size of the remaining stock will affect its availability in later years? Should we cut the timber this year, or is its growth rate high enough to justify waiting until some future year?

These are issues with a strong *intertemporal* dimension; they involve trade-offs between today and the future. Certain environmental problems are also like this, especially when dealing with pollutants that accumulate, or pollutants that require a long time to dissipate. What is in fact being depleted here is the earth's "assimilative capacity," the ability of the natural system to accept certain pollutants and render them benign or inoffensive. Some of the theoretical ideas about the depletion of natural resources are also useful in understanding environmental pollution. In this sense "assimilative capacity" is a natural resource akin to traditional resources like oil deposits and forests.

One feature of the modern world is that the dividing line between natural resources and environmental resources is blurring in many cases. Many resource extraction processes, such as timber cutting and strip mining, have direct repercussions on environmental quality. And there are plenty of instances where environmental pollution or disruption impacts resource extraction processes. Estuarine water pollution that interferes with the replenishment of fish stocks is an example, as is air pollution that reduces agricultural yields. And certain things, like wildlife, may be considered both natural resources and attributes of the environment. Despite these blurred edges, however, the distinction that economists have made between these two services of the natural world—as raw materials and as environment—is sufficiently strong and well developed that it makes sense for us to proceed with a book that focusses primarily on the latter. We will begin by considering a somewhat more complicated version of the simple diagram depicted above.

THE FUNDAMENTAL BALANCE

In this book you will find a lot of simple analytical "models" of situations that in reality are somewhat complex. A model is a way of trying to show the essential structure and relationships in something, without going into all of its details, much as a caricature of a person accentuates distinguishing features at the cost of all the details. Figure 2-1 is a more complex rendering of the relationships shown at the beginning of the chapter. The elements within the circle are parts of the economic system, the whole of which is basically encapsulated within the natural environment. The economy has been divided into two broad segments, producers and consumers. The "producers" category includes all the firms that take inputs and convert them to useful outputs, but it also includes units like public agencies, nonprofit organizations, and firms producing services, such as transportation; in short, all economic entities in the sys-

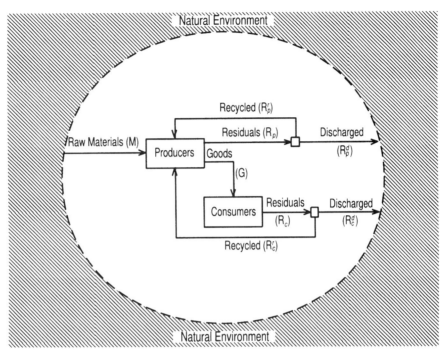

FIGURE 2-1   The Environment and the Economy.

tem up to the consumers themselves. The primary inputs from the natural environment to the producing sector are materials, in the form of fuels, minerals, and wood, fluids like water and petroleum, and gases of various types, like natural gas and oxygen. All goods and services are derived from materials with the application of energy inputs. The produced goods and services, embodying a portion of these materials and energy, then flow to consumers. One could argue that consumers utilize materials inputs directly from nature themselves without the intermediary of producers. Thus, we have water pumped from domestic wells or, in many countries, fuel wood harvested directly by householders. People also use the natural environment directly for pleasurable activities such as a walk in the woods, sport fishing, and bird watching. These activities do not necessarily involve any consumption of the natural environment. But in the interest of keeping it simple, these functions arc not directly drawn into the figure. In these cases we can consider producers and consumers as being the same people. Of course, in an even wider sense we need to keep in mind that "producers" and "households" actually consist of people, and in fact the same people in each case. The "us versus them" attitude that characterizes many environmental disputes is in fact an internal disagreement within a single group. Society as a whole is essentially in the same position as a single household that pumps water from its own well and discharges wastes into its own septic system, which happens to be near the well.

Production and consumption create "residuals," which is another way of saying leftovers. It includes all types of materials residuals that may be emitted into the air or water or disposed of on land. The list is incredibly long: sulfur dioxide, volatile organic compounds, toxic solvents, animal manure, pesticides, particulate matter of all types, waste building materials, heavy metals, and so on. Waste energy in the form of heat and noise, and radioactivity, which has characteristics of both material and energy, are also important production residuals. Consumers are also responsible for enormous quantities of residuals, chief among which are domestic sewage and automobile emissions. All materials in consumer goods must eventually end up as leftovers, even though they may be recycled along the way. These are the source of large quantities of solid waste as well as hazardous materials like toxic chemicals and used oil.

Let us first consider the question of production and consumption residuals from a strictly physical standpoint. Figure 2-1 shows materials and energy (M) being extracted from the natural environment and residuals (R_p^d and R_c^d) being discharged back into the environment. The first law of thermodynamics, the famous law on the conservation of matter, assures us that, in the long run, these two flows must be equal. In terms of the symbols of Figure 2-1:[1]

$$M = R_p^d + R_c^d$$

We must say "in the long run" for several reasons. If the system is growing, it can retain some proportion of the natural inputs, which go toward increasing the size of the system, through a growing population, the accumulation of capital equipment, etc. These would be disposed of if and when the system ceases to grow and through deterioration of capital equipment. Also, recycling can obviously delay the disposal of residuals. But recycling can never be perfect, each cycle must lose some proportion of the recycled material.[2] Thus, the fundamental materials balance equation must hold in the long run. This shows us something very fundamental: If we wish to reduce the mass of residuals disposed of in the natural environment, we must reduce the quantity of raw materials taken into the system.[3] We can look more closely at the options before us if we substitute for M. According to the flow diagram,

$$R_p^d + R_c^d = M = G + R_P - R_p^r - R_c^r$$

which says that the quantity of raw materials (M) is equal to output (G) plus production residuals (R_p), minus the amounts that are recycled from producers (R_p^r) and

---

[1] To make these direct comparisons all flows must be expressed in terms of mass.

[2] This is the second law of thermodynamics which says, with use, matter deteriorates over time into a lower grade. This is also known as the concept of entropy. Paper products can only be recycled several times before the fibres are too weak to be reused. The consumption of fossil fuels releases energy and by-products (carbon dioxide and other gases) that cannot be used again as energy sources.

[3] Note that $G = R_c$, i.e., everything that flows to the consumption sector eventually ends up as a residual from that sector.

consumers (R_c^r). There are essentially three ways of reducing M and, therefore, residuals discharged into the natural environment.

Reduce G   Assuming the other flows stay the same, we can reduce residuals discharged by reducing the quantity of goods and services produced in the economy. Some people have fastened on this as the best long-run answer to environmental degradation; reducing output, or at least stopping its rate of growth, would allow a similar change in the quantity of residuals discharged. Some have sought to reach this goal by advocating "zero population growth" (ZPG).[4]

A slowly growing or stationary population can make it easier to control environmental impacts, but does not in any way ensure this control, for two reasons. First, a stationary population can grow economically, thus increasing its demand for raw materials. Second, environmental impacts can be long run and cumulative, so that even a stationary population can gradually degrade the environment in which it finds itself. But it is certainly true that population growth will often exacerbate the environmental impacts of a particular economy. In the Canadian economy, for example, although the emissions of pollutants per car has dramatically decreased over the last few decades through better emissions-control technology, the sheer growth in the number of cars on the highways has led to an increase in the total quantity of certain automobile emissions in many regions, most particularly large cities such as Toronto, Montreal, and Vancouver.

Reduce R_p   Another way of reducing M, and therefore residuals discharged, is to reduce R_p. Assuming the other flows are held constant, this means essentially changing the amounts of production residuals produced for a given quantity of output produced. There are basically just two ways of doing this. We can invent and adopt new production technologies and practices that produce smaller amounts of residuals per unit of output produced. We can call this reducing the "residuals intensity" of production. When we discuss the global issue of CO_2 emissions and atmospheric warming, for example, we will see that there is much that could be done to reduce the CO_2 intensity of energy production, especially by shifting to different fuels but also by reducing (actually by continuing to reduce) energy inputs required to produce a dollar's worth of final output.

The other way of reducing R_p is to shift the internal composition of output. Output G actually consists of a large number of different goods and services, with great differences among them in terms of the residuals left after they are produced. So another way to reduce the total quantity of residuals is to shift the composition of G away from high- and toward low-residuals items, while leaving the total intact. The shift from primarily a manufacturing economy toward services is a step in this direction. Most developed, "industrial" economies have experienced relatively fast rates of growth in their service sectors over the last half century or so. The rise of the so-called "information sectors" is another example. It is not that these new sectors pro-

---

[4] For example, see Herman E. Daly, *Steady State Economics, Second Edition with New Essays*, Island Press (Washington, D.C.: Island Press, 1991).

duce no significant residuals; indeed, some of them may produce harsher leftovers than we have known before. The computer industry, for example, uses a variety of chemical solvents for cleaning purposes. But on the whole these sectors probably have a smaller waste-disposal problem than the traditional industries they have replaced.

Consumers can influence these production decisions by demanding goods that are more "environmentally friendly" than others. An environmentally friendly good releases fewer or less harmful residuals into the environment than more "pollution-intensive" goods. Examples are batteries that do not contain mercury, laundry detergents without phosphates, and energy-efficient appliances and vehicles.

Increase ($R_p^r + R_c^r$)   The third possibility is to increase recycling. Instead of discharging production and consumption residuals into the environment, we can recycle them back into the production process. What this shows is that the central role of recycling is to replace a portion of the original flow of virgin materials (M). By substituting recycled materials for virgin materials, we can reduce the quantity of residuals discharged while maintaining the rate of output of goods and services (G). In modern economics recycling offers great opportunities to reduce waste flows. But we have to remember the second law of thermodynamics, that recycling can never be perfect, even if we were to devote enormous resources to the task. Production processes usually transform the physical structure of materials inputs, making them difficult to use again. The conversion of energy materials makes materials recovery impossible. And recycling processes themselves can create residuals. But materials research will continue to progress and discover new ways of recycling. For a long time, automobile tires could not be recycled because the original production process changed the physical structure of the rubber. But recently a way has been found to overcome this problem, opening up the possibility that vast stockpiles of used tires with nowhere to go will no longer blight the landscape.[5]

These fundamental relationships are very important. We must remember, however, that our ultimate goal is to reduce the damages caused by the discharge of production and consumption residuals. Reducing the total quantity of these residuals is one major way of doing this, and the relationships discussed indicate the basic ways that may be done. But we can also reduce damages by working directly on the stream of residuals. We will look at this aspect of the problem, after a short pause to clarify terminology.

TERMINOLOGY

Throughout the chapters that follow we will be using the following terms:

• Ambient quality: "Ambient" refers to the surrounding environment, so ambient quality refers to the quantity of pollutants in the environment, for example, the concentration of SO_2 in the air over a city or the concentration of a particular chemical in the waters of a lake.

---

[5] "A Scrappy Stretch of Road: It's Made of a Mixture of Asphalt and Rubber from Recycled Tires." *Los Angeles Times*, June 8, 1992, B1.

• Environmental quality: A term used to refer broadly to the state of the natural environment. This includes the notion of ambient quality, and also such things as the visual and aesthetic quality of the environment.

• Residuals: Material that is left over after something has been produced; a plant takes in a variety of raw materials and converts these into some product; materials and energy left after the product has been produced are *production residuals. Consumption residuals* are what is left over after consumers have finished using the products that contained or otherwise used these materials.

• Emissions: That portion of production or consumption residuals that are placed in the environment, sometimes directly, sometimes after treatment.

• Recycling: The process of returning some or all of the production or consumption residuals to be used again in production or consumption.

• Pollutant: A substance, energy form, or action that, when introduced into the natural environment, results in a lowering of the ambient quality level. We want to think of this as including not only the traditional things like oil spilled into oceans or chemicals placed in the air, but also activities, like certain building developments, that result in "visual pollution."

• Effluent: Sometimes "effluent" is used to talk about water pollutants, and emissions to refer to air pollutants, but in this book these two words will be used interchangeably.

• Pollution: Pollution is actually a tricky word to define. Some people might say that pollution results when any amount, no matter how small, of a residual has been introduced into the environment. Others hold that pollution is something that happens only when the ambient quality of the environment has been degraded enough to cause some damage.

• Damages: The negative impacts produced by environmental pollution; on people in the form of health effects, visual degradation, etc.; on elements of the ecosystem through disruption of ecological linkages, species extinctions, etc.

• Environmental medium: Broad dimensions of the natural world which collectively constitute the environment, usually classified as land, water, and air.

• Source: The location at which emissions occur, such as a factory, an automobile, or a leaking landfill.

EMISSIONS, AMBIENT QUALITY, AND DAMAGES

Let us now focus on what happens at the end of those two discharge arrows at the right side of Figure 2-1. Very simply, emissions produce changes in ambient levels of environmental quality, which in turn cause damages to humans and nonhumans. Figure 2-2 shows one way of sketching out this relationship. It shows two sources of emissions; they might be private firms, government agencies, or consumers. Sources take in various inputs and goods and use different types of technologies in production and consumption. In the process they produce residuals. How these residuals are handled then has a critical effect on subsequent stages. Some may be recovered and recycled back into production or consumption. Many can be put

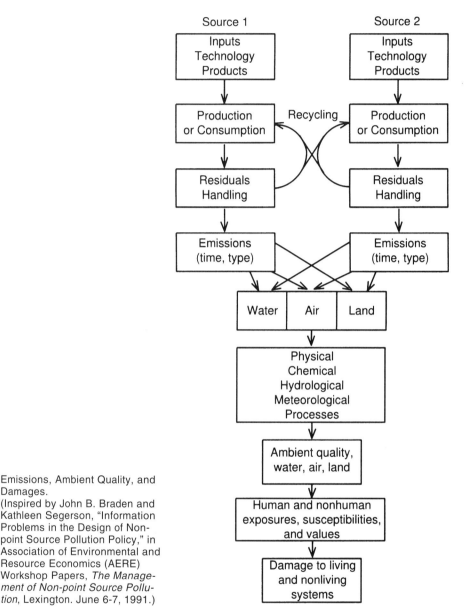

FIGURE 2-2   Emissions, Ambient Quality, and Damages.
(Inspired by John B. Braden and Kathleen Segerson, "Information Problems in the Design of Non-point Source Pollution Policy," in Association of Environmental and Resource Economics (AERE) Workshop Papers, *The Management of Non-point Source Pollution*, Lexington. June 6-7, 1991.)

through treatment processes (residuals handling) that can render them more benign when emitted. Some of these processes are strictly physical (mufflers on cars and trucks, settling ponds at wastewater treatment plants, catalytic converters); others involve chemical transformations of various types (advanced treatment of domestic wastewater).

All emissions must necessarily go into one or more of the different environmental media, and there is an important relationship among them. There is a natural tendency in policy deliberations to keep these different media in separate compartments, dealing with air pollution separately from water pollution, and so on. But they are obviously inteconnected; once residuals are produced, all that are not recycled must end up being discharged into one or more of the different media. Thus, for a given quantity of total residuals, if we reduce the amounts going into one medium, we must necessarily increase the amounts going into the others. When we remove sulfur dioxide (SO_2) from the stack gases of power plants, for example, we have not destroyed the sulfur compounds. Instead, we end up with a sulfurous sludge that must be disposed of some other way, perhaps by land burial. If we incinerate this material, we are in fact emitting some into the air, but we still end up with certain quantities of solid residuals that must be disposed of elsewhere.

The streams of emissions come from the two different sources, but once emitted they merge into a single flow. In the real world this mixing may be complete; for example, the effluent from two pulp mills located at the same point on a river may mix so thoroughly that a few kilometres downstream it is impossible to differentiate one source's effluent from the other's. When there are a million or so cars moving about an urban area, the emissions from all become uniformly mixed together. In other cases the mixing is less than complete. If one power plant is just outside the city and another is 30 km upwind, the closest plant will normally bear a greater responsibility for deteriorating air quality in the city than the other.

This mixing of emissions is a more significant problem than might first appear. With just a single source, the line of responsibility is clear, and to get an improvement in ambient quality we know exactly whose emissions we have to control. But with multiple sources, responsibilities become less clear. We may know how much we want to cut back total emissions, but we still face the problem of distributing this total reduction among the different sources. Each source then has an incentive to get the others to bear a larger share of the burden of reducing emissions. With every source thinking along the same lines, pollution control programs face a real problem of design and enforcement. We will run into this problem many times in the chapters to come.

Once a given quantity and quality of residuals has been introduced into a particular environmental medium, it is the physical, chemical, biological, meteorological, etc., processes of the natural system that determine how the residuals translate into particular ambient quality levels. For example, wind and temperature conditions will affect whether and how residuals emitted into the air affect nearby neighbourhoods, as well as people living farther downwind. And since these meteorological conditions vary from day to day, the same level of emissions can produce different ambient quality levels at different times. Acid rain is produced through chemical processes acting primarily on sulfur dioxide emissions emitted far upwind; smog is also the result of complex chemical reactions involving sunlight and quantities of various pollutants. Underground hydrological processes affect the transportation of materials disposed of in landfills. And so on. Thus, to know how particular emissions will affect ambient quality levels we must have a good understanding of the physical and chemical workings of the environment itself. This is where the natural and physical sciences come in, to study the full range of environmental phenomena, from small, localized models of groundwater flow in a particular aquifer, to complex models of large lakes and river basins, to studies of interregional wind patterns, to global climate models. The fundamental goal is to determine how particular patterns of emissions are translated into corresponding patterns of ambient quality levels.

Finally, we have damages. A given set of ambient conditions translates into particular exposure patterns for living and nonliving systems. Of course, these exposures are a function not only of the physical processes involved, but also of the human choices that are made about where and how to live, and of the susceptibilities of living and nonliving systems to varying environmental conditions. Lastly, damages are related to human values. Human beings do not have amorphous preferences over all possible outcomes of the economic/environmental interaction; they prefer some outcomes over others. A major part of environmental economics is trying to determine the relative values that people place on these different environmental outcomes, a subject to which we will turn in later chapters on benefit-cost analysis.

TYPES OF POLLUTANTS

Physically, the residuals identified in Figure 2-2 consist of a vast assortment of materials and energy flowing into the three environmental media. We will want to distinguish among broad types of emissions according to factors that critically affect their economic status.

Cumulative vs. Noncumulative Pollutants

One simple and important dimension of environmental pollutants is whether they accumulate over time or tend to dissipate soon after being emitted. The classic case of a noncumulative pollutant is noise; as long as the source operates, noise is emitted into the surrounding air, but as soon as the source is shut down, the noise stops. At the other end of the spectrum we have pollutants that cumulate in the environment in nearly the same amounts as they are emitted. Radioactive waste, for example, decays over time but at such a slow rate in relation to human life spans that for all intents and purposes it will be with us permanently; it is a strictly cumulative type of pollutant. Another cumulative pollutant is plastics. The search for a degradable plastic has been going on for decades, but so far plastic is a substance that decays very slowly by human standards; thus, what we dispose of will be in the environment permanently. Many chemicals are cumulative pollutants; once emitted they are basically with us forever.

Between these two ends of the spectrum there are many types of effluent that are to some extent, but not completely, cumulative. The classic case is organic matter emitted into water bodies; for example, the wastes, treated or not, emitted from municipal waste treatment plants. Once emitted the wastes are subject to natural chemical processes that tend to break down the organic materials into their constituent elements, thus rendering them much more benign. The water, in other words, has a natural assimilative capacity that allows it to accept organic substances and render them less harmful. As long as this assimilative capacity has not been exceeded in any particular case, we can shut off the source of the effluent, and in a few days or weeks or months the water quality will return to normal. Of course the fact that nature has some assimilative capacity doesn't automatically mean that we have a strictly non-cumulative pollutant. Once our emissions exceed the assimilative capacity we would move into a cumulative process. For example, the atmosphere of the earth has a given capacity to absorb CO_2 emitted by human and nonhuman activity, as long as this capacity is not exceeded. CO_2 is a noncumulative pollutant. But if the earth's assimilative capacity for CO_2 is exceeded, as it seems to be at the present time, we are in a situation where emissions are in fact accumulating over time.

Whether a pollutant is cumulative or noncumulative we still have essentially the same basic problem: trying to figure out the environmental damages and relating these back to the costs of reducing emissions. But this job is much more difficult for cumulative than for noncumulative pollutants. Consider the graphs in Figure 2-3. Panel (a) represents a noncumulative pollutant, while panel (b) depicts one that is cumulative. In panel (a) the graph begins at the origin, implying that current ambient concentrations are proportional to current emissions. Ambient concentrations are strictly a function of current emissions—reducing these emissions to zero would lead to zero ambient concentrations. But with cumulative pollutants the relationship is more complex. Today's emissions, since they accumulate and add to the stock of pollutant already existing, will cause damages not only today but also in the future, perhaps in the distant future. It also means that the current ambient quantity of an accumulating pollutant may be only weakly related to current emissions. The graph in panel (b) begins well up the vertical axis from the origin and has a flatter slope than the other. Thus

FIGURE 2-3   Relationship between Current Emissions and Ambient Pollution Concentration.

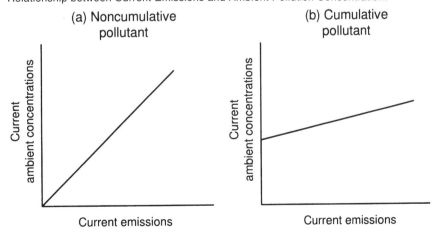

a cutback in today's emissions has only a modest effect on current ambient concentrations. Even if today's emissions were cut to zero, ambient quality would still be impaired because of the cumulative effect of past emissions. The fact that a pollutant cumulates over time in the environment has the effect of breaking the direct connection between current emissions and current damages. This has a number of implications. For one thing it makes the science more difficult. The cause-and-effect relationships become harder to isolate when there is a lot of time intervening between them. It also may make it more difficult to get people to focus on damages from today's emissions, again because there may only be a weak connection between today's emissions and today's ambient quality levels. Furthermore, cumulative pollutants by definition lead to future damages, and human beings have shown a depressing readiness to discount future events and avoid coming to grips with them in the present.

Local vs. Regional and Global Pollutants

Some emissions have an impact only in restricted, localized regions, while others have an impact over wider regions, perhaps on the global environment. Noise pollution and the degradation of the visual environment are local in their impacts; the damages from any particular source are usually limited to relatively small groups of people in a circumscribed region. Note that this is a statement about how widespread the effects are from any particular pollution source, not about how important the overall problem is throughout a country or the world. Some pollutants, on the other hand, have widespread impacts, over a large region or perhaps over the global environment. Acid rain is a regional problem; emissions in one region of the U.S. (and of Europe) affect people in other parts of the country or region. The ozone-depleting effects of chlorofluorocarbon emissions from various countries work through chemical changes in the earth's stratosphere, which means that the impacts are truly global.

Other things being equal, local environmental problems ought to be easier to deal with than regional or national problems, which in turn ought to be easier to manage than global problems. If a person smokes out the neighbour with a wood stove, we may be able to arrange a solution among ourselves, or we can call on local political institutions to do it. But if that person's behaviour causes more distant pollution, solutions may be more difficult. If we are within the same political system, we can call on these institutions to arrange solutions. In recent years, however, we have been encountering a growing number of international and global environmental issues. Here we are far from having effective means of responding, both because the exact nature of the physical impacts is difficult to describe and because the requisite international political institutions are only beginning to appear.

Point-Source vs. Nonpoint Source Pollutants

Pollution sources differ in terms of the ease with which actual points of discharge may be identified. The points at which sulfur dioxide emissions leave a large power plant are easy to identify; they come out the end of the smokestacks associated with each plant. Municipal waste treatment plants normally have a single outfall from which all of the wastewater is discharged. These are called *point-source pollutants*. On the other hand there are many pollutants for which there are no well-defined points of discharge. Agricultural chemicals, for example, usually run off the land in a dispersed or defused pattern, and even though they may pollute specific streams or underground aquifers, there is no single pipe or stack from which these chemicals are emitted. This is a *nonpoint source* type of pollutant. Urban storm water runoff is also an important nonpoint source problem.

As one would expect, point-source pollutants are likely to be easier to come to grips with than nonpoint source pollutants. They will probably be easier to measure and monitor and easier to study in terms of the connections between emissions and impacts. This means that it will ordinarily be easier to develop and administer control policies for point-source pollutants. As we will see, not all pollutants fit neatly into one or another of these categories.

Continuous vs. Episodic Emissions

Emissions from electric power plants or municipal waste treatment plants are more or less continuous. The plants are designed to be in operation continuously, though the operating rate may vary somewhat over the day, week, or season. Thus the emissions from these operations are more or less continuous, and the policy problem is to manage the rate of these discharges. We can make immediate comparisons between control programs and rates of emissions. The fact that emissions are continuous does not mean that damages are also continuous, however. Meteorological and hydrological events can turn continuous emissions into uncertain damages. But control programs are often easier to carry out when emissions are not subject to large-scale fluctuations.

Many pollutants are emitted on an episodic basis, however. The classic example is accidental oil or chemical spills. The policy problem here is to design and manage a system so that the probability of accidental discharges is reduced. But with an episodic effluent there may be nothing to measure, at least in the short run. Even though there have been no large-scale radiation releases from Canadian nuclear power plants, for example, we could still have a "pollution" problem if they are being managed in such a way as to increase the *probability* of an accidental release in the future. To measure the probabilities of episodic emissions we have to have data on actual occurrences over a long time period, or we have to estimate them from engineering data and similar information. We then have to determine how much insurance we wish to have against these episodic events.

Environmental Damages Not Related to Emissions

So far the discussion has focussed on the characteristics of different types of environmental pollutants as they relate to the discharge of residual materials or energy. But there are many important instances of deteriorating environmental quality that are not traceable to residuals discharges. The conversion of land to housing and commercial areas destroys the environmental value of that land, whether it be its ecosystem value, such as habitat or wetland, or its scenic value. Other land uses, such as logging or strip mining, can also have important impacts. In cases like these our job is still to understand the incentives of people whose decisions create these impacts, and to change these incentives when appropriate. Although there are no physical emissions to monitor and control, there are nevertheless outcomes that can be described, evaluated, and managed with appropriate policies.

SHORT-RUN AND LONG-RUN CHOICES—SUSTAINABILITY

Most of the discussion so far has focussed on the physical connections among inputs, residuals, emissions, and ambient quality levels. These relationships are of prime interest to the physical and natural scientists working on environmental issues. We can move the discussion more toward the economist's bailiwick by examining the trade-offs inherent in the relationship between market output and environmental quality. This will give us a way also of considering the differences between short-run and long-run environmental decisions.

The basic relationship is shown in Figure 2-4. This depicts several *production possibility curves* (PPCs) between marketed output and environmental quality. A PPC is a way of depicting diagrammatically the choice faced by a group of people between two desirable outcomes. Consider for the moment panel (a) of Figure 2-4. The vertical axis has an index of the aggregate economic output of an economy, that is, the total market value of conventional economic goods traded in the economy in a year. The horizontal axis has an index of environmental quality, derived from data on different dimensions of the ambient environment, for example, airborne SO_2 concentrations, urban noise levels, and water quality data. The curved relationship shows the different combinations of these two outcomes—marketed output and environmental quality—that are available to a group of people who have a fixed endowment of resources with which to work.[6]

The production possibility curve is determined by the technical capacities in the economy together with the ecological facts—meteorology, hydrology, etc.—of the natural system in which the country is situated. It says, for example, that if the current level of economic output is c_1, we can obtain an increase to c_2 only at the cost of a decrease in environmental quality from e_1 to e_2. But while the PPC itself is a technical constraint, where a society chooses to locate itself on its PPC is a matter of *social choice*. And this depends on the relative values that people in that society place on conventional economic output and environmental quality.

The current year production possibility curve depicts a competitive relationship between environmental quality and marketed output. More of one implies less of the

---

[6] At the extremes, the PPCs have been drawn with dashed lines. It's not clear what an outcome would be with "zero" environmental quality, nor what one would be with "zero" economic output. Thus, these extreme points are essentially undefined, and we will concentrate on points in the interior of the diagrams.

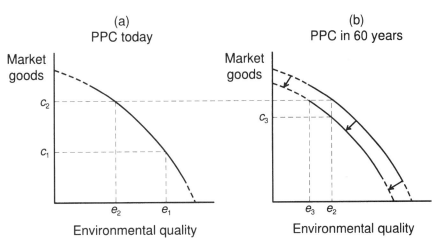

FIGURE 2-4   Production Possibility Curves for Current and Future Generations.

other. But if our concern is what happens over a relatively long period of time, the single PPC can be misleading. This is because in the long run, environmental quality may be less substitutive than complementary with conventional economic outputs. In the long run the natural environment plays the role of environmental capital input into the production system, and a significant drawing down of that environmental capital may have serious negative effects on the ability of the economic system to sustain itself. A production possibility curve depicts the trade-offs facing today's generation. But what about future generations? One way to think of this is to consider the impacts of our decisions today on the production possibility curves facing *future generations*. Consider panel (b) of Figure 2-4. It shows the production possibilities curve for people in, say, 60 to 80 years, the generation consisting of your great grandchildren. According to today's PPC we could choose combinations (c_1, e_1), or (c_2, e_2), or any others on the curve. But the future is not independent of the choice we make today. It's conceivable, for example, that degrading the environment too much today will affect future possibilities—for example by depleting certain important resources, or by pollution that is so high it causes irreversible damage, or simply by a pollutant that is very long-lived and affects future generations. In effect this could shift the future PPC back from where it otherwise would be. This is depicted in panel (b) of the diagram. Your grandchildren will be confronted with a reduced set of possibilities as compared to the choices we face today. The future generation, finding itself on the inner production possibilities curve, can still have the same level of marketed output we have today (c_2), but only at a lower level of environmental quality (e_3) than we have today. Alternatively, it could enjoy the same level of environmental quality, but only with a reduced level of marketed output (c_3).

We have to recognize, of course, that the influence of today's decisions on future production possibilities is much more complicated than this discussion might suggest. It's not only environmental degradation that affects future conditions, but also technical developments and changes in human capacities. Thus, today's decisions could shift the future PPC either in or out, depending on a great many dynamic factors that are hard to predict. But we need to be particularly alert to avoid decisions today that would have the effect of shifting the future PPC to the left. This is the essence of recent discussions about sustainability, a concept we introduced in Chapter 1. In terms of Figure 2-4, sustainability means simply that future production possibility curves are not adversely affected by what we do today. It does not mean that we must maximize environmental quality today, since that implies zero output of goods and services. It means simply that we reduce our environmental impacts enough today to avoid shifting future production possibilities curves back in comparison to today's production possibilities. As we said before, a sustainable economy will be one that maintains natural resource flows and environmental quality over time. We will meet the idea of sustainability throughout this book.

POLLUTION CONTROL IN THE CANADIAN ECONOMY

We will close this chapter by taking a general look at the Canadian economy and the role within it of pollution control. In 1989 Canadian gross national product (GNP) was $649 billion. Since the estimated population of the country in that year was around 26 million, the GNP per capita was about $25,000. If we again use the U.S. figure for estimated pollution-control costs as a percent of GNP of 2 percent, this means that Canadians were paying about $500 per capita for pollution control. The comparable figure for the U.S. is $460 per capita. The pollution-control costs measured in the U.S. include all the private costs of complying with pollution-control laws, that is, all the costs of purchasing, installing, operating, and maintaining pollution-control technology that firms need to be in compliance with these laws. It also includes the costs of changing internal operating procedures to meet pollution-control laws. Household and local government costs of such programs as trash collection and disposal are counted. Lastly, it includes all the public costs, at federal, state, and local levels, of administering and enforcing these pollution-control laws and regulations.[7]

Is the price high or low? It's impossible to answer that in an absolute sense, but we might be able to give it more meaning by making some comparisons. The following tabulation shows costs of certain categories of expenditures made by Canadians in 1989 as a percentage of personal income which totalled $552 billion in that year.

Clothing and footwear	2.8%
Food and nonalcoholic beverages	5.6
Motor vehicle fuel, repairs, parts	5.2
Durable goods (excluding motor vehicle repairs and parts)	4.0
Housing (gross rents)	8.3

[7] It does not include nonpollution-control environmental costs, however, like wildlife protection.

Other services	13.2
Transfers to government	21.3
Pollution-control costs	2.4

The figure for pollution control is quite approximate, as noted before. The calculation above assumes that households would pay for the entire costs of pollution control. The 2.4 percent figure probably overstates these costs because households are already paying for pollution control in their taxes ($118 billion of personal income represents transfers to governments), in the prices of goods and services they consume, and because part of the costs will be borne by industries and consumers of products exported from Canada. Of course, Canadian pollution-control costs may exceed those of the United States. If so, the percentage would rise. Nonetheless, these figures suggest that Canadian households are probably paying a small amount relative to their other expenditures for pollution control. Although pollution-control costs are expected to take a bigger share of GNP in future years, they may never get as large as the expenditures in basic consumer categories like clothing, housing, food, and transportation.

What are other countries spending on pollution-control costs as a percentage of GNP? The following tabulation shows pollution-control costs as a percentage of GNP in several countries for 1985:[8]

United States	1.67
Finland	1.32
France	1.10
West Germany	1.52
Netherlands	1.26
Norway	0.82
United Kingdom	1.25

These proportions range from 0.82 to 1.67 percent. We would expect Canada to lie somewhere within this range. One should be careful with numbers such as these. We can't infer directly that countries with higher pollution-control costs are enjoying a cleaner environment—less air pollution, cleaner water, and so on. Nothing is said here about the effectiveness with which pollution-control resources are being made in the different countries. It might be, for example, that although Norway spends less as a percentage of GNP on pollution control than the others, it spends it more effectively than the resources spent in other countries. Another factor that is not taken into account in simple comparisons is the severity of the pollution problems in different countries. Because of differences in industrial structure and differences in environmental resources (like meteorological patterns, geography, or assimilative capacity of the environment for example), it may cost more to reduce pollution to acceptable levels in one country than in another.[9] But the numbers are nevertheless

[8] U.S. Environmental Protection Agency, *Environmental Investments, The Costs of a Clean Environment, A Summary*, EPA-230-12-90-084 (Washington, D.C.: EPA) 4–7.
[9] We will discuss this question at greater length in Chapter 21.

interesting; it may be slightly surprising that most of these percentages are between 1.0 and 1.5.

Finally, Table 2-1 shows pollution abatement and control (PAC) costs for a survey of Canadian industries done by Statistics Canada for 1989. The table shows capital costs for the construction of pollution abatement and control facilities both in actual dollars and as a percent of total capital expenditures for plant and equipment in that year. It is interesting to note the sectors which appear to be the most pollution intensive, that is, who are incurring the largest costs of constructing abatement facilities. These would appear to be in the manufacturing sector, where total manufacturing has a ratio of PACs to total capital costs of 12.6 percent, compared to an economy-wide ratio of 6.2 percent. Within manufacturing, primary metals and petroleum and coal have the highest ratios at over 20 percent. Operating costs are also shown on the table, but unfortunately, no data was available which would allow a comarison of PAC costs to total operating costs for these industries. We have only one year of data for Canadian companies, so additional surveys are needed to provide more perspective on these figures.

One can take almost any position one wants on cost figures like these. Total pollution-control costs are many millions of dollars each year, but they are not enormous in comparison to many other types of expenditures. Certainly they are large enough

TABLE 2-1   POLLUTION ABATEMENT AND CONTROL (PAC) EXPENDITURES BY SECTOR, 1989

	(Millions of 1989 Dollars)		
Sector	PAC capital expenditures	PAC capital/ total capital expenditures	PAC operating expenditure
Forestry	X	X	X
Mining	69.9	4.7	76.8
Total manufacturing	702.1	12.6	468.6
Paper and allied products	292.8	12.4	NA
Primary metals	231.4	20.4	NA
Petroleum and coal	63.5	23.1	NA
Chemicals	56.1	9.8	NA
Utilities	85.0	1.3	X
Trade, finance and commercial	12.5	4.0	0.6
Institutions	3.9	0.9	0.8
Governments	X	X	X
Total costs	915.9	6.2	728.8

Notes: X = data confidential to meet secrecy requirements of the Statistics Act
NA = data not available
Source: Statistics Canada, Capital Expenditures Division, *Analysis of the 1989 Pollution Abatement and Control Survey* (Ottawa: Statscan, January 1992).

that we should be sensitive to the need for getting the most pollution-control impact for the money we are spending. A large part of what follows in this book is about designing efficient and effective pollution-control policy, as well as trying to measure some of the environmental values involved in this policy.

SUMMARY

The purpose of this chapter was to explore some basic linkages between the economy and the environment. We differentiated between the role of the natural system as a supplier of raw material inputs for the economy and as a receptor for production and consumption residuals. The first of these is normally called natural resource economics and the second environmental economics. After a very brief review of natural resource economics, we introduced the fundamental balance phenomenon, which says that in the long run all materials taken by human beings out of the natural system must eventually end up back in that system. This means that to reduce residuals flows into the environment we must reduce materials taken from the ecosystem, and we discussed the three fundamental ways that this can be done.

We then focussed more directly on the flow of residuals back into the environment, making a distinction among emissions, ambient environmental quality, and damages. The environmental damages from a given quantity of emissions can be very substantially altered by handling these emissions in different ways. Our next step was to provide a brief catalogue of the different types of emissions and pollutants, as well as nonpollution types of environmental impacts such as aesthetic effects. We then covered some ideas about how environmental quality and the output of conventional economic goods are related in the short and long run. Finally, we discussed pollution-control expenditures, comparing them to other cost categories as well as to expenditures in other developed countries. Our conclusion here was that although pollution-control expenditures are not large in comparison to other expenditure categories, they are large enough that we should be concerned about getting the greatest results possible in terms of improvements in environmental policy.

QUESTIONS FOR FURTHER DISCUSSION

1 How does population growth affect the balance of flows shown in Figure 2-1?
2 If all goods could be changed overnight so that they lasted twice as long as before, how would this change the flows of Figure 2-1 in the short and long runs?
3 A given quantity of a residual, discharged at one time and place, can be a pollutant; while if it is discharged at another time or place it may not constitute a pollutant. Why is this true?
4 Why are long-lived, cumulative pollutants so much harder to manage than short-lived, noncumulative pollutants?
5 Consider the visual pollution that is produced when an ugly factory is built in a scenic area; is that a cumulative or noncumulative pollutant? How about the scarred landscape of strip-mined land? Urban trash?

6 What considerations come into play when considering whether Canada or any other political entity is spending the "right" amount for environmental quality improvements?

SELECTED READINGS

Ayres, Robert U. *Resources, Environment and Economics, Applications of the Materials/Energy Balance Principle.* New York: John Wiley and Sons, 1978.

Baumol, William, and Wallace Oates. *Economics, Environmental Policy and the Quality of Life.* Englewood Cliffs, N.J.: Prentice-Hall, 1979.

Enthoven, Alain C., and A. Myrick Freeman III (eds.). *Pollution, Resources and the Environment.* New York: Norton, 1973.

Kneese, Allen V. *Economics of the Environment.* New York: Penguin Books, 1977.

Kneese, Allen V., and Blair T. Bower. *Environmental Quality and Residuals Management.* Baltimore, Md.: Johns Hopkins Press for Resources for the Future, 1979.

Krutilla, John V. "Conservation Reconsidered." *American Economic Review* 57(4) (September 1967): 777–786.

McKee, David L. *Energy, the Environment, and Public Policy: Issues for the 1990s.* New York: Praeger, 1991.

Ophuls, William. *Ecology and the Politics of Scarcity.* San Francisco: W. H. Freeman, 1977.

Organization for Economic Cooperation and Development: *The State of the Environment.* Paris: OECD, 1991.

Pearce, David, Anil Markandya, and Edward B. Barbier. *Blueprint for a Green Economy.* London: Earthscan Publications, 1989.

Wilson, Edward O. "Biodiversity, Prosperity and Value," in F. Herbert Bormann and Stephen R. Kellert (eds.). *Ecology, Economics, Ethics: The Broken Circle.* New Haven, Conn.: Yale University Press, 1991, 3–25.

SECTION **TWO**

ANALYTICAL TOOLS

Scientific analysis consists of giving coherent explanations of relevant events and of showing how other outcomes might have occurred if conditions had been different. It is to show connections among variables and to detail the ways in which they are interrelated. To do this, a science must develop a specialized vocabulary and conceptual structure with which to focus on its chosen subject matter. In this section we cover some of the basic ideas of economics and of their application to environmental matters. Those of you who have already been introduced to microeconomics can treat the next few chapters as a review. For those who are seeing this material for the first time, remember that the purpose is to develop a set of "analytical tools" which we can then use to focus on issues of environmental quality.

3

BENEFITS AND COSTS, SUPPLY AND DEMAND

In this and the next chapter we cover certain basic tools of microeconomics that we use in analyzing environmental impacts and policies. A key aspect of an economic approach to decision making is the evaluation of the benefits and costs of any action. Economic actions, including environmental actions, have two sides: on the one side they create value, and on the other side they encounter costs. We have to measure these costs and benefits and then evaluate the trade-offs that occur from every action. We look first at the question of value, later at costs.

WILLINGNESS TO PAY

The value side of our analysis is based on the fundamental notion that individuals have preferences for goods and services; given a choice they can express preferences for one good over another, or one bundle of goods over another bundle. In a modern economy there are thousands of different goods and services available, so let us focus on just one of them. The value of this good to a person is what they are willing and able to sacrifice for it. Sacrifice what? It could be anything, but it makes most sense to talk about sacrificing generalized purchasing power. Thus, the value of a good to somebody is what they are willing to pay for it. What is it that determines how much a person is willing to pay to obtain some good or service, or some environmental asset? It's partly a question of individual values. Some people are willing to sacrifice a lot to visit the Canadian Rockies, others are not. Some people are willing to pay a lot for a quiet living environment, others are not. Some people place a high value on trying to preserve the habitat of unique animal and plant species, others do not. It is obvious also that a person's wealth affects their willingness to sacrifice; the more wealthy a person is, the better they can afford to pay for various goods and services. Willingness to pay, in other words, also reflects ability to pay.

Let's consider the willingness to pay of a person for a particular good. Assume that the person has none of the good to begin with. We ask her, or perhaps deduce from watching her spend her money, how much she would be willing to pay for a single unit of a good rather than go without. Suppose this is some number, like $38 pictured in the top of Figure 3-1. We then ask, assuming she already has one unit of this good, how much would she be willing to pay for a second unit. According to Figure 3-1 her answer is $28. In similar fashion, her willingness to pay for each additional unit is shown by the height of the rectangle above that unit: $21 for unit 3, $14 for unit 4, and so on. These numbers depict a fundamental relationship of economics: the notion of diminishing willingness to pay. As the number of units consumed increases, the willingness to pay for additional units of that good normally goes down.

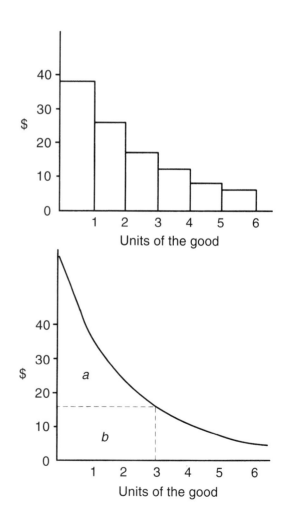

FIGURE 3-1   The Concept of Willingness to Pay.

It is not very convenient to work with diagrams that are stepped-shaped as in the top of Figure 3-1. If we now assume that people can consume fractions of items in addition to integer values (as in, e.g., the number of kilograms of potatoes consumed per week), a smoothly shaped willingness-to-pay curve, like the one pictured in the bottom of Figure 3-1 is obtained. On this smooth function we have singled out one quantity for illustrative purposes. It shows that at a quantity of three units, the willingness to pay for one more unit (the fourth) is $12.

We need to make a distinction here between *total* and *marginal*, since this is something we will be running into constantly in later chapters. Suppose a person is already consuming two units of this good; according to the willingness to pay curve, they would be willing to pay $17 for a third unit. This is the *marginal* willingness to pay, in this case, for the third unit. Marginal is thus a word that describes the *additional* willingness to pay of a person for one more unit. The height of the rectangles show in the top of Figure 3-1, or of the height of the curve in the bottom graph, is the marginal willingness to pay for this good.

The *total* willingness to pay for a given consumption level refers to the total amount a person would be willing to pay to attain that consumption level rather than go without the good entirely. Suppose the person is consuming at a level of three units; their total willingness to pay for consuming this quantity is $81, which is in fact the sum of the heights of the demand rectangles between the origin and the consumption level in question ($38 for the first plus $26 for the second plus $17 for the third, and so on). What this corresponds to in the smooth version of the willingness-to-pay function in the bottom is the whole area under the willingness-to-pay curve from the origin up to the quantity in question. For three units of consumption, the total willingness to pay is equal to an amount represented by the combined areas *a* and *b*.

Demand

There is another way of looking at these marginal willingness-to-pay relationships. They are more familiarly known as *demand curves*. An individual demand curve shows the quantity of a good or service that the individual in question would demand (i.e., purchase and consume) at any particular price. For example, suppose a person whose marginal willingness to pay/demand curve is shown in the bottom part of Figure 3-1 is able to purchase this item at a unit price of $15. The quantity they would demand at this price is three units. The reason is that their marginal willingness to pay for each of the first three units exceeds the purchase price. They would not push their consumption higher than this, since their marginal willingness to pay for additional quantities would be less than the purchase price.

An individual's demand/marginal willingness-to-pay curve for a good or service is a way of summarizing their personal consumption attitudes and capabilities for that good. Thus we would normally expect these relationships to differ somewhat among individuals, because individual tastes and preferences vary. Some individuals are willing to pay more for a given item than other people. People with high incomes have more to spend on goods and services. In Figure 3-2 there are displayed a number of

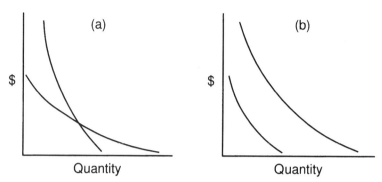

FIGURE 3-2   Typical Demand/Marginal Willingness-to-Pay Curves.

different demand curves. Panel (a) shows two demand curves, one steeper than the other. The steeper one shows a situation where marginal willingness to pay drops off fairly rapidly as the quantity consumed increases; with the other one marginal willingness to pay, though lower to begin with, goes down less rapidly as quantity increases. In panel (b) of Figure 3-2 there are also two demand curves; they have the same general shape, but one is situated well to the right of the other. The demand curve lying above and to the right shows a good for which the marginal willingness to pay is substantially higher than it is for the same quantity of the other good. In each case, the two demand curves could apply to two different people but the same product; or they might picture the case of one person but two different goods.

There is another way of looking at the two demand curves of panel (b), one that may be very important for the application of these ideas to environmental assets. Peoples' tastes depend on a lot of factors of a psychological and historical kind that are hard to pin down and describe but nevertheless real. They will depend in part on the experiences that people have and the information they gather over time about the qualities of different goods and how they feel about them. So, for example, the demand curve to the right could be the same consumer's demand curve for a good for which their appreciation has increased over time. These might be their demand curves for outdoor wilderness experiences, the one to the left applying before they knew much about this type of activity, and the one to the right applying to the situation after they had some wilderness experiences and learned to like them. Other factors are information and psychology; the demand curve on the right might be a person's demand for a food item before an announcement of the presence in it of pesticide residues, the curve on the left being the demand curve after the announcement.

Note that the demand curves are in fact curvilinear lines, rather than straight lines. A straight-line demand relationship would imply a uniform change in the quantity demanded as its price changes. For most goods, however, this is unlikely to be true. Consider water, for example. At low prices and high rates of consumption, studies have shown that relatively small increases in price will lead to substantial reductions in quantity demanded. At high prices and low quantity demanded, however, price increases have a much smaller effect, they produce much smaller reductions in quantity demanded. What this gives us is a demand relationship that is convex to the origin, that is, relatively flat at low prices and steep at higher prices.

Economics is sometimes misunderstood as assuming that people are driven only by thoughts of their own welfare, that they are complete egoists. Since these are individual demand curves, they do indeed summarize the attitudes of single individuals, but this does not imply that individuals make decisions with only themselves in mind. Some people may indeed act this way, but for most there are many other powerful motives that affect their demands for different goods, including altruism toward friends and relatives, feelings of civic virtue toward their communities, a sense of social responsibility toward fellow citizens, and so on. Individual tastes and preferences spring from these factors as well as from more narrow considerations of personal likes and dislikes.

AGGREGATE DEMAND/WILLINGNESS TO PAY

When we examine real-world issues of environmental quality and pollution-control policy, we normally focus our attention on the behaviour of groups of people rather than single individuals. Our interest is in the total, or aggregate, demand/marginal willingness to pay of defined groups of people.

An aggregate demand curve is the summation of a number of individual demand curves. What individuals are involved depends on which particular aggregation we want to look at: the demand of people living in the city of Montreal for brussels sprouts; the demand of people living in Toronto for clean water from Lake Ontario, the demand by people living in the entire country for public parks, and so on. An aggregate demand curve is simply the summation of the demand curves of all the people in the group of interest. The way in which these individual demand curves are summed up depends upon whether the good in question is a private or a public good.

Figure 3-3 depicts a very simple aggregate demand curve for a private good, one in which the "group" consists of only three people. At a price of $8, Person A demands 10 units of this good, while at the same price Person B demands 6 units and Person C demands 8 units of the good. Thus, the aggregate demand curve, pictured to the far right, shows an aggregate demand of 24 units for the price of $8. Note that we are summing these individual demand curves horizontally. Looked at in the other direction, we note that when Person A is consuming 10 units their marginal willingness to pay is $8, while when Persons B and C consume, respectively, at 6 units and 8 units their marginal willingnesses to pay are also $8. On the aggregate level, the marginal willingness to pay is also $8. If we make one more unit available to this aggregate, it must be distributed to Person A, Person B, or Person C, each of whom has a marginal willingness to pay of $8; thus, the aggregate marginal willingness to pay is also $8. At a price of $15, notice that Person B is not willing to buy the good at all. Aggregate demand is therefore only 7 units; the sum of Person A plus Person C's consumption of 4 and 3 units respectively.[1]

---

[1] Demand curves for public goods are examined in Chapter 4.

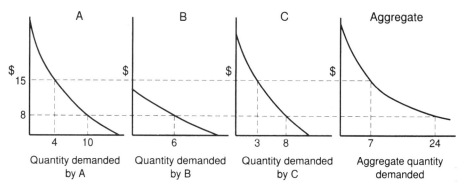

FIGURE 3-3   Aggregate Demand/Marginal Willingness-to-Pay Curves.

BENEFITS

The word "benefits" clearly implies being made better off; if someone is benefited by something, their position is improved, they are made better off. Conversely, if they are made worse off, it must be because benefits were somehow taken away from them. How do we confer benefits on somebody? By giving them something they value. How do we know that they value something? By the fact that they are willing to sacrifice, or willing to pay, for that something. According to this logic, then, the benefits that people get from something are equal to the amount they are willing to pay for that thing.

The logic behind this definition of "benefits" is quite strong. It means we can use ordinary demand curves to determine the benefits of making various things available to people. For example, in Figure 3-4 there are two demand curves shown, and on the horizontal axis two quantity levels are also indicated. Suppose we wish to estimate the total benefits to the two groups of people whose aggregate demand curves these are, of increasing the availability of this item from quantity q_1 to quantity q_2. According to our previous thinking, benefits are measured by willingness to pay, and we know that total willingness to pay is measured by areas under the demand curve, in this case the area under the demand curves between quantity q_1 and quantity q_2. So for the lower demand curve the benefits of such an increase in availability are equal to an amount shown by area b, while benefits in the case of the higher demand curve are equal to the total area $a + b$.

This apparently is as it should be. The people with the higher demand curve must place a greater value on this item; whatever it is, they are willing to pay more for it than are the people whose demand curve is the lower function. This is the fundamental logic underlying much of environmental economics. It underlies, for example, questions of how we place a value on the damage done to people when the natural environment surrounding them is degraded. It underlies the question of how we evaluate the impacts of environmental programs and policies undertaken by local, state and federal governments. This is its strength, the fact that it is based on a clear notion of the value that people place on different things.

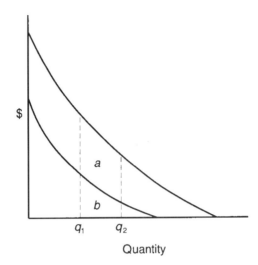

FIGURE 3-4   Willingness to Pay and Benefits.

But we must also recognize its shortcomings. For one thing demand, and therefore benefits, are often very hard to measure when it concerns environmental questions, as we will see in later chapters. For another, we have to remember that demand curves are critically affected by the ability to pay for something as well as preferences. In Figure 3-4, for example, the lower demand curve could represent a group of people with lower incomes than those with the higher demand curve. The logic of our argument would lead us to conclude that the increase in quantity of $q_2 - q_1$ would produce benefits that the lower income people value less than the higher income people. Thus, while the logic of the concept is clear, we have to be careful in using it, especially when we are dealing with groups of people with diverse income levels.

One other possible problem exists in using conventional demand curves to measure benefits. An individual's demand for something is clearly affected by how much they know about it; a person would not be willing to pay for a good if, for example, they were ignorant of its very existence. We don't fully understand many of the impacts that environmental degradation is having; furthermore, peoples' views about the importance of many of these impacts vary due to influences by the media, the scientific press, and so on. In some of these cases, we may want to be cautious about taking peoples' demand curves of the moment, influenced as they are by all kinds of real and imagined factors, as true expressions of the benefits of environmental actions.

COST

We now switch to the other side of the picture and consider costs. Any production process requires a variety of productive inputs—labour, machinery of various descriptions, energy, raw materials, waste handling equipment, and so on. Valuation of these inputs is straightforward for a private firm operating in a market economy: they are valued according to what they cost to procure in the markets for these items. However, a broader concept of cost is required. The costs of production are what could have been produced with productive inputs had they not been used to produce the good in question. The name for this is *opportunity cost*.

Opportunity Cost

The *opportunity* cost of producing something consists of the maximum value of other outputs we could and would have produced had we not used the resources to produce the item in question. The word "maximum" is in there for a reason. Productive inputs used to produce a particular good could have been used to produce a variety of other goods and services. Opportunity costs include out-of-pocket costs but are wider than this. Some inputs that are actually used in production may not get registered as cash costs. For example, people who volunteer their time to clean up trash in parks or on roadsides have an opportunity cost: they could have been working somewhere else at that time for wages. Even more importantly, manufacturing processes may produce waste products that are pumped into the environment. These production residuals produce environmental damage, which are real opportunity costs of producing goods and services, even though they do not show up as costs in a company's profit-and-loss statement.

Opportunity costs are relevant in any situation where a decision must be made about using productive resources for one purpose rather than another. For a public agency with a given budget, the opportunity costs of a particular policy are the value of alternative policies they may have pursued. For a consumer, the opportunity cost of spending time searching for a particular item is the value of the next most valuable thing to which they may have devoted their time.

How do we measure opportunity cost? It's not very useful to measure it in terms of the number of other physical items that could have been produced. Nor do we have enough information in most cases to be able to measure the value of the next best output that was foregone. In practice, therefore, we measure opportunity costs by the value of inputs used up in production. For this to work, we have to take care that the inputs have been correctly valued. If there are any distortions in markets, *shadow prices* will have to be used to measure opportunity costs. Shadow prices measure what the costs would be if markets operated perfectly. For example, volunteer labour must be valued at the going wage rate even though it is not paid in practice. If there are no markets, which may well be the case for many environmental goods, a price must be imputed. The effects on downstream water quality must be evaluated and included. Once all inputs have been accounted for and priced correctly, their total value may be taken as the true opportunity costs of production. This is an extremely important task for environmental economists.

Cost Curves

Cost information can be summarized with cost curves, which are geometric representations of production costs. And, just as in the case with willingness to pay, we will differentiate between *marginal costs* and *total costs*. Consider the cost curves in Figure 3-5. They are meant to apply to a single producing organization, a firm, or perhaps a public agency, that is producing some good or service. The graph is laid out, the same as we had earlier, with quantity on the horizontal axis and a monetary index on the vertical axis. The top panel shows marginal costs in terms of a stepped-shaped relationship. It shows that it costs $5 to produce the first unit of output. If the firm wants to increase output to two units it must spend an added $7. The addition of a third unit would add $10 to total costs, and so on. Marginal cost is a symmetrical measure; it is the added costs, the amount by which total costs increase, when output is increased by one unit. It is also the cost savings if production were to decrease by one unit. Thus, the reduction in output from four to three units would reduce total costs by $15, the marginal cost of the fourth unit.

It is inconvenient to work with stepped-shaped curves, so we make the assumption that the firm can produce intermediate quantities as well as integer values. This gives us a smooth marginal cost curve, as shown in the bottom panel of Figure 3-5. This curve now tells us the marginal cost—the added cost of one more unit of output—for any level of output. For example, at an output level of 4.5 units, marginal cost is $19.

We can use marginal cost curves to determine *total production costs*. On the stepped marginal cost curve of Figure 3-5, suppose we wish to know the total cost of

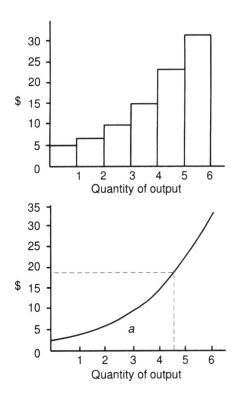

FIGURE 3-5   The Concept of Marginal Cost.

producing five units of this item. This is equal to the cost of the first unit ($5) plus that of the second ($7) plus that of the third ($10), and so on. This total is $60.00; geometrically we can see that it is equal to the total area of the rectangles above the first five units of output. Analogously, in the smoothly shaped marginal cost function in the bottom of the diagram, the total cost of producing a given quantity is the dollar amount equal to the area under the marginal cost curve between the origin and the quantity in question. The total cost of producing 4.5 units of output is thus given by the area marked *a* in the figure.

The Shapes of Cost Curves

The height and shape of the marginal cost curve for any production process will differ from one situation to another. A key determining factor is the technology utilized in production, and we will discuss this concept below. The price of inputs is also an important factor influencing the heights of marginal cost curves. In general, if input prices increase to a firm or group of firms, this will have the effect of shifting their marginal cost curves upward. Another important element is *time*, specifically the amount of time that a firm has to adjust to changes in its rate of output.

A typical short run marginal cost curve for an individual firm is shown in Figure 3-6; initially it declines as output increases but then eventually increases as output gets larger. The initial decline comes about because of basic efficiencies achievable with larger quantities at this level. Suppose our "output" refers to the quantity of wastewater handled in a municipal treatment plant. At very low levels of output the plant is not being fully utilized, thus output increases in this range are accompanied by less than proportionate increases in production cost, given marginal costs that diminish. But as output increases, the capacity of the plant is approached. Machinery must be worked longer, additional people must be hired, etc. Thus, marginal cost begins to increase. As the capacity of the operation is neared, these problems become more acute. To continue to increase output, more extraordinary measures are required, which can only be done at a high cost, thus, marginal cost increases even more. There may come a point

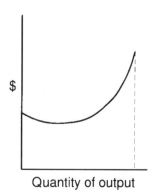

FIGURE 3-6   Typical Marginal Cost Curve.

where it becomes almost impossible to increase output further, which is the same as saying that the marginal costs of production at this point increase without limit.

This marginal cost curve depicts an important generic characteristic of all marginal cost curves, namely, that although they may initially decline, they will always increase, eventually, as output becomes large enough. These increases are related to certain underlying factors such as increased plant utilization, the need to reach farther away for raw materials, the inevitable higher management costs that accompany larger operations, and so on. Virtually all economic studies of particular operations and industries demonstrate eventually increasing marginal production costs, and this fact will be an important shaping element in our later discussions specifically related to environmental quality management.

The marginal cost curve in Figure 3-6 may be interpreted as a short-run or a long-run curve. In the short run, the wastewater treatment plant has a certain capacity that is fixed. In the long run, there is time to build a larger treatment plant with a larger capacity. At high output levels, the marginal costs of the larger plant will typically be lower than those of the smaller plant. But even in these long-run situations, marginal costs will eventually increase. In our subsequent discussions we assume that we are working with long-run marginal cost curves, unless we specify otherwise.

TECHNOLOGY

The most important factor affecting the shapes of marginal cost functions is the technology of the production process. By technology we mean the inherent productive capabilities of the methods and machines being employed. Any modern production requires capital goods (machinery and equipment) of various types and capacities, labour inputs, operating procedures, raw materials, and so on. The quantity of output a firm can get from a given set of inputs depends on the technical and human capabilities inherent in these inputs. Even within the same industry, marginal cost curves can differ among firms. Some firms will be older than others, meaning that they will perhaps be working with older equipment that has different cost characteristics. Even for firms of the same age, different production techniques may be available; past managerial decisions may have put them in different positions in terms of marginal production costs today.

This concept of technology is vitally important in environmental economics because we rely heavily on technological change to find ways to produce goods and services with fewer environmental side effects and also to handle better the quantities of production residuals that remain. In our simple cost model, technical advancement has the effect of shifting marginal cost curves downward. Technological progress makes it possible to produce a given increase in output at a lower marginal cost. It also reduces total production cost. Consider Figure 3-7. MC_1 is the firm's marginal cost curve before a technical improvement; MC_2 is the marginal cost curve after some technical improvement has been put into effect. The technical change, in other words, shifts the marginal cost curve downward. We can determine how much total production costs are reduced as a result of technological change. Consider output level

$q*$. With MC_1 the total cost of producing an output of $q*$ is represented by the area $a + b$, while after the reduction in the marginal cost curve to MC_2, the total cost of producing $q*$ is equal to area b. Thus, the reduction in total cost made possible by the technological change is equal to area a.

Technological change does not normally happen without effort, it normally requires research and development (R&D). R&D in environmental industries is obviously an important activity to promote, and one of the criteria we will need to use to evaluate environmental policies is whether they create incentives for individuals, firms, and industries to engage in vigorous R&D programs. In very simple terms, the incentive to do R&D is the cost savings that result from the new techniques, materials, procedures, etc., that are discovered in the effort. The cost-saving shown in Figure 3-7 (area a) shows part of this incentive. This is the cost savings that would result each year, and it is the accumulation of these annual cost savings that represents the full R&D incentive.

THE EQUIMARGINAL PRINCIPLE

We come now to the discussion of a simple but important economic principle, one that we will use repeatedly in chapters to come. It's called the "equimarginal" principle. To understand it, assume that we have a firm producing a certain product, and that the firm's operation is divided between two different plants. For example, suppose there is a single power company that owns two different generating plants. Each plant produces the same item, so that the total output of the firm is the sum of what

FIGURE 3-7   Technological Improvement.

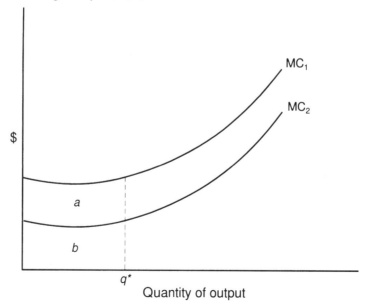

it produces in the two plants. But let us assume that the plants were built at different times and make use of different technology. The old one, plant "A" in Figure 3-8, has older technology; this gives a marginal cost curve that starts relatively low but rises steeply as production increases. The new plant, Plant "B" in Figure 3-8, uses newer technology; it has a higher marginal cost at low output levels, but marginal costs do not rise as steeply as production increases.

Consider now a situation where this two-plant firm wants to produce a total output of, say, 100 units. How many units should it produce in each plant, in order to produce the 100 units at the *least total cost*? Would it be best to produce 50 units in each plant? This is depicted in Figure 3-8; at an output of 50, Plant A has a marginal cost of $12 while Plant B has a marginal cost of $8. Total production costs are the sum of total costs at each plant, or $(a + b + c) + (d)$. But here is the important point: We can lower the total cost of our 100 units by reallocating production. Reduce production in Plant A by one unit; costs will fall by $12. Then increase the production in Plant B by one unit; costs there will rise by $8. We are still producing the 100 units as we have specified, but we have saved $12 – $8 = $4. Thus, our total cost, the sum of the costs in the two plants, has gone down.

As long as the marginal costs in the two plants differ from one another, we can continue to reallocate production—away from the high marginal cost plant—and toward the low marginal cost plant and get a reduction in total cost. In fact, our total costs of producing the 100 units in the two plants will be at a minimum only when the marginal costs of the two plants are equal—hence the "equimarginal principle." In the figure, this happens when the output in Plant A is 38 units and the output in Plant B is 62 units. Total costs in geometric terms are now $a + (d + e)$.

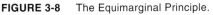 The equimarginal principle, therefore, says the following: If you have multiple sources to produce a given product or achieve a given goal, and you want to mini-

FIGURE 3-8   The Equimarginal Principle.

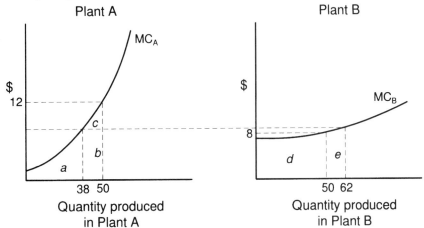

mize the total cost of producing a given quantity of that output, distribute production in such a way as to equalize the marginal costs between the production sources. There is another way of saying it that may look different but actually isn't: If you have a given amount of resources, and you want to maximize the total amount produced, distribute total production among the sources in such a way as to equalize marginal costs. This principle will be very valuable when we take up the issue of getting maximum emissions reductions from given amounts of resources.

MARGINAL COST AND SUPPLY

We will have many occasions to question whether private profit-seeking firms (as well as public, politically minded agencies) will produce the correct quantities of output from the standpoint of society in total, for conventional goods and services and the amount of environmental quality. To address this question we must understand how firms normally determine the quantities they will produce. The marginal cost of production is a key factor in determining the supply behaviour of firms in competitive circumstances. In fact, the marginal cost curve of a firm is its supply curve, showing the quantity of the good the firm would supply at different prices, assuming it can stay in business. Consider Figure 3-9. Assume that the firm with the indicated marginal cost curve is able to sell its output at a price of p^*. The firm will maximize its

FIGURE 3-9   Marginal Cost and Supply.

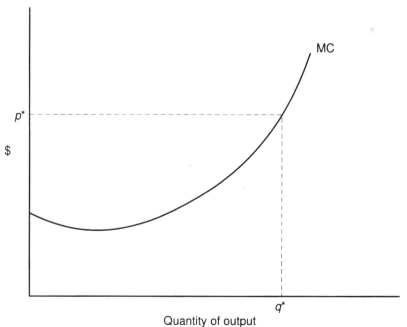

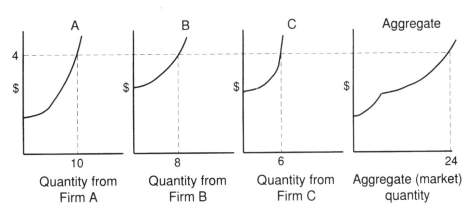

FIGURE 3-10   Deviation of Aggregate (Market) Supply from Individual Firm Supply Curves.

profits by producing that quantity of output where marginal cost is equal to p^*; that level is designated q^*. At any output level less than this, $MC < p^*$, so a firm could increase its profits by increasing output. At any output level above this, $p^* < MC$, so a firm is actually producing items the marginal cost of which is higher than price; in this case, the firm should reduce output if it wishes to maximize its profits.

We are often interested in the supply performance of industries composed of many firms rather than that of individual firms. In this case, the marginal cost/supply curve refers to a collection of firms all producing the same output. This is the concept of *market supply*, analogous to the concept of market demand we discussed previously. The market or aggregate supply curve of a group of firms is the summation of the individual supply curves of all the firms in the group. This is depicted in Figure 3-10. There are three firms, A, B, and C, with marginal cost curves as depicted in the first three panels of the figure. At a common price, say $4, Firm A supplies 10 units, Firm B supplies 8 units, and Firm C supplies 6 units. Thus, the aggregate supply at that price is 24 units, as depicted in the far right panel of Figure 3-10.

SUMMARY

In this chapter we have covered briefly some of the basic tools of microeconomics. The concepts covered were the following:

- Individual willingness to pay, marginal and total
- Individual demand
- Individual benefits, marginal and total
- Aggregate willingness to pay, demand, and benefits
- Opportunity costs
- Marginal and total production costs
- The equimarginal principle

• Supply
• Technological change.

We are going to be relying heavily on these ideas in the chapters to come, especially on the equimarginal principle and on graphs where we will want to jump back and forth between marginal and total measures. When we begin to look at real-world problems of environmental analysis and policy design, it is easy to get swept so far into the countless details that basic economic ideas get lost. It's the fundamental economic building blocks, such as those in this chapter, that allow us to identify the primary economic characteristics of these problems and proceed to develop solutions to them.

QUESTIONS FOR FURTHER DISCUSSION

1 What would happen to a demand curve showing aggregate quantity demanded per month of some good or service, if it became widely expected that the price of this item was going to be very high next year?

2 The logic of equating benefits with willingness to pay could lead us to the conclusion that cleaning the air to which low-income people are exposed would probably create fewer benefits than if it were done for high-income people. Does this undermine the idea of defining benefits as equal to willingness to pay?

3 Figure 3-10 illustrates the derivation of an industry supply curve, under competitive conditions where each firm receives the same price for its output. What is the relationship of this procedure to the equimarginal principle as discussed earlier in the chapter?

4 How do you think the shape of the long-run marginal cost curve for the production of electricity might differ from that of lawn-mowing services? From wastewater treatment plants?

5 For the marginal cost curve in Figure 3-6, draw the *total* cost curve, i.e., the cost curve showing the level of total cost at different rates of output.

6 Suppose that for a certain production process it is technically impossible to increase output beyond a level of 1,000 units per month. What would the marginal cost curve look like if all inputs are free?

SELECTED READINGS

The subjects treated in this chapter, demand, supply, willingness to pay, costs, etc., are treated in most introductory microeconomic texts. The best way to proceed, in order to get a somewhat deeper explanation of these concepts, or a slightly different perspective, is to consult the appropriate chapters of one of these books. Some of the more popular texts are the following:

Baumol, William J., Alan S. Blinder, and William M. Scarth. *Economics, Principles and Policy,* 4th ed. Toronto: Harcourt Brace & Company, Canada, Ltd. 1994.
Blomqvist, Ake, Paul Wonnacott, and Ronald Wonnacott. *Microeconomics*, 6th ed. Toronto: McGraw-Hill Ryerson Limited, 1993.
McConnell, Campbell R., Stanley L. Brue, and Thomas P. Barbiero. *Microeconomics,* 6th ed. Toronto: McGraw-Hill Ryerson Limited, 1993.

Parkin, Michael, and Robin Bade. *Economics: Canada in the Global Environment*, 1st ed. Toronto: Addison-Wesley Publishers Limited, 1991.

Lipsey, Richard G., Douglas D. Purvis, and Peter O. Steiner. *Economics*, 7th ed. New York: Harper Collins Publishers Inc., 1991.

Samuelson, Paul A., and William D. Nordhaus. *Microeconomics*, 6th ed. Toronto: McGraw-Hill Ryerson 1988.

4

ECONOMIC EFFICIENCY
AND MARKETS

In this chapter we do two things. We first develop the notion of economic efficiency, as an index for examining how an economy functions and as a criterion for judging whether it is performing as well as it might. We also discuss the relationship between economic efficiency and economic equity. We then ask the question whether a market system, left to itself, can produce results that are economically efficient. Economic efficiency is a simple idea but one that has much to recommend it as a criterion for evaluating the performance of an economic system or a part of that system. But it has to be used with care. A single firm or group of firms may be judged efficient when examining private costs and benefits from operations. But if we want to evaluate the *social* performance of these firms, we must use the idea of economic efficiency in a wider sense. To do this we must include all the social values and consequences of economic decisions, in particular environmental consequences. We will see that there are cases where a system of private markets will not normally be able to bring about results that are efficient in this wider sense. This will lead into the next chapter, where we will examine the policy question; that is, if the economy is not operating the way we want it to, especially in matters of environmental quality, what kind of public policy might we use to correct the situation?

Economic efficiency is a criterion that can be applied at several levels: to input usage and to the determination of output levels. We concentrate on the second of these because ultimately we want to apply the concept to the "output" of environmental quality. There are two questions of interest: (a) what is the quantity that ought to be produced, and (2) what is the quantity that is produced in fact? The first question deals with the notion of efficiency, the second with the way markets normally function.

ECONOMIC EFFICIENCY

In the preceding chapter we looked at two relationships, that between the quantity of output and willingness to pay, and that between output and marginal production costs. Neither of these two relationships can, by itself, tell us what is the most desirable level of output from society's standpoint. To identify this output level, we must bring these two elements together. The central idea of *economic efficiency* is that there should be a balance between the marginal benefits and marginal costs of production.

Efficiency must also have a reference point. What is "efficient" for one person, in the sense of balancing their costs and benefits, may not be "efficient" for somebody else. We want to have a concept of efficiency that is applicable to the economy as a whole. This means that, when we refer to marginal costs, we must include *all* the costs of producing the particular item in question, no matter to whom they accrue and whether these costs have a market-determined price or not. When we talk about marginal willingness to pay, we must insist that this represents accurately *all* of the value that people in the society place on the item including nonmarket values. This does not necessarily mean that all people will place a value on all goods, it means only that there are no missing sources of value.

How do we identify the rate of output that is socially efficient? We can look at this by bringing together the two relationships discussed in the last chapter. In Figure 4-1, we picture the aggregate marginal willingness-to-pay curve (labelled MWTP) and the aggregate marginal cost curve (MC), for the good in question. The efficient level of production for this item is the quantity identified by the intersection of the two curves, labelled q^e in the figure. At this output level the costs of producing one more unit of this good are just exactly equal to the marginal value of it, as expressed by the marginal willingness-to-pay curve. This common value is p^e.

FIGURE 4-1   The Socially Efficient Rate of Output.

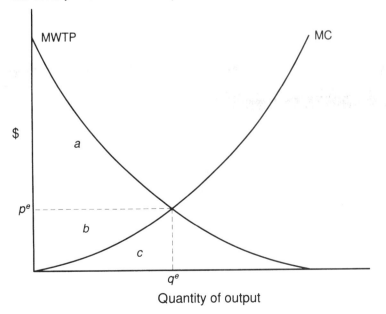

The equality of marginal willingness to pay and marginal production cost is the test for determining if output is at the socially efficient level. There is another way of looking at this notion of efficiency. When a rate of output is at the socially efficient level, the net value, defined as total willingness to pay minus total costs, is as large as possible. In fact, we can measure this net value on the diagram. At q^e we know that the total willingness to pay is equal to an amount corresponding to the area under the marginal willingness-to-pay curve from the origin up to q^e; this area consists of the sum of the three subareas: $a + b + c$. Total cost, on the other hand, consists of the area under the marginal cost curve, or area c. Thus, the surplus is $(a + b + c) - c = a + b$, which is the triangular area enclosed by the marginal willingness-to-pay curve and the marginal cost curve. At any other quantity the corresponding value of total willingness to pay minus total production costs will be less than this area $a + b$.

The models we examine in this book deal with economies at a point in time. While we discuss intertemporal aspects of environmental issues, developing models to explicitly address these effects is beyond the scope of the book. Efficiency in our models is *static efficiency*. That is, it deals with markets and actions at a point in time. *Dynamic efficiency* looks at the allocation of resources over time. While the two concepts both involve equating marginal benefits to marginal costs, dynamic efficiency will be more complex because intertemporal trade-offs involve questions of depletion of environmental capital stocks, irreversibilities, whether or not to discount future values, and so on. We address the issue of discounting in Chapter 6.

EFFICIENCY AND EQUITY

From the standpoint of society at large, production is at an efficient level when marginal benefits equal marginal production costs, that is, when net benefits are maximized, *no matter to whom those net* benefits accrue. Efficiency doesn't distinguish among people. A dollar of net benefits to one person is considered to be worth a dollar to anybody else. The term *Pareto optimality* refers to an equilibrium for which a stronger statement about the well-being of individuals can be made. A Pareto optimal equilibrium is one in which it is impossible to make any person better off without making someone else worse off. An efficient equilibrium is a Pareto optimum, as long as we mean by efficiency that no market failures of any kind exist. And, a Pareto optimum is an efficient equilibrium. We will continue to use the term efficiency to refer to outcomes that equate marginal benefits to marginal costs, recognizing that this equilibrium is also Pareto optimal.

In the real world an equilibrium may be efficient, but there is no explicit market mechanism by which the winners can compensate the losers. This is why the distribution of income and wealth is a concern to economists. An outcome that benefits very rich people at the expense of poor people would be regarded by most people as inequitable. Which is simply another way of saying that an outcome that is efficient in the above sense, need not be equitable in practice.

Equity is tied closely to the distribution of wealth in a society. If this distribution is regarded as essentially fair, then judgments about alternative output levels may justifiably be made using only the efficiency criterion. But if wealth is distributed unfairly, the efficiency criterion by itself may be too narrow. As well, the distribution of income and wealth can have effects on how resources are allocated. Having said this, however, we have to recognize that, in judging economic outcomes, the relative emphasis to be put on efficiency and equity is a matter of controversy. It is controversial in the political arena; it is controversial among economists themselves.

We will have much to say about distributional issues and equity throughout the book. In Chapter 6 we will develop terminology for describing the distributional impacts of environmental policies. And in Chapter 9 we will discuss the role of economic equity as a criterion for evaluating environmental policies.

MARKETS

Having specified what we mean by economic efficiency, we next ask the question, will a market system, a system where the major economic decisions about how much to produce are made by the more-or-less unhindered interaction of buyers and sellers, give us results that are socially efficient? In other words, if we rely entirely on the market to determine how much of this item gets produced, will it settle on q^e?

Why worry about this question? Why not simply jump to the question of public policy? Doesn't this question imply that, at bottom, we are committed to the market system, and isn't this the system that, from an environmental point of view, has gotten us into trouble in the first place? If the market doesn't do the job, maybe we should just ignore whatever the market does, and proceed through political/administrative means to bring about the desired rate of output.

The short answer to this is that, as a nation, we are in fact committed to a market-based economy. For all its faults, a market system will normally give us better economic results, overall, than any other system. Those who doubt this need only look at the environmental horror stories being uncovered in the countries of Eastern Europe following the communist era. Of course, we have to remember that although our system is "market based," we do not necessarily have to accept whatever results it gives us. The results are acceptable only if they are reasonably efficient and equitable. We will find that in the case of environmental quality, market institutions are not likely to give us results that are socially efficient.

The slightly longer answer to the question is that the market system contains within it certain incentive structures that in many cases can be harnessed toward the objective of improved environmental quality. One of these is the cost-minimizing incentive that stems from the competitive process. Another is the incentive provided through the rewards that may be reaped through initiative in finding better, that is, less expensive, technical, and organizational means of production. It will be far more effective in many cases to take advantage of these incentives than to try to do away with them. By altering them so that they take environmental values into account, we can often get more effective results than if we tried to jettison the whole system and adopt a different set of institutions.

A market is an institution where buyers and sellers of consumer goods, of factors of production, etc. carry out mutually agreed-upon exchanges. We normally expect that people, when they buy or sell on a market, are looking for the best terms they can get. Presumably buyers would like to pay a low price while sellers would prefer high prices. What brings all these conflicting objectives into balance is the adjustment of prices on the market. Equilibrium is established where supply is equal to demand. At this intersection, the equilibrium price and quantity produced is determined. This is illustrated in Figure 4-2.

For the market to work effectively there must be competition among sellers and among buyers. None can be large enough that their own performance affects market prices, or powerful enough that they can control how the market performs. Price must be allowed to adjust freely, so that it can "discover" the quantities that bring buyers and sellers into balance. At the quantity q^m there is an equality between the marginal willingness to pay by consumers for an additional unit of the item and the marginal costs of producing the item. These are equal at the value of p^m.

MARKETS AND SOCIAL EFFICIENCY

The next question is, do markets ordinarily produce results that are efficient from the standpoint of society. Compare Figures 4-1 and 4-2. They look the same, but there

FIGURE 4-2   The Market Model.

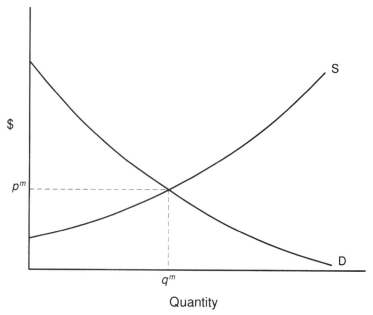

is actually a big difference. The first shows a socially efficient rate of output for a particular item, the second shows the rate of output and price that would prevail on a competitive market for that item. Are these two rates of output, labelled q^e and q^m, likely to be the same in the real world? The answer is yes *if*, and it's a big if, the market demand and supply curves, as pictured in Figure 4-2, are the same as the marginal cost and willingness-to-pay curves as shown in Figure 4-1. And here is the nub of the problem: When environmental values are concerned, there are likely to be very substantial differences between market values and social values. This is called *market failure*, and it will often call for public intervention, either to override the markets directly, or to rearrange things so that they will work more effectively.

In the rest of this chapter we will discuss the performance of markets when matters of environmental quality are involved. There are two phenomena to account for, one on the supply side and the other on the demand side. Environmental effects can drive a wedge between normal market supply curves and true marginal social cost curves. On the other side of the market, environmental effects can create a difference between market demands and true social marginal willingness to pay. On the supply side the problem is "external costs," while on the demand side the problem is "external benefits."

EXTERNAL COSTS

When entrepreneurs in a market economy make decisions about what and how much to produce, they will normally take into account the price of what they will produce and also the cost items for which they will have to pay: labour, raw materials, machinery, energy, and so on. We call these the *private* costs of the firm, they are the costs that show up in the profit-and-loss statement at the end of the year. Any firm, assuming it has the objective of maximizing its profits, will try to keep its production costs as low as possible. This is a worthwhile outcome for both the firm and society because inputs always have opportunity costs; they could have been used to produce something else. Furthermore, firms will be alert to ways of reducing costs when the relative prices of inputs change.

But in many production operations there is another type of cost that, while representing a true cost to society, does not show up in the firm's profit-and-loss statement. These are called *external costs*. They are called "external" because, although they are real costs to some members of society, they will not normally be taken into account by firms when they go about making their decisions about output rates. Another way of saying this is that there are costs that are external to firms but internal to society as a whole.[1]

One of the major types of external cost is the cost inflicted on people through environmental degradation. An example is the easiest way to see this. Suppose a paper

---

[1] External costs are sometimes called "third-party" costs. The first two parties are, respectively, producer and the consumer. So a third-party cost is one that is inflicted on people who are not directly involved in the economic transactions between buyers and sellers. They are also sometimes called "spillover" effects.

mill is located somewhere on the upstream reaches of a river and that, in the course of its operation, it discharges a large amount of wastewater into the river. The wastewater is full of organic matter that arises from the process of converting wood to paper. This waste material gradually is converted to more benign materials by the natural assimilative capacity of the river water but, before that happens, a number of people downstream are affected by the lower quality of water in the river. Perhaps the waterborne residuals reduce the number of fish in the river, affecting downstream fishers. The river may be also less attractive to look at, affecting people who would like to swim or sail on it. Worse, the river water perhaps is used downstream as a source of water for a public water supply system, and the degraded water quality means that the town has to engage in more costly treatment processes before the water can be sent through the water mains. All of these downstream costs are real costs associated with producing paper, just as much as the raw materials, labour, energy, etc., used internally by the plant. But from the mill's standpoint these downstream costs are *external costs*. They are costs that are borne by someone other than the people who make decisions about operating the paper mill. At the end of the year the profit-and-loss statement of the paper mill will contain no reference whatever to these real downstream external costs.

If we are to have rates of output that are socially efficient, decisions about resource use must take into account both types of costs—the private costs of producing paper plus whatever external costs arise from adverse environmental impacts. In terms of full social cost accounting:

Social Costs = Private Costs + External (Environmental) Costs.

This is pictured in Figure 4-3. The top panel shows the relationship between the rate of paper production and the occurrence of these downstream external costs. It shows that the marginal external costs increase as paper production increases. The bottom panel shows several things. It shows the demand curve for paper and the marginal private costs of producing paper. The intersection of these occurs at a price of p^m and a quantity of q^m. This is the price and quantity that would arise on a competitive market where producers pay no attention to external costs. But marginal social costs are in fact higher, as shown, since they contain both the marginal private costs and marginal external costs. Thus, the full socially efficient rate of output is q^*, and the associated price is p^*.

Compare the two rates of output and the two prices. The market output is too high compared to the socially efficient rate of output. And the market price is too low compared to the socially efficient price. It's not hard to understand the reason for this. In considering just its private costs the firm is essentially using a productive input they are not paying for. What is this unpaid input? The services of the river, which provide the firm with a cheap way to dispose of its production residuals. But while it may be cheap for the firm to do this, it may not be cheap to society; in fact, in this case we have costs being inflicted on downstream users that are being overlooked by the

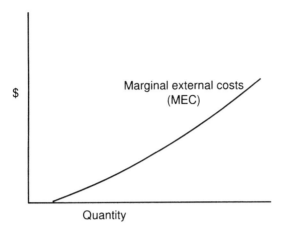

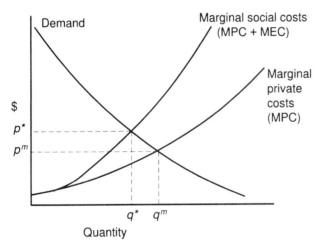

FIGURE 4-3 External Costs and Market Outcomes.

paper mill. So the private market system in this case produces too much paper at too low a price compared to socially efficient results.

Most of the cases of environmental destruction involve external costs of one type or another. Electricity generating plants emit airborne residuals that affect the health of people living downwind. Users of chemicals emit toxic fumes that affect people living in the vicinity. Developers build on land without taking into account the degradation of the visual environment of local inhabitants, and so on. Nor is it only businesses who are responsible for external environmental costs. When individuals drive their automobiles, exhaust gases add to air pollution, and when they dispose of solid waste materials (like old batteries), they may affect the quality of the local environment.

There are many different types of environmental externalities. Most, but not all, are expressed through physical linkages among parties involved, polluter and people damaged. The simplest is where there are just two parties involved—one polluter and one person suffering damages. An upstream pulp mill and a downstream firm that uses the river water in its production operations is an example. There are cases of single polluters and multiple damaged parties, such as a power plant that emits SO_2 affecting a group of community residents living downwind. Other cases involve multiple polluters but only one damaged party, for example, the runoff from many farms that affects the well water of a household. And finally there are many cases where both polluters and parties damaged are many in number, for example, urban air pollution stemming from automobile emissions; each driver is both a producer and a recipient of the externality. The same is true of global phenomena, such as the greenhouse effect.

There are some externalities that do not involve physical linkages. Degradation of the scenic environment through thoughtless land development is an example. And there are some externalities that involve neither physical linkages nor close proximity. People in one part of a country, for example, may feel loss when those in another region cause damage to an important environmental resource, for example, a unique species of animal or plant. This brings up a problem that we will state but not solve. What is the limit, if any, to be placed on external damage that people may legitimately claim? A person may suffer damages when someone in her vicinity plays their stereo too loudly, but can she legitimately claim that she suffers damages if, for example, they adopt a lifestyle with which she doesn't agree? If people in Victoria pollute the waters of their harbours, may residents in Edmonton claim that they have been damaged? If fishers in Newfoundland exhaust the cod stock to support their families, can people in Winnipeg justifiably claim that they have been damaged? The legal doctrine of "standing" is relevant to these situations. A private citizen may bring suit on environmental cases if that person is able to show that he or she is in fact being damaged by the activity in question. Few such suits for environmental damages have been initiated in Canada. For all the hypothetical situations noted above, it would be unlikely that standing would be granted by the courts because it would be difficult to show that individuals in a distant city were damaged. However, a resident of Victoria who operates a tourist business that has been adversely affected by the presence of sewage in Victoria waters would be more likely to be granted standing. These examples bring up a very important point. A person may feel worse off if fish stocks have been depleted or oceans polluted. They might even be willing to pay some amount of money to clean up the oceans or restock the fish. But, they still have no standing in the courts. The legal doctrine of standing is thus incompatible with the economist's use of willingness to pay as a measure of value. Values established through legal cases may not fully represent the value people are willing to pay for environmental quality.

Open-Access Resources

There is one source of external costs that has been widely studied by environmental economists (as well as natural resource economists): the case of open-access resources. An open-access resource is a resource or facility that is open to uncontrolled access by individuals who find it profitable or useful in some way to use the resource. A classic example is an ocean fishery, where anyone willing to buy a boat and take up fishing is free to do so. Other examples are a pasture that is open to anyone to graze their animals, or a forest where anyone may go and cut wood.

In these situations we have, in effect, problems in property rights—their definition, distribution, and/or enforcement. We discuss property rights in detail in Chapter 10. To illustrate the concept of open access and the inefficiencies created, consider the following example. Suppose there are four similar firms situated on a lake. The firms use the water of the lake in producing their output, and discharge emissions back into the lake. Because of the emissions, each firm must treat the water taken from the lake before they use it in production. The treatment costs of each firm depend on the ambient quality of the lake, which of course depends on the total emissions of the four firms. Suppose that the cost of intake water treatment is currently $40,000 per year for each firm. A new firm is contemplating starting operations on the lake. If it adds its untreated emissions to those of the current four, it will make ambient water quality worse and drive up the cost of water treatment for each firm to $60,000 per year. When the fifth firm makes its location and production decisions, it will take into account its various operating costs, which will include the $60,000 per year of water treatment costs. But the total social water-related costs of the firm's decisions are higher. There are also external costs inflicted on the other four firms, amounting to $20,000 each of added water treatment costs if the fifth firm locates on the lake. The social marginal costs of water supply when the new firm locates on the lake are $140,000, consisting of $60,000 internal costs of the new firm plus $80,000 ($20,000 × 4) of external costs inflicted on firms already on the lake. These are often called open-access externalities, because they result from the fact that the firms have uncontrolled access to the lake.

We have focussed on the externalities flowing from the fifth firm's decisions, but everything is symmetrical, in the sense that we could say exactly the same thing about each of the other firms. They will make their decisions without regard to the external costs inflicted on other firms. It is this reciprocal nature of these externalities that distinguishes them from the type we talked about before (e.g., the pulp mill upstream inflicting external costs on people downstream). But the effect is the same: When externalities are involved, market supply curves will understate social marginal production costs. If someone owns a pasture, or a forest, he or she will presumably keep out encroachers, or perhaps charge them for use of the resource or otherwise control their rate of access. But when a resource or facility is open to unrestricted access there is no way of ensuring that its rate of use is kept to the level that will maximize its overall value.

Let us demonstrate the logic of this in a simple way by using the example of a road that is open to access by anyone desiring to use it. A road is not a natural resource, but a person-made facility. But the essence of the uncontrolled-access problem is identical, and it perhaps is easier to understand with this particular example. It uses very simplifying assumptions so that we can highlight the basic issues. There is a road connecting two points, call them Point A and Point B. The figures in Table 4-1 show the average travel time it takes to get from Point A to Point B along this road, as a function of the number of motorists using the road. Thus, for example, if there is just one traveller on the road, it takes 10 minutes to get from A to B (we assume a speed limit that is enforced). Likewise, when there are either two or three motorists on the road the average travel time is still 10 minutes. But when the traffic increases to four travellers, the average travel time increases to 11 minutes. This is because of congestion, cars begin to get in each other's way and average speeds drop. As the number of motorists continues to increase, the congestion increases, thus driving up travel times even more.

Now suppose you are considering using this road to go from A to B, and that there are already five cars using it. Suppose, furthermore, that you have an alternative route that will take you 18 minutes. We assume you know the state of the traffic and the resulting travel times. Since taking the given road will save you 4 minutes over the alternative, your individual decision would be to use the road. But from the standpoint of "society," in this case consisting of you plus all the other motorists on the road, this is not efficient. When you enter the highway on which there are already five cars, the added congestion causes an increase in average travel times of 2 minutes to the people already using the road. Thus, your 4-minute individual saving is offset by added travel costs of 10 minutes (5 cars × 2 minutes per car) on the part of the other motorists, meaning, if we treat all minutes as equally valuable, a net social loss of 6 minutes when you decide to use the road.

TABLE 4-1   TRAVEL TIMES RELATED TO THE
NUMBER OF CARS ON THE ROAD

Number of cars	Average travel time between A and B
1	10
2	10
3	10
4	11
5	12
6	14
7	18
8	24

The problem arises because there is uncontrolled access to the road, and in using it people may inflict external costs on others, in the form of added congestion and higher travel times. The same kind of effect holds when a fisher enters a fishery; in catching a portion of the stock he leaves fewer to be caught by other fishers. When one farmer puts animals on a common pasture, and there are no rules regarding the use of that pasture he or she reduces the forage available to other herds on that pasture. We can see that this is related to the notion of external costs. The added costs that one user of an open-access resource inflicts on other users of that resource are in fact costs that are external to that user, but internal to the whole group of users. When a single individual is making a decision about whether and how much to utilize an open-access resource, they take into account the costs and benefits that impinge on themselves directly. Some might also altruistically take into account the externalities they inflict on others, but most will not. And the result will be, as it was with the road example, a rate of use that is higher than what is called for on grounds of social efficiency.

Thus, when external costs are present, private markets will not normally produce quantities of output that are socially efficient. This market failure may justify public policy to help move the economy towards efficiency. This may be done sometimes by changing rules, such as property rights rules, so that the market will function efficiently. Other cases may call for more direct public intervention. We will take up these matters again in Chapters 10 through 14. We must now move to the demand side of the market and consider another important source of market failure, that of external *benefits*.

EXTERNAL BENEFITS

An external benefit is a benefit that accrues to somebody who is outside, or external, to the decision about consuming or using the good or resource that causes the externality. When the use of an item leads to an external benefit, the market willingness to pay for that item will understate the social willingness to pay. Suppose a quieter lawn mower would provide $50 a year of extra benefits to whomever were to buy it. This is therefore the maximum that person would be willing to pay for this machine. But suppose that person's use of the new lawn mower would create $20 of added benefits to his or her neighbour, because of reduced noise levels in the course of the year. These $20 of benefits to the neighbour are external benefits for the owner of the lawn mower. The owner makes a purchasing decision on the basis of benefits accruing only to himself. Thus, the marginal willingness to pay for a quieter lawn mower is $50, whereas the social marginal benefits (where "society" in this case includes just the owner and neighbour) is $70 (the owner's $50 and the neighbour's $20).

As another example of an external benefit, consider a farmer whose land is on the outskirts of an urban area. The farmer cultivates the land and sells his produce to people in the city. Of course, the farmer's main concern is the income he can derive from the operation, and he makes decisions about inputs and outputs according to their effect on that income. But the land kept in agriculture produces several other bene-fits, including habitat for birds and other small animals, and scenic values for passers-by. These benefits, while internal from the standpoint of society, are exter-nal from the standpoint of the farmer. They don't appear anywhere in his profit-and-loss position; they are external benefits of his farming decisions. In this case the agri-cultural value of the land to the farmer understates the social willingness to pay to have the land in agriculture.

When economists discuss the rudiments of supply and demand, we usually use as examples very simple goods that do not have external benefits. Farmers produce and supply so many million apples per year. Individual and market demand curves for apples are easy to comprehend. If we want to know the total number of apples bought, we can simply add up the number bought by each person in the market. Each person's consumption affects no one else. In this case the market demand curve will represent accurately the aggregate marginal willingness to pay of consumers for apples. But in cases involving external benefits, this no longer holds. We can see this by consider-ing a type of good that inherently involves large-scale external benefits, what econ-omists have come to call "public goods."

Public Goods

Consider the provision of national defence services. Once the defence system with all its hardware and people are in place, everyone in the country receives the service. Once the services are made available to one person, others cannot be excluded from making use of the same services. This is the distinguishing characteristic of a *public good*. It is a good which, if made available to one person, automatically becomes available to others.

Another example of a public good is clean air. If the air around a city is free of serious contaminants, anyone in the city can breathe the air without diminishing its availability to all other people within the city. Note carefully that it is not the own-ership of the supplying organization that makes a public good public. Although our two examples require government involvement, a public good is distinguished by the technical nature of the good, not by the type of organization making it available. For example, radio signals are free to anyone with a receiver. But most radio stations are privately owned.

We are interested in public goods because environmental quality is essentially a public good. If the quantity of stratospheric ozone is increased, everyone worldwide benefits. Private markets are likely to undersupply public goods, relative to efficient levels. To see why, let's take another very simple example: a small freshwater lake on the shores of which there are three occupied homes. The people living in the houses use the lake for recreational purposes but, unfortunately, the water quality of the lake has been contaminated by an old industrial plant that has since closed. The contaminant is measured in parts per million (ppm). At present the lake contains 5 ppm of this contaminant. It is possible to clean the water by using a fairly expensive treatment process. Each of the surrounding homeowners is willing to pay a certain amount to have the water quality improved. Table 4-2 shows these individual marginal willingnesses to pay for integer values of water quality. It also shows the total marginal willingness to pay, which is the sum of the individual values.

The table also shows the marginal cost of cleaning up the lake, again just for integer values of water quality. Note that we have increasing marginal cost, as the lake becomes cleaner the marginal cost of continued improvement increases. Marginal cost and aggregate marginal willingness to pay are equal at a water quality of 2 ppm. At levels less than this (higher ppm), aggregate marginal willingness to pay for a cleaner lake exceeds the marginal cost of achieving it, hence from the standpoint of these three homeowners together, improved water quality is desirable. But at quality levels better than 2 ppm, total willingness to pay falls below marginal costs. Thus 2 ppm is the socially efficient level of water quality in the lake.

This is depicted graphically in Figure 4-4. The three top panels show the marginal willingness to pay by each of the three homeowners. When we summed individual demand curves for private goods, we could add together the individual quantities demanded at each price to get the aggregate quantity demanded. But with a public good people are, in effect, consuming the same units, so we must add together the individual marginal willingnesses to pay at each quantity to get the aggregate demand function. This is depicted in Figure 4-4. At a water quality level of 3 ppm, for example, the marginal willingnesses to pay are, respectively, $85, $30, and $20 for individuals A, B, and C. Thus the total marginal willingness to pay at this level of water quality is $135. The bottom panel of the graph shows the aggregate marginal willingness-to-pay/demand function labelled D, the marginal cost function (MC), and the efficient level of water quality.

Having identified the efficient level of water quality, could we rely on a competitive market system, where entrepreneurs are on the alert for new profit opportunities, to get the contaminant in the lake reduced to that level? Suppose a private firm attempts to sell its services to the three homeowners. The firm goes to person A and tries to collect an amount equal to that person's true willingness to pay. But that person will presumably realize that once the lake is cleaned up, it's cleaned up for everybody no matter how much they actually contributed. And so A may have the incen-

TABLE 4-2   INDIVIDUAL AND AGGREGATE DEMAND FOR LOWERING LAKE POLLUTION

| Level of Contaminant (ppm) | Marginal willingness to pay ($ per year) | | | | Marginal cost of cleanup |
	Homeowner A	Homeowner B	Homeowner C	Total	
4	110	60	30	200	50
3	85	30	20	140	65
2	70	10	15	95	95
1	55	0	10	65	150
0	45	0	5	50	240

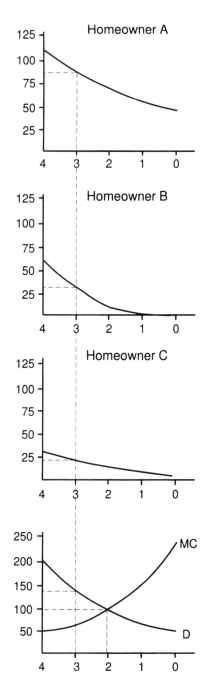

FIGURE 4-4   Aggregate Willingness to Pay for a Public Good.

tive to underpay, relative to their true willingness to pay, in the hopes that the other homeowners will contribute enough to cover the costs of the cleanup. But, of course, the others may react in the same way. When a public good is involved, each person may have an incentive to "free ride" on the efforts of others. A free rider is a person who pays less for a good than her/his true marginal willingness to pay, a person who underpays, that is, relative to the benefits they receive.

Free riding is a ubiquitous phenomenon in the world of public goods, or in fact any good the consumption of which produces external benefits. Because of the free-riding impulse, private, profit-motivated firms will have difficulty covering their costs if they go into the business of supplying public goods.[2] Private firms will be unable to determine a person's true willingness to pay for the public good. Thus, private firms will normally *undersupply* goods and services of this type, if they can supply the good or service at all. Environmental quality improvements are essentially public goods. Since we cannot rely on the market system to provide efficient quantities of "goods" of this type, we must fall back on some type of nonmarket institution involving collective action of one type or another. In the lake example, the homeowners may be able to act collectively, perhaps through a homeowner association, to secure contributions for cleaning up the lake. Of course, the free-rider problem will still exist even for the homeowner's association, but if there are not too many of them, personal acquaintance and the operation of moral pressure may be strong enough to overcome the problem. When there are many thousands or millions of people, however, as there usually are in most environmental issues, the free-rider problem may be handled effectively only with more direct collective action through a governmental body that has taxing power. It is not that we wish completely to replace market processes in these cases. What we want to do is add sufficient public oversight to the market system that we do finally end up with efficient levels of environmental quality that are equitably distributed. We will take a closer look at these questions in the next chapter.

SUMMARY

Our main goal in this chapter was to apply the market model to situations where environmental quality is an issue. Markets are places where buyers and sellers interact over the quantities and prices of particular goods or services. The intersection of supply and demand curves shows the unique quantity and price that can simultaneously satisfy both buyers and sellers. This we called the "efficient" level of output, since it was the only output level where marginal willingness to pay is equal to marginal costs of production.

We then discussed two main reasons why, when environmental quality issues are involved, market prices and quantities will not be fully efficient from a social stand-

---

[2] This sentence emphasizes the point made earlier: It is the technical nature of the good that makes it a public or private good, not whether the organization providing it is public or private. A lighthouse (a public good) might be operated by a private firm; insurance (a private good) might be provided by a public agency.

point. The primary reasons for this, on a conceptual level, are the existence of external costs and external benefits. In matters of the environment, external costs are the damages that people experience from environmental impacts that are not taken into account by the firms, public agencies, or consumers whose decisions produce them. A classic case is water pollution from an upstream pulp mill that damages people using the water downstream. Another important case is the external costs that users of an open-access resource inflict upon one another through uncontrolled use of the resource. External benefits are benefits accruing to people other than the direct buyers or recipients of a good. The classic case of external benefits is what are called public goods; these are goods or services which, when they are made available to one person, automatically become available to others.

Faced with external costs and benefits, public goods, and open-access resources, markets cannot be relied upon to supply efficient levels of environmental quality. Public environmental policies are called upon to rectify these market failures.

QUESTIONS FOR FURTHER DISCUSSION

1 Below are portions of the demand curves of three individuals for air quality in their neighbourhood. Air quality (integer values only) is measured in terms of $\mu g/m^3$ (micrograms of SO_2 per cubic metre of air). If the marginal cost of reducing ambient SO_2 is \$40 per $\mu g/m^3$, what is the socially efficient level of air quality, assuming that "society" in this case consists of just these three people?

Costs of sulfur removal (dollars per µg/m³)	Quantity demanded			Price of orange juice (cents per mL)
	A	B	C	
60	1,400	1,200	1,500	0
50	1,300	1,100	1,400	10
40	1,200	1,000	1,300	20
30	1,100	900	1,200	30
20	1,000	800	1,100	40
10	900	700	1,000	50
0	800	600	900	60

2 Suppose that Question 1 referred not to air quality but to ounces of orange juice demanded per year by the three individuals. In this case the price refers to cents per mL. Suppose the marginal cost of orange juice production is 40¢. What is the efficient aggregate level of orange juice production for these three people?

3 Considering the definition of public goods given in the chapter, are movie theatres public goods? Public telephones? Ski-hills?

4 It is easy to see why pulp-mill emissions may produce external costs, but what about loud radio music played by your neighbour? Your neighbour painting her house a colour you can't stand? Your neighbour watching a film that offends your values?

5 In the discussion of equity considerations we talked about wealth distributions as being fair or unfair, whereas one often hears such discussions carried out in terms of distributions that are equal or unequal. What is the difference?

6 What is the relationship between public goods and open-access resources?

7 Consider the example of the three homeowners around the lake. Suppose the lake was cleaned up to the efficient level, and that the total costs of this are shared equally among the homeowners (stick to integer values here). Will all three homeowners be better off? What problems does this bring up about sharing the costs of public goods?

SELECTED READINGS

The same comment is relevant here as appeared in the bibliography of the last chapter: consult the appropriate chapters of one of the popular microeconomics texts. In the present case you want to look specifically for "efficiency" and market failures in the face of externalities, public goods, and common-property resources. The best-known texts are:

Baumol, William J., Alan S. Blinder, and William M. Scarth. *Economics, Principles and Policy*, 4th ed. Toronto: Harcourt Brace & Company, Canada, Ltd. 1994.

Blomqvist, Ake, Paul Wonnacott, and Ronald Wonnacott. *Microeconomics,* 4th ed. Toronto: McGraw-Hill Ryerson Limited, 1994.

McConnell, Campbell R., Stanley L. Brue, and Thomas P. Barbiero. *Microeconomics*, 6th ed. Toronto: McGraw-Hill Ryerson Limited, 1993.

Parkin, Michael, and Robin Bade. *Economics: Canada in the Global Environment*, 1st ed. Toronto: Addison-Wesley Publishers Limited, 1991.

Lipsey, Richard G., Douglas D. Purvis, and Peter O. Steiner. *Economics*, 7th ed. New York: Harper Collins Publishers Inc., 1991.

Samuelson, Paul A., and William D. Nordhaus. *Microeconomics*, 6th ed. Toronto: McGraw-Hill Ryerson, 1988.

5

THE ECONOMICS OF
ENVIRONMENTAL QUALITY

In the preceding chapter we concluded that the market system, left to itself, will likely malfunction to some extent when matters of environmental pollution are involved. That is to say, it will not normally produce results that are socially efficient. Social efficiency is a *normative* concept in economics. It is a statement of what "ought to be." The determination of public policies to deal with environmental problems is another example of normative economics. If we don't like the fact that certain results occur in the economic real world, how should we change them? An example of a normative policy question is if our objective is to reduce the amount of SO_2 in the air, how should we go about doing so? *Positive economics* is the study of how events actually occur in the real world, how various outcomes come to pass. The quantity of output that actually occurs on a market, and its price, are matters of positive economics. This also includes questions like how much sulfur dioxide (SO_2) actually is produced from a group of power plants, how these are related to the fuel choices made by the utilities, and so on.

There are several normative policy problems to address. First is that of identifying the most appropriate level of environmental quality we ought to try to achieve. The second question is, how should we divide up the task of meeting environmental quality goals? If we have many polluters, how should we seek to allocate among them an overall reduction in emissions? Thirdly, we need to address the question of how the benefits and costs of environmental programs are distributed across society and whether this distribution is appropriate. In this chapter we take these issues up on a conceptual basis; in subsequent chapters we will look at specific policy alternatives.

Before developing our simple policy model we should stress again that effective public policy depends on good information on how economic and environmental systems actually work. We might call this the scientific basis of environmental policy: the study of how firms and consumers normally make decisions in the market economy, how residuals are emitted into the natural environment, and the ways in which these residuals behave in that environment to produce human and nonhuman damages. Thousands of scientists have worked on these issues, and continue to work to clarify these diverse linkages. Great effort will continue to be needed to expand the scientific base on which to develop environmental policy.

POLLUTION CONTROL—A GENERAL MODEL

Diverse types of environmental pollutants obviously call for diverse types of public policy, but in order to build up the required policy analyses we must start with a very simple model that lays out the fundamentals of the policy situation. The essence of the model consists of a simple trade-off situation that characterizes all pollution-control activities. On the one hand, reducing emissions reduces the damages that people suffer from environmental pollution; on the other hand, reducing emissions takes resources that could have been used in some other way.

To depict this trade-off consider a simple situation where a firm (e.g., a pulp mill) is emitting production residuals into a river. As these residuals are carried downstream, they tend to be transformed into less damaging chemical constituents, but before that process is completed the river passes by a large metropolitan area. The people of the area use the waters of the river for various purposes, including recreation (boating, fishing) and as a source for the municipal water supply system. When the river becomes polluted with industrial waste, the people downstream are damaged by the disruption of these and other services provided by the river. One side of the trade-off, then, is the damages that people experience when the environment is degraded.

Upstream, the offending pulp mill could reduce the amount of effluent put in the river, by treating its wastes before discharge, as well as by recycling certain materials that currently just run out the discharge pipe. This act of reducing, or abating, some portion of its wastes will require resources of some amount, the costs of which will affect the price of the paper it produces.[1] These abatement costs are the other side of the basic pollution-control trade-off.

Pollution Damages

By "damages" we mean all the negative impacts that users of the environment experience as a result of the degradation of that environment. These negative impacts are of many types and will of course vary from one environmental asset to another. In the river pollution example damages were to recreators, who could no longer use the river or who suffered a higher chance of picking up waterborne diseases, and to all the city dwellers who had to pay more to treat the water before they could put it into the public water mains. Air pollution produces damage through its impacts on human

---

[1] The word "resources" has a double meaning in economics. On the one hand it is a short-hand way of referring to "natural resources." More generally, it sometimes is used to refer to the inputs that are utilized to produce outputs.

health. Excess deaths from diseases such as lung cancer, chronic bronchitis, and emphysema are related to elevated levels of various pollutants, such as sulfur dioxide, asbestos fibres, and radon emissions. Air pollution can cause damages through the degradation of materials (all of the important outdoor sculpture from Renaissance Florence has had to be put inside to protect it from air pollution), and the deterioration of the visual environment. Besides damage to human beings, environmental destruction can have important impacts on various elements of the nonhuman ecosystem. Some of these, such as destruction of genetic information in plant and animal species driven to extinction, will ultimately have important implications for humans. Estimating environmental damages is one of the primary tasks facing environmental scientists and economists, and we will devote Chapter 7 to a discussion of this problem.

In general, the greater the pollution, the greater the damages it produces. To describe the relationship between pollution and damage, we will use the idea of a *damage function*. A damage function shows the relationship between the quantity of a residual and the damage that residual causes. We can distinguish *emission damage functions*, which show the relationship between the quantity of a residual emitted from a particular source or sources and the resulting damages, and *ambient damage functions*, which show how damages are related to the concentration of a residual contained in the ambient environment. Our primary graphical approach will be the *marginal damage function*, which shows the change in damages stemming from a unit change in emissions or ambient concentration. We can also use these to discuss total damages, since we know that, geometrically, the area under the marginal damage function is equal to total damages.

Several marginal damage functions are depicted in Figure 5-1. The top two are marginal emission damage functions; the horizontal axes measure the quantity of an effluent emitted into the environment during some specified period of time. The exact units (kilograms, tonnes, etc.) in any particular case depends on the specific pollutant involved. The vertical axes measure environmental damages. In physical terms, environmental damage can include many types of impacts: miles of coastline polluted, numbers of people contracting lung disease, numbers of animals wiped out, quantities of water contaminated, and so on. Every case of environmental pollution normally involves multiple types of impacts, the nature of which will depend on the pollutant involved and the time and place where it is emitted. To consider these impacts comprehensively we need to be able to aggregate them into a single dimension. For this purpose we use a monetary scale. It is sometimes easy to express damage in monetary units, for example, the "defensive" expenditures that people make to protect themselves against pollution (e.g., heavier insulation to protect against noise). But usually it is very difficult, as we will see below.

The marginal emission damage function in panel (a) of Figure 5-1 shows marginal damages increasing only modestly at the beginning but more rapidly as emissions get larger and larger. Work by environmental scientists and economists seems to suggest that this is a typical shape for many types of pollutants, though probably not for all of them. At low levels of emissions marginal damages may be comparatively small;

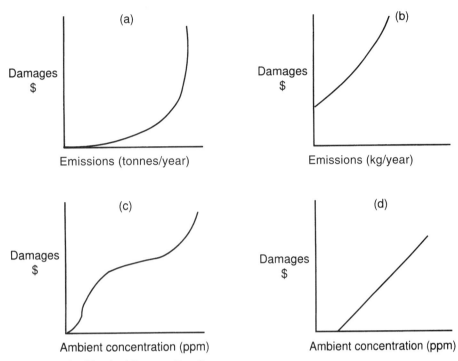

FIGURE 5-1   Representative Marginal Damage Functions.

ambient concentrations are so modest that only the most sensitive people in the population are affected. But when emission levels go higher, damages mount and at still higher levels of emissions, marginal damages become very elevated as environmental impacts become widespread and intense.

Panel (b) shows a marginal (emission) damage function that has the same general shape as panel (a) (i.e., it shows increasing marginal damage), but it begins much higher on the vertical axis and rises more sharply. It might represent a toxic substance that has a deadly effect even at very low levels of emission.

The two bottom relationships in Figure 5-1 are marginal ambient damage functions. While the vertical axes have a monetary index of damages, the horizontal axes have an index of ambient concentration, such as parts per million (ppm). Panel (c) shows a complicated function that increases at low concentrations, then tends to level off until much higher concentrations are reached, after which damages increase rapidly. This might apply, for example, to an air pollutant that causes marked damages among particularly sensitive members of society at relatively low concentrations, and among all people at very high concentrations, while in the middle ranges marginal damages do not increase rapidly. Panel (d) demonstrates an ambient marginal damage function that begins to the right of the origin and then increases linearly with ambient concentration.

Panels (a) and (d) show a characteristic that is in fact quite controversial. They have *thresholds*, that is, values of emissions or ambient concentrations below which marginal damages are zero. Thus, the pollutant can increase to these threshold levels without causing any increase in damages. As we will see in chapters to come, the assumed existence or nonexistence of a threshold in the damage functions for particular pollutants has had important impacts on real-world environmental control policies. There have been long, vigorous arguments about whether the damage functions of certain types of pollutants do or do not have thresholds.

We need to look deeper into the concept of the damage function because we will want to use it to express and analyze a variety of different types of pollution problems and public policy approaches. The analysis in the remainder of the chapter could be done either with ambient functions or emissions functions. We have chosen emissions relationships because we think it is easier to use these when we come to pollution control from particular sources of emissions. Accordingly, Figure 5-2 shows two marginal emissions damage functions. It is important to remember that, like the demand and supply curves we discussed earlier, these are time specific; they show the emissions and the marginal damages for a particular period of time. There are a couple of ways of thinking about this. One is to assume, for purposes of simplicity, that we have a strictly noncumulative pollutant. Thus, all damages occur in the same

FIGURE 5-2   Anatomy of a Marginal Damage Function.

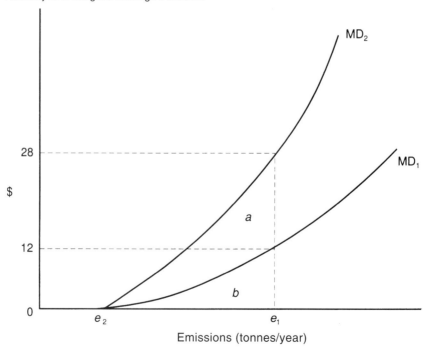

period as emissions. A somewhat more complicated assumption is that, for a pollutant that accumulates over time, the damage function shows the total value that people place on current and future damages. In Chapter 6 we will discuss the concept more fully.

Consider first just one of the marginal damage functions, say the lower one labelled MD_1. In previous chapters we discussed the relationship between marginal and total quantities, for example the relationship between marginal and total costs. We have the same relationship here. The height of the marginal damage curve shows how much total damages would change if there is a small change in the quantity of emissions. When the effluent level is at the point marked e_1, for example, marginal damages are $12. That is to say, if emissions were to increase by one tonne from point e_1, the damages experienced by people exposed to those emissions would increase by $12; by the same token, if emissions decreased by a small amount at point e_1, total damages would be reduced by $12. Since the height of the curve, as measured on the y-axis, shows marginal damages, the area under the curve between the point where it is zero and some other point, like the one labelled e_1, shows the total damages associated with that level of emissions. In the case of marginal damage function MD_1 and point e_1, total damages are equal to the monetary amount expressed by the triangular area bounded by the x-axis, the curve MD_1, and the effluent quantity e_1. That is area b in Figure 5-2. At this emission level the total damages that would occur if the damage function was MD_2 would be a sum equal to the area under MD_2, in this case $(a + b)$.

What factors might account for the difference between MD_1 and MD_2 in Figure 5-2? Let us assume that they apply to the same pollutant. We note that the one labelled MD_2 lies above MD_1, thus for any given level of emissions, marginal damages are higher for MD_2 than for MD_1. At emission level e_1, for example, a small increase in effluent would increase damages by $12 if the marginal damage function were MD_1 but by $28 if it is MD_2. Remember that any damage function shows the impacts of emitting a particular effluent in a particular time and place, so one possible explanation might be that MD_2 refers to a situation where there are many people who are impacted by a pollutant, like a large urban area, while MD_1 refers to a more sparsely populated rural area; fewer people, smaller damage. One major factor that moves damage functions upwards, in other words, is an increase in the number of people exposed to a particular pollutant.

Another possibility that might offer an explanation of why one marginal damage function lies above another is that, although they apply to the same group of people, they refer to different time periods. Damage results from ambient pollution, while what we have on the horizontal axis is quantity of emissions. The thing that connects these two factors is the functioning of the environment itself. Suppose the pollutant in question is some sort of material emitted into the air by industrial firms located near an urban area and that the damage functions refer to impacts felt by people living in that area. Marginal damage function MD_2 might be the situation when there is a temperature inversion that traps the pollutant over the city and produces relatively high ambient concentrations. MD_1 would be the damage function, on the other hand, when normal wind patterns prevail so that most of the effluent is blown downwind and out of the area. Thus the same emission levels at two different times could yield substantially different damage levels owing to the workings of the natural environment.

Having considered the concept of damages we must now look at the other side of the trade-off relationship mentioned above. It is tempting not to do this, to conclude instead that the damage functions themselves give us all the information we need to make decisions about pollution control. One might be tempted to say, for example, that society ought to strive for emission levels around point e_1, where marginal damages are zero, or perhaps even the origin, corresponding to a point where emissions are zero. There may be certain pollutants and situations where the efficient level of emissions is indeed zero. But to determine this we have to look at the other side of the problem: abatement costs.

Abatement Costs

Abatement costs are the costs of reducing the quantity of residuals being emitted into the environment, or of lowering ambient concentrations. Think of the pulp mill located upstream. In its normal course of operation it produces a large quantity of organic wastes. On the assumption that it has free access to the river, the cheapest way to get rid of these wastes is simply to pump them into the river. But technological and managerial means normally exist for the firm to reduce these emissions. The costs of engaging in these activities are called "abatement costs" because they are the costs of abating, or reducing, the quantity of residuals put in the river. These costs will differ from one type of effluent to another. The costs of reducing emissions of SO_2 from electric power plants will obviously be different from the costs of reducing, say, toxic fumes from chemical plants. Even for sources producing the same type of effluent the costs of abatement are likely to be different because of differences in the technological features of the operation. One source may be relatively new, using modern production technology, while another may be an old one using more highly polluting technology. In the discussion that follows keep in mind that "abatement" is used with the widest possible connotation and includes all the many ways there are of reducing emissions: changes in production technology, input switching, residuals recycling, treatment, abandonment of a site, etc.

As is our habit, we will represent this idea graphically. As usual also, it is more convenient to work with marginal abatement costs than with total abatement costs. The units on the axes are the same as before: quantities of pollutants on the horizontal axis and monetary value on the vertical axis. Marginal emission abatement costs show the added costs of achieving a one-unit decrease in emission level, or alternatively the costs saved if emissions are increased by a unit. On the horizontal axis, marginal abatement cost curves originate at the uncontrolled emission levels, that is, emission levels prior to undertaking any abatement activities. In general they slope upward to the left, depicting rising marginal abatement costs.[2]

---

[2] In Chapter 3, we showed marginal cost curves sloping upward to the right. The graph goes in the opposite direction because here the thing we are producing is *reductions* in emissions.

Figure 5-3 shows three alternative marginal abatement cost functions. The one in panel (a) depicts marginal abatement costs rising very modestly as emissions are first reduced, but then rising very rapidly as emissions become relatively small. Panel (b) shows marginal abatement costs that rise rapidly from the beginning. Panel (c) shows a marginal abatement cost curve that has an initial declining phase, followed by increasing values. This might characterize a situation where small reductions can only be handled with technical means that require substantial initial investment. For somewhat larger reductions the marginal costs may actually decline as it becomes possible to utilize these techniques more fully. Ultimately, however, marginal abatement costs increase. We have to keep in mind that in dealing with abatement costs we are dealing with a cost concept similar to that discussed in Chapter 3. The level of costs encountered when carrying out any particular task depends on the technology that one has available to do the task and also on the managerial skills that are applied to the job. It is quite possible to suffer extremely high abatement costs if the wrong technology is used or if what is available is used incorrectly.

To investigate more deeply the concept of marginal abatement cost, consider Figure 5-4, which shows two marginal abatement cost curves. For the moment we focus on the higher one, labelled MAC_2. It begins at an effluent level marked $\bar{e}$, the uncontrolled emission level. From there it slopes upward to the left. Beginning at the uncontrolled level, the first units of emission reduction can be achieved with a relatively low marginal cost. Think again of the pulp mill. This first small decrease might be obtained with the addition of a modest settling pond. But as emission levels are reduced further the marginal cost of achieving additional reductions increases. For example, to get a 30–40 percent reduction the pulp mill may have to invest in new technology that is more efficient in terms of water use. A 60–70 percent reduction in effluent might require substantial new treatment technology in addition to all the steps taken previously, while a 90–95 percent reduction might take very costly equipment for recycling virtually all of the production residuals produced in the plant. Thus the larger the reduction in emissions, the greater the marginal costs of producing further

FIGURE 5-3   Representative Marginal Abatement Cost Functions.

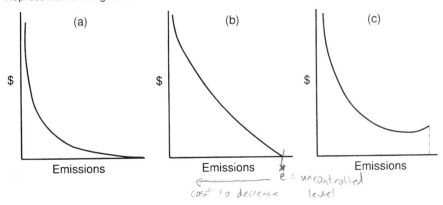

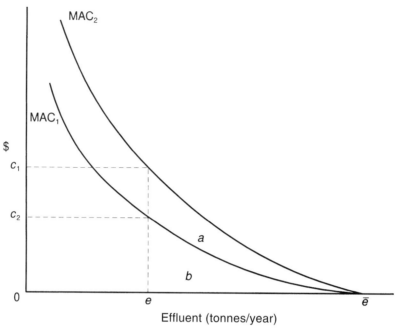

FIGURE 5-4   Anatomy of a Marginal Abatement Cost Curve.

reductions. This yields a marginal abatement cost function which gets steeper in slope as emissions are reduced.

Of course, there is an upper limit on these abatement costs. The extreme option for a single plant or pollution source is to cease operations, thereby achieving a zero level of emissions. The costs of doing this depend on circumstances. If the source was just one small plant within a large industry consisting of many such plants, the costs of actually closing it down may not be that great. In fact it may have very little impact on, say, the price to consumers of whatever is being produced (paper in the pulp mill example), though the local impact on jobs and community welfare may be substantial. But if we are talking about the marginal abatement costs for an entire industry, electric power production in Ontario, for example, the "shut-down" option, as a way of achieving zero emissions, would have enormous costs.

As with any marginal graph, we can depict not only marginal but also total values. If emissions are currently at e tonnes per year, the value on the vertical axis shows the marginal cost of achieving one more unit of emission reduction. The area under the marginal abatement cost curve, between its origin at point and any particular emission level, is equal to the total costs of abating emissions to that level. For example, with the curve labelled MAC_2, the total abatement cost of achieving an emission level of e tonnes per year is equal to the area under the curve between e and $\bar{e}$; the area $a + b$; remember we are reading the graph from right to left.

Consider now the other marginal abatement cost curve shown in Figure 5-4, labelled MAC_1. Its main feature is that it lies below MAC_2, meaning that it corresponds to a situation where the marginal abatement costs, for any level of emissions, are lower than in the case of MAC_2. At e tonnes per year of emissions, for example, the marginal costs of abating an extra ton are only c_2 in the case of MAC_1, which are substantially lower than the marginal abatement costs of MAC_2 at this point. What could account for the difference? Let us assume that we are dealing with the same pollutant in each case. One possibility is that these apply to different sources, say a plant that was built many years ago and another that was built more recently, and uses different production technology. The newer plant lends itself to less costly emissions reduction.

Another possibility is that MAC_1 and MAC_2 relate to the same pollutant and the same source, but at different times. The lower one represents the situation after a new pollution control technology has been developed, while the upper one applies before the change. Technological change, in other words, results in a lowering of the marginal abatement cost curve for a given pollutant. We can measure the annual cost that this source would save if it emitted at a rate e before and after the change. Before the firm adopted the new technology, its total abatement cost of achieving effluent level e was equal to $(a + b)$ per year, while after the change the total abatement costs are b per year. The annual cost savings from the technological change is thus a. This type of analysis will be important when we examine different types of pollution-control policies, because one of the criteria we will want to use to evaluate these policies is how much cost-saving incentive they offer to firms to engage in research and development to produce new pollution-control technologies.

Aggregate Marginal Abatement Costs

Our discussion of the last few pages has treated the marginal abatement cost function as something applying to a single firm, for example a single pulp mill on a river. Suppose, however, we want to talk about the marginal abatement cost of a group of firms, perhaps a group of firms in the same industry, or a group of firms all located in the same region. Most environmental policies, especially at provincial or federal levels, are aimed at controlling emissions from groups of pollution sources, not just single polluters. Suppose, furthermore, that the individual marginal abatement cost functions differ among the various firms. If we were trying to control organic pollutants in Hamilton Harbour, or Howe Sound, for example, we would be faced with a large variety of different sources, in different industries, with different production technologies, and therefore with very different individual marginal abatement cost functions. In this case we must construct the aggregate, or overall, marginal abatement cost function for the collection of firms by adding together the individual marginal abatement cost curves.

While this sounds simple, and it basically is, it nevertheless will lead us into one of the more important concepts underlying the design of effective environmental policy. We have to keep in mind the central idea of the abatement cost function. It is a function that shows the *least costly* way of achieving reductions in emissions for an individual firm if we are looking at an individual marginal abatement cost function, or for a group of polluting sources if we are interested in the aggregate marginal abatement cost function.

Figure 5-5 shows, on the left, two individual marginal abatement cost functions, labelled as "Source A" and "Source B." We note that they are not the same (although remember that the scales are the same, i.e., we are dealing with the same pollutant). MAC_A starts at 20 tonnes/week and rises rather rapidly as emissions are reduced. MAC_B also begins at the uncontrolled discharge level of 20 tonnes/week, but rises much less rapidly. Why the difference? Perhaps Source B is a newer plant with more flexible technological alternatives for pollution control. Or perhaps the two sources, although producing the same type of effluent, are manufacturing different consumer goods, using different production techniques. For whatever reason, they have different marginal abatement cost curves.

The aggregate marginal abatement cost curve is a summation, or aggregation, of these two individual relationships. But since the individual curves are different, it makes a great deal of difference how we add them together. The problem is that when we have two (or any other number greater than one) sources with different abatement costs, the total cost will depend on how we allocate the total emissions among the different sources. The principle we want to follow is to add together the two individual functions in such a way as to yield the lowest possible aggregate marginal abatement costs. The way to do this is to add them horizontally. Select a particular level of marginal abatement cost, for example the one marked w in Figure 5-5. This level of marginal abatement cost is associated with an effluent level of 10 tonnes/week from Source A, and an effluent level of about 7 tonnes/week from Source B. On the aggregate curve, thus, a marginal abatement cost of w would be associated

FIGURE 5-5   Aggregate Abatement Costs.

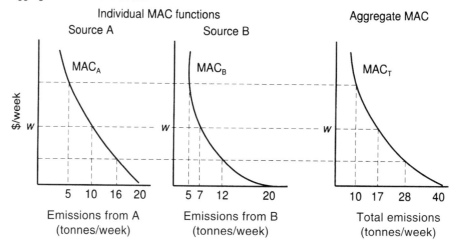

with an effluent level of 10 tonnes + 7 tonnes = 17 tonnes/week. All the other points on the aggregate marginal abatement cost are found the same way, by summing across horizontally on the individual marginal abatement cost curves.

In effect what we have done here is to invoke the important equimarginal principle, an idea that we introduced earlier in Chapter 4. If we are going to have the minimum aggregate marginal abatement cost curve, the aggregate level of emissions must be distributed among the different sources in such a way that they will all have the same marginal abatement costs. Start at the 10 tonnes/week point on the aggregate curve. Obviously, this 10-tonne total could be distributed among the two sources in any number of ways: 5 tonnes from each source, 8 tonnes from one and 2 from the other, etc. But only one allocation will give the lowest aggregate marginal abatement costs, this is the allocation that leads the different sources to the point where they have exactly the same marginal abatement costs. At the end of this chapter we will come back to this equimarginal principle, illustrating it with a simple numerical example.

The Efficient Level of Emissions

Having considered separately the marginal damage function and the marginal abatement cost function related to a particular pollutant being released at a particular place and time, we have now to bring these two relationships together to see what they tell us. This we do in Figure 5-6. This depicts a set of conventionally shaped marginal damage and marginal abatement cost curves labelled, respectively, MD and MAC. Marginal damages have a threshold at emission level $\hat{e}$, while the uncontrolled emission level is e'.

The "efficient" level of emissions is defined as that level where marginal damages are equal to marginal abatement costs. What is the justification for this? We note the trade-off that is inherent in the pollution phenomenon: higher emissions expose society, or some part of it, to greater costs stemming from environmental damages. Lower emissions involve society in greater costs in the form of resources devoted to abatement activities. The efficient level of effluent is thus the level where these two types of costs exactly offset one another, that is, where marginal abatement costs equal marginal damage costs. This is emission level e^* in Figure 5-6. Marginal damages and marginal abatement costs are equal to each other and to the value w at this level of emissions.

We can also look at this outcome in terms of total values, since we know that the totals are the areas under the marginal curves. Thus the triangular area marked a (bounded by points $\hat{e}$, e^* and the marginal damage function) depicts the total damages existing when emissions are at level e^*, while the triangular area b shows the total abatement costs at this level of emissions. The sum of these two areas ($a + b$) is a measure of the total social costs from e^* tonnes per year of this particular pollutant. The point e^* is the unique point where this sum is minimized. Note that area a need not equal area b.

You might get the impression, on the basis of where the point e^* is located on the x-axis, that this analysis has led us to the conclusion that the "efficient" level of emis-

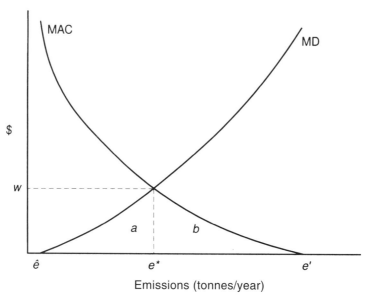

FIGURE 5-6   The Efficient Level of Emissions.

sions is always one that involves a relatively large quantity of emissions and substantial environmental damages. This is not the case. What we are developing,
rather, is a conceptual way of looking at a trade-off. In the real world every pollution problem is different. This analysis gives us a generalized way of framing the
problem that obviously has to be adapted to the specifics of any particular case of
environmental pollution. In Figure 5-7, for example, we have depicted three different situations that might characterize particular environmental pollutants. In each case
e^* depicts the efficient level of emissions and w shows marginal damages and marginal abatement costs at that quantity of emissions. In Panel (a) we have a pollutant
for which e^* is well to the right of zero (of course since the horizontal axis has no
units it's not clear exactly what "well to the right" actually means here). But marginal
damages at this point are quite small, so are total damages and abatement costs, as
shown by the small size of the triangles corresponding to these values. The reason
for this is that we have a pollutant where both marginal abatement costs and marginal
damages increase at first only very slowly.

Panel (b) shows a situation where the marginal abatement function rises moder-
ately, then rapidly, while the marginal damage function rises very rapidly from the
beginning. In this case e^* is to the right of zero, and w lies well above what it was in
the first diagram (assuming the vertical axis of these diagrams all have the same
scale). Note, however, that at e^* total abatement costs are substantially higher than
total damages, as is indicated by the relative sizes of the triangles that measure these
total values (a and b). What this emphasizes is that it is not the equality of total abate-

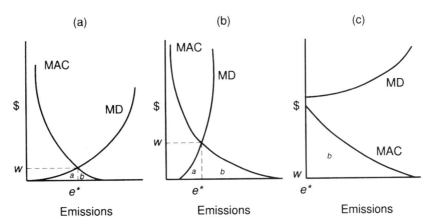

FIGURE 5-7   Efficient Emission Levels for Different Pollutants.

ment costs and total damages that defines the efficient level of effluent, but the equality of the *marginal* abatement costs and marginal damages.

In Panel (c) of Figure 5-7 we have a case where the efficient level of emissions is zero. There is no point of intersection of the two functions in the graph; area *a* does not even appear on the graph. The only way we could conceivably get them to intersect is if we could somehow extend them to the left of the vertical axis, but this would imply that emissions could actually be negative, which is an oddity that we will avoid. What makes $e^* = 0$ is that the marginal damage function doesn't begin at zero, but rather well up on the abscissa, implying that even the first small amount of this pollutant placed in the environment causes great damage (perhaps this diagram applies to some extremely toxic material). Relative to this the marginal costs of abatement are low, giving an efficient emission level of zero.

The real world is a dynamic place, and this is especially true of environmental pollution control. For our purposes this implies, for example, that the level of emissions that was efficient last year, or last decade, is not necessarily the level that is efficient today, or that is likely to be in the future. We know the factors that lie behind the marginal damage and marginal abatement cost functions, and thus we realize that when any of these underlying factors change, the functions themselves will shift and e^*, the efficient level of emissions, will thus change.

Before we take a look at this we need to remind ourselves of what we are doing. Remember the distinction we made earlier between positive and normative economics, between the economics of *what is* and the economics of *what ought to be*. The idea of the efficient level of emissions comes firmly under normative economics, under the idea of what ought to be. We are presenting emission level e^*, the level that balances abatement costs and damage costs, as a desirable target for public policy. We must not get this confused with the actual level of emissions; if the world worked so that the actual level of emissions was always equal to, or close to, the efficient level, we presumably would have no need to worry about intervening with environ-

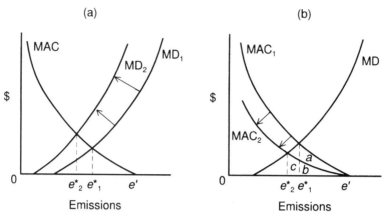

FIGURE 5-8   Changes in e*, the Efficient Level of Emissions.

mental policy of one type or another. Of course it doesn't, which is why we must turn to public policy.

In Figure 5-8 we analyze several ways in which $e*$ might change when underlying factors change. Panel (a) shows the results of a shift upward in the marginal damage function, from MD_1 to MD_2. One of the ways this could happen is through population growth. MD_1 might apply to a municipality in 1950, and MD_2 to the same municipality in 1990 after its population has grown. More people means that a given amount of effluent will cause more damage.[3] This leads us to a conclusion that is intuitively straightforward: the efficient level of emissions drops from e_1^* to e_2^*. With a higher marginal damage function, the logic of the efficiency trade-off would lead us to devote more resources to pollution control.

Panel (b) of Figure 5-8 shows the case of a shift in the marginal abatement cost function, from MAC_1 to MAC_2. What could have caused this? The most obvious, perhaps, is a change in the technology of pollution control. We noted above that abatement costs depend critically on the technology available for reducing effluent streams: treatment technology, recycling technology, alternative fuel technology, etc. New techniques normally arise because resources, talents and energy have been devoted to research and development. So the shift downward in marginal abatement costs depicted in Figure 5-8 might be the result of the development of new treatment or recycling technologies that make it less costly to reduce the effluent stream of this particular pollutant. It should not be too surprising that this leads to a reduction in the efficient level of emissions, as indicated by the change from e_1^* to e_2^*. We might

---

[3] This diagram could also apply, of course, to a different situation. MD_1 could be the damage function pertaining to a relatively sparsely settled rural region; MD_2 could be the marginal damage function pertaining to a more populous urban area. Everything we say about the relationship between e_1^* and e_2^* applies also to cases like this where we are comparing two different places at the same time, in addition to the above comparison of the same place at two different points in time.

note that this could lead to either an increase or decrease in the total cost of abating emissions. Before the change, total abatement costs were an amount equal to the area $(a + b)$, that is, the area under MAC_1 between the uncontrolled level e' and the amount e_1^*. After the change total abatement costs are equal to area $(b + c)$, and the question of whether total abatement costs at the efficient level of emissions have increased or decreased hinges on the relative sizes of the two areas a and c. This in turn depends on the shapes of the curves and the extent to which the marginal abatement cost curve has shifted; the more it has shifted the more likely the efficient level of total abatement costs after the change would exceed the costs before the change.[4]

A General Model of Pollution Control

Our simple model in this chapter focusses on the realistic situation in which polluters can invest in abatement technologies that reduce the emissions from their operation. Let's back up for a moment and look more generally at the trade-offs facing polluters. Assume that one unit of output produces one unit of pollution. Obviously we could complicate this relationship, but the basic principle is that pollution and output are related. In a world without any abatement technlogies, if a polluter is to reduce emissions, output must fall. Reductions in output impose a cost on polluters—the foregone profits they had from being able to discharge their waste products freely. In Figure 5-9, panel (a) we show the profit-maximizing solution for a firm operating in a competitive industry that is polluting. The firm maximizes profits where P = MC.

Panel (b) of Figure 5-9 graphs (P − MC) for all levels of Q. We see that marginal profits are greatest for the first unit of the good sold at the constant price of P, then fall until P = MC, at the competitive equilibrium. These marginal profits can also be interpreted as the *marginal benefits of pollution* (MBP) for the firm. That is, they represent the added profits a firm has by *not* incurring costs of treating its waste products in some way. If the firm has to take its pollutants into account, it will have to forego some of these profits.

Now suppose the firm is required to deal with its pollution, but there is no abatement technology available to treat wastes. The only way to reduce pollution is therefore to reduce output. The MBP curve shows what it costs the firm in the form of foregone profits for each unit of pollution reduced. We can now think of the horizontal axis in panel (b) as emissions, given our assumption of a one-to-one relationship between output and emissions. The MBP curve would then replace our marginal abatement cost (MAC) function examined in this chapter. The socially efficient equilibrium is where MBP = MD. Because MBP = P − MC, the equilibrium condition is: P − MC = MD, or P = MC + MD. A socially efficient equilibrium thus equates mar-

---

[4] These diagrams can also be used to examine some of the implications of making mistakes. For example, suppose we (i.e., the public control authorities) think that the real marginal abatement cost was MAC_1, but that, in fact, because there is a cheaper way of reducing this effluent that we don't know about, marginal abatement costs are actually MAC_2. Then we would conclude that the efficient level of effluent is e_1^* whereas it is actually e_2^*. We might be shooting at a target that involves excessive emissions.

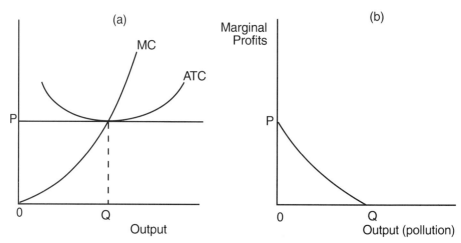

FIGURE 5-9   Profits from Pollution.

ket prices of goods to the social costs of production on the margin, where these social costs includes marginal costs of production plus marginal damages from production.

How does this relationship change when we introduce abatement into the model? Assume now that the firm has a choice of reducing pollution by reducing output or by incurring abatement expenses that reduce emissions per unit output. Total abatement may consist of both capital expenditures (fixed costs) and operating costs. The marginal abatement cost function of course does not include any fixed costs. Further assume that the firm's marginal abatement costs are equal to the profits foregone by reducing output to lower emissions. Obviously, this is a simplifying assumption. If the costs are different, firms will maximize profits by choosing some mix of output reduction and abatement, where marginal revenues equal the sum of marginal production plus marginal abatement costs. In practice this might lead to a situation where firms abate emisssions up to some level, then reduce output thereafter (or vice versa). For our purposes, the simplifying assumption is satisfactory. The MAC then becomes the MBP curve and gives analogous information. For each unit of emissions reduced, the firm incurs marginal abatement costs as shown in the diagrams in this chapter.

A simple algebraic model can represent the model presented in this chapter. Assume that both the MAC and MD curves are linear. Let:

$$MAC = a - be,$$

where a and b are positive parameters, e are emissions

$$MD = ce$$

where c is a positive parameter.

The socially efficient equilibrium is where MAC = MD. Substituting and solving these equations yields:

$$a - be = ce, \text{ and emissions are given by:}$$

$$e = a/(b+c)$$

The dollar value of marginal costs and damages at this equilibrium is $(ac)/(b+c)$. This algebraic relationship will be used in subsequent chapters to examine various types of policies that can be used to achieve the socially efficient equilibrium.

Enforcement Costs

So far we have considered only the private costs of reducing emissions. But emission reductions do not happen unless resources are devoted to enforcement. To include all sources of cost we need to add the marginal enforcement costs to the analysis. Some of these are private, such as added recordkeeping by polluters. But the bulk are public costs related to various components of the enforcement process. Figure 5-10 shows a simple model of pollution control with enforcement costs added. To the normal marginal abatement cost function has been added the marginal costs of enforcement, giving a total marginal cost function labelled MAC + E. The vertical distance between the two marginal cost curves equals marginal enforcement costs.

FIGURE 5-10   Enforcement Costs.

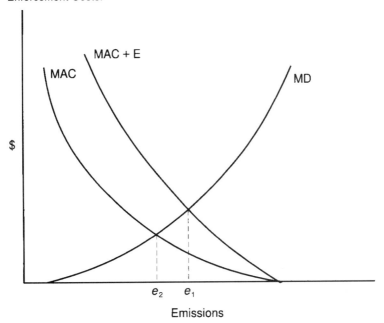

The assumption drawn into the graph is that marginal enforcement costs, the added costs of enforcement that it takes to get emissions reduced by a unit, increase as emissions decrease. In other words, the more polluters cut back emissions the more costly is it to enforce further cutbacks. We will have more to say about enforcement and its costs in later parts of the book.

In effect, the addition of enforcement costs moves the efficient level of emissions to the right of where it would be if they were zero. And this shows the vital importance of having good enforcement technology, because lower marginal enforcement costs would move MAC + E closer to MAC, decreasing the efficient emission level. In fact, technical change in enforcement has exactly the same effect on the efficient level of emissions as technical change in emissions abatement itself.

THE EQUIMARGINAL PRINCIPLE APPLIED TO EMISSION REDUCTIONS

Before going on we want to take a last, very explicit look at the equimarginal principle. One of its implications is that, if we have a situation with multiple sources of a pollutant, and we wish to reduce the overall level of emissions in the least costly way, we must arrange things so as to reduce the emissions from each source in accordance with the equimarginal principle. Achieving the lowest abatement costs or, alternatively, achieving the greatest emissions cutback for a given total cost, requires that we satisfy the equimarginal principle.

To illustrate this look at the numbers in Table 5-1. This shows explicitly the marginal abatement costs of each of two firms emitting a particular residual into the environment. If neither source makes any effort to control emissions, they will each emit 12 tonnes per week. If Plant A reduces its emissions by 1 tonne, to 11 tonnes per week, it will cost $1,000/week; if it reduces effluent further to 10 tonnes per week, its abatement costs will increase by $2,000/week, and so on. Note that the marginal abatement cost relationships of the two sources are different: that of Source B increases faster than that of Source A.

Suppose that initially each plant is emitting at the uncontrolled level; total emissions would then be 24 tonnes/week. Now let us assume that we want to reduce overall emissions to half the present level, or a total of 12 tonnes/week. One way to do this would be to have *equiproportionate* cutbacks; since we want a total reduction of 50 percent, we require each source to reduce by 50 percent. If Source A were cut 50 percent to 6 tonnes per week, its marginal abatement costs at this level would be $6,000/week, while at this level of emissions the marginal abatement costs of Source B would be $20,000 per week. Total abatement costs of the 12-tonne total can be found by adding up the marginal abatement costs; these are $21,000 per week for Source A [$1,000 + $2,000 + $3,000 + $4,000 + $5,000 + $6,000] and $56,000 per week for Source B [($2,000 + $4,000 + $6,000 + $10,000 + $14,000 + $20,000], or a grand total of $77,000 per week.

But we can achieve the overall reduction to 12 tonnes/week with a substantially lower total cost. We know this because with the equiproportionate reduction we are

TABLE 5-1   THE EQUIMARGINAL PRINCIPLE

Emissions (tonnes/week)	Marginal abatement costs ($1,000/week)	
	Source A	Source B
12	0	0
11	1	2
10	2	4
9	3	6
8	4	10
7	5	14
6	6	20
5	8	25
4	10	31
3	14	38
2	24	58
1	38	94
0	70	160

violating the equimarginal principle; marginal abatement costs are not equalized when each source reduces its effluent to 6 tonnes/week. What we seek are different emission rates for the two sources, where, simultaneously, they will emit no more than 12 tonnes of effluent and have the same marginal abatement costs. This condition is satisfied if Source A emits 4 tonnes and Source B emits 8 tonnes. These rates add up to 12 tonnes total and give each source a marginal abatement cost of $10,000/week. Calculating total abatement costs at these emission levels give $39,000/week for Source A [$1,000 + $2,000 + $3,000 + $4,000 + $5,000 + $6,000 + $8,000 + $10,000] plus $22,000/week for Source B [$2,000 + $4,000 + $6,000 + $10,000], or a grand total of $61,000/week. We have, by following the equimarginal principle, obtained our desired reduction in total emissions with a savings of $16,000/week over the case of an equiproportionate reduction.

Thus, we see that an emission reduction plan that follows the equimarginal rule gives emission reduction at minimum cost. Another way of saying this is that, for any particular amount of money devoted to effluent reduction, we can get the maximum quantitative reduction in total effluent if we follow the equimarginal principle. The importance of this principle cannot be overstated. When we defined the efficient level of emissions, we were going on the assumption that we were working with the lowest possible marginal abatement cost function. The only way we can achieve this is if we are controlling individual sources in accordance with the equimarginal rule. If we are designing public policy under the rule of equiproportionate reductions at the various sources, we will be working with a marginal abatement cost function that is higher than it should be. And one of the results of this is that we will define an "efficient" emission level that is higher than it should be, or, to say the same thing, we will seek smaller reductions in emissions than are socially efficient.

LONG-RUN SUSTAINABILITY

The model we have discussed in this chapter hinges on the idea of efficiency, where decisions are made through comparing costs and benefits—in the case of pollution control comparing marginal abatement costs and marginal damages. A question arises over whether this approach is consistent with the notion of long-run sustainability, as we discussed in Chapters 1 and 2. In comparing costs and benefits like this, are we not giving undue primacy to the people who are in the better position to have their values counted, namely present generations? Are we perhaps not giving enough consideration to future generations? They are not here to be heard from directly, so the only way they can be factored in is through the bequest motive of present generations, which may not be strong enough.

This would not be a problem if all environmental resources were renewable and all pollutants noncumulative. But these conditions don't hold. Species extinctions are forever. And certain long-lasting pollutants can accumulate to become legacies from the present generation to those of the future. In the history of the human race there have been many instances where very long-run negative environmental impacts have eventually undermined the productivity of a society's resource base.[5] Most of these have been regional or local in scope, for example, the salting of soils in the Tigris-Euphrates lowlands (1900–1600 BC).[6] Today these local and regional situations continue, and in addition we are concerned about long-run global sustainability.

The easy answer is to say that the marginal abatement cost and (especially) the marginal damage functions of our basic model must be interpreted as containing all impacts, both short and long run, insofar as we can predict them. Conceptually, this is correct, but in practice it may be difficult to do. It is much easier to estimate short-run costs and damages than costs and damages occurring well off in the future. The great uncertainty about future impacts often means that more weight is put on the better-known short-run impacts. The other problem is how to compare present and future effects. Should we treat a dollar's worth of damage that will occur 100 years from now as equivalent to a dollar's worth of damages incurred today?

Some have suggested that we might be able to identify an upper limit on damages strictly on physical grounds. Whatever the short-run trade-off we wish to make to achieve efficiency, we may be able to identify emission levels which, if exceeded, would severely degrade particular environmental resources over time. For certain renewable resources, like animal and plant species, we could perhaps identify this point with some level below which extinction would result. But for many environmental resources, we simply don't know what their physical limits are. All decisions, even when long-run impacts are involved, must incorporate human judgments to some extent. And where judgments are involved, trade-offs automatically become relevant. Conflicts between market-determined resource allocation and long-term sustainability may be inevitable.

[5] B. L. Turner II, ed., *The Earth as Transformed by Human Action* (Cambridge, England: Cambridge University Press, 1990), 36.

[6] Eric P. Eckholm, *Losing Ground: Environmental Stress and World Food Prospects* (New York: W. W. Norton), 1976.

SUMMARY

In this chapter we have looked at a simple model of pollution control. It is based on the notion of a trade-off of environmental damages and pollution abatement costs. We introduced the notion of a marginal damage function, showing the marginal social damages resulting from varying levels of residual emissions or ambient pollutant levels. Then we looked at marginal abatement cost relationships, first for an individual pollution source and then for a group of such sources. By bringing together these two types of relationships we then defined an efficient level of emissions: that level where marginal damages and marginal abatement costs are equal. At this level of emissions total social costs, the total of abatement costs and damages, is minimized.

The efficient level of emissions is subject to change as underlying factors shift. Population growth and the results of scientific studies can shift marginal damage functions, technological changes can cause marginal abatement cost functions to shift. One sometimes hears statements to the effect that "the optimal level of pollution can never be zero." While this may be true when considering all pollutants in the aggregate, it is most definitely not true when considering individual pollutants. We illustrated one case where the efficient level of a particular pollutant is zero. Finally, we reviewed the equimarginal principle as it applies to pollution control. That principle states that, with multiple sources having different marginal abatement cost functions, we achieve a given total emission reduction at least total abatement costs only if we distribute the emission reduction among the various sources in such a way as to equalize their marginal abatement costs.

A word of caution is appropriate. The model presented in this chapter is very general, and risks giving an overly simplistic impression of pollution problems in the real world. In fact, there are very few actual instances of environmental pollution where we know the marginal damage and marginal abatement functions with certainty. The natural world is too complex, and human and nonhuman responses are too difficult to identify with complete clarity. Furthermore, polluters come in all types and sizes and economic circumstances and it takes enormous resources to learn even simple things about the costs of pollution abatement in concrete instances. Pollution-control technology is changing rapidly, so what is efficient today will not necessarily be so tomorrow. Nevertheless, the simple model is useful for thinking about the basic problem of pollution control, and it will be useful in our later chapters on the various approaches to environmental policy. Before discussing complicated policy issues, it is appropriate to study the ways economists have tried to measure and make visible marginal abatement costs and marginal damages in specific cases of environmental quality changes.

QUESTIONS FOR FURTHER DISCUSSION

1 Prove (graphically) that the point labelled e^* in Figure 5-6 is indeed the point that minimizes total social costs, the sum of abatement and damage costs. (Do this by showing that at any other point, this total cost will be higher.)

2 Consider a large harbour through which many oil tankers pass on their way to and from an oil refinery. How would the efficient level of oil pollution in the waters of

the harbour be affected by: (1) the invention of better equipment for recovering spilled oil, (2) the redevelopment of the harbourside to make it more attractive to tourists, (3) the opening of a new refinery next to the existing one?

3 Suppose a new law is put into effect requiring oil tankers to use certain types of navigation rules in coastal waters of Canada. Suppose that the very next year there is a large tanker accident and oil spill in these waters. Does this mean that the law has had no effect?

4 In establishing the efficient level for emissions of any pollutant, what are the important roles to be played by physical scientists, natural scientists, economists, and policymakers?

5 Environmental economics is sometimes criticized because it seems to lead to the conclusion that the efficient level of all pollutants can never be zero. Comment on this.

6 How might equity considerations make the most "socially desirable" level of emissions different from the socially efficient level?

SELECTED READINGS

Freeman, A. Myrick, III, Robert H. Haveman, and Allen V. Kneese. *The Economics of Environmental Policy*. New York: John Wiley, 1973.

Hite, James C., et al. *The Economics of Environmental Quality*. Washington, D.C.: American Enterprise Institute, 1972.

Kneese, Allen V., and Charles L. Schultze. *Pollution, Prices, and Public Policy*. Washington, D.C.: The Brookings Institution, 1975.

Magat, Wesley A. *Reform of Environmental Regulation*. Cambridge, MA: Ballinger Publishing Company, 1982.

Mills, Edwin S., and Philip E. Graves. *The Economics of Environmental Quality*. 2nd ed. New York: Norton, 1986.

Pearce, David W., and R. Kerry Turner. *Economics of Natural Resources and the Environment*. Baltimore: Johns Hopkins Press, 1990.

ENVIRONMENTAL ANALYSIS

In the last few chapters we have used the concepts of "abatement costs" and "damages" without worrying too much about how we might measure their magnitudes in particular situations. In the next three chapters we will rectify this. Several types of analysis have been developed over the years to provide environmental, economic, and social information to the policy process. In the next chapter we will deal with these at the framework level. From the standpoint of economics, benefit-cost analysis is the primary analytical tool, and we will spend much of the chapter discussing its major elements. Then in the following two chapters we will look more closely at the methods available for estimating benefits and costs relevant to environmental policy decisions.

6

FRAMEWORKS OF ANALYSIS

Policy decisions require information and, although the availability of good information doesn't automatically mean that decisions also will be good, its *un*availability will almost always contribute to bad decisions. There are a variety of alternative frameworks for generating and presenting information useful to policymakers, calling for different skills and research procedures. We briefly review the most important of these, before focussing on benefit-cost analysis.

IMPACT ANALYSIS

"Impact" is a very general word, meaning the effects of any actual or proposed policy. Since there are many types of effects, there are many different types of impact analysis. We focus here on two of these: environmental impacts and economic impacts.

Environmental Impact Analysis

An Environmental Impact Analysis (EIA) is essentially an identification and study of all significant environmental repercussions stemming from a course of action. For the most part these focus on impacts that are expected to flow from a proposed decision, though retrospective EIAs are of great value also, especially when they are done to see if earlier predictions were accurate. EIAs can be carried out for any social action, public or private, industrial or domestic, local or national. They are frequently the work of natural scientists, who focus on tracing out and describing the physical impacts of projects or programs, especially following through the complex linkages that spread these impacts through the ecosystem. These types of EIAs do not address directly the issue of placing social values on these impacts.

Many countries have laws requiring environmental impact studies when substantial public programs and projects are under consideration, as well as private projects in some cases. In Canada, there is legislative mandate to do EIAs at the federal level and in most provinces. The current federal EIA process stems from the Canadian Environmental Assessment Act (CEAA) recently passed by Parliament (1993). The CEAA replaces a federal guideline to undertake EIA called the Environmental Assessment and Review Process (EARP).[1] The CEAA gives the federal government, through Environment Canada power to undertake an environment impact assessment for any development project located on federal lands, initiated by any federal department, and for any public project that has an area of federal responsibility. The Minister of the Environment can prohibit any activities associated with the project until the assessment is completed. This power is backed up by the Attorney General of Canada who can seek a court injunction against anyone not complying with the Minister's orders. Note that these powers only apply to public-sector projects. There is no federal review of privately initiated projects. Nor is there any review mandated of federal programs and/or policies. Some of the provinces, for example, British Columbia, do have EIA acts which assess certain private as well as public projects. The CEAA does not require environmental assessments for all projects. This is up to the discretion of the Minister of the Environment.

Economics has a distinct role to play as well in the EIA process. While natural scientists are essential to environmental assessment, it is not only ecological linkages through which environmental impacts spread; they spread also through economic linkages. Suppose, for example, it is proposed to build a dam that will flood a certain river valley, while providing new flatwater recreation possibilities. A substantial part of the environmental impact will stem from the inundation itself and the resulting losses in animals and plants, wild-river recreation, farmland, etc. But much also could come from changes in patterns of behaviour among people affected by the project. Recreators travelling into and out of the region could affect air pollution and traffic congestion. New housing or commercial development spurred by the recreation opportunities could have negative environmental effects. Thus, to study the full range of environmental impacts from the dam, it is necessary to include not just the physical effects of the dam and its water impoundment, but also the ways people will react and adapt to this new facility.

Economic Impact Analysis

When interest centres on how some action—a new law, a new technological breakthrough, a new source of imports—will affect an economic system, in whole or in terms of its various parts, we can speak of economic impact analysis. In most countries, especially developing ones, there is usually wide interest in the impact of environmental regulations on economic growth rates. Sometimes the focus will be on trac-

[1] We will examine Canada's federal EIA experience in more detail in Chapter 14.

ing out the ramifications of a public program for certain economic variables that are considered particularly important. One might be especially interested, for example, in the impact of an environmental regulation on employment, the impact of import restrictions on the rate of technological change in an industry, the effects of an environmental law on the growth of the pollution-control industry, the response of the food industry to new packaging regulations, and so on.

A good example of an impact analysis is a recent study by two Dutch environmental economists.[2] In the Netherlands there is an important problem with soil acidification, resulting in part from industrial emissions of sulfur dioxide (SO_2) and nitrogen oxides (NO_x), but also in part from agricultural practices in animal feeding and manure disposal. Various proposals have been made to reduce agricultural emissions of ammonia (NH_3). The objective of the researchers was to trace out the impacts of these proposed regulations on the agricultural sector. They concluded that the control program would lead to a decrease in net farm revenues of 35 percent over the period 1985–2010, a decline in the number of dairy cows, increases in yields per cow, declines in numbers of other animals, and a substantial reduction in the amounts of ammonia coming from the agricultural sector.

Economic impact analyses can be focussed at any level. Local environmental groups might be interested in the impact of a wetlands law on the rate of population growth and tax base in their community. Regional groups might be interested in the impacts of a national regulation on their particular economic circumstances. At the global level, an important question is how efforts to control CO_2 emissions might impact the relative growth rates of rich and poor countries. Whatever the level, economic impact analysis requires a basic understanding of how economies function, and how their various parts fit together.

COST-EFFECTIVENESS ANALYSIS

Suppose a community determined that its current water supply was contaminated with some chemical, and that it had to switch to some alternative supply. Suppose it had several possibilities: It could drill new wells into an uncontaminated aquifer, it could build a connector to the water supply system of a neighbouring town, or it could build its own surface reservoir. A cost-effectiveness analysis would estimate the costs of these different alternatives with the aim of showing how they compared in terms of, say, the costs per million gallons of delivered water into the town system. Cost-effectiveness analysis, in other words, essentially takes the objective as given, then costs out various alternative ways of attaining that objective. One might think of it as one-half of a benefit-cost analysis where costs, but not benefits, are estimated in monetary terms.

---

[2] Paul J. J. Veenendaal and Hoor M. Brouwer, "Consequences of Ammonia Emission Abatement Policies for Agricultural Practices in the Netherlands," in Frank J. Dietz et al. (eds.), *Environmental Policy and the Economy* (Amsterdam: North-Holland, 1991), chapter 12, 241–279.

Table 6-1 shows some of the results of a study done for a Remedial Action Plan to reduce phosphorous (P) concentrations in the Bay of Quinte in Lake Ontario. The study was done for the International Joint Commission (IJC) a bilateral organization that studies and makes recommendations to governments for water-related issues along the Canada–U.S. border. Phosphorous comes from leaching of fertilizers into waterways, from sewage treatment plants processing domestic household wastes, and from industrial sources. Excessive amounts of phosphorous lead to algal blooms and eutrophication of water bodies which depletes oxygen in the water and kills fish and other aquatic life. The secondary sewage treatment plants which currently exist in the region cannot remove enough of the phosphorous to prevent eutrophication. The results show the estimated costs of reducing phosphorous concentrations in a region of the bay by 1 microgram per litre (μg/L). It would appear, for example, that treatment of wastewater from water treatment plants is by far the most cost-effective alternative. A reduction of 1 μg/L costs $98 thousand as compared to a ten-fold next higher cost (diversion of Lake Ontario water). However, we have to interpret these cost coefficients with care. Although the wastewater treatment has the lowest costs per unit of phosphorous reduced, we can't conclude from this that the best way to reduce phosphorous concentrations in this bay is to concentrate solely on one approach. There are a number of additional concerns. Each of the technologies has limits as to the total amount of phosphorous it is capable of reducing, so, depending on what the desired total reduction is, different combinations of these techniques will have to be utilized. There may be other techniques that could be more cost effective, but were difficult to measure costs for. An example is phosphorous removal from industrial sources. These cost figures also involve quite different mixes of capital to operating costs. Treatment plants are capital intensive, while the diversions and alum treatment involve high operating costs. This might be an important budgetary con-

TABLE 6-1 COST EFFECTIVENESS OF DIFFERENT OPTIONS FOR REDUCING PHOSPHOROUS CONCENTRATIONS IN THE BAY OF QUINTE, LAKE ONTARIO

Strategy	Cost (in $ thousands) per microgram/litre reduction in phosphorous
Tertiary treatment at sewage treatment plants	$1078
Treatment of wastewater from water treatment plants	98
Reduction in phosphorous inputs from agricultural runoff	2033
Alum treatment of sediments in lake	2000
Diversion of 20 square kilometres of Lake Ontario into the upper bay	1104
Diversion of 35 square kilometres of Lake Ontario into the upper bay	978

Source: Adapted from Bay of Quinte Remedial Action Plan Committee, "Discussion Paper," September 1989.

cern for governments. Pollution problems may also be multifaceted. One technique (e.g., tertiary treatment plants) may have benefits in addition to phosphorous reduction, while others (dumping alum into the lake, for example) may have some other adverse environmental impacts. Cost-effectiveness is thus only one step in reaching a decision about environmental policy.

You may have noticed that cost-effectiveness analysis can be used along with the equimarginal principle, in this case as applied to comparisons across different emission-abatement technologies. In putting together an effective control program, authorities would want to choose techniques that have the lowest marginal abatement costs, and combine them in a way that satisfies the equimarginal principle. Of course, this leaves out the important prior question. In this example, how much ~~VOC~~ *phosphorus* reduction is efficient, in the light of damages done by these emissions? But you can see that the efficiency question is intertwined with the issue of cost-effectiveness. We can't answer the efficiency question until we know what emission-reduction costs are going to be, but these costs depend on the cost-effectiveness of the particular techniques chosen to reduce emissions. Another complication that may arise is the presence of nonconvexities in abatement costs (step functions, for example) and other functions. In these cases, it may be difficult to even find efficient solutions.

It may make good sense to do a cost-effectiveness analysis even before there is a strong public commitment to the objective you are costing out. In many cases people may not know exactly how much they value a given objective. Once a cost-effectiveness analysis is done, they may be able to tell, at least in relative terms, whether any of the different alternatives would be desirable. They may be able to say something like: "We don't know exactly how much benefits are in monetary terms, but we feel that they are more than the costs of several of the alternatives that have been costed out, so we will go ahead with one or both of them."

BENEFIT-COST ANALYSIS

Benefit-cost analysis is for the public sector what a profit-and-loss analysis is for a business firm. If an automobile company contemplated introducing a new car, it would want to get some idea of how its profitability would be affected. On the one hand, it would estimate costs of production and distribution: labour, raw materials, energy, emission-control equipment, transportation, etc.[3]

On the other hand, it would estimate revenues through market analysis. Then it would compare expected revenues with anticipated costs. Benefit-cost analysis is an analogous exercise for programs in the public sector. This means there are two critical differences between benefit-cost analysis and the car example. It is a tool for helping to make public decisions, done from the standpoint of society in general rather than from that of a single profit-making firm; and it usually is done for policies and

---

[3] Of course, it probably would not factor in the costs of air-pollution damage inflicted on people breathing the emissions of the new cars; if it did this without being required to, we probably wouldn't be here studying this topic.

programs that have *unmarketed* types of outputs like, for example, improvements in environmental quality.

Benefit-cost analysis has led two intertwined lives. The first is among its practitioners, economists inside and outside public agencies who have developed the techniques, tried to produce better data, and extended the scope of the analysis. The second is among the politicians and administrators who have set the rules and procedures governing the use of benefit-cost analysis for public decision making. In Canada, benefit-cost analysis has not been officially legislated for use by government agencies at the federal or provincial level. It has been used somewhat randomly and at times, for political self-interest, rather than as a technique for objective decision making. By contrast, in the U.S., benefit-cost analysis has a much stronger legislative history. It was first used in conjunction with the United States Flood Control Act of 1936. That act specified that federal participation in projects to control flooding on major rivers of the country would be justifiable *"if the benefits to whomever they accrue are in excess of the estimated costs."* In order to determine if this criterion was satisfied for any proposed flood-control dam or large levee project, procedures had to be developed to measure these benefits and costs.

The status and role of benefit-cost analysis in public natural resource and environmental decision making have been the subject of continuing discussions as well as political and administrative conflicts. Public agencies have often been taken to task by outsiders for trying to use benefit-cost analysis in ways that would help them justify ever-larger budgets. Some observers have taken the position that benefit-cost analysis is really an attempt to short-circuit the process of political discussion and decision that should take place around prospective public projects and programs. Perhaps because of these problems, benefit-cost analysis is not widely used in Canada. Some programs have been evaluated from a benefit-cost perspective, for example, the examination in the mid-1970s of the proposed MacKenzie Valley natural gas pipeline (which was not built), and resource development projects in British Columbia (such as Northeast coal which were undertaken). But, in recent years, little formal analysis has been done by government agencies. Nevertheless, benefit-cost analysis remains an important analytical tool that is used widely throughout the world.

The Basic Framework

As the name implies, a benefit-cost analysis involves measuring, adding up, and comparing all the benefits and all the costs of a particular public project or program. There are essentially four steps in a benefit-cost analysis:

1 Specify clearly the project or program.
2 Describe quantitatively the inputs and outputs of the program.
3 Estimate the social costs and benefits of these inputs and outputs.
4 Compare these benefits and costs.

Each of these steps incorporates a number of component steps. In doing a benefit-cost analysis, the very first step is to decide on the *perspective* from which the study is to be done. Benefit-cost analysis is a tool of public analysis, but there are actually many publics. If you were doing a benefit-cost study for a national agency, the "public" normally would be all the people living in the particular country. But if you were employed by a city or regional planning agency to do a benefit-cost analysis of a local environmental program, you would undoubtedly focus on benefits and costs accruing to people living in those areas. At the other extreme, the rise of global environmental issues has forced us to undertake some benefit-cost analyses from a worldwide perspective.

When we have decided on the perspective from which to do a study, step 1 also includes a complete specification of the main elements of the project or program: location, timing, groups involved, connections with other programs, etc. We can distinguish between the two primary types of public environmental programs for which benefit-cost analyses are done:

1 *Physical projects* that involve direct public production: public waste treatment plants, beach restoration projects, hazardous-waste incinerators, habitat improvement projects, land purchase for preservation, and so on.

2 *Regulatory programs* that are aimed at enforcing environmental laws and regulations, such as pollution-control standards, technological choices, waste disposal practices, restrictions on land development, and so on.

When we have specified the basic project or program the next step is to determine the relevant flows of inputs and outputs. For some projects this is reasonably easy. If we are planning a wastewater treatment facility, the engineering staff will be able to provide a full physical specification of the plant, together with the inputs required to build it and keep it running. For other types of programs it is much harder. A restriction on development in a particular region, for example, can be expected to deflect development elsewhere into surrounding areas. These must be predicted with tolerable accuracy. It is in this step that we first have to recognize the great importance of time. Environmentally related projects or programs do not usually last for a single year, but are spread out over long periods of time. So the job of specifying inputs and outputs involves predictions of future events, often quite remote in time. This puts a premium on having a good understanding of things like future growth patterns and future rates of technological change and possible changes in consumers' preferences.

The next step is to put values on input and output flows; that is, to measure costs and benefits. We could do this in any units we wish, but normally we try to measure benefits and costs in monetary terms. This does not mean in market-value terms, because in many cases we will be dealing with effects, especially on the benefit side, that are not directly registered on markets. Nor does it imply that only monetary values count in some fundamental manner. It means that we need a single metric into which we can try to translate all of the impacts of a project or program, in order to make them comparable among themselves as well as with other types of public activities. Ultimately, certain environmental impacts of a program may be irreducible to monetary terms because we cannot find a way of measuring how much people value these impacts. In this case we must supplement the monetary results of the benefit-cost analysis with estimates of these intangible impacts.

Finally, we must compare benefits and costs. To understand what is involved in very general terms consider the numbers in Table 6-2. They are meant to illustrate the estimated benefits and costs of a regulatory program to control various airborne and waterborne pollutants coming from a group of pulp mills. These emissions reduce downstream water quality in the river on which they are located and contribute to serious air pollution in the vicinity of the plants. The numbers pertain to the totals of the various cost and benefit categories over the life of the program. Compliance costs in the industry consist of $580 million of capital equipment costs and $560 million of operating costs. Public-sector monitoring and enforcement required to achieve an acceptable level of compliance total $96 million. There are three major benefit categories. Downstream recreators (fishers and boaters) are benefited from the improved water quality: The value of these benefits is $1,892 million. Agricultural operators in the vicinity of the plants are expected to suffer $382 million loss in damages to crops and livestock because of reduced airborne emissions. Finally, there are intangible benefits which we have found no way of measuring in monetary terms. These are shown simply as some quantity "A."

We can compare total benefits and costs in several ways. One way is to subtract the total costs from total benefits to get "*net benefits.*" In Table 6-2 the net benefits are shown as $1,042 million ($2,278 − $1,236), together with an indeterminate allowance for intangible benefits. Another criterion is the *benefit-cost ratio*, found by taking the ratio of benefits and costs. This shows the benefits the project will produce for each dollar of costs; in Table 6-2 the benefit-cost ratio is 1.8 (2,278 ÷ 1,236), together with an indeterminate adjustment (indicated as "a") for the intangible benefits.

TABLE 6-2   ILLUSTRATIVE RESULTS FROM A BENEFIT-COST ANALYSIS OF A PROPOSED EMISSION REDUCTION PROGRAM FOR A GROUP OF PULP MILLS

	Totals over life of the program
Costs	($1,000,000)
Private compliance	
Capital equipment	580
Operating	560
Public monitoring and enforcement	96
Total	1,236
Benefits	
Increased benefits to recreators from improved water quality	1,896
Reduced damages to agricultural crops and livestock	382
Intangible	A
Total	2,278 + A
Net benefits: $1,042 + A	
Benefit-cost ratio: 1.8 + a	

Scope of the Project

This example, simple as it is, illustrates a number of problems in benefit-cost analysis. One important one is deciding on the scope of the project or program. How can we be sure that this one is the appropriate size—that a somewhat more restrictive or, alternatively, less restrictive program might not be better? The basic problem here is reconciling the fact that in reality it is always possible to vary the scope of a program—to make it larger or smaller by any amount, whereas in doing a benefit-cost analysis we have to focus on a program of a specific size.

To explore this issue consider Figure 6-1. It shows our standard emission-control model as developed in the last chapter, with marginal damage (MD) and marginal abatement cost (MAC) functions. Let us assume that the current level of emissions is e_1, that is, emissions are essentially uncontrolled. A control program is proposed that would lower emissions to e_2. For this program, total benefits (total damages reduced) are equal to $(a + b)$ while total abatement costs are equal to b. Net benefits are therefore equal to area a.

For an emission reduction program to give maximum net benefits, however, it would have to reduce emissions to e^*, the level at which MD = MAC. Here, net benefits would equal $(d + a)$. We can define the area $(d + a)$ as the change in *social welfare* that arises from the emission reduction program. The problem is, when we do a benefit-cost analysis of a specific proposal, how can we be sure that we are dealing with one such as e^* in the figure, and not one such as e_2? For example, how can we be sure that the program analyzed in Table 6-2 represents one that is close to efficient size?

FIGURE 6-1   Establishing the Size of a Public Program.

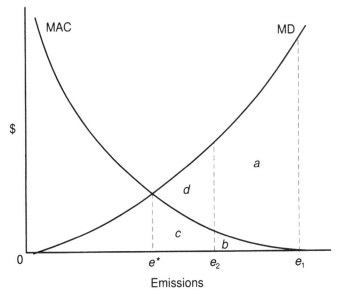

The general procedure here is to carry out *sensitivity analyses* on these results. This means recalculating benefits and costs for programs somewhat larger and somewhat smaller than the one shown in the table. We would analyze a program that has somewhat more restrictive emission reductions, with appropriate enforcement resources, and one that is somewhat less restrictive. If our chosen program is indeed appropriately scaled, each of the variations will produce lower net benefits.

The benefit-cost ratio is often used in public debates in describing environmental projects or programs. But the efficient program size is not the one that gives the maximum benefit-cost ratio. At emission level $e*$ the benefit-cost ratio is equal to $(a + b + c + d) \div (b + c)$. At emission level e_2, the benefit-cost ratio is $(a + b) \div b$, which is higher than that at $e*$. The benefit-cost ratio may be used to make sure that, at the very least, benefits exceed cost, but beyond this it is a misleading indicator in planning the appropriate scope of public programs.

Under some circumstances, there may be grounds for sizing programs at less than that which maximizes net benefits. Suppose you are a regional public agency in charge of enforcing air-pollution laws in two medium-sized urban areas. Suppose further that you have a fixed and predetermined budget of $1 million to spend. You have two possibilities: (1) put it all in one enforcement program in one of the cities or (2) divide it between two programs, one in each city. Suppose the numbers are as follows:

	Costs	Benefits	Net benefits	Benefit/cost ratio
One-city program	$1,000,000	$2,000,000	$1,000,000	2.0
Two-city program				
City A	500,000	1,200,000	700,000	2.4
City B	500,000	1,200,000	700,000	2.4

In this case we do better with our fixed budget by putting it into two half-sized programs rather than just one. In this case what we want to do is allocate our resources so that the net benefits produced by the total budget are maximized.

Discounting

We turn now to the important problem of how we compare costs and benefits that occur at very different points in time. If we institute a pollution-control policy, how do we weigh the high initial-year capital costs of abatement equipment and the long-run costs of maintaining it? In the global warming problem, how do we compare the very high costs today of controlling CO_2 emissions with the benefits that won't really start accruing for several decades? Suppose we have two programs, one with relatively high net benefits that materialize well into the future, and another with smaller net benefits that occur in the near future. How do we compare these two options?

The standard way to address problems like these is through *discounting*, a technique employed to add and compare costs and benefits that occur at different points in time. Discounting has two facets: first, the mechanics of doing it; then, the reasoning behind the choice of discount rates to be used in specific cases. We take these up in turn.

A cost that will occur 10 years from now does not have the same significance as a cost that occurs today. Suppose, for example, that one has incurred a cost of $1,000 that she must pay today. To do that she must have $1,000 in the bank, or her pocket, with which to pay the obligation. On the other hand, suppose she has a commitment to pay $1,000, not today, but 10 years from now. If the rate of interest she gets in a bank is 5 percent, and she expects it to stay at that level, she can deposit $613.90 in the bank today and it will compound up to $1,000 in 10 years, exactly when she needs it. The formula for compounding this sum is:

$$\$613.90(1 + .05)^{10} = \$1,000$$

We can now turn this around and ask: What is the *present value* of this $1,000 obligation 10 years from now? Its present value is what would have to put in the bank today to have exactly what is needed in 10 years, and we get this by rearranging the above expression:

$$\text{Present value} = \frac{\$1,000}{(1 + .05)^{10}} = \$613.90$$

The present value is found by discounting the future cost back over the 10-year period at the interest rate, now called the discount rate, of 5 percent.[4] If it were higher—say, 8 percent—the present value would be lower—$463.20. The higher the discount rate, the lower the present value of any future cost.

The same goes for a benefit. Suppose you expect someone to give you a gift of $100, but only at the end of 6 years. This would not have the same value to you today (i.e., the same present value) as $100 given to you today. If the applicable discount rate is 4 percent, the present value of that future gift would be:

$$\frac{\$100}{(1 + .04)^6} = \$79.03$$

Discounting is used extensively in benefit-cost analyses. Its main role is to help in aggregating a series of costs or benefits that are strung out over the life of a project or program. Consider the following illustrative numbers, showing benefits for two different programs over their short lives:

---

[4] In general, the discount formula is $PV = m/(1 + r)^t$, where m is the future value, r is the discount rate, and t is the number of years involved.

	Benefits ($) in year:			
	1	2	3	4
Project A	20	20	20	20
Project B	50	10	10	10

If we simply add these benefits across the four years for each project, they have the same total: $80. But Project A has a series of equal annual benefits, while B has substantial benefits in the first period and lower annual benefits thereafter. To compare the total benefits of the two projects, we must calculate the present value of total benefits for each program. For illustrative purposes we used a discount rate of 6 percent.

$$PV_A = \$20 + \frac{\$20}{1 + .06} + \frac{\$20}{(1 + .06)^2} + \frac{\$20}{(1 + .06)^3} = \$73.45$$

$$PV_B = \$50 + \frac{\$10}{1 + .06} + \frac{\$10}{(1 + .06)^2} + \frac{\$10}{(1 + .06)^3} = \$76.73$$

Note first of all that both present values are less than the undiscounted sums of benefits. This will always be true when a portion of a program's benefits accrues in future years. Note also that the present value of benefits for B exceeds that of A, which is what we would expect because more of B's benefits are concentrated early in the life of the program. That is to say, the time profile of B's benefits is more heavily concentrated in earlier years than the time profile of A's benefits.

Similar calculations are made for costs if we wish to know the present value of the stream of annual costs of a program. And the same reasoning applies; discounting reduces the present value of a dollar of cost more the further out in the future that cost will be incurred. The present value of the stream of benefits minus the present value of costs gives the present value of net benefits. Alternatively, we could calculate for each year of the life of a project its *net benefits*, then calculate the present value of this stream of net benefits in the same way, by summing their discounted values.

Since discounting is a way of aggregating a series of future net benefits into an estimate of present value, the outcome depends importantly on which particular discount rate we use. If we were to use a very low rate, we would essentially be treating a dollar in one year as very similar in value to a dollar in any other year. If we use a very high rate, we are saying that a dollar in the near term is much more valuable to us than one later on. Thus, the higher the discount rate, the more we would be encouraged to put our resources into programs that have relatively high payoffs (i.e., high benefits and/or low costs) in the short run. The lower the discount rate, on the contrary, the more we would be led to select programs that have high net benefits in the more distant future.

Choice of the Discount Rate

The choice of a discount rate has been a controversial topic through the years, and we can only summarize some of the arguments here. Firstly, we have to keep in mind the difference between *real* and *nominal* interest rates. Nominal rates are what you actually see on the market. If you take a nominal rate and adjust it for inflation, you get a real interest rate. Suppose you deposited $100 in a bank at an interest rate of 8 percent. In 10 years your deposit would have grown to $216. But this is in monetary terms. Suppose over that 10-year period prices increase 3 percent per year on average. Then the real value of your accumulated deposit would be less; in fact, the real interest rate at which your deposit would accumulate would only be 5 percent (8 percent – 3 percent), so in real terms your deposit would be worth only $161 after the 10 years.[5] So we have to be careful about the interest rate we use for discounting. If the cost estimates we are using are expected real costs, i.e., adjusted for expected inflation, we want to use a real interest rate for discounting purposes. If our cost estimates are nominal figures, then we use a nominal interest rate in the discounting analysis. If cost estimates are for a number of years and inflation is expected to occur, then these costs should be adjusted for inflation (deflated by an appropriate index such as the gross national expediture deflator or a selling price index for intermediate goods) and discounted by a real discount rate.

The discount rate reflects the current generation's views about the relative weight to be given to benefits and costs occurring in different years. But even a brief look will show that there are dozens of different interest rates in use at any one time—rates on normal savings accounts, certificates of deposit, bank loans, government bonds, etc. Which rate should we use? There are essentially two schools of thought on this question. The first is that the discount rate should reflect the way people themselves think about time. Any person normally will prefer a dollar today to a dollar in 10 years; in the language of economics, they have a positive rate of time preference. We see people making savings decisions by putting money in bank accounts that pay certain rates of interest. These savings account rates show what interest the banks have to offer in order to get people to forgo current consumption. We might, therefore, take the average bank savings account rate as reflecting the average person's rate of time preference.

The problem with this is that there are other ways of determining peoples' rates of time preference, and they don't necessarily give the same answer. Economists at Resources for the Future[6] recently completed a large survey in which they asked individuals to choose between receiving $10,000 today and larger amounts in 5 or 10 years. The responses yielded implied rates of discount of 20 percent for a 5-year time

---

[5] These are slight approximations. The deposit would actually be worth $160.64 and the real rate of accumulation would be 4.89 percent..

[6] Resources for the Future (RFF) is a well-known Washington organization that specializes in natural resource and environmental economics research. It publishes a quarterly newsletter discussing its work. This information comes from RFF, *Resources*, No. 108 (Summer 1992) 3.

horizon and 10 percent for a 10-year horizon. These were substantially higher than bank savings rates at the time of the survey.

The second approach to determining the "correct" rate of discount is based on the notion of investment productivity. When investments are made in productive enterprises, people anticipate that the value of future returns will offset today's investment costs; otherwise, these investments would not be made. The thinking here is that when resources are used in the public sector for natural resource and environmental programs, they ought to yield, on average, rates of return to society equivalent to what they could have earned in the private sector. Private-sector productivity is reflected in the rates of interest banks charge their business borrowers. Thus, by this reasoning, we should use, as our discount rate, a rate reflecting the interest rates that private firms pay when they borrow money for investment purposes. These are typically higher than savings account interest rates.

With the multiplicity of interest rates the real world offers, and these different arguments for choosing a discount rate, practices could differ among agencies in the public sector. To reduce the potential for a multiplicity of rates being used, the federal Treasury Board has set a real rate of 10 percent as the official discount rate to be used by all agencies and ministries of the federal government. There is a difficulty with a fixed rate when economic conditions are changing such as in the early 1990s when inflation fell substantially and nominal interest rates decreased as well. We can conclude that although discounting is widely accepted, the rate controversy is far from being resolved.

Discounting and Future Generations

The logic of a discount rate, even a very small one, is inexorable. A billion dollars, discounted back over a century at 5 percent, has a present value of only slightly over $7.6 million. The present generation, considering the length of its own expected life, may not be interested in programs having very high, but long-run, payoffs like this.

The logic is even more compelling if we consider a future cost. One of the reasons that environmentalists have looked askance at discounting is that it can have the effect of downgrading future damages that result from today's economic activity. Suppose today's generation is considering a course of action that has certain short-run benefits of $10,000 per year for 50 years, but which, starting 50 years from now, will cost $1 million a year *forever*. This may not be too unlike the choice faced by current generations on nuclear power, or on global warming. To people alive today the present value of that perpetual stream of future cost discounted at 10 percent is only $85,000. These costs may not weigh particularly heavily on decisions made by the current generation. The present value of the benefits ($10,000 a year for 50 years at 10 percent, or $99,148) exceeds the present value of the future costs. From the standpoint of today, therefore, this might look like a good choice, despite the perpetual cost burden placed on all future generations.

The problems associated with using positive discount rates for environmental programs with long-run impacts are difficult to resolve. Exhibit 6-1, is a news clip illustrating some of the differences on this point among economists. Many take the view that for long-run environmental projects the appropriate discount rate is zero. But we

EXHIBIT 6-1

WHAT A DIFFERENCE A DISCOUNT MAKES

Bruce Stokes

In 1908, when Thomas Jefferson planted the stately tulip poplars that grace the west front lawn at Monticello, he did so knowing full well that he would never benefit from their shade on a muggy Virginia summer afternoon. By the time the poplars' boughs spread their leafy canopy over Monticello's lawn, Jefferson would long be dead.

For his investment of time and money, the immediate return he received was nil. Yet, by all accounts, Jefferson never once considered not planting the poplars.

Jefferson's paradox—investments in the environment often cannot be justified on purely economic grounds—is at the heart of today's debate between environmentalists and economists over what to do about global warming.

In assessing the costs and benefits of building a factory, erecting a bridge or putting a scrubber on a smokestack, it is standard practice for economists to compare the benefits to be gained from the investment with the potential return that might be generated if the money were used in some other way. That estimated rate of return is called the discount rate. Corporations frequently use a 15 percent discount rate to weigh new investments. The World Bank uses double-digit rates, and the U.S. government often relies on rates of more than 10 percent.

The choice of a discount rate can make or break the case for investing in the environment. Suppose, for example, that scientists agree that a particular pollutant will cause $100 million in damage in the year 2092. Society has two economic choices: invest now in pollution abatement technology to avoid the damage, or channel the investment elsewhere on the assumption that a century from now, the economy will be richer as a result and thus will be better able to absorb the costs of any damage to the environment.

In weighing this decision, if policy makers assume that for every $1 they invest now, they can get $1.10 next year (applying, in essence, a 10 percent discount rate), it would be fiscally irresponsible to spend more than $7,305 on pollution control now to avoid $100 million in cleanup costs 100 years from now. If the current pollution control costs are even a dollar higher, economists conclude that it would be better to invest the money in roads or education (which have a higher return) and compensate the victims of pollution down the road.

The assessment of the proposed pollution abatement action changes radically, however, if a 2 percent discount rate is used. At that assumed rate of return, nearly $14 million in expenditures for pollution control are economically justifiable today to avoid $100 million in costs a century from now.

"This illustrates," said William R. Cline, a senior fellow at the Institute for International Economics, "that those who prefer discount rates of 10 percent can, for all practical purposes, dismiss global warming 100 years from now, because however catastrophic it might be, it is worth only a few dollars today to try to avert it."

In his recent book, *Global Warming: The Economic Stakes* (Institute for International Economics, 1992), Cline suggests using a 2 percent discount rate—a figure based on the expected future growth in per capita income, plus an allowance for the cost of capital—to justify an aggressive and expensive effort to slow global warming.

Nobel prize-winning economist James Tobin, a professor emeritus at Yale University, concurred with Cline's choice of a discount rate. "For long-run things, one should not use interest rates set in the market," Tobin said. The use of current interest rates to assess the economics of environmental projects only "reflects the impatience of those on the globe who would like their goodies now," he added.

Lawrence H. Summers, the chief economists at the World Bank, disagrees. He argued that the compelling needs of the poor and the uncertainty over future climate changes justify using the same discount rate for global warming projects as is applied to sanitation or education projects in the Third World.

"Do I sacrifice to help those in the future or help the one billion extremely poor people who share the planet Earth with me today?" Summers said. "I hold no greater grief for people who will die 100 years from now from global warming than for people who will die tomorrow from bad water."

have to be very careful here. A great deal of harm has been done to natural and environmental resources by using very low discount rates to evaluate development projects. With low discount rates, it's often possible to justify very disruptive public infrastructure projects because enough distant and uncertain benefits can be accumulated to outweigh the tremendous near-term costs.

One factor that comes into play, and that is hard to pin down, is the extent to which the current generation is sensitive to the needs of future generations as it makes its decisions. Clearly it has, to some extent, through regard for future family members, the desire to leave something for descendants, and generally a social conscience that leads people to care about the distant future. But are these motives strong enough to be sure that future generations are adequately represented today?

Given these uncertainties about discounting when looking at very long-run environmental impacts, we may want to fall back on additional criteria to help us in making current decisions. One of these might be the concept of sustainability that we have discussed in earlier chapters. Sustainability connotes the idea that we should avoid courses of action that reduce the long-run productive capabilities of our natural and environmental resource base. In practice the concept is very difficult to pin down, and we will have much more to say about it in a later chapter on environment and economic development.

Distributional Issues

The relation of total benefits and total costs is a question of economic efficiency. Distribution is a matter of who gets the benefits and who pays the costs. In public-sector programs, distributional matters must be considered along with efficiency issues, which implies that benefit-cost analyses must incorporate studies of how net benefits are distributed among different groups in society. In this section we introduce some of the main concepts of distribution analysis.

The distribution of benefits and costs is primarily a matter of equity, or fairness. There are two main types of equity: horizontal and vertical. Horizontal equity is a case of treating similarly situated people the same way. An environmental program that has the same impact on an urban dweller with $20,000 of income as on a rural dweller with the same income is horizontally equitable. Consider the following numbers; they refer to the annual values of a particular program accruing to three different individuals who, we assume, all have the same income. Abatement costs show the costs of the program to each individual; these may be higher prices on some products, more time spent on recycling matters, higher taxes, or other factors. The reduced damages are measures of the value of the improvements in environmental quality accruing to each person.

	Person A	Person B	Person C
Reduced environmental damages ($/year)	60	80	120
Abatement costs ($/year)	40	60	80
Difference	20	20	40

Costs and reduced damages are different for individuals A and B, but the difference between them ($20/year) is the same; hence the difference as a proportion of their income is the same. With respect to these two people, therefore, the program is horizontally equitable. It is not, however, for individual C, because this person experiences a net difference of $40/year. Since Person C is assumed to have the same income as the other two people, he or she is clearly better off as a result of this program; horizontal equity in this case has not been achieved.

Vertical equity refers to how a policy impinges on people who are in different circumstances, in particular on people who have different income levels. Consider the numbers in Table 6-3. These show the impacts, expressed in monetary values, of three different environmental quality programs on three people with, respectively, a low income, a medium income, and a high income. In parentheses next to each number is shown the percentage that number is of the person's income level. Note, for example, the "difference" row of Program 1; it shows the difference between how much the person benefits from the program (in terms of reduced environmental damages impinging on him) and how much it will cost him (in terms of the extent to which he will bear a part of the abatement costs of the program). Note that this net difference represents 1 percent of the income of each person. This is a *proportional impact*; i.e., it affects the people of each income level in the same proportion.

Program 2, on the other hand, is *regressive*; it provides higher proportional net benefits to high-income people than to low-income people. Program 3 has a *progressive* impact because net benefits represent a higher proportion of the lower-income person's income than it does of the rich person's income. Thus an environmental program (or any program for that matter) is proportional, progressive, or regressive, according to whether the net effect of that policy has proportionally the same, greater, or less effect on low-income people as on high-income people.

TABLE 6-3   VERTICAL EQUITY*

	Person A		Person B		Person C	
Income	5,000		20,000		50,000	
Program 1						
Reduced damages	150	(3.0)	300	(1.5)	600	(1.2)
Abatement costs	100	(2.0)	100	(0.5)	100	(0.2)
Difference	50	(1.0)	200	(1.0)	500	(1.0)
Program 2						
Reduced damages	150	(3.0)	1,400	(7.0)	5,500	(11.0)
Abatement costs	100	(2.0)	800	(4.0)	3,000	(6.0)
Difference	50	(1.0)	600	(3.0)	2,500	(5.0)
Program 3						
Reduced damages	700	(14.0)	2,200	(11.0)	3,000	(6.0)
Abatement costs	200	(4.0)	1,000	(5.0)	1,500	(3.0)
Difference	500	(10.0)	1,200	(6.0)	1,500	(3.0)

*Figures in the table show annual monetary values. Numbers in parentheses show the percentage of income these numbers represent.

We need to note also that although the net effects of a program may be distributed in one way, the individual components need not be distributed in the same way. For example, although the overall effects of Program 2 are regressive, the abatement costs of that program are in fact distributed progressively (i.e., the cost burden is proportionately greater for high-income people). In this case damage reduction is distributed so regressively that the overall program is regressive. So also in Program 3; although the overall program is progressive, abatement costs are distributed regressively.

These definitions of distributional impacts can be misleading. A program that is technically regressive could actually distribute the bulk of its net benefits to poor people. Suppose a policy raised the net income of one rich person by 10 percent, but raised each of the net incomes of 1,000 poor people by 5 percent. This policy is technically regressive although more than likely the majority of its aggregate net benefits go to poor people.

It is normally very difficult to estimate the distributional impacts of environmental programs, individually or in total. To do so requires very specific data showing impacts by income groups, race, or other factors. In general, environmental and health data have not been routinely collected by income and race. Thus, data on environmentally related diseases don't typically allow the comparison of differences across socioeconomic and racial groups. Nor is it easy to estimate how program costs are distributed among these groups, because these depend on complex factors related to tax collections, consumption patterns, the availability of alternatives, and so on. Despite the difficulties, however, benefit-cost analyses should try to look as closely as possible at the way in which the aggregates are distributed through the population. We will meet up with distributional issues throughout the later chapters of the book.

Uncertainty

In applications of benefit-cost analysis to natural and environmental resources we are projecting events well off into the future, and when we do this we run squarely into the fact that we have no way of knowing the future with certainty. Our uncertainty can arise from many sources. We may not be able to predict the preferences of future consumers, who may feel very differently than we do about matters of environmental quality. For studies of the long-run impacts of global warming, future population growth rates are important, and it is impossible to know these with certainty. Uncertainty may arise from technological change. Technical advancement in pollution-control equipment or in the chemistry of materials recycling could markedly shift future costs of achieving various levels of emission control. Nature itself is a source of uncertainty. Meteorological events can affect the outcomes of pollution-control programs; for example, in some cases we are still uncertain of the exact way human activities impact natural phenomena.

How should we address the fact that future benefits and costs are uncertain; that is, that future outcomes are "probabilistic"? If we know something about how these future probabilities manifest themselves, we may be able to estimate the "most likely" or "expected" levels of benefits and costs. Consider the problem of predicting the effect of certain policy changes on oil spills. In any given year we may have no tanker accidents, or one, or several; the exact number is uncertain. But we want a way to talk about the annual number of spills we could anticipate under different types of oil-spill control policies. One way of doing this is to estimate the *expected value* of oil spills we would anticipate in a year's time. Where would we get the information for this? If we have been collecting data over a long period of time, we might know something about actual long-run averages. If we don't have information like this, we might have to fall back on estimates provided by engineers, scientists, or people familiar with the problem. Assuming we can get information of this type, we could develop a *probability distribution* of the number of oil tanker accidents, as shown in Table 6-4. This shows the probabilities of having different numbers of tanker accidents in a year.[7] For example, the probability is .77 that we will have no tanker accidents, .12 that we will have one accident, .07 that we will have two accidents, and so on. Having obtained probabilities, we can then calculate the *expected value* of oil spills in a year's time. In effect this is the average number of oil spills we would experience each year over a period of time many years long. This is done by calculating a weighted average, as shown in Table 6-4. According to this calculation, the expected number of tanker accidents is .39 per year. We could then go on and estimate the expected quantity of oil that will be spilled and, perhaps, the expected value of damages. Thus, in this case of uncertainty, we are able to proceed by estimating expected values of probabilistic events, in particular the expected values of benefits and costs.

This approach is appropriate if we have reliable estimates of the probabilities of future events. But in many cases these may not be available, because we have not had enough experience with similar events to be able to know the future probabilities of different outcomes with any degree of confidence. One possibility here, made possible by the modern computer, is to carry out a *scenario analysis*. Suppose we are trying to predict the long-run costs of reducing CO_2 emissions as a step toward lessen-

---

[7] These are illustrative numbers only.

TABLE 6-4   CALCULATING THE EXPECTED NUMBER OF "LARGE" OIL SPILLS

Number of spills	Probability	Expected value of the number of oil spills
0	.77	$0 \times .77 = 0$
1	.12	$1 \times .12 = .12$
2	.07	$2 \times .07 = .14$
3	.03	$3 \times .03 = .09$
4	.01	$4 \times .01 = .04$
Over 4	—	—
		Expected value: .39

ing the greenhouse effect. These costs depend critically on the future pace of technological developments affecting the energy efficiency of production. We have little experience with predicting technical change over long periods of time, so it is unrealistic to try to estimate the probabilities that technical change will occur at different rates. Instead, we run our analysis several times, each time making a different assumption about the rate at which technical change will occur. Thus, our results might consist of three scenarios, with different results based on whether future technical change is "slow," "moderate," or "fast."

There is another difficulty that you should be aware of in using expected values on which to base decisions. These are appropriate if we are analyzing a relatively large number of recurrent situations, where good results in some will outweigh bad results in others. In the oil-spill case, we expect the annual number of spills to approach its expected value. But for unique events that will occur only once, we may want to look beyond expected values decisions. Consider the following numbers:

Program A		Program B	
Net benefits	Probability	Net benefits	Probability
$500,000	.475	$500,000	.99
$300,000	.525	−$10,000,000	.01
Expected value:	$395,000	Expected value:	$395,000

These two programs have exactly the same expected value. But suppose we had only a one-time choice between the two; perhaps it relates to the choice of a nuclear versus a conventional power plant to generate electricity. With A the net benefits are uncertain, but the outcomes are not extremely different and the probabilities are similar—it's very nearly a 50-50 proposition. Program B, on the other hand, has a very different profile. The probability is very high that the net benefits will be $500,000, but there is a small probability of a disaster, where there would be large negative net benefits. If we were making decisions strictly on the basis of expected values, we would treat these projects as the same; we could flip a coin to decide which one to choose. If we did this, we would be displaying *risk*-neutral behaviour-making decisions strictly on the basis of expected values. On the other hand, if this is a one-shot decision, we might decide that the low probability of a large loss in the case of project B represents a risk to which we do not wish to expose ourselves. In this case, we might be *risk averse*, preferring Project A over B.

There are many cases in environmental pollution control where risk aversion is undoubtedly the best policy. The rise of planetary-scale atmospheric change opens up the possibility of catastrophic human dislocations in the future. The potential scale of these impacts argues for a conservative, risk-averse approach to current decisions. Risk-averse decisions are also called for in the case of species extinction; a series of incremental and seemingly small decisions today may bring about a catastrophic decline in genetic resources in the future, with potentially drastic impacts on human welfare. Global issues are not the only ones where it may be prudent to avoid low risks of outcomes that would have large negative net benefits. The contamination of an important groundwater aquifer is a possibility faced by many local communities. And in any activity where risk to human life is involved, the average person is likely to be risk averse.

RISK ANALYSIS

The importance of risk in environmental management has led in recent years to modes of analyses specifically directed at this dimension of the problem. *Risk analysis* essentially covers two types of activities: *risk assessment* and *risk management.*

Consider the case of a hazardous waste dump into which a hazardous chemical has been dumped over the years. Suppose also that the people of a nearby community rely on a groundwater aquifer for their water supply. In a situation like this a risk assessment can be carried out to determine the size and significance of the risk the site poses to people in the community. One part of this is to determine the risks that the chemical might end up contaminating the aquifer. This requires engineers, hydrologists, etc., who can study the physical aspects of the landfill and surrounding area. A second element is to study the likely impacts on the health of community residents if the aquifer is contaminated. This involves taking the predicted chemical levels to which people in the community would be exposed if contamination occurred, and estimating the resulting health effects, such as, for example, the expected number of increased cases of cancer. This would call on *dose-response* relationships that scientists have developed in analyzing this particular substance. Often this type of information will come from laboratory studies with animals, the results of which are then extrapolated to human beings.

Economics comes into risk assessment in determining how much people value alternative situations involving differing risk levels. In our terminology, this is the estimation of peoples' willingness to pay for changes in levels of risk to which they are exposed. Experience has shown that the scientific results of relative risks stemming from different sources may not agree very well with how people actually feel about different types of risk. For example, people may be willing to pay substantial sums to have a chemical taken out of their water supply even though the health risk is relatively low; whereas they may not be willing to pay much for improved seat belts, which would reduce their overall risk by a great deal.

Risk management refers to public policies that have as their objective the reduction of risks to which humans are exposed. In the landfill example, after the levels and significance of the risk have been established, the problem becomes one of considering different policy options for managing the landfill and the water supply system. This could call upon *comparative risk analysis*, the investigation of different policy options and the levels of risk each would produce.

Risk management also calls on *risk-benefit analysis*. Suppose an administrative agency, such as the EPA, is considering whether a particular pesticide should be allowed on the market. It might do a study comparing the benefits farmers and consumers would gain, in the form of production cost savings, when the pesticide is used, to the increased health risks to farm workers, who must handle it, and possibly to consumers if there are pesticide residues on the marketed crop. In essence this is a benefit-cost analysis in which the cost side is treated more explicitly in terms of risk.

SUMMARY

In previous chapters we put the issue of environmental improvement in a trade-off type of format, where we have willingness to pay (benefits) on one side and abatement costs on the other. In this chapter we started to focus on the problem of measuring these benefits and costs. To do this researchers have to use some underlying analytical framework to account for these benefits and costs. We considered several types of frameworks (impact analysis and cost-effectiveness analysis), then settled on the primary approach used in resource and environmental economics: benefit-cost analysis. The rest of the chapter was devoted to a discussion of the main conceptual issues involved in benefit-cost analysis. These are:

- The basic analytical steps involved,
- Determining the appropriate size of a project or program,
- The difference between net benefits and the benefit-cost ratio as a decision criterion,
- Discounting,
- Distributional issues, and
- Uncertainty.

Having discussed the basic structure of benefit-cost analysis, we will turn now to problems of actually measuring the benefits and costs of specific environmental programs.

QUESTIONS FOR FURTHER DISCUSSION

1 In the section on choosing the current size of a project or program we mentioned the problem of a regional planning agency allocating its budget among several programs in different cities. What is the relevance here of the equimarginal principle?

2 When setting public policy on environmental risks, should we base it on the levels of risk to which people think they are exposed or on the risk levels scientists have determined them to be in fact?

3 Suppose we are comparing two ways of protecting ourselves against mobile-source air pollution: putting additional controls on the internal combustion engine or developing an entirely different type of engine that is cleaner. How would changes in the discount rate be likely to affect the comparison between these two options?

SELECTED READINGS

Abelson, Peter. *Cost-Benefit Analysis and Environmental Problems*. Farnborough, England: Saxon House, 1979.

Coker, Annabel, and Cathy Richards. *Valuing the Environment, Economic Approaches to Environmental Evaluation*. London and Boca Raton: Belhaven Press, Fl., 1992.

Dasgupta, Ajit K., and D. W. Pearce. *Cost-Benefit Analysis: Theory and Practice*. New York: Barnes and Noble, 1972.

Freeman, A. Myrick, III. *Air and Water Pollution Control: A Benefit-Cost Assessment*. New York, John Wiley, 1982.

Kneese, Allen, and Blair Bower. *Environmental Quality Analysis*. Baltimore, Md.: Johns Hopkins Press, 1972.

Lave, Lester B. *The Strategy of Social Regulation: Decision Frameworks for Policy*. Washington, D.C.: The Brookings Institution, 1981.

Lind, Robert C. "Reassessing the Government's Discount Policy in Light of New Theory and Data in a World Economy with a High Degree of Capital Mobility." *Journal of Environmental Economics and Management* 18(2) (March 1990): S-29 to S-50.

Russell, Clifford S., and V. Kerry Smith. "Demands for Data and Analysis Induced by Environmental Policy," in Ernst R. Berndt and Jack E. Triplett (eds.). *Fifty Years of Economic Measurement*. University of Chicago Press, Chicago: National Bureau of Economic Research, Studies in Income and Wealth, 1990, 299–340.

Sugden, Robert, and Alan Williams. *The Principles of Practical Benefit-Cost Analysis*. Oxford, England: Oxford University Press, 1978.

Tolley, George S., Philip F. Graves, and Glenn C. Blomquist. *Environmental Policy, Elements of Environmental Analysis*. Vol. I. Cambridge, Mass: Ballinger Publishing Company, 1981.

7

BENEFIT-COST ANALYSIS: BENEFITS

We have already made the connection between benefits and willingness to pay. The benefits of something are equal to what people are willing to pay for it, remembering the provisos about the distribution of income and the availability of information. If we want to estimate peoples' willingness to pay for potatoes, we can go and observe them buying potatoes—so many potatoes at such-and-such prices—and develop a good idea of the value people place on this item. But we can't do this when valuing changes in environmental quality. There are no markets where people buy and sell units of environmental quality, so we can't measure consumer benefits directly the way we can with potatoes. Instead, we have to fall back on indirect means. As one environmental economist has put it: "benefit estimation often involves a kind of detective work for piecing together the clues about the values individuals place on [environmental services] as they respond to other economic signals."[1]

The measurement of benefits is an activity pursued on many levels. For an analyst working in an environmental agency, it can turn into a plug-in-the-numbers exercise. So many acres of clambed destroyed (information provided by a marine biologist) times the going price of clams (provided by a quick trip to the local fish market) equals damages of water pollution in the "X" estuary. At the other extreme, for an environmental economist whose interest is in extending the technique, it can be an excursion into sophisticated means of squeezing subtle information from new sets of data. Our path in this chapter will lie between these extremes. We will review the main techniques environmental economists have developed to measure the benefits of improvements in environmental quality. We will try to understand the economic

---

[1] Myrick Freeman III, "Benefits of Pollution Control," in U.S. Environmental Protection Agency, *Critical Review of Estimating Benefits of Air and Water Pollution Control* (Washington, D.C.: EPA 600/5-78-014, 1978), II-16.

logic lying behind these techniques, without getting bogged down in all the theoretical niceties and statistical details.[2]

MEASURING DAMAGES DIRECTLY

When environmental degradation occurs, it produces damages; our emissions control model of Chapter 5 is based in part on the relationship between emissions and marginal damages. So in a very direct sense the benefits of improved environmental quality come about because of reduced damages. To measure a complete emissions damage function, it is necessary to go through the following steps:

1 Measure emissions,
2 Determine the resulting ambient quality,
3 Estimate human exposure,
4 Measure impacts (health, aesthetic, recreation, etc.),
5 Estimate the values of these impacts.

The first three of the steps are largely the work of physical scientists. Models that show the relation between emissions and ambient levels are often called *diffusion models*. Step 4 involves economists to some extent, but also biological scientists and epidemiologists. The linkage of Steps 3 and 4 is often called a *dose-response* function. This means estimating the response in terms, for example, of human mortality and morbidity to varying exposure levels to environmental pollutants. Step 5 is where economics comes strongly into play, in estimating the values associated with different impacts as identified in the previous step. It might appear easy to measure benefits by measuring damages directly, but this will turn out not to be the case. To understand this let us look at several approaches that have been made in the past to measuring damages directly.

Health Damages

Some of the most important damages caused by environmental pollution are those related to human health. Air pollution, especially, has long been thought to increase mortality and morbidity among people exposed to it, certainly in the episodic releases of toxic pollutants, but also from long-run exposure to such pollutants as SO_2 and particulate matter. Diseases such as bronchitis, emphysema, and lung cancer are thought to be traceable in part to polluted air. Estimates of the health costs of air pollution suggest that many billions of dollars are lost each year. Water pollution also produces health damages, primarily through contaminated drinking water supplies. So the measurement of the human health damages of environmental pollution is a critical task for environmental economists.

---

[2] There are a number of recent books reviewing the current state of environmental benefits measurement. These are listed in the bibliography at the end of the chapter.

Fundamental to this work is the underlying dose-response relationship showing the relationship between human health and exposure to environmental pollution of various types. Many factors affect human health—lifestyles, diet, genetic factors, age, etc.—besides ambient pollution levels. To separate out the effects of pollution, one has to account for all the other factors or else run the risk of attributing to pollution effects that are actually caused by something else. This calls for large amounts of accurate data on health factors as well as the numerous suspected causal factors. Some of this—air or water quality, mortality statistics, etc.—may be available from published sources, but these may be too highly aggregated to give accurate results. Similarly, although published data may give us information on, for example, average air-pollution levels in certain areas of a city, it doesn't give completely accurate exposure data because that depends on how long individuals have lived in that environment. In a mobile society it's hard to develop accurate exposure data for people, since they may have lived in a variety of places throughout their lives. Epidemiologists have developed extensive experience with panel data, information developed through in-depth interviews with people about their lifestyles, consumption habits, locational history, etc.

The first major study of air pollution and human health was done in the U.S. by Lave and Seskin in the 1970s.[3] The data were for 1969 and refer to published information on standard metropolitan statistical areas (SMSAs). They concluded that, in general, a 1 percent reduction in air pollution produces a .12 percent reduction in death rates. Since that study, researchers have examined these and other data on health and pollution to improve the statistical procedures and add new explanatory variables. One conclusion is that the results one gets are very sensitive to the data used and the way they are handled, which means we are still very uncertain about the exact links between air pollution and human mortality rates.

The same conclusion holds for the dose-response function with respect to human morbidity. Morbidity refers to the incidence of disease, so it can be expressed in different ways. One study looks at the relationship between air pollutants and morbidity expressed in two ways: (1) days absent from work and (2) days affected by ill health.[4] The author found no connection between these variables and sulfur pollution but did find an effect for total suspended particulates. Other morbidity studies have been carried out on air pollution and water pollution, but there is certainly no consensus yet on the underlying relationships. Much more work remains to be done.

The main work of economists comes after the dose-response research, in putting values on the various health impacts. How should we approach placing a value on a life prematurely shortened or on a debilitating illness suffered as a result of exposure to environmental pollutants? Your first reaction may be that it's a dubious moral exercise to try to attach a monetary value to a human life. Isn't life "priceless"? In a sense

[3] Lester B. Lave and Eugene P. Seskin, *Air Pollution and Human Health* (Baltimore, Md.: Johns Hopkins Press, 1977).

[4] Bart D. Ostro, "Air Pollution and Morbidity Revisited: A Specification Test," *Journal of Environmental Economics and Management* 14(1) (March 1987): 87–98.

it is. If you stop a person in the street and ask her how much her life is worth, you may not get an answer because the question seems to violate a common moral standard. Nevertheless, society as a whole—that is, all of us acting collectively—doesn't behave that way. In fact, through our collective decisions and behaviour, we implicitly assign values to human lives. The clearest place to see this is in traffic control. Each year thousands of people are killed on the nation's highways. Yet we do not see a massive outpouring of funds to redesign highways, slow traffic, make substantially safer cars, etc. This is because we are making an implicit trade-off between traffic deaths and other travel-related impacts, especially the benefits of reasonably fast and convenient travel. The same may be said of other risky technologies and practices of which modern life is replete. Thus, despite the moral prescriptions about the ultimate values of human life, it makes sense to examine the values that society actually places on lives and human health in the everyday course of its operation.

For some years it was standard procedure to estimate health damages by looking at such things as increased monetary expenditures on health care and reductions in worker productivity accompanying deteriorated health and shortened lives. For example, we might try to measure the value of a human life by looking at the economic contribution that society forgoes when that life is stopped. Over their working lives people contribute to the production of useful goods and services enjoyed by others in society. When they die, this productivity ceases; thus, we might estimate the cumulative value of production that they would have produced had they lived. Lost productivity would vary among individuals, as a function of their age, skills, employment history, etc., so we might take averages for people in different categories. Using the same logic, we might estimate the value of reduced morbidity by measuring the value of increased production this would make possible.

Another direct approach at measuring health damages is to look at medical expenditures. As health is affected by increasing pollution we would expect increased medical expenditures, on hospitals, doctors, rehabilitation, etc. Reducing pollution would, therefore, lead to a reduction in medical expenditures, which can be counted as a benefit of the environmental change.

Other Types of Damages

Some types of air pollution have been implicated in damages of agricultural crops. One way of measuring these might be to take the dose-response information developed by physical and natural sciences and use it to predict the increased yields resulting from the amelioration of a particular case of air pollution. These increased yields would then be multiplied by the market price of the item to get a measure of the benefits of the improved air quality.

Another type of direct damage estimation might be applied to materials damage. Air pollution in urban areas has been shown to lead to deterioration in exposed materials, from buildings to outdoor sculpture. These damages might be measured by looking at the increased maintenance costs required to keep these materials from deteriorating.

Problems with Direct Damage Approaches

The basic problem with direct damage estimates like this is that they are almost always seriously incomplete. Consider the case of measuring health damages by lost productivity and medical expenditures. We note, first, that these are market measures. They measure the value of marketed goods and services a person might, on average, produce. So the many nonmarket contributions people make, both inside and outside the home, don't get counted. This method would also assign a zero value to a student unable to work, or a retiree. There is also the question of whether a person's consumption should be subtracted from his production to measure his actual net contribution. This might seem reasonable but, if we do this, we would be forced into awkward conclusions, such as that the premature death of a welfare recipient would be a benefit to society. There are numerous monetary, as well as psychic, benefits received by others—friends and relatives, for example—that the productivity measure does not account for. Nor does it account for the pain and suffering of illness. Thus, although the productivity approach may be useful in some circumstances, it can give misleading results in others. The same may be said of using medical expenditures to estimate damages from reduced environmental quality. Suppose we estimate the damages to a woman of getting a head cold. We come up with an estimate of $1.27, the cost of the aspirin she will consume to reduce the discomfort. This probably would be a serious understatement of the true damages of the cold. If she were asked how much she would be willing to pay to avoid the cold, the answer is likely to be substantially more than the cost of the aspirin. This is perhaps an unfair example because major medical expenditures for a person suffering from air pollution-induced lung cancer are much more significant than a bottle of aspirin. Nevertheless, because of problems like these we must turn back to our fundamental concept for determining value: willingness to pay.

WILLINGNESS TO PAY

The problem with the direct approach to damage estimation discussed above is that it is usually incomplete. This is a difficulty with measurement, not with the concept. A marginal damage function shows the changes in damages suffered by people or other elements of the ecosystem when exposed to pollution or environmental alteration. We must think of "damages" in the broad sense; it includes what we would think of as direct physical damage, such as health impacts, but also such impacts as degradation of the aesthetic quality of the environment (e.g., lowered visibility or psychic damage). In other words, "damages" include all the negative effects of the airborne emissions. Looked at from a different perspective, the marginal damage function for increases in emissions is the same as the demand/willingness-to-pay function for decreases in emissions. If a small increase in emissions causes a person $10 in increased damages, the maximum he would be willing to pay to decrease emissions by that small amount would presumably be $10. We want to focus, therefore, on willingness to pay for environmental improvements.

There are essentially three ways of trying to find out how much people are willing to pay for improvements in environmental quality. We can illustrate them by considering a case of noise pollution. One feature of the modern world is high-speed roadways (highways, expressways, freeways, and turnpikes), and a major characteristic of these roads is that the traffic on them creates noise. Thus, the people who live nearby suffer damages from this traffic noise. Suppose we would like to estimate the willingness to pay of people living near highways to reduce traffic noise. How might we do this?

1 The homeowners themselves may have made expenditures to reduce the noise levels inside their homes. For example, they may have installed additional insulation in the walls of their homes or put double-thick glass in the windows. When people make expenditures like this, they reveal something about their willingness to pay for a quieter environment. In general, then, if we can find cases where market goods are purchased in order to affect a consumer's exposure to the ambient environment, we may be able to analyze these purchases for what they say about the value people place on changes in that ambient environment.

2 The noise in the vicinity of the road may have affected the prices that people have paid for the houses there. If two houses have exactly the same characteristics in all respects but the level of exterior noise, we would expect the one in the noisier environment to be less valuable to prospective buyers than the one in the quieter environment. If the housing market is competitive, the price of the noisier house would be lower than the other one. Thus, by looking at the difference in house prices we can estimate the value people place on reduced noise pollution. In general, therefore, any time the price of some good or service varies in accordance with its environmental characteristics, we may be able to analyze these price variations to determine people's willingness to pay for these characteristics.

3 Both of the foregoing techniques are indirect, in the sense that they look for ways of analyzing market data to find out what they imply about the willingness to pay of people for closely associated environmental characteristics. The third way is deceptively direct. We could conduct a survey among homeowners and ask them how much they would be willing to pay for reductions in noise levels around and inside their homes. This direct survey approach has received a lot of attention from environmental economists in recent years, primarily because of its flexibility. Virtually any feature of the natural environment that can be described accurately to people can be studied by this method.

In the remainder of the chapter we will examine some of the ways these approaches have been applied to estimate the benefits of improvements in environmental quality.

WILLINGNESS TO PAY: INDIRECT METHODS

The thought behind these indirect approaches is that when people make market choices among certain items that have different characteristics related to the environment, they will reveal the value they place on these environmental factors. Perhaps the most important is what they reveal about the values of health and human life.

The Value of Human Health as Expressed in "Averting" Costs

Air and water pollution can produce a variety of adverse health conditions, ranging from slight chest discomfort or headaches all the way to acute episodes requiring hospital care. People often make expenditures to try to avoid, or avert, these conditions, and these averting costs are an expression of their willingness to pay to avoid them. A number of studies have been done in which these averting expenditures have been analyzed for what they tell about willingness to pay.[5] One study was done of a sample of people in the Los Angeles area in 1986 looking at expenditures they made to avoid a variety of respiratory symptoms. Expenditures included such things as cooking with electricity rather than gas, operating a home air conditioner, and driving an air-conditioned car. Their estimates of the willingness to pay to avoid various respiratory symptoms ranged from $0.97 for shortness of breath to $23.87 for chest tightness.

The Value of Human Life as Expressed in Wage Rates

Diminished air quality and contaminated water can lead to deteriorated health and death. How are these impacts to be valued? It is tempting to say "human life is beyond measure," but that is not the way people behave in the real world. We can see by casual observation that individuals do not, in fact, behave as if prolonged life, or the warding off of disease, is in some sense an ultimate end to which all their resources must be devoted. We see people engaging in risky activity, in some sense trading off risk for the benefits received. Almost everybody drives a car, some people smoke, some rock climb, many strive to get tans, and so on. We also see people allocating portions of their income to reducing risk; buying locks, installing smoke alarms, staying away from dark places at night. And we observe people making differential judgments of their own worth; parents with children buying more life insurance than single people, and so on. All of which suggests that people treat the risk of death in a reasonably rational manner, and that we could use willingness to pay as a way of evaluating the benefits of reducing the risk of death or illness.

But we must be clear on exactly what is involved. There is a joke about the stingy millionaire, walking down a street, who gets held up. The robber points a gun at her and says, "Your money or your life," and the victim replies: "Ah, let me think about that." Estimating the willingness-to-pay value of a human life does not involve this kind of situation. We do not ask people to express their willingness to pay to save their own lives. Under some circumstances a person presumably will be willing to

[5] These are reviewed in Maureen L. Cropper and A. Myrick Freeman III, "Environmental Health Effects," in John B. Braden and Charles D. Kolstad (eds.), *Measuring the Demand for Environmental Quality* (Amsterdam: North-Holland, 1991), 200–202.

give everything he owns. But these are not the kinds of situations people normally face. When one expresses a willingness to pay for reducing air pollution, the relevant concept is the value of the *statistical life*, not the life of some particular individual. This does not imply that people are assumed to care only about the average, or random, person, and not certain specific people. People obviously feel closer to their relatives, friends, and neighbours than to strangers. What is involved is the value of rearranging the living conditions of a large group of people by, for example, reducing their exposure to environmental pollutants, in order to lower the probability that some randomly determined individual from the group will suffer illness or premature death. Suppose that the average person in a group of 100,000 people would be willing to pay $5 to lower the probability of a random death among members of that group from 7 in 100,000 to 6 in 100,000. Then the total willingness to pay is $5(100,000) = $500,000, which is the value of a statistical life based on willingness to pay.[6]

Using willingness to pay to measure health benefits has the virtue of being consistent with other types of economic demand studies, and it recognizes that even with something as important as health care, it is peoples' evaluations of its worth that should count. But we need to use the concept with care. In any real-world situation, willingness to pay implies ability to pay; one cannot express a willingness to pay for something if one lacks the necessary income or wealth. So we must be sensitive to the income levels of people whose demand we are trying to measure. If, in our analysis, we have included a substantial number of people with low incomes, the measured willingness to pay we obtain may be lower than justified. We may not want to lower the estimated health benefits of an environmental program simply because the target population has lower than average incomes.

Another feature about health care as a normal economic good is that people may be willing to pay for the health of others. Parents may not care if their daughter eats meat; her own willingness to pay is a good expression of her demand for meat. But they do care about her health and, to her own willingness to pay for good health, they would be willing to add a substantial sum of their own. Thus, strictly individualistic measures of willingness to pay for health improvements may underestimate the true benefits of programs that increase health.

The most fully developed approach to measuring the willingness to pay for reducing risk to life is through *industrial wage rate studies*. In work situations, whether industrial, agricultural, mining, or marine, pollutants are often present in concentrated form because of seriously diminished ambient conditions in the vicinity of the production process, because production requires workers to handle relatively large amounts of potentially harmful substances, or because accidents can lead to high-level exposure of workers to pollutants of various types. Many pollutants that pose few threats when dispersed throughout the general population may have substantial impacts in the concentrated amounts in which they occur in the workplace. Many cases of workplace exposure and damage have come to light in recent decades. "Black

---

[6] This example comes from A. Myrick Freeman, *The Benefits of Environmental Improvement: Theory and Practice* (Baltimore, Md.: Johns Hopkins Press for Resources for the Future, 1979).

lung" from working in mines, "brown lung" from working in cotton mills, and severe lung damage from working with asbestos are examples. Agricultural workers handling pesticides are at risk from exposure to these toxic chemicals.

If we study wage rates among different jobs that expose workers to different pollution-exposure risk, we may be able to measure the value people put on these reduced health risks. It's hard to get good data on workplace exposure to various pollutants. Where wage rate studies have been used more effectively is in measuring the value of reducing the risk of premature death. They have been used, in other words, to get at the problem of the value of a statistical life. Suppose there are two jobs similar in all respects except that in one, because of the type of machinery used, the risk of death is somewhat higher than in the other. Suppose that initially the wage rates in the two industries were the same. In this case it would obviously be preferable to work in the safer industry—same wage, lower risk. Workers would then seek to move from the dangerous to the safer industry. This would tend to drive down the wage in the safer industry and increase the wage in the other, as firms sought to keep workers from leaving that industry. Thus, a wage differential would evolve between the two industries; the amount of that differential would show how workers valued the differences between them in terms of risk of death. By analyzing wage differences like this, we can get a measure of the benefits people would get from reducing pollution-related premature deaths.

Table 7-1 summarizes some of the recent results of wage-rate studies done for the United States and United Kingdom aimed at estimating the value of a statistical life. Note that the estimates vary widely. What accounts for these differences? Different data and statistical techniques probably account for most of them. These studies are difficult because there are many other factors that have to be taken into account and because it is hard to get exactly the right data. For example, most worker accident and wage data apply to industry groupings, and within these groups there may be substantial variation among individual firms, not only because of technological differences among them but also because some firms may have done a lot more than others to make the workplace safer. It's also the case that wage-rate studies like this are predicated on the reasonably efficient working of the labour market, and this may not be the case in some industries. Union agreements, collusion among firm managers, and lack of information can upset the competitive wage-making process in some industries. Another problem is that the analyst may have an objective measure of risk to health, but the risk perceived by the worker could be quite different. This again breaks the link between wage rates and the benefits people get from lower pollution levels. These problems do not mean that these studies are not useful, only that we have not yet reached a point where they are giving us a consistent story.

The Value of Environmental Quality as Expressed in House Prices

The wage-rate studies above estimate the willingness to pay to be exposed to lower risk of death; that is, the willingness to pay for a specific consequence of being

TABLE 7-1   VALUE OF LIFE IN OCCUPATIONAL RISK STUDIES: THE UNITED STATES AND THE UNITED KINGDOM

Study	Best estimate of value of a statistical life (U.S. = $ mil; UK = mil; 1982 prices)
United States	
Arnould/Nichols (1983)	0.64
Dillingham (1979)	0.40
Olson (1981)	7.10
Smith, R. (1976)	3.30
Thaler/Rosen (1975)	0.57
Viscusi (1978)	2.90-3.90
United Kingdom	
Marin/Psacharopoulos (1982)	1.64
Velijanovski (1981)	3.39-4.59
Needleman (1979)	0.13-0.72

Sources: Richard Arnould and Len Nichols, "Wage Risk Premiums and Workers' Compensation: A Refinement of Estimates of Compensating Wage Differential." *Journal of Political Economy* 91(2), (April 183): 332–340; A. Dillingham, "The Injury Risk Structure of Occupations and Wages," Ph.D. dissertation, Cornell University, 1979; Alan Marin and George Psacharopoulos, "The Reward for Risk in the Labor Market: Evidence from the United Kingdom and a Reconciliation with Other Studies," *Journal of Political Economy* 90(4) (August 1982): 827–853; L. Needleman, "The Valuation of Changes in the Risk of Death by Those at Risk," Working Paper 103, University of Waterloo, 1979; Craig Olson, "An Analysis of Wage Differentials Received by Workers on Dangerous Jobs," *Journal of Human Resources* 16(2) (Spring 1981): 167–185; Robert Smith, "The Feasibility of an Injury Tax Approach to Occupational Safety," *Law and Contemporary Problems* 38(4) (1974): 730–744; Richard Thaler and Sherwin Rosen, "The Value of Saving a Life: Evidence from the Labor Market," in Nester Terleckyj (ed.), "Regulating Industrial Accidents: An Economic Analysis of Market and Legal Responses," Ph.D. thesis, University of York, 1981; W. Kip Viscusi, "Health Effects and Earnings Premiums for Job Hazards," *Review of Economics and Statistics*, 60(3) (August 1978): 408–416.

exposed to higher levels of environmental pollution. But there are wider benefits to a cleaner environment than health benefits. A more inclusive approach to take is to examine peoples' willingness to pay to live in a less polluted environment. This would include the health effects but also other dimensions such as aesthetic impacts.

Suppose you had two houses that were exactly the same in terms of all their physical characteristics—number of rooms, floor area, age, etc.—as well as in locational factors—distance to neighbours, distance to shopping facilities, etc. But assume one house is located in an area of substantial air pollution, while the other is located in an area with relatively clean air. We would expect the market prices of these two houses to differ because of the air quality difference. This conclusion generalizes to a large housing market involving many properties. The surrounding air quality is essentially a feature of the location of a house so, as houses are bought and sold in the house market, air quality differences would tend to get "capitalized" into the market prices of the houses.[7] Of course, homes differ in many respects, not just in terms of air quality. So we must collect large amounts of data on many properties, then

[7] By "capitalized" we mean that house prices adjust to reflect the present value of the stream of future damages to which homeowners would be exposed if they lived in the various houses.

use statistical techniques to identify the role played by air pollution, as well as of other factors. The technical name for this type of approach is "hedonic" analysis. When the price of something is related to the many characteristics it possesses, we can study patterns of price differences to deduce the value people place on one of those characteristics.

The derivation a hedonic price function is done using statistical techniques. The analyst typically collects data on a sample of housing units sold over a particular time period. The relationship between housing prices and all the possible characteristics that might influence people's willingness to pay for each house is then estimated statistically. We can graph what is called a *hedonic price function* for a particular characteristic, say air quality (measured by an air quality index or AQI), holding all other characteristics constant. Figure 7-1 panel (a) illustrates this relationship. The hedonic price function is shown as P(AQI; z) where z is all other characteristics that are held constant. The function is not a straight line to show that for most people, their marginal willingness to pay for a characteristic changes as more of the characteristic is supplied. At low levels of air quality, people willingness to pay for a small increase in air quality might be quite high. But if the level of air quality is already high, a small increase will not yield a large increase in willingness to pay. If we then take the slope of this hedonic price function for different levels of air quality, we obtain the hedonic demand function for air quality which depicts the marginal willingness to pay for each increment in air quality, again remembering that all other characteristics are held constant.[8]

Panel (b) of Figure 7-1 illustrates a hedonic demand function, D(AQI;z). AQI is still on the horizontal axis, but the vertical axis now measures willingness to pay for air quality (AQ). This demand function can then be interpreted in the usual way to

---

[8] For those familiar with calculus, the hedonic demand function is found by taking the derivative of the hedonic price function with respect to the characteristic one wishes to examine. In this case, it is the API.

FIGURE 7-1   Derivation of a Hedonic Demand Curve for Air Quality.

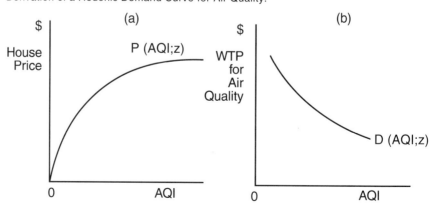

estimate benefits of improving environmental quality. For a change in air quality from AQ_0 to AQ_1, the area under the hedonic demand curve between these two levels shows the total benefits from that air quality improvement.

Table 7-2 shows results from a number of studies in which economists have looked for impacts of air pollution on property values. The results are given in terms of elasticities, that is, percentage change in house prices for a 1 percent change in air pollution. Note that there have been numerous types of air pollutants studied, with similar results for different ones. They show that for sulfur pollution a 1 percent increase in ambient concentration is associated with a change in house prices of between .06 and .12 percent. For particulates the sizes of the elasticities are quite similar.

The same kind of approach might be used with some cases of water pollution. In Chapter 4 we used lake pollution to introduce the concept of a public good. Suppose a lake is surrounded by a number of residences. The market price of these homes will be affected by many things—their age, size, condition, etc. They will also be affected by the water quality of the lake. If this water quality degrades over time, we would expect the market values of the surrounding properties to go down. The deteriorating water quality means that homeowners will obtain less utility from living in that vicinity, other things remaining equal, and this will get capitalized into the values of the houses. One way we might approach measuring the benefits of cleaning up the lake is to estimate the overall increase in property values among the homes in the vicinity of the lake. We have to remember, however, that this is likely to be only a partial estimate of total benefits. If nonresidents have access to the lake or park, they

TABLE 7-2   HOME PRICES AND AIR POLLUTION

City	Year	Pollutant	Results*
St. Louis	1960	Sulfation†	.06–.10
	1963	Particulates	.12–.14
Chicago	1964–1967	Particulates and sulfation	.20–.50
Washington	1970	Particulates	.05–.12
	1967–1968	Oxidants	.01–.02
Toronto	1961	Sulfation	.06–.12
Philadelphia	1960	Sulfation	.10
	1969	Particulates	.12
Pittsburgh	1970	Dustfall and sulfation	.09–.15
Los Angeles	1977–1978	Particulates and oxidants	.22

*Percentage reduction in value of house per 1 percent increase in ambient concentration of pollutant.
†A measure of SO_2 using the lead peroxide candle method.
Sources: A. Myrick Freeman III, *The Benefits of Environmental Improvement: Theory and Practice* (Baltimore, Md.: Johns Hopkins Press for Resources for the Future, 1979), 156–160; David S. Brookshire, Mark A. Thayer, William D. Schulze, and Ralph C. D'Arge, "Valuing Public Goods: A Comparison of Survey and Hedonic Approaches," *American Economic Review* 72(1) (March 1982): 165–171; David W. Pearce and Anil Markandya, *Environmental Policy Benefits: Monetary Valuation* (Organization for Economic Cooperation and Development, 1989), 31.

would also be gaining benefits, but these would not show up in property value changes. Property value changes to measure benefits from pollution reduction can also be used in other situations; for example, in valuing the damage from noise around airports and major highways and in measuring the benefits flowing from urban parks.

The Value of Environmental Quality and Intercity Wage Differentials

We talked about using wage-rate differences among jobs to measure the value of reducing health risks from pollution. Wage-rate studies have also been used to estimate the value of living in a cleaner environment. Suppose there were two cities, alike in every respect, but one has higher air pollution than the other. Suppose that initially wage rates in the two cities were equal. Since everything else is exactly the same, it would be more desirable to work in the less polluted city—same wage but less air pollution. Workers would, therefore, migrate to the cleaner city. In order to keep a labour force in the dirty city, one of two things must happen: the air must be cleaned up or a higher wage must be offered to offset the damages of living in more polluted air. So we could study wage-rate differentials among cities with different degrees of, say, air pollution to measure the value that people place on cleaner air. And this would give us a way of estimating the benefits of cleaning up the air in the more polluted cities.

The Effects of Pollution on Production Costs

Air pollution can reduce crop yields on exposed farms; it can also reduce the growth rates of commercially valuable timber. Water pollution can adversely affect firms and municipalities that use the water for production purposes or for domestic use. Diminished water quality can also have a negative impact on commercial fishing industries. Soil contamination can have serious impacts on agricultural production. Pollution in the workplace can reduce the effectiveness of workers and can often increase the rate at which machinery and buildings deteriorate. In these cases the effects of pollution are felt on the production of goods and services. The damage caused by the pollution comes about because it interferes in some way with these production processes, in effect making it more costly to produce these outputs than it would be in a less polluted world.

How we actually measure production-related benefits of reducing pollution depends on circumstances. Suppose we are looking at a small group of agricultural producers living in a certain region who will be affected by reduced airborne emissions coming from an upwind factory. Pollutants from the factory have depressed yields, so reducing emissions will cause yields to increase. The crop being produced is sold in a national market, and its price will be unaffected by the output changes in this one region. This situation is depicted in Figure 7-2. In this diagram, S_1 is the supply curve for this group of farms before the improved air quality; S_2 is the supply curve after the improvement.[9] Price of the output is p_1. Before the change, these farm-

[9] See Chapters 3 and 4 for a discussion of supply curves.

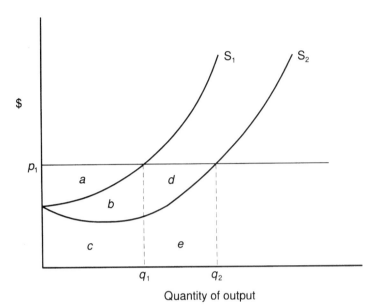

FIGURE 7-2   Benefits from Reduced Production Costs.

ers produce at an output level of q_1, while after the improvement their output increases to q_2.

One way of approximating the benefits of this environmental improvement is to measure the value of increased output produced by this group of farms. The increased output is simply multiplied by the price of the crop. This gives an estimate corresponding to the area $(d + e)$ in Figure 7-2.

A number of studies have been done along these lines.[10] Moskowitz et al.[11] studied the effects of air pollution on alfalfa in the U.S. They measured the quantity of production lost because of air pollution and valued this loss at the going price of alfalfa. They found that air pollution was responsible for a loss in 1974 of between $24 million and $210 million. The difference between these figures comes about because of uncertainties over the actual pollution dose the alfalfa received in that year. Another study was done by Page et al.[12] to measure crop-related air-pollution losses in a six-state area. They estimated annual losses in the production of soybeans,

[10] These are reviewed in Gardner M. Brown, Jr., and Mark L. Plummer, "Market Measures of User Benefits," in *Acid Deposition: State of Science and Technology*, Report 27, Methods for Valuing Acidic Deposition and Air Pollution Effects (Washington, D.C., U.S. Superintendent of Documents: National Acid Precipitation Assessment Program, 1990) 27-35 to 27-73.

[11] Paul D. Moskowitz et al., "Oxidant Air Pollution: A Model for Estimating Effects on U.S. Vegetation," *Journal of Air Pollution Control Association* 32(2) (February 1982): 155–160.

[12] Walter P. Page et al., "Estimation of Economic Losses to the Agricultural Sector from Airborne Residuals in the Ohio River Basin," *Journal of Air Pollution Control Association*, 32(2) (February 1982): 151–154.

wheat, and corn and then aggregated these to see what the present value of total losses would be over the period 1976–2000. They came up with an estimate of about $7 billion.

Several Canadian studies have been done on the effects of ground-level ozone on crops.[13] Ozone is seen as the most damaging air pollutant to crops in Canada. The value of reduced crop yields per year in southern Ontario ranges from $17 to $70 million, depending on the year chosen. The reason the range is so large is that the number of severe ozone days varies per year. In the Fraser Valley of B.C., estimates of lost production are approximated at $8.8 million annually.

A more refined approach to estimating the value of reducing pollution is possible. The problem with taking just the value of the increased output is that production costs may also have changed. When air pollution diminishes, farmers may actually increase their use of certain inputs and farm this land more intensively. How do we account for this possibility? Note that we can analyze the full change in the following way, using net incomes of the farmers (total value of output minus total production costs).

Situation before the change:

Total value of output: $a + b + c$

Total costs: $b + c$

Net income: a

Situation after the change:

Total value of output: $a + b + c + d + e$

Total costs: $c + e$

Net income: $a + b + d$

Thus, the improvement in net incomes is $(a + b + d) - a$, or an amount equal to area $b + d$ in the diagram.

How we measure this amount depends on how much information we are able to get. If we have studied these farms and know their supply curves before and after the change, we can measure the increased net income directly. If we don't know the supply curves, another possibility might be to look at the increased values of agricultural land in the area. In many cases, added net incomes of this type will get capitalized into land values, and we can use the increased land values to estimate the benefits of the environmental improvements.

---

[13] These studies are cited in Environment Canada, *Ground-Level Ozone in Canada,* A State of the Environment Fact Sheet, No. 92-1, Catalogue No. EN1-12/92-1E (Ottawa: Ministry of Supply and Services, 1992), 4.

Materials Damage

Air pollutants cause damage to exposed surfaces, metal surfaces of machinery, stone surfaces of buildings and statuary, and painted surfaces of all types of items. The most heavily implicated pollutants are the sulfur compounds, particulate matter, oxidants, and nitrogen oxides. For the most part, the damage is from increased deterioration that must be offset by increased maintenance and earlier replacement. In the case of outdoor sculpture, the damage is to the aesthetic qualities of the objects.

In this case the dose-response relationship shows the extent of deterioration associated with exposure to varying amounts of air pollutants. The basic physical relationships may be investigated in the laboratory, but in application to any particular area one must have data on the various amounts of exposed materials that actually exist in the study region. Then it is possible to estimate the total amount of materials deterioration that would occur in an average year of exposure to the air of the region with its "normal" loading of various pollutants. One must then put a value on this deterioration. Taking a strict damage-function approach, we could estimate the increased cost of maintenance (labour, paint, etc.) made necessary by this deterioration.[14] But this would be an underestimate of the true damages from a willingness-to-pay perspective. Part of the damages would be aesthetic, the reduced visual values of less sightly buildings and painted surfaces. We might get at these values through contingent valuation methods, discussed below. The maintenance cost approach would not be complete also if pollution causes builders to switch to other materials to reduce damages.

The Value of Environmental Amenities as Expressed in Travel Costs

One of the first approaches that environmental economists use to estimate the demand for environmental amenities is a method that takes travel costs as a proxy for price. Although we don't observe people buying units of environmental quality directly, we do observe them travelling to enjoy, for example, recreation experiences in national and provincial parks, swimming and fishing experiences in lakes and streams, and so on. Travel is costly; it takes time as well as out-of-pocket travel expenses. By treating these travel costs as a price that people must pay to experience the environmental amenity, we can under some circumstances estimate a demand function for those amenities.

By getting travel cost data for a large number of people, we can build up estimates of the aggregate willingness to pay for particular environmental amenities. Of course, we must get information on more than just their travel costs. Families will differ in terms of many factors, not just in terms of their travel costs to this park. They will have different income levels, they will differ in terms of the presence of alternative

---

[14] This approach is taken from R. L. Horst et al., *A Damage Function Assessment of Building Materials: The Impact of Acid Deposition* (Washington, D.C.: U.S. Environmental Protection Agency, 1986).

parks and other recreational experiences available to them, and so on. So surveys have to collect large amounts of data on many visitors in order to be able statistically to sort out all these various influences on park visitation rates.

We can use this approach to estimate the benefits of improving the quality of the environment at the visitation site; for example, by improving the water quality at a recreation lake so that fishing is better. To do this we must collect information not only on the travel costs of recreators to a single recreation site, but on the travel costs to many different sites with differing natural characteristics. Then we can parse out the effects on visitation of various qualitative aspects of different sites. From this we can then determine their willingness to pay for improvements in these qualitative changes.

WILLINGNESS TO PAY: DIRECT METHODS

We come now to the direct approach to estimating willingness to pay, called the "contingent valuation" method. Contingent valuation (CV) is based on the simple idea that if you would like to know the willingness to pay of people for some characteristic of their environment, you can simply ask them. The word "simply" is a little extreme because it turns out not to be so simple, even though the basic idea seems straightforward. The method is called "contingent" valuation because it tries to get people to say how they would act if they were placed in certain contingent situations. Going back to our potatoes example, when we want to measure peoples' willingness to pay for potatoes, we can actually station ourselves at stores and see them choosing in real situations. But when there are no real markets for something, like an environmental quality characteristic, we can only ask them to tell us how they would choose *if* they were placed in certain situations; that is, *if* they were faced with a market for these characteristics.

Contingent value studies have been done to date for a long list of environmental factors: air quality, the value of view-related amenities, the recreational quality of beaches, preservation of wildlife species, congestion in wilderness areas, hunting and fishing experiences, toxic waste disposal, preservation of wild rivers, and others.[15] In fact, CV methods have spread into nonenvironmental areas such as the value of programs for reducing the risks of heart attacks, the value of supermarket price information, and the value of a seniors companion program. Over time the method has been developed and refined to give what we think are reasonably reliable measures of the benefits of a variety of public goods, especially environmental quality.

The steps in a CV analysis are the following:

1 Identification and description of the environmental quality characteristic to be evaluated.

---

[15] For a review of many of these studies and of the general problems of CV analysis, see Robert Cameron Mitchell and Richard T. Carson, *Using Surveys to Value Public Goods: The Contingent Valuation Method* (Washington, D.C.: Resources for the Future, 1989); and Ronald G. Cummings, David S. Brookshire, and William D. Schulze, *Valuing Environmental Goods: An Assessment of the Contingent Valuation Method* (Totowa, N.J.: *Rowland and Allanheld Publishers*, 1986).

2 Identification of respondents to be approached, including sampling procedures used to select respondents.

3 Design and application of a survey questionnaire through personal, phone, or mail interviews (in recent years, focus groups have sometimes been used).

4 Analysis of results and aggregation of individual responses to estimate values for the group affected by the environmental change.

We can best appreciate the nature of CV analysis by looking more closely at the questionnaire design phase.

The Questionnaire

The questionnaire is designed to get people to think about and reveal their maximum willingness to pay for some feature of the environment. It has three essential components:

1 A clear statement of exactly what the environmental feature or amenity is that people are being asked to evaluate.

2 A set of questions that will describe the respondent in economically relevant ways, e.g., income, residential location, age, and use of related goods.

3 A question, or set of questions, designed to elicit willingness-to-pay responses from the respondent.

The central purpose of the questionnaire is to elicit from respondents their estimate of what the environmental feature is worth to them. In economic terms this means getting them to reveal the maximum amount they would be willing to pay rather than go without the amenity in question. A number of techniques have been used to get at this response. The most obvious is to ask people outright to provide the number with no prompting or probing on the part of the interviewer. Other approaches include using a bidding game, where the interviewer starts with a bid at a low level and progressively increases the value until the user indicates that the limit has been reached. Alternatively, the interviewer could start with a high figure and lower it to find where the respondent's threshold value is located. Another method is to give the respondents printed response cards with a range of values, then ask the respondents to check off their maximum willingness to pay. Exhibit 7-1 presents some examples of questions used in several contingent valuation studies.

Some Results

One great advantage of contingent valuation is that it is flexible and applicable to a wide range of environmental amenities, not just those that can somehow be measured in conjunction with some marketable good. Virtually anything that can be made comprehensible to respondents can be studied with this technique.

CV was pioneered in the United States. In 1963 Davis estimated the benefits of outdoor recreation opportunities in the Maine backwoods. He found that the modal

EXHIBIT 7-1

SAMPLE OF QUESTIONS USED IN SEVERAL CONTINGENT VALUATION STUDIES

Study to Estimate Benefits of National Freshwater Quality Improvements

1   How many people in this household are under 18 years of age?

2   During the last 12 months, did you or any member of your household boat, fish, swim, wade or water-ski in a freshwater river, lake, pond, or stream?

Here are the national water pollution goals:

Goal C—99 percent of freshwater is at least boatable.
Goal B—99 percent of freshwater is at least fishable.
Goal A—99 percent of freshwater is at least swimmable.

3   What is the highest amount you would be willing to pay each year:

a   To achieve Goal C?
b   To achieve Goal B?
c   To achieve Goal A?

4   Considering the income classes listed in the accompanying card, what category best describes the total income that you and all the members of the household earned in 19__?

Study to Estimate the Value of Salmon Restoration

Suppose that all funding to restore Atlantic salmon in New England is stopped. Without this funding, there will be no organized effort to restore or preserve Atlantic salmon in New England and Atlantic salmon will be extinct in most New England rivers. Now suppose an independent private foundation is formed to restore Atlantic salmon in New England. The foundation's activities will include maintaining and restoring Atlantic salmon habitats and reintroducing infant salmon into selected waters. Please assume that the foundation will be able to restore the Atlantic salmon to all New England's major river systems in the next five years providing they receive adequate funds.
  The foundation will be funded by private donations over the next five years. All contributors will be provided with information, at no cost, on how the Atlantic salmon are doing in New England, which rivers provide opportunities to see Atlantic salmon, and where in New England Atlantic salmon may be fished for.
  Would you contribute $ __ per year for the next 5 years, to help restore Atlantic salmon in New England? (Please circle the number of your choice.)

1   YES—I WOULD CONTRIBUTE THIS AMOUNT, IN FACT, I WOULD DONATE UP TO $__ PER YEAR OVER THE NEXT 5 YEARS. (Write in the highest dollar amount you would pay.)

2   NO—I WOULD NOT CONTRIBUTE THIS AMOUNT. IF NOT, WHY?

a   THE AMOUNT IS TOO HIGH, BUT I WOULD DONATE $ __ PER YEAR OVER THE NEXT 5 YEARS. (Please write in the highest amount you would pay.)

Sources: Water quality: Robert Cameron Mitchell and Richard T. Carson, *Using Surveys to Value Public Goods: The Contingent Valuation Method.* (Washington, D.C.: Resources for the Future, 1989). Salmon restoration: Tim Hager, Tom Stevens, and Cleve Willis, *Economic Benefits of Salmon Restoration in Massachusetts,* Massachusetts Agricultural Experiment Station, Research Bulletin No. 726. December 1989.

willingness to pay per family for the use of a wilderness recreation area was between $1.00 and $2.00 per day.[16]

A number of U.S. researchers have used the approach to estimate willingness to pay to avoid ill health. For example, Chestnut et al. asked respondents how much they would be willing to pay to reduce by half the number of bad asthma days experienced each year.[17] The mean response per asthma day was $10.

Several CV studies have been done to measure the willingness to pay for increased visibility of the air in urban areas of the U.S. The results that researchers have obtained vary a lot; for a 10 percent increase in visual range, estimates of the annual willingness to pay per household (in the early to mid-1980s) vary from $7 to $101, although most of the results are in the $20 to $40 range.[18]

Schulze and his coworkers did a CV study to see how much people would be willing to pay for an increase in air visibility in the Grand Canyon. The average willingness to pay among their respondents was $9.20 for an iterative bidding approach and $5.69 for a payment card approach.[19]

Desvouges, Smith, and McGivney used CV to estimate the value of water quality improvements for water-based recreational purposes. They found that users of the recreation sites they sampled would on average be willing to pay $12.30 per person to increase the water quality from "boatable" to "fishable" and $29.60 per person to go from "boatable" to "swimmable" water.[20] Brookshire et al. used CV to measure the benefits of improving air quality. For the people in their study they found a mean willingness to pay of $14.50 per month to go from "poor" to "fair" quality air and $20.30 per month to go from "fair" to "good" quality air.[21]

Boyle and Bishop used CV methods to investigate the benefits of undertaking steps to preserve the bald eagle. Their results varied from $11.84 to $75.31 per person, depending on whether they had ever travelled to view bald eagles and whether they had ever contributed to Wisconsin's Endangered Resources Donation program.[22]

Randall and his associates used CV to estimate the benefits people would get from reducing the environmental damages stemming from large power plants in the four-

[16] Robert K. Davis, "The Value of Big Game Hunting in a Private Forest," in *Transactions of the Twenty-ninth North American Wildlife Conference* (Washington, D.C.: Wildlife Management Institute, 1964).

[17] Lauraine G. Chestnut et al., *Heart Disease Patient's Averting Behaviour, Cost of Illness and Willingness to Pay to Avoid Angina Episodes*, U.S. Environmental Protection Agency, EPA/230/10-88/042, (Washington, D.C.: 1988).

[18] Gardner M. Brown, Jr., and J. M. Callaway, *Acid Deposition: State of the Science and Technology*, National Acid Precipitation Assessment Program, Report 27 (Washington, D.C.: U.S. Government Printing Office, 1990), 27–164.

[19] William D. Schulze et al., "The Economic Benefits of Preserving Visibility in the National Parks of the Southwest," *Natural Resources Journal* 23(1) (January 1983): 149–173.

[20] William H. Desvouges, V. Kerry Smith, and Matthew P. McGivney, *A Comparison of Alternative Approaches for Estimating Recreation and Related Benefits of Water Quality Improvements*, Environmental Protection Agency, EPA/230/05-83/001 (Washington, D.C.: 1983).

[21] David Brookshire, Mark A. Thayer, William D. Schulze, and Ralph C. d'Arge, "Valuing Public Goods: A Comparison of Survey and Hedonic Approaches," *American Economic Review* 72(1) (March 1982): 165–171.

[22] Kevin J. Boyle and Richard C. Bishop, "Valuing Wildlife in Benefit-Cost Analysis: A Case Study Involving Endangered Species," *Water Resources Research* 23(5) (May 1987): 943–950.

corners area of the U.S. (New Mexico, Colorado, Utah, Arizona). These were amenity damages from reduced visibility and the visual aspects of transmission lines. Respondents were shown pictures representing a situation of no control, one of moderate control, and one representing high levels of control for airborne emissions and location of transmission lines. For moderate levels of control the aggregate willingness to pay was $11,250,000, while for high levels of control it was $19,310,000.[23]

Brookshire and Coursey did a CV study to determine people's willingness to pay for a change in tree density in an urban park from 200 to 250 trees per acre. The median willingness to pay among their respondents was $9.30. In eliciting these responses researchers showed respondents pictures of the park with different tree densities.[24]

These are just a few of the hundreds of contingent valuation studies that have been done in the U.S. and other countries for the purpose of measuring the benefits of environmental improvements. The technique is still evolving and will undoubtedly lead to more accurate estimates of the values people place on environmental assets of all types.

Problems of CV Analysis

The most problematic aspect of contingent valuation is its hypothetical character. When people buy potatoes, to go back to our example, they have to "put their money where their mouth is," as the saying goes. It's a real situation and if the wrong choices are made, people suffer real consequences. But in a CV questionnaire the same real-world implications are not present. People face a hypothetical situation, to which they may give hypothetical responses, not governed by the discipline of a real marketplace. In thinking about this, two types of questions come up: First, will people know enough about their real preferences to be able to give valid responses and, second, even if they know their preferences, will they have incentives to misrepresent them to the investigator?

Everyone develops experience buying some things, but not others, on the market. In seventeenth-century New England, people were used to buying and selling pews in the church. In some countries official papers from public officials require standard monetary bribes. In contemporary society there are going prices for cantaloupes and cars. When people face market prices for a good or service over a period of time, they have time to learn about their values, adjust their purchases, and settle on a willingness to pay that accurately represents their preferences. But when asked to place a monetary value on something that does not normally carry a price, it may be much more difficult to state one's true willingness to pay. What would you be willing to pay for 10 more beautiful sunsets per year? People also develop ideas over time about the appropriate extent of the market in allocating certain goods and services; when

---

[23] Alan Randall, Berry Ives, and Clyde Eastman, "Bidding Games for Valuation of Aesthetic Environmental Improvements," *Journal of Environmental Economics and Management* 1(2) (August 1974): 132–149.

[24] David S. Brookshire and Don L. Coursey, "Measuring the Value of Public Goods: An Empirical Comparison of Elicitation Procedures," *American Economic Review* 77(4) (September 1987): 554–566.

asked to put a value on something that is currently beyond the market, their answers may reflect not just the value of a particular item, but something about what kind of an economic system they want to live in, which is a much broader question.

The other question is whether respondents could normally be expected to have incentives to misstate their true willingness to pay. Environmental quality characteristics are public goods, as we saw in Chapter 4. People can be expected to understate their preferences for these kinds of goods when they expect that their answers will be used to establish payment schedules for the goods. But in CV studies, there is no threat that responses could be used, for example, to set taxes to pay for the item being evaluated. So, perhaps, this source of bias is unlikely. The opposite bias may be more likely. People may be led to give an inflated estimate of their willingness to pay hoping, perhaps, that others will do the same thing, realizing that their share of the cost of making the item available will, in any case, be very small.

PROBLEMS IN BENEFIT ESTIMATION

Many problems remain in estimating the benefits of improved environmental quality. Good data are always hard to come by. Better techniques are always useful to separate out the effects of other factors and isolate the true environmental impacts. More thought has to be given to the conceptual problems that remain. We will very briefly indicate some of the latter.

Discounting

One of the most important is the matter of *discounting*. Should we discount future benefits, as we talked about in the last chapter about discounting costs and, if so, what discount rate should we use? When we discount the future value of something, we reduce its present value, and the further into the future we go the lower the present value. So in discounting future benefits we tend to decrease the relative value of programs that produce benefits far in the future and increase those that produce benefits in the next few years. This might make sense when we talk about certain types of benefits. People today presumably would put more value on reducing environmentally related premature deaths next year than they would on premature deaths 50 years from now. But there are some significant environmental issues, like global warming, where substantial impacts are expected to occur in the distant future, and in this case discounting tends to reduce substantially the importance of programs addressing this problem.

There is no easy answer to this problem. We cannot simply reject discounting altogether; even future generations would be unlikely to agree with that if they could make their wishes known. But in ordinary affairs the present generation is undoubtedly too oriented to the short run; too much reliance is placed on recent history and not enough on future possibilities. For society as a whole a longer-run perspective is appropriate. As we mentioned in the last chapter, perhaps the best approach is to combine discounting with the idea of sustainability.

Willingness to Pay vs. Willingness to Accept

We have used throughout the notion of willingness to pay as a measure of benefits. Willingness to pay, besides reflecting a person's tastes and preferences, also reflects her income level. Another way of approaching the problem of valuing environmental improvements is to ask people how much they would be willing to accept to give up some environmental amenity. To value better air quality we could ask either how much people would be willing to pay for a small improvement or how much they would have to receive to compensate them for a small reduction in air quality. Suppose public authorities are contemplating locating a hazardous waste incinerator in a particular community. As a measure of the damages suffered by the community, we could take the amount of money required to get the community willingly to accept the incinerator (rather than, in other words, the amount they would be willing to pay to keep it out).

Clearly, willingness to accept is not constrained by one's income, as is willingness to pay. So it may be no surprise that when people are asked willingness-to-accept questions, their answers are usually higher than their willingness-to-pay responses for the same item. To some extent it may depend on what they are asked. For a small change we would expect the two measures to be close. Suppose what is involved is a single cantaloupe. If a person is willing to pay $1.49 for one more cantaloupe, that is also probably close to what it would take to compensate for his or her loss of a single cantaloupe. Even in cases involving small changes, researchers have found that willingness to accept exceeds willingness to pay. In surveys and experimental work, people are found to compare gains and losses relative to a reference point. They value losses from this reference point much more than gains. The minimum compensation demanded has been found to be several times larger than the maximum amount they are willing to pay.[25]

Canadian students participated in a number of experiments measuring willingness to pay versus compensation demanded. The commodities exchanged were chocolate bars and coffee mugs. These are not goods which we would expect people to have strong divergences between willingness to pay and willingness to accept, but they do!

For large changes (what are called "nonmarginal" changes) the divergences may be even more substantial. If we are talking, for example, of large changes in air pollution in a neighbourhood that will substantially change one's welfare, the two measures may be quite different.

Economists have taken several approaches to resolving this problem. One is to look closely at the questionnaire and the way questions are asked of respondents. Experience has shown that responses will differ according to how questions are phrased, so one possibility is that the differences between willingness to pay and willingness to accept are traceable primarily to the way questions are being framed. The other

---

[25] See the work done by Jack Knetsch and others, for example, "Environmental Policy Implications of Disparities between Willingness to Pay and Compensation Demanded Measures of Values," *Journal of Environmental Economics and Management 18* (1990): 227–237, and the references in that article.

approach is to replace the standard economic principles, which imply that there should be no difference between these two measures, with new concepts that can explain the difference. This is a matter of current controversy and much importance for environmental policy. If the two measures are quite different in practice, policy prescriptions should take into account both willingness to pay and compensation demanded valuations.

Nonuse Values

When people buy potatoes, we assume that they do so because they expect to eat them; the value of potatoes to people lies in their *use* value. This reasoning extends also to environmental assets, but in this case there may be more. When people voluntarily donate money for the preservation of unique environmental assets that they may never even see, except perhaps in photographs, something other than use value must be involved. Peoples' willingness to pay for these environmental characteristics must also involve certain nonuse values. One possibility is that although perhaps not currently in a position to experience directly a particular environmental asset, people often want to preserve the option to do so in the future. *Option value* is the amount a person would be willing to pay to preserve the option of being able to experience a particular environmental amenity in the future. People may even be willing to pay to preserve a species or ecosystem, even if they never see or use it directly—African wildlife, for example. In this case, we may measure an *existence value*, a willingness to pay simply to help preserve the existence of some environmental amenity. Such altruistic values may be focussed to some extent on future generations, in which case they might be called *bequest values*. One of the reasons contingent valuation studies have become more common is that questions can be phrased so as to get at these nonuse values.

NATURAL RESOURCE DAMAGES

The United States has a law that may require parties who injure public natural resources through releases of oil or other hazardous substances to make compensatory payments equal to the damages caused by these releases.[26] The payments are to be used by states or the federal government to restore, replace, or acquire the equivalent of the damaged resources. The U.S. Department of Interior was assigned the job of determining how "damages" are to be measured in these cases.

They concluded that damages should be equal to the lesser of: (1) the lost resources use value, as measured by willingness to pay, or (2) the value of restoring the resource to its former state. Consider the following figures, representing willingness to pay and restoration values, for several cases:

---

[26] This is the Comprehensive Environmental Response, Compensation and Liability Act, known as CERCLA, which we discuss in Chapter 18.

	A	B
Willingness to pay	$1.2 million	$1.6 million
Restoration cost	$0.6 million	$3.8 million

For case A, willingness to pay to avoid the oil or hazardous waste release is $1.2 million, but the cost of restoring the resource to its former state is only $0.6 million, so the latter is taken as the true measure of damages. In case B, willingness to pay, at $1.6 million, is substantially less than restoration costs, so the former would be used to assess damages.

On the surface it might seem easier to measure restoration costs than willingness to pay for damaged environmental resources. Restoration appears to involve primarily engineering actions based on knowledge from physical and biological sciences. But "restoration" is in fact a rather complicated idea. In some cases restoration may be technically impossible, for example, when there is some element of uniqueness in the destroyed resource. Restoration of the physical values of a resource (e.g., soil pH, water temperature, amount of tree cover) may not restore all of its ecological characteristics. Experience with this law and its legal clarification is just beginning to develop.[27] As it does, it will be necessary to come to grips with the fact that it is impossible to discuss restoration in physical terms without considering its monetary costs.

SUMMARY

Benefit measurement is a major focus of study within environmental economics. New techniques are being developed to uncover values that previously were hidden from view. From legislatures and courts a brisk demand has arisen for benefits information on which to base laws and legal settlements. Public environmental agencies have devoted considerable time and effort to generating benefits estimates in order to justify their policy rulings. After reviewing briefly what we mean by "benefits," we discussed some of the main techniques environmental economists use to measure these benefits. Health impacts, previously assessed by direct damage estimation, are now more frequently pursued through willingness-to-pay procedures, especially wage-rate studies showing how people value risks to health. We also covered house-price studies, production cost studies, and travel cost studies. Finally, we reviewed the recently popular technique of contingent valuation. This technique allows us to measure the benefits of a much wider range of environmental phenomena than traditional techniques permitted. Indeed, contingent valuation techniques allow us to push beyond traditional "use values" and explore some of the less tangible, but no less real, sources of environmental benefits, like "option value," and "existence value."

---

[27] See, for example, Ellen Louderbough, "The Role of Science in Valuing Natural Resources after State of Ohio vs. Department of Interior, 880F. 2nd 432 (D.C. Cir. 1989)," *Natural Resources Journal* 32(1), (Winter 1992): 137–148.

QUESTIONS FOR FURTHER DISCUSSION

1 Suppose you were hired by the homeowners located around a lake to determine the benefits of improving the water quality in the lake. How might you go about doing it?

2 Suppose the city council in a particular city votes to spend $5 million to improve air quality in the city. Is this a useful measure of the benefits of cleaner air in that city?

3 When the "average" person considers how much she or he is willing to pay to have environmental pollution reduced, do you think that person considers the views of unborn future generations?

4 Suppose you want to find out what value people place on increasing the expected human life span by one year. What ways can you think of to accomplish this?

5 Suppose you want to determine the aggregate willingness to pay among students at your school for reducing litter on the school grounds. How might you do this?

6 Many people object to trying to estimate the "value" of a human life, on the grounds that life is "priceless." What are the strengths and weaknesses of that viewpoint?

SELECTED READINGS

Bentkover, Judith D., Vincent T. Covello, and Jeryl Mumpower (eds.). *Benefits Assessment: The State of the Art.* Dordrecht, Holland: D. Reidel Publishing Company, 1986.

Braden, John B., and Charles D. Kolstad (eds.). *Measuring the Demand for Environmental Quality.* Amsterdam: North-Holland, 1991.

Desaiques, Brigitte, and Patrick Point. *Economie du Patrimoine Naturel, La Valorisation des Bénéfices de Protection de L'environnement.* Paris: Economica, 1993.

Dixon, John A., and Paul B. Sherman. *Economics of Protected Areas, A New Look at Benefits and Costs.* Washington, D.C.: Island Press, 1990.

Freeman, A. Myrick, III. *The Benefits of Environmental Improvement: Theory and Practice.* Baltimore, Md.: Johns Hopkins Press for Resources for the Future, 1979.

Hall, Jane V., Arthur M. Winer, Michael T. Kleinman, Frederick W. Lurmann, Victor Brajer, and Steven D. Colome. "Valuing the Health Benefits of Clean Air." *Science* 255 (February 14, 1992): 812–817.

Kneese, Allen V. *Measuring the Benefits of Clean Air and Water.* Washington, D.C.: Resources for the Future, 1984.

Knetsch, Jack L. "Environmental Policy Implications of Disparities between Willingness to Pay and Compensation Demanded Measures of Values." *Journal of Environmental Economics and Management* 18 (1990): 227–237.

Krutilla, John V., and Anthony C. Fisher. *The Economics of Natural Environments.* Baltimore, Md.: Johns Hopkins Press for Resources for the Future, 1975.

Mitchell, Robert Cameron, and Richard T. Carson. *Using Surveys to Value Public Goods: The Contingent Valuation Method.* Washington, D.C.: Resources for the Future, 1989.

Organization for Economic Cooperation and Development. *Benefits, Estimates and Environmental Decision Making.* Paris: OECD, 1992.

Pearce, David W., and Anil Markandya. *Environmental Policy Benefits: Monetary Valuation.* Paris: Organization for Economic Cooperation and Development, 1989.

Rowe, Robert D., and Lauraine G. Chestnut. *The Value of Visibility: Theory and Application*. Cambridge, Mass.: Abt Books, 1982.

Schelling, Thomas. "The Life You Save May Be Your Own," in Samuel Chase (ed.). *Problems of Public Expenditure Analysis*. Washington, D.C.: Brookings Institution, 1968, 127–158.

Smith, V. Kerry, and William H. Desvouges. *Measuring Water Quality Benefits*. Boston, Mass.: Kluwer-Nijhoff Publishing, 1986.

8

BENEFIT-COST ANALYSIS: COSTS

In this chapter we look at the cost side of benefit-cost analysis. The importance of accurate cost measurement has often been underestimated. It is a full half of the analysis, the results of which can as easily be affected by, for example, overestimating costs as by underestimating benefits. In developing countries, where people place a high priority on economic growth, it is critically important to know how environmental programs will affect that growth rate and how costs are distributed among different social groups. In industrialized countries opposition to environmental policies frequently centres on their estimated costs, which means that those doing benefit-cost analyses of these programs are well advised to get the cost estimates right. In this chapter we will first take up some general considerations about costs, then look at some specific issues and examples of cost estimation.

THE COST PERSPECTIVE

Cost analysis can be done on many levels. At its simplest, it focusses on the costs to a single community or firm of an environmental program, or of a single environmental project like a wastewater treatment plant, incinerator, or beach restoration project. The reason for calling these the simplest is that they usually proceed by costing out a definite engineering specification that has clear boundaries, and for which the "rest of the world" can rightly be assumed to be constant. At the next level we have costs to an industry, or perhaps to a region, of meeting environmental regulations or of adopting certain technologies. Here we can no longer rely on simple engineering assumptions; we must do things like predict with reasonable accuracy how groups of polluting firms will respond to changes in laws on emissions or how they will respond to changes in recycling regulations. Problems will arise because not all firms will be alike—some small, some large, some old, some new, etc.—and each of them will usually have multiple possibilities for reacting to regulations. At a still higher level, our concern may be with the costs to an entire economy of achieving stated environmental goals. Estimating costs at the national level calls for an entirely different approach. Here everything is connected to everything else; when pollution-control regulations are imposed, adjustments will reverberate throughout the economy. To trace them out we must deal with macroeconomic data and usually fairly sophisticated aggregate models. In the following pages we will deal with cost estimation at these different levels.

OPPORTUNITY COSTS

In economics the most fundamental concept of costs is *opportunity costs*. The opportunity cost of using resources[1] in a certain way is the highest valued alternative use to which those resources might have been put and which society has to forego when the resources are used in the specified fashion. Note the word "society." Costs are incurred by all types of firms, agencies, industries, groups, etc. Each has its own perspective, which will focus on those costs that impinge directly on them. Suppose a community is contemplating building a bicycle path to relieve congestion and air pollution downtown. Its primary concern is what the town will have to pay to build the path. Suppose it will take $1 million to build it, but 50 percent of this will come from the provincial or federal government. From the town's perspective the cost of the bike path will be a half million dollars, but from the standpoint of society the full opportunity costs of the path are $1 million.

The trouble is that when most people think of cost they usually think of money expenditure. Often the monetary cost of something is a good measure of its opportunity costs, but frequently it is not. Suppose the bike path is going to be put on an old railroad right-of-way that has absolutely no alternative use, and suppose the town must pay the railroad $100,000 for this right-of-way. This money is definitely an expenditure the town must make, but it is not truly a part of the opportunity costs of building the path, because society gives up nothing in devoting the old right-of-way to the new use.

Environmental Costs

It may seem paradoxical to think that environmental protection control programs might have environmental costs, but this is in fact the case. Most of our specific emissions-reduction programs are media based; that is, they are aimed at reducing emissions into one particular environmental medium like air or water. So when emissions into one medium are reduced, they may increase into another. Reducing untreated domestic waste outflow into rivers or coastal oceans leaves quantities of solid waste that must then be disposed of—perhaps through land spreading or incineration.

---

[1] Remember that "resources" is a word that can have two meanings: It can be a short way of saying "natural resources" or a general reference analogous to the word "inputs." Here we are using it in the second sense.

Reducing airborne SO_2 emissions from power plants by stack-gas scrubbing also leaves a highly concentrated sludge that must be disposed of in some way. Incinerating domestic solid waste creates airborne emissions.

Media switches are not the only source of environmental impacts stemming from environmental improvement programs. There can be direct effects; for example, sediment runoff from construction sites for new treatment plants or sewer lines. There can also be unforeseen impacts when firms or consumers adjust to new programs. Gasoline producers reduced the amounts of lead in their product but, since consumers still insisted on high-powered performance, they added other compounds, which ended up having environmental impacts in their own right. With the beginning of community programs to charge consumers for solid-waste disposal, some have been faced with substantial increases in "midnight dumping," that is, illegal dumping along the sides of roads or in remote areas.

Some of the potential environmental impacts from these public projects or programs can be *mitigated*; that is, steps can be taken to reduce or avoid them. More enforcement resources can help control midnight dumping, extra steps can be taken to reduce construction-site impacts, special techniques may be available to reduce incinerator residuals, and so on. These mitigation costs must be included as part of the total costs of any project or program. Beyond this, any remaining environmental costs must be set against the overall reduction in environmental damages to which the program is primarily aimed.

No-Cost Improvements in Environmental Quality

Sometimes environmental improvements can be obtained at zero *social* cost, except the political cost of making the required changes in public laws or regulations. In virtually any type of political system, usually some laws and administrative practices are instituted primarily to benefit certain groups within society for political reasons, rather than to move toward economically efficient resource use or achieve deserving income redistributions. These regulations, besides transferring income to the favoured groups, often have negative environmental effects. Of course, changing these regulations may entail substantial private costs to the individuals affected. This may require some form of compensation for losses. Compensation for the introduction of environmental regulation or changes in other regulation is a topical and controversial issue at present.

Consider some examples of zero social cost changes. During the 1970s, the federal government introduced a two-price system of oil and natural gas pricing. The policy was designed to help Canadian energy consumers cope with the rapid increase in energy prices which occurred in the 1970s. Domestic prices for oil and natural gas were held below world prices. Energy consumers in Canada received a subsidy and no doubt were better off than they would have been had they faced the higher world prices. However, these subsidies slowed the Canadian economy's adjustment to a world with higher energy prices. Canadians continued to consume more energy per capita than in any other developed nation, and as a result, incurred greater adverse environmental impacts from energy consumption and production than would have been the case had energy prices risen more quickly. After the two-price system was abolished in the early 1980s, Canadian energy consumption per capita declined until the late 1980s. Final energy consumption per capita for residential and agricultural sectors declined by almost 6 percent from the period 1975–79 to 1980–84.

There are many other examples like this. Agricultural subsidies in many developed countries have provided the incentive to develop intensive, chemical-based production methods, which has resulted both in increased agricultural output and in the non-point source water and air pollution to which these methods lead. Reducing these agricultural subsidies would increase national income and reduce the environmental impacts, though of course many farmers would be worse off.

Enforcement Costs

Environmental regulations are not self-enforcing. Resources must be devoted to monitoring the behaviour of firms, agencies, and individuals subject to the regulations, and to sanctioning violators. Public environmental facilities, such as wastewater treatment plants and incinerators, must be monitored to be sure they are being operated correctly.

There is an important application of the opportunity idea in the enforcement phenomenon. Many environmental laws are enforced by agencies whose enforcement budgets are not strictly tailored to the enforcement responsibilities they are given. Thus, budgets can be stable, or even declining, at the same time that new environmental laws are passed. Enforcing the new laws may require shifting agency resources away from the enforcement of other laws. In this case the opportunity costs of new enforcement must include the lower levels of compliance in areas that now are subject to less enforcement.

COSTS OF SINGLE FACILITIES

Perhaps the easiest type of cost analysis to visualize is that for a single, engineered project of some type. There are many types of environmental quality programs that involve publicly supported construction of physical facilities (although the analysis would be the same whatever the ownership), such as public wastewater treatment plants, of which hundreds of millions of dollars worth have been built over the last few decades. Other examples include flood control projects, solid-waste handling facilities, hazardous-waste incinerators, beach-restoration projects, public parks, wildlife refuges, and the like.

Facility-type projects like this are individualized and substantially unique, though of course they have objectives and use technology that is similar to that used for many other projects. To estimate their costs, primary reliance is placed on engineering and technical specifications, developed largely through experience with similar types of facilities. Consider the simple example shown in Table 8-1. It gives the estimated costs of a new wastewater treatment plant for a small community. The plant is expected to use standard technology, as specified in the engineering plans for the

TABLE 8-1   PROJECTED COSTS OF A SMALL WASTEWATER TREATMENT PLANT ($1,000)

	Construction Costs			
	Initial cost	Life (years)	Replacement costs	Salvage value
Treatment plant				
Mechanical	1,104	20	125	—
Structural	1,296	40	—	544
Engineering (15%)	360	—	—	—
Contingencies (10%)	240	—	—	—
Total	3,000	60	125	544
Conveyances				
Pumping station	245	15	245	164
Metering station	40	40	—	7
Piping	1,028	40	—	480
Engineering (15%)	195	—	—	—
Contingencies (10%)	131	—	—	—
Total	1,639	95	245	651
Sludge-disposal works (land spreading)				
Site work	254	40	—	—
Piping	228	40	—	95
Land purchase	350	40	—	—
Other	150	40	—	—
Total	982	—	—	95
Mitigation of construction-related environmental costs	24	40	—	

Annual Costs				
Operation and maintenance (O&M)		Environmental costs		
Pumping station	21	Mitigation costs		8
Treatment plan		Unmitigated environmental costs		46
Labour	60			
Electric power	45			
Parts and supplies	13			
Chemicals	6			
Other	7			
Sludge disposal	4			
Total	156			

Present Values		
Cost item	Total	Present value (@8%)
Construction	5,645	5,656
Replacement	370	107
Salvage values	−1,290	−320
Annual O&M	156	1,860
Annual environmental	54	644
Total		7,936

Source: Adapted from U.S. Environmental Protection Agency and Wisconsin Department of Natural Resources, Environmental Impact Statement, Wastewater Treatment Facilities at Genwa Lake Area, Walworth County, Wisconsin, Washington, D.C., June 1984.

treatment plant, collector lines, and other essential parts of the system. It will be built by a private firm but owned and operated by the town.

There are three types of construction costs: the treatment plant proper, conveyances, and sludge-disposal works. The latter refers to disposal of the solid waste produced at the plant. The waste materials extracted from the wastewater stream don't just disappear; these heavily treated substances must be disposed of in some fashion. There are various ways of doing this (composting, land spreading, incineration). In the case of land spreading, the costs involve buying a large area of land on which the sludge will be spread and allowed to decompose and mix with the soil. The assumed life of the plant is 40 years. Some portions of the plant—for example, certain pieces of equipment—will wear out and have to be replaced during this period. The costs of this are listed under "replacement costs." Additionally, certain parts of the plant and conveyance system are expected to have a salvage value at the end of the 40 years; these are shown in the last column. Note that allowances have been made for engineering work and construction contingencies. An estimate has also been included of the initial costs of some environmental mitigation activities.

Annual costs are divided into operation and maintenance (O&M) of the treatment plant, O&M of the pumping station, sludge disposal operation, and environmental costs. The latter includes certain mitigation costs, together with some remaining, or unmitigated, environmental costs. The latter might refer, for example, to odour problems at the plant and on the sludge disposal lands. These are, in fact, environmental damages, which might be estimated, for example, with contingent valuation techniques.

The last section of Table 8-1 includes the present values of the costs, evaluated with a discount rate of 8 percent. Replacement costs are discounted to the present from the year in which they are expected to be required. Salvage values are discounted back from the end of the project's life, in this case 40 years. These appear with negative signs because they act to lower the total cost of the project. The present value of annual environmental costs is also included.

With the exception of unmitigated environmental costs, these items are all expenditure figures, and only close inspection can tell if they represent true social opportunity costs. Suppose, for example, that in the construction phase a number of local unemployed people are hired. Although the construction costs include their wages, their opportunity costs would be zero because society had to give up nothing when they went to work on the plant. It might be that the land on which the plant is to be placed is town land that is to be donated. In this case there will be no specific cost entry for land, but there will be an opportunity cost related to the value the land could have had in its next best use. Suppose that the construction firm, because it is working on a public project, is able to get subsidized loans from local banks (i.e., borrow money at lower than market rates). Then the true opportunity costs of construction will be higher than the monetary costs indicated. There are no specific rules for making these adjustments; only a knowledge of the specific situations can reveal when it is important enough to make them and where sufficient data are available to do the job.

COSTS OF A LOCAL REGULATION

Environmental regulations are frequently enacted at the local level and impact on local firms. In fact, in the political economy of pollution control, it is often the fear of these local impacts that deters communities from enacting the regulations. Fears of lost payrolls and the secondary losses to other firms from shrinking local markets loom large at the local level; from a national perspective the opportunity costs are less severe.

Suppose in a particular small town there is a large apple orchard that provides substantial local employment. Suppose further that presently the orchard managers use relatively large applications of chemicals to control apple pests and diseases, and that the chemical runoff from this activity threatens local water supplies. Assume the community enacts an ordinance requiring the orchard to practise "integrated pest management" (IPM), a lower level of chemical use coupled with other means to compensate for this reduction. Assume further, for purposes of illustration, that the IPM practices increase the costs of raising apples in this orchard.[2] What are the costs of this regulation?

If the orchard raises and sells the same number of apples it previously did, the true social opportunity costs of the regulation are the increased production costs. If local consumers are willing to pay somewhat higher prices for locally grown apples, some of this cost gets passed on to these consumers. But suppose competitive conditions make it impossible for the orchard to sell its apples for any higher price than pertained before. In this case the higher production costs must be reflected in lower incomes of either the apple orchard owners themselves, or perhaps orchard workers, if they will accept lower wages.

But suppose the orchard was just breaking even before the local IPM ordinance, and that the statute leads to such cost increases that production is substantially curtailed; in fact, assume for purposes of argument that the orchard goes out of business. Clearly there will be local costs: lost payrolls of orchard workers, lost income to the local orchard owners, lost income to local merchants because their markets shrink. But these lost incomes are not likely to be social opportunity costs in their entirety, unless the workers become permanently unemployed. Assuming they transfer to other job opportunities (this requires obviously that the economy be operating at full employment), their new incomes will offset, at least partly, the lost incomes they had been earning previously. There may be certain valid opportunity costs in the form of adjustment costs, as workers and owners have to move to new places of employment.

What about the value of the apples no longer produced in this orchard? If we assume that there are many other orchards in neighbouring towns and other regions to take up the slack with essentially no cost increases, then this lost production is offset by others, consumer prices are stable, and the social opportunity costs of this marginal rearrangement of apple production are basically nil. Of course, if the orchards

---

[2] In fact, various authorities and scientific studies suggest that IPM practices can actually lower costs relative to chemical-intensive growing techniques.

in the other regions are still using pollution-intensive techniques, the social costs of environmental degradation remain.

To summarize, when we are dealing with a single local ordinance affecting one firm and the economy is at or near full employment, ensuing resource adjustments ensure that social opportunity costs are small, limited to the costs of actually carrying out the adjustments. From the standpoint of the affected community, of course, costs will seem high, because of lost local incomes brought about by the increased apple production costs.

COSTS OF REGULATING AN INDUSTRY

These conclusions do not follow when we impose an environmental regulation on an entire industry. Higher production costs for the industry are true social opportunity costs, because they require added resources that could have been used elsewhere. But when we deal with whole industries, we can't make the assumption, like we did with the one apple orchard, that its production could easily be picked up by the others. For an industry we may have to make many adjustments in order to get from higher production costs to social opportunity costs.

We will consider first the standard approach to estimating increased industry production costs, which is to measure the added expenditures that an industry would have to make to come into compliance with an environmental regulation. Cost estimation in this case requires the analyst to predict how polluters will respond to environmental regulations, and then to estimate the costs of this response. If the regulation is very specific, requiring for example that manufacturing firms install a certain piece of pollution-control equipment or that farmers adopt certain cultivation practices to avoid soil runoff, the cost estimation may be fairly straightforward. But if the regulation leaves the polluters considerable latitude in making their response, it may be hard to predict exactly what they will do and, therefore, what their costs will be.

Suppose, for example, a group of pulp mills are required to reduce their emissions by some percentage, and that we (a public agency) wish to estimate the impact of this on the production costs of the firms in the industry. In effect, we want to estimate the aggregate marginal abatement cost function for this group of firms. To do this with reasonable accuracy, we have to know enough about the pulp business to be able to predict how the firms will respond, what treatment techniques they will use, how they might change their internal production processes, and so on. Or suppose we wanted to estimate the costs among farmers of a ban on a certain type of pest control chemical. We would need to know what alternatives farmers had available to replace this chemical, what impacts this would have on yields, how much additional labour and other inputs they would use, and so on. We don't often have all this information in the detail we would like. The example below illustrates the type of data that is available.

An Example

The Canadian pulp and paper industry is currently undergoing major changes because of environmental regulation. An important industry to many regions of the country, it is facing more stringent regulation at the federal and provincial levels. As well, it is likely to feel the impact of recycling legislation in the United States (and proposed for Canada) that requires particular percentages of recycled fibre in newsprint and other paper products. New regulations will require pulp and paper companies to modify their capital stock and operating procedures, incurring expenditures that could be quite large. Statistics Canada has examined the cost to the industry of complying with the 1992 federal regulations.[3] The study looks at the how the age of the mill affects potential expenditures; whether compliance costs vary with type of treatment facility, by region, capacity, profitability, and other characteristics of firms in the industry. As is true of most studies of regulatory impacts, there were too many firms in the industry to do a technical study of each one. A common way of addressing this problem is to estimate costs for the "average" or "representative" or "model" plant, one that corresponds to typical operating conditions in the industry but not to any particular plant. But in this case, as in most cases, the size and technical heterogeneity of plants in the industry made it necessary to specify a number of representative plants, each of which corresponded to one portion of the firms in the industry. Abatement costs are shown in Table 8-2 for six different plant sizes, where "size" is given by the capacity in tonnes of output per day from the plants in each group. The first

[3] See Craig Gaston, "Pulp and Paper Industry Compliance Costs" in Statistics Canada, National Accounts and Environment Division, *Environmental Perspectives 1993, Studies and Statistics,* Catalogue No. 11-528E, March 1993.

TABLE 8-2   ESTIMATED COSTS OF COMPLIANCE WITH 1992 FEDERAL PULP AND PAPER REGULATIONS, 1989 DOLLARS

	Capacity of Plants (tonnes per day)					
	620–800	800–1000	Over 1000	Under 200	200–300	300–620
Number of Plants in Size Class	4	8	34	9	14	17
Average BOD (kg per tonne)	13.8	21.1	32.3	43.4	33.9	24.0
Average Investment Costs ($ millions)	6.2	7.9	21.0	39.0	28.7	38.3
Annual Costs ($ millions)						
Capital Costs*	0.3	0.4	1.1	2.0	1.4	1.9
Depreciation†	0.6	0.8	2.1	3.9	3.0	3.8
Operating Costs	0.8	1.0	1.9	3.1	2.3	3.5
Total	1.7	2.6	5.1	9.0	6.7	9.2

Note:*10% of average investment costs. Annual investment each year of the project is equal to original investment minus depreciation. Average investment is the mean of these annual investments. Since depreciation is 10-year straight-line, average investment is actually equal to one-half of the original investment.
†Straight-line depreciation—10-year life.
Source: Adapted from Statistics Canada, *Environmental Perspectives, 1993,* Catalogue 11-528E (Ottawa: Statistics Canada, 1993).

row shows the number of plants in each size class. Note that the majority of plants are in the 300 to 620 tonnes per day category, with the second highest number in the largest category (over 1,000 tonnes per day) .

The first section in the table shows investment costs needed to install the new equipment that will allow the firms to reduce their emissions flows. These are the "up-front" investment costs of new buildings, equipment, and the land to put them on. The second part of the table shows annualized costs. These are operating costs which include conventional items like energy, labour, and materials, and also the annual-ized investment costs. In the waste treatment plant example above, we aggregated dis-counted annual operating costs and added these to initial investment costs to get the present value of total costs. The other way of adding initial investment costs and annual operating costs is to "annualize" the investment costs, that is, spread them out over the years of life that the investments are assumed to have. This is done in Table 8-2. Annualized investment costs consist of two parts: the opportunity costs of the capital, and depreciation. The former is the forgone return that one could earn if the investment were made in some other industry. Depreciation is the cost associated with the progressive using up of the equipment and buildings over their useful life.

Total annual costs are shown for each of the representative plants. If we wanted to have an estimate of the total costs of meeting the emission standard for the entire industry, we could calculate a weighted total:

Size to Firm Total Costs (Capacity in tonnes per day)	Annual costs ($ millions)	Number of Firms	Total Costs ($ millions)
Under 200	1.7	4	6.8
200–300	2.6	8	20.8
300–600	5.1	34	173.4
600–800	9.0	9	81.0
800–1000	6.7	14	93.8
Over 1,000	9.2	17	156.4
Total Costs			532.2

Thus, the anticipated total annual cost of this industry to meet the emission-reduction standards is $532.2 million (in 1989 dollars). We might note that these costs are incomplete in at least one sense. In regulatory programs of any type, public enforcement resources are required if we expect to get large-scale compliance by the regulated firms. Table 8-2 contains nothing about these costs, but in a full social benefit-cost analysis, they would obviously have to be included.

Where does one get the cost data necessary to construct these representative firms? Many of the basic data are generated through *cost surveys* of existing firms. In effect, questionnaires are sent out to these firms, asking them to supply information on num-ber of employees, processes used, costs of energy and materials, etc. With a suffi-ciently detailed questionnaire and a reasonably high response rate by firms, researchers can get a good idea of basic cost conditions in the industry and how they might be affected by environmental regulations.

One problem with cost surveys is that they are usually better at getting information on past cost data than on future costs under new regulations. Firms can probably report past cost data with more reliability than they can estimate future costs of meeting environmental constraints. Historical data may not be a good guide to the future, especially since environmental regulations almost by definition confront firms with novel situations. In these cases it is common to supplement survey data with technical engineering data that can be better adapted to costing out the new techniques and procedures that firms may adopt. Surveys are also problematic because they rely on accurate responses. If firms know that the results of the survey are to be used in developing an environmental control program, they may have a strong incentive to overstate their costs. Or they may substantially understate their current emissions, which would lead administrators to overestimate the costs of achieving particular emission standards.

The "representative firm" approach, while dictated by the large number of firms in an industry, has its own problems, especially when those firms are substantially heterogeneous among themselves. In following this procedure all researchers run into the problem of whether costs of the real plants in the industry, each of which is to some degree unique, can be accurately represented by a composite cost estimate. Government agencies have to be particularly careful if regulations will be based on these estimates. They do not want to incur legal and/or political problems that could arise if individual firms argue that their own unique cost situations are misrepresented by the figures for the "representative" firm. This has been a problem in the United States.

Actual vs. Minimum Pollution-Control Costs

The costs shown in Table 8-2 show the estimated costs of the pulp and paper industry meeting the federal environmental standards imposed by law. There is an important question of whether these costs are the *least costs* necessary to achieve the emission reductions sought in the law. This is an important point because, as we saw in Chapter 5, the efficient level of emissions or ambient quality is defined by the trade-off of emission abatement costs and environmental damages. If abatement costs used to define the efficient level are higher than they need to be, the point so defined will be only a pseudoefficient outcome.

When there is a single facility involved, we must rely on engineering judgment to ensure that the technical proposal represents the least costly way of achieving the objectives. When what is involved is an entire industry, both technical and economic factors come into play. We saw earlier that in order for the overall costs of a given emission reduction to be achieved at minimum cost, the equimarginal principle has to be fulfilled. Frequently, environmental regulations work against this by dictating that different sources adopt essentially the same levels of emission reductions or install the same general types of pollution-control technology. As we will see in later chapters, many environmental laws are based on administratively specified operating decisions that firms are required to make. These decisions may not lead, or allow, firms to achieve emission abatement at least cost. Thus, industry costs such as those depicted in Table 8-2 may not represent minimum abatement costs.

There is no easy way out of this dilemma. If one is called on to do a benefit-cost analysis of a particular environmental regulation, one presumably is committed to evaluating the regulation as given. But in cases like this it would no doubt be good policy for the analyst to point out that there are less costly ways of achieving the benefits.

The With/Without Principle

There is an important principle that has to be kept in mind in this work. In doing a benefit-cost analysis of how firms will respond to new laws, we want to use the "with/without" approach and not the "before/after" approach. We want to estimate the differences in costs that polluters would have with the new law, *compared to what their costs would have been in the absence of the law*. This is not the same as the difference between their new costs and what their costs used to be before the law. Consider the following illustrative numbers, applying to a manufacturing firm for which a pollution-control regulation has been proposed:

Estimated production costs:

Before the regulation: $100
In the future without the regulation: $120
In the future with the regulation: $150

It would be a mistake to conclude that the added costs of the pollution-control regulation will be $50 (future costs with the regulation minus costs before the law). This is an application of the before/after principle and does not accurately reflect the true costs of the law. This is so because in the absence of any new law, production costs are expected to increase (for example, because of increased fuel costs, unrelated to environmental regulations). Thus, the true cost of the regulation is found by applying the with/without principle. Here these costs are $30 (costs in the future with the regulation minus future costs without the regulation). Of course this makes the whole job of cost estimation harder because we want to know not historical costs of a firm or an industry but what its future costs would be if it were to continue operating without the new environmental laws.

Output Adjustments

The increase in abatement expenditures may not be an accurate measure of opportunity costs when an entire industry is involved. This is because market adjustments are likely to alter the role and performance of the industry in the wider economy. For example, when the costs of a competitive industry increase, the price of its output increases, normally causing a reduction in quantity demanded. This is pictured in Figure 8-1, which shows supply and demand curves for two industries. For convenience the supply curves have been drawn horizontally, representing marginal production costs that do not vary with output. Consider first panel (a). The initial supply func-

tion is C_1, so the initial quantity produced is q_1. The pollution-control law causes production costs to rise, represented by a shift upward in supply from curve C_1 to C_2.
Suppose we calculate the increased cost of producing the initial rate of output. This
would be an amount equal to the area $(a + b + c)$. The comparable cost in panel (b)
is $(d + e + f)$. But this approach to measuring costs will overstate the true cost increase
because when costs and prices go up, quantity demanded and output will decline.

How much output declines is a matter of the steepness of the demand curve. In
panel (a), output declines only from q_1 to q_2. But in panel (b), with the flatter demand
curve, output will decline from r_1 to r_2, a much larger amount. The correct measure
of the cost to society is $(a + b)$ in panel (a) and $(d + e)$ in panel (b). Note that the original approach to cost estimation, calculating the increased cost of current output, is

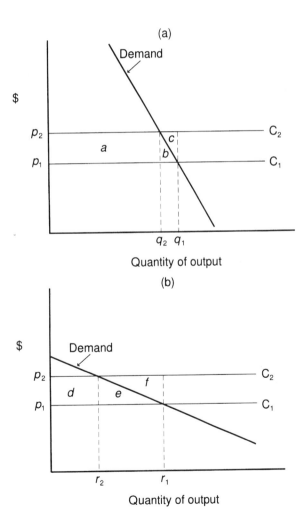

FIGURE 8-1   Output Adjustments in Industries Subject to Pollution-
Control Regulations.

a much better approximation to the true burden on society in panel (a) than in panel (b). This is because the output adjustment is much larger in the latter. The lesson here is that if increased expenditures are to be taken as true opportunity costs, they must be calculated taking into account price and output adjustments that occur in the industries affected by the environmental regulations.

The graphs in Figure 8-1 can help us understand something about the *incidence* of pollution-control costs. By incidence we mean who actually ends up paying the costs. Firms in the affected industries bear these costs in the beginning, but the final burden depends on how the cost increase is passed forward to consumers or backward to workers and shareholders. We note that in both panels (a) and (b) the market prices of the goods increased by the amount of the cost increase. But the response is quite different. In panel (a) consumers continue buying close to what they did before; little adjustment is called for in terms of output shrinkage in the industry. Thus, workers and shareholders in this industry will be little affected, in relative terms. In panel (b) the same price increase leads to a large drop in output. Consumers have good substitutes to which they can switch when the price of this output goes up; in effect, they can escape the full burden of the price increase. On the other hand, the industry adjustment is large. Resources, particularly workers, will have to flow out of the industry and try to find employment elsewhere. If they can, the costs may be only temporary adjustment costs; if not, the costs will be much longer run.[4]

Long-Run Adjustments

In the foregoing example cost estimation required that we predict the effect of emission-control regulations on a group of existing firms, most of which were expected to continue operating in the future. But environmental regulations could have long-run effects on the very structure of an industry, that is, on the number and size of firms. In this case, long-run prediction requires that we be able to predict these "structural" changes with some accuracy.

In Canada, there have been few regulations with the potential to alter industry structure until quite recently. Therefore, no studies on this issue exist for Canada. However, it is important to see what might happen as a result of our newer, more rigorous policies. Experience from the U.S. might provide some insight. One study looks at changes in the number of plants, the average size of the plant, and other measures of industrial structure for a sample of pollution-intensive industries compared to industries with less pollution per unit output.[5] Pollution intensity of an industry is

---

[4] Recall from Chapter 7 that the change in consumer surplus—the area under the demand curve between the two prices—measures the change in welfare associated with the policy. Note that the loss in consumer surplus is larger for the good with few substitutes (area *a* + *b* in panel (a) of Figure 8-1), than it is for the good with the many substitutes (area *d* + *e* in panel (b) of Figure 8-1). Remember that these figures only measure the costs of the policy, not the benefits in the form of higher environmental quality.

[5] See B. P. Pashigian, "The Effect of Environmental Regulation on Optimal Plant Size and Factor Shares," *Journal of Law and Economics* 27 (1984): 1–28.

measured by the ratio of pollution abatement and control expenditures to value added in the industry. The study found that pollution-intensive industries grew faster over the period 1958 to 1972 than did industries with lower pollution expenditures. However, the pollution-intensive industries had a decrease in the number of plants operating. This means that average output per plant must have risen, that is, plant size had risen. These are the type of changes one might expect with regulation. Another study looked at just one industry—pulp and paper mills in the U.S. to see if pollution abatement requirements increased the minimum efficient scale in the industry.[6] If an industry has a large minimum efficient scale of operation, if may make it difficult for new plants to enter. The industry will thus be less competitive than one with a lower minimum efficient scale. While there were some statistical difficulties with the study, it was found that the minimum efficient scale did increase as the stringency of the pollution regulation rose.

These two examples suggest that industries will not remain static in their structure as a result of environmental regulation. The very nature of the industry may also change. Regulation may eliminate the production of certain products and stimulate others. We see that to analyze the impact of environmental policy we will want to study the economics of the industry, or potential industry, that will develop in response to the regulations.

Another very important long-run impact is on technological change in the industry affected by pollution-control requirements. When firms are subject to emission-reduction requirements, they have an incentive to engage in research and development (R&D) to find better emissions-abatement technology. There is some evidence that in reality this may draw resources away from output-increasing R&D efforts, thereby affecting the firm's ability to reduce costs in the long run. On the other hand, there is evidence also that environmental regulations have led to unanticipated, marketable products or processes stemming from their research. And some studies have even shown that after investing in pollution-control R&D some firms have reduced their long-run production costs. In cases like this the short-run cost increases arising from pollution-control regulations are not accurate estimates of the long-run opportunity costs of these regulations.

COSTS AT THE NATIONAL LEVEL

We finally come to the most aggregative level for which cost studies are normally pursued, the level of the national economy. The usual question of interest is the extent of the macroeconomic cost burden of the environmental regulations a country imposes, or might be planning to impose, in a given period of time. Sometimes interest centres on the totality of the regulations put in place. Sometimes the focus is on specific regulations which will nevertheless impact broadly on a national economy, such as a program of CO_2 emissions reduction.

[6] See R. W. Pittman, "Issues in Pollution Control: Interplant Cost Differences and Economies of Scale," *Land Economics* 57 (1981): 1–17.

Considered as a single aggregate, an economy at any point in time has available to it a certain number of inputs—labour, capital, equipment, energy, materials, etc.—which it converts to marketed output. Suppose the firms in the economy are subject to a variety of environmental regulations requiring them, or inducing them, to devote a portion of the total inputs to reductions in emissions. Marketed output must go down (assuming full employment) because of the input diversion. By how much will it drop? There are two answers to this, one applicable to the short run and the other to the long run.

In the short run, marketed output must drop because a portion of total resources is devoted to pollution control rather than to the production of marketed output. But if we simply add up the pollution-control expenditures made by all the industries subject to environmental controls, we may not get an accurate picture of how these controls are affecting the national economy. Expenditures for plant, equipment, labour, and other inputs for reducing emissions can affect other economic sectors not directly covered by environmental regulations, and macroeconomic interactions of this type need to be accounted for to get the complete picture. An industry subject to environmental controls and trying to lower its emissions puts increasing demand on the pollution-control industry, which expands output and puts increasing demands on other sectors—for example, the construction sector—which responds by increasing output.

Another economy-wide adjustment is through prices. Increased pollution-control expenditures lead to increased prices for some items, which leads to reductions in quantity demanded, which leads to lower outputs in these sectors and thus to lower production costs. Total employment will also be affected by pollution-control expenditures. On the one hand, diverting production to pollution control will lower employment needs in the sector producing marketed output. On the other, it will increase employment in the pollution-control industry. So the net result cannot be predicted in the absence of relatively sophisticated macroeconomic modelling.

In the long run, more complicated macroeconomic interactions are at work. Long-run economic change—growth or decline—is a matter of the accumulation of capital: human capital and inanimate capital. It also depends on technical change, getting larger amounts of output from a given quantity of inputs. So an important question is how environmental laws will affect the accumulation of capital and the rate of technical innovation. Diverting inputs from conventional sectors to pollution-control activities lowers the rate of capital accumulation in those conventional sectors. This can be expected to reduce the rate of growth of productivity (output per unit of input) in the production of conventional output and thus slow overall growth rates. The impacts on the rate of technical innovation in the economy are perhaps more ambiguous, as mentioned above. If attempts to innovate in pollution control reduce the efforts to do so in market production, the impact on future growth could be negative. But some people think that efforts to reduce emissions can have a positive impact on the overall rate of technical innovation, which would have a positive impact. Needless to say, the last word on the matter has not yet been spoken.

The standard way to proceed in working out these relationships is through macroeconomic modelling. Mathematical models are constructed using the various macro-

TABLE 8-3 EFFECT OF ENVIRONMENTAL REGULATIONS ON GROSS
DOMESTIC PRODUCT, SELECTED OECD COUNTRIES

	Percentage difference of GDP with environmental regulations compared to without
Austria (1985)	−.2
Finland (1982)	.6
France (1974)	.1
Netherlands (1985)	−.6
U.S. (1987)	−.7

Source: Organization for Economic Cooperation and Development.
(Paris: OECD, 1985), 27.

economic variables of interest, such as total output, perhaps broken down into several economic subsectors, employment, capital investment, prices, pollution-control costs, etc. The model is then run using historical data, which show how various underlying factors have contributed to the overall rate of growth in the economy. Then the model is rerun under the assumption that the pollution-control expenditures were in fact not made. This comes out with new results in terms of aggregate output growth, employment, and so on, which can be compared with the first run. The differences are attributed to the pollution-control expenditures.

Table 8-3 shows a few results of a recent review study done by the Organization for Economic Cooperation and Development (OECD) pertaining to the macroeconomic costs of environmental expenditures in a number of developed countries. They show the percentage difference in gross domestic product (GDP) with environmental regulations compared to what it would have been without the regulations. Two things stand out. One is that in several countries GDP was actually higher in the year indicated under environmental controls than it would have been without them. This is attributed to the fact that these years were relatively early in the life of the environmental programs, when the stimulating effect of pollution-control expenditures were still somewhat dominant. The other conclusion is that for countries whose GDP was lower as a result of the environmental programs, the effect was quite small. These results confirm what others have found—that environmental regulations have lowered the growth rates of the countries applying them, but only by relatively small amounts.

SUMMARY

In this chapter we reviewed some of the ways that costs are estimated in benefit-cost studies. We began with a discussion of the fundamental concept of opportunity costs, differentiating this from the notion of cost as expenditure. We then looked at cost estimation as it applied to different levels of economic activity. The first was a cost analysis of a single facility, as represented by the estimated costs of a wastewater treatment facility. We then considered the costs of an environmental regulation undertaken by a single community, distinguishing between costs to the community and opportunity costs to the whole society.

We then shifted focus to cost estimation for an entire industry. We put special attention on the difference between short-run and long-run costs and the problem of achieving minimum costs. We finally expanded our perspective to the national economy as a whole, where cost means the loss in value of marketed output resulting from environmental regulations.

QUESTIONS FOR FURTHER DISCUSSION

1 Suppose that in the example of the waste treatment plant depicted in Table 8-1, the town donated the sludge-disposal land to the operators of the plant at no financial cost. Does this mean that the total opportunity costs of this project would now be $350,000 lower?

2 Suppose that in the local apple orchard problem, the cessation of production by the orchard led to much more land being put on the local market, producing a drop in local land prices. Is this reduction in the value of land in the community a part of the social opportunity cost of the IPM regulation?

3 "Environment Canada has estimated that a certain pesticide used by farmers leads to an average of 2.1 excess deaths per year among farm workers. This means that banning the pesticide could be expected to lower farm worker deaths by 2.1 per year." Comment on this statement.

4 Suppose that a certain environmental regulation results in the closing down of many firms in an industry, leaving just two or three dominant firms. How might this affect the long-run costs of the regulation?

5 A wastewater treatment plant is built for a community, thereby improving the water quality in a nearby river. But the plant is a scenic disaster. How might we measure the costs of the plant in terms of losses in scenic quality?

6 "The costs of achieving emission reductions in the future will depend importantly on the types of policies used to reduce emissions today." Explain.

SELECTED READINGS

Babcock, Lyndon R. "Costs of Pollution Abatement," in George S. Tolley, Philip E. Graves, and Glenn C. Blomquist (eds.). *Environmental Policy, Volume I.* Cambridge, Mass.: Ballinger, 1981, 75–91.

Christiansen, G. B., and T. H. Tietenberg. "Distributional and Macroeconomic Aspects of Environmental Policy," in Allen V. Kneese and James L. Sweeney (eds.). *Handbook of Natural Resource and Energy Economics*, Vol. 1. Amsterdam: North-Holland, 1985, 345–393.

Kneese, Allen V. "Costs of Water Quality Improvement, Transfer Functions and Public Policy," in Henry M. Peskin and Eugene P. Seskin (eds.). *Cost Benefit Analysis and Water Pollution Policy.* Washington, D.C.: The Urban Institute, 1975, 175–206.

Palmer, Karen L., and Alan J. Krupnick. "Environmental Costing and Electric Utilities' Planning and Investment," *Resources, 105*, Washington, D.C.: Resources for the Future, Fall 1991.

ENVIRONMENTAL POLICY ANALYSIS

The public policy problem arises when there is a discrepancy between the actual level of environmental quality and the preferred level. How to change this state of affairs? Something has to be done to change the incentives people face on both the production and consumption sides of the system. The available public policy approaches for doing this are as follows:

Liability laws
Property rights
Moral suasion
Standards
Incentive-based policies
    Taxes and subsidies
    Transferable discharge permits.

In the chapters of this section we will discuss each of these policy approaches. But before that we must address briefly a prior question: What criteria do we use to evaluate alternative policies and identify the one best suited to any particular environmental problem? We consider a number of these criteria in the next chapter, then analyze in depth the specific policy approaches listed above.

9

CRITERIA FOR EVALUATING ENVIRONMENTAL POLICIES

One way of thinking of different environmental policies is along a centralized/decentralized continuum. A centralized policy requires that some central administrative agency take the lead in determining what is to be done and how. A decentralized policy derives results from the interaction of many individual decision makers, each of whom is essentially making his or her own assessment of the situation. The classic case of a centralized system is that of environmental *standards*, established and enforced by central authorities. At the other end of the spectrum are *property-rights approaches*; basic laws establish the initial distribution of rights, then individual decisions reallocate theses rights and determine what the effect will be on environmental quality. The significance of this difference will come out more as we discuss the specific criteria for evaluating policy, which are:

- Their ability to achieve efficient and cost-effective reductions in pollution.
- Their fairness.
- The incentives they offer to people to search for better solutions.
- Their enforceability.
- The extent to which they agree with certain moral precepts.

EFFICIENCY

By "efficiency" we mean the balance between abatement costs and damages. An efficient policy is one that moves us to, or near, the point (either of emissions or of ambient quality) where marginal abatement costs and marginal damages are equal. To discover where this point is we must know both costs and damages. In a centralized policy approach the burden is usually on an administrative agency to make this determination. In policies that rely on decentralized decisions information about costs and damages arises out of the interactions of the people involved.

It is often the case that we cannot effectively measure damages produced by environmental degradation. This pushes us back to the use of cost-effectiveness as a primary policy criterion. A policy is cost-effective if it produces the maximum environmental improvement possible for the resources being expended or, equivalently, it achieves a given amount of environmental improvement at the least possible cost. For a policy to be efficient it must be cost-effective, but not necessarily vice versa. A policy might be cost-effective even if it were aimed at the wrong target. Suppose we decided to clean up the St. Lawrence River, regardless of what the benefits are. We would still be interested in finding policies that did the job cost-effectively. But for a policy to be socially efficient, it must not only be cost-effective, it must also balance costs with benefits. To be efficient, the river-cleaning project must balance marginal benefits with marginal cleanup costs.

The capability of a policy to achieve cost-effective emission reductions, besides yielding the maximum improvement for the resources spent, is also important for another reason. If programs are not cost-effective, the policymakers and administrators will be making decisions using an aggregate abatement cost function that is higher than it needs to be, leading them to set less restrictive targets in terms of desired amounts of emission reductions. This is shown in Figure 9-1, for a case of SO_2 emissions. With a cost-*in*effective policy the perceived marginal abatement cost is the higher one, labelled MAC_1, whereas with a cost-effective approach marginal abatement costs would be MAC_2. Thus, with the MD function as shown, the emissions level a_1 appears to be the efficient level of pollution, whereas with a cost-

FIGURE 9-1   Mistaking the Efficient Emissions Level When Abatement Technologies Are Not Cost-Effective.

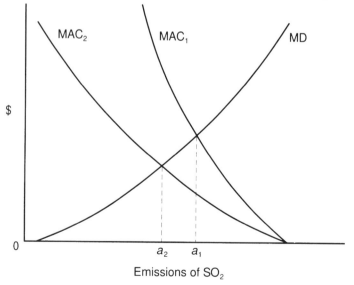

effective program the efficient level would be a_2.[1] The real problem with having costs higher than they need to be is that we will be inclined to set our objectives too low in terms of the amount of emission reduction we seek.

Efficiency and cost-effectiveness are important because, although preserving environmental resources is critically important, it is only one of the many desirable things that people seek. Advocates are usually convinced that their objectives are automatically worth the cost, but success depends on persuading large numbers of other people that environmental policies are efficiently designed. Thus, the resources devoted to environmental quality improvement ought to be spent in ways that will have the greatest impact. This is especially important in less developed economies, where people have fewer resources to put in environmental programs and can ill-afford policies that are not cost-effective and efficient. Cost-effectiveness also becomes an important issue in industrialized countries during times of recession or economic stagnation.

FAIRNESS

Fairness, or equity, is another important criterion for evaluating environmental policy (or any policy, for that matter). Equity is a matter of morality and the regard that relatively well-off people have for those less fortunate. In a sense it is also a concern for policy effectiveness, because policies may not be supported as enthusiastically in the political arena if they are thought to be inequitable. Having said this, however, we have to recognize that there is no agreement on how much weight we should put on the two objectives: efficiency and distribution. Consider the following hypothetical numbers, which might relate, for example, to the costs and benefits of several alternative approaches to air-pollution control in a given region.

Program	Total costs	Total benefits	Net benefits	Distribution of net benefits	
				Low income	High income
A	50	100	50	25	25
B	50	100	50	30	20
C	50	140	90	20	70
D	50	140	90	40	50

The first three columns show total costs, total benefits, and net benefits, respectively. Programs A and B have the same net benefits, but these are distributed more progressively in B than in A. We might agree that B is preferable to A because it has

---

[1] We show the marginal damages in this and subsequent chapters as a rising function. As we discussed in Chapter 5, the marginal damage function could take on a variety of shapes (and even be constant), depending on the impact of the pollutant on people and ecosystems. The MAC function could also take on a different shape than we have shown.

the same net benefits and "better" distributional effects. But compare Programs B and C. The net benefits of Program C are much higher than in B. Unfortunately, they are not distributed as progressively as those of B; in fact, they are distributed more toward higher-income people. If we had to choose between B and C, which should we pick? Some might argue that we should take B for distributional reasons, others might argue for C on overall efficiency grounds. Or compare Programs B and D. In this case, D has the advantage in overall efficiency, although, as in the case of C, more of the net benefits go to higher-income people. But here we also see that low-income people would be better off in absolute terms, though not relatively, with D than with B. On these grounds we might prefer D.

It is an open question how much emphasis we should put on the distributional impacts of environmental policy compared to their other characteristics. On one side is the argument that environmental degradation is so pervasive that we should focus primarily on policies that are the most efficient, that give us the most impact for the resources spent. On the other is the position that we should avoid policies, even efficient ones, that have a strongly regressive impact. Whatever one feels about these distributional impacts, and it does depend on personal values to a great extent, we need to keep in mind that distributional considerations should have some weight in the selection of environmental policies.

Equity considerations also loom large in the making of international environmental policy. As we will discuss later in chapters on global and international environmental problems, countries at different stages of development have different views on how the burdens of international pollution-control programs should be distributed. These views are driven by considerations of what seems fair in the light of the wide economic disparities around the globe.

It is usually very difficult to determine the ultimate distributional impacts of any environmental policy. Take, for example, the regulations of airborne emissions from electric power plants. These regulations will increase the costs of electricity, and it may not be too hard to estimate the effect on different income groups because we have pretty good data on electricity consumption by these groups (but suppose the item is something like apples, about which very little relative consumption information is available?). Of course, even here we would run into some difficulty, because consumers will engage in some amount of energy conservation to escape the effects of the higher price. On the benefit side, we have to know how much the regulation will change ambient conditions for people in different income groups, and this kind of information is very difficult to obtain.

The relative scarcity of information on the distributional impacts of environmental policies argues for putting more effort into finding out what they are. To date, benefit-cost analysis with measurement of the distributional effects of any policy is not a part of official federal government policy in Canada. Some provinces are moving in this direction with recently passed environmental impact assessment legislation. There is increasing pressure from environmental groups and others to show how the total benefits and costs of a regulation are distributed among various income, ethnic, and racial groups within society. If this effort is pursued with vigour, we should be able over time to build up a body of results about efficiency-equity trade-offs in environmental policies.

INCENTIVES FOR IMPROVEMENTS

In studying environmental policy much of the focus normally gets cast on the performance of public officials, since they appear to be the source of that policy. We need to keep clearly in mind, however, that it is private parties, firms, and consumers whose decisions actually determine the range and extent of environmental impacts,[2] and the incentives facing these private parties determine how and where these impacts will be reduced. Thus, a critically important criterion that must be used to evaluate any environmental policy is whether that policy provides a strong incentive for individuals and groups to find new, innovative ways of reducing their impacts on the ambient environment, that is, does it stimulate technological progress in this area. Does the policy place all the initiative and burden on public agencies, or does it provide incentives for private parties to devote their energies and creativities to finding new ways of reducing environmental impacts? When we look at these changes over time, it is an issue of dynamic efficiency.

We can miss the importance of this sometimes when we concentrate on the abatement cost and damage functions in our standard analysis. These show the efficient level of emissions according to the current functions, but over the longer run it is important that we try to shift the functions. It's especially important to try to shift downward the marginal abatement cost function, to make it cheaper to secure reductions in emissions, because this will justify higher levels of environmental quality. Technological change, flowing from programs of research and development (R&D), shifts the marginal abatement cost function downward. So do education and training, which allow people to work and solve problems more efficiently. So ultimately we want to know whether, and how much, a particular environmental policy contains incentives for polluters to seek better ways of reducing pollution. The greater these incentives, the better the policy, at least by this one criterion.

ENFORCEABILITY

Imposing regulations and ensuring that they are met requires resources of people, time, and institutions. There perhaps is a natural tendency among people to think that enacting a law automatically leads to the rectification of the problem to which it is addressed. It is unlikely that polluters will more or less automatically comply with whatever laws are enacted, even in countries that have relatively strong legal traditions and institutions. Policies have to be enforced through the monitoring of emissions or technologies used, negotiations with polluters about timetables for compliance, and the legal system used to address violations of a law. Unfortunately, there

---

[2] Though we must keep in mind that many serious cases of environmental destruction have been caused by public agencies.

will always be people whose interests lie in not having environmental policies enforced. All these actions are the administrative costs that must be incurred with any policy.

The reason for pursuing this is that policies differ in terms of how easy it is to enforce them. Some may require sophisticated technical measures to get reasonable enforcement, others may be enforceable at much lower cost. There is no sense in attempting a dazzling new policy approach if it is essentially impossible, or very costly, to enforce. We may be better off settling for a less perfect policy that is more easily enforceable. There are two main steps in enforcement: *monitoring* and *sanctioning*. Monitoring refers to measuring the performance of polluters in comparison to whatever requirements are set out in the relevant law. Sanctioning refers to the task of bringing to justice those whom monitoring has shown to be in violation of the law. The objective of enforcement is to get people to comply with an applicable law. Thus, some amount of monitoring is normally essential; the only policy for which this does not hold is that of moral suasion. Monitoring polluting behaviour is far more complicated than, say, keeping track of the temperature. Nature doesn't really care, and so it won't willfully try to outwit and confound the monitoring process. But polluters, who are intelligent human beings and who may stand to lose money if environmental laws are vigorously enforced, can usually find many ways of frustrating the monitoring process. And the more sophisticated and complicated that process, the easier it may be for polluters to find ways of evading it.

The other main part of enforcement is sanctioning polluters who are in violation of the law. This may sound like a simple step; if violators are found, we simply take them to court and levy the penalties specified in the relevant law. But things are much more complicated than this. Court cases take time and energy and resources. With many laws and many more violators, the burden on the legal system of trying to bring all violators to justice may be overwhelming. Violators are also reluctant participants; they may devote many resources to fighting the sanctions, turning the procedure into long, drawn-out, costly court battles. In many cases the data underlying the sanctions will be imperfect, leading to challenges and costly conflicts. To create a demonstration effect it may be desirable for authorities to sanction only a few of the most egregious violations, but this opens up the problem of trying to determine just which violators to single out. It is perhaps no wonder that in the real world many violators, especially first-time violators, are not sanctioned with the full penalties allowed by the law. Very often authorities try to achieve voluntary compliance and encourage violators to remedy the situation without penalty.

There is a paradox built into the sanctioning process. One might think that the greater the potential sanctions—higher fines, long jail terms for violators, etc.—the more the law would deter violators. But the other side of the coin is that the higher the penalties the more reluctant courts may be to apply them. The threat to close down violators, or even to levy stiff financial penalties, can in turn threaten the economic livelihoods of large numbers of people. Courts are usually reluctant to throw a large number of people out of work, and so may opt for less drastic penalties than allowed by the law. A trade-off exists between the size of the penalty and the probability that it will be imposed. So the sanctioning process can become much more complicated than the simple model implies.

We have very little information in Canada about these administrative costs. The size of the budgets for environmental ministries at the federal and provincial level are known, but how do we tell what proportion of the costs of the legal system represent environmental compliance costs? We have some sketchy data on enforcement activities—the number of investigations, warnings, prosecutions, convictions and so on, but it isn't clear what this data tells us about compliance. The data indicates that enforcement activity is occurring, but also that very few prosecutions and convictions resulted. Does this mean that compliance with the regulation is high or that violations aren't being detected? Or, does it simply mean that compliance is obtained through methods other than legal enforcement activities? In Canada, negotiation between polluters and government agencies is a common method of obtaining compliance.

Perhaps we can learn from the experiences in the United States. The few studies that have been done there show that there is cause for concern. In a 1983 study the General Accounting Office surveyed a large number of major wastewater dischargers in the country to determine if they were complying with existing laws. They found that a substantial fraction (more than one-third) of the sources were not in compliance.[3]

Other studies of enforcement activities by U.S. states, which are often relied upon to enforce both state and federal environmental laws, show that enforcement activity is far less energetic than we might hope, certainly far less than would be required to ensure a high rate of compliance. The reason, of course, is that enforcement is costly.

Environmental economists at Resources for the Future (RFF) surveyed a large number of U.S. state enforcement agencies to determine common practices and costs associated with enforcing pollution-control regulations.[4] A very widespread practice is for agencies to require self-reporting of emissions by firms, with the public authorities carrying out periodic audits of these records and perhaps also periodic testing of emissions. Table 9-1 shows some of the results of the RFF survey. The number of sources for which enforcing agencies were responsible varied enormously, with an average of 4,550 for air-pollution sources and 1,770 for sources of water pollution. The costs per audit visit depended on whether the visit included the measurement of emissions along with the investigation of the firm's own records. The costs per visit averaged $155 and $301 for, respectively, air and water sources, when there was no emission monitoring. But these jumped to $1,725 for air and $955 for water sources when emission measurement was also carried out. There was an enormous variation in these costs among agencies, however.

These results show that enforcement costs are an important segment of environmental quality programs. Public agencies virtually everywhere face budget strin-

---

[3] U.S. General Accounting Office, *Wastewater Discharges Are Not Complying with EPA Pollution Control Permits* (Washington, D.C., 1983).
[4] Clifford Russell, Winston Harrington, and William J. Vaughan, *Enforcing Pollution Control Laws* (Washington, D.C.: Resources for the Future, 1986).

TABLE 9-1 SURVEY INFORMATION ON STATE ENFORCEMENT AGENCIES, 1982

	Number of sources for which agency was responsible		Costs per audit visit	
Type of source	Average	Range	When no discharges were measured	When discharges were measured
Air	4,550	40–8,140	$155 ($129)*	$1,725 ($1,042)
Water	1,770	220–3,900	$301 ($324)	$ 955 ($932)

*Numbers in parentheses are standard deviations.
Source: Clifford S. Russell, Winston Harrington, and William J. Vaughn, *Enforcing Pollution Control Laws.* (Washington, D.C.: Resources for the Future, 1986), 50–57.

gencies, but also responsibilities which are large and continually growing. Thus, the costs of enforcement, though perhaps not as large as overall compliance costs in most cases, are critical to the success of environmental quality programs and ought to be treated explicitly in evaluating the overall social costs of these programs.

MORAL CONSIDERATIONS

We earlier discussed questions of income distribution and the impacts of different environmental policies on people with different levels of wealth. These are ethical issues on which different people will feel differently, but they are important to discuss when deciding on alternative public policies. But moral considerations extend beyond these distributional questions. The innate feelings that people have about what is right and wrong undoubtedly affect the way they look at different environmental policies. These have to be weighed in the balance along with the more technical criteria we have discussed above.

Take, for example, the question of choosing between effluent taxes and effluent subsidies. Both are economic incentive-type policies, and both might have roughly the same effect in given cases of pollution control. From the standpoint of effectiveness, one might argue that subsidies would be better. Polluters might very well respond quicker and with greater willingness to a subsidy program than to one that is likely to cost them a lot of money. Strictly from the standpoint of getting the environment cleaned up as soon as possible, subsidies might be the most effective. But this may run counter to the ethical notion that people who are causing a problem ought not to be "rewarded" for stopping, which is how subsidies are sometimes viewed.

Some people would take this idea further, arguing that, since we should regard polluting behaviour as essentially immoral to begin with, we should adopt policies that tend to recognize it as such.[5] By this criterion, policies that declare outright that certain types of polluting behaviour are illegal are to be preferred to policies that do not.

[5] Steven Kelman, *What Price Incentives? Economists and the Environment* (Boston: Auburn House, 1981).

Another idea grounded in morality is that those who cause a problem ought to bear the major burden of alleviating it. We see this, for example, in discussions of global environmental issues. The industrial nations, especially the most economically developed among them, are largely responsible for the atmospheric buildup of CO_2, and the deterioration of the protective ozone layer. Many people take the view that these countries ought to bear the major burden in rectifying the situation.

With these criteria in hand, we are now ready to launch into a study of different types of environmental policies. We begin with several traditional decentralized approaches, after which we investigate the use of environmental standards, the approach most frequently resorted to in the past. Finally, we look at what are called economic-incentive types of policies.

QUESTIONS FOR FURTHER DISCUSSION

1 "Efficiency implies cost-effectiveness but cost-effectiveness does not imply efficiency." Explain this statement.

2 If the net benefits of a particular environmental program were found to be regressively distributed among different income groups, would this be sufficient grounds to oppose the program?

3 Besides having different impacts on people at different income levels, environmental policies could also have varying impacts in different regions of a country. How might a federal policy, applied uniformly across a country, have different impacts in different regions?

4 Some people have stressed that "political feasibility" ought to be a criterion in designing environmental policies. Discuss this.

5 Ultimately, it is the policy process itself that must determine the weight to be put on different policy criteria. What is the role of the policy analyst in facilitating this decision?

SELECTED READINGS

Bernstein, Janis. "Alternative Approaches to Pollution Control and Waste Management: Regulatory and Economic Instruments," Discussion Paper INU 79. Washington, D.C.: World Bank, Infrastructure and Urban Development Department, May 1991.

Bohm, Peter, and Clifford S. Russell. "Comparative Analysis of Alternative Policy Instruments," in Allen V. Kneese and James L. Sweeney (eds.). *Handbook of Natural Resources and Energy Economics*, Vol. 1. Amsterdam: North-Holland, 1985, 395–460.

Dewees, Donald N. "Instrument Choice in Environmental Policy." *Economic Inquiry* 21(1) (January 1983): 53–71.

Environment Canada. *Economic Instruments for Environmental Protection*, Discussion Paper, catalogue no. En21-1199/1992E. Ottawa: Supply and Services, 1992.

Eskeland, Gunnar, and Emanuel Jimenez. *Choosing Among Policy Instruments in Pollution Control: A Review*. World Bank, Country Economics Department, June 20, 1990.

Organization for Economic Cooperation and Development. *Environmental Policies for Cities in the 1990s*. OECD: Paris, 1990.

Ruff, Larry E. "The Economic Common Sense of Pollution." *The Public Interest*, No. 19 (Spring 1970): 69–85.

10

DECENTRALIZED POLICIES: LIABILITY LAWS, PROPERTY RIGHTS, MORAL SUASION, GREEN GOODS

By "decentralized" policies we mean policies which essentially allow the individuals involved in a case of environmental pollution to work it out themselves once a set of clearly defined rules of procedures and rights have been established by regulation and/or through the legal system. Think back to the example we used in previous chapters of water quality in a lake. Suppose there are several industrial plants around the lake. One is a food-processing plant, and the water of the lake is an important input in its operation. The other is an industrial operation that uses the lake for waste disposal. How can we balance the pollution damage suffered by the first firm with the abatement costs of the second? A decentralized approach to finding the efficient level of ambient water quality in the lake is simply to let the two plants work it out between themselves. They might do this either through informal negotiations or through more formal interaction in a court of law. There has been much discussion in the economics and law literature about the impact the different distributions of rights and rules have on the ultimate outcomes reached. We examine some of these issues in this chapter. Decentralized approaches have the advantage that the people directly involved are the ones who may know the most about damages and abatement costs, and therefore can presumably find the right balance between them. Sometimes decentralized approaches can be very effective. But not always.

Property rights must be defined and distributed before any sort of decentralized process can occur. In the case of the environment, the basic decision that must be made by society through its governments and legal system is who should have the right to environmental quality. As you might expect, it is difficult to define this sort of right. But the basic issue is whether people have the right to a particular level of environmental quality or whether those who discharge wastes can do so freely. We will talk about the rights to the environment as "belonging" to the polluter or the pollutee. Once this decision is made, the next decision is how rights will be protected: through liability laws or property rules. We begin with liability laws because they are familiar to most people.

LIABILITY LAWS

Almost everybody has an intuitive notion of liability and compensation. To be liable for some behaviour is to be held responsible for whatever untoward consequences result from that behaviour. Questions of liability are usually worked out in the courts. The party claiming damage proceeds against the party it believes to be responsible, and judges and juries decide according to whatever provisions of common and statutory law are applicable. The courts will also decide the value of the damages. As we'll see below, this is in contrast to property rights, where the value of the damages is determined by the parties themselves.

One approach to environmental issues, therefore, is to rely on liability laws. This would work simply by making polluters liable for the damages they cause. The purpose of the laws is not just to compensate people after they have been injured, though that is important. The real purpose is to get would-be polluters to make careful decisions. Knowing that they will be held liable for environmental damages in effect internalizes what would otherwise be ignored external effects.

Consider Figure 10-1. It's our familiar model of environmental pollution showing marginal abatement costs and marginal damages, both related to the rate at which some production residual is emitted. Suppose that the actual emission rate is initially at e_1, substantially above the efficient rate e^*. Suppose further that we now invoke a liability law that requires polluters to compensate those damaged in an amount equal to the damages caused. The effect of the law is to internalize the environmental damages that were external before the law. They now become costs that polluters will have to pay, and so will want to take into account when deciding on their emission rate. At e_1 the total damages, and hence the amount of the compensation payment, would be a monetary amount equal to the area $b + c + d$. This polluter could reduce its compensation payments by reducing emissions. As it does that, of course, its marginal abatement costs increase. But as long as the marginal abatement costs are less than marginal damages, it would have an incentive to move to the left; that is, to reduce its rate of emissions. In theory, then, a liability system could automatically lead this polluter to emission level e^*. We say "automatically" because it would not require any centralized control authorities to intervene and mandate emission reductions. It requires rather a system of decentralized courts and liability laws that would permit those damaged by pollution to seek compensation for damages suffered.

Theoretically, this approach appears to address the incentive question—getting people to take into account the environmental damages they may cause—as well as the question of compensating those who are damaged. It also appears to solve the

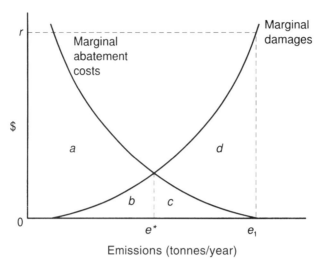

FIGURE 10-1   Policy Options: Liability and Property-Rights Approaches.

problem of determining just where e^* is along the emission axis. This would be discovered as a result of the interactions in court of polluters and those damaged. Both sides would present evidence and claims which, assuming the court is impartial, would lead to something approaching the efficient level of emissions.

The requirement that polluters be held liable for damages may be part of a country's basic legal code, or it could be provided through special statutory enactments. In common-law countries such as Canada (outside of Quebec), the U.S. and the United Kingdom, doctrines of nuisance and liability have been developed through the evolution of court decisions. This law now recognizes the difference between *strict liability*, which holds people responsible for damages regardless of circumstances, and *negligence*, which holds them responsible only if they did not take appropriate steps to avoid damage. A firm disposing of hazardous materials might be held strictly liable for damages done by these wastes. Thus, any damages that resulted, regardless of how careful the firm had been in disposing of the waste, would require compensation. On the other hand, negligence would hold it responsible only if it failed to take appropriate steps to ensure that the materials did not escape into the surrounding environment.

In civil-law countries and jurisdictions such as Quebec, liability requirements may be written into the appropriate parts of the code. And in any country environmental laws may specify conditions under which polluters may be held liable for damages. We will talk in Chapter 20 about the pollution-liability laws of Japan and the Netherlands. Many countries, individually and in international agreements, have sought to use liability policy to address the problem of maritime oil spills. Several international conventions have been devoted to specifying the liability requirements of companies whose tankers release, accidentally or not, large quantities of oil into the sea. And many countries have individually enacted laws specifying liability of their oil companies for damages from spills in coastal waters. One particularity of oil tanker spills is that it is very difficult to monitor the behaviour of the polluters in this case. It is an episodic emission, so there is no continuous flow to measure, and spill probabilities depend on many practices (navigation, tanker maintenance, etc.) that are difficult for public authorities to monitor continuously. When polluter behaviour is extremely difficult to monitor, we nevertheless would like to know that the polluters have undertaken all appropriate steps to reduce the probability of accidents. To provide the incentive for this, the most appropriate response may be to rely on a system of strict liability.

But a number of factors work against a wholesale reliance on liability to solve environmental problems. The critical factors in a liability system are where the burden of proof lies and what standards have to be met in order to establish that proof. In Canada, those who believe they may have been injured by pollution must file an action within a specified time period, and then in court must establish a direct causal link between the pollution and the damage. This involves two major steps: first to show that the polluting material was a direct cause of their damage, and then that the material did in fact come from the specific defendant that appears in court. Both steps are difficult because the standards of proof required by the courts may be more than current science can supply. Most chemicals, for example, are implicated in increased disease only on a *probabilistic* basis; that is, exposure to the substance involves an increased probability of disease, not certainty. Even though we "know" that smoking "causes" lung cancer, for example, this causal link remains probabilistic; an increased number of people will get lung cancer if they smoke, but we can't tell exactly which ones. In parts of rural Ontario, contamination of well water was estimated by some epidemiologists to have contributed to excess cases of leukemia in the areas affected. But under traditional standards of proof, a plaintiff could not conclusively prove that a *specific* cancer was caused by the water contamination. In other words, without being able to show explicitly how the polluting material operated in a particular body to produce cancer, the plaintiff cannot meet the standard of proof historically required in our courts.[1]

The other link in the causal chain is to show that the material to which one was exposed came from a particular source. This won't be difficult in some cases; the oil on the Alaskan shoreline definitely came from the Exxon *Valdez* wreck, the sulphur smells in in Prince George definitely come from the pulp and paper mills, etc. But in many cases this direct linkage is unknown. For an urban dweller in Montreal or Toronto, which specific industrial plant produced the SO_2 molecules that a particular person may have breathed? For the people living in cities and towns taking their drinking water from Lake Ontario, which specific companies were responsible for the

---

[1] In some cases the law is beginning to change to recognize the special characteristics of pollution-caused damage. For example, statutes of limitation are being changed to count from the time the disease first becomes apparent, in recognition of the fact that many pollution-caused diseases may not show up for many years after exposure. Some courts are also beginning to allow statistical cause-and-effect linkages.

chemicals that showed up in their water supply? Without being able to trace a polluting substance to specific defendants, those who have been damaged by it may be
unable to obtain compensation.

Another major point to make about liability systems can best be understood by
introducing the concept of *transactions costs*. In general terms transactions costs are
the costs of reaching and enforcing agreements. The concept was first introduced in
economics to apply to the costs that buyers and sellers encounter in making a successful transaction—costs of searching out information, costs of bargaining over
terms, and costs of making sure an agreement is actually carried out. But the transactions costs also apply to liability systems where plaintiffs and defendants are competing in a court of law to determine the question of liability and the appropriate
amounts of compensation. In this case transactions costs are all the legal costs associated with gathering evidence, presenting a case, challenging opponents, awarding
and collecting damages, etc.

If we are dealing with simple cases, with one party on each side and a reasonably
clear case of damage, the liability system may function, with a minimum of transactions costs, to give something approaching the efficient level of emissions. In the case
of the two small factories on a small lake, the two can go to court and argue about
the economic values to each of them of using the lake for their purposes. And since
these values are comparable, it presumably would not be too difficult for a judge to
determine the extent of the damages that the one firm is inflicting on the other. But
things are very different when large numbers of people are involved on one or both
sides of an issue. In the case of the Exxon *Valdez* oil spill, for example, probably tens
of thousands of people regard themselves as having been directly damaged, hundreds
of lawyers represent all the different sides, and numerous environmental groups, government organizations, and business groups are involved, as Exhibit 10-1 makes clear.
At the end of a very long series of court battles some compensation will be paid. But
the transactions costs will be enormous, and at the end of the process the compensation probably won't accurately reflect real damages. This is no doubt why the major
parties tried to settle this case with a lump-sum agreement relatively early in the
process, although continuing lawsuits are not ruled out.

We may rely on private liability arrangements to identify efficient pollution levels when relatively few people are involved, causal linkages are clear, and damages are
easy to measure. These conditions may be met in some localized cases of pollution,
but for most cases of environmental externalities they are not, and so we must consider
other means of arranging relationships between polluters and the people they affect.

PROPERTY RIGHTS

In the previous section we discussed the case of a small lake which one firm used for
waste disposal and another for a water supply. On deeper thought we are led to a more
fundamental question: Which one of the firms is really causing damage and which
firm is the one suffering damages? This may sound counterintuitive because you
might naturally think that the waste-disposing firm is of course the one causing the

EXHIBIT 10-1

EXXON VALDEZ'S SEA OF LITIGATION

Bickering among lawyers has added to the tension.

By Barnaby J. Feder

Can a bartender in Anchorage claim damages for tips he might have received from fishermen thrown out of work as a result of the Exxon *Valdez* spill?

What about California drivers who had to pay sharply higher gasoline prices after the *Valdez* grounding temporarily closed the port of Valdez and interrupted the flow of North Slope oil to California refineries?

And how about citizens of other states who have no plans to ever visit Alaska, but who, because of the spill, no longer have the knowledge that they could visit an unsullied region. What of the "bequest value" such knowledge would bring to future generations?

These are just a few of the legal questions stemming from the grounding of the *Valdez* in Prince William Sound on March 24 and the disgorgement of 11 million gallons of Alaskan crude oil into its pristine waters. The lawsuits began proliferating within days of the spill as lawyers from across the nation rushed to the scene.

"One of the mayors up there told me that the only thing worse than the oil hitting the shore was the wave of gray-flanneled lawyers that came next," said T. Barry Kingham, a lawyer with the New York firm of Curtis, Mallet-Prevost, Colt and Mosie. Mr. Kingham is not involved with the Exxon litigation but is one of the many lawyers who expects it to drag on into the next century. And he is in a better position than most to know why. He represents the French fishermen and villagers suing Amoco in the still unsettled litigation in the United States District Court in Chicago that began 11 years ago when the Amoco *Cadiz* ran aground off the Brittany coast.

The Amoco *Cadiz* case involved a spill seven times larger than the one in Alaska, but the latter may well involve more extensive environmental damage and more complicated interactions between state and Federal law. Already, it involves far more types of plaintiffs and byzantine negotiations among high-powered law firms from all over the country over how to share both the work and control over litigation strategy. "You have to ask whether the legal system is set up to cope with something like this," Mr. Kingham said.

"It will be a fun case, a chance to do some good for the public, but I don't think it's going to be very remunerative for plaintiffs' lawyers," said Stephen D. Susman, a Houston lawyer who was an early leader among the class-action plaintiffs' lawyers but was forced to drop out because of a conflict.

"Alaska is a funny place—they love the environment but they also love the oil industry and they won't want to punish it too badly," Mr. Susman said. "Spill cases tend to have their maximum value in the early days when there are dead birds on television. There's going to be real questions in this case on how you measure damages."

That issue alone may drag out the case, and delay the day when lawyers are paid. One solution, according to Mr. Gerry, may be to treat the spill as a running nuisance case in which damages are reexamined and new payments made every few years. "It would be unfair to both Exxon and plaintiffs to try to settle some things quickly because it would be sheer guesswork," said Mr. Gerry.

Whatever the complications, many lawyers believe the *Valdez* case is unlikely to set any lasting standard for how much it costs the legal system to sort out liabilities after environmental disasters. "Look at Chernobyl," said Professor Schoenbaum, referring to the devastation caused by the 1987 failure of a Soviet nuclear reactor. "It is hard to imagine the legal impact of something like that if it occurred in the United States. We haven't scratched the surface."

damage. But we might argue just as well that the presence of the food-processing firm inflicts damages on the waste-disposing firm because its presence makes it necessary for the latter to take special efforts to control its emissions. (Assume for purposes of argument that there are no other people, like homeowners or recreators, using the lake.) The problem may come about simply because it is not clear who has the initial right to use the services of the lake; that is, who effectively owns the property rights to the lake. When someone owns a resource, she has a strong incentive to see to it that it is managed in a way that gives it the maximum value. To solve the problem of lake pollution, therefore, it is necessary to specify clearly who has the rights of ownership to the lake. Whether or not the specification of ownership rights is also sufficient to solve the problem and reach a socially efficient equilibrium is the topic of this section.

Private-property rights are, of course, the dominant institutional arrangement in most developed economies of the West. Developing countries also are moving in that direction, as are even the ex-socialist countries. So we are familiar with the operation of that institutional system when it comes to person-made assets such as machines, buildings, and consumer goods. Private property in land is also a familiar arrangement. If somebody owns a piece of land, he has an incentive to see to it that the land is managed in ways that maximize its value. If somebody comes along and threatens to dump something onto the land, the owner may call upon the law to prevent it if he wants to. By this diagnosis, the problem of the misuse of many environmental assets comes about because of imperfectly specified property rights in those assets.

Consider again the case of the lake and the two firms. Apparently we have two choices for vesting ownership of the lake. It could be owned either by the polluting firm or by the firm using it for a water supply. How does this choice affect the level of pollution in the lake? Would it not lead to zero emissions if owned by the one firm, and uncontrolled emissions if owned by the other? Not if we allow owners and nonowners to negotiate. Of course, this is the very essence of a property-rights system. The owner decides how the asset is to be used, and may stop any unauthorized use, but may also negotiate with anybody else who wants access to that asset.

Look again at Figure 10-1. Suppose the marginal damage function refers to all the damages suffered by the brewery—call this Firm A. Assume the marginal abatement cost curve applies to the firm emitting effluent into the lake—call this one Firm B. We have to make some assumption about who owns the lake, Firm A or Firm B. We will see that, *theoretically*, we will get the same quantity of emissions in either case, provided that the two firms can come together and strike a bargain about how the lake is to be used.

In the first case, suppose we assume that Firm B owns the lake. For the moment we need not worry about how this came about, only that this is the way it is. Firm B may use the lake any way it wishes. We can suppose that emissions initially would be at e_1. Firm B is initially devoting no resources at all to emissions abatement. But is this where matters will remain? At this point marginal damages are r, while marginal abatement costs are nil. The straightforward thing for Firm A to do, therefore, is to offer Firm B some amount of money to reduce its effluent stream; for the first tonne any amount agreed upon between 0 and r would make both parties better off. In fact, they could continue to bargain over the marginal unit as long as marginal damages exceeded marginal abatement costs. Firm B would be better off by reducing its emissions for any payment in excess of its marginal abatement costs, while any payment less than the marginal damages would make Firm A better off. In this way, bargaining between the owners of the lake (here Firm B) and the people who are damaged by pollution would result in a reduction in effluent to e^*, the point at which marginal abatement costs and marginal damages are equal.

Suppose, on the other hand, that ownership of the lake is vested in Firm A, the firm that is damaged by pollution. In this case we might assume that the owners would allow no infringement of their property; that is, that the emission level would be zero or close to it. Is this where it would remain? Not if, again, we allow bargaining between owners and others who would like to use the lake. In this case Firm B would have to buy permission from Firm A to place its wastes in the lake. Any price for this lower than marginal abatement costs but higher than marginal damages would make both parties better off. And so, by a similar process of bargaining with, of course, payments now going in the opposite direction, the emissions level into the lake would be adjusted from the low level where it started toward the efficient level e^*. At this point any further adjustment would stop because marginal abatement costs, the maximum the polluters would pay for the right to emit one more tonne of effluent, are equal to marginal damages, the minimum Firm A would take in order to allow Firm B to emit this added tonne. The key point here is that individuals determine the value of damages and compensation through their bargaining process. The owner of the property right has the power to stop the other party's actions that are deleterious to it. It can also sell this right if a price is established that both parties agree to. Recall again the difference between property rights and liability rules. In the case of liability rules, the courts determine whose rights are violated and what the amount of compensation will be. The property right allows the parties involved to attempt to reach a mutually agreeable level of pollution and compensation for damages.

It is important to note that the gains to each party associated with different property rights need not be identical. This can be easily shown in Figure 10-2 which is identical to Figure 10-1 except that more areas are identified. As before, the efficient level of emissions is e^* regardless of whether we start at the low level shown or e_1, but the net gains to the individuals involved differ. Suppose we start at e_1 and Firm B has the property rights and Firm A is offering to make a payment of r^* per unit emissions reduced. We know that r^* is the efficient payment because it is the point where marginal damages and marginal abatement costs are equal. Firm B will now incur abatement costs equal to area d. But Firm B gains a payment from Firm A equal to area $d + e$ when Firm A pays r^* per unit emissions reduced. Firm B's net gain is area e. But Firm A, the party afflicted by the pollution, also gains. When emissions were e_1, its total damages were areas $c + d + e + f$. At e^*, the total damages are only equal to area c. Firm A's net gain at point e^* is area f which is its damages foregone (areas $d + e + f$) minus its payment to Firm B (areas $d + e$). Net gains to "society," which in our case is Firms A and B, is equal to areas $e + f$.

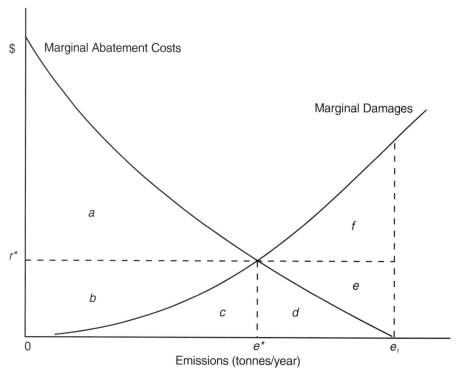

FIGURE 10-2   Gains from Alternative Property-Right Assignments.

Suppose now that Firm A owns the lake and Firm B must pay Firm A to be allowed to discharge emissions into the lake. Again, the efficient payment will be r^* per unit discharged, and equilibrium is at e^*. Now Firm A receives a payment equal to areas $b + c$ to compensate for incurring total damages equal to area c. Its net gain is therefore area b. Firm B is allowed to pollute to level e^*, so saves having to incur abatement expenses equal to area $a + b + c$. It pays Firm A area $b + c$, so its net gain is area a. Net gains to both parties then total areas $a + b$. As the figure is drawn, areas $a + b$ do not equal areas $e + f$. There is no reason to expect them to be equal as this will depend on the shapes of the marginal abatement cost and marginal damage function. Thus "society" may well be better off under one property-right assignment than another, even though either assignment will be efficient.

So, as we have seen in this example, if we clearly define who has the property right over the environmental asset and then allow bargaining among owners and prospective users, we will arrive at the efficient level of effluent irrespective of who was initially given the property right. In fact, this is a famous theorem, called the "Coase theorem," after the economist who invented it.[2] The wider implication is that by defining

[2] Ronald H. Coase, "The Problem of Social Cost," *Journal of Law and Economics*, Vol. 3 (October 1960): 1–44.

private-property rights (not necessarily individual property rights because private *groups* of people could have these rights), we can establish the conditions under which decentralized bargaining can produce efficient levels of environmental quality. This has some appeal. The good part of it is that the people doing the bargaining may know more about the relative values involved—abatement costs and damages—than anybody else, so there is some hope that the true efficiency point will be arrived at. And since it would be a decentralized system, we would not need to have some central bureaucratic organization making decisions that are based mostly on political considerations instead of the true economic values involved. Ideas like this have led some people to recommend widespread conversion of natural and environmental resources to private ownership as a means of achieving their efficient use.

How well is this property-rights approach likely to work in practice? As we saw with liability laws, something that looks good in theory may not work well when faced with the complexities of the real world. In order for a property-rights approach to work right—that is, to give us something approaching the efficient level of environmental pollution—essentially three main conditions have to be met:

1 Property rights must be well defined, enforceable, and transferable.

2 There must be a reasonably efficient and competitive system for interested parties to come together and negotiate about how these environmental property rights will be used.

3 There must be a complete set of markets so that private owners may capture all social values associated with the use of an environmental asset.

If Firm A cannot keep Firm B from doing whatever the latter wishes, of course a property-rights approach will not work. In other words, owners must be physically and legally able to stop others from encroaching on their property. Owners must be able to sell their property to any would-be buyer. This is especially important in environmental assets. If owners cannot sell the property, this will weaken their incentives to preserve its long-run productivity. This is because any use that does draw down its long-run environmental productivity cannot be punished through the reduced market value of the asset. Many economists have argued that this is a particularly strong problem in developing countries; since ownership rights are often "attenuated" (that is, they do not have all the required characteristics specified above), people do not have strong incentives to see that long-run productivity is maintained.

We saw above that the efficient use of the lake depended on negotiations and agreement between the two interested firms. Negotiating costs, together with the costs of policing the agreement, could be expected to be fairly modest. What we are referring to here is transactions costs, the idea that we introduced in the preceding section. In the simple lake case, transactions costs would probably be low enough that the firms would be able to negotiate on the efficient level of emissions. But suppose we replace Firm A, the firm using the lake as a water supply source, with a community of 50,000 people who use it not only for a water supply, but also for recreational purposes. Now the negotiations must take place between a single polluting firm on one side and 50,000 people, or their representatives, on the other side. For each of these individuals the value of improved water quality is small relative to the value to the firm of polluting the lake. Moreover, the level of water quality in the lake is a public good for these individuals. This seriously increases the transactions costs of negotiating an agreement among different users.

To make matters worse, suppose we replace the one polluting firm with 1,000 polluting firms, together with a few thousand homeowners who are not yet hooked into the public sewer system and so are using septic tanks on the shores of the lake. Here the possibilities of vesting the ownership of the lake in one person, and expecting negotiations between that person and prospective users to find the efficient levels of use, essentially vanish. This is another way of saying that in large and complex cases of environmental degradation, where free-rider problems abound, very high transactions costs will seriously reduce the potential of the private-property approach to identify the efficient level of emissions.

For private-property institutions to ensure that an environmental asset is put to its best use, the process must also work in such a way that the owner is able to capture the full social value of the resource in that use. Suppose you own a small island in the Thirty Thousand Islands in Lake Huron. There are two possible uses: Develop a resort hotel or devote it to a wildlife refuge. If you build the hotel, you get a direct flow of monetary wealth because the tourism market is well developed in that part of the world and you can expect customers to find your hotel and pay the going rate for your services. But there is no comparable "market" for wildlife refuge services. The value of the island as refuge may well be much higher than its value as resort, in terms of the actual aggregate willingness to pay of all the people in the country and the world. But there is no good way for them to be able to express that value; there is no ready market like the one in the tourism market where they can in effect bid against the tourists who would visit the island. You might think that a nature conservancy could buy up the island if its value as refuge really is higher than its value as hotel. But the nature conservancy runs on the basis of voluntary contributions, and islands and other lands are in effect public goods. We saw earlier that when public goods are involved, voluntary contributions to make something available are likely to be a lot less than its true value, because of free-riding behaviour. The upshot is that, while you as an owner could certainly expect to reap the full monetary value of the island as resort, you would not be able to realize its full social value if you held it as a preserve.

Exhibit 10-2 shows a real-world example of this problem. It is about a person in the state of Kansas who owns a piece of land that was one of the largest remaining stretches of virgin land in the country. An 80-acre piece, it had never known the plow. As such it probably had important ecological as well as historical value. But these values, though we all recognize their validity and importance, cannot very well be captured by a private landowner. The basic problem is that there is no way for the full ecological values to be made apparent and expressed in a direct way. Although a private group bid for the land,[3] without success, its budget was limited by its vol-

---

[3] The group is the Nature Conservancy, which seeks to protect sensitive resources from damage by buying them outright. Over the last few decades it has acquired more than 5.5 million acres of land in Canada and the U.S.; some has been transferred to other public and private conservation groups; the rest still belongs to the Nature Conservancy.

EXHIBIT 10-2

IGNORING PLEAS OF ENVIRONMENTALISTS, KANSAS MAN DIGS UP VIRGIN PRAIRIE

Special to The New York Times

LAWRENCE, Kan., Nov. 22—The largest remaining stretch of virgin prairie in northeast Kansas disappeared under the plow this week after futile attempts by the Nature Conservancy and local environmentalists to buy it.

The plowing of the 80-acre Elkins Prairie was first noticed soon after sunrise on Sunday, and the news quickly spread to a community group that had worked for two years to preserve the land, one of the few remaining unspoiled pieces of the 200 million acres of tall grass prairie that once covered North America.

Environmentalists hurried to the site and pleaded with the landowner to stop his tractor. The Douglas County Commission called an emergency meeting and after negotiating half the night offered to pay the landowner $6,000 an acre within six months, the equivalent of what developers had recently paid for nearby land.

But the owner, Jack Graham, rejected the offer and resumed plowing. By late Monday, only a small strip of virgin prairie remained.

Home to 150 Plant Species

It's heart-wrenching," said Joyce Wolf, leader of a group that had hoped to buy the land for an environmental education area. "He has stolen a resource from a community."

Mr. Graham, a 39-year-old businessman who bought the land five years ago, declined to comment on his action. His lawyer, Thomas Murray, said Mr. Graham and his family "simply wanted to make their property more productive," but he would not elaborate.

Only about 2 percent of the original tallgrass prairie in North America remains, and Craig Freeman, coordinator of the state's Natural Heritage Program, said the Elkins stretch, about a mile outside this booming college town, was a particularly fine example of the complex prairie ecosystem. It was home to 150 species of plants, including two threatened species. Mead's milkweed and the western prairie fringed orchid.

Federal plant protection laws do not apply to private property that receives no Federal money.

Last year the Nature Conservancy, a national land preservation organization, offered to buy the Elkins Prairie for $3,500 and acre within a year, Ms. Wolf said, a bid that had unintended consequences. The organization's failure to offer a higher price. Mr. Murray said, convinced the Grahams that the land was not as environmentally important as many Lawrence residents believed.

The Kansas director of the conservancy, Alan Pollom, defended the offer, saying it was based on an appraisal. "We can't unjustifiably enrich someone using the funds of a nonprofit organization," he said.

In the past few years Lawrence residents have tried to balance urban growth and preservation of the environment. Home to the University of Kansas, Lawrence has grown 23 percent to nearly 65,000 people since 1980, but development has been tempered by strong community support for preservation.

Philosophy on the Highway

Throughout the day on Monday, people gathered on a corner across the busy two-lane highway from the Elins Prairie, talking as they watched the tractor work its way back and forth across the land.

"I question the wisdom of plowing up good prairie, but I would defend his right to do it," said Larry Warren, a farmer and neighbor. "It's his land: it's his prerogative."

But Buzz Hoagland, a biology professor at the University of Kansas, argued that individuals have a responsibility to preserve the environment, even at the expense of their own profits.

"It took a couple of million years for this land to evolve to the state it is in today, and it took 48 hours to destroy it," Dr. Hoagland said.

untary character and the free-rider problems inherent in preserving what are in effect public goods. But development values are real and immediate. Thus, the private landowner opted for development, in spite of the ecological and historical value of the property.

This example is actually a local version of a larger problem that has global significance. Much attention has been focussed in recent years on biological diversity and the stock of unique genetic material contained in the millions of animal and plant species worldwide. A disproportionately large share of these species is located in developing countries. But these are countries also where development pressures have led to high rates of land clearance and habitat destruction. When landholders in these countries are considering their options, they weigh the value of the land in different uses. Unfortunately, there is no way at present that they can capture the value of the land left as species habitat. No ready economic markets exist where these services can be sold; if they did, landholders could reap private benefits from keeping land undeveloped or using land in ways that are consistent with the preservation of species.

One role for public authorities in this situation might be to create the demand side for such a market. This could be done by offering to pay the landowners an amount equal to the wider ecological value of the land, provided these ecological values were not impaired by the landholders' use of the land. Of course, this would involve enormous difficulties in measuring these ecological values with some degree of accuracy, as well as in finding sources of funds to pay for these services. But without these kinds of market or marketlike institutions, private-property-rights institutions are unable to give society the fully efficient amounts of preservation and environmental quality.[4]

MORAL SUASION

By "moral suasion" we mean programs of persuasion that appeal to a person's sense of moral values or civic duty, to get him or her to refrain voluntarily from doing things that degrade the environment. The classic case of this is the success of public pressure against littering. While there are fines and penalties for doing these things, antilittering campaigns were not based on threats of penalties as much as on appealing to people's sense of civic morality.

In the early days of recycling, communities often mounted voluntary efforts, where appeals were made on the basis of civic virtue. In some cases these efforts were successful; in others they fell flat. Today we are moving in the direction of more mandatory recycling programs, though it is true that they still must rely heavily on moral suasion to get high rates of compliance. Other situations clearly exist where appeals to civic morality may be effective public policy. This is especially the case with emissions as in litter, where violators are normally scattered throughout a population in a way that makes it impractical to monitor them and detect violations as they occur.

The good thing about moral suasion is that it may have widespread spillover effects. Whereas an effluent tax on a single type of effluent will have no impact on

---

[4] Recently a private U.S. drug company agreed to pay the government of a Latin American country certain sums of money for plant species useful in drug development. We will discuss this in Chapter 22.

emissions of other types of waste products, appeals to civic virtue for one problem may produce side effects on other situations. People who, through a special publicity campaign, are brought to feel a greater sense of civic virtue when they refrain from littering in cases where they clearly could get away with it may find themselves having the same feelings when they, for example, refrain from sneaking used motor oil into their household waste, or keep the pollution-control systems on their cars in a higher state of repair.

There are problems, however, with relying on moral suasion as a primary policy approach. Not all people are equally responsible from an ethical standpoint. Some people will respond to moral arguments; others will not. The burden of this policy will fall, therefore, on the part of the population that is morally more sensitive; those who respond less to moral arguments will be free riding on the others, enjoying the benefits of others' moral restraint but escaping their rightful share of the burden. What is especially bad about this is the long-run demonstration value. If those who would be responsive to moral arguments are confronted with the sight of widespread moral free riding, this may in the long run tend to erode the general level of civic and moral responsibility. Thus, appeals to the moral responsiveness of people, although perhaps effective in the short run, could actually have the opposite effect in the long run. This is similar to the cynicism that people often feel when new environmental laws are continually put on the books but never enforced.

While moral virtue is its own reward, it is even better if other people know about it. Moral suasion will be more effective in deterring pollution if information is readily available about emission levels and changes in them.[5] Thus, as a counterpart to campaigns of moral suasion, efforts to measure and publicize emission levels and efforts people take to reduce these emissions are an important adjunct. These factors lie behind the recent attempt by environmental groups in Canada and the U.S. to develop an antipollution code of conduct to which companies could voluntarily subscribe. As indicated in the news clipping of Exhibit 10-3, these "Valdez Principles" involve voluntary disclosure of operations that might cause harm to the environment.[6]

It is easy to be cynical about moral suasion as a tool for environmental improvement. In this era of increasing mass society and heightened environmental destruction, tough-minded policymakers are naturally drawn toward environmental policies that have more teeth in them. This would probably be a mistake. It perhaps is true that we cannot rely very heavily on moral suasion to produce; for example, a significant reduction in air pollution in the Windsor to Montreal corridor or substantial drops in the use of groundwater-contaminating farm chemicals. But in our search for new and effective, concrete public policy devices to address specific pollution problems, we perhaps underestimate the contribution of the overall climate of public morality and civic virtue. A strong climate in this sense makes it possible to institute new policies and makes it easier to administer and enforce them. From this we can

---

[5] Much like the United Way uses the large red thermometer to show the progress of community fund drives.

[6] There may be more than moral suasion involved here; the article mentions the possibility of such things as boycotts and shareholder actions, which have more direct economic implications for targeted companies.

EXHIBIT 10-3

JOAN BAVARIA'S CRUSADE FOR THE ENVIRONMENT

Social Activist Is Driving Force Behind the Valdez Principles,
a Corporate Code of Conduct.

By Stan Hiden

When the Exxon *Valdez* tanker plowed into a reef in March 1989 and spilled millions of gallons of crude oil into the pristine waters of Prince William Sound, the massive damage to the Alaskan environment set off angry cries across America.

One of the anguished voices belonged to an idealistic Boston money manager named Joan Bavaria, who has spent a decade on the front line of social investing, searching out companies that make safe products and pursue worthy social goals.

Within months of the *Valdez* spill, as the cries of anger turned to cries for action, the 47-year-old social activist emerged as the driving force behind a new and potent alliance of investors and environmentalists that was formed to force corporations to accept more responsibility for their environmental conduct. The members of the coalition, called Ceres, hold millions of shares of stock in major corporations.

Out of their alliance came the Valdez Principles—a tough 10-point code of conduct that asks corporations to disclose their environmental problems and act decisively to remedy them.

"We are trying, in a very fundamental way, to change the way corporations look at the environment and at their practices around the environment," said Bavaria, whose coalition controls $150 billion in pension and mutual funds and represents environmental groups with some 10 million members.

The stringent standards of the Valdez Principles, the heightened public concern about pollution and new federal cleanup laws have all combined to put environmental issues on the front burner in the board rooms of America.

In the coming year, more than 50 major corporations will get shareholder resolutions from environmental and church groups, asking the companies to sign the Valdez Principles. Boiled down, they ask corporations to end air and water pollution, conserve energy, market safe products, pay for damages to the environment and make public reports on their progress.

That is more than many corporations are willing to promise—primarily because they fear they might open themselves to legal problems.

But the principles fit neatly with Bavaria's vision of the future, which is that U.S. corporations will learn to live with tough environmental standards—just as they now live with tough accounting standards.

Bavaria's battle to make the Valdez Principles the standard for corporate behavior will be opposed by many in the corporate world. But few companies and industries will ignore the steadily growing public concern about global warming, acid rain and toxic waste.

Many corporate officials share the view of Harvey Alter, manager for resources policy at the U.S. Chamber of Commerce who said the Valdez Principles showed that Ceres was "naive" about the way companies operate and that companies could achieve the same environmental goals on their own.

"Ceres," he said, "has put up a litmus test in which a company has to say 'yes' or 'no'. It's not that easy."

Up to this point, Bavaria and her colleagues at Ceres (short for Coalition for Environmentally Responsible Economies) have been using persuasion and the threat of shareholder action to gain signers for the Valdez Principles. Bavaria said any thoughts of boycotts would be far in the future.

In the coming year, each of the Fortune 500 companies will be asked by Ceres to fill out a 37-page questionnaire about their environmental problems and policies.

Among the environmental groups that belong to Ceres are the Sierra Club, Friends of the Earth, the National Audubon Society, the National Wildlife Federation and the Wilderness Society.

One of the most powerful demands for corporations to sign the Valdez Principles has come from the $16.4 billion New York City Employees Retirement System fund. The fund has asked the Exxon Corp., Occidental Petroleum Corp. and Champion International Corp. to sign the Valdez Principles.

also deduce the importance of politicians and policymakers in doing things that replenish this moral climate rather than erode it.

MARKET RESPONSES TO ENVIRONMENTAL POLLUTION: GREEN GOODS

Once property rights have been clearly established that limit the amount of pollution emitted or specify some level of environmental quality, we expect that some markets will arise to supply environmental quality. Suppose consumers are willing to pay for goods that give them the same level of pleasure but involve less environmental damage either in the production process or in use than ordinary goods. If firms can produce such items, a market in so-called "green goods" might arise. In Canada, a number of green goods are currently being sold. They include, for example, household items such as no-phosphate laundry detergent, batteries not containing mercury, paper products made from recycled fibre, and appliances such as energy-efficient refrigerators and furnaces. There may also be green inputs into production processes. How do green goods reduce pollution?

Consider Figure 10-3. Panel (a) shows the market for paper products made using virgin fibre. Panel (b) illustrates the market for paper products made using recycled fibres. We assume that recycled fibres result in a less pollution-intensive process than virgin fibres. In each panel two supply curves are shown: S_p is the curve that reflects the marginal private costs of production; S_s the marginal social costs (which are the sum of marginal private costs plus marginal external costs as we saw in Chapter 4, page 71). The pollution intensity of the two types of good is reflected in the higher marginal social costs for paper produced with virgin fibre. Now let's add some demand curves. Suppose the market is originally supplied only with paper from the

FIGURE 10-3   Marginal Social Costs with Green Goods vs. Pollution-Intensive Goods.

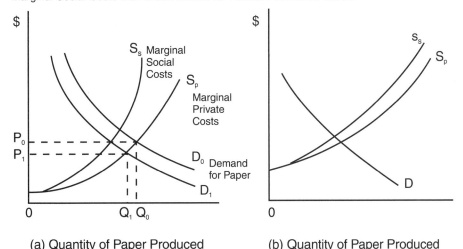

(a) Quantity of Paper Produced
using Virgin Fibre

(b) Quantity of Paper Produced
using Recycled Fibre

pollution-intensive process. Given a demand curve for paper, D_0, an equilibrium price of P_0 is established and quantity Q_0 is produced, as shown in panel (a). Now producers of less-pollution-intensive paper enter the market. If consumers feel that recycled paper products are a good substitute for ordinary paper products, there will be some demand for recycled paper goods. If the two goods are substitutes the demand for pollution-intensive paper will shift to the left with the introduction of the recycled paper. A new equilibrium price will be established where there is less production of ordinary paper (Q_1) and it is sold at a lower price (P_1). There will be some demand for recycled paper. The more consumers wish to substitute recycled for ordinary paper, the greater the leftward shift of the demand curve in panel A. The extent of this shift is dependent upon consumers' tastes, the marginal private costs of production, etc.

If recycled paper goods capture some of the market, pollution must decrease. This occurs because the marginal abatement cost function shifts down. Why? Think back to our derivation of the aggregate marginal cost of abatement curve (MAC) in Chapter 5, pages 91–93. Instead of having one type of production with a lot of pollution per unit output, we now have the output of paper coming from two types of producers; one with much lower emissions per unit output. If total output of paper stays the same, then total pollution must fall. This is shown in Figure 10-4, where MAC_1 is the

FIGURE 10-4   How Green Goods Affect the Marginal Abatement Cost Curve.

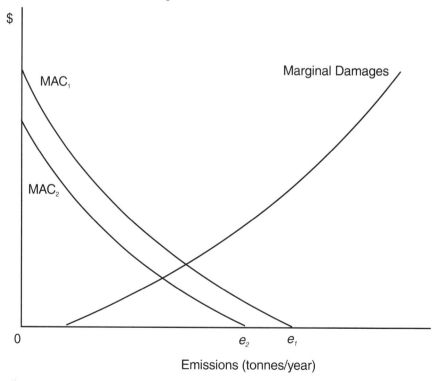

aggregate MAC with only pollution-intensive suppliers; and MAC_2 is the new curve obtained when some of the suppliers have much lower levels of emissions per unit output. We see that maximum pollution levels fall from e_1 to e_2. This means that regardless of where the marginal damage function is located, pollution is lower even without any government policy designed to reach the efficient level of emissions. Note that the MD function does not shift because the relationship between each unit of emissions and environmental damage does not change. An economy with a higher proportion of its production and consumption coming from green goods will thus have less pollution than an economy using more pollution-intensive goods. Government policy can of course stimulate the production of green goods. We will talk more about this in Chapter 12 on incentive-based strategies. The point here is that even without government intervention, if there is demand for green goods and it is technologically possible to produce them, environmental quality will be higher if these goods are produced and consumed.

SUMMARY

In this chapter we began our exploration of different types of public policies that might be used to combat environmental pollution. We began the chapter with a brief discussion of the criteria we might use to evaluate the effectiveness of alternative environmental policies. While the most important may be the ability of policies to attain efficient levels of emissions, there are other important criteria such as equity considerations, the ability to create incentives for future changes, and enforceability.

In the chapter we discussed two main decentralized types of approaches to environmental quality improvement. The first was to rely on liability rules, which require polluters to compensate those they have damaged. In theory, the threat of liability can lead potential polluters to internalize what would ordinarily be external costs. By weighing relative compensation and abatement costs, polluters would be brought to efficient emission levels. While liability doctrines may work well in simple cases of pollution where few people are involved and cause-and-effect linkages are clear, they are unlikely to work reliably in the large-scale, technically complicated environmental problems of contemporary societies.

The second major approach we discussed was reliance on the institution of private-property rights. Looked at from this perspective, environmental externalities are problems only because ownership of environmental assets is often not clearly defined. By establishing clear property rights, owners and others who would like to use environmental assets for various purposes can negotiate agreements that balance the relative costs of different alternatives. Thus, negotiations among parties could theoretically bring about efficient emission rates. But problems of transactions costs, especially related to the public goods aspects of environmental quality, and lack of markets for environmental services work against relying primarily on traditional property-rights institutions in environmental quality issues. We will see in a subsequent chapter, however, that some new types of property-rights approaches may hold greater promise.

We mentioned the idea of moral suasion, which may be useful when it is impossible to measure the emissions stemming from particular sources. The problem of free riding was discussed, as was the problem of public disclosure as a means of encouraging ethical behaviour in environmental matters.

Finally, we discussed the introduction of green goods into an economy by the private sector in response to consumer demands for less-pollution-intensive products. We showed that the greater the proportion of green goods in an economy's output, the lower the level of emissions and higher the level of enviromental quality.

QUESTIONS FOR FURTHER DISCUSSION

1 Neighbours could, relatively easily, negotiate with one another to settle questions of externalities, such as excessive noise or incompatible property development. So why do most communities rely on local laws and regulations to manage these externalities?

2 In the case of a pollutant which has an uncertain effect on people, the courts could put the burden of proof either on the people damaged to show that they indeed were injured or on the polluters to show that the pollutant is not harmful. What difference would this make to the working of the liability system?

3 Suppose a community weighed each resident's solid-waste disposal when it was picked up and published the individual totals each year in the local newspaper. Do you think this would lead to a reduction in the total quantity of solid waste disposed of in the community?

4 In the negotiations among property owners and potential users, how are future generations taken into account?

5 Accidents with trucks carrying hazardous wastes have become fairly common. Suppose the perpetrators of any accident of this type are held liable for a sum equal to the average damages done in all such accidents. Would this lead trucking companies to take the efficient amount of precautions against such accidents?[7]

6 Explain and illustrate how the degree of substitution between green goods and pollution-intensive goods affects the level of environmental quality.

SELECTED READINGS

Anderson, Terry L. "The Market Process and Environmental Amenities," in Walter E. Block (ed.). *Economics and the Environment: A Reconciliation*. Vancouver: The Fraser Institute, 1990, 137–157.

Anderson, Terry L., and Donald R. Leal. *Free Market Environmentalism*. San Francisco: Pacific Research Institute, 1991.

Coase, Ronald H. "The Problem of Social Cost." *Journal of Law and Economics*, Vol. 3 (October 1960): 1–44.

Dales, J. H. *Pollution, Property and Prices*. Toronto: University of Toronto Press, 1968.

Hoffman, W. Michael, Robert Frederick, and Edward S. Petry, Jr. (eds.). *The Corporation, Ethics, and the Environment*. New York: Quorum Books, 1990.

---

[7] This question is based on a similar one in Tom Tietenberg, *Environmental and Natural Resource Economics*, 3rd ed. (New York: Harper Collins, 1992), 71.

Kneese, Allen V., and William D. Schulze. "Ethics and Environmental Economics," in Allen V. Kneese and James L. Sweeney (eds.). *Handbook of Natural Resource and Energy Economics*, Vol. 1. Amsterdam: North-Holland, 1985, 191–220.

Rothbard, Murray N. "Law, Property Rights, and Air Pollution," in Walter E. Block (ed.). *Economics and the Environment: A Reconciliation*. Vancouver: The Fraser Institute, 1990, 233–279.

Singer, Steven T. "An Analysis of Common Law and Statutory Remedies for Hazardous Waste Injuries." *Rutgers Law Journal* 12 (Fall 1980): 117–150.

11

COMMAND-AND-CONTROL STRATEGIES: THE CASE OF STANDARDS

A "command-and-control" (CAC) approach to public policy is one where, in order to bring about behaviour thought to be socially desirable, political authorities simply mandate the behaviour in law, then use whatever enforcement machinery—courts, police, fines, etc.—are necessary to get people to obey the law. In the case of environmental policy, the command-and-control approach consists of relying on *standards* of various types to bring about improvements in environmental quality. In general, a standard is simply a mandated level of performance that is enforced in law. A speed limit is a classic type of standard; it sets maximum rates that drivers may legally travel. An emission standard is a maximum rate of emissions that is legally allowed. The spirit of a standard is, if you want people not to do something, simply pass a law that makes it illegal, then send out the authorities to enforce the law.

Figure 11-1 is our familiar graph showing marginal abatement costs and marginal damages related to the rate at which some production residual is emitted into the environment. The target level of emissions is set at e^*, where marginal damages equal marginal abatement costs. This socially efficient level of emissions thus minimizes the sum of abatement plus damage costs. Suppose that initially the actual level of effluent is at e_1, a rate substantially above the efficient rate of e^*. To achieve e^* the authorities set an emission standard at that level; e^* becomes a mandated upper limit for the emissions of this firm. To enforce this standard we would then send out various enforcement authorities to measure and detect any possible violations of the standard. If infractions are found, the source is fined or subject to some other penalty. Assuming the firm reduces emissions in accordance with the standard, it would be paying an amount equivalent to area a per year in total abatement costs. These total abatement costs can be called the *compliance costs* of meeting the standard.

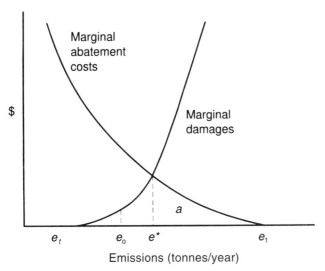

FIGURE 11-1 Emission Standards.

ENVIRONMENTAL POLICY ANALYSIS

Standards are popular for a number of reasons. They appear to be simple and direct. They apparently set clearly specified targets. They appeal, therefore, to the sense that everybody has of wanting to come directly to grips with environmental pollution and get it reduced. Standards also appear to be congenial to our ethical sense that pollution is bad and ought to be declared illegal. The legal system is geared to operate by defining and stopping illegal behaviour, and the standards approach conforms to this mindset. We will see, however, that the standards approach is a lot more complex than might first appear. In fact, a very practical reason for the popularity of standards is that they may permit far more flexibility in enforcement than might be apparent. What appears to be the directness and unambiguousness of standards becomes a lot more problematic when we look below the surface.

TYPES OF STANDARDS

Any action you can think of could be the subject of a standard, but in environmental matters there are three main types of standards: ambient, emission, and technology.

Ambient Standards

Ambient environmental quality refers to the qualitative dimensions of the surrounding environment; it could be the ambient quality of the air over a particular city, or the ambient quality of the water in a particular river. So an *ambient standard* is a never-exceed level for some pollutant in the ambient environment. For example, an ambient standard for dissolved oxygen in a particular river may be set at 3 parts per million (ppm), meaning that this is the lowest level of dissolved oxygen that is to be allowed in the river. Ambient standards cannot be enforced directly, of course. What can be enforced are the various emissions that lead to ambient quality levels. To ensure that dissolved oxygen never falls below 3 ppm in the river, we must know how the emissions of the various sources on the river contribute to changes in this measure, then introduce some means of controlling these sources.

Ambient standards are normally expressed in terms of average concentration levels over some period of time. For example, the current national ambient air quality objective for sulfur dioxide (SO_2) is 23 parts per billion (ppb) on the basis of an annual arithmetic mean and 115 ppb on a 24-hour average basis.[1] The standard, in other words, has two criteria: a maximum annual average of 23 ppb and a maximum 24-hour average of 115 ppb. The reason for taking averages is to recognize that there are seasonal and daily variations in meteorological conditions, as well as in the emissions that produce variations in ambient quality. Averaging means that short-term ambient quality levels may be worse than the standard, so long as this does not persist for too long and so long as it is balanced by periods when the air quality is better than the standard.

Emission Standards

Emission standards are never-exceed levels applied directly to the quantities of emissions coming from pollution sources. Emission (or effluent) standards are normally expressed in terms of quantity of material per some unit of time; for example, grams per minute or tonnes per week. Continuous emissions streams may be subject to standards on "instantaneous" rates of flow; for example, upper limits on the quantity of residuals flow per minute or on the average residuals flow over some time period.

It is important to keep in mind the distinction between ambient standards and emission standards. Setting emission standards at a certain level does not necessarily entail meeting a set of ambient standards. Between emissions and ambient quality stands nature, in particular the meteorological and hydrological phenomena that link the two. The environment usually transports the emissions from point of discharge to other locations, often diluting and dispersing them along the way. Chemical processes occur in all environmental media that often change the physical character of the pollutant. In some cases this may render the emitted substance more benign. Organic wastes put in rivers and streams will normally be subject to natural degradation processes, which will break them down into constituent elements. Thus, the ambient quality of the water at various points downstream depends on the quantity of emissions as well as the hydrology of the river—its rate of flow, temperature, natural reaeration conditions, and so on.

---

[1] These are the maximum acceptable concentrations. There are two other target concentrations for ambient air quality. We will examine these targets in Chapter 16.

Sometimes the environment will convert a certain type of pollutant into something more damaging. Research to link emission levels and ambient quality levels is a major part of environmental science.

The link between emissions and ambient quality can also be vitally affected by human decisions. A classic case is automobiles. As part of the mobile-source air-pollution program, we establish emission standards for new cars in terms of emissions per kilometre of operation. But since we have no way of controlling either the number of cars on the roads or the total number of hours each is driven, the aggregate quantity of pollutants in the air and, thus, ambient air quality, is not directly controlled. Emission standards can be set on a wide variety of different bases; for example:

1 Emission rate (e.g., kilograms per hour),

2 Emission concentration (e.g., parts per million of biochemical oxygen demand, or BOD, in wastewater),

3 Total quantity of residuals (rate of discharge times concentration times duration),

4 Residuals produced per unit of output (e.g., SO_2 emissions per kilowatt hour of electricity produced),

5 Residuals content per unit of input (e.g., sulfur content of coal used in power generation),

6 Percentage removal of pollutant (e.g., 60 percent removal of waste material before discharge).

In the language of regulation, emission standards are a type of *performance standard*, because they refer to end results that are meant to be achieved by the polluters who are regulated. There are many other types of performance standards; for example, workplace standards set in terms of maximum numbers of accidents or levels of risk to which workers are exposed. A requirement that farmers reduce their use of a particular pesticide below some level is also a performance standard, as is a highway speed limit.

Technology Standards

There are numerous standards that don't actually specify some end result, but rather the technologies, techniques, or practices that potential polluters must adopt. We lump these together under the heading of "technology-based standards," or TBEs. The requirement that cars be equipped with catalytic converters, or seat belts, is a technology standard. If all electric utilities were required to install stack-gas scrubbers to reduce SO_2 emissions,[2] these would be in effect technology standards, since a particular type of technology is being specified by central authorities. This type of standard also includes what are often called "design standards" or "engineering standards." There are also a variety of product standards specifying characteristics that

[2] A "scrubber" is a device that treats the exhaust gas stream so as to remove a substantial proportion of the target substance from that stream. The recovered material must then be disposed of elsewhere.

goods must have, and input standards that require potential polluters to use inputs meeting specific conditions. Technology standards often specify that polluters use the "best available" technology, known as BAT, the best practicable technology (BPT), or best available technology "economically achieveable," BATEA. Other acronyms may also be used. BPTs generally refer to technologies that are known and can be implemented immediately. BATs are the best possible technology whether there are any practical applications in use at the time or not. A BATEA allows some recognition of abatement costs and effect of the technology standard on a firm's profits. We will analyze and evaluate TBEs in more detail in Section V.

At the edges the difference between a performance standard and a technology standard may become blurred. The basic point of differentiation is that a performance standard, such as an emission standard, sets a constraint on some performance criterion and then allows people to choose the best means of achieving it. A technology standard actually dictates certain decisions and techniques to be used, such as particular equipment or operating practices to be used by polluters. In Canada there are a wide variety of federal and provincial regulations apply to specific industries. For example, under the Canadian Environmental Protection Act (CEPA), there are emission guidelines or regulations for Arctic mineral extraction, asbestos mines and mills, the asphalt paving industry, chloralkali mercury releases, pulp and paper mill effluent, lead, and vinyl chloride, to name a few. Technology standards under CEPA apply to a number of industries including the energy sector, pulp and paper mills, mineral smelters, and many more. This is just one act.

THE ECONOMICS OF STANDARDS

It would seem to be a simple and straightforward thing to achieve better environmental quality by applying standards of various types. But standards turn out to be more complicated than they first appear. In the rest of this chapter we will discuss some of these complications, which we will encounter directly when we get to the chapters on specific pollution-control policies. Understanding the way standards work, helps us examine the costs of reaching a socially efficient equilbrium using this policy instrument. We can then compare standards to other policy instruments using the criteria developed in Chapter 9.

Setting the Level of the Standard in Practice

Perhaps the first issue is where to set the standard. We saw in the case of the decentralized approaches to pollution control—liability laws and property-rights regimes—that there was, at least, the theoretical possibility that the interactions of people involved would lead to efficient outcomes. In theory, setting the level of the standard is even more straightforward. As noted many times, the socially efficient standard equates marginal damages to marginal costs. But in practice, standards are often set by examining a narrower set of criteria. Standards emanate from a political/administrative process that may be affected by all kinds of considerations.

What are some of the approaches that have been taken in practice, and how do they relate to social efficiency? Look again at Figure 11-1, particularly at the marginal damage function. One approach in standard setting has been to try to set ambient or emission standards by reference only to the damage function. A reason for this may be that regulators do not have information about the marginal abatement cost function. Thus, one looks at the damage function to find significant points where marginal damages change substantially. One approach has been to set the standard at a "zero-risk" level, that is, at the level that would protect everyone, no matter how sensitive, from damage. This would imply setting a threshold level, labelled e_t in Figure 11-1. This standard is clearly not socially efficient if the MAC is as shown. Another difficulty is determining whether or not a threshold exists. Recent work by toxicologists and other scientists, seems to indicate that there may be no threshold for many environmental pollutants; that in fact marginal damage functions are positive right from the origin. Exhibit 11-1 discusses new findings on the impacts of ground-level ozone. What were once considered "safe" levels of ozone may not be. This suggests that regulators might want to consider a more stringent ozone standard. In fact, if we followed a "zero-risk" approach, we would have to set all standards at zero. This may be appropriate for some substances—certain highly toxic chemicals, for example, where marginal damages are everywhere greater than marginal abatement costs. But for many pollutants, a zero level of emissions would not be socially efficient, and difficult or impossible to achieve. We might decide, therefore, that we could accept some "reasonably small" damages, in which case we might set it at a place like e_0, the point where the marginal damage function begins to increase very rapidly. Here again, however, we would be setting the standard without regard to abatement costs.

You should note that there is, in effect, a certain amount of "balancing" going on when standards are set on the basis of an average over some time period. In this case short-run periods, when ambient quality is relatively low, are considered acceptable as long as they do not last "too" long. A judgment is being made, in effect, that it is not necessary to install enough abatement technology to hold ambient quality within the standard under all conceivable natural conditions. In other words, an implicit trade-off is being made between the damages that will result from the temporary deterioration of ambient quality below the standard and the high costs that would be necessary to keep ambient quality within the standard under all conditions.

Perhaps the most fundamental aspect of standards is their all-or-nothing quality. Either the standard is being met or it isn't. If it isn't, the implication is that it should be, regardless of the cost of doing so. If it is being met, the implication is that it is not necessary to do any better, even though the cost of doing so may be quite low.

Uniformity of Standards

A very practical problem in standard setting is whether it should be applied uniformly to all situations or varied according to circumstances. We can illustrate this using the problem of the spatial uniformity of standards. The ambient air quality standards in the U.S., for example, are essentially national. The problem with this is that regions

EXHIBIT 11-1

GROUND-LEVEL OZONE AND HEALTH

During the spring and summer months in Canada, ground-level ozone concentrations can reach levels high enough to adversely affect human health, vegetation, and cause damage to materials such as rubber tires and fabrics. The problem is particularly serious in the lower mainland of B.C., the corridor from Windsor to Quebec City, and some Maritime cities.

Ground-level ozone is formed when volatile organic compounds and nitrogen oxides combine with sunlight and warm temperatures. The primary sources of these compounds which create ozone are motor vehicles and industrial emissions. It persists in regions where winds aren't able to disperse the pollutants.

There is increasing evidence that ozone at levels generally considered safe remains a health hazard. Lung function in young, normal subjects were adversely affected when they exercised for six hours in concentrations of ozone as low as the present Canadian objective for one hour of 82 parts per billion (ppb). When ozone levels exceed 82 ppb, more people are admitted to hospitals with acute respiratory diseases. A recent study conducted by scientists at the University of Toronto found that when patients inhaled air with 120 parts per billion of ozone (which is the health standard for

the U.S.), their sensitivity to allergens that may cause asthma attacks doubled. It had been thought previously that at levels below 120 ppb, it was only people with lung conditions or those who exercised strenuously who were at risk. Children, because they have less lung capacity and spend more time outdoors than adults, are also at greater risk.

In the United States, the American Lung Association has been calling for stricter standards in that country. In Canada, the objective is to consistently achieve the one-hour air quality objective of 82 ppb. Most of Canada's largest cities exceed that standard on many days. For example, at the eastern end of the Burrard Inlet in Vancouver (where mountains traps the ozone), the maximum one-hour ozone concentration in any year averages about 150 ppb, but concentrations of over 200 ppb have been measured. Between Windsor and Toronto, annual maximum readings are between 110 and 160 ppb for a one-hour period. Similar readings are obtained for Montreal.

Sources: Environment Canada, *Ground-Level Ozone in Canada*, A State of the Environment Fact Sheet No. 92-1, Catalogue No. EN1-12/92-1-E (Ottawa: Ministry of Supply and Services: 1992); "Link Between Asthma and 'Safe' Ozone Levles is Studied," *New York Times*, July 6, 1991.

may differ greatly in terms of the factors affecting damage and abatement cost relationships, so that one set of standards, uniformly applied across these local variations, may have serious efficiency implications.

Consider Figure 11-2. It shows two marginal damage functions, one of which (labelled MD_u) is assumed to characterize an urban area, while the other (labelled MD_r) applies to a rural area. MD_u lies above MD_r because there are many more people living in the urban area, so the same quantity of emissions will affect the health of more people there than in the rural region. We assume that marginal abatement costs (labelled MAC) are the same in the two regions. We might suppose, for example, that we are analyzing a production process that also produces emissions of benzene, a carcinogenic substance. The marginal costs of reducing emissions are the same in each area. Since the marginal damages are much higher in the urban than in the rural area, the efficient level of ambient benzene is much lower in the former than in the latter region; the efficient level is e_r in the rural region and e_u in the urban area.

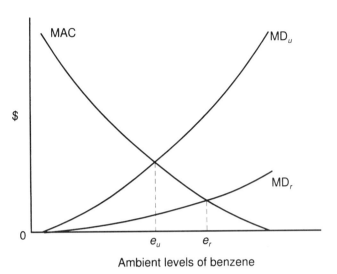

FIGURE 11-2   Regional Variation in Efficiency Levels.

Thus a single, uniform standard cannot be efficient simultaneously in the two regions. If it is set at e_u, it will be overly stringent for the rural area, and if it is set at e_r, it will not be tight enough for the urban region. The only way to avoid this would be to set different standards in the two areas. Of course, this confronts us with one of the great policy trade-offs: The more we try to tailor a policy so that it applies to different and heterogeneous situations, the more efficient it will be in terms of its impacts, but also the more costly it will be in terms of getting the information needed to set the diverse standards and enforcing them once they have been established. The curves in Figure 11-2 could be used to represent other heterogeneous situations as well as differences in geographical regions. For example, MD_u might represent marginal damages in a particular region under some meteorological conditions, or in one season of the year, while MD_r could represent the marginal damage function for the same area but under different meteorological conditions or at a different time of year. Now a single standard, enforced throughout the year, cannot be efficient at all points in time; if it is efficient at one time, it won't be at the other.

When marginal damages for a particular pollutant differ among sources of the emisssions, we will see a dispersion of pollution across sources or regions because the pollutants are not uniformly mixed. This means that regulatory authorities have to monitor ambient environmental quality at different receptor points or monitoring stations within their jurisdiction. A socially efficient equilibrium then requires the marginal costs of abatement be equal to the marginal damages at each receptor point. This equilibrium can be obtained in theory by imposing standards that reflect the marginal damages of each source at each receptor. Pollution from each source will be translated into ambient concentrations of pollution at each site by using what are called transfer coefficients. A transfer coefficient converts emissions from source i into an impact on environmental quality at site j, and is determined by scientific factors such as meteorological relationships and physical/chemical properties of the pollutant. Air-pollution dispersion models have been developed for a number of major urban areas. In practice, as noted above, pollutants which are not uniformly mixed create a much more difficult and costly regulatory environment. Section V illustrates examples of standards that are specific to pollution sources. Evidence from the United States suggests that these policies have high compliance costs.

Standards and the Equimarginal Principle

Having discussed the issue of setting the standard at the efficient level of emissions, we must remember that the efficient level itself is defined by the minimum marginal abatement cost function. And where there are multiple emissions sources producing the same effluent,[3] the equimarginal principle must hold. The principle states that in order to get this outcome, the different sources of emissions must be controlled in such a way that they have the same marginal abatement costs. This means that different sources of a pollutant would normally be controlled to different degrees, depending on the shape of the marginal abatement cost curve at each source. A major problem with standards is that there is almost always an overwhelming tendency for authorities to apply the same standards to all sources. It makes their regulatory lives much simpler, and it gives the impression of being fair to everyone, since all are apparently being treated alike. But identical standards will be cost-effective only in the unlikely event that all polluters have the same marginal abatement costs.

Consider Figure 11-3, showing the marginal abatement cost relationships for two different sources, each emitting the same waste material. Note that the marginal abatement cost functions differ; for Firm A they increase much less rapidly as emissions are reduced than they do for Firm B. Why the difference? They may be producing different outputs with different technologies. One firm might be older than the other, and older technology may be less flexible, making it more costly to reduce emissions than at the plant with the newer equipment. One plant may be designed to use a different type of raw material input than the other. This, in fact, mirrors the situation in the real world. Normally one can expect considerable heterogeneity in abatement costs among groups of firms even though they are emitting the same type of residual.

Assume that emissions are currently uncontrolled. Thus, they are 20 tonnes/month at each firm, or a total of 40 tonnes/month. Let us assume now that authorities wish to reduce total emissions to 20 tonnes/month by setting emission standards. How should the standards be set? The procedure that may seem most obvious—it certainly has to most environmental regulators—is to apply the same standard to each source; in this case, 10 tonnes/month. This has the superficial appearance of being fair, of treating these sources alike, since each would be reduced in the same proportion from their current levels. Of course, the problem is that the sources are economically *unlike*

---

[3] That is, in cases of "uniformly mixed" emissions.

Emission level (tonnes/month)	Marginal abatement costs ($)	
	A	B
20	0.00	0.00
19	1.00	2.10
18	2.10	4.60
17	3.30	9.40
16	4.60	19.30
15	6.00	32.50
14	7.60	54.90
13	9.40	82.90
12	11.50	116.90
11	13.90	156.90
10	16.50	204.90
9	19.30	264.90
8	22.30	332.90
7	25.50	406.90
6	28.90	487.00
5	32.50	577.00
4	36.30	677.20
3	40.50	787.20
2	44.90	907.20
1	49.70	1037.20
0	54.90	1187.20

FIGURE 11-3   Marginal Abatement Costs for Two Sources.

in that they have significantly different marginal abatement costs. By applying uniform standards to dissimilar sources we violate the equimarginal principle and end up getting far less total emission reduction than we might for the costs involved. At emission levels of 10 tonnes/month Source A has marginal abatement costs of $16.50/tonne while Source B has marginal abatement costs of $204.90/tonne. Remembering that total costs are the sums of the marginal costs, we calculate total compliance costs as $75.90 for A and $684.40 for B, or a grand total of $760.30.

How much higher is this than the costs that would result from a program satisfying the equimarginal principle? A look at Figure 11-3 shows that we can achieve the total reduction we want and satisfy that principle by having Firm A cut its emissions to 5 tonnes/month and Firm B to 15 tonnes/month. At these levels their marginal abatement costs would be the same ($32.50/tonne) and the total cost of the cutback would be $272.30 ($204.40 for A and $67.90 for B), a 64 percent reduction in total costs from the equal-standards case. To put it perhaps more dramatically, for the $760.30 cost of the equal-standards case, we could achieve a much larger reduction in total emissions if we cut back in accordance with the equimarginal principle. In fact, cutting Firm A back to zero emissions (total cost: $430.70) and Firm B back to emissions of 12 tonnes/month (total cost: $322.60) would give total compliance costs about the same as the equal-standards case but with substantially lower total emissions (12 tonnes/month rather than 20 tons/month).

To summarize: Standards are usually designed to be applied uniformly across emission sources. This practice is almost inherent in the basic philosophy of the standards approach, and to many people this strikes them as an equitable way to proceed. But if marginal abatement costs in the real world vary across sources, as they usually do, the equal-standards approach will produce less reduction in total emissions for the total compliance costs of the program than would be achieved with an approach that satisfied the equimarginal principle. The greater the differences in marginal abatement costs among sources, the worse will be the performance of the equal-standards approach. We will see in the chapters ahead that this difference can be very large indeed.

Could standards be set in accordance with the equimarginal principle? Unless the applicable law required some sort of equiproportional cutback there may be nothing to stop the authorities from setting different standards for the individual sources. To get an overall reduction to 20 tonnes/month in the example above, they could require Source A to reduce to 5 tonnes/month and Source B to cut back to 15 tonnes/month. The difficult part of this, however, is that, to accomplish this, the authorities must know what the marginal abatement costs are for the different sources. We need to stress this strongly. For almost any real-world pollution problem there will normally be multiple sources. For a public agency to set individual standards in accordance with the equimarginal principle *it would have to know the marginal abatement cost relationship for each of these sources.* It would take a prodigious effort for any agency to get high-quality information on marginal abatement costs for many different sources, each perhaps producing different outputs using different production technology and methods. The primary source of data would have to be the polluters themselves, and there is no reason to believe they would willingly share this information. In fact, if they realize, as they certainly would, that the information would be used to establish individual source standards, they would have every incentive to provide the administering agency with data showing that their marginal abatement costs rise very steeply with emission reductions. Thus, there are real problems with authorities attempting to establish source-specific emission standards. *Nevertheless*, a considerable amount of this is done informally, through the interactions of local pollution-control authorities, charged with enforcing common standards, and local sources, each of whom is in somewhat different circumstances. We will come back to this below when we discuss issues of enforcement.

STANDARDS AND THE INCENTIVES FOR FURTHER IMPROVEMENTS

One of our criteria for evaluating alternative types of environmental policies is the strength of the incentives they produce for discovering and adopting better technical and managerial means for controlling pollution. The management of production and consumption residuals is not a static pursuit; it is subject to change and improvement through human energy and creativity. But improvements don't just happen randomly; they appear when the appropriate incentives exist.

It is easy to deal with the case of technology standards. Here the incentives to find cheaper ways (considering all costs) of reducing emissions are effectively zero. If control authorities dictate in detail the specific technology and practices that polluters may legally use to reduce emissions, there are no rewards to finding better approaches. In fact, they may be motivated to avoid other techniques in order to protect themselves against charges of noncompliance, even if these other approaches showed considerable promise. Better to play it safe, adopt the technology specified by the standard, and let the public control authorities themselves be saddled with the job of defending the correctness of the choice. Rather than leave firms free to use their own creativity in devising the technological means to achieve a goal, a technology standard instead places the burden on the public authority to make the correct technology decisions.

Now consider emission standards. Figure 11-4 shows marginal abatement costs of a firm in two situations: MAC_1 refers to such costs before a given technological improvement; MAC_2 is the marginal abatement cost curve the firm could expect to have after investing some large amount of resources in an R&D effort to develop better treatment or recycling technology. Without any pollution-control program at all there is absolutely no incentive to spend the money on the R&D. But suppose the firm is now faced with having to meet emission standards of e_2 tonnes/year. With the original marginal abatement costs the total annual cost of compliance for this firm is ($a + b$) per year. If the R&D program is successful, its compliance costs would be only

FIGURE 11-4   Cost Savings from Technological Change: The Case of Standards.

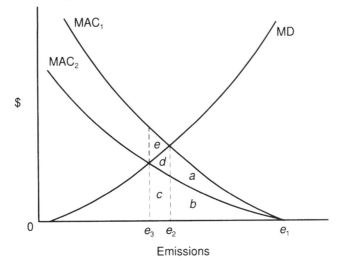

b/year. The difference, *a*/year, is the amount by which compliance costs would be reduced and represents, in fact, the incentive for engaging in the R&D effort. We will see in the next chapter that this is a weaker effect than is provided by economic-incentive types of programs. Nevertheless, it is an incentive, which is more than we could say for technology standards.

Nevertheless, the complete logic of standard setting may do much to undermine this incentive. Suppose authorities are making every effort to set the standard at something approaching the efficient level of emissions. In Figure 11-4, e_2 is their view of the efficient level before the technical change. But the new technology lowers the marginal abatement cost curve, and we know from Chapter 5 that this will reduce the efficient level of emissions. Suppose the authorities estimate that, given their view of marginal damages, the new technology shifts the efficient emission level to e_3 in Figure 11-4, and that they now change the standard to reflect this. Now the firm's compliance cost will be $(b + c)$ per year. The difference is now $(a - c)$. So the firm's cost savings will be substantially less than when the standard was unchanged; in fact, compliance costs may actually be higher than before the R&D program. In other words, the firm could suppose that because of the way regulators may tighten the standards, they would be worse off with the new technology than with the old methods. The standard-setting procedure in this case has completely undermined the incentive to produce new pollution-control technology.

If emission standards create incentives for technological change, is it not desirable to establish very stringent standards so as to increase that incentive? If, in Figure 11-4, the standard is set at e_3 right at the beginning, this would mean cost savings of $(a + d + e)$ with the new technology rather than just a as it would be with the standard set at e_2. This type of approach goes under the heading of "technology forcing." The principle of technology forcing is to set standards that are unrealistic with today's technology in the hope that it will motivate the pollution-control industry to invent ways of meeting the standard at reasonable cost. By "unrealistic with today's technology," we mean simply so costly that it would lead to widespread economic hardship.

But stricter standards also create another incentive, the incentive for polluters to seek relief from public authorities through delaying the date when they become applicable. In an open political system, firms may take some of the resources that might have gone for pollution-control R&D and devote them instead to influencing political authorities to delay the onset of strict standards. The stricter and more near-term the standards, the more of this activity there is likely to be. Thus, technology forcing is another one of those strategies where the effectiveness of moderate amounts does not imply that more will be even more effective.

We have to remember also that to a significant extent new R&D for pollution control is carried out by a pollution-control industry rather than the polluting industries themselves. Thus, to draw conclusions about the incentives of pollution-control policy for technological change means to predict how these policies will contribute to the growth and productivity of the pollution-control industry. Technology standards are stultifying on these grounds because they substantially drain off the incentives for entrepreneurs in the pollution-control industry to develop new ideas. Emission standards are better in this respect, as we have seen. The evidence for this is the fact that representatives of the pollution-control industry usually take the side politically of stricter environmental standards; in fact, they see the fortunes of their industry tied almost directly to the degree of stringency in the emissions standards set by public authorities.

THE ECONOMICS OF ENFORCEMENT

The typical pollution-control law incorporates standards calling for some degree of emissions reduction from current levels, or the adoption of specified pollution-control technologies. When we evaluate these policies ex ante we often assume implicitly that the penalties written into the law will be sufficient to produce complete compliance. But this is in fact never the case. Pollution-control laws, like any others, require enforcement, and this takes resources. Since public enforcement agencies always work under limited budgets, it is not a forgone conclusion that enough resources will ever be devoted to enforcement to achieve acceptable levels of compliance. In fact, the notion of "acceptable" is itself subject to debate.

Like lots of other problems in economics and the allocation of resources, enforcement involves a trade-off, here between the resources used for this activity, which have opportunity costs, and benefits in the form of greater degrees of compliance. We picture this trade-off in Figure 11-5. MD is the relevant marginal damage curve for this case, while MAC is the conventional marginal abatement cost function, showing the marginal costs required by sources to reduce emissions. The curves labelled C_1 and C_2 are curves that combine marginal abatement costs and marginal enforcement costs. Note that these begin at e_0, which is somewhat to the left of the uncontrolled emission rate e. When an emission standard is set at e^*, some degree of voluntary compliance may be expected to occur—in this case from e to e_0. But to get emission reductions beyond e_0 requires explicit enforcement resources. Curves C_1 and C_2 correspond to different technologies of enforcement. We have normally thought of e^* as the efficient level of emissions, but when enforcement costs are present this is no longer the case. With relatively high enforcement costs (curve C_1), the socially efficient rate of emissions is e_1. At this point total emission reduction costs are equal to $(a + b)$ of enforcement costs and $(c + d)$ of abatement costs. The technology of enforcement includes many things: the monitoring of equipment, the expertise of personnel, the operation of the court system, etc. When changes occur in any of these factors, the effect is to shift the combined cost curve; in Figure 11-5 it shifts to C_2. This leads to a change in the efficient level of emissions to e_2; at this point, total emission reduction costs would be made up of $(e + b)$ of enforcement costs plus $(f + c + d)$ of abatement costs.

When enforcement costs are included in the analysis, it brings up the question of whether standards should be set, at least in part, with enforcement costs in mind. Stricter standards may involve larger enforcement costs because they require larger operating changes on the part of sources. Less strict standards may be achievable with fewer enforcement resources, for the opposite reason. Public environmental agencies

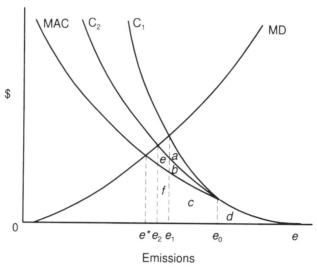

FIGURE 11-5   The Economics of Enforcement.

are usually faced with budget stringencies. In some cases, greater overall reductions in emissions may be obtained by using less strict standards that can be easily enforced than by stricter standards involving higher enforcement costs.

However, it needs to be stressed that the "strictness" of the standard is not the only factor affecting enforcement costs. A critical element in enforcement is the size of the sanction written into the laws. Most pollution-control statutes contain provisions on the size of the fine (or jail term) that may be levied against violators, if and when they are caught and found guilty. In many cases, especially when legislation was first introduced, fines have been set too low, lower than the abatement costs required to meet the standards. In these situations firms can actually save money by dragging their feet on compliance. With low sanctions like this, enforcement is therefore likely to be much more difficult and costly than if sanctions are higher. Sources faced with the possibility of having to pay substantially higher fines would presumably have a stronger incentive to come into compliance. In recent years, penalties for failure to comply with Canadian environmental regulations have increased dramatically and there is evidence that the sanctions are providing sufficient incentives to comply with legislation. We need to keep in mind, however, the paradoxical effect mentioned earlier: If laws attempt to set fines that are extremely high, this could actually dissuade local administrators and courts from pursuing violators vigorously, because of the economic dislocation that would result.

Stringency in enforcement budgets helps explain the attractiveness of public authorities to policies of standards. The essential characteristic of most standards approaches is that they do not require, nor automatically commit, a public agency to a costly enforcement process, especially a costly monitoring program. It is true that the more resources devoted to enforcement the more likely it is that the standards will be met. But standards programs can be put on the books while still leaving open the question of how much money and effort will be put into enforcement. Consider an emission standard that specifies an upper limit on the daily or hourly emission rate. To enforce this perfectly one would have to monitor the emission rate continuously. For a public agency charged with monitoring thousands of sources, this would be totally impossible. In Canada, this has led to a system of self-monitoring, where sources themselves keep the books on emissions flows over time. This permits the agencies to visit periodically to audit the records at each source. Agencies can also make random checks to measure emissions. The rate of auditing and random visits can be varied according to agency budgets. Needless to say, the rate of compliance would worsen as fewer resources are devoted to monitoring, but tolerable levels of compliance may still be attainable with fairly modest efforts at monitoring. A cynic, or a political realist, might conclude that standards approaches are favoured because of the very fact that in the real world of tight public agency budgets, they permit partial or incomplete compliance.

One very common feature of environmental standards is that they are usually set and enforced by different groups of people. Standards are often set by national authorities; enforcement is usually done by local authorities. For example, the air quality standards established under the Canadian Environmental Protection Act are set at the federal level, but much of the enforcement is carried out by provincial agencies. This has a number of important implications. One is that standards can be set without much thought to costs of enforcement; it is more or less assumed that local authorities will find the necessary enforcement resources. Of course, this is not the case in practice. With limited enforcement budgets, local authorities may react to new programs by reducing resources devoted to other programs. Another implication is that, in practice, environmental policies incorporating standards end up having a lot more flexibility than might at first appear. Laws written at national levels are specific and apparently applicable everywhere. But at the local level, "where the rubber meets the road," as they say, it's a matter of local pollution-control authorities applying the law to local sources, and in this process there can be a great deal of informal give-and-take between the authorities and local plant managers, with participation by local environmental groups as well.

Technology standards allow the same flexibility in enforcement. Here we have to distinguish between *initial compliance* and *continued compliance*. Initial compliance is where a polluter charged with meeting a particular technology standard installs the appropriate equipment. To monitor initial compliance it is necessary to have inspectors visit the site, check to see that the equipment is installed, and make sure it will operate in accordance with the conditions of the standard. Having ascertained this, the administering agency can then give the firm the necessary operating permit. But this does not ensure that the equipment will continue to be operated in the future in accordance with the terms of the permit. It may deteriorate through normal use, it may not be maintained properly, future operating personnel may not be properly trained, etc. Without some amount of monitoring, therefore, there is no assurance that the source will continue to be in compliance. But here again the administering agency has great flexibility in setting up a monitoring program. It can vary from very infrequent visits to randomly selected sites all the way up to permanent observers stationed at each source. While more monitoring will undoubtedly lead to higher rates of compliance, the standards approach essentially leaves open the question of the amount of time, effort, and money to be put into enforcement. It is clearly one of the advantages (some might say disadvantages) of the standards approach that it permits this flexibility in monitoring and enforcement. It is important to note however that all policies require monitoring to ensure compliance. As we'll see, policies may differ in terms of the amount and nature of the monitoring required. This is turn affects compliance costs.

SUMMARY

The most popular approach to environmental pollution control historically has been the setting of standards. This has been called the "command-and-control" approach because it consists of public authorities announcing certain limits on polluters, then enforcing these limits with appropriate enforcement institutions. We specified three primary types of standards: ambient, emission, and technology. Initial discussion centred on the level at which standards should be set and the regional uniformity of standards.

A leading problem with standard setting is the question of cost-effectiveness and the equimarginal principle. In most standards programs the administrative bias is to apply the same standards to all sources of a particular pollutant. But pollution control can be cost-effective only when marginal abatement costs are equalized across sources. When marginal abatement costs differ among sources, as they almost always do, uniform standards cannot be cost-effective. In practice, differences among sources in their marginal abatement costs are often recognized informally by local administrators in applying a uniform national standard.

We dealt at length also with the question of the long-run impact of standards through their effects on the incentives to look for better ways of reducing emissions. Technology standards completely undermine these incentives. Emission standards do create positive incentives for R&D in pollution control, though we will see that these are weaker than those of economic-incentive types of pollution-control policies, the subject of the next two chapters. Finally, we discussed the all-important question of enforcement.

QUESTIONS FOR FURTHER DISCUSSION

1 Environmental protection programs are frequently designed to require all polluters to cut back emissions by a certain percentage. What are the perverse incentives built into this type of program?

2 Would it be better to set less restrictive standards and enforce them vigorously, or tighter standards and enforce them more loosely? What are the important factors bearing on this question?

3 What are the factors determining how stringent emission standards should be set in order to have the right degree of "technology forcing"?

4 If emission standards are ruled out because of, for example, the impossibility of measuring emissions (as in nonpoint source emissions), what alternative types of standards might be used instead?

5 In Figure 11-2, show the social cost of setting a uniform national standard, applicable to both rural and urban areas (to do this you can assume that the national standard is set at either e_u or e_r).

6 Consider the example of Figure 11-3. Suppose we define as "fair" a cutback in which the two sources have the same total costs. Would an equiproportionate reduction be fair in this sense? A reduction meeting the equimarginal principle? Is this a reasonable definition of "fair"?

7 Numerous people have suggested that the most equitable way to resolve the trade and environment problem would be for all countries to adopt the same emission standards. What are the pros and cons of this from an economic standpoint?

SELECTED READINGS

Crandall, Robert W. *Controlling Industrial Pollution.* Washington, D.C.: The Brookings Institution, 1983.

Hawkins, Keith. *Environment and Enforcement.* Oxford, England: Clarendon Press, 1984.

McKean, Roland N. "Enforcement Costs in Environmental and Safety Regulation." *Policy Analysis* 6(3) (Summer 1980): 269–289.

Richardson, Genevra, with Anthony Orgus and Paul Burrows. *Policing Pollution.* Oxford, England: Oxford University Press, 1983.

Russell, Clifford S. "Monitoring and Enforcement," in Paul Portney (ed.). *Public Policies for Environmental Protection.* Washington, D.C.: Resources for the Future, 1990, 243–274.

Russell, Clifford S., Winston Harrington, and William J. Vaughan. *Enforcing Pollution Control Laws.* Washington, D.C.: Resources for the Future, 1986.

Viscusi, W. Kip. *Risks by Choice: Regulating Health and Safety in the Workplace.* Cambridge, Mass.: Harvard University Press, 1983.

12

INCENTIVE-BASED STRATEGIES: EMISSION TAXES AND SUBSIDIES

If we wanted to build a house, we would have to buy some building materials; nobody is likely to give them to us free. If we want to have architects and carpenters work on the house, we will have to hire them; they won't ordinarily work for nothing. In other words, in order to use the services of these inputs, we have to pay for them. We are used to doing this because they are bought and sold in well-developed markets. The fact that we have to pay for them gives us an incentive to use the inputs as sparingly and efficiently as possible. The economic incentive approach to environmental policy works in much the same way. Until recently people have been able to use the waste-disposal services of the environment virtually without cost, so there has been little incentive for them to think about the environmental consequences of their actions and to economize on the use of these environmental resources. The incentive approach seeks to change this situation.

There are basically two types of incentive policies: (1) taxes and subsidies and (2) transferable discharge permits. Both require some administering agency to put the program into effect and to monitor outcomes. Regulators set a price for pollution via taxes and subsidies and quantities of allowed emissions with transferable discharge permits. The market determines the price of pollution under the permit approach. Under each policy, polluters make their own decisions about the amount of pollution to emit based on the prices per unit pollution they face. While there are few Canadian policies that currently involve economic incentives, governments are contemplating their wider use.[1]

In the U.S., environmental laws have begun to incorporate many types of transferable discharge permit systems. In other countries, particularly those of Europe,

---

[1] See Environment Canada, *Economic Instruments for Environmental Protection*, Discussion Paper, Catalogue No. En21-119/1992E (1992).

greater reliance is being put on programs of emission taxes. In the present chapter we will examine the economics of emission charges and subsidies. In the next chapter we will consider the technique of transferable discharge permits.

Environmental economists have long favoured the idea of incorporating incentive-based policies more thoroughly into environmental policies. These can serve to put more teeth into environmental policies in many cases and substantially improve the cost-effectiveness of these policies. But keep in mind something we said before: No single type of policy is likely to be the best in all circumstances. Incentive-based policies are no exception. They have strengths and they have weaknesses. The strengths are sufficiently strong to encourage greater reliance on them in many circumstances. But there are many types of environmental problems where they may not be as useful as other approaches.

EMISSION TAXES

The most straightforward incentive-based approach to controlling emissions of a particular residual is to have a public agency offer a financial incentive to change those emissions. This can be done in two ways: by taxing each unit of emissions, or by giving a subsidy for each unit of emissions that the source cuts back.

We deal first with emission taxes, sometimes also called "emission charges." In a tax system we say to polluters: "You may discharge any amount of residuals you wish, but your emissions will be measured and you will be required to pay a certain tax for every unit (e.g., tonne) of effluent you discharge." For example, Canada has contemplated introducing a tax on the carbon content of fuels as a means of reducing carbon dioxide emissions and ameliorating global warming. When an emission tax is put into effect, firms responsible for emissions must essentially pay for the services of the environment transportation, dilution, chemical decomposition, etc. just as they must pay for all other inputs used in their operations. And just as they have always had an incentive to conserve on scarce labour and other conventional production inputs, they will now have an incentive to conserve on their use of environmental services. How do they do this? Any way they wish (within reason). This may sound flippant but in fact it represents the main advantage of this technique. By leaving polluters free to determine how best to reduce emissions, we call into play their own energy and creativity, and their desire to minimize costs, to find the least-cost way of reducing emissions. It could be any combination of treatment, internal process changes, changes in inputs, recycling, shifts to less polluting outputs, etc. The essence of the tax approach is to provide an incentive for the polluters themselves to find the best way to reduce emissions, rather than having a central authority determine how it should be done.

The Basic Economics

The essential mechanics of an emission tax are depicted in Figure 12-1. The numbers refer to a single source of a particular pollutant. The top panel shows the analysis numerically while the bottom shows essentially the same information graphically. The tax has been set at $120 tonnes/month. The second column shows the firm's marginal abatement costs and the third column total abatement costs. The last two columns show the total monthly tax bill the firm would pay at different emission levels, and the total cost, consisting of the sum of abatement costs and the tax bill. We see that the minimum total cost of $850 occurs at an emission rate of 4 tonnes/month. Let's pursue the logic of this by considering marginal abatement costs. Suppose the firm

FIGURE 12-1   An Emissions Tax.

Emissions (tonnes/month)	Marginal abatement cost	Total abatement cost	Total tax bill at $120/tonne	Total costs
10	0	0	1,200	1,200
9	15	15	1,080	1,095
8	30	45	960	1,005
7	50	95	840	935
6	70	165	720	885
5	90	255	600	855
4	115	370	480	850
3	135	505	360	865
2	175	680	240	920
1	230	910	120	1,030
0	290	1,200	0	1,200

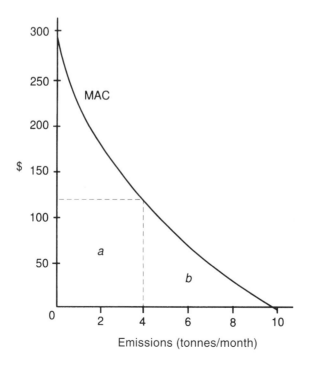

is initially emitting 10 tonnes/month; if it were to cut emissions to 9 tonnes, it would cost $15 in abatement costs, but on the other hand it would save $120 in taxes, clearly a good move. Following this logic, it could improve its bottom line by continuing to reduce emissions as long as the tax rate is above marginal abatement costs. The rule for the firm to follow is, thus: reduce emissions until marginal abatement costs are equal to the emissions tax rate. This is shown diagrammatically in the bottom part of Figure 12-1. With a continuous marginal abatement cost function it's possible to talk about fractions of tonnes of emissions, something we could not do in the upper panel. So the graph is drawn to agree with the integer values above, for example, the tax of $120 leads the firm to reduce emissions to exactly 4 tonnes/month.

After the firm has reduced its emissions to 4 tonnes/month, its total (monthly) tax bill will be $480. Its monthly abatement costs will be $370. Graphically, total abatement costs correspond to the area under the marginal abatement cost function, labelled *b* in the figure. The total tax bill is equal to emissions times tax rate, or the rectangle labelled *a*. Under a tax system of this type, a firm's total cost equals its abatement costs plus the tax payments to the taxing authority.

Why wouldn't the firm simply disregard the tax, continue to pollute like it has been, and just pass the tax on to consumers in the form of higher prices? If the firm stayed at 10 tonnes of emissions, its total outlay would be $1,200 per month, consisting entirely of tax payment. This is much higher than the $850 it can achieve by cutting back to 4 tonnes/month. If a firm operates in a perfectly competitive environment, it survives by maximizing its profits. Emission taxes raise the costs of the firm. Therefore to maximize profits, the firm must do whatever it can to minimize its total costs inclusive of the emission taxes. However, we must recognize that if firms do not operate in perfectly competitive markets, a tax will not work in the way we have shown. Electric power plants, for example, are usually operated by provincial crown corporations, whose activities, until recently have not been subject to much scrutiny. They may not respond to taxes on SO_2 emissions in the same way as firms who operate in more competitive economic climates.

For competitive firms, the amount of the response will depend on several factors. The higher the tax, the greater the reduction, and vice versa. In the example of Figure 12-1, a tax of $50 would have led the source to reduce emissions only to 7 tonnes/month, while a tax of $180 would have produced a cutback to 2 tonnes/month, etc. Also, the steeper the marginal abatement cost function, the less will emissions be reduced in response to a tax. We will come back to this below.

Compare the tax approach with an emission standard. With the tax the firm's total outlay is $850. Suppose that, instead, the authorities had relied on an emission standard to get the firm to reduce emissions to 4 tonnes/month. In that case the firm's total outlay would be only the $370 of abatement costs. Thus, the tax system ends up costing the firm more than the standards approach. With a standard the firm has the same total abatement costs as in the tax system, but it is still essentially getting the services of the environment free, while with a tax system it has to pay for those services. But while polluting firms would thus prefer standards to emission taxes, there are good reasons, as we shall see, why society would often prefer taxes over standards.

The Level of the Tax

In competitive situations, higher taxes will bring about greater reductions in emissions, but just how high should the tax be set? If we know the marginal abatement cost and marginal damage function, the economist's answer is to set the tax so as to produce the efficient level of emissions, as in Figure 12-2. At a tax rate of t^*, emissions are e^*, and marginal damages equal marginal abatement costs. The firm's total costs of emission control are divided into two types: total abatement costs (compliance costs) of e and total tax payments of $(a + b + c + d)$. The former are the costs of whatever techniques the firm has chosen to reduce emissions from e_0 to e^*, while the latter are payments to the control agency covering the tax on the remaining emissions. From the standpoint of the firm, of course, these are both real costs that will have to be covered out of revenues. From the standpoint of *society*, however, the tax payments are different from the abatement costs. While the latter involve real resources and therefore real social costs, the taxes are actually *transfer payments*, payments made by the firms (ultimately by people who buy the firms' output), to the public sector and eventually to those in society who are benefited by the resulting public expenditures. When a firm considers its costs, it will include both abatement costs and tax payments; when we are considering the social costs of a tax program, we must exclude transfer payments.

The reduction of emissions from e_0 to e^* has eliminated damages of $(e + f)$. Remaining damages are $(b + d)$, an amount less than the firm pays in taxes. This underscores the idea that the emission tax is based on the right to use environmental

FIGURE 12-2   An Efficient Emission Tax.

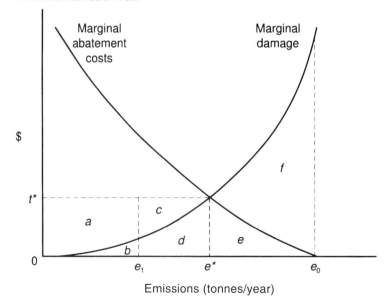

resources, not on the notion of compensation. But a "flat tax" like this (one tax rate for all emissions) has been criticized because it would often lead to situations where the total tax payments of firms would substantially exceed remaining damages. A way around this is to institute a *two-part emission tax*. We allow some initial quantity of emission to go untaxed, applying the tax only to emissions in excess of this threshold. For example, in Figure 12-2 we might allow the firm e_1 units of emissions free of tax, and apply the tax rate of t^* to anything over this. In this way the firm would still have the incentive to reduce emissions to e^*, but its total tax payments would be only $(c + d)$. Total abatement costs, and total damages caused by the e^* units of emissions, would still be the same.

How might we set the tax if we did not know the marginal damage function? We know that emissions are connected to ambient quality; the lower the emissions the lower the ambient concentration of the pollutant, in general. So one strategy might be to set a tax and then watch carefully to see what this did in terms of improving ambient quality levels. We would have to wait long enough to give firms time to respond to the tax. If ambient quality did not improve as much as desired, increase the tax; if ambient quality improved more than was thought appropriate, lower the tax. This is a successive approximation process of finding the correct long-run emissions tax. It is not all clear whether this approach would be practicable in the real world. In responding to a tax, polluters would invest in a variety of pollution-control devices and practices, many of which would have relatively high up-front costs. This investment process could be substantially upset if, shortly afterwards, the authorities shift to a new tax rate. Any agency trying to use this method to find the efficient tax rate would undoubtedly find itself embroiled in a brisk political battle over the matter. Rather than planning to make successive adjustments in the tax rate, there would be a strong incentive for policymakers to determine the correct tax rate at the beginning. This would put a premium on prior study to get some idea of the shapes of the aggregate abatement and damage cost curves.

Emission Taxes and Efficiency

Perhaps the strongest case for a policy of effluent taxes is to be made on grounds of cost effectiveness, that is when controlling multiple sources of emissions in a way that satisfies the equimarginal principle. If we apply the same tax rate to different sources with different marginal abatement cost functions, and each source reduces its emissions until their marginal abatement costs equal the tax, then marginal abatement costs will automatically be equalized across all the sources.

This is depicted in Figure 12-3.[2] We assume here that there are two sources of a particular type of emission, labelled Source A and Source B. We also assume that these emissions, after they leave the respective sources, are uniformly mixed together, so that the emissions of the two plants are equally damaging in the downstream, or downwind, impact area. The marginal abatement costs for the two sources are the

---

[2] We have seen this graph several times before, e.g., in Figures 11-4 and 11-5.

FIGURE 12-3   Emission Taxes and the Equimarginal Rule.

Emission level (tonnes/month)	Marginal abatement costs	
	Source A	Source B
20	0.0	0.0
19	1.0	2.1
18	2.1	4.6
17	3.3	9.4
16	4.6	19.3
15	6.0	32.5
14	7.6	54.9
13	9.4	82.9
12	11.5	116.9
11	13.9	156.9
10	16.5	204.9
9	19.3	264.9
8	22.3	332.9
7	25.5	406.9
6	28.9	487.0
5	32.5	577.0
4	36.3	677.2
3	40.5	787.2
2	44.9	907.2
1	49.7	1,037.2
0	54.9	1,187.2

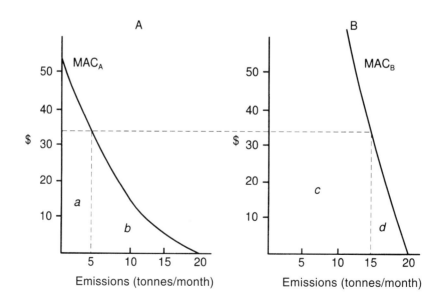

same as those we used in the last chapter. They are shown in graphical form at the bottom of Figure 12-3. The marginal abatement costs of Source A increase much less rapidly with reductions in emissions than do those of Source B. In the real world, differences like this are normally related to the fact that the firms are using different production technologies. They may be producing different outputs (e.g., a pulp mill and a food-canning firm), or they may be plants in the same industry but using different production techniques (e.g., coal-fired and hydroelectric power plants). According to the graphs, the production technology used by Source B makes emission reduction more costly than it is at Source A. If we impose an effluent tax of $33/tonne on each source, the operators of Source A will reduce their emissions to 5 tonnes/month, those at Source B will cut back to 15 tonnes/month (dealing only with integer values). After these reductions, the two sources will have the same marginal abatement costs. The total reduction has been 20 tonnes/month, which the effluent tax has automatically distributed between the two firms in accordance with the equimarginal principle.

Note very carefully that the emission tax has led Source A to reduce its emissions by 75 percent while Source B has reduced its emissions by only 25 percent. The emissions tax leads to larger proportionate emission reductions from firms with lower marginal abatement costs. Conversely, firms having steeper marginal abatement costs will reduce emissions less, in proportionate terms. Suppose that instead of the tax the authorities had instituted a *proportionate* cutback, on the grounds that "everybody should be treated alike," so they require each source to reduce emissions by 50 percent. Our two sources in Figure 12-3 both reduce emissions to 10 tonnes/month. At this point their marginal abatement costs would be different. Furthermore, we can calculate total abatement costs, by remembering that total cost is the sum of marginal costs. Thus, for example, for Source A the total costs of 10 tonnes of emissions would be $(1.0 + 2.1 + \ldots + 16.5 = 75.9)$.

The following tabulation compares the compliance costs of the equiproportionate reduction that would occur under a standard with the effluent tax.

	Total Compliance Costs ($/month)	
	Uniform Standard (equiproportionate reduction)	Effluent Tax
Source A	75.9	204.4
Source B	684.4	67.9
Total	760.3	272.3

The big thing is to note how much the totals differ. The total compliance cost of an equiproportionate cutback is about 2.8 times the total cost of an emission tax. The simple reason is that the equiproportionate cutback violates the equimarginal principle; it requires the same proportionate cutback regardless of the height and shape of a firm's marginal abatement costs. The difference in total costs between these two approaches is quite large with these illustrative numbers. We will see in later chapters that in the real world of pollution control these differences have often been much larger.

The higher the tax rate the more will emissions be reduced. In fact, if the tax rate were increased to something over $55/tonne, Firm A would stop emitting this residual entirely. The marginal abatement cost function for Firm B increases so rapidly, however, that an extremely high tax (over $1,187/tonne) would be required to get this source to reduce emissions to zero. A single effluent tax, when applied to several firms, will induce a greater reduction by firms whose marginal abatement costs increase less rapidly with emission reductions than from firms whose marginal abatement costs increase more rapidly. Since the firms are paying the same tax rate, they will have different total abatement costs and different tax bills. In Figure 12-3 the total abatement costs are equal to area b for Source A and area d for Source B. On the other hand, the monthly tax bill sent to Source A would be only *a*, compared to a bill of *c* sent to Source B. Thus, the less steeply the marginal abatement cost of a firm increases, the larger will be that firm's emission reduction and the smaller its tax bill.

We need to emphasize that the cost effectiveness of the emission tax approach (that is, that it satisfies the equimarginal principle) are achievable *even though the administering agency knows nothing about the marginal abatement costs of any of the sources*. This is in clear contrast with the standards approach, where the public agency has to know exactly what these marginal abatement costs are for each firm in order to have a fully efficient program. In a tax approach the only requirement is that firms pay the same tax and that they are cost minimizers. After each one has adjusted its emissions in accordance with its marginal abatement costs (which we can expect them to know themselves), they will all be emitting at the appropriate rates to satisfy the equimarginal principle.

Emission Taxes and Nonuniform Mixing of Emissions

So far we have proceeded under the assumption that the emissions of all sources are uniformly mixed together, that is, the emissions from one source have the same marginal impact on ambient quality levels as those from other sources. In the real world this is not always the case, as we noted in the last chapter. Very often the situation is something like, though of course more complicated than, that depicted in Figure 12-4. Here we have two sources. Source A, however, is about twice as far away from the centre of population as Source B. This means that emissions from Source A do not produce as much damage in the urban area as do emissions from Source B. If the two sources are emitting some material into a river that flows toward the city, the emissions of Source A have a longer time in the water to be broken down and rendered less harmful than do the emissions from Source B. Or if it is an air-pollution problem, Source A is much farther upwind than Source B, so there is more time for its emissions to be spread out and diluted than the emissions from Source B. There could be other reasons than location differences for the different impacts, for example, they may emit residuals at different times of the year when wind patterns are dif-

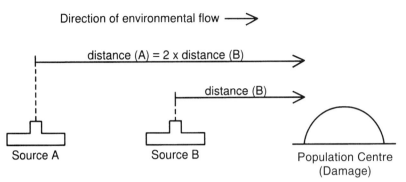

FIGURE 12-4   Nonuniform Emissions.

ferent. Studying the location problem will allow us to examine the general problem of nonuniform mixing of emissions.

In this case a single emission tax applied to both sources would not be fully efficient. A single tax addresses only the problem of differences in marginal abatement costs, not differences in damages caused by the emissions from different sources. In Figure 12-4 a one-unit reduction in emissions from Plant B would improve environmental quality (reduce damages) in the urban area more than a one-unit reduction in emissions from Plant A, and this fact must be taken into account in setting emission tax rates. Suppose emission reductions at Source B are twice as effective at reducing damages than reductions in emissions at Source A. This means, in effect, that the effluent tax paid by Source B must be twice as high as the effluent charge paid by Source A.[3] Thus, after adjusting to these tax levels the marginal abatement cost of Source B would be twice the marginal abatement cost of Source A. But the damage reduction *per dollar spent in reducing emissions* would be equalized across the two sources.

The logic of the preceding discussion would seem to lead us to the conclusion that in these cases we would have to charge different emission taxes to each source. To do this we would have to know the relative importance of the emissions from each source in affecting ambient quality. This is analogous to the problem we discussed in Chapter 11 where individual standards have to be based on the transfer coefficients of polluters. But finding out exactly what these relative differences are among polluters would be a difficult job, as would the administrative task of charging a different tax rate to each firm. The best response here might be to institute what is called a *zoned emission tax*. Here the administering agency would divide a territory into sep-

---

[3] The technical concept here is called a "transfer coefficient." A transfer coefficient is a number that tells how the emissions from any particular source affect ambient quality at some other point. In the simple example above, suppose one tonne of SO_2 emitted by B would increase SO_2 concentration over the urban area by 0.1 ppm. Then a tonne emitted from Source A would increase the ambient concentration by 0.05 (assuming an effect that is strictly proportional to distance). If the transfer coefficient for Source B is 1, that for Source A is 1/2, so the tax at A has to be 1/2 the tax at B.

arate zones; the actual number of zones would depend on the circumstances of the case. Within each zone the agency would charge the same emission tax to all sources, while it would charge different taxes in different zones. Naturally the zones would be identified by grouping together sources whose emissions have similar effects on ambient quality levels. Figure 12-5, for example, shows the schematic of a river with a dozen different sources of emissions and one urban area where water quality is measured and water quality targets are established. The ten upstream sources are strung along the river at increasing distances from the urban area. Thus each has a different impact on measured water quality at the monitoring station, and a fully cost-effective program of emissions reductions would have to account for this fact, *in addition to* their different marginal abatement costs. But it would be administratively very costly to apply a different emissions tax to each source. We might, in this case, fall back on a zoned emission tax. We first define different zones along the river, then apply the same tax to all sources within the same zone, but different taxes to sources in different zones. Each zone would contain sources whose emissions have roughly the same impact on measured water quality. In Figure 12-5, for example, there are sketched out four upstream zones along the river. The three sources in Zone 1 would get the same tax, as would the four sources in Zone 2, etc. Sources 11 and 12 are downstream from the urban area and may not get taxed at all. Of course, this is a simplified diagram to show the basic idea; in the real world, there would also very likely be downstream damages. By using a zone system we can achieve a certain amount of administrative simplification while recognizing differences in the locations of different groups of sources.

Emissions Taxes and Materials Balance

It's important at this point to remind ourselves about the fundamental materials balance aspects of residuals. Given a certain quantity of residuals, if we reduce the flow going into one environmental medium, we have to increase the flow going to others. If we forget this, we might run into situations in which, for example, firms respond to a tax on a certain waterborne residual by adopting a relatively cheap (from their

FIGURE 12-5   Zoned Emissions Tax.

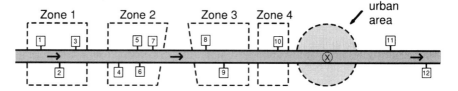

Key: ▢   Emission sources
       ⊗   Water quality monitoring station

standpoint) method of incineration that substantially increases airborne emissions. This implies that if taxes are put on residuals going into one environmental medium, we have to have some means of coordinating this with discharges of these emissions to other media. This could be done in several ways. We might simply put the same tax on a residual no matter which medium it was discharged into. But if the marginal damages of the residual were different across media, we would want to charge different taxes for different media, if we had enough information to determine what they should be. If the administering agency couldn't do this, it might fall back on simply proscribing certain courses of action; it might, for example, simply rule out any increases in airborne emissions from sources subject to a tax on waterborne emissions of the same residual. This should alert us to the problems of coordination that the materials-balance principle makes necessary.

Emissions Taxes and Uncertainty

Pollution-control policies have to be carried out in a world of uncertainty. We don't know exactly what damages stem from diminished ambient water quality. Administrating agencies often do not know exactly what emissions are being produced by each source nor exactly what the human and ecosystem impacts are. Another source of uncertainty is the shape of the marginal abatement cost curve of the sources subject to control; these may be known reasonably well by the polluters themselves but administrators will usually be very unsure of how high they are, how steep they are, how much they differ from source to source, and so on. It is one of the advantages of emissions taxes that they can bring about cost-effective results even within that state of uncertainty.

Nevertheless, when administrators set taxes at certain levels, they will normally be uncertain how much emission reduction will ensue, for that depends on how sources respond to the tax. This is one of the drawbacks of emission taxes. We can't predict exactly how much total emissions will decrease because we don't know the exact marginal abatement cost relationships. Observe Figure 12-6. It shows two different marginal abatement cost functions, a steep one (MAC_1) and one that is much less steep (MAC_2). They cross at a tax rate of t per kilogram. Consider MAC_1. If we set a tax at the relatively high rate of t_h, this source would reduce emissions to e_3, while if we had set it at the low rate of t_1, it would adjust emissions to e_2. These two emission rates are relatively close together; in other words, whether the tax is high or low the emissions rate of this source would not vary much; we could count on having an emissions rate of something around e_1.

But for the firm with the less steep marginal abatement costs (MAC_2) things are much more unstable. If the tax were set low, it would change emissions to e_4, while with a high tax emissions would go all the way down to e_5. In other words, for given changes in the tax rate, this firm would respond with much larger changes in emission rates than would the source with the steeper MAC curve.

The upshot of this discussion is that if most firms in a particular pollution problem have relatively flat MAC functions, we may have trouble finding the tax rate that

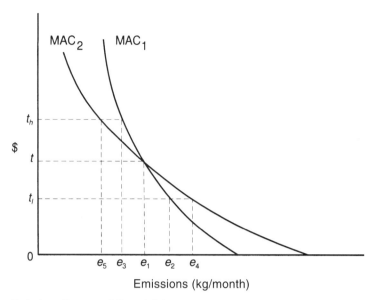

FIGURE 12-6   Emissions Taxes and Uncertainty.

will give us just the amount of reduction in total emissions we want. Since we don't know exactly where the MAC functions really are, we don't know exactly how high to set the tax. If we set it a little high or a little low, these firms will respond with large changes in their emissions. This is one of the main reasons why administrators opt for standards: they seem to offer a definite control on quantities of emissions produced. In the next chapter, we will discuss an incentive approach that addresses this problem.

Emission Taxes and the Incentives to Innovate

In a dynamic world, it is critical that we adopt environmental policies that encourage technological change in pollution control. One of the main advantages of emission taxes is that they provide strong incentives for this. This is shown in Figure 12-7, which shows two marginal abatement cost curves for a single firm. MAC_1 represents the current condition. It shows the costs the firm would experience in cutting back its emissions with the particular technology it presently uses. MAC_2, on the other hand, refers to abatement costs that the firm would experience after engaging in a relatively expensive R&D program to develop a new method of reducing emissions. We assume the firm has a reasonably good idea of what the results of the R&D will be, though of course nothing is ever a sure thing. We can use it to measure the strength of the incentives for this firm to put money into the R&D program.

Suppose the firm is subject to an effluent tax of t per tonne of emissions. Initially it will reduce emissions to e_1; at this point its total pollution-related costs will consist of $(d + e)$ worth of abatement costs and a tax bill of $(a + b + c)$. If it can lower its marginal abatement cost curve to MAC_2 through the R&D activities, it would then

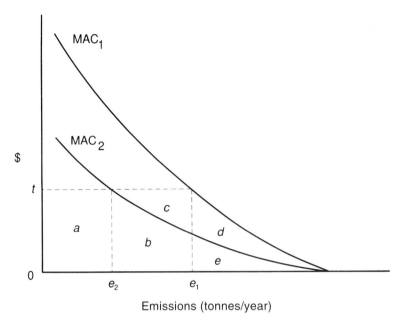

FIGURE 12-7   Emission Taxes and the Incentive for R&D.

reduce its emissions to e_2. At this point it would pay $(b + e)$ in abatement costs and a in taxes. The reduction in total costs has been $\$(c + d)$. If the firm had instead been faced with an emissions standard of e_1, its cost savings with the new technology would have been only d, as we saw in the last chapter. Also, as we saw in the last chapter, if public authorities shift the standard to e_2 when the new technology becomes available, (giving the same emissions reduction as the tax would have) the firm could actually experience an *increase* in costs because of its R&D efforts.

Thus, the firm's R&D efforts will lead to a bigger reduction in its pollution-control related costs (abatement costs plus tax payments) under a policy of emission taxes than under a standards approach. *Additionally, under the tax system the firm would automatically reduce its emissions as it found ways to shift its marginal abatement cost function downward, whereas under the standard no such automatic process would result.* The difference is that under a tax approach, polluters must pay for emissions as well as for abatement costs, while with standards they need pay only abatement costs. So, their potential cost savings from new pollution-control techniques are much larger under the tax program.

Emission Taxes and Enforcement Costs

Taxes pose a different type of enforcement problem than standards. Any tax system requires accurate information on the item to be taxed. If emissions are to be taxed, they must be measurable at reasonable cost. This means that residuals flowing from a source must be concentrated in a small enough number of identifiable streams that monitoring is possible. This rules out most nonpoint-source emissions because they are spread thinly over a wide area in a way that makes them impossible to measure. It would normally be impossible to tax the pollutants in agricultural runoff because the diffuse nature of the "emissions" makes them impossible to measure. However, if there is a well-defined relationship between agricultural input use and emissions, an input tax may be easy to impose and enforce. Certain toxic chemical emissions may also be difficult to tax because in addition to being nonpoint sources, there are often such small quantities that their flow rates are difficult to measure.

With emission taxes the taxing authorities would be sending a tax bill to the polluting firms at the end of each month or year, based on their total quantity of emissions during that period. So the agency would require information on cumulative emissions from each source. This is more involved than just information on rate of discharge, because cumulative discharge is rate times duration. There are several ways of getting this information. Perhaps the most ideal would be to have permanent monitoring equipment that measures emissions continuously over the time period in question. Lacking such technology, one could fall back on periodic checking of the rate of emissions, with an estimate of the duration based on normal business considerations or perhaps self-reporting by firms. Alternatively, engineering studies might be carried out to determine prospective emission quantities under specified conditions of operation, inputs used, etc.

Are the monitoring requirements of an emissions tax policy more stringent than those for the typical standards program? If the tax is on emissions per day, while a standard is based on annual emissions, the tax policy will have higher enforcement costs. But it is possible that monitoring must be done on exactly the same basis to ensure compliance with the tax or the standard. The frequency of monitoring required will be a function of the the environmental characteristics of the pollutants. The frequency of monitoring in practice will often be constrained by government budgets. A question we pose, but cannot answer is if frequency of monitoring affects whether polluters are more likely to comply under a standard or a tax. Polluters, of course, have incentives to find ways, legal and otherwise, to get their tax bills reduced or to avoid meeting a emission target under a standard. One way to do this is to influence the monitoring process enough so that reported emissions are smaller. Once they do get their tax bills, recipients will have every incentive to contest them if they appear to be based on uncertain data or have other technical weaknesses. But if they receive a fine for failure to meet a standard, the same incentives apply.

Other Types of Taxes

So far we have discussed only one type of tax, an effluent or emissions tax. Since it is the emission of residuals that leads directly to environmental pollution, taxes on emissions presumably have the greatest leverage in terms of altering the incentives of polluters. But there are many situations where it is impossible or impractical to levy taxes directly on emissions. In cases where we can't measure and monitor emissions at reasonable cost, taxes, if they are to be used, would obviously have to be applied to something else. A good case of this is the problem of water pollution from fertilizer runoff in agriculture. It is impossible to tax the kilograms of nitrogen in the runoff because it is a nonpoint-source pollutant and thus not directly measurable. The same problem applies to agricultural pesticides. What may be feasible instead is to put taxes on these materials as they are bought by farmers, that is, a tax per tonne of fertilizer or per 100 kilograms of pesticide purchased. The tax is to reflect the fact that a certain proportion of these materials ends up in nearby streams and lakes. By raising the prices of these items, farmers would have the incentive to use them in smaller quantities. The higher price also creates the incentive to use the fertilizer in ways that involve less wastage, for example by reducing the amounts that run off.

Placing a tax on something other than emissions is usually a "second-best" course of action made necessary because direct emissions can't be closely monitored. In cases like this we have to watch out for distortions that can come about as people respond to the tax, distortions that can substantially alleviate the effects of the tax, or can sometimes make related problems worse. We mentioned in Chapter 1 the move by many U.S. and some Canadian communities to tax household trash. One of the techniques we discussed is to sell stickers to the residents and require each bag of trash have a sticker on it. The rate of tax is determined by the price of the stickers, and it is relatively easy to monitor and enforce the system through the curb-side pickup operations. But the per-bag tax will produce an incentive to pack more into each bag, so the reduction in total quantity of trash may be less than the reduction in the number of bags collected.

Another example. Suppose we put a tax on new cars on the basis of their emissions of residuals like nitrogen oxides and hydrocarbons. The tax on any car is determined by the quantity of emissions per kilometre that car produces, as determined by testing at the plant. Our objective is to raise the price of heavily polluting cars relative to less polluting ones, thus giving people more incentive to shift to the latter when they make their new car purchases. The tax is linked to the quantity of residuals emitted during a typical mile travelled. But the factor we really wish to control is the total quantity of residuals emitted. We have the following relationship:

$$\begin{pmatrix} \text{Total emissions} \\ \text{per year} \end{pmatrix} = \begin{pmatrix} \text{Emissions} \\ \text{per kilometre} \end{pmatrix} \times \begin{pmatrix} \text{Number of kilometres} \\ \text{driven per year} \end{pmatrix}$$

In fact, the number of kilometres driven is as important a factor in determining annual emissions as is the emissions rate of the car. Although consumers might shift to cars that have lower emission rates, they will have absolutely no incentive to look around for ways of driving fewer kilometres each year; taking fewer trips, living closer to work, etc. So total emissions may go down very little despite the tax on new car emissions. The point is that this tax is being put on something other than what we want to control, so it will have less "leverage" and produce smaller results than if it had been put directly on total emissions.[4]

---

[4] See Robert Crandall, "Policy Watch: Corporate Average Fuel Economy Standards," *Journal of Economic Perspectives* 6 (Spring 1992): 171–180 for an interesting discussion of this same problem arising from technological regulations.

Distributional Impacts of Emission Taxes

There are two primary impacts of effluent taxes on the distribution of income and wealth: impacts on prices and output, and the effects of the expenditures made from the tax revenues. Businesses subject to a tax will experience an increase in costs, because of both abatement costs and the tax payments. From the firm's standpoint these would constitute increases in production cost, which they would presumably pass on to consumers like any cost of production. Whether and how much they can do this depends on competitive conditions and the conditions of demand. If the tax is applied to a single firm or small group of firms within a competitive industry, it will not be able to push its price up above the industry price, and so will have to absorb the cost increase. In this case the impacts will be felt entirely by owners of the firm and the people who work there. Many firms fear or pretend to fear being in precisely this situation, and base their public objections to taxes on this outcome. If the tax is applied to an entire industry, then prices will go up and consumers will bear part of the burden. How much prices go up depends on demand conditions.[5] Price increases are often thought of as regressive because, for any given item, an increase in its price would affect poor people proportionately more than higher-income people. For something that both poor and well-off people consume, like electricity, this conclusion is straightforward. For price increases in goods consumed disproportionately by more well-to-do people (e.g., airline travel), however, the burden would be mostly on them.

The burden on workers is tied closely to what happens to the rate of output of the affected firms. Here again, the extent of the output effect depends on competitive conditions and the nature of demand for the good. If the emission tax program is applied to a single firm in a competitive industry, or if the demand for the output of an industry is very responsive to price, output adjustments will be relatively large and displaced workers could result. The long-run burden is then a matter of whether good alternative sources of employment are available.

While burdens because of price and output changes may be real, we have to remember, that on the other side, the tax program is creating substantial benefits in the form of reduced environmental damages. To know how a program affects any particular group we would have to account also for how these benefits are distributed.

Effluent taxes also could involve substantial sums running from consumers of the goods produced by the taxed industry to the beneficiaries, whoever they may be, of the funds collected by the taxing authorities. These funds could be used for any number of purposes; how they were used would determine impacts. They might, for example, be distributed to lower-income people to offset the effects of price increases. They might even be returned in part to the firms paying the effluent taxes. This is done in some European countries to help finance the purchase of pollution-control technology. As long as the return payments do not make the marginal emissions tax rate effectively lower, the incentive effects of the tax are not affected. Alternatively, they

---

[5] This was discussed in greater detail in Chapter 8.

might be used to pay for other environmental initiatives in places where direct public action is called for. They might even be used to reduce overall budget deficits, with benefits flowing to general taxpayers.

One final note on tax revenues. The emission taxes we have talked about in this section are designed to induce polluters to use environmental resources more sparingly. The taxes essentially correct the distorted pattern of resource use that results when environmental resources may be used as free inputs. The other feature of emission taxes that ought to be stressed is as revenue source. This suggests the possibility that is open to governments of replacing certain other taxes, which have distorting effects on the economy, with emission taxes, which are designed to reduce resource-use distortions. For example, many countries have payroll taxes, levied on firms and workers to provide revenues for a variety of purposes, such as social insurance. These taxes have the effect of making labour more expensive, and so cause a reduction in the quantity of labour hired and a reduction in jobs. If this were replaced in whole or in part by an emissions tax, there would be desirable effects both in the labour market and in the reduction of environmental externalities.

ABATEMENT SUBSIDIES

An emission tax works by placing a price on the environmental asset into which emissions are occurring. Essentially the same incentive effects would result if, instead of a tax, we instituted a subsidy on emissions. Here a public authority would pay a polluter a certain amount per tonne of emissions for every tonne they reduced, starting from some benchmark level. The subsidy acts as a reward for reducing emissions. More formally, it acts as an opportunity cost; when a polluter chooses to emit a unit of effluent, they are in effect foregoing the subsidy payment they could have had if they had chosen to withhold that unit of effluent instead. Table 12-1 shows how this works in principle, using the same numbers as in the preceding discussion on emission taxes. The firm's base level is set at its current emissions rate: 10 tonnes/month. It receives $120 per tonne for every tonne it cuts back from this base. The third column shows its total subsidy revenues, and the last column shows total subsidies minus total abatement costs. This net revenue peaks at 4 tonnes/month, the same emissions level the firm would choose with the $120 tax. In other words, the incentive for the firm is the same as for the tax.

Many of the points we made earlier about emission taxes also apply to emission subsidies. The job of monitoring emissions would be essentially the same. There would undoubtedly be great difficulties in establishing the original base levels from which reductions are to be measured. Each source would wish to have this base level set as high as possible. Perverse incentives might be present in the planning stages because sources might try to increase their emissions in the hopes of increasing their base. There is however an additional problem with subsidies not faced by taxes. To be able to pay subsidies to polluters, governments will have to raise revenue in some way. The extra revenue needed for subsidies could come from more government debt, higher income or sales taxes, and so on. If governments can't raise revenues, they

TABLE 12-1   AN ABATEMENT SUBSIDY

Emissions (tonnes/month)	Marginal Abatement Cost	Total Abatement Cost	Total Subsidy at $120/tonne	Total Subsidy Minus Total Abatement Costs
10	0	0	0	0
9	15	15	120	105
8	30	45	240	195
7	50	95	360	265
6	70	165	480	315
5	90	255	600	345
4	115	370	720	350
3	130	500	840	340
2	180	680	960	280
1	230	910	1,080	170
0	290	1,200	1,200	0

have two other options. They could cut back on expenditures in other programs or forego revenues if the subsidy takes the form of a tax write-off, say for investment in pollution abatement equipment. In each of these situations, it is likely that undesirable effects on the economy will occur. Given the current difficult fiscal situation in most jurisdictions, subsidies are generally not seen as viable environmental policies, except in special circumstances.

A further difficulty with subsidies is on their effect on total emissions from an industry. Although an emission subsidy like we have described would have the same incentive for each individual source, total emissions may actually increase. To understand why, note the difference in the financial position of this firm when it emits 4 tonnes of pollutant under the two programs: with the tax it has total costs of $850 while with the subsidy it has a total *revenue* of $350. Thus, the financial position of the firm is much different. In effect, it will be earning higher profits after the imposition of the subsidy, and this can have the effect of making this industry more attractive for potential new firms. We have the possibility, in other words, of having the emissions per firm go down but the number of firms in the industry, and therefore total emissions, increase. This feature is a major drawback of simple subsidies like this.

Deposit-Refund Systems

One place where subsidies may be more practical is in deposit-refund systems. A deposit-refund system is essentially the combination of a tax and a subsidy. For example, a subsidy is paid to consumers when they return an item to a designated collection point. The purpose of the subsidy is to provide the incentive for people to refrain from disposing of these items in environmentally damaging ways. The funds for paying the subsidy are raised by levying taxes on these items when they are purchased. In this case, the purpose of the tax is not necessarily so much to get people to reduce the consumption of the item, but to raise money to pay the subsidy. Of course, the tax is called a deposit and the subsidy a refund, but the principle is clear.

Deposit-refund systems are particularly well suited to situations where a product is widely dispersed when purchased and used, and where disposal is difficult or impossible for authorities to monitor. In Canada, several provinces including British Columbia, Alberta and Saskatchewan have enacted deposit-refund systems for beverage containers, both to reduce litter and to encourage recycling. This approach has also been widely used in Europe. But many other products could be handled effectively with this type of system.

In the late 1960s, Germany instituted a deposit-refund on waste lubricating oil. Each year very large quantities of waste oil are disposed of improperly, putting many air, water, and land resources under threat. In the German system, new lubricating oil is subject to a tax (a deposit), the proceeds of which go into a special fund. This fund is then used to subsidize (the refund side) a waste oil recovery and reprocessing system. The terms of the subsidy are set so as to encourage competition in the recovery/reprocessing system, and to provide an incentive for users to reduce the extent to which oil is contaminated during use.[6]

In Sweden and Norway deposit-refund systems have been instituted for cars. New car buyers pay a deposit at time of purchase, which will be refunded when and if the car is turned over to an authorized junk dealer. Experience with these systems shows that success depends on more than just the size of the deposit-refund. For example, it is essential that the collection system be designed to be reasonably convenient for consumers.

Other items for which deposit-refund systems might be appropriate are consumer products containing hazardous substances, such as batteries containing cadmium and car batteries, or for products containing chlorofluorocarbons such as refrigerators and air-conditioning units. Automobile tires might also be handled this way. The deposit-refund system might also be adaptable to conventional industrial pollutants. For example, users of fossil fuels might pay deposits on the quantities of sulfur contained in the fuels they purchase; they would then get refunds on the sulfur recovered from the exhaust gas. Thus, they would lose their deposit only on the sulfur that went up the stacks.

SUMMARY

Emission taxes attack the pollution problem at its source, by putting a price on something that has been free and, therefore, overused. The main advantage of emission taxes is their efficiency aspects: If all sources are subject to the same tax, they will adjust their emission rates so that the equimarginal rule is satisfied. Administrators do not have to know the individual source of marginal abatement cost functions for this to happen; it is enough that firms be faced with the tax and then left free to make their own adjustments. A second major advantage of emission taxes is that they produce a strong incentive to innovate, to discover cheaper ways of reducing emissions.

---

[6] Peter Bohm, *Deposit-Refund Systems* (Baltimore, MD: Johns Hopkins Press for Resources for the Future, 1981), 116–120.

The apparent indirect character of emission taxes may tend to work against their acceptance by policymakers. Standards have the appearance of placing direct control on the thing that is at issue, namely emissions. Emission taxes, on the other hand, place no direct restrictions on emissions but rely on the self-interested behaviour of firms to adjust their own emission rates in response to the tax. This may make some policymakers uneasy because firms apparently are still allowed to control their own emission rates. It may seem paradoxical that this "indirect" character of effluent taxes can sometimes provide a stronger inducement to emission reductions than seemingly more direct approaches.

But emission taxes require effective monitoring. They cannot be enforced simply by checking to see if sources have installed certain types of pollution-control equipment. If emission taxes are to have the appropriate incentive effects, they must be based closely on *cumulative emissions*. Thus, point sources where emissions can be effectively measured are the likely candidates for pollution control via emissions taxes.

An advantage of emission taxes is that they provide a source of revenue for public authorities. Many have recommended that tax systems be changed, relying less on taxes that have distorting economic effects and more on emissions taxes. This requires that authorities be able to predict with accuracy the effects of particular emissions taxes on rates of emissions.

Emissions subsidies would have the same incentive effect on individual polluters, but they could lead to increases in total emission levels. One place where subsidies have been used effectively is in deposit-refund systems, which are essentially tax and subsidy systems in combination.

QUESTIONS FOR FURTHER DISCUSSION

1 In order to carry out a program of subsidizing emission reductions it would be necessary to start from some baseline level of emissions. What problems are presented in establishing these baselines for different sources?

2 What are the problems and potential of using a deposit-refund system to address the problem of newspaper disposal?

3 How might we design an emission charge program for the control of automobile emissions?

4 Suppose that we institute an emission charge on a particular pollutant, and we use the proceeds of the tax to help subsidize the short-term capital costs by firms in the same industry of installing emission-reduction equipment. Will this approach upset the incentive effects of the emission tax?

5 Opponents of emission charges often say that polluters will simply pay the taxes and pass the cost on to consumers without reducing emissions. Is this correct?

6 Emission charges are sometimes seen as creating a "double burden": Firms must pay the costs of reducing emissions and also pay the government for polluting discharges. How might a charge system be designed to reduce this "double burden"?

7 Suppose the federal government proposes a tax on SO_2 emissions. The tax is to be levied on the sulfur content of the fuel used by utilities and other industries. But in cases where firms have ways of measuring the SO_2 content of exhaust gases, the tax will be levied on the SO_2 content of the gases. What do you think the effect of this system might be?

SELECTED READINGS

Ackerman, Bruce A., and Richard B. Stewart. "Reforming Environmental Law: The Democratic Case for Market Incentives." *Columbia Journal of Environmental Law* 13 (1988): 171–199.

Anderson, Frederick R., et al. *Environmental Improvements Through Economic Incentives*. Baltimore, Md.: Johns Hopkins University Press, 1978.

Anderson, Robert C., Lisa A. Hofmann, and Michael Rusin. *The Use of Economic Incentive Mechanisms in Environmental Management*. Washington, D.C.: American Petroleum Institute, June 1990.

Bohm, Peter. *Deposit-Refund Systems: Theory and Application to Environmental, Conservation and Consumer Policy*. Baltimore, Md.: Johns Hopkins Press for Resource for the Future, 1981.

Breger, Marshall J., et al. "Market-Oriented Regulation of Environmental Problems in the Netherlands." *Law and Policy* 11(2) (April 1989): 215–239.

Brown, Gardner M., Jr., and Ralph Johnson. "Pollution Control by Effluent Charges: It Works in the Federal Republic of Germany, Why Not in the U.S.?" *Natural Resources Journal* 24(4) (October 1984): 929–966.

Costanza, Robert and Charles Perrings. "A Flexible Assurance Bonding System for Improved Environmental Management." *Ecological Economics* 2(1) (February 1990): 57–75.

Hahn, Robert W. and Robert N. Stavins. "Incentive-Based Environmental Regulation: A New Era from an Old Idea?" *Ecology Law Quarterly* 18(1) (1991): 1–42.

James, D. E., H. M. A. Jansen, and J. B. Opschoor. *Economic Approaches to Environmental Problems: Techniques and Results of Empirical Analysis*. Amsterdam: Elsevier Scientific Publications, 1978.

Moore, John L., Larry Parker, John E. Blodgett, James E. McCarthy, and David E. Gushee. *Using Incentives for Environmental Protection: An Overview*. Washington, D.C.: U.S. Congressional Research Service, June 1989.

Nichols, Albert L. *Targeting Economic Incentives for Environmental Protection*. Cambridge, Mass.: MIT Press, 1984.

Ontario Fair Tax Commission: *Final Report—Environment and Taxation*. Toronto: Environment and Taxation Working Group, 1992.

Organization for Economic Cooperation and Development: *Economic Instruments for Environmental Protection*. Paris: OECD, 1989.

Organization for Economic Cooperation and Development: *Taxation and the Environment, Complementary Policies*. Paris: OECD, 1993.

Schelling, Thomas E. (ed.). *Incentives for Environmental Protection*. Cambridge, Mass.: MIT Press, 1983.

Tietenberg, Tom H. "Economic Instruments for Environmental Regulation." *Oxford Review of Economic Policy* 6(1) (Spring 1990): 17–33.

U.S. Environmental Protection Agency. *Economic Disincentives for Pollution Control: Legal, Political and Administrative Dimensions*. Washington, D.C.: EPA (EPA-600/5-74-026), 1974.

U.S. Environmental Protection Agency: *Economic Incentives, Options for Environmental Protection*. Washington, D.C.: EPA (21P-2001), March 1991.

13

INCENTIVE-BASED STRATEGIES: TRANSFERABLE DISCHARGE PERMITS

An effluent tax requires that some central public authority establish a tax rate, monitor the performance of each polluter, and then collect the tax bills. It is essentially an interaction between polluters and public authorities in which we might expect the same type of adversarial relationship we get in any tax system. In this chapter we will take a look at a policy approach which, while incorporating economic incentives, is designed to work in a more decentralized fashion. Rather than leaving everything to a centralized public agency, it works through the decentralized market interactions of polluters themselves. It's called the system of "transferable discharge permits."

GENERAL PRINCIPLES

In a transferable discharge permit (TDP) system a new type of property right is created. This property right consists of a permit to emit pollutants. Each permit entitles its holder to emit one unit (kilogram, tonne, however the permit is calibrated) of the waste material specified in the right. Rights holders would ordinarily have a number of such permits at any point in time. If a discharger owned 100 permits, for example, it would be entitled to emit, during some specified period of time, a maximum of 100 units of the designated type of effluent. Thus, the total number of permits held by all sources puts an upper limit on the total quantity of emissions. These discharge permits are *transferable*; they can be bought and sold among anybody allowed to participate in the permit market, at whatever price is agreed upon by the participants themselves.

A TDP program begins by a centralized decision on the total number of discharge permits to be put into circulation. These permits are then distributed among the sources responsible for the emissions. Some formula must be used to determine how many permits each source will receive; we will come back to this problem below. Again, an economist would advocate using social efficiency as the criterion for determining the number of permits chosen. Setting marginal damages equal to marginal abatement costs determines the optimal amount of emissions. The socially efficient TDPs then must specify this amount of emissions. Assuming that the total number of permits is less than current total emissions, some or all emitters will receive fewer permits than their current emissions.

Suppose, for example, that we have a TDP program to reduce the amount of sulfur emitted by a group of power plants. Current total emissions are, say, 150,000 tonnes of sulfur per year, and policymakers have decided that this must be reduced to 100,000 tonnes/year. Let's focus on the situation of one of the power plants, which we suppose to be emitting 7,000 tonnes of sulfur currently. This plant is initially given 5,000 discharge permits. The plant manager now has three choices. The first is simply to reduce the emissions to the level covered by the number of permits the plant was initially given, or 5,000 tonnes/year. The second is to buy additional permits and emit at higher levels; for example, it might *buy* an additional 1,000 permits, giving it a total of 6,000 permits. In this case it would reduce its emissions from 7,000 tonnes to 6,000 tonnes/year. The third option is to reduce its emissions below the 5,000 tonnes for which it has permits and then *sell* the permits it doesn't need. For example, if it reduced its emissions to 4,000 tonnes, 1,000 of its original allocation would not be needed; these could be sold.

It may not be obvious that the buying and selling of permits among polluters (and perhaps others) would lead to the distribution of total emissions among polluters in a way that satisfies the equimarginal principle. We can examine this with the help of Figure 13-1. Here we have pictured two polluters whose emissions are uniformly mixed together (we will treat the case of nonuniformly mixed emissions below). They have different marginal abatement costs; costs go up much more rapidly for B than for A as emissions are reduced. Assume that initially neither firm is controlling any of its emissions, so total emissions are 210 tonnes/year, 120 tonnes from A and 90 tonnes from B. Suppose we now wish to reduce total emissions by 50 percent, to 105 tonnes/year. We create 105 transferable discharge permits, each one of which entitles its possessor to emit 1 tonne/year. We distribute these permits to the two sources, using some agreed-upon allocation rule. Let's assume that each is allocated permits in proportion to its current emission rates. Thus, A gets 60 permits and B gets 45 permits in the original distribution.

Firm A will have to cut back to 60 tonnes/year and Firm B will have to reduce to 45 tonnes/year, unless they can agree to redistribute the permits among themselves through buying and selling. Suppose Firm B were to cut back to 45 tonnes; at this point its marginal abatement costs would be $4,000/tonne. If it could buy an extra discharge permit for some price less than $4,000, it would be better off because this would allow it to save the difference in abatement costs. Firm A's marginal abatement cost, on the other hand, would be $1,200/tonne if it reduces emissions in accordance with its original holding of 60 permits. If A could sell a permit for some price above $1,200, it would be better off because the revenue from the sale would more

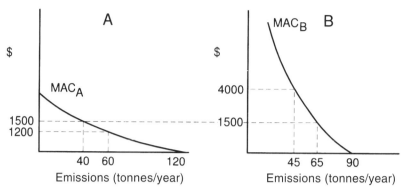

FIGURE 13-1   How Transferable Discharge Permits Work.

than cover the added abatement costs required to reduce its emissions by that unit. Thus, A would be willing to sell a permit for anything above $1,200 and B would be willing to buy a permit for anything below $4,000. Each would obviously be better off by trading the permit, at whatever price they could agree upon between these two extremes. A way of saying this is that there are "gains from trade" for these two polluters in trading a permit from A to B.

After this trade, A will be emitting 1 tonne less, or 59 tonnes/year; and B will be emitting 1 tonne more, or 46 tonnes. But in this situation their marginal abatement costs will still be different. As long as this is true, there will continue to be gains from trade for each of them through trading additional permits. Gains from trade would continue to exist and permits would continue to be traded until marginal abatement costs are equalized. This occurs at emission levels of 40 tonnes for A and 65 tonnes for B. At this point Source A has reduced its holdings of discharge permits to 40 (the 60 permits it was initially awarded minus the 20 sold to B), while B has increased its holdings to 65 permits (45 from the original allocation plus the 20 bought from A). Note, however, that as long as the *total* number of permits in circulation is constant, *total* emissions will be constant. Of course, in the bargaining process between A and B it is unlikely that they would have proceeded just one permit at a time. More than likely they would have some idea of the prices for which permits could be bought and sold and the level of their marginal abatement costs, so they could trade blocks of permits for agreed-upon prices. But the essential point is that as long as marginal abatement costs are unequal between these sources, they can both become better off by trading permits at some price between these marginal abatement costs. Thus, in the trading of permits and the adjusting of emissions in accordance with their permit holdings, these sources would be led to an outcome that satisfies the equimarginal principle.

When a large number of firms is involved, the TDP system works in the same way, but trading patterns, of course, will be more complicated. The initial distribution of emission rights will now include many firms, with many potential buyers and sellers. Exhibit 13-1 shows a news clip about proposed transferable discharge

EXHIBIT 13-1

AQMD OFFICIALS PROPOSE POLLUTION RIGHTS MARKET

Smog: Incentive Concept Would Let Emitters
Direct Own Cleanup Efforts and, if Successful,
Sell Excess Shares.

By Judy Pasternak, Times Staff Writer

After two years of studying the pros and cons, the staff of the South Coast Air Quality Management District on Wednesday recommended establishing a revolutionary "smog exchange" that would replace many of the agency's traditional stringent regulations with a trading market in pollution rights.

The prospect previously has generated dire warnings from environmentalists about gambling with public health and excited talk by industry about new freedom and economic relief for recession-weary businesses.

The AQMD staff believes a market would provide incentives to clean the air faster than under the current regulatory system, while saving industry hundreds of millions of dollars. The AQMD board must approve the concept for it to move forward. But if the go-ahead is given as expected in March, trading by 2,000 polluters could begin in 1994.

It would be by far the nation's largest experiment ever in using financial incentives to cut pollution. The progress of the market would be watched closely across the country.

The big question now is what form the "smog exchange" will take, and at a meeting of an AQMD advisory group Wednesday, the staff revealed its blueprint.

About 2,000 facilities that emit hydrocarbons and 700 that emit nitrogen oxides would be eligible to trade under the plan. Some facilities emit both pollutants.

In all, about 24,000 facilities send smog-forming pollutants into the region's air. About 17,000 are regulated by the AQMD. The staff proposal suggests exemptions beyond those for polluters that emit less than four tons of hydrocarbons or nitrogen oxides.

Although the hydrocarbon and nitrogen oxides markets would be separate, they would work in essentially the same way; Polluters would be issued an initial number of shares, based on past emissions. Each share would be worth a pound of pollutant per month of per quarter—a detail yet to be decided.

Over the first 10 years, the value of each share would decline by 5.8% annually for hydrocarbons and by 8% for nitrogen oxides—in theory, forcing cleanup.

In exchange for their participation in the market, businesses would no longer be subject to about 40 existing or proposed AQMD rules that specify certain equipment or methods to reduce pollutants. They could meet their emissions target however they chose, giving them the flexibility they say they need.

Some businesses would benefit more from a market than others, according to an analysis by the AQMD staff. The analysis found that refineries, for example, would spend $253 million less in 1994 under a market than under the regulatory structure. But the furniture industry, which has complained bitterly about the cost of complying with regulations, would spend about $92 million more in a market than in the current system. Under regulations now in place, furniture makers are allowed an escape hatch if cleaner wood coatings are not developed. The market would require continued emissions reductions regardless of available technology.

Regionwide, the agency predicts, compliance costs under a market system would fall by $427 million in 1994 alone.

Although environmentalists did not object to the nitrogen oxides market, they suggested postponing the market for hydrocarbons for two to three more years, saying it is too difficult to track those emissions.

permit systems, covering emissions of hydrocarbons and nitrogen oxides, in the Los Angeles area. About 2,000 sources are expected in the hydrocarbon market, and 700 sources in the NO_x market. The expectation is that these markets can achieve emission-reduction goals at substantial savings in costs over traditional programs; the article mentions an estimated saving of $427 million in 1994 alone. It also mentions concerns that some observers have about how effectively the markets will operate, especially considering the problems of monitoring emissions. We will discuss this below.

In order for the equimarginal principle eventually to be satisfied in this case it is obviously necessary that all permit buyers and sellers be trading permits at the same price. What this requires is a single overall market for permits where suppliers and demanders may interact openly and where knowledge of transactions prices is publicly available to all participants. We can then expect that the normal forces of competition would bring about a single price for permits. The permits would in general flow from sources with relatively low to those with high marginal abatement costs. Although the example above shows how two sources would redistribute permits among themselves, we would expect that in markets with many sources participating, trading would continue in the future, because of the built-in incentive for polluters to look for better ways of reducing emissions and because of natural changes in a growing economy. We would also anticipate the development of standard market institutions—permit brokers and bankers, permit trading on stock exchanges, etc.—that develop on any market dealing with rights like this, giving us a fully developed market in traded discharge permits, as pictured in Figure 13-2. The demanders in this market would be new firms that wish to begin operations in the trading area or existing sources that wish to expand their operations and require more permits to cover expected increases in emissions. Supplies of permits would include firms leaving the area or going out of business, and most especially firms who have invested in better abatement techniques and now have excess permits to sell. In any particular year there would be a tendency for a market price to establish itself, such as p^* in Figure 13-2, and for a certain number of permits to change hands, such as q^* in the figure.

In recent years the idea of transferable discharge permits has become quite popular among some environmental policy advocates, as well as among policymakers themselves. Unlike effluent tax approaches, which basically make people pay for something they were once getting free, TDP programs begin by creating and distributing a new type of property right. These property rights will have a market value as long as the total number of permits created is limited. From a political standpoint it is perhaps easier for people to agree on a pollution-control policy that begins by distributing valuable new property rights than by notifying people they will be subject to a new tax. Of course, like any pollution-control policy, TDP programs have their own set of problems that have to be overcome if they are going to work effectively. What looks in theory like a neat way of using market forces to achieve efficient pollution reduction must be adapted to the complexities of the real world.

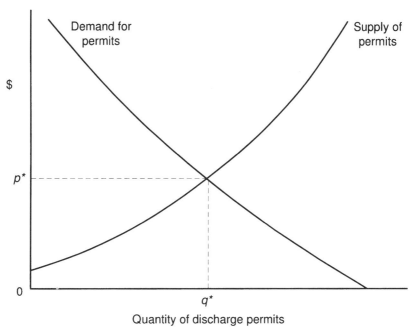

FIGURE 13-2   A Market for Discharge Permits.

The Initial Rights Allocation

The success of the TDP approach in controlling pollution depends critically on limiting the number of rights in circulation. Since individual polluters will no doubt want as many as they can get in the first distribution, the very first step of the program is one of potentially great controversy: what formula to use to make the original distribution of emission rights. Almost any rule will appear to have some inequities. We might contemplate distributing them equally among all existing sources of a particular effluent. But this would encounter the problem that firms vary a lot in size. Some pulp mills are larger than others, for example, and the average size of pulp mills, in terms of value of output, may be different from the average size of, say, soda bottling plants. So giving each polluter the same number of permits may not be fair at all.

We might allocate permits in accordance with the existing emissions of a source. For example, each source might get permits amounting to 50 percent of its current emissions. This may sound equitable but, in fact, it has built-in incentive difficulties. A rule like this does not recognize the fact that some firms may already have worked hard to reduce their emissions. One could easily argue that those firms who have already, out of a good conscience, or for any reason, invested in emission reduction, should not now be penalized, in effect, by receiving emission permits in proportion to these lower emission levels. This tends to reward firms who have dragged their feet in the past.[1] It could go even further. If polluters believe that permits will soon be allocated in this way, they may have the incentive to *increase* today's emission rate because this would give them a larger base for the initial allocation of permits.

Each allocation formula has its problems, and policymakers must find some workable compromise if the approach is to be widely accepted. Closely related to this issue is the question of whether the rights should be given away or perhaps sold or auctioned. In principle it doesn't matter as long as the permits get distributed fairly widely. Subsequent market transactions will redistribute them in accordance with the relative marginal abatement costs of polluters whatever the original distribution may have been. What a sale or auction would do, however, is transfer some of the original value of the rights into the hands of the auctioning agency. This might be a good way for public agencies to raise funds for worthy projects, but it has to be recognized that a plan like this would create political objections. A hybrid system would be to distribute a certain number of permits free, and then auction some number of additional permits. Or a small surcharge might be put on permits in the original distribution.

Establishing Trading Rules

For any market to work effectively, clear rules must exist covering who may trade and the trading procedures that must be followed. Furthermore, the rules should not be so burdensome that they make it impossible for market participants to gauge accurately the implications to them of buying or selling at specific prices. This implies a "hands-off" stance by public agencies after the initial distribution of the rights. Working against this is the normal tendency for environmental agencies to want to monitor the market closely and perhaps try to influence its performance. The supervising agency, for example, may want to have final right of approval over all trades, so as to be able to stop any trades it considers undesirable in some way. But this intervention in the permits market is likely to be counterproductive. The problem with this is that it is likely to increase the uncertainty among potential traders, increase the general level of transactions costs in the market, and interfere with the efficient flow of permits. The general rule for the public agency should be: set simple and clear rules and then allow trading to proceed.

One basic rule that would have to be established is who may participate in the market. Is this to be limited to polluters, or may anyone trade? For example, may environmental advocacy groups buy permits and retire them as a way of reducing total emissions? One's first reaction is to say that such groups ought to be permitted to buy permits, because that is evidence that society's willingness to pay for lower total emission levels exceeds the price of the permits, which should be the same as marginal abatement costs. This conclusion is probably valid if we are dealing with a local or regional environmental group whose membership is roughly coincidental with the

---

[1] This is just another example of the perverse incentives built into any program that asks everybody to cut their consumption by *x* percent from their current rate. It favours those who have consumed at high rates in the past and hurts those who have tried hard to live frugally.

trading area, and which has raised money specifically to buy discharge permits in that region. There may however be problems if large national advocacy groups were to use their resources to buy permits on a regional market for strategic or political reasons that do not reflect the willingness to pay of the people in the region.

These and other trading rules will have to be worked out for particular programs in particular circumstances. A body of common law governing discharge permit transactions will also develop over time. For the rest of this chapter we will deal with some of the important economic dimensions of these trading institutions.

Nonuniformly Mixed Emissions

Suppose we are trying to design a TDP program to control total airborne SO_2 emissions in a region where there are numerous different sources, power plants, industrial plants, etc., scattered rather widely around the area. A schematic of this situation is depicted in Figure 13-3. All the emission points are not equally situated relative to the prevailing wind or to the area of highest population density. Some sources are upwind, others are downwind, of the populated area. We assume they are not all equal in terms of marginal abatement costs, but neither are they equal in terms of the impact of their emissions on ambient SO_2 levels over the populated area. They have different transfer coefficients linking their own emissions with damages in the urban area. Having distributed discharge permits we now allow them to be traded. As long as the number of permits in circulation is held constant, we have effectively controlled total SO_2 emissions. But if we allow straight trading, unit for unit, of permits among all sources, the damage caused by that total could change. For example, if a downwind

FIGURE 13-3   Nonuniform Emissions and TDP Programs.

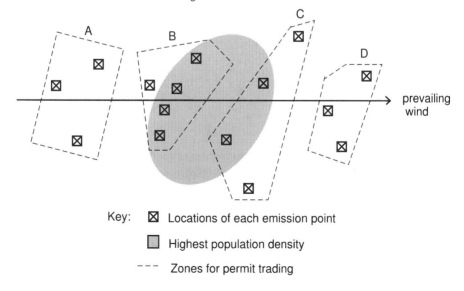

Key: ⊠   Locations of each emission point

▨   Highest population density

- - -   Zones for permit trading

firm sold permits to an upwind firm, the total number of permits would remain the same but there would now be more emissions upwind of the population and, therefore, more damage.[2]

The problem is similar to the one we encountered under uniform standards and the effluent tax policy; in effect each firm is differently situated relative to the damage area, so the emissions of each will have a different impact on ambient quality in that area. If the program were simply to allow trading of permits among all sources on a one-for-one basis, it could easily come to pass that a firm or group of firms with higher transfer coefficients, whose emissions therefore have a greater impact on ambient quality, could accumulate larger numbers of permits. One way to avoid this would be to adjust the trading to take into account the impacts of individual sources. Suppose the emissions from Source A were twice as damaging as the emissions of Source B simply because of the location of the two sources. Then the administrators of the program might set a rule that if Source A is buying permits from Source B, it must buy two permits to get one.

If we extend this into a situation with many sources, things can quickly get very complicated. Authorities would have to determine, for each source, how many permits would have to be purchased from each other source in order for the purchasing source to be credited with one new permit. If there were five sources, the agency would have to figure out only 10 such trading ratios, but if there were 20 different sources, it would have to estimate 190 of these ratios.[3] One way around this would be to use a zoned system, analogous to the zoned effluent charge we talked about earlier. Authorities would designate a series of zones, each of which would contain sources that were relatively similar in terms of their location and the impact of their emissions on ambient quality. Four such zones are shown in Figure 13-3. We could then do one of two things: allow trading by firms only with other firms in the same zone, or make adjustments for all trades across zone boundaries similar to the technique discussed above. Thus, for example, if sources in Zone A were judged to have transfer coefficients twice the size, on average, as sources in Zone B, any trade between sources in these two zones would be adjusted by that same factor of two: Any firm in Zone A buying permits from any firm in Zone B would have to buy two permits in order to get credit for one new one; any source in Zone B would have to buy only half a permit from a firm in Zone A to get credit for one new permit.

TDPs and Problems of Competition

The question of allowing trading across zone boundaries or, on the contrary, restricting it to within zones has a much wider importance than might first appear. TDP programs work through a trading process, where buyers and sellers interact to transfer title to valuable property rights. Markets work best when there is substantial com-

---

[2] This is sometimes called the "hot spot" problem.
[3] In general, if there were n sources, there would have to be $[n(n-1)]/2$ trading ratios established.

petition among buyers and among sellers; they work much less well if there are so few buyers or sellers that competitive pressures are weak or absent. In cases where there are few traders, one of them, or perhaps a small group, may be able to exercise control over the market, colluding on prices, perhaps charging different prices to different people, using the control of discharge permits to gain economic control in its industry, etc. From the standpoint of fostering competition, therefore, we would like to set our trading zones as widely as possible, to include large numbers of potential buyers and sellers.

But this may work against the ecological facts. In many cases there may be meteorological or hydrological reasons for limiting the trading area to a relatively narrow geographical area. If we are interested in controlling airborne emissions affecting a particular city, for example, we would probably not want to allow firms located there to trade permits with firms in another city. Or if our concern is controlling emissions into a particular lake or river, we could not allow sources located there to trade permits with sources located on some entirely different body of water. Thus, for environmental reasons we may want to have trading areas restricted, while for economic reasons we would want to have trading areas defined broadly. There is no magic rule to tell us exactly how these two factors should be balanced in all cases. We can only look at specific cases as they come up and weigh the particularities of the environmental features with the subtleties of the competitive conditions in the industries where trading will occur.

TDP Programs and Enforcement

The directly controlling aspect of a TDP program is that sources are constrained to keep their emissions at a level no greater than the total number of discharge permits in their possession. Thus an administering agency would essentially have to keep track of two things: the number of permits in the possession of each source and the quantity of emissions from each source. Since the initial permit distribution will be well known, the agency must have some way of keeping track of permit transactions among market participants. Trades could, in fact, become complicated with multiple buyers and sellers, and with different types of transactions like temporary rentals and long-term leases in addition to permanent transfers. Since permit buyers (or renters) would have a strong incentive to have their purchases revealed to the agency, and since all purchases imply sellers, a system of self-reporting, coupled with modern means of information transfer, may be sufficient to provide reliable information on which sources have the permits.

As regards monitoring, the administrative agency must be able to monitor polluters to see whether emissions at each source exceed the number of permits it holds. If permits are expressed in terms of total emissions over some period of time, a means has to be available to measure cumulative emissions at each source. This is the same requirement as with an effluent tax. If there were reasonable certainty that emissions were fairly even throughout the year, authorities could get a check on cumulative emissions by making spot-checks of instantaneous rates. For most industrial sources of pollution, however, there is considerable daily, weekly, or seasonal variations in emissions, so more sophisticated monitoring would be required.

One desirable feature of TDP programs is that there may be an incentive for sources to monitor each other, at least informally. When, and if, some sources emit more than they have permits for, they are essentially cheating by not buying sufficient permits to cover all of their emissions. In effect this reduces the demand for permits below what it would otherwise be. And this has the effect of lowering the market price of permits. This clearly works against the interest of any firm holding large numbers of permits, which gives it an incentive to see that other firms don't cheat on emissions.

TDPs and the Incentive for R&D

One of our main criteria for judging an environmental policy is whether or not it creates strong incentives for firms to seek better ways of reducing emissions. Emission standards were weak in this regard, while emission taxes were much stronger. TDP programs in this respect are identical to the emissions tax, at least in theory. Consider the firm in Figure 13-4. Suppose that at present the firm's marginal abatement cost function is MAC_1. Emission permits sell for p each, and let us assume that this price is not expected to change. The firm has adjusted its holdings so that it currently owns e_1 permits.[4] Its emissions are therefore e_1 and its total abatement costs are $(a + b)$. The incentive to do R&D is to find a less costly way of controlling emissions, so the firm can cut emissions and sell the surplus permits. How much would it be worth to get marginal abatement costs shifted to MAC_2? With MAC_2, the firm would shift to an emissions level of e_2. Its total abatement costs here would be $(b + d)$, but it would be able to sell $(e_1 - e_2)$ permits for a revenue of $p(e_1 - e_2) = (c + d)$. The change in its position would thus be:

$$\text{Total abatement costs with } MAC_1 - \text{Total abatement costs with } MAC_2 + \text{Receipts from TDP Sales}$$

or $(a + b) - (d + b) + (c + d)$. Check this with the savings under an effluent tax (above, pp. 236–237). It is exactly the same. The market price of the permit has the same incentive as a pollution tax; by not reducing their emissions, firms are foregoing the increased revenues they could have obtained by selling some of their permits.

SUMMARY

Transferable discharge permits are being used more frequently in North America. As we'll see in Chapter 22, Canada's implementation of the Montreal Protocol for chlorofluorocarbon elimination is a type of TDP. Several programs are already in place

---

[4] These marginal abatement cost functions apply to a year; i.e., they are the costs per year of changing emissions. The price p is therefore a one-year purchase (or sale) price, what it would cost to buy or sell a permit for just one year. If a firm is buying a permit to hold permanently, the price will be some multiple of the annual value, much as the purchase price of a rental house is some multiple of its annual rental income.

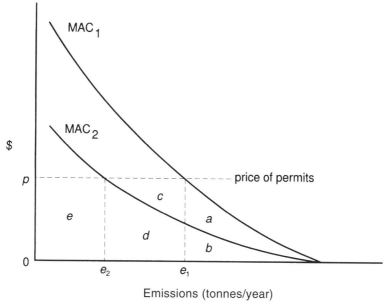

FIGURE 13-4 TDP and Technological Change.

in the United States, for example, a TDP program for SO_2 reduction among electric power producers. TDP programs are being contemplated in Canada for nitrogen oxide and volatile organic compounds. There is the expectation that this approach could give us pollution control at a substantially lower cost than the current system of performance and technology-based effluent standards, and also a sense that, politically, they would be more acceptable than emission taxes.

But TDP programs come with their own set of problems. Most especially, TDP programs take some of the burden of pollution control out of the hands of engineers and place it under the operation of a market. How that market operates is obviously critical to whether this type of policy will work. There is a host of important factors: who gets the permits at the beginning, the strength of their incentives to minimize costs, the degree of competition in the market, the transaction rules set by the administering public agency, the ability to monitor and enforce compliance, and so on. Nevertheless, the transferable discharge permit system seems to be an idea receiving a lot of attention.

Both transferable discharge systems and emission tax systems seek to take the burden and responsibility of making technical pollution-control decisions out of the hands of central administrators and put them into the hands of polluters themselves. They are not, we should stress, aimed at putting pollution-control *objectives* themselves into the hands of the polluters. It is not the market that is going to determine the most efficient level of pollution control for society. Rather, they are means of enlisting the incentives of the polluters themselves in finding more effective ways of meeting the overall objective of reducing emissions.

QUESTIONS FOR FURTHER DISCUSSION

1 In discussing emission taxes we considered the "two-part tax," where sources would pay a low, or zero, tax on some initial quantity of emissions, and a higher tax on anything over this level. How might the same feature be designed into a program of transferable emission permits?

2 What are the pros and cons of letting *anybody* (banks, private citizens, environmental groups, government agencies, etc.) buy and sell transferable discharge permits, in addition to emission sources themselves?

3 How might you design a transferable discharge permit system for solid waste? For phasing out of use a certain type of plastic? For phasing in a program of using recycled newsprint in newspapers?

4 What would the effect on a TDP market be if it were subject to the oversight of a committee which frequently changed the rules governing trades?

5 What do you think the effect on a TDP market would be if a judge decided that purchasers of discharge rights could be held liable if the sources that sold them the rights did not reduce their emissions commensurate with the sale?

SELECTED READINGS

Brady, Gordon L. "Emissions Trading in the United States: An Overview and Technical Requirements." *Journal of Environmental Management* 17(1) (1983): 63–79.

Clark, Timothy B. "A New Approach to Regulatory Reform—Letting the Market Do the Job." *National Journal* 11(32), (August 11, 1979): 1316–1322.

Dales, John. *Pollution, Property and Prices*. Toronto: University of Toronto Press, 1968.

Hahn, Robert W. "Economic Perspectives for Environmental Problems: How the Patient Followed the Doctor's Orders." *Journal of Economic Perspectives* 3(2) (Spring 1989): 95–114.

———. *A Primer on Environmental Policy Design*. Chur, Switzerland: Harwood Academic Publishers, 1989.

Hahn, Robert W., and Gordon L. Hester. "Marketable Permits: Lessons for Theory and Practice." *Ecology Law Quarterly* 16(1) (Winter 1989): 361–406.

Hahn, Robert W., and Roger G. Noll. "Designing a Market for Tradeable Emission Permits," in Wesley Magat (ed.). *Reform of Environmental Regulation*. Cambridge, Mass.: Ballinger Publishing Company, 1982, 119–146.

Project 88—Round II Incentives for Action: Designing Market-Based Environmental Strategies. A Public Policy Study sponsored by Senators Timothy E. Wirth and John Heinz, Washington, D.C., May 1991.

Roberts, Marc J. "Some Problems in Implementing Marketable Pollution Rights Schemes: The Case of the Clean Air Act," in Wesley A. Magat (ed.). *Reform of Environmental Regulation*. Cambridge, Mass.: Ballinger Publishing Company, 1982, 93–118.

Rose-Ackerman, Susan. "Market Models for Water Pollution Control: Their Strengths and Weaknesses." *Public Policy* 25(3) (Summer 1977): 383–406.

Tietenberg, Tom H. *Emissions Trading: An Exercise in Reforming Pollution Policy*. Washington, D.C.: Resources for the Future, 1985.

Tripp, James T. B., and Daniel Dudek. "Institutional Guidelines for Designing Successful Transferable Rights Programs." *Yale Journal of Regulation* 6(2) (Summer 1989): 369–392.

U.S. Environmental Protection Agency. *An Evaluation of Marketable Effluent Permit Systems*. Washington, D.C.: EPA-600/5-74-030, 1974.

14

GOVERNMENT POLICIES
IN PERSPECTIVE[1]

The last three chapters have introduced command-and-control and incentive-based policies: standards, taxes and subsidies, and transferable discharge permits. We take the analysis a step further in this chapter by contrasting the policies in a number of ways. Numerical examples and simple algebra are used. In the first section, a simple model is used to derive cost-effective solutions for all the policies. The private and social costs of compliance with each policy are examined. The second section introduces uncertainty about the shape and location of the marginal abatement cost and marginal damage function into the model. Uncertainty can prevent the attainment of a socially efficient equilibrium. Another criterion for choosing among policies is introduced—minimizing the social costs of being at an inefficient level of emissions. We conclude with a discussion of the incentives created by each policy to reveal information about the shape of the MAC curve.

PRIVATE AND SOCIAL COSTS OF COMPLIANCE

A simple model can be used to illustrate a variety of points about the cost-effectiveness of policies and the costs of compliance with the policy from the viewpoint of the polluter. Suppose there are two firms with different marginal costs of abatement. In our example, Firm L has low marginal costs of abatement, Firm H has high marginal abatement costs. Both operate in a perfectly competitive market. There are no distortions in the economy except for pollution from these firms. We also assume that the pollutant in question is uniformly mixed. If there are spatial dimensions to the pollutant, the analysis becomes much more complex. Let:

---

[1] The material in this chapter is somewhat more advanced than in the preceeding chapters. This chapter may be omitted without affecting subsequent chapters.

$$MAC^L = 900 - 15e \qquad (1)$$

$$MAC^H = 2000 - 25e \qquad (2)$$

If there is no regulation against pollution, each firm will incur zero costs of abatement. Emissions from the low-cost firm will equal 60, those from the high-cost firm equal 80. These emission levels are found by setting each of equations (1) and (2) equal to zero and solving for e. Total emissions without regulation are 140. Figure 14-1 illustrates the MACs for each polluter.

Suppose the regulator wants to achieve a 40 percent reduction in emissions. The target level of emissions is therefore 84 units. This target level could represent the socially efficient equilbrium, or be the regulator's best guess at such a point. In the discussion that follows, social efficiency is not crucial to any arguments. Each policy can reach 84 units of emissions. If that target is socially efficient, so is each policy. What will differ among the policies is whether or not they are cost-effective, that is, do they minimize the social costs of obtaining the target level of pollution. We focus on cost-effectiveness in this chapter.

First, we need to define two costs of compliance with a policy. Private compliance costs measure the total costs of abatement. At whatever level of emissions chosen,

FIGURE 14-1   Cost-Efficient Emissions.

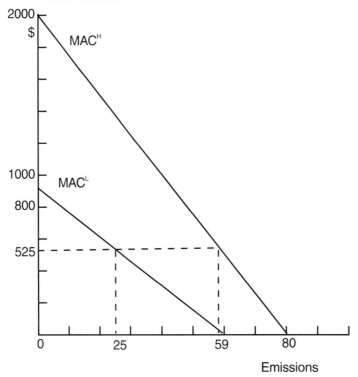

we assume the polluter pays the area under its marginal abatement cost curve between its initial pollution level and the pollution level chosen after the policy. If the policy is a pollution tax, the private compliance costs also include the total tax payment to the government. In the case of TDPs, private compliance costs include the total cost of any permits purchased either from the government or another polluter, or any revenues received from the sale of permits. The social costs of compliance are defined as the private compliance costs borne by the polluter net of any redistribution back to polluters of tax or discharge permit revenues collected by the government. These revenues will not influence any decisions on the margin, if they are given back to polluters in lump sums, that is, not dependent on the amount of abatement/emissions.

From society's viewpoint, the social abatement costs are what matters. We calculate private compliance costs because they illustrate quite clearly some political economy features of the policies. When private costs of a policy are high, we can expect a lot of resistance by polluters to the implementation of that policy. The identification of two polluters with different MACs allows us to show that policies can have a different impact on firms operating within the same industry.

When there is more than one polluter, it is easier to use simple algebra to solve for a cost-effective solution than to depend on a graph. The equilibrium is found where two conditions are met:

$$e^L + e^H = 84 \qquad (3)$$

$$\text{MAC}^L = \text{MAC}^H \qquad (4)$$

This ensures that total emissions equal the pollution target and that marginal abatement costs are equal across polluters at the equilibrium level of emissions. Substituting equations (1) and (2) into equation (4), and then, substituting equation (3) into equation (4), we find that:

$$e^L = 25$$

$$e^H = 59, \text{ and}$$

$\text{MAC}^L = \text{MAC}^H = \$525$ at the cost-effective level of emissions for each polluter. Because initial emissions were 60 for L and 80 for H, this means that total abatement is equal to 35 units for L and 21 units for H.

Which of the policies we have examined can obtain this cost-effective equilibrium? The only policy that fails to achieve cost-effectiveness is the uniform standard, as noted in Chapter 11. The uniform standard would require each firm to reduce its emissions by 40 percent, to a level of $e^L = 36$ and $e^H = 48$. At these emission levels, MAC^L would be \$360 and $\text{MAC}^H = \$800$. This cannot be cost-effective because the marginal abatement costs of the two firms are not equal at this equilibrium. An individual standard, set at the efficient levels of emissions, a tax set at the efficient price, and marketable permits, are all cost-effective.

Table 14-1 shows the private and social compliance costs for each policy (we discuss the other columns below). As is illustrated, the social costs of compliance are identical for all policies except for the uniform standard. The cost-effective total social costs are $14,700. The table clearly shows that the uniform standard achieves the emission target at total costs in excess of all other policies. Next, note the differences in private control costs among the policies and between the two types of firms. The policies can be ranked from lowest to highest private costs for each type of polluter. For the low-cost polluter, the preferred policies in order from lowest to highest cost are: TDP that is initially allocated without any charge, the uniform standard, the individual standard, then the uniform tax and TDP that is auctioned by the government. For the high-cost polluter, the ranking is: individual standard, TDP that is not auctioned, uniform standard, then tax and auctioned TDP. The standards thus have a different impact depending on whether the polluter is high or low cost. But the TDP that is initially allocated without charge is the policy with either the lowest or the second-lowest private costs. This may help to explain why there is growing support for the implementation of TDPs among polluters. The asymmetry of the impact of the standards is also interesting and may help explain support for different policies. The high-cost polluter clearly favours individual standards. If the high-cost polluter also rep-

TABLE 14-1   CONTROL COSTS OF POLLUTION POLICIES

POLICY

	Private control costs	Social control costs	Technological incentive	Information required
Uniform standard				
Low-cost polluter	$ 4320	$ 4320	Weak	Low
High-cost polluter	12,800	12,800	Strong	Low
Total costs	17,120	17,120		
Individual standard				
Low-cost polluter	9187.50	9187.50	Weak	High
High-cost polluter	5512.50	5512.50	Weak	High
Total costs	14,700	14,700		
Uniform tax				
Low-cost polluter	22,312.50	9187.50	Strong	High/medium
High-cost polluter	36,487.50	5512.50	Strong	High/medium
Total costs	58,000	14,700		
TDPs (given away)				
Low-cost polluter	3412.50	3412.50	Strong	Low/medium
High-cost polluter	11,287.50	11,287.50	Strong	Low/medium
Total costs	14,700	14,700		
TDPS (auctioned)				
Low-cost polluter	22,312.50	9187.50	Strong	Low
High-cost polluter	36,487.50	5512.50	Strong	Low
Total costs	58,800	14,700		

resents the existing firms in the industry, it is obvious that they will oppose any policies that have uniform standards. If new firms can enter the industry *and* have lower MACs, a uniform standard will clearly disadvantage the old firms. Thus, when we see standards in practice, they are frequently one standard for existing firms, and a tougher standard for new firms that enter the industry. The table also clearly shows that polluters will resist the implementation of taxes and TDPs that are auctioned because of their high private costs relative to the other policies.

The columns called Technological Incentives summarize the information presented in Chapters 11 through 13 about the incentive each policy creates to invest in more effective pollution abatement equipment. We note here the asymmetry under uniform standards for low-versus high-cost polluters. The high-cost polluter has a strong incentive to invest in abatement equipment that lowers its MACs. It's private control costs could fall substantially, making it likely that the rate of return on investing in abatement technology will be high. For the low-cost polluter, the return to investment in abatement may simply not be as high because they already have low private control costs. The incentives to invest under individual standards is weak for both types of polluters. The lower each firm's costs of abatement, the greater share of total abatement it may have to incur, other things equal. Each polluter even has an incentive to misreveal its abatement costs, hoping to convince the regulatory authorities that they are higher than these costs actually are. The regulator interested in cost-effectiveness would then assign the polluter a more lenient standard. In the next section of this chapter, we illustrate graphically the incentives to misreveal information under standards versus taxes. For all the other policies, there are strong incentives to invest in abatement equipment, because for each unit of pollution reduced, the total private or social costs of the policy decline.

The final column gives an indication of the amount of information regulators require to determine the target level of emmissions. We do not consider information required to enforce each policy. Two policies are ranked "low." Uniform standards and auctioned TDPs require the least amount of information. In the case of the uniform standard as defined above (a given percentage reduction in emissions), the regulator does not need to know anything about individual firms. The same is true for TDPs that are auctioned. The regulator simply annouces an auction and the market takes care of the rest. The allocated TDPs are rated low to medium. This is because some means of initially distributing the permits must be established. For example, regulators may use each polluter's share of total pollution. We rate the uniform tax at medium to high. To compute the cost-effective tax, the regulator has to solve for the cost-effective solution. This means it must know the MACs for all polluters. If there are many polluters, the information costs would be quite high. The reason we've given it a medium is that the regulator may iterate to an efficient tax by setting the tax rate, observing total emissions, then raising or lowering the rate until the target level of emissions is reached. We illustrate this is the section below on uncertainty and information. The individual standard requires a large amount of information. Like the cost-effective tax (that isn't set by iteration), the MACs of all polluters must be known to determine each's individual standard. Unlike the tax, there is no way to iterate to the cost-effective solution. Once the polluters comply with a given standard, the regulator will get no information about their MAC curves.

UNCERTAINTY AND INFORMATION

Uncertainty about the MD and MAC Curves

We have assumed thus far that regulators know precisely the equations for the MAC and MD curves. This information enables them to determine the socially efficient policy. But, in practice, it is likely that information about these curves will not be known with certainty. In this section, we examine the policy options regulators have when there is uncertainty about the MD and MAC curves. The policies considered are a uniform tax, uniform standard, and tradeable discharge permits.[2] When there is uncertainty about the MAC or MD curve, it is generally impossible to achieve a socially efficient equilibrium. There will typically be some *social loss* associated with the use of any policy. We assume the objective of regulators is to choose the policy that *minimizes the social loss* obtained as a result of the uncertainty. The social loss is defined as the loss of real resources devoted to too much or too little pollution control relative to the socially efficient level. It is measured as the area between the MD and MAC curves from the actual pollution level to the socially efficient pollution level. Of course, regulators do not know the socially efficient level of pollution. The theoretical model developed below allows them under certain circumstances to predict the relative size of social losses without this information.

We begin with the case where the regulator is uncertain about the location of the MD curve, but knows the MAC curve with certainty. We continue to assume that pollution is uniformly mixed, but return to a case where all polluters have identical MACs. Figure 14-2 illustrates. Two MD curves are shown. MD^E is the curve estimated by regulators; MD^T is the "true" curve that is not observed. The socially efficient equilibrium is at e^*; e' is the level of emissions the regulators have estimated as the intersection of the MD and MAC curves. The regulator would then set the standard or number of permits at e'. The uniform tax would be set at t'. The choice of policy instrument will not affect the size of the social loss in this case. Under a standard or TDP, the total emissions are e'. Under a tax set at t', the total emissions are also e' because the polluter sets t' equal to its true MAC. The social loss is identical for all policies and equal to the shaded area abc. The level of emissions is too low relative to the socially efficient equilibrium. Thus, if there is uncertainty about the MD curve, no policy dominates another in terms of minimizing social losses. The economist cannot help the regulator choose a preferred policy.

Now, assume that the uncertainty is about the MAC curve. Figure 14-3 illustrates this case. We assume the regulator knows the actual amount of emissions when no

---

[2] The article that stimulated much of the work on this topic is by Martin Weitzman, "Prices versus Quantities," *Review of Economic Studies* 41 (1974): 477–491.

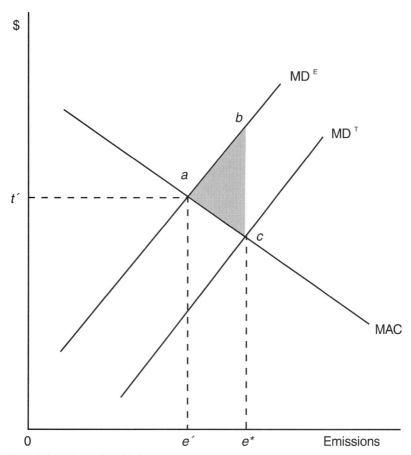

FIGURE 14-2   Uncertainty about the MD Curve.

policy is in place. Initial emissions are e_0. The uncertainty about the MAC is therefore about its slope.[3] MAC^T is the true curve; MAC^E the estimated curve. Again, we show the socially efficient equilibrium as e^* and the estimated equilibrium as e'. The standard or number of TDPs is set at e'; the tax set at t'. The equilibrium under the standard or TDPs is at e', with a social loss equal to the shaded area abc. But now, the use of an emission tax at rate t' will lead to a different equilibrium than under the standard or TDPs. The polluter sets t' equal to its true MAC. Emissions under the tax are e'', which is greater than the socially efficient level of e^*. The social loss under a tax is shaded area adf.

[3] It is possible that the regulator knows neither the slope of the MAC nor the initial level of emissions. The basic analysis in this section is the same.

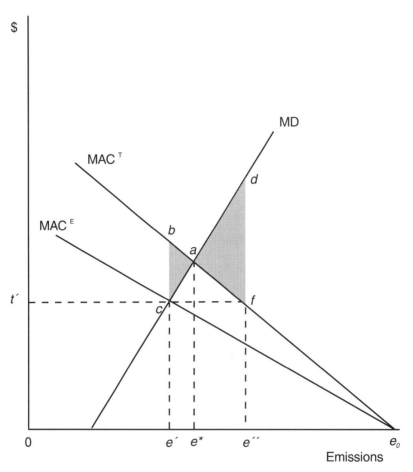

FIGURE 14-3   Uncertainty about the MAC Curve: Steep MD.

We now have the means to compare policies in terms of which ones lead to the lowest social loss, by examining the relative sizes of area *abc* to area *adf*. But recall that the regulator doesn't know where point e^* is or where MAC^T actually lies. So how can areas *abc* and *adf* be measured? The regulator cannot measure these areas precisely but can determine their relative size if they have some information about the slopes of the MD and MAC curve. In Figure 14-3, the MD curve is relatively steep. Even though the regulator doesn't know the exact slope of the MAC, suppose he or she knows the MD is steeper than the MAC. In this case, area *abc* is less than area *adf*. A uniform standard or TDP will minimize the social losses. The intuition behind this result is that whenever MDs rise considerably as emissions increase, social losses will be larger the farther away actual emissions are from e^*. The equilibrium under a tax is less predictable than with a standard or TDPs. If MAC^E lies below

MAC^T, the tax will lead to too high a level of emissions and large social damages. If MAC^E lies above MAC^T, the tax will overcontrol emissions and will lead to large social losses due to too little production of pollution-generating goods. In the extreme case where the MD curve is vertical, it is obvious that the socially efficient policy is a standard or TDP set at e^*.

Figure 14-4 illustrates the case where the MD curve is flat relative to the MAC curves. In this situation, the tax is the policy that minimizes the social losses of failing to be at the socially efficient equilibrium, e^*. Area adf is now smaller than area abc. Again the intuition is straightforward. If the MD curve were horizontal, the socially efficient policy would be a tax. Uncertainty about the MAC curve wouldn't matter as the tax rate would be set at the level of MD. Therefore, the flatter the MD curve, a tax will be closer to the socially efficient equilibrium than a standard or TDP program.

FIGURE 14-4   Uncertainty about the MAC Curve: Flat MD.

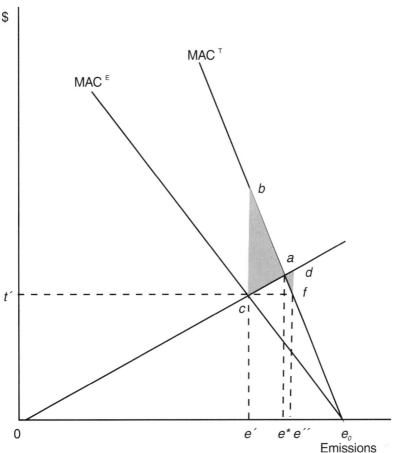

Information Revelation under Taxes, Standards, and TDPs

We continue the model developed above to see whether the policy instrument used will reveal to the regulator any information about the slope of the MAC curve. As well, we consider how the policy chosen affects the polluter's incentives to reveal information to the regulator. Assume in all cases that the regulator and all polluters know the MD curve with certainty. Consider first the case of a standard, as shown in Figure 14-5. The regulator has set the emissions standard at e'. First note that the standard reveals no information to the regulator about the polluter's true MAC. If the polluter complies with the standard, actual emissions are what the regulator expected. But standards create incentives for the polluter to reveal information to the regulator. The polluter knows the socially efficient level of emissions is at e^*, so under the standard set at e', it will be incurring very high marginal abatement costs (shown as

FIGURE 14-5   Incentives to Overstate MACs under a Standard.

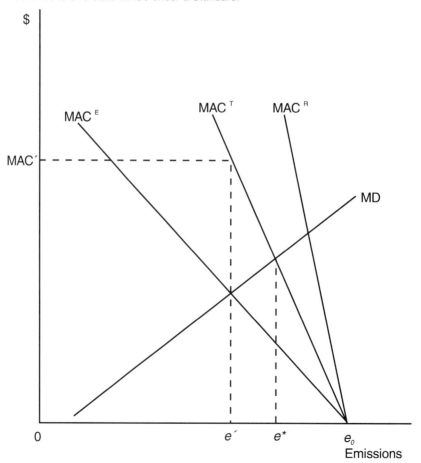

MAC′ on Figure 14-5), if it complies with the regulation. The polluter wants to minimize its abatement costs, so it has an incentive to tell the government that its MACs are higher than the regulator estimated at MAC^E. But, what is to prevent the polluter from telling the regulator that its MACs are even higher than MAC^T? Suppose it tries to convince the regulator that its "true" marginal abatement costs are MAC^R. If a standard is used, the polluter will then have to control far fewer emissions than under the regulator's initial estimate of MAC^E. Under a standard then, the polluter has an incentive to reveal an MAC that is higher than its true MAC.

What about a tax? Figure 14-6 illustrates this case. Again we start with an estimated MAC that lies below the true MAC. The regulator sets the tax equal to t'. The polluter sets t' equal to its true MAC and releases emissions equal to e'', where e'' exceeds both the socially efficient level of emissions (e^*) and the regulator's antic-

FIGURE 14-6   Iteration to Socially Efficient Tax Rate.

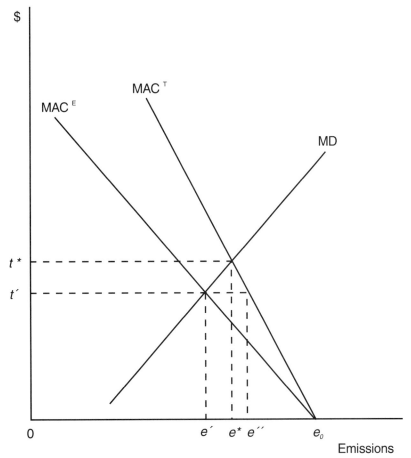

ipated emission levels given its estimate of MAC (e'). First note that the level of emissions provides the regulator with information. Assuming the regulator can monitor emissions, if e'' exceeds e', the regulator knows the tax rate has been set too low. The regulator now has two points on the polluter's true MAC curve, found from e_0 and e'' (MAC equal to zero and to t'). If MACs are linear, this is all the information needed to go directly to the socially efficient tax of t^*. If MACs are not linear, and the regulator can adjust tax rates, an iterative process can be followed to reach t^*. The regulator adjusts the tax rate, measures emissions, then maps out more of the MAC curve.

Does the tax provide any incentives for the polluter to reveal true or misleading information to the regulator? This case is more complex than that of the standard. To calculate the incentives for the polluter, the total abatement costs plus the tax bill under different tax rates have to be calculated. The polluter has no incentive to reveal an excessively high MAC as in the case of MAC^R under the standard. This would result in a very high tax rate and thus tax bill (t' times the level of emissions), and more emissions controlled than if the true MAC curve were revealed. Does the polluter have an incentive to try to convince the government that its MACs are as the regulator estimated, below the true MAC? The answer here is possibly, yes. Suppose the polluter does not equate the estimated tax of t' to its true MAC, but to the regulator's estimated MAC^E. This is shown in Figure 14-7. The question is whether the polluter is better off by following this strategy rather than equating t' to MAC^T. At t' and e', the polluter pays a tax bill equal to the area $0t'ae'$. If the polluter sets t' equal to MAC^T its tax bill is higher and equal to area $0t'be''$. The difference between the two tax bills is area $abe''e'$, which represents the gain from "pretending" that MAC^E is the true MAC. However at e' emissions, the polluter will incur total abatement costs equal to area $e'e_oc$. If it sets t' equal to its true MAC, total abatement costs equal area $e''e_ob$. The difference between the total abatement costs is area $e'e''bc$, which represents the savings in total abatement costs if the polluter sets t' equal to MAC^T. We can now compare the net costs to the polluter under the two options shown. If it sets the estimated tax equal to its true MAC, the savings in abatement costs exceed the savings in the tax bill if it sets t' equal to MAC^E. Area abc is the net gain by setting t' equal to MAC^T.

Recall that eventually the regulator will iterate to the socially efficient tax rate of t^*. Does it still pay the polluter to reveal its true MAC, knowing that the tax rate won't stay at t'? Following the same type of analysis, we now compare total abatement costs and tax bills under t' to those with t^*, the socially efficient tax rate. We can no longer predict without knowing the exact slopes of the MAC curves whether or not the polluter will reveal its true MAC. Refer again to Figure 14-7. The net gain to polluters from being at the inefficient tax of t' relative to the efficient tax of t^* is equal to the difference between any saving in the tax bill (area $0t^*fe^*$ minus area $0t'ab$) and the difference in the total abatement costs (area $e'e_oc$ minus $e''e_ob$). Whether or not the polluter reveals its true MAC then depends on the size of area cdf to area $t't^*da$, which in turn depends on the tax rate set by the regulator and the polluter's true MAC. In the case illustrated, the polluter will gain by pretending its MAC is MAC^E.

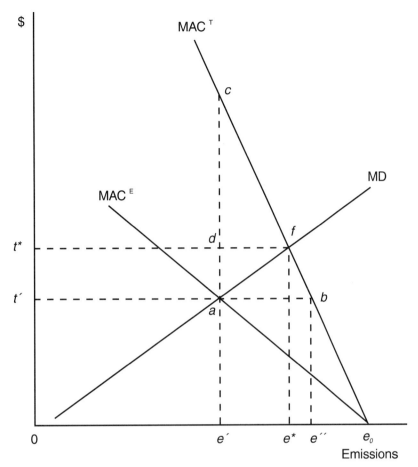

FIGURE 14-7   Incentives to Reveal True MAC under a Tax.

Finally, we come to the case of TDPs. To keep the analysis simple, we still look at only one MAC that represents the entire industry. Figure 14-8 illustrates this case. Suppose the regulator sets the number of permits at e' which is too low a level relative to the socially efficient number. This is analogous to the cases we have examined above. Assume the regulator attempts to auction the permits. It would expect the permit market to clear at a price equal to p' if the efficient number of permits had been distributed. If there are too few permits, their market-clearing price will be p'' which is above p'.[4] Like the tax, permit prices give information about the true MACs. The

---

[4] If the regulator initially distributes the permits without charge, it will have to monitor subsequent permit prices in the TDP market to obtain information about whether there is an excess supply of or excess demand for permits.

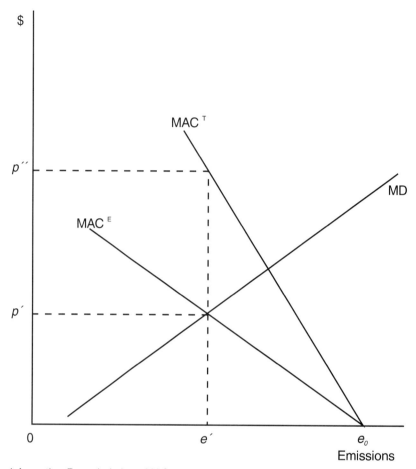

FIGURE 14-8   Information Revealed about MACs under a TDP.

regulator could then adjust the number of permits to iterate to the socially efficient equilibrium. Will individual polluters have incentives to reveal false information about their MACs to the regulator for the initial trades and to other polluters for other trades? Analogous to the tax, there is no incentive to reveal an MAC that is higher than the true MAC, for this would simply raise the permit price the polluter would have to pay. If one polluter pretends its MAC is lower than the true one and others don't, the one that revealed false information won't be able to buy sufficient permits in the market to cover its emissions. With our simple analysis, it appears that TDPs, if used in perfectly competitive markets, are likely to reveal information that results over time in the attainment of a socially efficient equilibrium. However, we caution that what is required in a full analysis of TDPs is a game theoretic framework. This a subject for a more advanced course.

SUMMARY

Regulatory policies are compared using a simple algebraic model of two polluters with different MACs. All policies have the potential to achieve a socially efficient equilibrium, and all are cost-effective except for the uniform standard. Policies differ in terms of the private costs of compliance. These differences help explain polluters' support for or opposition to the implementation of policies. We also discussed the incentives created by each policy to invest in pollution abatement equipment, and the information required by regulators to implement the policy. These criteria can help regulators choose a policy for each particular pollution problem. No single policy is appropriate for all types of pollution.

When uncertainty exists about the MAC and MD curves, regulators may no longer be able to reach a socially efficient level of emissions, but can enact policies that minimize the social losses of having too high or low a level of emissions. If there is uncertainty about the MD curve, all regulatory policies lead to equal social losses and some other criteria must be used to choose among them. If the uncertainty is about the MAC curve, we saw that taxes will minimize the social losses when the MD curve is relatively flat compared to the MAC curve and standards or TDPs will minimize social losses when the MD curve is relatively steep.

Incentive-based policies reveal information about the MAC curve of the polluter, while standards do not. Under a tax, a socially efficient policy can be reached by iteration of the tax rate. Under a TDP, social efficiency can be reached by adjusting the number of permits. Standards create an incentive for polluters to reveal a MAC curve that is steeper (higher) than their true marginal abatement costs. Taxes and TDPs do not create this incentive. Taxes may however induce polluters to reveal to regulators a MAC that is lower than their true curve. It is unlikely that this will occur with TDPs.

QUESTIONS FOR FURTHER DISCUSSION

1 Why is cost-effectiveness a desirable goal of environmental policy? How is it achieved?

2 Why do pollution taxes have a more uncertain impact on the level of pollution than does a standard?

3 Suppose you are a government regulator that is trying to design a pollution-control policy for a nondegradable water pollutant such as dioxin. Your objective is to get an immediate reduction in emissions plus provide an incentive to firms to switch to production technologies that yield fewer emissions of these compounds. Which ONE of the following three policies would you recommend and why? The policies are: uniform standard, uniform tax, or individual standard.

4 You are a polluter with a steep marginal cost of abatement curve that is positively sloped and linear. You would prefer to be allowed to freely dump your wastes, but recognize that the government will impose environmental regulation of some sort. Rank, from best to worst, the policies you would like to see imposed, and explain the reasons for your ranking.

5 Suppose the government cannot accurately measure and monitor the pollution emissions from each polluter, but it knows the marginal damages per unit pollution

and these are relatively constant per unit pollution. What policy or policies would you recommend that government implement? Explain why.

6 Assume that the government does not know the location of the polluter's marginal cost of abatement curve. The government plans to impose an emissions tax. Would the polluter have an incentive to reveal their MAC curve to the government? Could an efficient equilibrium be reached? Explain why or why not.

7 How do market-based policies differ from command-and-control policies with regard to incentives created by the policy to reveal information about the polluter's marginal costs of abatement curve to the regulator?

SELECTED READINGS

Adar, Z. and J. M. Griffin. "Uncertainty and the Choice of Pollution Control Instruments." *Journal of Environmental Economics and Management* 3 (1976): 178–188.

Baumol, William J. and Wallace E. Oates. *The Theory of Environmental Policy*, 2nd ed. Cambridge: Cambridge University Press, 1988, Chapters 6–8, 14.

Cropper, Maureen L. and Wallace E. Oates. "Environmental Economics: A Survey." *Journal of Economic Literature* 30 (1992): 675–740.

Dewees, Donald. "Instrument Choice in Environmental Policy." *Economic Inquiry* 21 (1983): 53–71.

Pezzey, John. "The Symmetry between Controlling Pollution by Price and Controlling it by Quantity." *The Canadian Journal of Economics* 25 (1992): 983–991.

Watson, W. D. and R. Ridker. "Losses from Effluent Taxes and Quotas Under Uncertainty." *Journal of Environmental Economics and Management* 11 (1984): 310–326.

Weitzman, Martin L. "Prices versus Quantities." *The Review of Economic Studies* 41 (1974): 477–491.

ENVIRONMENTAL
POLICY IN CANADA

In the preceeding chapters, we have seen how and why markets fail to achieve social efficiency when externalities associated with the natural environment exist. Chapter 10 looked at the extent to which decentralized policies can work out socially efficient solutions to environmental problems. Chapters 11 through 14 examined the economics of specific government policies designed to achieve social efficiency. In this section, Chapter 15 provides an introduction to some key characteristics of Canadian environmental policy—the constitution and important features of the parliamentary system of government in a federal system. In the four chapters that follow, we examine specific environmental policies that have been used by governments in Canada to deal with environmental problems—water and air pollution, toxic substances and solid wastes. The analytical tools developed in the previous sections are used to evaluate these policies. Canadian policies are contrasted with those in the United States to get a perspective on where we stand relative to other industrialized countries.

15

ENVIRONMENTAL POLICY IN CANADA: AN OVERVIEW

Some general observations about environmental policy in Canada are presented in this chapter to help focus the discussion in the chapters that follow. It is much more difficult in practice to achieve social efficiency than our economic models suggest. There are many reasons for this. In this chapter, we examine several of these factors. Others are addressed in subsequent chapters.

GENERAL POINTS ABOUT CANADIAN ENVIRONMENTAL POLICY

1 Incentive-based policies have rarely been used. There are a few examples of specific taxes and tax write-offs for investment in pollution abatement equipment, but all levels of government rely primarily on command-and-control polices.

2 There has been a reluctance to impose specific standards. Most regulation has been in the form of guidelines that suggest a range of pollution targets. Both ambient and emission guidelines and standards are used. In recent years, there has been a tendency to use technology-based standards to achieve environmental targets.

3 Environmental legislation in Canada has been based on a cooperative model of negotiation between the government regulator and the polluting party. There are many examples of contracts between specific polluters and government.

4 Negotiation and moral suasion have been used to achieve compliance with environmental policies. Recently, there has been increasing use of the legal system.

5 Environmental legislation in Canada has been primarily enabling rather than mandatory. What this means is that officials are authorized to develop regulations. They rarely have the obligation to act. This is quite different from the United States where regulations passed by Congress generally require implementation of specific policies.

6 Jurisdiction over the environment is not always well defined. Conflict among the levels of government and inaction can arise as a result.

7 Lack of information on pollution sources and environmental science has been a handicap to policymakers in the past. While information flows are improving, there remains a reliance on polluting sources for much information.

8 The amount of public scrutiny of government decision making in setting environmental policy has been minimal until the 1990s. Most policy decisions during the 1960s to 1980s were made without public input.

Economic efficiency is only one possible objective of environmental policy. Other motivations include political factors such as vote seeking on the part of politicians, responses to pressure groups, ideological beliefs, and so on. Governments are also constrained by constitutional powers, legislative constraints, and the presence or absence of particular institutions. While it is beyond the scope of this text to address all these factors, in this chapter we examine briefly the legal powers of Canadian governments and political constraints imposed by our parliamentary system. This information helps explain why certain policies have been enacted and others not, and why some of the points raised above arise. This chapter looks first at the role of the constitution and conflicts that arise from the division of powers over environmental policy. We then look at some of the features of the parliamentary system that inhibit the development of environmental policies. The chapter concludes with an overview of Canada's major federal environmental legislation, the Green Plan.

CONSTITUTIONAL POWERS OVER THE ENVIRONMENT[1]

Section 91 of the Constitution Act (1967) establishes federal powers over ocean and inland fisheries (section 91[12]), navigation and shipping (section 91[10]), and over federal lands and waters. Each of these powers has been used by the federal government to enact legislation that has some element of pollution control. For example, under its fisheries powers, one of the strongest and most utilized environmental regulations, the Fisheries Act, was promulgated. The federal government enacted under its navigation and shipping powers, the Navigable Waters Protection Act, and the Arctic Waters Pollution Prevention Act. The Northern Inland Waters Act comes from its powers over federal lands and waters. The federal government also has powers to enter into international agreements and has done so on many occasions in matters that involve environmental concerns. Examples of international agreements regarding the environment are the Montreal Protocol, Basil Convention on toxic wastes, and many others. Finally, there is a provision that is increasingly serving as a basis for federal government regulation regarding the environment. This is the preamble to section 91 of the Constitution Act that gives the federal government the power to enact legisla-

---

[1] This section of the chapter is based largely on the readings in Robert Boardman, ed., *Canadian Environmental Policy: Ecosystems, Politics, and Process* (Toronto: Oxford University Press, 1992). We will deal with local government powers in Chapter 19.

tion in the interests of "peace, order, and good government." The widely used acronym for this is POGG. The major piece of federal legislation relating to toxic materials, the Canadian Environmental Protection Act, was based on POGG power. The federal government also has the power over interprovincial and international trade, and the power to levy taxes and to make expenditures. Its taxation powers have rarely been used to justify environmental policy.

The key to understanding Canadian environmental policy is to recognize that it is with the provincial governments that most regulatory powers applicable to the environment lie. Most of these powers come from section 92 of the Constitution. Under section 92, the provinces have power over local works (section 92[10]), property and civil rights within the provinces (section 92[13]), matters of a local or private nature (section 92[16]), and authority over provincially owned lands and resources (section 92[5]; 109). This last authority is extremely significant, as it gives the provinces the right to regulate their natural resource industries. These industries can involve significant environmental trade-offs in their development and use of the natural environment. As well, most publicly held land in the country is in the provinces, so whatever policies provincial governments enact will tend to have larger environmental impacts than federal policies related to lands. A 1982 amendment to the Constitution Act (section 92A) strengthened the provincial powers over its natural resources. Under 92A, each province has exclusive jurisdiction over the development, conservation, and management of its nonrenewable resources, which have been interpreted to include energy resources, forests, and hydroelectric power facilities. Each province has established an environmental regulatory regime that contains provisions for procedures and statutes controlling various sources of pollution and addressing ambient environmental quality.

Having looked at these constitutional powers, it is tempting to generalize by saying that with the exception of fisheries, the federal government is responsible for federal lands and international aspects of the environment, while the provinces are responsible for intraprovincial environmental quality. Unfortunately, the situation is not this simple. The regulation of specific environmental problems in Canada tends to be done at *both* the federal and provincial levels. The Constitution does not explicitly prohibit this. For example, provincial water-pollution regulations overlap with federal fisheries regulations. Both have regulations for accidental spills into waterways as well as air-pollution regulations. Pesticide distribution, use, and sale is regulated by the federal government. Provinces have their own pesticide regulations. This leads to the possibility that certain pesticides may be legal to produce in Canada, but not able to be sold in a particular province.

Another indeterminate area of constitutional powers concerns *inter*provincial pollution flows. In principle, one would expect that the federal government would have regulatory power when pollution flows across provincial boundaries. This would be analogous to its international and interprovincial powers in other matters. However, federal extrajurisdictional powers can be in conflict with section 92A powers of the provinces. Interprovincial environmental problems remain an area of potential federal-provincial tension. Several examples are presented later in this chapter.

Finally, there are even unresolved issues with the federal government's treaty-making powers. While the federal government clearly has the power to negotiate an international treaty, implementing a treaty would be a provincial matter if section 92A and other provincial powers apply. There is the possibility that provinces may refuse to cooperate with the federal government. Individual provinces may also want to make separate arrangements about the conditions of implementation with the federal government, or even act independently for political or other reasons. It is not necessarily a bad thing to have different arrangements with each province because environmental quality and pollution problems differ widely across the country. But, it can lead to unequal and unjust burdens in different provinces, or even thwart the federal government's efforts. If each province enacts its own legislation, this also raises the compliance costs of dealing with a myriad of regulations. Suppose, for example, the federal government signs an international treaty to reduce carbon emissions and imposes a tax on the carbon content of fuels. In principle, this incentive-based policy could meet the obligations of the treaty. But Alberta and some other provinces may not want to impose costs on its energy industry that the carbon tax would entail. Will the federal government force some unliked policy on Alberta? Will it make arrangements with Alberta to soften the burden on its economy? Or, will it simply spread the burden of meeting its treaty obligations among the remaining provinces? In each case, federal-provincial tensions arise. Many provinces remain wary of federal regulation. It is difficult to see how these sorts of problems can be avoided in our type of federal system.

The third set of players in Canadian environmental regulations are the courts. With respect to the Constitution, their role is to establish principles for interpreting the powers of each level of government through litigation dealing with these powers.[2]

The types of rulings the courts must make include determining if only one level of government has the exclusive power (under section 91 or 92) to enact particular legislation. If, for example, the subject matter of a law does not come within section 92 powers, a provincial law is said to be *ultra vires*, which means beyond its power. The other type of ruling concerns cases where both levels of government have laws pertaining to the environment. This is allowed as long as the laws are not in direct conflict. The court's job is to determine whether or not the laws conflict. The term used to describe the situation where both levels of government have laws over the same thing is "concurrency." If the laws are in conflict, the federal law has precedence over the provincial law. This is called the doctrine of "paramouncy." The legal system is driven by cases. Even though there is the potential for conflict between the levels of government, a suit must be launched to generate a legal interpretation of the powers of each government. Very few legal decisions regarding environmental legislation have been rendered. The one exception is in the management of fisheries. However, it is expected that more challenges may emerge as environmental legislation in Canada moves from the level of suggested guidelines to specific standards

---

[2] We have already discussed in Chapter 10 the role of the legal system in environmental issues that involve property rights and liability laws, i.e., actions taken by private individuals or companies. We won't discuss these issues further in this chapter.

and/or incentive-based policies. One potential area of conflict is the Canadian Environmental Protection Act (CEPA) mentioned above.

Many aspects of the constitutional powers over the environment remain unclear. The delegation of the powers between the federal and provincial governments can be ambiguous and has in the past contributed to conflict in the development and implementation of environmental policy. Let's look at some of these problems in more detail.

Constitutional Powers in Conflict

In this section, we highlight two types of problems that have arisen in environmental policy that stem from our Constitution and federal system. These are:

1 Lack of clarity and overlap of jurisdictional responsibilities.
2 Conflicting objectives between the federal and provincial governments.

Lack of Clarity and Overlap of Jurisdictional Responsibilities   As noted above, the Constitution does not clearly spell out distinct jurisdictional responsibilities for each level of government. Their responsibilities can overlap, causing the potential for uncertainty as to which level of government has the authority to regulate for specific environmental problems and objectives. The overlap may be sustainable with both levels of government concurrently regulating some sector of the economy. We will see many examples of this in the chapters on specific pollution problems. If concurrent regulations are consistent in that they have identical objectives and use similar policy instruments, conflict is less likely. For example, if the province of Nova Scotia and the federal government both require a permit for industries to dump wastes into a waterway and the allowed amount of wastes is identical, conflict and confusion over the concurrent policies are unlikely. However, if the province issues a permit and the federal government prohibits dumping, obvious problems arise. There are examples of conflicts such as this that have gone to the courts for adjudication as to which level of government has the authority to regulate.

As we discussed, the federal government has constitutional powers over water in the area of fisheries, navigation and shipping. The provinces have the power to manage and conserve natural resources. When we are then dealing with natural resource management that affects federal water powers, who can regulate? This is an evolving area for the courts. Their legal decisions are basically shaping the conditions for one level of government to have supremacy. Several examples illustrate this point. The Supreme Court of Canada ruled many years ago (in 1929) in *The Water Power Reference* that the federal government may restrict or even prohibit provincial water developments to preserve federal navigation and fisheries rights. Many years later, in 1980, the Supreme Court upheld a federal prosecution against a company that spilled oil into an inlet in British Columbia on the grounds that the federal government had the right to protect fisheries. The company responsible for the spill had argued that the province had the sole authority to regulate pollution under its property and civil rights power. Other cases have put conditions on federal powers over water. In a case involving the discharge of logging debris into any waterway, the

Supreme Court ruled that a section of the federal Fisheries Act was beyond the power of the federal government because logging regulation was a provincial power under the property and civil rights clause. This ruling might at first be seen as contradictory to the previous ruling. However, the court noted that the federal government had failed to meet certain conditions in this regulation. First it did not show that timber debris had a specific deleterious effect on fish. Second, the regulation was too broad. It had no specific limitation on the amount of debris. By implication then, any amount of debris was deleterious to fish. Clearly, this is unlikely to be the case. Third, the regulation covered all waterways, some of which may not have a fishery. Finally, all aspects of logging operations were covered by the regulation. This is where the conflict with provincial powers emerged. Other cases have reinforced aspects of this case, for example, overturning convictions under the Fisheries Act when the federal government failed to show that discharges went into rivers frequented by fish. So while the courts have interpreted federal water rights as allowing the federal government to impose pollution regulation, certain conditions have to be satisfied to prevent infringement of provincial constitutional rights.

The Supreme Court also appears to have given the federal government the power to regulate pollution when the pollution flows outside provincial boundaries even if the federal government has not shown harm to fish or navigation and shipping. The federal right to regulate transboundary pollution was based on the Peace, Order and Good Government power in the Constitution. Ironically, the 1988 case that generated this decision again involved the dumping of logging debris, this time into an ocean cove in British Columbia.[3] The federal policy in question was the Ocean Dumping Control Act that required a permit for discharge into the ocean. The defendant in the case did not have a permit. The key aspect of the ruling was the court's decision that the federal government has regulatory power under POGG to enact regulations when there is "national concern" about pollution. The court ruled that marine pollution was a matter of national concern because marine waters are an indivisible resource, whereas fresh waters are not. If a province failed to control pollution into the marine environment, other provinces or countries could be affected. Thus, the federal government had the authority to enact environmental regulations.[4]

Unfortunately, decisions such as the two cases described above have not completely clarified federal versus provincial powers. The term "national concern" was defined somewhat vaguely. The court noted that a matter of national concern must have a "singleness, distinctiveness, and indivisibility that clearly distinguishes it from provincial concern."[5] To help decide whether a pollution problem met these criteria, the court added that measurement should be made of any extraprovincial effects that occurred when a province failed to regulate pollution within its own boundaries.

---

[3] The case is *Regina vs Crown Zellerbach Canada*.

[4] The federal government also has power to intervene with regulation when there is seen to be a national environmental emergency.

[5] Supreme Court of Canada, 1 S.C.R. 401 (1988), as cited in David VanderZwaag and Linda Duncan, "Canada and Environmental Protection" in Robert Boardman, *Canadian Environmental Policy: Ecosystems, Politics, and Process* (Toronto: Oxford University Press, 1992).

There is certainly room for disagreement as to what is a national concern. As well, the court acknowledged in this case that provinces may be granted concurrent jurisdiction to protect local interests. Ambiguity and the scope for conflict remain. We may see legal challenges of current and pending legislation once specific regulations are approved. CEPA is an example of a federal regulation that uses the concept of national concern as a basis for regulation. The pollutants of national concern in this case are toxic substances. Few specific regulations have been brought in under CEPA. At present, the federal and provincial governments appear to be cooperating in the setting of regulatory instruments. However, if the federal government attempts to impose national standards or regulations that conflict with provincial interests, it is more likely that the provinces may challenge the federal government's right to do so.

An Example of Government Conflict: Environmental Impact Assessment
Federal and provincial interests are most likely to conflict when environmental protection and sustainable development objectives of the federal government confront the provincial right to manage and develop their natural resources. The provinces are concerned that the federal government will effectively control the economic development of their natural resources through environmental policy. The arena where these conflicts have emerged most vividly is over federal environmental impact assessment of provincial development projects. In Chapter 6, we talked generally about environmental impact analysis, and noted briefly the differences between Canadian and U.S. approaches. In this section, we review and discuss Canadian experience with federal EIA in some detail. The objective is to point out some of the difficulties with EIA in a federal system. As we noted before, many provinces also have environmental impact assessment legislation.[6]

The federal government initiated the environmental assessment process with the creation of a board called the Federal Environmental Assessment and Review Office (FEARO) in the early 1970s. FEARO was not given any explicit regulatory powers through legislation. Rather, its activities were spelled out with federal cabinet administrative directives in 1973 and 1977 called the Environmental Assessment and Review Process (EARP). The purpose of EARP was to ensure that all federal departments and agencies took environmental matters into account when planning and implementing projects. In 1984, a Guidelines Order was published in the *Canada Gazette*. The 1984 Guidelines Order is the date the courts have recognized as the date that federal regulations regarding environmental assessment began. Because the 1973 and 1977 guidelines were internal documents and not published in the *Canada Gazette*, they did not have any force of law.

The 1984 guidelines specified that a broad set of development projects could be subject to federal review. These included projects located on federal lands, those involving a federal financial commitment, those having an environmental impact on an area of federal responsibility, and projects initiated by a department of the federal

---

[6] These provinces include British Columbia, Alberta, Ontario, Manitoba, Newfoundland, Nova Scotia, and Saskatchewan.

government. Very few reviews were ever done under EARP. In the almost 20 years that FEARO has been in existence, a total of 35 panel reviews were undertaken. By contrast, under the National Environmental Policy Act in the United States, the act requiring the environmental impact statements for federal legislation and actions that significantly affect the environment, over 400 assessments are done per year.[7] While the U.S. economy is quite a bit larger than Canada's, this wide disparity in EIA suggests the policies of the two countries are quite different.

EARP had procedural difficulties in addition to the small number of assessments done. Responsibility for the initiation of a review resided with the federal department responsible for the project. No external oversight existed. Even when external pressure was brought by the public or other departments to have a hearing, the initiating department still had the right to refuse to carry one out. When public hearings did occur, their recommendations were advisory, not binding in any way. The federal government was clearly not engaging in aggressive environmental impact assessment. They generally deferred to the processes existing in the provinces. In this way, the federal government avoided any potential conflict between the environment and development of natural resources in the provinces. It was up to the provinces to make these trade-offs. Many critics of the policy feared that the provincial decisions tended to favour development without sufficient concern for adverse impacts on the environment.

In the 1980s, several river development projects in the Prairie provinces triggered a chain of events that pitted the federal government against the provinces and led to a change in federal environmental assessment policy. Exhibit 15-1 summarizes the interaction between the federal and provincial governments, the courts and the public in one of these projects: the Rafferty and Alameda dams.

A similar process occurred in the case of the Oldman River Dam in Alberta. In both cases, the court decisions did not ultimately affect the construction of these dams because the provinces ignored them. However the stage was set for a different relationship between the federal and provincial governments over environmental assessments. Provinces responded to the court rulings in different ways. Some decided to cooperate more closely with the federal government to ensure that these sorts of problems would not arise. British Columbia said they would submit all their public projects to federal environment officials before any project commenced. Alberta and the federal government established a federal-provincial review panel to assess a controversial pulp and paper project. However, the federal and Quebec governments became involved in a not-so-cordial dispute about the James Bay II–Great Whale project. Provinces were concerned that a new era of federal involvement in provincial affairs could arise (reminiscent of federal energy policy in the 1970s and early 1980s).

The courts subsequently ruled that the federal government did not have an obligation to undertake an environmental assessment in all provincial development projects

---

[7] George Hoberg, "Comparing Canadian Performance in Environmental Policy," in Robert Boardman, *Canadian Environmental Policy: Ecosystems, Politics, and Process* (Toronto: Oxford University Press, 1992), 259.

EXHIBIT 15-1

THE RAFFERTY AND ALAMEDA DAMS

Rafferty and Alameda Dams 'Hands off, leave environmental reviews to the province' aptly describes the federal government's initial attitude towards the Saskatchewan government's proposal to construct two dams on the Souris River rising in Saskatchewan and flowing into North Dakota and then northward to Manitoba. On 4 August 1987, the Souris Basin Development Authority, a provincial Crown corporation, submitted an environmental impact statement to the Minister of the Environment for Saskatchewan. Following public hearings as part of a provincial environmental review, the Minister of the Environment granted approval on 15 February 1988 for the project to proceed. Even though the environmental impact assessment prepared in Saskatchewan did not assess impacts on North Dakota or Manitoba, on 17 June 1988 the federal Minister of the Environment issued a licence pursuant to the International River Improvements Act, allowing the project to go ahead....

In a lawsuit brought by the Canadian Wildlife Federation the federal government's regulatory reluctance became clear.... The federal Crown argued that since the project was a provincially funded initiative, located on provincial lands and subjected to a formal review by the provincial Department of the Environment and Public Safety, a federal environmental assessment review would be an unwarranted duplication.... The Court, however, declared the Order to be binding on the federal government, quashed the license, and ordered compliance with the Guidelines Order.... Regardless of this clear judicial opinion of the binding nature of the EARP Order, the federal assessment as ordered was conducted without formal public hearings and the licence was reissued. A public hearing panel was appointed only following further litigation by the Canadian Wildlife Federation to obtain a court order for its appointment....

Political dealings and wranglings followed, further shaking the credibility of the environmental assessment process. In late January, 1990, the federal Minister of the Environment and Saskatchewan reached an agreement for construction to be postponed. Ottawa would pay Saskatchewan $1 million a month for up to ten months to cover the extra costs of halting the project during a formal review.... On 4 October 1990, the environmental review panel, established in response to the court ruling in December, wrote to the Minister of the Environment that the panel's terms of reference were being violated by Saskatchewan's initiation of channelization downstream of the dam and proposed tree-clearing above. On 11 October Premier Devine instructed the Souris Basin Development Authority to begin or resume construction on all aspects of the Rafferty-Alameda project. On 12 October the panel tendered its resignation....

Federal respect for the environmental assessment process was also called into question by the Government of Canada's signing an agreement with the United States in October, 1990, assuring the US of dam completions. In return for approximately $41 million (US) the Government of Canada agreed to expeditiously provide the US with flood control storage fro the Rafferty and Alameda dams and pledged to ensure the dams would be designed to have a hundred-year project life... The Canadian Government was subsequently severely criticized for not itself referring the agreement for public process and hearings....

Source: David VanderZwaag and Linda Duncan, "Canada and Environmental Protection: Confident Political Faces, Uncertain Legal Hands," in Robert Boardman (ed.), *Canadian Environmental Policy: Ecosystems, Politics, and Process* (Oxford: Oxford University Press), 1992, 11–12.

---

with the potential for major environmental effects. Exhibit 15-2 illustrates the difference between a hydroelectric project in James Bay and the dams in Alberta and Saskatchewan. The Eastman project in James Bay had been approved by the federal government before the 1984 EARP guidelines existed. The court ruled that the 1984 guidelines could not be applied retroactively.

EXHIBIT 15-2

HYDRO PROJECT REVIEW FAULTED

OTTAWA LACKS POWER IN CASE, COURT RULES

Canadian Press

OTTAWA—The federal government has no power to do an environmental assessment of the $1.5-billion Eastmain hydro-electric project in northern Quebec, the Federal Court of Appeal has ruled.

In a 3–0 decision released Friday, the appeal court overturned a lower court ruling that ordered Ottawa to do a full impact study of the work, which is part of the James Bay hydro project.

James Bay Crees immediately said they would appeal the ruling to the Supreme Court of Canada.

They said the decision has broad implications because it runs counter to recent Supreme Court rulings that favored environmental assessments and expanded recognition of native rights.

"It's a devastating attack on aboriginal people and the environment," said Bill Namagoose, of the Grand Council of the Crees of Quebec.

"They've clearly given a licence to Hydro Quebec just to go in there and destroy the environment in northern Quebec."

Ottawa had already started organizing an environmental review of the project, which involves flooding 700 square kilometres of territory along the

Eastman River in the James Bay region. It is part of the original James Bay hydro project, rather than the $12.6-billion expansion known as the Great Whale project.

A federal environment department spokesperson said the ruling is being studied to determine its impact.

With the appeal court ruling, the Eastmain project will be subject to provincial, but not federal, environmental review.

The appeal court ruled Ottawa had no power to do a review because the Eastmain work is part of the James Bay project, which the federal government authorized in the 1975 James Bay and Northern Quebec Agreement.

Federal environmental review regulations cannot be retroactively applied to government decisions made before the regulations came into effect in 1984, the court said in a ruling written by Justice Robert Decary.

Source: The Canadian Press, November 21, 1992.

The federal government ultimately responded to these cases and other concerns about EARP by tabling new environmental impact legislation in 1990, the Canadian Environmental Assessment Act (CEAA). It was approved by Parliament in 1993. The federal government touted the act as ensuring that environmental assessment would occur. The act gives the federal government explicit powers to prohibit any construction or development activities on a project until an environmental assessment is complete. The Minister of the Environment has such authority and she or he can be backed up by court injunctions requested by the Attorney General of Canada if any contravention of the order occurs. These provisions would seem to strengthen the powers of the government compared to EARP. However, other features of the act seem to point to a weakening of federal powers. Perhaps the most significant and the one some feel was designed to appease the provinces, prohibits private actions from forcing the federal government to carry out an environmental assessment. If this provision had been part of EARP, the Rafferty-Alameda and Oldman Dam cases presumably could not have occurred. The act also removed the part of EARP that required assessment of the environmental impacts of a project that has an impact on an area of federal responsibility. This could mean that some provincial projects, even those affecting federal government authority over the environment could avoid federal scrutiny. For example, certain types of regulatory and licensing decisions that gave the federal government assessment authority under EARP for the dam projects in Saskatchewan and Alberta are excluded under the CEAA. Other features of EARP that limited federal involvement are retained such as restricting assessment to projects not policies or programs, and giving the Minister of Environment discretion in which projects to review. Public reviews still result only in nonbinding recommendations. There remains no external oversight. One is left with the impression that the federal government wants to defer to the provinces for most environmental assessment. Environmental impact assessment could be a cooperative process between the federal and provincial governments. It could also be used to promote development consistent with sustainability. Time will tell if this will occur.

ENVIRONMENTAL REGULATION IN A PARLIAMENTARY SYSTEM

Overview

Environmental policy in any country is greatly affected by its political system. In this section, we briefly note some of the implications for environmental policy of Canada's parliamentary democracy. The Canadian situation is also compared to the policy process in the United States. We make several simple points. First, under a parliamentary system with a majority government, the governing party has a lot of control over the legislative agenda. Our system of government is very good at getting legislation approved that is supported by the party in power. The converse is also true. In the past 10 years, we have seen environmental issues go from a very low priority for the federal party in power at the time to something they very much wanted to be seen as supporting. Environmental policies and, more importantly, action on these policies by the federal government, track quite well the level of environmental concern of the public and the party.

Second, there are few, if any, checks and balances in a parliamentary system. There is nothing equivalent to the two different branches of government in the United States, the executive branch and legislative branch, Congress. The U.S. Congress may have one or more of its houses controlled by the party which is not that of the president. Congress writes and passes laws that need not have the support of the executive branch. In the parliamentary system, this is generally impossible. The executive and legislative branches under a majority government are essentially one. If the federal government wants to drag its feet on dealing with environmental problems, it can. Public pressure plays a very important role, as it does in all democratic political systems. And, the government is ultimately accountable at election times. However, a five-year maximum term gives the party in power a lot of time to avoid confronting issues if this is what it wants to do.

The parliamentary system can also curtail public debate and scientific inquiry into environmental issues through its control of the federal bureaucracy. In Canada, the party in power basically controls the federal bureaucracy, and the federal bureaucracy controls research and legislative agendas. Environmental research is essential for undertaking regulation. For example, a standard cannot be imposed until there is evidence on what the level of emissions or ambient quality should be. Until quite recently, scientific and economic environmental research was not a high priority of the federal government. An example is the budget cuts of the early Mulroney years that threatened the monitoring of toxic chemicals in waterfowl. There is no other body independent of the federal government that can initiate large and potentially expensive studies. Academic research exists, but it too is largely dependent on grants from governments, especially in science and to do empirical economic research. By contrast, there are many examples of research on environmental issues done for the U.S. Congress that influence policy. In our federal system, the one check we have is the provinces. They can have different priorities and public pressures than the federal government. For example, Ontario typically led the country in environmental initiatives from the 1960s to 1980s.

Third, with the legislative and executive branches combined, environmental legislation takes on quite a different character in Canada than it does in the United States. The process for setting standards and designing regulations is said to be "far more informal, discretionary and closed than that in the United States."[8] This is true for the provinces as well. Federal environmental regulations are typically prepared by Environment Canada. The ministry has quite a bit of discretion in the scope and formulation of the laws and regulations it proposes to Cabinet. This is quite different from the situation in the U.S., where typically Congress initiates a bill that *requires* their environmental agency, the Environmental Protection Agency (EPA) to develop regulations within specified time periods, impose those regulations, report back to Congress on progress, and sometimes even to achieve specific targets such as zero discharge by specific dates. In Canada, because Environment Canada designs the legislation without conditions imposed by another political body, it is much less likely to propose a law that binds it to specific timetables, procedures, and so on. In practice, Canadian environmental laws are much more vague than their U.S. counterparts. They authorize or permit Environment Canada to do something, but do not compel it to act. Once a regulation is designed by Environment Canada, its path into application is much less arduous than typically is the case in the United States. In Canada, the only procedural requirement for imposing federal regulations is that they be published in the *Canada Gazette*. This is what was done with the EARP policies discussed above. Committees of Parliament may review the regulations "gazetted," but typically don't do so until after the regulation is adopted. Environment Canada consults with affected parties, other ministries, and the provinces prior to the adoption of the regulation. In the past, environmental groups were left out of this consultation

---

[8] Don Dewees, *Reducing the Burden of Environmental Regulation* (Kingston: School of Policy Studies, Queen's University, Government and Competitiveness Discussion Paper, 1992), 22.

process, but that has changed in recent years. There are now regular meetings of what are called "stakeholder's" groups that include public- and private-sector representatives as well as those from nongovernmental organizations (NGOs). They discuss not only regulation but all aspects of environmental policy. In the U.S., the whole system is much more litigious. Federal agencies must publish a notice of proposed regulation in the *Federal Register*, allow interested parties to comment on it, then publish reasons for the final regulation. The regulations must be supported by what's called "substantial evidence." The courts are the judges of what is substantial. There are many legal challenges to regulations in the United States, and very few in Canada. It is important to note that despite these significant differences in policy-making between the two countries, the U.S. is not more successful than Canada in reducing pollutants or achieving higher levels of environmental quality. In the U.S., battles within Congress or between the legislative and executive branches and the large amount of litigation that occurs can impede effective implementation of policies. Our often more cooperative process of regulation-setting might lead to higher compliance.

A Sketch of the Regulatory Activities of Environment Canada

To understand the regulatory process at the federal level in Canada more fully, we provide a brief history of Environment Canada, Canada's federal environment ministry.[9] Environment Canada (EC) was created in 1971 to bring together a number of different federal agencies that had environmental responsibilities. New responsibilities were also intended for the agency, notably environmental protection through the creation of the Environmental Protection Service, and coordination of federal efforts at preserving environmental quality and/or controlling pollution. There were high hopes at the beginning of the 1970s that Environment Canada would be a world leader in protecting the environment. A number of factors combined to prevent that realization from the time of its creation until the end of the 1980s.

First, Environment Canada had a number of bureaucratic difficulties. From the period 1971 to 1986, it had 10 different ministers and many reorganizations. At one point, it was under the jurisdiction of the federal fisheries department. It has not been a high profile ministry. Perhaps some of this was intentional policy on the part of the federal Cabinet; to have in place the institution for environmental policy, but not let it do very much. Evidence for this is in some of Environment Canada's powers and its political influence relative to other federal ministries. For example, EC was limited to duties, powers and functions not by law assigned to any other department, branch or agency of the federal government. This meant that if Agriculture Canada had regulations about water use (that might have significant environmental impacts),

---

[9] This section is based on material in M. Paul Brown, "Target or Participant? The Hatching of Environmental Industry Policy" in Robert Boardman, *Canadian Environmental Policy: Ecosystems, Politics, and Process* (Toronto: Oxford University Press, 1992).

EC couldn't also intervene. Secondly, a number of its initiatives were stopped by budget cuts. EC had designed a program to deal with environmental aspects of federal operations on Indian reserves. This was terminated in the mid 1970s by budget reductions, and not reinstated until the federal Green Plan in 1990. Further evidence of EC's weak regulatory role comes from a study of the federal bureaucracy done at the end of the Trudeau government. The study identified 82 pieces of federal legislation that had a bearing on the environment. Of these, EC was responsible for 13. The Department of Indian and Northern Affairs had more. Environment Canada was typically thwarted in its efforts because its responsibilities overlapped with other federal agencies, and because these agencies had greater political and statutory powers.

Environment Canada was also adversely affected by the federal budgetary process. The allocation of the federal budget among its ministries and agencies is done by placing each agency into a particular "envelope" based on its principal tasks. Environment was in the "social development" envelope that included health and welfare, a major recipient of federal funds (some 35 percent of total federal spending in the 1970s to 1980s). Social development also included statutory transfers to the provinces and to individuals. By the time these two activities received their budgets, there was not much left for Environment Canada. The other significant aspect of placing environment into social development was that it separated it from economic agencies and more importantly, treated the environment as a social not an economic issue. When social policies started to be hit hard in the federal budgets of the 1980s, EC sank with them to some extent. This separation of economic policy from environmental policy has had a bearing on the type of policies enacted as well. As we'll see in later chapters, there has been virtually *no use of economic incentives* for environmental improvement at the federal level.

Not all the early activities of Environment Canada were dismal. The early to mid 1970s saw the delivery of a number of environmental policies, which we examine in the next three chapters. EC had an agreement with the Department of Fisheries and Oceans to allow it to administer the section of the federal Fisheries Act that dealt with pollution of fish habitats. Similar agreements with Transport Canada existed for the shipping of hazardous wastes, and with Agriculture Canada for pesticide regulation. But many areas of regulation were essentially left to other agencies. We must not forget as well the powers of the provincial governments over environmental policy. Overall, the period from the mid-1970s to late 1980s is one of missed opportunity to act for the federal government.

By the mid-1980s, public opinion about the environment began to force some changes in federal policy. Public opinion polls started consistently putting environmental concerns at the top of people's lists. Some recognized that environmental protection did not necessarily mean losing one's job. The publication of the Brundtland Commission's *Our Common Future* in 1986 focussed attention on the concept of "sustainable development." The Mulroney government found this concept appealing (at least as rhetoric) and moved to create a stronger environmental ministry. The Canadian Council of Resource and Environment Ministers was created in 1986. Its task was to establish a National Task Force on Environment and the Economy. This council was later changed to the Canadian Council of Ministers of the Environment (CCME), a federal-provincial group that now meets regularly to discuss shared environmental concerns (the resource ministers have their own organization). Various "round tables" on the environment, economy and sustainable development arose at the provincial levels as well by the end of the 1980s.

New environmental legislation emerged in the late 1980s with the appoval of CEPA by Parliament in 1988. The Canadian Environmental Assessment Act also emerged in this period. In January of 1989, the Cabinet Committee on the Environment was created and chaired by the Minister of the Environment. The other departments on this committee included Health and Welfare, Energy, Mines and Resources, Department of Fisheries and Oceans, Transport Canada, Forestry Canada, Consumer and Corporate Affairs, Labour, Agriculture, Science and Technology, and the Atlantic Canada Opportunities Agency. Curiously absent (again) were the "economic" ministries—the Department of Finance and Investment Canada. The mandate of the Cabinet committee was to "manage the government's environmental agenda." The Minister of the Environment was also given a seat on the influential Priorities and Planning Committee and the Operations Committee. Whether these changes were merely window dressing or will result in substantive changes in the way the environment is integrated into federal decision making, remains to be seen. The biggest test of this may be in the success of the major policy initiative coming out of Environment Canada since its invigoration—the 1990 "Green Plan." We look now at the Green Plan in more detail, as it sets the agenda for federal environmental policy.

Canada's Green Plan

Canada's Green Plan is the national strategy and action plan for sustainable development launched by the federal government on December 11, 1990. The Green Plan was developed through extensive consultations with Canadians from all sectors—government, business, interest groups and the public. The Green Plan's goal is "to secure for current and future generations a safe and healthy environment, and a sound and prosperous economy." It represents a fundamental shift in the way the federal government views economic development and environmental protection: they are inextricably linked; both are critical to the health and well-being of Canadians. Thus, while continuing action on a wide range of specific issues from depletion of the ozone layer to protected spaces, the Green Plan also addresses the fundamentals of sustainable development—the need to incorporate sustainability into all aspects of decision-making at all levels of society. The Green Plan also establishes the basis for new and stronger partnerships for sustainable development. We all have a role to play in meeting our environmental challenges; we all have to work together to make sustainable development a reality.[10]

---

[10] Government of Canada, *Canada's Green Plan: The Second Year*, Catalogue No. En21-110/1993E (Ottawa: Minister of Supply and Services, 1993), 4. This report is the source for the information on the Green Plan discussed below.

This quotation provides a succinct description of the overall objectives of the Green Plan. Brought in initially with a financial commitment of $3 billion (since reduced), the Green Plan was heralded as a major breakthrough in environmental policy; a recognition that the economy and environment were linked. The Green Plan establishes seven goals that are:

1 Clean air, water and land;
2 Sustainable use of renewable resources;
3 Protection of our special spaces and species;
4 Preserving the integrity of our North;
5 Global environmental security;
6 Environmentally responsible decision making;
7 Minimizing the impact of environmental emergencies.

The Green Plan primarily sets an agenda; it does not prescribe many specific regulations. Although the plan has only been in effect for a short time, some progress on these goals has been made, which we note below. There remain many skeptics who feel that the plan delivers more rhetoric than substance. Exhibit 15-3 is an example of the concerns expressed about the Green Plan during its first year. Some of the Green Plan is simply a consolidation of activities that already existed. Other aspects do represent new initiatives. What it brings to environmental policy is a comprehensive envelope for addressing environmental concerns, not simply a listing of individual, and at times, unconnected policies. So while there is optimism about environmental policy in the country, many concerns remain. The economic recession of the 1990s has greatly curtailed government spending powers. Environment Canada was protected from some of the early budget cuts, but current reorganization of bureaucracies and restrictions on spending may adversely affect the government's ability to reach these targets.

We now examine the Green Plan's progress toward meeting its seven targets. We look at each target and note some of the specific policies that have emerged.

Goal 1: Clean Air, Water and Land   This goal is clearly the most traditional for environmental ministries, and includes a lot of initiatives, some old, others new. Most of the activities have not yet culminated in specific regulation and legislation. Some of the programs grouped under this goal are the following.

1 *The Action Plan on Health and the Environment.* This plan was released in 1991 and covers four broad areas: regulation and monitoring to identify and respond to health risks; protecting groups at significant risks, including aboriginal peoples living on particular diets, infants and children; facilitating community and individual action plans; and supporting international initiatives. Specific actions grouped under this heading include CEPA and its Priority Substances List (of toxic compounds); collaborative studies on health risks with the provinces in Windsor, Ontario, and the Fraser Valley in B.C.; ongoing activities in the St. Lawrence Health Effects program (risk from eating fish); working with Native Peoples to establish safe drinking water standards; work on databases of health hazards, reports on health and the environ-

EXHIBIT 15-3

MOSS GROWS ON GOVERNMENT'S GREEN PLAN

Anne McIlroy
Southam News

OTTAWA—With three months left in Year One of the Green Plan, the federal government has a slew of promises that remain unfulfilled.

Unveiled in December, the $3-billion ecological master plan got scathing reviews because it outlined more than 100 initiatives without saying how much each would cost or what they would entail.

Then environment minister Robert de Cotret said there would be a flood of detailed announcements—perhaps as many as one a week. That flood has been little more than a trickle, closer to one a month.

Over the past nine months, 10 announcements have been made. They account for $637 million of the $3 billion the government has pledged to spend, and included $25 million for pollution prevention in the Great Lakes, $275 million for water and sewage treatment on native reserves and $100 million for the Fraser River cleanup.

More than 30 promises have yet to be implemented. That works out to two a week if the government is to complete the list by the end of December—more if MPs take three weeks off for Thanksgiving and Christmas as planned.

"I don't think they can do it," says David Runnalls with the Institute for Research on Public Policy. Stephen Hazell, a lawyer with the Canadian Arctic Resources Committee, will also be surprised if the government makes it.

"We're rooting for them and all that but there is a serious morale problem in the department and it is hard to get things done with continuing staff cuts."

In the February budget, the government proclaimed the Green Plan would become longer and thinner, with the money spent over six years. So far,

the government has paid at least $6 million developing and selling the Green Plan, including millions on outside consultants who provided communications advice.

Opposition critics charge that the Green Plan is little more than a slush fund, claiming that the money will be spent in Conservative ridings to help win the next election.

Environment Minister Jean Charest's press secretary didn't return phone calls last week and a departmental spokesperson said she couldn't comment.

Among the initiatives that are still promised for 1991:

- A comprehensive Code of Environmental Stewardship that will cover all areas of federal operations.
- A health and environment action plan with the detailed measures needed to identify and address human health problems associated with pollution.
- A new Drinking Water Safety Act.
- Improved regulations to prohibit the ocean disposal of industrial wastes.
- A discussion paper on economic instruments that could be used to achieve environmental objectives.
- To start a comprehensive review of the environmental implications of existing statutes, policies, programs and regulations.
- Issue the first annual report on the state of Canada's climate.

Source: Vancouver Sun, September 16, 1991.

ment; and guidelines for ground water management. Note that with the exception of CEPA, which was passed before the Green Plan, most of the activities involve studies and intentions to regulate.

2 *Native Health and Water.* This involves the establishment and improvement of water and sewage treatment services on reserves. The projects will be administered and implemented by the Native communities. Work on providing these services to all Natives is proceeding with a target of reducing backlogs of undone work by 50 percent by 1996–97.

3 *Fraser River Basin Action Plan.* This plan was also introduced in 1991 and attempts to promote sustainable development of the Fraser River Basin ecosystem through partnerships with all affected parties living and working in the river basin. The plan's objectives are to clean up past pollution problems and prevent new ones through existing legislation (the Fisheries Act and CEPA), enhance fisheries, protect wildfowl and their habitats, and ensure water quality objectives are set and maintained. Federal, provincial and local governments have since formed a Fraser Basin Management Board that is now working on a plan.

4 *Atlantic Coastal Action Program.* This is analogous to the Fraser River Plan except that it deals with ecosystems at 13 different sites in Atlantic Canada. These sites have been identified and multisector community-based programs have been initiated at 12 of the 13 sites.

5 *Great Lakes–St. Lawrence Pollution Prevention Plan.* This plan was introduced in 1991 and complements efforts under individual plans for the Great Lakes and St. Lawrence River that began in 1988. A Great Lakes Pollution Prevention Centre opened in Sarnia, Ontario, in 1992. It will ultimately become "arm's length" from governments and will promote pollution prevention initiatives through information, education, and outreach programs. There has also been some substantive regulatory work done. In May 1992, a memorandum of understanding was signed between Environment Canada, Ontario's Ministry of the Environment, and Ford, Chrysler, and General Motors to reduce toxic substances and other contaminants from their operations, and to verify these activities. A memorandum of understanding is a commonly used agreement between governments and the private sector to achieve a particular goal, in this case, reduction of emissions. This allows the government to achieve pollution targets without passing specific regulations. However, it may also thwart achieving these targets. If there is a memorandum of understanding, a company cannot be prosecuted for failure to comply if it has notified the government that it needs more time, for example, to install pollution abatement equipment or if adverse economic conditions prevent compliance. This has enabled some companies to delay compliance for fairly long periods of time. Other activities under this plan include the signing of a bilateral agreement with the U.S. to restore and protect Lake Superior and initiation of a consultation process with stakeholders over a pollution protection strategy for 10 socioeconomic sectors in the St. Lawrence basin.

6 *Control of Ocean Dumping.* This action plan, introduced in 1991, has the objective of improving regulations under CEPA to enhance surveillance of oceans and to reduce the presence of persistent plastics in oceans. Amendments to ocean dumping regulations were to be published in 1993. These amendments actually have a fee attached to application forms to discharge wastes. This fee creates the potential to introduce economic incentives. There are also plans to release a discussion paper on new environmental assessment procedures and standards for the marine environment.

7 *Toxic Substances.* This program has a number of initiatives. We will have more to say about these in Chapter 18. The goal is to step up efforts to reduce or eliminate toxic substances. The Priority Substances List was first introduced in 1989 (i.e., before the Green Plan) with 44 substances that were to be monitored and assessed for their environmental and health impacts. By March 1993, six assessments had been completed and reports were to be released for comment. If any of these substances were declared "toxic," consultations on control options would begin. The goal is to publish a revised list of substances in 1994 and new lists every three years thereafter. One hundred assessments are to be completed by the year 2000. These targets appear to be very optimistic. Other intiatives include the Pulp and Paper Regulatory Package (which we discuss in Chapter 18) which requires the industry to change its technologies to prevent the formation of dioxins and furans, to reduce organochlorine levels, and to strictly control other conventional pollutants. This came into effect in December 1992, but certain mills have been given an extension of the time to meet the emission standards.

8 *Smog.* The national smog program was introduced in 1991 to begin the process of negotiating agreements with the provinces on NOx-VOC emission targets. A NOx-VOC management plan is also under way. Progress toward these agreements has been greatest with B.C. and Ontario, but none have yet been signed. In 1992, the federal government and automobile industry agreed to establish more stringent exhaust emission controls for new passenger cars. These will be phased in for the 1994 and 1995 model years. Full compliance is expected by the 1996 model year. Economic incentives have been investigated. Studies on emissions trading for Ontario and British Columbia were completed in 1992.

9 *Waste Reduction and Management.* The Canadian Council of Ministers of the Environment is in the process of developing national action plans for solid and hazardous waste reduction. A Federal Waste Reduction Plan was released in 1991 that is to create the first national inventory of wastes. An Office of Waste Management has been established as part of this plan to promote the "four Rs"—reduce, reuse, recycle, and recover. A goal of 50 percent reduction in hazardous wastes (presumably from its 1990 level) by the year 2000 also exists. Work on how to achieve this goal is under way. A regulatory package on the export and import of hazardous wastes was published in December 1992. This will enable Canada to implement a United Nations convention on hazardous wastes (the Basil Convention, which Canada ratified in August of 1992). The regulations keep track of movements of hazardous wastes. The federal government is also looking at remediation of sites contaminated by toxic wastes, and released a report in 1992 about these sites. Site remediation is to occur at some 30 high-risk sites that have not been cleaned up or will not be cleaned up by the polluters of these sites.

10 *Low-Level Radioactive Waste.* The government initiated a program to store these wastes in 1988. While there is no specific Green Plan commitment to this program, it seems to fall under the Green Plan umbrella. Essentially what this program entails is attempting to find a place to store these wastes (currently in Port Hope, Ontario). The NIMBY (not-in-my-backyard) problem is severe in this situation.

We have covered the Green Plan activities in this area of clean air, water and land in some detail because they are key components of any environmental policy. They also represent most of the Green Plan's initiatives. As we noted above, the plan still is in the formative stages. For the other goals, this is even more the case.

Goal 2: Sustaining Our Renewable Resources   Sustainable development initiatives for forests, agriculture, and fisheries are under way in cooperation with the other federal and provincial ministries responsible for these natural resources. An improved regulatory program for pesticide registration was announced in 1992. Draft legislation is in the works.

Goal 3: Our Special Spaces and Species
1 *Protected Species*. The Green Plan established a target of setting aside 12 percent of the country as protected space. Protected spaces include national parks, marine parks, wildlife areas and migratory-bird sanctuaries. A number of new sites have since been created, as well as programs launched to better conserve existing sites (such as wetlands). *Canada's Green Plan: The Second Year* does not indicate what progress has been made toward this goal.
2 *Wildlife Strategy*. The National Wildlife Strategy was introduced in 1991 with the goal of protecting wildlife diversity, conserving wildlife habitat, and safeguarding healthy ecosystems. Funds for wildlife toxicology were renewed in 1992, research centres and networks are planned, and financial assistance for private efforts to protect endangered species has been given. A National Enforcement Strategy for migratory bird protection is being developed. Canada ratified the United Nations Convention on Biological Diversity in 1992, and a strategy for meeting this convention is being developed with the provincial and territorial governments.

Goal 4: Preserving the Integrity of Our North   This involves the development of an Arctic Environmental Strategy in partnership with the territorial governments, Native organizations, and other residents. The components of the strategy (which was introduced in 1991) are to call for action on contaminants, waste cleanup, water quality, and to integrate economic and environmental objectives. Research and data collection on all of these are under way. Assessment of waste cleanups was accomplished on more than 100 sites and cleanup activities are under way.

Goal 5: Global Environmental Security   We will have more to say about most of the activities related to this goal in Chapters 22 and 23. A number of important policies have been initiated in this area. These include:
1 *Federal-Provincial Greenhouse Gas Emission Agreements*. Action programs to limit greenhouse gases are to be announced separately by the federal, provincial, and territorial governments. The federal government plans to enter bilateral agreements with the provinces and territories to create a comprehensive inventory and reporting system for greenhouse gases.

2 *Global warming*. An Efficiency and Alternative Energy Program has been set up to improve energy efficiency throughout the country. The *Energy Efficiency Act* came into force on January 1, 1993, with regulations expected to follow. Energuide labelling for home appliances is being improved with new labels to be released. A new Energy Code for buildings is being developed. Other activities include more research on technologies and programs to enhance energy efficiency. One specific economic incentive was announced. The federal budget of February 1992 removed an excise tax on ethanol-methanol portions of blended fuels produced from grains and agricultural wastes. This tax encourages substitution of ethanol-methanol for fossil fuels that are more carbon dioxide and monoxide intensive. Economic incentives could play a major role in altering energy consumption.

3 *Tree Plan Canada*. This is a community-level tree planting program begun in 1992. The federal government's role is to encourage privately funded tree planting projects across the country. Many such projects have begun.

4 *Global Warming: Reducing Uncertainties*. A Global Warming Science Program was created to do research, monitor climate data, and disseminate information in cooperation with the provinces and scientific community. Efforts on all fronts are underway.

5 *Climate Change Convention*. Canada signed the U.N. Framework Convention on Climate Change in 1992 (at the United Nations Conference on the Environment in Rio de Janeiro, Brazil); 150 other countries also signed. Canada is encouraging other countries to ratify this convention so that specific actions can be undertaken.

6 *Ozone Depletion*. An acceleration of the phase-out of ozone-depleting substances agreed to in the Montreal Protocol of 1987 was announced by the CCME in 1992. Completion of the phase-out is to occur no later than December 31, 1995. Environmental Indicator Bulletins on stratospheric ozone depletion are now being produced annually by a division of Environment Canada, State of the Environment Reporting. We discuss these issues more fully in Chapter 22.

7 *Acid Rain*. Most of the activity surrounding Canada's acid rain problems—a transboundary pollutant between Canada and the U.S., occurred prior to the Green Plan. We discuss acid rain in detail in Chapter 17. The Green Plan extends acid rain research, monitoring, and control efforts from previous federal and provincial actions.

8 *Building International Partnerships*. The Green Plan's goals are to be integrated into Canada's foreign policy in the form of multilateral, bilateral, and commercial partnerships. Canada provides funding to international organizations such as the United Nations to meet our commitments under international agreements and to promote Canadian interests.

Goal 6: Environmentally Responsible Decision Making   This is a rather broad goal that attempts to promote the provision of timely, accurate, and accessible information to assist in environmental decision making. The government created a division of Environment Canada called State of the Environment Reporting (SOER). Its goal is to provide Canadians with credible and comprehensive environmental information that is linked with socioeconomic factors to help make informed choices on sustainable development concerns. A State of the Environment Report was released in April 1992.[11] The report provides a comprehensive assessment of the state of Canada's environmental and natural resources and our progress toward sustainable development goals. The document was seen as a very useful aid to decision makers in all sectors. The next State of the Environment Report will be released in 1996. SOER has also produced a number of environmental indicator bulletins on selected environmental problems such as ozone depletion, water quality, urban pollution, and others. The goal is to update these indicator bulletins annually. They are developing a national set of environmental indicators. As we discuss in Chapter 20, SOER also works with Statistics Canada to incorporate environmental factors into Canada's System of National Accounts. In addition to SOER, a number of other initiatives exist with community groups, universities, the United Nations, the Royal Society of Canada, and the private sector. We also see explicit mention of economic incentives in this section of the Green Plan. A program was established in 1991 to support applied research into the use of economic instruments. An Environment Canada discussion paper on economic instruments was released in 1992.[12] Further efforts on economic incentives are expected. Environment Canada has funded some university research and private-sector consultant's reports on economic instruments.

Goal 7: Minimizing the Impact of Environmental Emergencies

1 *Marine Environmental Emergencies Response Strategy.* This was introduced in 1991 and aims to protect Canada's oceans, coastline, and inland waters from oil and chemical spills. There are three components to the strategy: prevention of spills, emergency preparedness, and the introduction of legislation to encourage safety and ensure that polluters pay for environmental damages associated with spills. Many of the activities in this area include greater monitoring efforts, stricter standards for vessel construction, and research on oil spills. After July 1993, oil tankers are required to have double hulls or the equivalent when they are operating in Canadian waters. Amendments to the Canada Shipping Act have been proposed to impose tougher fines and sentences for pollution offenses. New safety regulations for shipping are to be implemented.

2 *Hazardous Spills Prevention and Response Program.* The goal of this program is to develop measures for spill prevention, emergency preparedness, public education, and contingency planning. Canada signed in 1992 an International Convention on the Transboundary Effects of Industrial Accidents. The objective here is for countries to cooperate with neighbouring states on transboundary accidents. Efforts to negotiate a bilateral agreement with the U.S. on inland pollution spills are under way.

3 *Prediction and Warning.* The goal here is to provide more effective and timely detection and warning of severe weather conditions, other natural hazards, and atmospheric pollution emergencies.

---

[11] This was the second State of the Environment Report. The first was done prior to the Green Plan.
[12] Government of Canada, *Economic Instruments for Environmental Protection*, Catalogue No. En21-119/1992E (Ottawa: Ministry of Supply and Services, 1992).

SUMMARY

In this chapter, we have examined the constitutional basis for environmental regulation by the federal and provincial governments. Each level of government has unique powers that can be applied to the environment. The federal government has the power to legislate over ocean and inland fisheries, navigation and shipping, over federal lands and waters, to negotiate international treaties, and national concerns under Peace, Order, and Good Government. The provinces have power over local works, property and civil rights within the provinces, matters of a local or private nature, and authority over provincially owned lands and resources. The last right gives each province exclusive jurisdiction over the development, conservation, and management of its nonrenewable resources. These powers do not necessarily mean that only one level of government will enact environmental regulations for a particular problem such as air or water pollution. There are many examples of concurrent regulation, which is allowed under the Constitution unless the laws are in direct conflict. If that is the case, the federal government is said to have supremacy and its laws prevail. Concurrent legislation can lead to overlap in regulation and the potential for confusion and high costs of compliance to polluters. In this federal system, there is also the possibility of conflict between the federal and provincial governments over the interpretation of their constitutional powers. A number of court cases have occurred which have helped to define the powers of each level of government with regard to the environment. Sometimes these strengthened the federal powers. Other decisions imposed restrictions on federal powers.

The regulatory process in Canada is highly dependent on the interests of the party in power under our parliamentary system. Because the legislative and executive branches of government are not separate when there is majority rule, the party in power controls the legislative policy agenda. Public pressure can influence policy, but there has been little public involvement in the policy process. The history of Environment Canada illustrates many of the difficulties of introducing environmental policies into a highly bureaucratic federal government. The federal Green Plan of 1990 is the first comprehensive policy statement of Environment Canada. It contains many ambitious goals to secure a sustainable environment and economy.

QUESTIONS FOR FURTHER DISCUSSION

1 Would you change any of the powers of the federal and/or provincial governments in our Constitution to facilitate the design and implementation of environmental policy?

2 Some people think that incentive-based environmental policies create more federal/provincial conflict than command-and-control policies. Why might this be the case?

3 Should environmental impact analysis be a federal or a provincial responsibility?

4 "Canadian environmental policy is constrained by its political system." Why is this the case and what can be done about it?

5 Think about the goals of Canada's Green Plan for clean air, water, and land and how you would design incentive-based policies to accomplish these goals.

6 The theme of sustainable development underlies the entire Green Plan. This is something to keep in mind as you are reading the chapters that follow. Evaluate whether or not our environmental policies contribute to this sustainability as you read.

SELECTED READINGS

Boardman, Robert. *Canadian Environmental Policy: Ecosystems, Politics, and Process.* Toronto: Oxford University Press, 1992.

Doern, G.B. *Shades of Green: Gauging Canada's Green Plan.* Toronto: C.D. Howe Institute, 1991.

Fenge, Terry, and L. Graham Smith. "Reforming the Environmental Assessment and Review Process." *Canadian Public Policy* 12 (1986).

Government of Canada. *Canada's Green Plan.* Ottawa: Supply and Services, 1990.

_____. *Canada's Green Plan: The Second Year.* Catalogue No. En21-110/1993E. Ottawa: Supply and Services, 1993.

Macdonald, Doug. *The Politics of Pollution.* Toronto: McClelland & Stewart, 1991.

Nemetz, Peter. "Federal Environmental Regulation in Canada," *Natural Resources Journal* 26 (1985): 578–590.

16

FEDERAL AND PROVINCIAL WATER POLLUTION-CONTROL POLICY

Water is biologically necessary for life but, beyond this, water resources play a vital and pervasive role in the health and welfare of a modern economy. Water for direct human consumption is a small but critical part of the domestic system, which also includes water used in food preparation, cleaning, and sewage disposal. Water is an essential element in many industrial and commercial production processes, again both as an input and as a medium of waste disposal. Large amounts of water are used by farmers for irrigation, especially in the Prairie provinces. And in recent decades water-based sports and recreation, both freshwater and saltwater, have become very popular.

The water resource system itself consists of a vast array of interconnected components, from the grandiose to the tiny. The surface-water system includes the huge main-stem rivers, the Great Lakes, other large lakes, James Bay, as well as the thousands of small neighbourhood streams and ponds. Add to these the innumerable person-made components, from the mill ponds of the first industrial era to the vast reservoirs and canals of today. Swamps and wetlands abound. And then there is the vast, but unseen, system of groundwater aquifers, typically exceeding surface waters in terms of sheer quantity of water. Saltwater resources are also of vital importance. Marshes and coastal lowlands are critical for fish and wildlife resources; beaches and scenic coasts are important recreational resources; coastal waters provide transportation and pleasure boating services; and saltwater fisheries are a major source of food.

Efforts to protect these water resources have gone on for a long time but with increasing vigour in the last few decades. In this chapter we will look at federal and provincial water pollution-control policies. Our objective is to review the main elements of these policies with the economic concepts we have developed in preceding chapters. While our primary focus is on Canada, we will look briefly at some recent policy innovations in the United States that seek to make use of economic incentives to achieve improvements in water quality.

TYPES OF WATER POLLUTANTS

One way to categorize waterborne pollutants is by their chemical and physical nature.[1]

• Organic wastes: degradable wastes such as domestic sewage, residuals from pulp mills, food-processing plants; chemicals such as pesticides, detergents, solvents, oil.
• Inorganic substances: chemicals such as toxic metals, salts, acids; plant nutrients such as nitrate and phosphorous compounds.
• Nonmaterial pollutants: radioactivity, heat.
• Infectious agents: bacteria, viruses.

Waterborne emissions include all the different types of discharges discussed in Chapter 2. *Point sources* include outfalls from industry and domestic wastewater treatment plants. *Nonpoint sources* include agricultural runoff of pesticides and fertilizers and the chemicals and oils that are flushed off urban streets by periodic rains. Many sources, especially point sources, have *continuous* emissions, related to the rate of operation of the industrial plant or the domestic sewer system. There are also many *episodic* emissions, such as accidental releases of toxic materials, oil-tanker accidents, or occasional planned releases of industrial pollutants.

In Chapter 2 we also spoke of cumulative and noncumulative pollutants. In water-pollution control it is more common to speak of *persistent* and *degradable* pollutants. Degradable waterborne pollutants undergo a variety of biological, chemical, and physical processes that change their characteristics after emission. Especially important are the oxygen-using chemical processes that rely on the oxygen contained in receiving waters to degrade the wastes.[2] The reason for focussing on oxygen requirements is that oxygen plays a critical role in water quality. High levels of dissolved oxygen (DO) are usually associated with high-quality water, water that will support high-quality recreational uses, and that can be used in domestic water supply systems.

Since DO is used up in the degradation process, one way of measuring the quantity of waste emitted is through "biochemical oxygen demand," or BOD, the amount of oxygen required to decompose the organic material under specified conditions of temperature and time.[3] A substantial proportion of the BOD load introduced into the water resources of the country comes from municipal waste treatment plants. Much

---

[1] G. Tyler Miller, Jr., *Resource Conservation and Management* (Belmont. Calif.: Wadsworth Publishing Company, 1990), 201.

[2] Degradable wastes also include a variety of infectious bacterial agents that can cause such diseases as typhoid, cholera, and dysentery. Waste heat is also a degradable pollutant; it comes mostly from large-scale industrial processes that use water for cooling purposes.

[3] For example, 10 pounds of BOD_{10} is a quantity of material requiring 10 pounds of oxygen in order to be completely converted to its constituent elements over a period of 10 days and at a temperature of 20°C.

of this consists of wastewater from treated domestic waste, which contains a variety of degradable organic compounds. Industrial sources also contribute large amounts of BOD, some stemming from the sanitary facilities within the plants, but more importantly from the great variety of water-using steps in the production processes, such as cleaning, product formation, waste removal, and product transport.

When a BOD load is put into a river or body of water, it produces a temporary reduction in the DO level of that water, as the oxygen is used up to degrade the waste. But over time, through natural aeration processes, the DO content of the water will normally recover. The DO "profile" would thus look like Figure 16-1 (where the discharge point is marked *x*). We could think of this as the average DO level at various distances downstream from the point at which a BOD load is introduced, or the DO level at various times after a BOD load has been introduced into a lake. This is called a DO "sag," and illustrates the degradation process by which the water body is assimilating the BOD load. The important thing to see is that the DO reduction is reversible. It is also noncumulative—if the BOD source were stopped, the DO sag would shortly disappear.

Early water pollution-control efforts were centred on conventional pollutants like BOD, suspended solids, etc., for which there are common water quality measures such as DO, turbidity, acidity, and coliform count. Attempts to reduce these pollutants was primarily through greater use of sewage treatment plants throughout the country and guidelines for discharges of these conventional pollutants into waterways. However, it became increasingly clear over the 1970s and 1980s that *toxic* pollutants had the potential to become a serious problem for the health of water ecosystems as well as of people making use of them. Toxics include heavy metals such as mercury, pesticides, polychlorinated biphenyls (PCBs), dioxins and other industrial chemicals. Toxicity is often a matter of concentration; substances that are toxic at high concentrations may not be at low concentrations. This implies that the diluting ability of water is a valuable quality in addition to its capacity to transform degradable substances.

FIGURE 16-1   Dissolved Oxygen Profile in Water after a BOD Load Has Been Introduced.

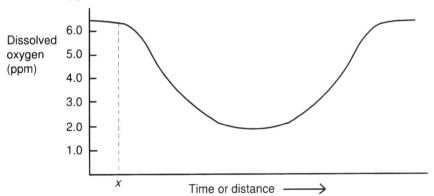

Persistent water pollutants are those that remain for a long period of time, either because they are nondegradable or because the rate of degradation is very slow. This category includes thousands of inorganic and organic chemicals of various descriptions, the wastes of a modern, chemical-based economy. Industrial wastes contain many such persistent pollutants. Wastes from mining operations can contain various metals as well as acid-mine drainage. Agriculture is the source of a variety of pesticides, fertilizers, and soil runoff. The concept of "persistent" does not mean permanent in a technical sense; many chemicals, oils, solvents, etc., break down, but over a long period of time. In the process they pose a persistent threat. Radioactive waste is physically degradable over very long periods, but measured in terms of a human scale it is essentially a persistent pollutant. Viruses are apparently also in this category.

FEDERAL AND PROVINCIAL POLICIES: HISTORICAL PERSPECTIVES

In this section, we examine some of the environmental policies developed at the provincial and federal level. Some themes from Chapter 15 are revisited; new ones added. The federal Fisheries Act of 1868 was Canada's first legislation with a potential environmental application. The clause that banned the discharge of substances deleterious to fish has been the basis of much federal water-pollution legislation beginning in the 1970s. However, the first environmental legislation was at the provincial, not the federal level of government, beginning in Ontario. Regulation of water pollution began in Ontario with the creation of the Ontario Water Resources Commission (OWRC) in 1956.[4] (See Table 16-1 on page 305 for further acronymns needed for this chapter.) Its mandate was to assist municipalities in financing the construction of their sewage and water treatment plants. The OWRC also had the authority to regulate direct discharges of liquid industrial and municipal wastes, that is, those not going through a sewage treatment process. By 1966, most of the other provinces had followed Ontario in setting up an independent commission to regulate water quality, although some used their provincial health departments for this task. OWRC's powers by the end of the 1960s included setting water quality objectives and working to meet these through the licensing of polluting industries, and by using administrative orders to enforce pollution abatement requirements. The first type of policy implemented was an emission or discharge standard imposed in the form of a license to emit a specific concentration of a compound. By the end of 1971, 497 industries were discharging wastes into Ontario waters under these permits.[5]

Enforcement of the standards was negotiated. Even when charges were laid, they were often withdrawn as soon as the polluter agreed to specified actions in reducing

---

[4] Pollution-control policy is rife with acronyms. In the text we use acronyms frequently, but have also occasionally included the complete phrase as a reminder.

[5] Doug Macdonald, *The Politics of Pollution* (Toronto: McClelland & Stewart, 1991), 138.

TABLE 16-1   GLOSSARY OF ACRONYMS USED IN THIS CHAPTER

BAT	Best available technology
BATEA	Best available technology economically achievable
BOD	Biochemical oxygen demand
BPT	Best practicable technology
DO	Dissolved oxygen
EPA	U.S. Environmental Protection Agency
MISA	Municipal-Industrial Strategy for Abatement (Ontario)
MOE	Ministry of Environment (provincial)
NPS	Nonpoint source of pollution
OWRC	Ontario Water Resources Commission
POGG	Peace, order and good government (federal power)
TBES	Technology-based effluent standards
TSS	Total suspended solids

their emissions. The OWRC estimated that on average 60 percent of those regulated met the effluent guidelines.

Alberta set water quality objectives for two rivers in its province, the Saskatchewan and North Saskatchewan in 1967. Under its Department of Health, objectives were set for 10 compounds including BOD, coliforms, odour, oil and grease, heavy metals, and other deleterious substances. They based their guidelines on U.S. standards. The Alberta government also set up a Department of the Environment in 1971 (just before a similar action by the federal government).

Quebec created an Environment Department in 1972, while the remaining seven provinces had environmental activities combined with those of other agencies. In most of the provinces, environment was combined with agencies responsible for natural resource management and development. There is thus the potential for conflict or cooperation between economic and environmental objectives.

The federal government did not play a major role in water-pollution regulation in the 1960s and 1970s. It had no quarrel with letting provinces do the regulation. Public pressures to act on the environment stimulated a modest amount of federal regulatory activity. One of the first federal actions was the establishment in 1968 of the *Guidelines for Canadian Drinking Water*. These guidelines covered 50 substances. No specific regulation of pollution discharges into waters used for drinking occurred. The Canada Water Act was approved in 1970. An important goal of this act was to set the foundation for amicable federal/provincial cooperation over environmental policy. This goal was realized, at least in part. The federal and provincial governments negotiated a number of agreements during the 1970s regarding the division of environmental responsibilities. The act had two parts. Part 1 provided funds to assist municipalities in the construction of sewage treatment plants, and to undertake research on water quality issues. Part 2 provided for Water Quality Management Authorities to set up regional water quality boards in cooperation with the provinces. These boards were to establish water quality management plans. They also had the power to implement these plans, for example, by charging fees, monitoring discharges, imposing standards, and so on. None of these agencies or plans were ever created. The boards appear to have been doomed by the terms of the act. From the federal point of view the problem was the act constrained their ability to respond to severe water-pollution cases. The federal government could act only when water quality had deteriorated to the point of "urgent national concern." Note here the use of the term national concern to elicit the federal government's POGG power. Even then, the federal government could intervene only with the permission of the provinces. From the provincial point of view, the act threatened their jurisdiction over environmental problems. The federal government would have the right to unilaterally address water quality issues for that region if, after signing an agreement with a province, the two governments could not agree on what standards to impose. The provinces thus felt more threatened if they agreed to joint management than if they did not.

Part 2 of the act was used to enact the Phosphorous Concentration Control Regulations. This has been a successful program. High phosphorous concentrations in the Great Lakes were a major concern in the 1960s and early 1970s. As we discussed in Chapter 6, phosphorous contributes to eutrophication of lakes. Lake Erie, by the late 1960s, was choked with algae. This eutrophication was destroying fish populations, commercial fishing operations, and generally creating a very odorous lake unappealing for any uses. Phosphorous control in Canada was coordinated with that in the United States. Canadian federal regulations imposed limits on phosphorous concentrations. Because it is shallow, Lake Erie's water quality improved dramatically in a relatively short amount of time. Subsidies for sewage treatment plants also helped improve water quality. Gradually over the 1970s and 1980s, the proportion of municipal wastewater that is untreated has fallen from over 50 percent to less than 20 percent. We discuss sewage treatment further in Chapter 19.

The 1971 amendments to the Fisheries Act were the other major federal initiative at this time. The Fisheries Act contains a clause that prohibits the dumping of "deleterious substances into waters frequented by fish." Regulation of the effluent from pulp mills is based on this clause. The act has been amended a number of times. The 1991 amendments increase the penalties for violations. There is now a maximum penalty upon indictment of up to $1 million for the first and each subsequent offense, and a maximum jail sentence of up to three years. Other specific standards brought in under the Fisheries Act include discharge standards for the following industries: chloralkali plants which release mercury as a by-product of their production of chlorine and caustic soda, processors of meat and poultry products, metal mining operations, petroleum refining, and as mentioned, pulp and paper mills. The Fisheries Act thus acts as a standard set at zero discharges of substances deemed deleterious. This standard is socially efficient if the marginal damage function lies above the marginal abatement cost function for all possible levels of emissions. Figure 16-2 illustrates a socially efficient standard set at zero emissions. While the MD and MAC functions

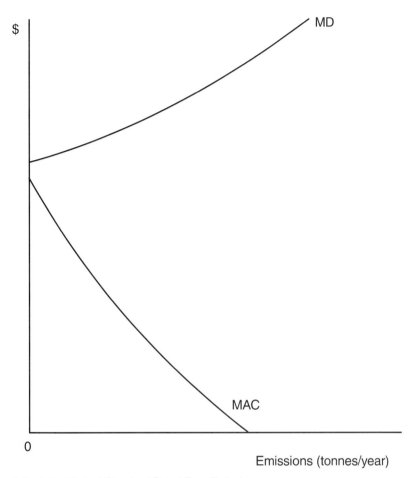

FIGURE 16-2 A Socially Efficient Standard Set at Zero Emissions.

could look this for a number of toxic compounds, it is likely for other pollutants that the MD intersects the MAC at a level of emissions greater than zero. Note that the MAC shown in Figure 16-2 has a positive intercept. This means that it is technically feasible to prevent the discharge of any emissions. This may not be the case in practice.

Enforcement of the Fisheries Act has not been consistent. The responsibilities for enforcement are shared by Environment Canada, the federal Department of Fisheries and Oceans, and provincial agencies. Not surprisingly, this has led to a rather awkward and at times, very inefficient process. A number of reports found that inconsistent application of the act has lead to small-scale polluters being charged, while large ones have not. There is evidence that Environment Canada's enforcement efforts were thwarted by other branches of the government. For example, after a major fish kill occurred in Nova Scotia near a large paper mill, the Department of Justice wouldn't act on Environment Canada's attempt to bring charges against the mill. Between 1978 and 1983, a total of 38 convictions were registered under the Fisheries Act. Of these, only 8 resulted in fines of over $5000.[6] Provincial enforcement of water pollution regulations was also far from zealous. In Ontario over the period 1972–1980, there were 69 convictions. This changed after the mid-1980s when Ontario created a branch of investigations and enforcement, headed by people with law enforcement experience. From April 1988 to March 1989, there were 169 convictions in Ontario.[7]

From the 1970s to 1990s, all the provinces introduced environmental legislation for water pollution and some form of administrative system to deal with environmental regulations. For example, in Ontario a detailed policy of water management was brought in. This was its 1978 *Water Management: Goals, Policies, Objectives and Implementation Procedures of the Ministry of the Environment*. The Ontario Water Resources Act followed in 1980. These policies set out 52 ambient water quality objectives covering all the conventional pollutants plus metals such as cadmium, copper, iron, lead, zinc, and selenium, pesticides, and a number of organic compounds produced by industry. The objectives have not led to explicit emission standards. They are guidelines for control. Most of the guidelines apply to all polluters, new and old sources. There are specific guidelines for the pulp and paper, petroleum refining and mineral industries. Some control orders for specific sites have been issued to achieve provincial ambient water quality objectives or to comply with federal guidelines. The guidelines were based primarily on U.S. experience. A similar process was initiated by the other provinces.

Since the 1970s, water pollution policies have basically stagnated. There were few specific standards and no innovative policies. Exhibit 16-1 illustrates a recent controversy over water quality regulation. We have already discussed the features of the Green Plan that deal with water quality, and must wait to see what comes of that. New pulp and paper regulations have been produced by the federal and several provincial governments. This process has been very contentious because the regulations, especially in British Columbia are quite stringent. For example, they require very large capital expenditures to build mills able to meet the zero discharge of dioxin-forming compounds. The pulp and paper case is discussed in more detail in Chapter 18. We turn now to a discussion of one further policy as it sets the stage for an examination of the economic issues that are involved in water-pollution management. This is Ontario's *Municipal and Industrial Strategy for Abatement*, known as MISA.

The Municipal and Industrial Strategy for Abatement (MISA)

In the mid-1980s, Ontario initiated a major program to deal with all types of water pollutants; conventional discharges, toxics, metals, and organic chemicals. The goal

---

[6] David VanderZwaag and Linda Duncan, "Canada and Environmental Protection: Confident Political Faces, Uncertain Legal Hands" in Robert Boardman, *Canadian Environment Policy: Ecosystems, Politics, and Process* (Toronto: Oxford University Press, 1992), 16.

[7] Doug Macdonald, *The Politics of Pollution* (Toronto: McClelland and Stewart, 1991), 146. Prior to 1988, enforcement was done by the same people responsible for regulations and negotiating emission reductions with polluters.

EXHIBIT 16-1

CLEAN UP GREAT LAKES, WATCHDOG DEMANDS

Chlorine cited in new report as key pollutant

Brian McAndrew
Environment Reporter

A Great Lakes watchdog agency is hanging tough in its demands that Canada and the United States rid the world's largest body of fresh water of the worst toxic chemicals.

The International Joint Commission repeated its demand for a greater effort at toxic pollution cleanup in a report released today in Ottawa and Washington. The report calls on the governments to pay especially close attention to ending the industrial use of chlorine.

The commission, a bilateral agency established by the two countries to monitor Great Lakes water issues, maintained its stand despite massive pressure from chlorine manufacturing and chlorine-using industries.

More than 300 industry representatives were among the record-setting 1,700 people attending the commission's biennial meeting last fall in Windsor.

The commission's report calls on the two countries to develop a common strategy within two years to stop the dumping of "persistent toxic substances" in the Great Lakes.

Eight of the 11 most persistent toxic substances —chemicals that remain for lengthy periods in the water—contain chlorine or chlorinated compounds including dioxins, PCBs (polychlorinated biplenyls), DDT, and hexachlorobenzene. The chemicals have been linked with health problems in fish, wildlife and humans including cancer, reproductive troubles, declining learning performance and increasing behavioral problems among children, the report says.

"Surely there can be no more compelling self-interest to force us to come to grips with this problem than the spectre of damaging the integrity of our own species and its entire environment," the report says.

A coalition of enviromental groups will send a letter today to federal Environment Minister Sheila Copps urging the government to adopt the commission's recommendations. The letter says there was an "urgent need for your government to develop a national strategy for sunsetting persistent toxic substances such as the use of chlorine and chlorine-based compounds in industrial processes." It adds: "To date, Canada has failed to develop an adequate regulatory response to the public health and ecological danger presented by persistent toxic substances."

The seven groups signing the letter were Greenpeace, Pollution Probe, Great Lakes United, Canadian Environmental Law Association, Sierra Club, Canadian Institute for Environmental Law and Policy and Quebec's Society to Vanquish Pollution.

Environment Canada, shortly before the federal election, took a stand against the commission's proposals.

Source: The Toronto Star, February 17, 1994, p. A17. Reprinted with permission—The Toronto Star Syndicate.

---

of MISA "is the virtual elimination of toxic contaminants in municipal and industrial discharges into waterways."[8] MISA is a very ambitious environmental policy. It is to cover over 300 industrial dischargers and around 400 sewage treatment plants. However, MISA also entails a significant departure from the type of regulation undertaken previously. The major change is in the regulatory instrument used. Emission

---

[8] Ontario Ministry of Environment, *Municipal-Industrial Strategy for Abatement (MISA)* (Toronto: Ministry of Environment), 7.

and ambient standards are to be supplanted by limits on maximum allowable concentrations per day that are based on the technology available for pollution control from each type of source. The term used in MISA is "best available technology economically achievable" (BATEA). The intent is to base the standard on technologies for pollution control that take into account economic conditions in each industry. It is unlikely that BATEA will be socially efficient when a standard is based on what is technically feasible, rather than marginal benefits and damages. It is also unclear in practice what role economic achievability plays in establishing the standard. Economic achievability could include the same factors that are measured by the MAC curve. It may also incorporate more politically motivated factors such as the number of jobs lost in the industry at different levels of environmental control. Without some link to MAC and MD, we cannot tell whether elimination of contaminants is socially efficient, even if it is technically feasible.

The key features of the strategy for industrial polluters are as follows.

1 Each plant in the nine industrial sectors covered monitors its effluent for 12 months to measure a wide range of contaminants.

2 Regulations will be developed based on the data gathered and estimates of BATEA.

3 Joint technical committees consisting of government (federal, provincial, and municipal) and industry representatives will be established to review the proposed regulations and make recommendations about specific standards that are BATEA.

4 All recommended standards will be reviewed by a MISA advisory committee that contains industry and government people plus representatives of public interest groups. The draft regulations will also be released to the public for comment.

5 Enforcement activities will be introduced to ensure that compliance occurs.

6 Over time, the standards will be tightened as technological changes permit greater control of emissions.

Progress on MISA has been slower than the Ontario government expected. Monitoring was to be completed by mid-1988. Some sectors were just beginning to monitor in 1990. No effluent regulations had been adopted by 1992. The process is also proving to be very expensive. Between 1986 and 1990, the MOE spent over $43 million on MISA.[9] The nine industrial sectors covered by MISA estimated $73 million was spent in the initial monitoring and that annual costs of the program could cost them around $50 million.

This type of regulation raises many important issues and questions. These include: definition of "virtual elimination"; establishment of rules for monitoring and interpreting the data obtained; determination of what chemicals should be monitored and regulated; how to verify industry data; how to define BATEA; how to translate BATEA into an effluent limit; what to do for water bodies of very different initial water quality; what constitutes compliance with the regulation; when the regulations

---

[9] The source for this and other figures noted in this paragraph is Burkhard Mausberg, *Still Going to BAT for Water Quality?* (Toronto: Canadian Institute for Environmental Law and Policy, 1990).

are to be reviewed and revised and what new compounds should be added to the initial list. It will take years before we know the outcome of this program. However, MISA is based on the federal water-pollution policy of the United States that began in the early 1970s. The U.S. has now had 20 years of experience with a technologically-based standard. We look briefly at their experience and in doing so will address many of the issues listed above.

THE U.S. EXPERIENCE WITH TECHNOLOGY-BASED WATER-POLLUTION POLICIES

The 1972 Water Pollution Control Act Amendments set a goal of zero discharges to be attained by 1985. Federal authorities were to set specific effluent standards for individual sources. There would be a system of federally issued discharge permits. Each source of waterborne emissions would require a permit specifying the time, place, and maximum quantity of emissions. To provide the basis for these permits, the EPA would promulgate *technology-based effluent standards* for all sources discharging wastes into the nation's waters. These are similar to MISA's BATEAs.

While these regulations are still in place in the U.S., considerable difficulties in implementation have occurred. It became clear soon after the 1972 law was enacted that the deadlines were impossibly short; they required the EPA to establish effluent limitations within one year of that act. But setting standards that would withstand court challenge took much longer than this. The 1977 Clean Water Act pushed the deadlines back a number of years and relaxed the basis for establishing standards for conventional, but not toxic, pollutants. The 1987 act also pushed back the target deadlines for the adoption of technology-based effluent standards and gave some recognition to the growing concern about nonpoint-source water pollution. We now want to look in more detail at the economics of technology-based effluent standards

Technology-Based Effluent Standards

As we noted in Chapter 11, a technology-based effluent standard (TBES) is an effluent standard set at the level of emissions that a source would produce if it were employing a particular type of abatement technology. Firms emitting waste materials or energy usually face a choice among different technologies and methods for reducing emissions. From among the possibilities each source must choose one particular package, which may involve, for example, particular types of equipment, raw materials, internal operating procedures, recycling machinery, treatment processes, or effluent removal techniques. Different packages of technologies and operating procedures lead to different costs as well as a different level of emissions. TBEs will be established in Ontario following the MISA procedures described above, that is, after industry self-monitoring and data collection.

It would require enormous effort to establish effluent standards for each and every individual source. Thus, in the U.S., the EPA sets standards for categories of polluting sources. Suppose, for example, we are concerned with vegetable-processing plants. This is a process that uses a large amount of water for cleaning and processing purposes; thus, the wastewater may contain large amounts of suspended solids and BOD. Table 16-2 shows hypothetical costs and emissions performance of five different technology options for plants in this industry. These are not costs and emissions for any particular plant; they are anticipated costs and emissions for a "representative" plant of each type. Each technological option refers to a particular collection of treatment equipment, operating procedures, fuels, etc., that the plants might adopt. The EPA or the Ministry of Environment in Ontario, after having developed these estimates must now choose a particular level of emissions for the standard.

Clearly, lower levels of emissions can be obtained with greater costs; in fact, emissions into water bodies could be reduced to zero at a very high cost. To pick one set of emission levels for the standard requires the use of some sort of criterion. The first criterion in the U.S. was meant to be an interim one, followed by a stricter standard. Initially, standards would be based on the "best practicable technology" (BPT) currently available to the firms. This would be followed in later years by standards based on best available technology (BAT).

The determination of BPT or BAT is open to interpretation, since the notions of "practicable" and "available" are not precise by any means. "Practicable" apparently refers to technology that is reasonably well known and readily available without excessive costs. Suppose EPA decides that technology C, with an estimated cost of $23.4 million per year, represents the best practicable technology for this type of processing industry. Then it would set emission standards at 1.05 kg/kkg for BOD and 1.02 kg/kkg for total suspended solids. All vegetable-processing plants would then be subject to this emission standard. Then it has to determine the best available technology. BAT would appear to imply a more stringent standard than BPT, since all technologies that are available are included whether or not they are practicable. But the U.S. rules also specify that BAT has to be "economically achievable," that is, BATEA. On this basis, technology E in Table 16-2 might be regarded as the BATEA for vegetable-processing plants. On the other hand, some (especially those in the industry) might argue that technology doesn't realistically exist, that it is

TABLE 16-2   ESTIMATED TOTAL COSTS AND EMISSIONS FROM VEGETABLE-PROCESSING PLANTS USING ALTERNATIVE EMISSION ABATEMENT TECHNOLOGY

	No control	Technological option				
		A	B	C	D	E
Emissions (kg/kkg of raw product processed)						
BOD*	5.8	3.6	2.2	1.05	.23	0.0
TSS†	10.2	5.7	2.5	1.02	.30	0.0
Total costs ($ mil/year)	0.0	8.0	14.4	23.40	36.50	78.8

*Biochemical oxygen demand.
†Total suspended solids.

too costly to be considered "available" in any economic sense, in which case D is the BATEA.

Setting technology-based effluent standards for an industry is obviously a time-consuming business. It requires large amounts of economic analysis and hinges on an agency judgment about what "available" and "practicable" mean when applied to pollution-control technology. In the U.S., it is also politically controversial, with industries ready to challenge in court when they feel the standards are too constraining. It is no wonder that the EPA made very slow progress in setting TBESs after the 1972 law was enacted. In the 1977 Clean Water Act the criteria for selecting emission standards were changed. After 1984 sources were to meet standards based on "best conventional technology" (BCT). The notion of "conventional" technology is different, and weaker, than the idea of "available" technology; it presumably allows more weight to be put on the costs of installing and operating the technology. In some cases the EPA has set BCT equal to BPT.

Technology-based effluent standards to control water pollution stem from the desire—widespread in the twentieth century—to find a technological fix for pollution problems. The original notion behind the 1972 act in the U.S. was that enlightened engineering studies by the EPA would identify preferred pollution-control technologies, and that since emission standards would be based on these technologies, there would be few practical obstacles in the way of their timely adoption by firms. In fact, the very ambiguity of words like "practicable," "conventional," and "economically achievable" means that a great amount of discretion and judgment must be used by people developing the standards. Over the years EPA has struggled valiantly to clarify the role of discretion and judgment in setting the standards. Industrial firms also have had views about what these words mean, which has led through the years to vast amounts of conflict and litigation. Will Ontario now have to go through this same process?

TBESs and Water Quality

The justification for emission standards is presumably that they will lead to better ambient levels of water quality. But, compliance with the technology-based effluent standards does not necessarily imply that certain levels of ambient water quality have been attained, because the standards are set by reference to available technology and not by reference to the ambient quality of receiving waters. In the U.S., over the decade 1978–1987, water quality improved, but not for all pollutants. While there was substantial improvement in phosphorous and considerable improvement in three others (suspended solids, oxygen deficit, and fecal coliform bacteria), there was substantial worsening of readings in dissolved solids and nitrogen.

Efficiency and Cost-Effectiveness of TBESs

For a policy to be efficient it must balance damages and control costs. The technology-based effluent standards are designed, however, to be applied in the U.S. on a national basis; in Ontario on a provincial basis. The same standards for, say, leather-processing plants, will be applied to all leather plants in the province, whether they are located on a river just upstream from a large urban area or on a river in some remote part of the province. It is unlikely that MDs are identical across the province or the country, and even more unlikely that MACs are identical for all pollution sources. A totally technology-based approach to pollution control thus excludes questions of economic efficiency from consideration.

Cost-effectiveness, as we have discussed many times so far, is a question of whether we are getting the maximum effect, in terms of reduced emissions, for the money spent. The simple key to this question is whether the policy is designed so that when sources are in compliance they will have the same marginal abatement costs. There is nothing in the logic of the TBES process that moves water-pollution sources in the direction of meeting the equimarginal condition. The procedure leads instead to the application of the same standards to all firms within each subcategory. For example, all vegetable-processing plants in the province are subject to the same effluent standards. These will be cost-effective only if all individual plants in each category have exactly the same marginal abatement costs. This is unlikely to be the case. There are thousands of individual industrial water-pollution sources, so some of the subcategories must contain very large numbers of sources. There can be little doubt that the sources in most subcategories are heterogeneous in terms of the production technology they are using, so we would expect them to be heterogeneous in terms of their marginal emission abatement costs. Thus, applying the same emission standards to each firm cannot be cost-effective.

The cost *in*effectiveness of equal treatment-type programs like TBESs has been examined directly in a series of river basin studies in the U.S. carried out by teams of economists and environmental scientists. These use large-scale models of individual river basins, incorporating the different estimated marginal abatement costs of various sources of pollution, together with the main hydrological features of the basins' water resources. They compare the costs of water pollution-control programs in which all sources were treated alike to those where sources are controlled in accordance with relative marginal abatement costs.

The best-known of these studies is the Delaware estuary study, and although the results are now over 25 years old, they nevertheless continue to illustrate very well the issues involved. The lower Delaware River runs through the heavily industrialized sections around Philadelphia and southwestern New Jersey, then opens out into the broad and shallow Delaware Bay. Wastewater emissions contribute to serious water quality problems in the estuary, both in the traditional measures of dissolved oxygen (DO) and in other types of organic and inorganic wastes. Investigators used a water quality model that predicted the effects of changing waste loads in any part of the estuary on water quality elsewhere in the estuary. Superimposed on this was a mathematical model showing the relationship of abatement costs at any of the large effluent outfalls on the estuary to emission levels at those outfalls. By operating these models together researchers could estimate the costs of meeting water quality goals by controlling emissions at each of the various sources.

The main results are summarized in Table 16-3. These show the costs of reducing BOD emissions from sources on the Delaware estuary so as to achieve given target levels of DO in the waters of the estuary. The exact levels of costs are not as important as the comparison of different types of policy approaches. The table shows two alternative target levels, one at 2 parts per million (ppm) and a higher one at 3–4 ppm of DO. To meet the lower DO target with a uniform treatment approach—that is, a policy of reducing emissions at each source in the same proportion—would have cost $5 million per year, while the costs of an equal treatment program attaining DO levels of 3–4 ppm would have cost an estimated $20 million annually. We note immediately that we have increasing marginal abatement costs: To reach the higher water quality levels requires substantially larger costs. But the same DO targets could be reached at much lower cost by reducing emissions in a cost-effective way. The costs of a program designed to meet the targets with a set of emission controls satisfying the equimarginal principle were $1.6 million for 2 ppm and $7.0 million for 3–4 ppm DO. Note that these costs are roughly *one-third* of the costs of the uniform treatment program or, to put it another way, the uniform treatment approach would cost about three times more than a fully cost-effective program.[10]

To impose a least-cost approach by specifying allowable emissions at each source would, of course, require an administering agency to have an enormous amount of knowledge about marginal abatement costs at each of the sources. Alternatively, authorities could achieve cost-effective emission reductions by imposing an effluent tax on emissions. Researchers investigated several approaches to emission taxes in the Delaware study. One was a single emissions tax (in this case a single tax on BOD emissions) levied on all sources throughout the estuary. The annual costs of this sin-

[10] Similar results have been obtained in other studies; for example, for the Willamette River: Kenneth D. Kerri, "An Economic Approach to Water Quality Control," *Journal of the Water Pollution Control Federation* 38(12) (December 1966): 1883–1897; the Miami River in Ohio: M. W. Anderson, "Regional Water Quality Management in the Miami Basin" (Ph.D. thesis, Carnegie Mellon University); and the Merrimack Valley of Massachusetts: Alvin S. Goodman and William Dobbins, "Mathematical Model for Water Pollution Control Studies," *Journal of the Sanitary Engineering Division, Proceedings ASCE* 92[SA6], (December 1966): 1–9.

TABLE 16-3   SUMMARY OF RESULTS OF THE DELAWARE ESTUARY WATER QUALITY CONTROL STUDY

DO objective	Uniform treatment program	Least-cost program	Effluent charge program	
			Single	Zoned
		Million Dollars per Year		
2 ppm	5.0	1.6	2.4	2.4
3-4 ppm	20.0	7.0	12.0	8.6

Source: Allen V. Kneese and Blair T. Bower, *Managing Water Quality: Economics, Technology, Institutions* (Baltimore, Md.: Johns Hopkins Press for Resources for the Future, 1968), 162.

gle tax approach were estimated at $2.4 million for the 2 ppm target and $12.0 million for the target of 3–4 ppm. Why aren't the costs of the single emissions tax as low as the least-cost program? The problem here is that sources are differently situated on the Delaware estuary, so the emissions of each source do not have the same impact on water quality targets.[11] The single emission tax would lead all sources to reduce emissions to the point where all marginal abatement costs were fully equalized, but a single tax is not able to account for the fact that some sources are more important than others in causing water quality problems. To respond fully to these locational factors an administering agency would have to charge a unique effluent tax to each source, taking into account both its marginal abatement costs *and* its location relative to other sources. Of course, this would be a totally unrealistic administrative burden, given the hundreds of different BOD sources on the Delaware estuary. There is a trade-off, in other words, between lower control costs on one side and administrative complexity on the other.

As we discussed in Chapter 12, one answer to this is to institute a zoned emission tax. Here the sources are grouped into zones, and all sources in the same zone are charged the same tax, while sources in different zones are taxed at different rates. In the Delaware estuary study, the zoned emission charge has the same annual costs as a single tax approach for the lower DO target, but is substantially less costly for the higher DO target of 3–4 ppm. What this shows in effect is that the larger the improvement we want to achieve in water quality the greater the difference it makes to have a cost-effective program. Applying this to our discussion of TBESs leads us to the following conclusion: This type of system, where all sources are required to meet the same standard and all are encouraged to adopt the same effluent control technology, may be reasonable in terms of cost if we are seeking only a modest improvement in water quality. But if we wish to have substantial improvements, the TBES approach will normally be a lot less cost-effective than better designed programs.

TBESs and Technological Improvements

We saw in Chapter 12 that emission standards lead to weaker incentives to innovate in pollution control than economic incentive-type policies. In the case of TBESs, incentives are made even weaker by linking the emission standards to particular control technologies. When polluters are faced with this type of technology-linked standard, compliance tends to become a matter of adopting the technology the authorities have used to set the standard. Since permanent emissions monitoring is quite costly, administering authorities can check compliance by making periodic inspections to ascertain whether sources are using approved emissions-control technology.

---

[11] Technically, they have different transfer coefficients with respect to the various points where water quality was measured.

In order to minimize the risk of being penalized for noncompliance, polluters have the incentive to adopt the particular technology that the government used to establish the standard. The result is that although the TBESs are nominally just emission standards, they end up tending to dictate the particular effluent control technologies chosen by firms. This substantially undermines any incentives to search for other, cheaper ways to meet the standards.

There is another dimension to these incentive effects. We mentioned above the importance, in designing a pollution-control program, of placing the control on the right element in the total input-production-emission process. This goes for any program, whether it uses standards or an incentive approach. The technology-based effluent standards in water-pollution control are normally expressed in terms of quantity of emissions per unit of raw material input used in production. But the real pollution-control issue is the total quantity of emissions during a given time period. The connection between these two factors can be shown as follows:

$$\text{Total emissions} = \text{Output} \times \frac{\text{Input}}{\text{Output}} \times \frac{\text{Emissions}}{\text{Input}}$$

"Output" refers to what the firm produces, "input" to the productive inputs used in the production process. TBE standards apply only to the last expression in this equation. Another way for a firm to reduce its total emissions, however, is to reduce raw product (input) per unit of output; for example, by installing more efficient production equipment or better operating procedures. Still another way of reducing total emissions is to reduce total output, the first term in the expression above. For example, electric power companies can reduce total emissions by promoting energy conservation among their customers. The basic problem, as we can see from the formula, is that the incentive has to be put on the right thing. In this case, expressing the standard in terms simply of total emissions would at least provide incentives to make improvements in all the factors of the equation, not just the last one.

TBESs and Enforcement

Effluent standards are enforced through a system of discharge permits in the U.S. This is also what is planned for Ontario. In order to discharge wastes into a river or body of water a firm must have a permit. The permit specifies the allowable emissions the source may make, and is subject to enforcement by state (or provincial) authorities. Given the enormous number of discharge points and the difficulties of monitoring emissions, enforcement becomes a critical program element. One response in the U.S. has been to distinguish between major and minor emitters, using criteria like quantity, toxicity, conventional pollution load, and impact of emissions. In this way more enforcement resources can be devoted to the major sources, which account for the largest proportion of total emissions.

Lacking high-quality techniques for monitoring emissions, control authorities are forced back on some other means of ensuring compliance. When emission standards are tied to certain technologies, enforcing authorities can try to confirm compliance simply by checking to see if firms have put in place the criterion technology.[12] The problem here is that there is a difference between *initial* compliance and *continued* compliance. The fact that a firm has installed certain pollution-control equipment does not necessarily mean that this equipment will be operated efficiently in the years to come. If operating costs are substantial and if nobody is effectively monitoring emissions, the incentive will be to save on operating costs and let emissions increase. It's very difficult to get good information on these matters, but several studies indicate that this is probably a substantial problem. In 1983 the General Accounting Office (GAO) reported that there was widespread failure of sources to meet the conditions of their discharge permits.[13] Of the 531 large wastewater treatment plants surveyed, the GAO found that 31 percent had significantly exceeded the permitted levels of discharge.[14] The actual level of noncompliance may be higher than this because the GAO results used self-reported data from polluters, who no doubt have an incentive to understate their violations. Studies by environmental economists have also concluded that noncompliance is a significant problem.[15] New and better ways of emissions monitoring are being developed. Pollution-control efforts will be considerably enhanced when they become inexpensive and accurate.

Technology-based effluent standards have an aura of concreteness and directness. What better way to get pollution reduced than simply to require polluters to adopt certain types of pollution-control technology? But this engineering-based approach is far less effective than it appears. We have seen how, from an economic standpoint, it is likely to be seriously cost *in*effective; for the money that is being devoted to pollution control under this system, substantially greater improvements in water quality could be achieved with other policy approaches. The apparent technological definiteness of the approach (BATEA, BPT, etc.) is, in fact, far less effective in practice. Countless engineering decisions are required in order to develop these standards. Not only is this very difficult for an administrating agency, but each of these decisions is a place where political interests can focus influence. The apparent concreteness of technology-based effluent standards is also substantially undermined by the monitoring and enforcement problem. What looks like a straightforward technological fix becomes, in reality, a policy with a great deal of hidden flexibility.

---

[12] The word "simply" in this sentence may be misleading. Nothing is simple in the world of pollution control. Polluters have challenged virtually every part of the U.S. federal pollution-control program, including enforcement procedures. Thus, over the years, legal doctrine has developed regarding such things as the specific procedures for visiting sources to check for compliance.

[13] U.S. General Accounting Office, *Wastewater Dischargers Are Not Complying with EPA Pollution Control Permits* (Washington, D.C., 1983).

[14] Technically, their discharge levels were at least 50 percent above permitted levels of at least one quality parameter (e.g., BOD emissions) for at least four consecutive months.

[15] Clifford S. Russell, Winston Harrington, and William J. Vaughan, *Enforcing Pollution Control Laws* (Washington, D.C.: Resources for the Future, 1986).

RECENT POLICY INNOVATIONS IN WATER-POLLUTION CONTROL IN THE U.S.

A national or provincial system of technology-based effluent standards has been criticized from its beginnings, especially by economists, for its relative inflexibility and cost ineffectiveness. The premise of these programs that all sources should be subject to the same standards is bound to make water quality improvements much more costly than they have to be. In recent years, the United States has adopted some innovative programs that try to build in flexibility and adaptability to local conditions. Most have been based on emission permit trading among sources on particular bodies of water. The localized scope of these new programs is appropriate. Most water-pollution problems are local in nature; they centre on the water quality problems of particular rivers or lakes that result from the waste-disposal activities of a geographically limited group of polluters. So it stands to reason that localized programs, on the level of a single river basin or lake or bay, can be designed to take advantage of local conditions in a way that a nationally mandated, technologically oriented policy cannot. As people gain more experience with these new types of programs, we will undoubtedly see a lot more of them, especially if the hoped-for cost savings materialize. Canadian policymakers can learn from the cases noted below.

Fox River (Wisconsin) Emission Permits

In 1981 the state of Wisconsin initiated a limited program of tradable BOD emission permits on the Fox River. This river is used for wastewater disposal by numerous groups, especially pulp mills and municipal treatment plants. Emissions to the river were already subject to control through the regular EPA technology-based effluent standards and emission permits. Allowable discharges vary over the year because variations in temperature and stream flow alter the river's BOD assimilative capacity. The goal of the trading program is to get the same level of water quality improvement at a substantially reduced cost.

The trading scheme is aimed solely at BOD discharges. Initial distribution of emission rights was based on historic levels of emissions by the major polluters. The rights were distributed free and they are valid only for five years; after that they must be reissued by the administering agency. Traded emission permits also have a maximum life of five years.[16] The designers of the plan hoped that by allowing permits to be traded, firms or municipalities with relatively high marginal BOD abatement costs would buy permits from those with low marginal abatement costs. Some researchers had estimated that this would result in substantial cost savings in cleaning up the river.[17]

---

[16] See Martin H. David and Erhard F. Joeres, "Is a Viable Implementation of TDP's Transferable?" in Erhard F. Joeres and Martin H. David (eds.), *Buying a Better Environment, Cost Effective Regulation Through Permit Trading* (Madison, Wisc.: University of Wisconsin Press, 1983), 233–248.

[17] William B. O'Neil, "The Regulation of Water Pollution Permit Trading Under Conditions of Varying Stream Flow and Temperature" in ibid., 219–232.

To date there have been relatively few trades of BOD emission permits among dischargers on the Fox River. A major difficulty with the Fox River program has been the relatively small number of potential participants. The pulp mills are few enough in number that they can potentially act as oligopolists instead of competitive bidders.[18] The municipalities are also relatively few in number, coupled with the fact that being publicly controlled wastewater treatment facilities, they don't necessarily have to make decisions on the basis of strict cost minimization objectives. Municipal dischargers could also qualify for public subsidies, further undermining the incentives to minimize costs.

Another important factor working against trades was that the original permit allocations were too liberal. If polluters are to have incentives to trade, the quantity of permits initially allocated must be substantially less than current, or easily achievable, emission levels. In the Fox River case the number of permits given out did not imply a significant reduction of BOD emissions beyond what could be obtained by standard and easily available control techniques. In addition, municipal dischargers had historically been able to get waivers of emission limitations if they found them too costly to achieve. Also working against permit trades have been the rules that administrative authorities have established to govern transactions. In principle, trades should be allowed whenever market participants wish to make them; it is their cost calculations and objectives that should be allowed to govern their market participation. In the Fox River case, however, firms are required to justify the need for permits, and trades that "simply" reduce operating costs are not allowed.[19] This substantially limits the number of potential traders. In addition, the fact that the administering agency must reissue permits every five years creates uncertainty over whether purchased permits will be counted in a firm's new base when reauthorization occurs. All these factors have worked to reduce the number of trades that might otherwise have occurred. We can perhaps look at the Fox River case as providing a good laboratory for learning about designing and administering transferable discharge permit programs.

Point-Source/Nonpoint-Source Emission Trading

Nonpoint-source (NPS) emissions account for a substantial amount of the water pollution in Canada and the United States. In the U.S., more than half of the BOD, suspended solids and in some regions phosphorous and nitrogen come from nonpoint sources. Similarly, nonpoint sources contribute large amounts of toxic pollutants to the country's water resources. Major nonpoint sources are agricultural runoff, urban

---

[18] An "oligopoly" is an industry containing just a few firms. The auto and airline industries are oligopolies. In this example, although there may be many pulp mills nationwide, the Fox River TDP market included a relatively small number of them.

[19] Robert W. Hahn, *A Primer on Environmental Policy Design* (Chur, Switzerland: Harwood Academic Publishers, 1989), 34.

street runoff, and activities related to land clearance and building construction. The EPA has initiated, in cooperation with the states, a National Estuaries Program to develop better pollution-control efforts in the major estuaries and bays of the coastal U.S. One result of water quality studies done under this program is to demonstrate how much of the remaining water quality problems in these areas is related to non-point-source pollutants. The fact that NPS emissions are diffuse and not concentrated into specific outfalls has made them very difficult to control. NPS pollutants are also normally very weather related, which makes the runoff patterns more difficult to monitor. Traditional approaches like emission standards are problematic because it is difficult to measure emissions accurately. Emissions taxes would run into the same problem. This means that the locus of control will normally have to be pushed back directly onto the practices and technologies that typically lead to substantial nonpoint-source runoff.

This suggests what we earlier called "design standards." These are standards that require certain techniques or practices to be used by sources whose activities lead to nonpoint-source emissions. Standards that rule out agricultural cultivation on steep, easily eroded land, standards specifying the design of urban storm sewers, and standards requiring home builders to take certain steps to control construction site runoff are types of design standards. The 1987 Water Quality Act, for example, establishes a program of federal subsidies for farmers to adopt "best management practices" (BMPs) to control agricultural pollution. While design standards may be necessary in the case of NPS emissions, we should keep in mind the difficulties inherent in their use. They require administrative determination of what particular technologies and techniques will be allowed in different circumstances. The danger is that they will undermine the incentives among polluters to find new and better ways of reducing NPS emissions.

Another method of controlling NPS emissions is to tax those activities or materials that lead to the emissions, rather than the emissions themselves, if possible. Taxes might be put on fertilizer used by farmers, for example, or on lawn chemicals used by suburban dwellers. The objective in this case is to induce a reduction in the use of materials that may ultimately end up in rivers, lakes, or groundwater aquifers.

Difficulties of control explain why NPS pollution has not been addressed as vigorously as point-source emissions, despite their importance. Early federal water quality laws directed state agencies to consider nonpoint-source pollution in their water quality programs, but did not require that specific steps be taken. The 1987 law gives it somewhat more prominence and authorizes federal money to subsidize local efforts to control NPS pollution. In fact, there is a major contrast between the national, uniform policy that has been followed to control point- source emissions and the policy for nonpoint-source pollution. In the latter case federal authorities have essentially thrown the problem into the hands of the states. Their reasoning is that "the application of uniform technological controls . . . is not appropriate for the management of non-point sources. Site specific decisions must consider the nature of the watershed, the nature of the water body, . . . and the range of management practices available to control non-point source pollution."[20] So in this case there is a recognition that a uniform national program is not appropriate.

There are many areas of the country where point sources and nonpoint sources exist in close proximity, essentially contributing to the same water quality problems. The equimarginal principle would say in this case that the control of point and non-point sources should be balanced so that the marginal emission reduction costs are the same in the two cases. Historically, however, point sources have been controlled much more vigorously than nonpoint sources. What this means is that there may be many regions of the country where shifting more of the burden onto nonpoint sources would be an effective way of lowering the costs of water quality improvements. One way of doing this is the trading of emission reduction credits between point sources and nonpoint sources, a program that is being tried in several parts of the country.

The best-developed trading program is that involving Dillon Reservoir in Colorado. The large impoundment is a major water source for Denver. In the early 1980s it was recognized that phosphorous loadings in the reservoir were causing water quality problems. While some of the phosphorous was of natural origin, about half was from human activity. Somewhat more than half of this was from nonpoint sources—urban runoff, golf courses, construction sites, septic tanks, etc. The rest was from four municipal waste treatment facilities. Researchers determined that point-source control by itself would not be sufficient to avoid water quality problems; even if municipal phosphorous emissions were reduced to zero, there would still be enough phosphorous to cause eutrophication in the reservoir.[21] Besides the very high direct abatement costs it would require, this would severely constrain future population growth in the county, which in the 1970s was the fastest growing county in the country.

The answer has been to initiate a phosphorous trading program between point and nonpoint sources of phosphorus. The program allocated baseline phosphorous loads to different polluters and then allowed phosphorous emission permits to be traded. The intention is to allow point sources, especially the municipal treatment plants, to buy phosphorous emission permits from nonpoint-source polluters whose marginal phosphorous abatement costs are lower. Those responsible for nonpoint-source emissions have a variety of means available to reduce their phosphorous loadings, such as sewering housing developments that are now using septic tanks, routing underground storm sewers through a series of storage tanks, and detention basins. Of course, the trading program requires that administrative authorities be able to monitor the nonpoint-source emissions at reasonable cost. To date (1991) several trades have been made, under the management of the Summit Water Quality Committee, composed of representatives from towns in the region as well as other public agencies. If the full trading potential is realized, it has been estimated that the trading program will allow the participants to solve the phosphorous problem in the reservoir at

[20] U.S. Environmental Protection Agency, *Non-Point Source Pollution in the U.S., Report to Congress* (Washington, D.C.: EPA, 1984), xiii–xiv.
[21] Lane Wyatt, *A Basinwide Approach to NPS Management* (Northwest Colorado Council of Governments, n.d.).

a cost savings of more than $1 million a year. Similar point/nonpoint-source trading programs have been initiated in the Cherry Creek reservoir of Colorado and the Tar-Pamlico basin of North Carolina. The idea is also being explored in other regions.[22]

SUMMARY

Canadian environmental regulation is a complex mix of federal and provincial policies that rely primarily on command-and-control instruments in the form of guidelines and objectives. There are few specific standards. Cooperation between the levels of government and between government and industry is sought. Public involvement has been minimal until recently. Most water-pollution policies are at the provincial level. The federal government uses its powers under the Fisheries Act to suggest ambient guidelines and impose some specific discharge standards, notably for pulp and paper mills. Ontario has turned to a technology-based effluent standard (TBES) in its MISA policy. Under MISA, emission standards based on the "best available technology economically achievable (BATEA) are to be designed in cooperation with industry. The Ontario policy is based on federal water-pollution regulations in the United States. We saw that these technology-based standards, though appealing as "technological fixes," have a number of drawbacks. They are likely to give far less pollution control for the money spent than alternative approaches, because they normally violate the equimarginal principle. They also have negative impacts through reducing the long-run incentives polluters might have to find better ways of controlling waterborne emissions.

We also examined some incentive-based policies used or proposed in the United States. The basic problem with emissions trading approaches is that they require relatively larger numbers of participants if competitive permit markets are to develop. But most water-pollution problems are local, or at most regional, in nature. Thus, the potential number of traders is likely to be too small for effective trading. This perhaps implies that more emphasis should be put on the use of emission taxes as a means of attaining cost-effective water pollution-control programs.

QUESTIONS FOR FURTHER DISCUSSION

1 Most technology-based effluent standards have focussed on "end-of-the-pipe" treatment technology. What is the reason for this, and what has been the likely impact?

2 Can you think of a way of designing a water pollution-control policy that combines a media-based approach with a technology-based approach?

3 Water pollution has been dealt with primarily by the provinces. Would you advocate a larger role for the federal government? If so, what types of policies would you recommend. If not, how do you think water quality objectives for our major interprovincial waterways such as the St. Lawrence River should be achieved?

[22] David Letson, "Point/Non-Point Source Pollution Reduction Trading: An Interpretive Survey," *Natural Resources Journal* 32(2) (Spring 1992): 219–232.

4 Controlling the residuals from the production of bleached tissue paper is about five times costlier than controlling the residuals from unbleached tissue paper. Analyze this difference with our standard pollution-control model. What does it suggest in terms of public policy toward water-pollution control?

5 To date, there have been few Canadian policies dealing with water-pollution problems stemming from nonpoint-source emissions. How might the different types of pollution-control policies be employed in the case of nonpoint-source emissions?

SELECTED READINGS

Dewees, D. "The Effect of Environmental Regulation: Mercury and Sulphur Dioxide" in M. L. Friedland (ed.). *Securing Compliance: Seven Case Studies*. Toronto: University of Toronto Press, 1990.

Feenberg, Daniel, and Edwin S. Mills. *Measuring the Benefits of Water Pollution Abatement*. New York, Academic Press, 1980.

Freeman, A. Myrick, III. "Water Pollution Policy," in Paul R. Portney (ed.). *Public Policies for Environmental Protection*. Washington, D.C.: Resources for the Future, 1990, 97–149.

Government of Ontario. *The Public Review of MISA White Paper and the Ministry of the Environment's Response to It*. Toronto: Ministry of the Environment, 1990.

Harrington, Winston, Alan J. Krupnick, and Henry M. Peskin. "Policies for Nonpoint-Source Water Pollution Control." *Journal of Soil and Water Conservation* 40(1) (January–February 1985): 27–32.

Kneese, Allen V., and Blair T. Bower. *Managing Water Quality: Economics, Technology, and Institutions*. Baltimore, Md.: Johns Hopkins Press for Resources for the Future, 1968.

Luken, Ralph A. *Efficiency in Environmental Legislation: A Benefit-Cost Analysis of Alternative Approaches*. Boston: Kluwer Academic Publishers, 1990.

Magat, Wesley A., Alan J. Krupnick, and Winston Harrington. *Rules in the Making: A Statistical Analysis of Regulatory Agency Behavior*. Washington, D.C.: Resources for the Future, 1986.

McGarity, Thomas O. "Media-Quality, Technology, and Cost-Benefit Balancing Strategies for Health and Environmental Regulation." *Law and Contemporary Problems* 46(3) (Summer 1983): 159–233.

Webb, Kernabham. *Pollution Control in Canada: The Regulatory Approach in the 1980s*. Ottawa: Law Reform Commission of Canada, 1988.

17

FEDERAL AND PROVINCIAL AIR POLLUTION-CONTROL POLICY

As it travels through space, planet earth takes along with itself an enveloping, but relatively thin, layer of gases, without which it would be a cinder. That layer of atmospheric gases provides two critical services: direct life support for living organisms on the earth's surface and control over the radiation exchange between earth and space. Both of these services can be upset by human activity.

For human beings and other living organisms the air is what water is for fish. Unless you wear a gas mask, there is no escaping what the air has to offer. The surface air (the "troposphere") normally contains about 78 percent nitrogen, 21 percent oxygen, small amounts of other gases, and varying amounts of water vapour. It may also have many, many other things put there through special acts of nature and the activities of human beings. The upper layers of the earth's atmosphere (the "stratosphere") contain only about 5 percent of the planet's air, but it has a critical role to play in making it habitable. Trace gases in the stratosphere, particularly ozone, filter out about 99 percent of incoming ultraviolet radiation, acting like a giant sun block, without which we would be exposed to damaging levels of radiation. Other trace gases in the stratosphere provide greenhouse services; they trap some of the infrared radiation that is reflected back from the earth's surface, warming it and making it more hospitable to living organisms. As we have recently found out, both of these vital phenomena can be disrupted by human activity.

Human disruptions of the atmosphere are not new; instances of local smoke pollution have occurred for centuries. But in the last few decades the potential severity of air-pollution problems has grown more acute, owing to the sheer scale of airborne residuals released and the exotic nature of some of the emitted substances. There are thousands of potential air pollutants—for example, oxides of carbon, nitrogen and sulfur, volatile organic compounds, suspended particulate matter, photochemical oxidants, radioactivity, heat, and noise. These pollutants cause a diverse set of damages. Perhaps the most important are human health impacts. Prolonged exposure to airborne substances can lead to lung cancer, bronchitis, emphysema, and asthma; accidental releases can have acute impacts. Air pollution also causes damage to plants, as in, for example, the destruction of forests and reduced crop yields stemming from acid deposition. Air pollution can lead to severe damage of exposed materials, such as the surface erosion and discolouration of stone and concrete work and the corrosion of metals. Stratospheric ozone depletion and enhanced global warming have significant implications for the sustainability of humans and the earth's ecosystem. Not all air pollution is outdoors; in fact, indoor air pollution is a critical problem in many homes, factories, mines, and farms.

Many airborne pollutants are emitted on a continuous basis. The sulfur dioxide (SO_2) emissions from coal-fired electric power plants, for example, are continuously produced as long as the plants are in operation. For individual motor vehicles, emissions start and stop with their operation, although for an entire urban area, auto and truck emissions vary continuously throughout the days and seasons according to the rhythms of economic activity. Episodic, especially accidental, emissions have been the cause of severe air-pollution incidents; for example, the Bhopal disaster in India and, to a much lesser degree, the numerous transportation accidents that occur in many countries. The links between emissions and ambient air quality levels can be complicated because of the complexities of meteorological phenomena. The best-known example of this is the creation of local weather conditions that trap air pollutants, sometimes for extended periods of time. The infamous "temperature inversions" over urban areas are well known.

What has been the impact on the environment of federal and provincial policy for air-pollution control? Table 17-1 shows Canadian emissions for major air pollutants in 1970, 1976, 1980, and 1985. These are divided into emissions from stationary sources and emissions from mobile sources. SO_2 emissions are largely from stationary sources; these emissions have fallen continuously over the time period, so that they were almost 50 percent lower in 1985 than in 1970. The pattern from mobile sources is more erratic. Nitrogen oxides from stationary sources fell from 1970 to 1980, but then rose again in 1985. Mobile sources of nitrogen oxides rose by over 60 percent from 1970 to 1980, then dropped somewhat in 1985. Stationary sources of particulates show a continual decline, while mobile sources rise. A big concern is carbon monoxide. Total emissions have not declined over the period. Volatile organic compounds are a concern, but we do not have enough data to track them over time. The biggest success story is in lead emissions, with a vast decrease in emissions from mobile sources. This is due to the virtual elimination of leaded gasoline as a result of government policies.

Figure 17-1 on page 328 illustrates trends in ambient air quality in Canada over the past 15 years in terms of how close they are to an air quality guideline. All except ozone meet or exceed the commonly used federal guideline for air quality. The other pollutants show declines, but at relatively modest rates. We can conclude that air quality has generally improved in Canada over the last 15 years relative to our current fed-

TABLE 17-1   STATIONARY AND MOBILE-SOURCE EMISSIONS OF AIR POLLUTANTS IN CANADA: 1970, 1976, 1980, 1985

	Annual Emissions (kilotonnes)			
	1970	1976	1980	1985
Sulfur dioxide				
Stationary	6,600	5,250	4,400	3,550
Mobile	100	150	200	150
Nitrogen oxide				
Stationary	975	800	675	700
Mobile	800	1,150	1,300	1,250
Particulates				
Stationary	2,025	1,800	1,800	1,575
Mobile	50	75	100	125
Carbon monoxide				
Stationary	2,100	2,300	2,650	3,600
Mobile	7,900	8,200	7,750	7,150
Lead*				
Stationary	NA	5.2	4.4	4.3
Mobile	NA	9.4	7.2	2.2
Hydrocarbons				
Stationary	900	1,025	1,035	1,375
Mobile	1,200	1,175	1,090	925

*Lead emission figures are for the years 1978, 1982, and 1987. No figures are available for volatile organic compounds until 1985. In that year, stationary sources emitted approximately 1,000 kilotonnes, mobile sources 750 kilotonnes.

Sources: Government of Canada, *State of the Environment* (Ottawa: Ministry of Supply and Services, 1991), 12–18, 14–8, 14–9, 14–10; Environment Canada, *Ground-Level Ozone in Canada*, A State of the Environment Fact Sheet, No. 92-1. Catalogue No. EN1-12/92-1-E (Ottawa: Ministry of Supply and Services: 1992).

eral guidelines, although there are a number of problem pollutants and locations in the country. No doubt this is related to the various air pollution-control programs we have put in place. Some questions arise. Have the sums of money the nation has put into air-pollution control bought as much improvement in air quality as they could have? Are the guidelines we have sufficient to protect health and environmental quality, especially in our urban areas? To answer this we look more closely at the policies themselves. Ideally, a benefit-cost study of policies would be in order. Unfortunately, we don't have sufficient data to do this.

FEDERAL AND PROVINCIAL AIR POLLUTION-CONTROL POLICIES: A BRIEF SKETCH

As with the case of water pollution, there was little federal concern or statutory activity in air-pollution matters prior to the late 1960s. Ontario again led the country with the first regulatory actions pertaining to air pollution. It formed a committee on air pollution in 1957 to investigate and recommend steps for the protection of Ontario's air quality. In their 1957 report to the Ontario legislature, municipal waste incineration and motor vehicle exhaust were identified as problem areas. The committee called for the creation of an air pollution-control commission with regulatory powers. This sort of commission was not created, but responsibility for air pollution was turned over to the Department of Public Health in 1957. In 1959, the Ontario Air Pollution Control Act (APCA) was enacted. As in chapter 16, a table (Table 17-2) provides a list of acronyms used in this chapter.

The APCA gave the municipalities the legislative authority to pass by-laws regulating air pollution. This presumably was because of the identification of municipal waste incineration as a major pollutant. It is however a curious choice for level of responsibility for a mobile source of pollution such as motor vehicles. The munici-

FIGURE 17-1   Trends in Canadian Air Quality, 1974–89.

The graph shows yearly average pollutant concentrations for all stations in the NAPS (National Air Pollution Surveillance) Network, as a percentage of the maximum acceptable level of the national ambient air quality objectives for each pollutant, with the exception of lead. Because no percentages have been established for lead, the annual averages have been indexed by setting the 1974 value at 100. For most pollutants the annual average recorded at the station is shown; however, peak eight-hour and one-hour averages for carbon monoxide and ozone, respectively, are better indicators of the effects of these pollutants.

Average pollutant concentrations in the atmosphere have generally fallen over the last 15 years, with a levelling off of some in recent years. All the pollutant indicators, save ozone, are well-within the acceptable level of the air quality objectives. Hot, dry weather in summer 1988 contributed in the high ozone levels recorded that year.

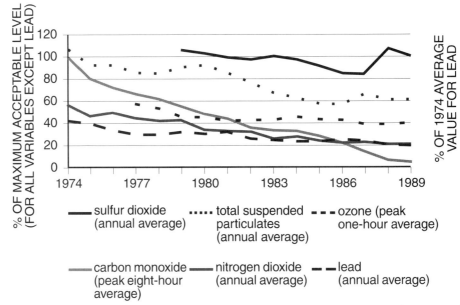

Source: T. Furmanczyk, Environment Canada, personal communication, as cited in Government of Canada, 1991, *The State of Canada's Environment.* 2–12.

TABLE 17-2 GLOSSARY OF ACRONYMS USED IN THIS CHAPTER

APCA	Air Pollution Control Act (Ontario)
CAA	Clean Air Act (Canada and United States)
CFC	Chlorofluorocarbon
CO_2	Carbon dioxide
ERC	Emission reduction credit
LAER	Lowest achievable emission rate
NAAQS	National ambient air quality standards (U.S.)
NAAQOS	National ambient air quality objectives (Canada)
NO_x	Nitrogen oxides
NSPS	New-source performance standards
NSR	New-source review
PSD	Prevention of serious deterioration
RACT	Reasonably available control technology
SO_2	Sulfur dioxide
TSP	Total suspended particulates
VOCs	Volatile organic compounds

palities did not have jurisdiction for long. In 1963, the provincial government declared it had control over all "new" sources of air pollution, that is, new enterprises of any sort. In 1967, the APCA was amended to transfer all regulatory power back to the province. By this time, the provincial regulators had begun to recognize that air-pollution problems "spill over" municipal boundaries. The first specific air-pollution standards were established at this time. Under APCA, maximum concentrations for 13 substances were established at the "point of impingement" for stationary sources of pollution. This is defined as the point where pollutants from a factory stack or other discharge point first encountered the ground, a building or other object. Point of impingement is therefore an ambient standard that is applied to all pollution sources. No source can release emissions that result in a concentration exceeding the standard at each point of impingement.

In 1972, these regulations became Regulation 308 of Ontario's Environmental Protection Act (passed in 1971). The number of substances regulated had grown to 20. By 1974, the list of regulated substances reached 100. The key difference between air-pollution regulations in Ontario and its water-pollution regulations is that the former apply to *any* source. Recall that water-pollution discharge guidelines have been in the form of negotiated licences between the government and specific polluters. Air-pollution regulation covers emissions from all sources. The allowable concentrations for each pollutant are set by a committee consisting of the MOE and Ontario Ministry of Labour. There was no public input into the decision making nor independent review of the recommendations from the committee. Since 1983, the province has been revising its regulations. It is moving from point of impingement standards based on scientific and health studies to BATEA standards, analogous to those planned under MISA. Draft regulations were released in 1990. We have already dealt at length with the problems of BATEA standards in Chapter 16.

As of 1992, Ontario, Newfoundland, and Manitoba are the only provinces that use point of impingement concentrations for their air quality regulations. Saskatchewan sets ambient standards that specify maximum concentration levels for pollutants such as particulates, oxidants, and nitrogen dioxide. If there are multiple sources of a pollutant, the aggregate discharge from all sources must not exceed the ambient standards. These standards are thus analogous to point-of-impingement regulations. British Columbia, and Nova Scotia have air quality objectives. Alberta, Quebec and New Brunswick have imposed regulations. These objectives and regulations are based primarily on federal objectives (discussed below). Task forces consisting of the federal and provincial governments and sometimes industry worked together to establish these policies. Alberta, for example, sets emission limits for visible emissions, particulates, lead from secondary smelters, and vinyl chloride. There are guidelines for the fertilizer industry, asphalt plants, and ammonia storage. The guidelines and standards are based on BPT—best practicable technology.

Federal regulation of air quality began in the early 1970s as did water-pollution regulation. The federal government has objectives (targets) for ambient air quality, and guidelines and some standards for specific air-pollution emissions. We focus first on ambient air quality policies. The Clean Air Act (CAA) was enacted in 1971. This act was repealed in 1988, when ambient air quality objectives became part of the Canadian Environmental Protection Act (CEPA). However, the features of the Clean Air Act remain as part of CEPA.

The Clean Air Act gave the federal government the authority to:

1 Conduct a national program of air-pollution surveillance;
2 Establish air quality objectives (i.e., targets);
3 Establish regulations including standards at the source; and
4 Establish guidelines which were recommended limits on pollutants.

Under the CAA, the federal government adopted national ambient air quality objectives (NAAQOs) for the "conventional" air pollutants—sulfur dioxide, nitrogen dioxide, carbon monoxide, ozone, and particulates. These objectives were developed by a Federal-Provincial Advisory Committee on Air Quality that began its work in the late 1960s. As noted above, the provinces can adopt these NAAQOs as objectives or enforceable standards if they wish. Until recently, most have chosen to adopt them as guidelines. The objectives are set at three levels. The "maximum desirable level" is the long-term goal for air quality. It provides a basis for preventing degradation of air quality in relatively unpolluted parts of the country. The next lower level of air quality is the "maximum acceptable level." It is seen as the level of air quality needed to provide adequate protection against adverse effects of air pollutants on human health and comfort, soil, water, vegetation, animals, materials, and visibility. This is the target against which Environment Canada typically reports ambient air quality, for example, as in Figure 17-1. Finally, there is the "maximum tolerable level" which represents the lowest boundary before immediate action is required to protect the health of the general population. As we saw in Figure 17-1, only ground-level ozone exceeds the maximum acceptable level. Table 17-3 lists the current NAAQOs for the five pollutants covered. These objectives are not enforceable against any polluter. They were designed to stimulate the provinces to enact their own regulations. Thus, we again find the federal government treating the provinces as the primary jurisdiction for pollution control in the period from the 1970s to 1980s. The federal-provincial committees apparently reviewed scientific information, as well as economic, social and technological factors in establishing these objectives. The deliberations of these committees were not public, so we cannot be sure how a particular air quality objective was chosen. The NAAQOs are the only ambient air quality policy at the federal level. There are no ambient standards for any pollutants, not even toxic chemicals. The article in Exhibit 17-1 illustrates some of the frustration felt by environmental groups about the lack of regulation.

New initiatives on ambient air quality are under way, but most are still in the planning phases. Under the Canadian Council of Ministers of the Environment (CCME), a national management plan for NO$_x$ and VOCs has been developed in consultation with industry, public interest groups and environmental groups. Its aim is to achieve an ambient air quality objective of 82 parts per billion (ppb) by the year 2005. Recall from Table 17-2 that this is the maximum acceptable concentration for ground-level ozone. Thus, this plan is simply trying to achieve the existing objective for air quality. Implementation is supposed to occur in three phases. Phase I (to be in place by 1995) involves:

1 *A National Prevention Program.* This program involves 31 initiatives that attempt to reduce NOx/VOCs emissions through energy conservation and improve-

TABLE 17-3   CANADA'S NATIONAL OBJECTIVES REGARDING AMBIENT AIR QUALITY

Pollutant	Averaging time	Maximum desirable concentration	Maximum acceptable concentration	Maximum tolerable concentration
Sulphur	annual	11 ppb	23 ppb	—
dioxide	24-hour	57 ppb	115 ppb	306 ppb
	1-hour	172 ppb	344 ppb	—
Suspended	annual	60 µg/m^3	70 µg/m^3	—
particulates	24-hour	—	120 µg/m^3	400 µg/m^3
Ozone	annual	—	15 ppb	—
	1-hour	50 ppb	32 ppb	153 ppb
Carbon	8-hour	5 ppm	13 ppm	17 ppm
monoxide	1-hour	13 ppm	31 ppm	—
Nitrogen	annual	32 ppb	53 ppb	—
dioxide	24-hour	—	105 ppb	160 ppb
	1-hour	—	213 ppb	532 ppb

Source: Reproduced from Government of Canada, 1991, *The State of Canada's Environment*, 2–11.

EXHIBIT 17-1

MINISTERS PROMISE AIR-QUALITY PLAN

National scheme announced hours after governments criticized for inaction

By James Rusk
Environment Reporter with Canadian Press

Canada's environment ministers announced yesterday they hope to work out a national air-quality plan next year, bringing all air-pollution programs under a single umbrella for the first time.

The promise came hours after Pollution Probe released a report saying that thousands of tonnes of toxic air pollutants are drifting down onto Canadian soils, crops and waterways, and that efforts to control city smog are failing.

Federal Environment Minister Jean Charest did not dispute the findings of the Toronto-based environmental group. But he said the national plan will deal with all air pollutants, including toxic chemicals, smog and greenhouse gases.

"We are hoping for an umbrella air-quality accord for all of Canada," he told a news conference in Aylmer, Que. at the conclusion of a meeting of federal and provincial environment ministers.

The Pollution Probe report said Ottawa and the provinces have shirked their responsibility to protect the air Canadians breathe.

"Despite fine-sounding promises and public pronouncements, they [federal and provincial governments] continue to ignore health and environmental threats, including urban smog and airborne toxic contaminants," Janine Ferretti, executive director of the environmental group, said at a news conference in Toronto yesterday.

Because there was no overview of how effectively governments have been protecting air quality, the group undertook to prepare one by collecting the latest data through interviews with numerous government officials. Ms. Ferritti said, "Frankly, what we discovered surprised even us."

The report cites a number of alarming findings that indicate that Canadians are breathing what Ms. Ferretti described as "chemical soup."

Among these are:

- At least once each year, more than half of all Canadians are exposed to unhealthy levels of ground-level ozone, a principal ingredient in smog.
- No one knows how many tonnes of toxic pollutants are dumped in the air each year, but the incomplete data collected by Pollution Probe puts it in the thousands.

Government negligence is indicated by two key indicators: the low funding priority given to air issues and the lack of standards for air quality, the 161-page report says.

Most provinces do not even spend 4 per cent of their environmental budgets on air quality, and most do not routinely monitor concentrations of toxic substances in the air, the report says.

When they do collect information, most provinces delay publishing it for two to four years, some do not bother to make it public. Quebec and Nova Scotia have not published air-quality reports since the mid-1980s, the report notes.

Nationally, there are "virtually no Canadian ambient-air standards or even guidelines" for toxic contaminants, the report says.

Source: The Globe and Mail, November 27, 1992.

ments in products to reduce emissions upon use; public education about such things as driving habits, energy conservation in homes and business, use of energy-efficient products; and initiatives to control emissions at the source. This last effort involves tightening of standards for new motor vehicles and emission guidelines for new sources (power plants, chemical processes, printing, dry cleaning, etc.). Note that these initiatives pick up on a Green Plan theme to involve the public in changing their actions to help protect the environment. It will be interesting to see if information and moral suasion work. There are a variety of economic incentives, for example, excise taxes on pollution-intensive products, that also could be used to address ground-level ozone problems. Whether governments adopt any of these remains to be seen.

2 *Remedial Programs.* Working with the regions most adversely affected (the Lower Fraser Valley, Windsor-Quebec corridor, Southern Atlantic Region), these initiatives involve installation of emission-control technologies for existing sources of the pollutants.

3 *Studies.* Twenty-four research initiatives are planned to study the most effective ways to control ground-level ozone. These include technical research on monitoring and air diffusions, as well as studies on incentive-based environmental policies. Two reports on the potential for using marketable permits to control NOx-VOCs have been done.

4 *Federal-Provincial Agreements.* Responsibilities for remediation actions must be determined for both levels of government. These agreements are also supposed to determine interim targets for emission reductions.

All of this is Phase I. At the time of writing, it is not clear how much of Phase I has been accomplished. Phases II and III of the plan are supposed to establish emission limits for problem regions for the years 2000 and 2005. The program sounds ambitious, but there is no clear indication that specific regulations will be in place soon. There is the usual abundance of study and negotiation, and if previous experience is a guide, delays in all these initiatives will occur. The government is hoping for a 15 to 35 percent reduction in maximum ground-level ozone concentrations by 2005.[1]

By contrast, there are guidelines *and* standards for emissions of certain air pollutants. Under the Clean Air Act (now CEPA), emission guidelines were created for the cement industry, coke ovens, asphalt paving, mining in the Arctic, types of incinerators, the wood pulp industry, and thermal power generators. In each case, there is a distinction between old and new plants. The guidelines are less stringent for old plants, that is, those already in existence at the time the guidelines were introduced. In some cases, the old plants are required to meet the guideline, but are given a longer time in which to do so than the new plants. There are federal standards for lead from secondary smelters, asbestos from mining and milling, mercury from chloralkali plants, vinyl chloride from vinyl chloride and polyvinyl chloride manufacturing. Note the overlap between this list and that of the federal water-pollution standards. In the case of these standards, old and new plants are treated symmetrically. This might be because some of these compounds, such as mercury, are quite toxic.

The federal government also regulates emissions from new motor vehicles under the Motor Vehicle Safety Act, which was administered by Transport Canada until recently. Under the Green Plan, administration of motor vehicle emissions has been

---

[1] Environment Canada, *Ground-Level Ozone in Canada*, State of Environment Fact Sheet No. 92-1, Catalogue No. EN1-12/92-1E (Ottawa: Minister of Supply and Services, 1992), 10.

shifted to Environment Canada. There are specific standards for three pollutants. For oxides of nitrogen the limit is 3.1 grams per kilometre; hydrocarbons, 2.0 grams per kilometre; and carbon monoxide, 25.0 grams per kilometre. The automobile industry has recently agreed to phase in more stringent controls starting with 1994 model cars. The reason the regulation is only on new cars stems from the federal government's constitutional powers regarding trade and commerce. It can only regulate interprovincial or international trade and commerce (and even interprovincial is tenuous). Therefore, once a car leaves the assembly line, the provinces are responsible for any air-pollution regulations that apply. Most provinces have not regulated emissions of vehicles once in use. However, starting in 1992, British Columbia introduced mandatory testing of all light-duty vehicles registered in the Lower Mainland that were more than a few years old. Emission standards for these vehicles have been imposed. Vehicles not meeting the standards must be repaired or will not be granted a licence to operate. The program got off to a shaky start due to continual breakdowns in the monitoring equipment, long queues, and angry motorists.

There is a fundamental problem with all these regulations. They are based on the emissions per kilometre travelled, there is no control for the *total* number of kilometres driven. Pollution may therefore initially decrease as emissions per car fall, but if there is an increase in the number of cars driven each year, and/or an increase in the number of kilometres driven, emissions may start rising again. One Canadian study expected NOx and VOCs to rise over the period 1985 to 2005 unless additional regulation of some sort occurred. To illustrate these points in more detail, we can express the total quantity of mobile-source emissions in a given period in the following way:

$$\begin{array}{c} \text{Total quantity} \\ \text{of emissions} \end{array} = \begin{array}{c} \text{Number of} \\ \text{vehicles} \end{array} \times \begin{array}{c} \text{Average kilometre} \\ \text{travelled} \end{array} \times \begin{array}{c} \text{Emissions} \\ \text{per kilometre} \end{array}$$

If we were devising a cost-effective way of reducing the total quantity of emissions, we would want to balance the three factors on the right side of this equation according to the equimarginal principle. In fact, the federal motor vehicle emission standards focus only on the last of these factors. And a major reason air pollution is still a serious problem in many regions is that although we have been diligently trying to produce cars with ever smaller emissions per kilometre, the first two factors in the equation have continued to grow relentlessly and virtually without control. Another problem is with the maintenance of motor vehicles. As a car ages and accumulates kilometres, emissions can increase unless the equipment is properly maintained. This is why programs such as those in B.C. are important in dealing with mobile sources of urban air pollution.

Policies which rely on technological fixes to solve a massive air-pollution problem do little to address the basic attachment to the multiple-car family, high-performance vehicles, and the fully mobile lifestyle. The technological fixes are meant to be as invisible as possible, in order not to disrupt these lifestyle factors. Some people have long-run visions of a complete conversion to electric vehicles, so that we might continue to accumulate cars and continue to drive many kilometres, but without emissions. This is a will-o'-the-wisp. Uncontrolled growth in the numbers of vehicles will lead to increasingly congested urban highways. In addition, the switch to electric cars means simply that much of the airborne emissions will move to the power stations that are required to generate the added electricity. The basic fact is that mobile-source air emissions are linked not only to the technical characteristics of cars and the fuel system, but also to the millions of decisions that individuals make about where, when, and how to travel. Without reshaping these decisions in the urban areas where air quality is seriously degraded, significant long-run improvements will be impossible.

This argues for more direct incentive-based approaches to mobile-source emissions. One approach that has been suggested is to levy a significantly higher tax on motor vehicle fuels. With these fuels being more expensive, motorists would have the incentive to think more about their driving habits, organize their driving more coherently, reduce total kilometres travelled, shift to more fuel-efficient vehicles, use mass transit to a greater extent, etc. The effects of the higher fuel price would filter throughout the transportation system and lead people to shift their behaviour in places where the marginal costs of doing so are lowest, much as they did in the energy "crisis" of the 1970s. There are however powerful political forces against such a tax.

Another suggestion is to place a tax directly on vehicle emissions. As part of each province's annual vehicle licensing, the total kilometres that a vehicle had been driven could be recorded. This total could be multiplied by the emissions per kilometre, also measured at the time of licensing (as in B.C.), to yield an estimate of total emissions in the preceding year. A tax could then be levied on these emissions. Unlike a fuel tax, which would have no direct incentive for drivers to worry about emissions, a tax on emissions would create an incentive to look at all the ways of lowering them, including reducing total kilometres driven, driving low-polluting vehicles, and so on. One attractive aspect of this approach is that the tax could be varied among regions to match the severity of regional air quality problems. What is clear is that innovative approaches that go beyond technology standards will be required to meet air-pollution problems from mobile sources. An example of the use of incentives in air-pollution regulation were the actions taken on lead in gasoline.

The federal government regulates the lead content in gasoline. Airborne lead was seen by the 1970s as a serious health threat, especially to children. In 1976, the lead content in gasoline was limited to 0.77 grams per litre. In 1990, this was reduced to 0.26 grams per litre. That limit, combined with federal taxation of gasoline, effectively eliminated lead as a fuel additive for automobiles. Some lead is still used in fuel for farm equipment, trucks, and fishing boats. The innovative part of the federal government's policy with respect to lead in gasoline was that it used an excise tax to speed the switching by motorists to unleaded fuel. When unleaded gasoline first appeared on the market, it was more expensive than leaded. Motorists whose vehicles were supposed to burn unleaded fuel had an incentive to "misfuel" by buying leaded fuel instead. Many did. In 1989, the federal government announced a 1 cent per litre additional excise tax on leaded gasoline. Six provinces followed suit by increasing their own taxes on leaded gas. The tax differential between leaded and unleaded gasoline ranged from 1.5 to 3 cents per litre. Not only did misfueling disappear, but most motorists switched to the now cheaper unleaded gasoline. By 1992, leaded gasoline had disappeared from the retail market.[2]

AIR-POLLUTION POLICY IN THE UNITED STATES: CONTRASTS AND LESSONS

As in Chapter 16, we look briefly at the U.S.'s experience with air-pollution control because Canadian policies are frequently based on those in the U.S., and because air pollutants can readily flow between the two countries. The U.S. has also recently introduced a tradable discharge program for sulfur dioxide. Air-pollution control policies of the U.S. federal government have been in the form of uniform national ambient air quality standards (NAAQS), some technology-based emission standards, and emission standards for new cars (upon which ours are based). Canada's ambient emission guidelines are basically weaker versions of the U.S. ambient standards. The U.S. has however done more than Canada about the problem of preventing degradation of areas with air quality better than the national standards. There was widespread concern that cities in areas with air quality already better than the national ambient standard could compete unfairly for new industrial development. New firms might be attracted to these areas by the promise of less strict emissions controls than firms would face in areas where air quality was already worse than the standards. In 1977, amendments to their Clean Air Act differentiated "PSD" areas (PSD stands for "prevention of serious deterioration"), and "nonattainment" areas. Stricter technology-based effluent standards would apply to PSD regions, where air quality was already better than the standard, than to nonattainment regions.

After the 1977 act there were no new federal air-pollution statutes until 1990, a reflection of the Reagan administration's desire to reduce the "burden" of regulations on the U.S. economy. There were, however, some significant policy innovations that occurred during this period within the existing laws. These were the "bubble" and "offset" programs for air-pollution control, which we will discuss in some detail below. In 1990, after many years of negotiation and political conflict, Congress passed, and the president signed, the Clean Air Act Amendments of 1990. This statute contains five main sections, dealing with: (1) motor vehicles and fuels, (2) acid rain, (3) urban air quality, (4) air toxics, and (5) stratospheric ozone problems. The law is notable for including an innovative transferable discharge permit system for SO_2 emissions. As well, taxes and quotas are used to reduce and ultimately eliminate the use of ozone-depleting compounds. The other sections of the act continue to rely on the typical command-and-control approaches that have characterized federal pro-

---

[2] In the U.S., a lead-trading system was used for refineries in their transition from leaded to unleaded gasolines. It should also be noted that eliminating lead as an additive to gasoline may reduce one environmental problem while creating others. Benzene, toluene, and xylenes are added to motor vehicle fuels to help engine performance. Each of these are known carcinogens and also increase emissions of VOCs.

grams to date. The law also attempts to deal more directly with toxic air pollutants, a problem it, like Canada, had made very little progress in addressing.

The 1990 act seeks to come to grips with the continuing nonattainment problem. In the 1977 law the metropolitan areas of the country had been given until 1987 to come into compliance with ambient standards. Although some progress had been made, many cities still failed to meet the standards at the end of the 1980s. Previous laws treated all these regions alike, but in 1990 an effort was made to recognize degrees of nonattainment. A system was established in the law to classify cities in terms of the severity of their air-pollution problems. The law specifies five classifications for ozone, two for carbon monoxide, and two for particulate matter. Control programs of increasing severity are specified for cities in increasingly serious nonattainment categories. These might be what the CCME has in mind for NO_x-VOCs in Canada. The law then specifies increasingly stringent control techniques for cities according to which category they are in. These techniques are based primarily on the enforcement of technology-based effluent standards and the outright specification of technologies that must be adopted in the various regions. In the next few sections we will look more some of the economic issues related to the U.S.'s and Canada's air pollution-control program (the discussion of the CFC phaseout is in Chapter 22).

National Ambient Air Quality Standards or Objectives

In Chapter 11 we discussed the question of uniformity in standards. Unless marginal damage and marginal abatement costs happen to be the same in all regions, uniform national standards will not be efficient. They will be overly stringent where marginal damages are relatively low and/or marginal abatement costs relatively high; or not stringent enough where marginal damages are relatively high and/or marginal abatement costs relatively low. Thus, standards cannot in general be efficient unless they are established with an eye toward both marginal benefits and marginal control costs. The U.S. 1970 Clean Air Act, however, expressly forbade the EPA from taking abatement costs into account in setting the ambient standards. It is doubtful that in Canada, these costs were considered either. The 1970 law mandated that the EPA set standards for criteria pollutants *strictly on the basis of damages*. The standards as set imply that the damage functions associated with these criteria pollutants have *thresholds*, below which damages are minimal or nonexistent. When the standards were set, relatively little was known about the damage functions. Even today we are unsure if these thresholds exist. Recent results suggest that they may not, that in fact damages may occur even at very low levels of these pollutants, especially among particularly sensitive individuals in the population. But the costs of achieving zero levels of these pollutants would be enormous.

The implication of this is that in setting the national standards some informal recognition was undoubtedly given to abatement costs. Implicit concern with abatement costs has also occurred in enforcement. Despite the unambiguous nature of the standards, there are many urban areas of the United States where ambient air quality is still worse than the standards, two decades after their establishment. Strict enforcement of the standards in a short period of time would simply have cost too much. Enforcement has involved an implicit trade-off of marginal damages and marginal abatement costs, according to the particularities of the different urban areas, the appearance of new abatement technology, and the willingness to pay for air-pollution control, as manifested primarily in the ongoing political struggle in local areas.

Technology-Based Effluent Standards

The U.S. regulates emissions from stationary sources of air pollution with several different types of TBESs. The standards differ between existing and new sources and between nonattainment and PSD regions. In Canada, many regulations also distinguish between "old" and "new" sources of pollution. This is a prominent feature in environmental control programs. New sources, or existing sources that are modified in some major way, are usually held to stricter standards than existing, established sources. In the U.S. air quality program, new sources in nonattainment areas are subject to a LAER (lowest achievable emission rate) standard,[3] which is meant to be more restrictive than the RACT (reasonably available control technology) standard applied to existing sources in those areas. In PSD regions new sources are held to standards based on BACT (best available control technology), while existing sources are in effect not subject to any standard.[4]

The case for holding new sources to stricter standards (a *new-source bias*) than those applied to existing sources is usually made on the basis of cost; it normally costs more to retrofit existing plants with pollution-control equipment than to incorporate the equipment into new plants when they are being built. In effect the argument is that the marginal abatement costs of existing plants are normally higher than those of new plants, so cost-effectiveness justifies more restrictive emission standards for the former than for the latter. To a large extent, this is probably an economic argument being used to justify a course of action that is politically expedient. It is easier to put stricter limits on new sources than on existing ones because, by definition, the former will have less political clout than the latter. And existing firms may not be so opposed to applying stricter controls that make it relatively costly for new competitors to get into business. Exhibit 17-2 illustrates examples from England of existing firms who lobby government for stronger environmental standards. Their motivation is not always altruism as the article explains.

---

[3] LAER is defined as the lowest emission rate specified in any state implementation plan, whether or not any source is currently achieving that rate.

[4] In the U.S., the states have the primary responsibility to set TBESs. Because of this, there was some fear among federal policymakers that economic competition among them would motivate some to set less restrictive standards to attract business. Thus, the EPA is empowered to set a floor level for standards applying to new or modified stationary sources. These are called new-source performance standards (NSPS).

From an administrative standpoint a new-source bias is also easy to understand. In any given year there are many times more existing sources than there are new or modified sources, so more administrative resources may be concentrated on the latter. A focus on new sources also implies a gradualist approach, since it means that stricter standards will gradually spread through the various industries as old capital is replaced with new.

But the price paid for holding new sources to stricter standards may be high. The problem is that a new-source bias creates incentives to hold on to existing plants because they will be subject to less strict environmental standards than new or modernized plants. So in trying to ease the transition to lower pollution levels through a new-source bias, we may inadvertently slow up the rate of adoption of pollution-withholding technology. This is no doubt one of the main reasons so many urban regions of the U.S. continue to suffer from substantial air-pollution problems many years after the beginning of the federal program. Canada may have similar problems.

Virtually all of the observations we made about technology-based effluent standards in water-pollution control are also applicable to air pollution-control policy. It is an approach that tends to put the initiative and responsibility for pollution control in the hands of administrative agencies rather than the polluters themselves. Too much of the energy and creativity of polluting firms is devoted to finding ways of avoiding compliance rather than devising better means of controlling emissions. The incentives for R&D to develop new techniques of pollution control or to reach back into the production process to reduce residuals in the first place are weakened. But most importantly, TBESs have the effect of encouraging uniform compliance measures among sources. In a world where marginal abatement costs differ substantially across sources, this cannot be a cost-effective policy.

Numerous studies have been done by environmental economists to estimate excess costs of the command-and-control approach to air-pollution control inherent in technology-based effluent standards. These studies involve complex models that incorporate economic factors, such as control costs at each source, with emission and meteorological factors that show how ambient air quality is affected by various patterns of emissions. The models can be run to determine the costs and ambient quality levels achieved with the CAC approach, then run again without the TBESs to see what the total control cost would be of a program that achieved the same ambient air quality but with a cost-effective distribution of emission reductions among firms. Table 17-4 on page 343 summarizes the main results of some of the studies. The last column shows the ratio of the CAC program costs, incorporating various technology-based effluent standards, as indicated, to least-cost programs that would provide the same improvement in air quality. If the actual programs were also cost-effective, these ratios would be at or near 1.0. In fact, they vary from 1.07 to 22.0.

Four of the studies show CAC/least-cost ratios between 1.0 and 2.0. These are CAC programs that also come close to achieving minimum costs. The most likely explanation for this is that these cases involve multiple sources that have relatively small differences in marginal abatement costs. Most of the other ratios, however, are around 4.0 to 6.0, meaning that the actual programs involving TBESs were four to

EXHIBIT 17-2

REGULATE US, PLEASE

Managers are supposed to abhor government intervention. Not if their business owes its existence to regulation.

They have a saying in the waste-management industry: the more government interferes in business, the more money business makes. On both sides of the Atlantic, angry waste-management companies are complaining that government is not intervening enough—and, in America, even allying themselves with green lobbyists. Indeed, in many environmental industries, regulation offers ways not just to create markets but also to compete with rivals.

As environmental laws have become tougher, firms have learned to lobby for rules that bring them benefits. Paul Portney of Resources for the Future, an American think-tank, lists three variants:

• Established companies in slow-growing industries may lobby for stricter standards, knowing that these will mainly affect new entrants. In the United States, the old industrial states helped to win tighter national pollution limits for electrical utilities and metal-smelters, thus making life harder for younger rivals in the southern and western states.
• Companies lobby for standards which they can meet, but which they know will impose high costs on competitors. Thus in the 1980s Chrysler, which makes lots of small cars, supported high fuel-economy standards which its rivals opposed.
• Companies press for regulations that will create a market for their products. As an example, take the way companies selling low-sulphur coal have rooted for legislation to reduce acid rain—caused

partly by burning high-sulphur fuels. Or take the waste-management business.

In Britain, the big waste managers have had a miserable few months. The January issue of the magazine of the National Association of Waste Disposal Contractors writes of "the year that never was", when "fears grew of a wholesale dismantling of environmental-protection regulations." What was this horror? Twice, the government postponed a new licensing scheme which would drive the smallest, cheapest waste managers out of business. Now the scheme is expected to start in May—more than a year late. First results from a study by KPMG Management Consulting suggest that the delay has postponed about 1 billion ($1.5 billion) of investment.

One of Britain's largest waste-management companies, Shanks & McEwan, has been urging the waste-regulation authorities (WRAS) to tighten the rules on what can be put in rubbish dumps. Britain, almost alone in the industrial world, allows "co-disposal": the mixing of hazardous and non-hazardous muck in landfills. Shanks & McEwan, Britain's biggest landfiller, does plenty of co-disposing itself. But it recently published a paper arguing that some types of hazardous waste were not suitable for landfill, but should be treated or incinerated instead.

David Fitzsimmonds, the company's business policy adviser, says that Shanks & McEwan has no

six times more costly than they would have been had they been designed to be cost-effective. The problem with this is not just that we are paying much more than is necessary to get the improvements in air quality, though this is certainly a serious shortcoming. The real problem is that since the actual control programs are so much more costly than they need be, we are in fact working with an aggregate marginal abatement cost function that is much higher than it need be, and therefore we are probably settling for smaller improvements in ambient quality than we might achieve if control programs were fully cost-effective.

intention of refusing to landfill most of the materials listed as unsuitable (although it tries to persuade customers to plump for safer methods). If it did, customers would simply turn to more compliant disposers. But it would be delighted if WRAS would apply tighter rules to all landfills.

Selfless environmentalism? Not quite. In 1991 the company bought—expensively—two of Britain's four main hazardous-waste incinerators. In May the British government will allow local authorities to ban imports of hazardous waste. As a result, the company fears that its incinerators will lose 40% of their turnover. If all WRAS took the company's advice, then an extra 100,000 tonnes of hazardous waste would need to be treated or incinerated each year, providing domestic business to replace lost imports.

The match would not be perfect: imports are much more lucrative than the extra domestic business would be. But the company also argues that more incineration is in the long-term national interest. A new Brussels directive on landfills is likely to restrict or outlaw co-disposal. That will eventually force Britain to incinerate much more hazardous waste. Yet the country has far less incineration capacity than other big European countries.

Bring in the Greens

A glance at America shows that an alliance between the more reputable waste managers and the more moderate environmentalists can bring benefits to both. As in Britain, tougher standards for all rubbish dumps were first promised and then repeatedly postponed. Rules proposed under the Solid Waste Disposal Act were opposed by small operators which could not afford to meet them. Waste Management, America's biggest rubbish company, "helped to develop the rules, and then spent many tens of millions of dollars to put our own

facilities into compliance," says Bill Brown, the company's director of environmental affairs. The company teamed up with several environmental groups, including National Audubon and the Sierra Club, to lobby for the rules, which finally began to come into force in October 1993.

In the case of landfill regulations, the big waste-management companies were demanding tougher standards for smaller competitors in their own industry. But in the case of hazardous-waste incineration, some big companies want to use green standards as a weapon against rivals from other industries.

Having invested in expensive incinerators, American waste managers have found that the recession has reduced the amount of hazardous waste; and that many companies have invested in ways to produce less waste. They also grumble that industrial boilers and cement kilns have been burning hazardous waste as fuel with fewer controls. Now the Hazardous Waste Treatment Council, which campaigns on behalf of the industry, has joined forces with environmentalists to badger the government into imposing tighter standards on these competitors.

In Britain, cement kilns are starting to bid fiercely for hazardous waste. Lower standards mean that they can undercut the waste-management companies. The amount of hazardous waste incinerated in cement kilns is likely to double in 1994 from its 1993 total of 35,000 tonnes. Already the European waste-management industry is starting to lobby for tighter environmental controls on cement kilns when they burn hazardous waste.

NEW DIRECTIONS IN AIR-POLLUTION CONTROL

Emission Reduction Credits

It was recognized very early in the U.S., that the CAC types of policies favoured by current laws would produce far less improvement in ambient quality for the money spent than would be obtained with more efficient policies. In the mid-1970s the EPA began to experiment with alternatives that might be more flexible and cost-effective in meeting air quality goals. The 1977 Clean Air Act authorized a limited type of emission permit trading, and several other approaches were developed on the initiative of EPA. These plans were, and are, meant to be strictly secondary to the primary approach based on technology-based emission standards. More recently, the interest in market-incentive approaches to pollution control, together with their acceptance by a number of the large environmental advocacy groups, led to the 1990 Clean Air Act Amendments, which specifically incorporates a new permit trading scheme for the control of airborne SO_2 emissions.

The earlier programs allow the trading of what are called "emission reduction credits" (ERCs). An ERC is essentially the same as what we have called a transferable discharge permit. Sources obtain ERCs by reducing their emissions below a given baseline level specified by administrative authorities. In order for an ERC to be tradable, the EPA rules require that it be "surplus," "enforceable," "quantifiable," and "permanent."[5] This does not mean that all trades must be permanent, only that the emission reductions giving rise to the ERC be permanent. There are four subprograms of the ERC trading program: offsets, bubbles, banking, and netting.

Offsets   This is a system designed to apply to nonattainment regions in order to accommodate economic growth while still making progress on cleaning up the air. It allows new sources, or major modifications of existing sources, to begin operations in a nonattainment area if the new emissions they will produce are offset by decreases in emissions among existing sources of the same pollutant in that area. The way this is done is for the new source to purchase ERCs from existing sources. In effect, the new sources help to finance existing sources to reduce their emissions below their baseline levels. In order to qualify for the right to buy ERCs, new sources must conform to the LAER standards set by EPA; that is, they must have emissions that do not exceed this standard. Offset transactions can occur among sources within the same firm or among different firms. If offsets are traded one for one, there will be no net change in total emissions as trades are made. If the emissions target was initially *not* set at the socially efficient level, offset trading can also be used to "ratchet down" the total quantity of emissions. This can be done by requiring buyers to obtain more than one offset for each unit of added emissions. Thus, for example, purchasers might be required to buy 1.5 ERCs for each unit increase in emissions.[6]

Bubbles   The bubble system is primarily meant for *intra*firm transactions. Suppose one firm has multiple sources of an air pollutant. This is common among large industrial operations like refineries, whose plants often spread over a relatively large area. Instead of holding each source at the plant to the applicable TBES, the entire plant is treated as a single source, and an effluent standard is applied to this single

---

[5] Arlene R. Borowsky and Howard M. Ellis, "Summary of Final Federal Emissions Trading Policy Statement," *Journal of Air Pollution Control Administration* 37(7) (July 1987): 789–790.

[6] In the 1990 Clean Air Act Amendments a system of "exchange rates" is adopted for some offset trades; for "moderate" areas in terms of ambient ozone, new sources must obtain 1.15 ERCs for each additional unit of VOCs it expects to emit; for "extreme" areas this ratio is 1.5 to 1, and the ratio varies between these limits for areas in the intermediate categories.

TABLE 17-4   COMPARISON OF CAC CONTROL COST WITH LEAST-COST PROGRAMS IN AIR-POLLUTION CONTROL

Study	CAC benchmark	Ratio of CAC costs to least cost
1 Particulates, St. Louis (1974)	SIP regulations	6.00
2 Sulfur dioxide, four corners region (Utah, Colorado, Arizona, and New Mexico) (1981)	SIP regulations	4.25
3 Sulfates, Los Angeles (1982)	Applicable Clean Air Act emission standards	1.07
4 Nitrogen dioxide, Baltimore (1983)	RACT regulations	5.96
5 Nitrogen dioxide, Chicago (1983)	RACT regulations	14.40
6 Particulates, Baltimore (1984)	SIP regulations	4.18
7 Sulfur dioxide, Delaware Valley (1984)	Uniform percentage reduction	1.78
8 Particulates, Delaware Valley (1984)	Uniform percentage reduction	22.00
9 Airport noise, U.S. (1983)	Mandatory retrofit	1.72
10 Hydrocarbons, all domestic DuPont plants (1984)	Uniform percentage reduction	4.15
11 CFC emissions, U.S. (nonaerosol) (1980)	Proposed emission standards	1.96

Source: Adapted from T. H. Tietenberg, *Emissions Trading: An Exercise in Reforming Pollution Control* (Washington, D.C.: Resources for the Future, 1985), 42–43. Individual studies are as follows: **1** Scott E. Atkinson and Donald H. Lewis, "A Cost-Effective Analysis of Alternative Air Quality Control Strategies," *Journal of Environmental Economics and Management* 1(3) (November 1974): 237–250; **2** Fred Roach et al., "Alternative Air Quality Policy Options in the Four Corners Region," *Southwestern Review* 1(2) (Summer 1981): 44–45; **3** Robert W. Hahn and Roger G. Noll, "Designing a Market for Tradeable Emission Permits" in Wesley A. Magat (ed.), *Reform of Environmental Regulation* (Cambridge, Mass.: Ballinger, 1982), 132–133; **4** Alan J. Krupnick, *Costs of Alternative Policies for the Control of NO₂ in the Baltimore Region,* (Washington, D.C.: Resources for the Future, 1983): 22; **5** Eugene P. Seskin, Robert J. Anderson, Jr., and Robert O. Reid, "An Empirical Analysis of Economic Strategies for Controlling Air Pollution," *Journal of Environmental Economics and Management* 10(2) (June 1983): 117–120; **6** Albert M. McGartland, "Marketable Permit Systems for Air Pollution Control: An Empirical Study" (Ph.D. dissertation, University of Maryland, 1984): 67a; **7** Walter O. Spofford, Jr., *Efficiency Properties of Alternative Source Control Policies for Meeting Ambient Air Quality Standards: An Empirical Application to the Lower Delaware Valley* (Washington, D.C.: Resources for the Future, 1984), 77; **8** Ibid.; **9** David Harrison, Jr., "Case Study 1: The Regulation of Aircraft Noise" in Thomas C. Schelling (ed.), *Incentives for Environmental Protection* (Cambridge, Mass.: MIT Press), 81–96; **10** Michael T. Maloney and Bruce Yandle, "Estimation of the Cost of Air Pollution Control Regulation," *Journal of Environmental Economics and Management* 11(3) (September 1984): 244–264; **11** Adele R. Palmer et al., *Economic Implications of Regulating Chlorofluorocarbon Emissions from Nonaerosol Applications,* Rand Corporation, Report No. R-2524-EPA (June 1980): 225.

consolidated source. This allows the firm to rearrange emission reductions among their various sources in accordance with the equimarginal principle.

Banking   In 1979 the EPA gave states the right to create ERC banks, making it possible for sources to bank and save for future use any ERCs they had produced by reducing their emissions. States are required to develop a system where ERCs can be deposited and to develop procedures for transferring ERCs into and out of the appropriate bank accounts. Banked ERCs can be used for future offset and netting transactions.

Netting   Netting transactions, like most bubble arrangements, are *intra*firm transactions applying to the modification of existing sources. They arise when existing firms are considering an expansion of their operations that would increase emissions enough to trigger a new source review (NSR). These NSRs are relatively involved, time consuming, and costly. Firms may be able to avoid NSRs if the increase in emissions in the part of the plant that is to be expanded can be offset by reductions elsewhere in the plant, so that the *net* increase in total emissions falls below the NSR-triggering level. The new source must still meet NSPS, but with netting the firm may be able to avoid certain requirements like having to find external offsets to cover their increased emissions.

These emission permit transfer programs were developed by the EPA in the 1970s and refined over the next decade. The "final" guidelines in trading rules were published in 1986, and they apply both to criteria pollutants and to listed hazardous air pollutants. There was reasonably widespread enthusiasm for their development, especially among environmental economists,[7] and an expectation that they would be useful in making the air pollution-control program more cost-effective. The actual results are more ambivalent. While there has been a relatively large number of transactions, there are many who feel that their full potential has not yet been reached.

Table 17-5 shows the number of ERC transactions that took place from the time the various systems were initiated until 1986, and the estimated cost savings they have made possible. Cost savings are the difference between control costs using the transfer programs and what costs would have been had these programs not been available. Several things stand out from these figures. The most obvious is that virtually all transactions have been internal, where individual firms have adjusted emissions among the several sources at their plants to lower compliance costs. This has made it possible for individual firms to move toward more cost-effective emission reduction. On the other hand, firms have not taken the opportunity to obtain cost savings that *interfirm* trading could bring about. The economists who estimated these numbers concluded that the uncertainties about the legal status of the ERCs and the costs of finding outside demanders and suppliers of credits led most firms to rely mostly on intrafirm trades.

A contributing factor was that few firms engaged in ERC banking, and those that did chose to bank their credits in internal accounts rather than at a central depository. Again, the uncertainty about the property-right status of the ERCs and the fear that banked credits might be confiscated by administrative authorities under pressure to reduce air pollution may have led them to avoid depositing excess credits in a central account. A more visible bank of excess emission credits might have contributed to the development of a more active external market for credits, with more informa-

---

[7] But not among many environmental advocates, who inclined toward the position that permit trading would weaken the effort to control emissions in nonattainment areas.

TABLE 17-5   EMISSIONS TRADING ACTIVITY FROM INCEPTION OF PROGRAMS TO 1986

| Type of trade | Estimated number of transactions | | Estimated cost savings (millions) |
	Internal	External	
Offsets	1800	200	Probably large, but difficult to measure
Bubbles	129	2	$435
Banking	< 100	< 20	Small
Netting	5,000 to 12,000	0	$25 to $300 in permitting costs; $500 to $12,000 in control costs

Source: Robert W. Hahn and Gordon L. Hester, "Where Did All the Markets Go? An Analysis of EPA's Emission Trading Program," *Yale Journal of Regulation* 6(1) (Winter 1989): 138.

tion about present and expected future prices. This, in turn, would have fostered more external market transactions.

We should note also the great popularity of netting transactions compared to bubble arrangements. The explanation for this is that netting involves modified sources while bubbles apply to existing sources. When firms modify one of their sources, they may trigger the costly and lengthy permitting procedures that apply to new sources of emissions, procedures that do not apply to existing sources. Netting has become a reasonably popular way of trying to avoid this; a firm searches for sources elsewhere in its operations where it can cut back emissions so that the net increase in emissions will be small enough to avoid the need for a new or modified-source approach.

These emission reduction credit trading procedures have become a permanent part of the stationary-source air pollution-control program in the U.S. For a time there will be a built-in conflict between administrative needs to change rules so that markets may work more effectively and the needs of market users, for whom stability and certainty about future rules and accepted procedures are paramount. We would expect firms increasingly to take advantage of them as these administrative uncertainties are reduced.

Acid Rain: A Transboundary Pollution Problem

Sulfur dioxide is a transboundary pollutant in North America. The most serious problems occur in the eastern parts of Canada and the United States. In these regions, sulfur dioxide is responsible for the acidic precipitation that lowers the pH of susceptible lakes, damages forests and buildings, and may also contribute to health problems of susceptible individuals. The flow of sulfur dioxide both ways across the Canada–U.S. border has been the source of a political struggle between the two countries. There are many barriers to an efficient solution to this cross-border pollution problem. Many levels of government are involved. The distribution of benefits and costs of reducing sulfur dioxide emissions are unequal across jurisdictions. Scientific information about damages took time to be established, and was debated by the various interest groups.

In Canada, the primary sources of sulfur emissions are metal smelting companies in Sudbury, Ontario. The Ontario government began regulating these companies in the early 1900s.[8] It wasn't until the 1970s, that acid rain became a topical issue in Canada. The major contributor to sulfur dioxide emissions in Ontario was from Inco, Ltd., the major producer of nickel in the world. The area around Inco's smelter in Sudbury was largely barren due to sulfur dioxide emissions. The Ontario provincial government responded by requiring Inco to lengthen the height of the stack on its smelter. This regulation reflected thinking at the time that "the solution to pollution was dilution." The "super stack," as it was called, did result in fairly rapid improvement in Sudbury's air quality. Scientists then began discovering that lakes in the Canadian Shield downwind of the superstack were becoming acidified and fish stocks were threatened. These lakes were susceptible because they lacked buffering capacity. The Great Lakes, for example, are not susceptible to acidification because their bedrock is mostly limestone, a highly alkaline mineral that neutralizes the sulfuric acid created by the sulfur dioxide emissions.

Canada saw acid rain as a bilateral issue because other than Sudbury, major sources of acid precipitation came from the coal-fired power plants in the midwestern states, primarily along the Ohio Valley of the United States.[9] Until the 1990 amendments to the U.S. Clean Air Act, Canada took the position that the U.S. was not "doing its share" in regulatory actions to protect the environment from acid rain. Even though this was a bilateral problem, U.S. "exports" of sulfur dioxide to Canada exceeded our exports to them. Canada's position was that the ambient air quality standards in the U.S. weren't strong enough. One reason for this was that certain states were not implementing the national standards. Another problem was the very slow phase-in of technology standards for existing plants. By the early 1980s, it was clear that strong actions from the U.S. were unlikely. This position reflected in part the fact that Canada would benefit more than the U.S. from sulfur dioxide controls, while the U.S. would bear the largest proportion of control costs. The official view of the U.S. federal administration was that not enough was known about the problem and additional scientific research was needed before more stringent regulations would be passed.

In Ontario, acid rain was a major issue. Many environmental groups took part under the umbrella of an organization called the Canadian Coalition on Acid Rain (CCAR). The CCAR began a massive lobbying effort in Canada and the U.S. that ultimately succeeded in accomplishing the regulatory targets it had established. Its efforts were supported by the federal and Ontario governments who were happy to keep the attention focussed on the U.S. as the main culprit. Canada became increasingly frus-

---

[8] See Don Dewees, "The Efficiency of the Common Law: Sulphur Dioxide Emissions in Sudbury," *University of Toronto Law Journal* 42 (1992): 1–22, for a discussion of the early legal actions regarding metal mining and smelting and air pollution.

[9] The other major Canadian source of sulfur dioxide are the coal-fired plants of Ontario Hydro.

trated with the lack of action in the United States, and began taking unilateral action, while continuing scientific studies to document damages. Ontario imposed increasingly strict emission limits on Inco and Ontario Hydro. In 1982, the federal government announced a federal-provincial agreement (for all provinces east of Saskatchewan) to cut sulfur dioxide emissions by 50 percent of the 1980 levels by 1990. This plan was to be contingent on the U.S. following suit. The U.S. federal government rejected the plan, again arguing that it was too costly and that not enough was known about the problem to justify action.[10] This plan did not proceed until the election of the Mulroney government in 1984. Mulroney had made a campaign promise to bring in a Canadian acid rain program within six months of taking office, regardless of how the U.S. responded. Essentially the same federal-provincial program devised in 1982 was proclaimed as a unilateral Canadian action in February 1985. The 50 percent reduction remained the target and the federal government was to contribute $150 million to assist the mining industry in complying. Provincial subsidies were also forthcoming. Later in 1985, the new Liberal government in Ontario extended its acid rain commitments to include all major sources of SO_2, and brought in regulations that would reduce emissions by 67 percent of their 1980 levels by 1994. The other eastern provinces implemented regulations over the next few years. The Canadian program has succeeded in significantly reducing emissions. It is currently believed that the target reductions will be met in 1994. The U.S. finally cooperated with Canada's requests for action in 1990 when newly elected President Bush signed the 1990 Clean Air Act. We now turn to the innovative features of this act.

The Transferable Discharge Program of the U.S. Clean Air Act of 1990

The 1990 Clean Air Act contains a program that represents a major innovation in pollution-control regulation. It is a transferable emission permit plan for controlling SO_2 emissions from U.S. power plants. The EPA is to issue a quantity of emission permits to designated power plants. Each permit will allow the release of 1 ton of sulfur dioxide from that plant; thus, if, for example, operators of a particular plant have 20,000 permits, this plant would be allowed to emit a maximum of 20,000 tons of sulfur per year. The permits may be traded at prices agreed upon between buyer and seller. As we discussed in detail in Chapters 13 and 14, the purpose of a TDP program like this is to achieve a reduction in total SO_2 emissions at much lower cost than if all plants were required to meet the same proportionate reductions or if all firms were held to the same TBESs. The law calls initially for a reduction of approximately 20 percent from estimated total sulfur emissions of 1980, and a further 20 percent reduction in later years. The program represents a very substantial departure from the command-and-control approaches of the past. If it works according to expectations, at least the expectations of many environmental economists, it should save consid-

---

[10] New England was the principal region of the U.S. harmed by acid precipitation.

erable amounts of money and give a big boost to the application of incentive-type measures to other environmental problems.

Initial Permit Distribution   The program has two phases. The first will run from 1995 to 2000 and will be limited to 110 electric utility plants located in 21 eastern and midwestern states. The plants involved are large coal-burning plants that currently emit more than 2.5 pounds of SO_2 per Btu of fuel used. Each of these plants will be allocated a prescribed number of permits (or "allowances," as they are called by the EPA). These allocations were calculated with the following formula:

$$\frac{\text{Number of}}{\text{permits}} = \frac{\text{Average Btus of fuel used}}{\text{1985–1987 (in millions)}} \times \frac{\text{2.5 pounds of } SO_2}{\text{per million Btus}}$$

The formula gives more permits to larger plants, as measured by the average quantity of fuel used during the base period 1985–1987. It is not exactly an equiproportionate system, but it moves in that direction by using a common sulfur conversion factor—2.5 pounds of SO_2 per million Btus of fuel—to calculate initial allowances. Two plants burning the same amount of fuel end up with the same permit allocation, even though one of them may have put more effort than the other into reducing SO_2 emissions. But since the plants are all large coal-burning plants, the formula in effect treats them roughly the same.

This initial allocation totals 5,489,335 permits. About 57 percent of these will go to power plants in five states: Ohio, Indiana, Georgia, Pennsylvania, and West Virginia. An additional special Phase I allocation of permits will be given to power plants in Illinois, Ohio, and Indiana.[11] The EPA will also hold back large quantities of permits. It will have a "bonus reserve" of up to 3.5 million permits, which can be used to allow certain states to accommodate growth in their electricity producing sectors or to provide temporary delays to power plants that wish to install scrubbers[12] to reduce SO_2 emissions. It also may auction off a number of permits, as well as sell a certain number at a fixed (real) price of $1,500/permit. The EPA will have an additional reserve of permits that it may allocate to utility firms that undertake approved programs in energy conservation or renewable energy development.

In Phase II, starting in 2000, the program is to be expanded to cover power plants throughout the country. At this point it is expected to cover about 1,000 power plants burning coal, oil, or natural gas. The formula for allocating permits will be much the same as in Phase I except that the SO_2 index will be lowered to 1.2 pounds of SO_2 per million Btus of fuel used. Furthermore, in Phase II there is to be an overall cap of 8.95 million permits given out by the EPA.

---

[11] The initial allocation of permits was probably the most controversial issue when the law was being hammered out because it determines how the overall cost burden of SO_2 reduction will be distributed among plants, states, and regions. The extra allocation to the three midwestern states was simply a way to help get their political support for the program.

[12] A "scrubber" is a device for treating stack gases; it can remove up to 95 percent of the sulfur in the gas.

Trading Rules   Emission permits are tradable. Managers of an individual plant may do one of three things. They may simply hold on to the permits they were originally allocated and reduce their sulfur emissions to or below that level.[13] They could reduce their emissions below their permit holdings and sell the surplus permits. Or they could reduce their emissions to something more than their initial permit holdings and buy extra permits to cover the overage. Thus, market participants—buyers and sellers—will consist of these 110 utility plants adjusting their permit holdings to match their emission rates. But other participants may buy and sell permits. Other utilities that might wish to expand their electricity output, but are held in check by SO_2 emission limitations, may buy additional permits, as may new plants starting operations after the program is put into effect. The law also allows permits to be traded and held by private citizens, brokers, speculators, environmental groups, other types of business enterprises, etc. As an environmental group, you might wish to buy permits simply to try to get total SO_2 emissions reduced. As a manufacturer of pollution-control equipment, you might wish to buy a stock of permits that you could lend to your customers while they were installing your equipment. As a speculator, you might want to buy and hold permits because you think their price is going to rise.

The Role of the EPA   The role of the EPA is designed to be much more modest than in typical command-and-control type pollution-control programs. It is to keep track of permit trades so that it knows at all times how many emission permits are held by each plant. It must also monitor emissions to ensure that no plant emits more than it is entitled to by the number of permits it holds. The law specifies that each source is to install and maintain continuous monitoring devices. In theory the EPA will be concerned only with whether emissions exceed allowances, its only direct control over technology choices is to approve for each plant "a compliance plan that specifies the company's choice of one or more of the compliance methods authorized under the act."[14] Penalties for plants emitting more than they have permits to cover are set at $2,000/ton/year of excess emissions.

Will It Work?   Will the program run smoothly and produce reductions in SO_2 emissions at a substantial cost savings over a CAC-type program? The program is too new to know exactly how successful it will be. Much depends on the role that the EPA chooses to play over the years, and whether the inevitable adjustments that will have to be made in market rules are made with an eye toward increasing efficiency or toward giving one group of participants an additional advantage over others. A key is for the EPA to refrain from trying to dictate technology choices made by utilities to reduce their SO_2 emissions. The market will work best if utilities are allowed to use whatever means they find the cheapest (within reason) to reduce SO_2 emissions

---

[13] They might reduce emissions below their permit holdings in order to have a reserve of surplus permits in hand for future contingencies.

[14] *EPA Journal* 17(1) (January/February 1991): 23.

and then take advantage of this flexibility by buying or selling emission permits.[15] One problematic factor in this program is that the main participants, electric utilities, may not have the "correct" economic incentives. Programs of transferable discharge permits are based on the assumption that polluters will be rational cost minimizers, and this is reasonably assured if they are operating in competitive industries. But the electric power industry in the U.S. is not a competitive industry. Electric utilities are instead regulated monopolies, individual plants with no competitors that are regulated by public utilities commissions. So, in fact, the public utility commissions in the various states will have a lot to say about how their power plants respond to the opportunities of the program, and we do not yet know how public utility commissioners will behave toward the program. Remember that even if the industry operating with TDPs is not perfectly competitive, the pollution target set by the initial number of permits cannot be exceeded.

Despite these possible problems, the program represents a considerable innovation in U.S. pollution-control policies. It is the first large-scale example of a system of transferable discharge permits tried in the United States and, in that sense, represents a kind of laboratory for environmental economists, who have been talking for many years about the advantages of moving to economic incentive programs to combat pollution.[16]

SUMMARY

Air-pollution control in Canada, like water-pollution control, is primarily a provincial responsibility. Ambient and emission guidelines (and some standards) exist. The federal government has played a strong advisory role with the creation of the NAAQOs—national ambient air quality objectives. The federal objectives are not binding on any polluter. It is up to each province to enact its own regulations. Most provinces have chosen to use the federal objectives as the basis for their guidelines and standards. A new federal/provincial initiative is under way for NO_x-VOC emissions. The focus is on remedial actions in regions with the most severe problems and on activities that reduce emissions through private actions (energy conservation, moral suasion), and imposition of design and emission standards. Some provinces (for example, Ontario) are basing their emission standards for all air pollutants on BATEAs. Vehicle emissions from new cars are controlled by federal design standards. Provinces have the authority to regulate emissions from mobile sources of air pollution. British Columbia has moved to an annual system of vehicle exhaust

---

[15] As the quote in the previous paragraph makes clear, however, some control over choices may be necessary. We have to remember the materials balances principle. If some utilities use stack-gas scrubbers to reduce their SO_2 emissions, they will end up with large quantities of sulfur sludge. This must be disposed of in a socially efficient way.

[16] To date, several trades have been made and others are pending. The trades are generating some public controversy. See, for example, "Lilco's Emissions Sale Spurs Acid Rain Concern,"*New York Times*, March 18, 1993.

inspections as part of vehicle licensing requirements. Little attention has been given to the important problem of reducing total vehicle kilometres in urban areas with seriously degraded air quality. The federal and some provincial governments used an incentive-based policy, an excise tax on leaded gasoline, in combination with a standard to eliminate the use of leaded gasoline in Canada.

Federal air-pollution policies in the U.S. were noted to illustrate some important problems. Their national ambient air quality standards were established, not on the basis of efficiency considerations as we have discussed them, but "to protect the public health," with an "adequate margin of safety," irrespective of the costs. In fact, the essential trade-offs between costs and benefits were left for administrators to work out behind the scenes. A distinction is made between nonattainment areas, where ambient standards are not met, and PSD regions, where they are. To meet the ambient standards, primary reliance is placed on technology-based emission standards. Most economic studies of these TBESs in air-pollution control show that for the total amount of money spent on pollution control, they achieve only a fraction of the emission reduction that a fully cost-effective program would attain.

The bilateral problem of acid rain has led to unilateral command-and-control actions by Canada in the 1980s to reduce domestic emissions. The U.S. finally agreed in 1990 to significant reductions in their emissions with the use of an innovative national program of transferable emission permits for sulfur dioxide emissions from large power plants. Emission permits are to be allocated to existing power plants; these permits may then be traded. The objective is to achieve a roughly 50 percent reduction in total SO_2 emissions in a cost-effective way. Substantial uncertainties surround this new market for discharge permits, and additional regulatory oversight and legal evolution will determine how well the system succeeds.

QUESTIONS FOR FURTHER DISCUSSION

1 How might one design a system of transferable discharge permits to control emissions from automobiles? Would this help reduce ground-level ozone?

2 The federal regulation of emissions from new automobiles and light trucks means that those vehicles sold in rural regions meet the same emissions standards as ones sold in urban areas. Since there are a lot fewer vehicles in rural areas, this means that air quality will be a lot better there than in the cities. Is this efficient? Is it equitable?

3 What are the advantages and disadvantages of a "new-source" bias in stationary-source air-pollution control? Consider especially its impacts on the incentives of the operators of existing sources.

4 Most of the firms included in the SO_2 emission permit trading program of the 1990 CAA Amendments are public utilities rather than profit-maximizing firms in the conventional sense. What effects might this have on the operation of the trading program?

5 What are the advantages and disadvantages of dealing with mobile-source emissions by instituting a substantial tax on gasoline, but not all motor vehicle fuels?

SELECTED READINGS

Crandall, Robert W., Howard K. Gruenspecht, Theodore E. Keeler, and Lester B. Lave. *Regulating the Automobile.* Washington, D.C.: Brookings Institution, 1986.

Dewees, Donald. *Reducing the Burden of Environmental Regulation*, Discussion Paper, Government and Competitiveness Reference. Kingston, Ontario: Queen's University School of Policy Studies, 1992.

Doern, G.B. *Getting it Green: Case Studies in Canadian Environmental Regulation.* Toronto: C.D. Howe Institute, 1990.

Downing, Paul B., and William D. Watson, Jr. "Cost Effective Enforcement of Environmental Standards." *Journal of the Air Pollution Control Association* 25(7) (July 1975): 705–710.

Hahn, Robert W., and Gordon L. Hester. "Where Did All the Markets Go? An Analysis of EPA's Emission Trading Program." *Yale Journal of Regulation* 6(1) (Winter 1989): 109–153.

Hahn, Robert W., and Roger G. Noll. "Barriers to Implementing Tradeable Air Pollution Permits: Problems of Regulatory Interactions." *Yale Journal on Regulation* 1(1) (1983): 63–91.

Harrison, David, Jr. *Who Pays for Clean Air: The Cost and Benefit Distribution of Federal Automobile Emissions Standards.* Cambridge, Mass.: Ballnger, 1975.

House of Commons, Special Committee on Acid Rain. *Report of the Special Committee on Acid Rain*, 2nd Session, 33rd Parliament, Ottawa, September 1988.

Krupnick, Alan J., and Paul R. Portney. "Controlling Urban Air Pollution: A Benefit-Cost Assessment." *Science* 252 (April 26, 1991): 522–528.

Liroff, Richard. *Reforming Air Pollution Regulation.* Washington, D.C.: Conservation Foundation, 1986.

Long Range Transport of Air Pollutants Steering Committee. *Management Plan for Nitrogen Oxides and Volatile Organic Compounds.* Ottawa, March 1990.

National Research Council. *Rethinking the Ozone Problem in Urban and Regional Air Pollution.* Washington, D.C.: National Academy Press, 1991.

Portney, Paul R. "Air Pollution Policy" in Paul R. Portney (ed.). *Public Policies for Environmental Protection.* Washington, D.C.: Resources for the Future, 1990, 27–96.

Tietenberg, Tom H. *Emissions Trading, An Exercise in Reforming Pollution Policy.* Washington, D.C.: Resources for the Future, 1985.

Wolozen, Harold (ed.). *The Economics of Air Pollution.* New York: W. W. Norton, 1966.

18

FEDERAL AND PROVINCIAL POLICY ON TOXIC AND HAZARDOUS SUBSTANCES

Within the general domain of environmental analysis and policy there is a class of pollutants that have come to be called "toxic" substances and "hazardous" materials. While all pollutants are damaging to some extent, these have been singled out for their special short- or long-run potency. Most are chemicals, the person-made organic and inorganic compounds that are now ubiquitous throughout all industrialized economies, and even widespread in developing countries. Today chemicals and chemical products have permeated into every corner of the economy. In product improvements, new materials, food safety, health innovations, and many other dimensions, chemicals have enriched the lives of almost everyone. There is, however, a downside. A large number of these substances may cause human and ecosystem damages, certainly from exposure to concentrated doses, but also from long-run exposure to the trace amounts that show up virtually everywhere in workplaces, consumer products, and the environment.

The call to arms on chemicals in the environment was made by Rachel Carson in her book *Silent Spring*. She documented the ecosystem damage caused by the popular pesticide DDT and was largely responsible for getting it banned in the U.S., Canada and many other countries. Other events have multiplied concern. Health damages to workers exposed to chemicals in the workplace, such as vinyl chloride and certain potent agricultural chemicals, have occurred with disconcerting frequency. In 1978, in the celebrated case of Love Canal, people found chemicals oozing into their houses built on top of an abandoned hazardous waste disposal site. Accidental releases of chemicals have become a growing problem, from the large-scale episodes like those in Milan, Italy, in 1976 and Bhopal, India, in 1984, to innumerable smaller airborne and waterborne accidents. There is rising concern about the damages from long-term exposure to chemical residues in food, clothing, and other consumer products.

The primary concern is the impact of chemicals on human health. The EPA, for example, has developed a rough estimate of 2,000 excess cancer deaths a year in the U.S. from toxic airborne pollutants (compared to total annual cancer deaths of about half a million).[1] Health damages from accidental releases and workplace exposure are relatively easy to identify. Those from long-run exposure to trace amounts of chemicals in water, air, and soil are much harder to measure. Ecosystem damages are also important. Accidental waterborne chemical releases have wreaked havoc among fish and other organisms in enclosed bodies of water. Agricultural and industrial runoff has substantially damaged many rivers and estuaries around the world.

Hazardous and toxic materials have characteristics that present unique problems for monitoring and control.

1 They are ubiquitous in the modern economy; each year sees the development of new chemicals. This makes it difficult even knowing what substances are being used and in what quantities. It accounts for the fact that much public policy has been directed at simply getting better information about quantities of hazardous and toxic materials at various places in the system.

2 With the thousands of substances in use, each with different chemical and physical properties, it is virtually impossible to be fully informed about the levels of danger that each one poses to humans and other parts of the ecosystem.

3 In many cases the quantities used are relatively small, as are the quantities that end up as effluent. This substantially increases monitoring problems. It also makes it easier for users to carry out surreptitious disposal. It is easy to see the plume of smoke coming out of the stack of an industrial plant; it is harder to track the much smaller quantities of chemicals used in production.

4 The damages caused by exposure to hazardous materials can often take many years, even decades, to show up. And whenever there is a long time gap between cause and effect, there is a tendency to downgrade the overall seriousness of the problem. Exhibit 18-1 illustrates the human and ecological tragedy that can arise from a toxic compound.

In the next few sections we will consider government policy on hazardous and toxic substances and some of the major economic issues in the management of these materials. Canada has only recently begun to develop policies. There is, as always, scope for conflict and cooperation. But all levels of government face a situation where thousands of different substances are in use, hundreds more introduced each year, massive uncertainties exist about the human and nonhuman effects of most of them, and public concerns flare up and die down in unpredictable ways.

FEDERAL AND PROVINCIAL POLICIES TO REDUCE EMISSIONS OF TOXIC SUBSTANCES

Toxic emissions come in a great variety of forms, from small airborne releases of cleaning fluid from dry cleaning establishments to large-scale releases of toxics from

---

[1] U.S. Council on Environmental Quality, *Environmental Quality, 1984* (Washington, D.C., 1985), 58.

EXHIBIT 18-1

MERCURY POISONING OF THE WABIGOON-ENGLISH RIVER SYSTEM

Pijibowin: the poisoning of the Wabigoon—English River system

Pijibowin—the Ojibwa word for poison. In 1970 it took on a terrible relevancy for the residents of Grassy Narrows and White Dog in northwestern Ontario when scientists discovered that the river that ran through the two Ojibwa communities, and had been their economic lifeblood, was polluted with mercury—*pijibowin.*

From 1963 to 1970, a pulp and paper plant in Dryden that produced chlorine from a mercury cell had discharged approximately 9–11t of mercury into the Wabigoon-English River system (Canada-Ontario Steering Committee 1983). Fish in the Wabigoon-English River system had accumulated concentrations of mercury up to 30 times that considered "safe".... As a result, local Ojibwa people of the White Dog and Grassy Narrows communities, many of whom were fishing guides and heavy fish-eaters, themselves had accumulated unacceptably high levels of mercury in their blood....

It is impossible to separate the direct debilitating medical effects of mercury poisoning on the people of White Dog and Grassy Narrows—their degree is still a matter of scientific debate—from the devastating impacts of mercury on their economic, social, and psychological well-being. Pollution of the Wabigoon-English River system meant lost income from guiding, abrupt separation from lifestyles based on fish consumption, and a loss of faith in nature and its ability to provide.

The gradual recovery of the Wabigoon-English River system is illustrated in Figure 3.B4, which charts the decline in mercury concentrations found in the tail muscle of crayfish taken from Cray Lake, Ontario. However, cases of high mercury levels (more than 6 ppm) keep turning up in the population—most recently in a 3-year-old girl whose grandmother fed her fish frequently. Twenty years after the pulp and paper mill stopped discharging mercury into the river, provincial and federal ministries continue to advise people to restrict their intake of fish from lakes and rivers in the region....

Source: Reproduced from Government of Canada, 1991, *The State of Canada's Environment.*

Concentrations of Mercury in Crayfish from Cray Lake on the Wabigoon-English River System, Ontario, 1970–90.

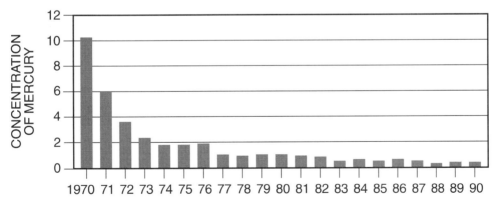

Note: Point source at Dryden reduced by approximately 95% in 1970 and reduced to virtually zero in 1975.
Source: G.P. MacRae. Freshwater Institute, personal communication, as cited in Environment Canada, *The State of Canada's Environment*, Supply and Services, 1991, p. 3–21.

substantial industrial plants. Also included are the concentrated accidental releases that have helped in the past to spur public concern about toxics in the environment. Not all toxics are chemicals; some, like heavy metals (mercury, cadmium, etc.), are by-products of various industrial and mining operations. Emissions-control policies at the federal and provincial levels have focussed largely on the management of conventional airborne and waterborne pollutants. For air this meant the criteria pollutants—SO_2, CO, O_3, NO_x, total suspended particulates, and lead—and for water it meant BOD, suspended solids, coliform count, etc. However, it was known during the initial regulatory days that there was a potentially serious class of toxic emissions stemming from industrial production operations, as well as from household sources. But the difficulties with even enumerating all of the possible substances involved, and of knowing what impacts each might have, essentially led to postponing coming to grips with the problem. In addition, the control of conventional pollutants has been effective to some extent in controlling toxics, since they are often closely associated. In recent years, however, more effort has gone into specific toxic emissions reduction programs, but as of now, little has been accomplished compared to efforts in other environmental areas.

There is a short list of laws and regulations that pertain to toxic substances in Canada. Table 18-1 lists the federal regulations. The provinces have a few policies, typically combined with existing air- and water-pollution regulations. Our discussion of toxic policies is divided into two topics—policies dealing with the emission of toxic substances and the management of the disposal and storage of toxic substances. In this section we focus on strategies to reduce emissions. Two federal policies, the Environmental Contaminants Act (ECA) of 1975 (which was replaced by CEPA), and the Canadian Environmental Protection Act of 1988 (CEPA), are discussed. We then turn to a discussion of the regulation of toxic compounds from the pulp and paper industry (which entails federal and provincial legislation).

Federal Policies on Toxic Substances

The objective of the Environmental Contaminants Act was to prevent "dangerous contaminants" from entering the environment. Federal powers under the act included:

1 The right to obtain information from manufacturers, processors, and importers of substances Environment Canada thinks are dangerous;

2 The power to conduct research on dangerous substances in cooperation with provincial governments; and

3 The right to prevent discharges of substances authorized jointly by the Minister of the Environment and Minister of Health and Welfare which "pose a significant danger to human health or the environment."

Once a substance has been so designated, it cannot be released into the environment without a special permit. Under the Environmental Contaminants Act, only five compounds ever made it to the prohibited or restricted list: polychlorinated biphenyls (PCBs), polybrominated biphenyls (PBBs), polychlorinated triphenyls (PCTs), mirex,

TABLE 18-1   FEDERAL LAWS AND REGULATIONS COVERING TOXIC SUBSTANCES

Atomic Energy Control Act
   Transport packaging of radioactive materials regulation
   Uranium and thorium mining regulations

Canadian Environmental Protection Act
   Chloralkali mercury release regulations
   Chlorobiphenyls regulations
   Contaminated fuel regulations
   PCB waste export regulations
   Pulp and Paper mill effluent chlorinated dioxins and furans regulations
   Vinyl chloride national emission standards regulations
   Vinyl chloride release regulations

Environmental Contaminants Act
   Mirex regulations

Fisheries Act
   Chloralkali mercury liquid effluent regulations
   Metal mining liquid effluent regulations
   Petroleum refinery liquid effluent regulations
   Pulp and paper effluent guidelines and regulations

Hazardous Materials Information Review Act

Hazardous Products Act

Pest Control Products Act

Transportation of Dangerous Goods Act

and CFCs. As illustrated in Figure 16-1 of Chapter 16, a total ban on release of these compounds is socially efficient if the MD curve lies everywhere above the MAC. The determination of the MD is clearly crucial to determining efficient regulations.

The government's powers under the ECA enable it to act only after it has shown that a danger to health or the environment exist. This means that the burden of proof is on the government to get information about substances and determine their toxicity. Companies are thus allowed to produce the compounds and release them into the environment without proving that they aren't dangerous. If the government then regulates the substance, it may be (and generally is) years after it has been in use. This is like the old expression "shutting the barn door after the horse is out." The policy is thus *reactive* not *proactive*. The legislation is very different from that of other chemical compounds entering our environment. For example, pharmaceuticals cannot be licensed for human use until extensive tests are done to show that they deal with the problem they are designed for without endangering human health. Food additives undergo a similar process. Even pest control products have to be registered before being sold (but do not have to verify safety). While testing prior to release for sale is not foolproof, it is more proactive than waiting until the compound is in use. It might have been a more prudent policy to require chemical compounds to go through a similar process.

In the late-1980s as part of the resurgence of Environment Canada, the Environmental Contaminants Act was absorbed into the Canadian Environmental Protection Act. The powers regarding toxics are the same under CEPA as they were under the ECA. Then Minister of the Environment at the time said that CEPA represented the toughest environmental legislation in the world. The environmental lobby did not respond with the same enthusiasm, recalling the slow progress made by the ECA. By the early 1990s, under first, ECA, then CEPA, a total of 13 compounds have been regulated. Among those compounds added to the list were dioxins and furans in pulp mill discharges. These were to be eliminated by 1994. As noted in earlier chapters, CEPA established a federal presence in an area that might be construed by the provinces as their jurisdiction. Toxic materials were called a matter of national concern. The act also covers ocean dumping, transboundary air pollutants, and flows of fertilizers. These types of pollution problems are clearly within the federal domain. Federal-provincial cooperation is called for in the act to help alleviate provincial concerns.

Another feature of the act was the creation of a "Priorities Substance List" (PSL) in 1989. The PSL was to identify compounds of immediate concern that would then receive detailed assessments. One or more of the following criteria must be present for a substance to be nominated to the PSL.[2] These are:

1 Once released into the environment, they are persistent in the ecosystem. They are highly resistant to chemical and biological breakdown by natural processes.

2 They are harmful, and may therefore pose a threat to human health and/or the environment.

3 They accumulate in the food chain, causing adverse effects at higher trophic levels.

4 They are widely used or used in large quantities, and have the potential to cause significant contamination if released into the environment.

5 They are already present in the environment and are suspected of causing damage to it.

So again we see that the burden of proof is on the government to identify substances with these characteristics. Once substances are on the list, they are studied. Only after this process, do regulations occur. The regulations may take the form of voluntary actions, guidelines, codes of good practice, and/or regulations to ban the substance, or limit its use or discharge into the environment. Regulations can be immediate, or phased in, and applied to all aspects of a compounds manufacture and use. Thus CEPA and its PSL offers no more or no less than most other Canadian environment policies.

Forty-four substances and classes of substances have been adopted by the Ministers of the Environment and Health and Welfare Canada, in consultation with an advisory panel. Assessment is to occur by February 1994. Under the Green Plan (as noted

---

[2] The source for this list and other information about the PSL is Environment Canada and Health and Welfare Canada, *Preparing the Second Priority Substances List*, An Invitation to Stakeholders to Comment on the Federal Government Proposals (April 1993): 2–4.

in Chapter 15), the federal government is committed to publish a revised PSL every three years thereafter. The goal is to assess 100 substances by the year 2000. Efforts are now under way to prepare the second PSL.

The Regulation of Toxic Compound's from Canada's Pulp and Paper Industry

Much has been written about the regulation of toxic compounds coming from pulp mills. Some governments and environmental organizations offer studies which show that the chlorinated organic compounds in mill effluent are very dangerous compounds that should be banned. The forest industry counters with research that says the other studies are inconclusive; that chlorine bleaching in their pulping process isn't necessarily the guilty technology, and that they are already spending large amounts of money to control their wastes. Exhibit 18-2 illustrates these opposing viewpoints.

Federal pulp and paper regulation began under the Fisheries Act in the early 1970s with standards that divided the pollutants in the mill effluent into three categories: total suspended solids (TSS), biochemical oxygen demand (BOD), and acute toxicity.[3] We have already dealt with TSS and BOD pollutants in Chapter 16. Our concern here is with toxicity, defined in the regulations as the unknown mix of chemicals lethal to fish and other organisms in the immediate vicinity of the effluent outfall. The federal regulations were in the form of standards based on best-practicable technology. The federal government had to be careful not to impinge on provincial powers, so it tried to "sell" the standards to the provinces as minimal national standards that would ensure that no one region of the country would become a haven for polluters. As well, existing mills were exempted from the standards, thus reducing the burden for provinces where pulp mills were a significant contributor to local economies. Once again, the ability to control emissions and political factors were criteria used for regulation, not a balancing of the marginal benefits and costs of control. Throughout this early process the industry remained the source of information on what was practicable technology. It was said that government regulators at the time had no way of checking the industry's information. The toxic regulations were in the form of discharges per unit of output produced. There were no absolute limits on total loadings to the environment. The test of acute toxicity was pass/fail, based on fish mortality.

Once the regulations were promulgated, implementation was another story. The pulp and paper industry was reluctant to spend money on processes that did not contribute to output in some way. This continued to be a problem into the 1980s.[4] The standards were enforceable by the provinces. Compliance with the regulations was

---

[3] Information for this section comes from Doug Macdonald, *The Politics of Pollution* (Toronto: McClelland & Stewart, 1991), 225–240.

[4] See William F. Sinclair, *Controlling Pollution from Canadian Pulp and Paper Manufacturers: A Federal Perspective* (Environment Canada, 1990), for a very detailed examination of the industry's spending on capital improvements to expand production capacity versus expenditures for pollution abatement.

EXHIBIT 18-2

MILL TOXINS REPORTED WIDESPREAD

Glenn Bohn
Sun Environment Reporter

Three-quarters of Canada's chlorine-consuming pulp mills are dumping fish-lethal wastes into our rivers and seas, spreading poisons as far as 1,400 kilometres away from their source, a new federal government report warns.

Dilution of the wastes is no solution, according to scientists in the federal health, environment and fisheries departments.

Their report, Ottawa's official assessment of the risks of releasing chlorinated organics into the environment from Canada's 47 bleaching pulp mills, says the mills' effluents remain deadly to fish even at concentrations as low as three-per-cent waste and 97-per-cent water.

At even lower concentrations—as little as one-half of one-per-cent effluent—there are sub-lethal effects such as reproductive problems.

The report concludes what environmental groups warned of before Canada's first dioxin-triggered fisheries closure in 1988 at Howe Sound—that the chlorinated organic wastes dumped by pulp mills that bleach with chlorine are, in the scientists' words, causing "immediate and long-term harmful effect on the environment."

The report estimates that Canadian mills dump one million tonnes of chlorine-based wastes into the environment annually—a soup of at least 250 compounds, some still unidentified.

The scientists found that chlorinated organics were "toxic" as defined by the Canadian Environmental Protection Act—a ruling that empowers the federal environment and health ministers to impose pollution laws with $1-million-a-day fines and jail terms for violators.

That conclusion triggered new demands Thursday that the federal government enact a pollution law that restricts the dumping of all chlorinated organics, not just dioxins and furans, the most notorious members of the family of man-made chemical compounds.

Federal environment ministers promised a law would be in force in 1990, then in early 1991, then in late 1991.

"It's very clear they're under a lot of pressure from the forest industry to take the 'more research' approach," said Lynn Jamieson, a Greenpeace pulp-and-paper campaigner.

"The industry feels that, if they do more research, they can water the (proposed law) down, to the point where they won't actually have to eliminate chlorine and chlorine-based compounds."

A B.C. pulp-industry spokesman complained the federal report is "off the mark" when it comes to B.C.'s 18 chlorine-bleaching pulp mills.

Brian McCloy of the Council of Forest Industries of B.C. said all the B.C. mills with secondary treatment pass the toxicity tests, and he said all the remaining mills will pass proposed federal pollution standards by 1993 or 1994, when all have secondary treatment.

He said the industry is spending $1.2 billion in B.C. to cut water pollution, so the new federal report was "certainly not true in a B.C. context."

Al Colodey, an Environment Canada scientist and one of the report's authors, said the government has promised to regulate dioxins, but the authors could not establish a scientific basis for setting legal limits for chlorinated organics.

Source: Glenn Bohn, *The Vancouver Sun,* November 1, 1991, page A3.

sought through individual negotiation with each company; prosecution was not used until later years. Over the period 1969 to 1982, a large number of mills were not meeting the toxicity requirements even though the industry received considerable financial assistance from the federal government. Between 1971 and 1979, this amounted to $10.6 million under accelerated capital cost (depreciation) allowances in the federal corporate income tax. Another $3 million was given to the industry in the form of direct support for installing pollution abatement equipment in a program begun in 1975. Between 1979 and 1985, the industry received a total of $544 million from the federal government and the provinces of Ontario, Quebec, New Brunswick, Nova Scotia, and Newfoundland, under the Pulp and Paper Modernization Program. This program was designed to assist the industry in improving its capital stock to be more competitive with pulp and paper producers in other countries. Of the industry's total spending on capital improvements over this period, 18 percent was spent on pollution abatement equipment. It is thus somewhat difficult to accept the industry's repeated insistence that it was unable to comply with pollution regulations due to its fierce competitive environment. Significant gains were made in BOD and TSS reductions. This happened in part because of greater technical efficiency in using its wood inputs.

Public pressure against the industry intensified in the late 1980s when Greenpeace stepped up its campaign to eliminate emissions of chlorine compounds associated with dioxin and other chlorinated organic compounds. A flurry of research was done on dioxin concentrations and their likely impact on ecosystems and human health. An expert committee investigating pulp effluent in Ontario reported in 1988 that the health threat of dioxins and furans was overstated. The real problem was that 97 percent of the chemicals in the waste products had never been analyzed or even identified. The committee recommended that steps be taken to reduce the total quantity of organochlorine emissions. This illustrates an important point with the regulation of any compound when it is released with a number of other contaminants: focussing on a few such compounds may not result in an improvement in the ecosystem and human health if you haven't controlled *all* the compounds responsible for adverse effects. Environmental policy is then seen as a useless expense. The Ontario committee's recommendation is rarely taken into account in environmental regulation. The committee also found that cost of pollution control was not prohibitive given the industry's financial situation.

Finally, in 1989 continued pressure from the public, environmental groups and a report by Environment Canada on the pulp and paper industry, led to an announcement of new dioxin and furan regulation under CEPA.[5] Later that year, B.C., Ontario, Quebec, and Alberta announced they would be bringing in regulations within several years. In 1990, Environment Canada announced that organochlorine discharges would be added to the regulations and that the Fisheries Act would be amended to make these standards or guidelines applicable to all plants, regardless of when built. Environment Canada said the discharge requirements would be met though provincial regulation and enforcement where equivalency of standards for the two levels of government was met. If there was no equivalency, Environment Canada would enforce the requirements. The new regulations have three components.

---

[5] This Environment Canada report was known as the Sinclair Report, after its author, William Sinclair, who was cited above.

1 Under the Fisheries Act, new limits for toxic discharges, BOD, and TSS are set. By 1994, the new regulations plus those imposed in 1971 would be applied to all mills. (As of 1990, only 11 out of 155 mills in the country were covered by the 1971 regulations.)

2 Under CEPA, dioxin and furan discharges from plants using chlorine bleaching are to be "virtually eliminated." The regulation is to be in force by 1994.

3 Other regulations for organochlorine discharges will be developed. No specific date was given.

Needless to say, the industry responded that these regulations will cost a lot of money. Their estimate was $5 billion. Statistics Canada estimates the total capital costs of compliance at $2.2 billion, with a lot of variation in costs across mills of different sizes and vintages. The costs per mill could vary from over $100 thousand to $100 million.[6] Average annual investment from 1978 to 1989 by mills in the study done by Statistics Canada was $16.8 million per mill (in 1989 dollars). The average capital cost of compliance per mill (for those not already in compliance) is estimated at $25.7 million over the life of the equipment. These costs can thus be thought of as consuming about 1.5 years of what would be ordinary investment. This can also be converted into an annualized cost over the life of the capital asset. Statistics Canada estimates the average annualized cost per mill at $4.4 million which represents just under 8 percent of their average annual surplus. Annual surplus is defined as the value of shipments minus the cost of energy, materials, and labour. Surplus therefore includes head office overhead, some purchased services, depreciation, and profit. The political debate will no doubt continue. What is needed now for an economic assessment is more quantitative evidence on the marginal damages from the mill effluent and MAC for different levels of control so that a socially efficient level of emissions can be calculated.

ECONOMIC ISSUES IN TOXIC WASTE MANAGEMENT

The early policies on hazardous waste were aimed at managing the flow of hazardous emissions coming from firms, in order to reduce potential impacts, especially on human health. In this respect it mirrored the approach taken in conventional pollutants. But toxic emissions are more difficult to manage. Smaller quantities make them much more difficult to monitor, even though in many cases small quantities can be quite damaging. This has led policymakers to think about attacking the toxics problems by "moving back up the line"; that is, by trying to reduce the amounts of material that are in need of disposal. This can be done in two ways: (1) by recycling residuals back into the production process, and (2) by shifting technologies and operations

---

[6] Craig Gaston, "Pulp and Paper Industry Compliance Costs" in Statistics Canada, *Environmental Perspectives, 1993*, Catalogue No. 11-528E Occasional (Ottawa: Statistics Canada, March 1993), 20. This is the source for all the numbers reported in this section.

so that the amount of residuals actually generated by firms is reduced. We will call these methods "waste reduction."[7]

Waste Reduction

The thought behind waste reduction is that by changing production processes and adopting new technologies and operating procedures, firms can substantially reduce the quantities of hazardous waste they produce per unit of final product. For example, a firm might find a new way to operate a materials cleaning process to get the same effect but with less cleaning solvent. Or a firm might shift from using a process requiring a toxic material to one involving a nontoxic substance. Or an end product might be redesigned in a way that permits its fabrication using smaller quantities of hazardous materials. These are industrial counterparts to our discussion on "green" consumer goods in Chapter 10. Waste reduction is obviously very complicated and firm-specific. Different processes lend themselves to different waste reduction procedures, and the costs of achieving significant waste reduction in one situation will be very different from the costs of other cases.[8] This is a setting where it is essentially impossible to achieve efficient controls by having a regulatory agency dictate particular technology choices for firms using toxic substances. The technical aspects of production processes and the situation of each firm are too heterogeneous for this approach. Instead, more effective means need to be found that will give firms themselves strong incentives to reduce toxic emissions in cost-effective ways.

How to give firms the appropriate incentives for waste reduction? Changes in hazardous-waste disposal laws might make a difference. With waste disposal more difficult, firms will be motivated to search for better ways of reducing the quantities of waste requiring disposal. A major flaw in this approach, however, is that the vast majority of hazardous waste is not subject to disposal regulations because it never leaves the premises of the firms where it is used. We will come back to this below.

To what extent might we rely on liability and compensation laws to provide the necessary incentives? We discussed the issue of liability conceptually in Chapter 10. By requiring polluters to compensate those whom they have damaged, these costs can become internalized, which would lead firms to take them into account in making their decisions. This could also operate through an insurance market, if premiums for hazardous-waste damage policies could be set so as to reflect accurately the risks of damage associated with a firm's hazardous waste actions. The real problem is whether we know enough about risks to be able to rely on an efficient insurance market and compensation system. Although there are thousands of chemicals in use, we have very little hard information on exactly how much damage they may cause to humans; most of the dose-response information we have comes from studies on ani-

---

[7] Some people prefer to distinguish between "waste reduction" and "recycling" as separate processes, but in our discussion we will lump them together.

[8] For some examples see Office of Technology Assessment, *Serious Reduction of Hazardous Waste* (Washington, D.C., 1986).

mals, especially mice. Under the circumstances, there is not enough information about risks and the damages to be able to establish consistent compensation awards or insurance premium rates that reflect true risks. This lack of information also impedes the use of all regulatory instruments.

In the case of conventional pollutants we have discussed using incentive mechanisms like emission taxes. In applying this to toxics the biggest problem is accurate emissions monitoring. The widespread dispersion of these materials throughout the economic sector, together with the fact that many are emitted in nonpoint modes, makes widespread monitoring by third parties essentially impossible. Also, taxing emissions would provide a strong incentive for firms to dispose of toxics illegally, which would usually be difficult to detect because of the relatively small volumes involved. Taxes on waste disposal, however, may be somewhat more feasible, as we will discuss below. Another possibility is to levy a tax on the feedstocks used to manufacture chemicals, since these would be fewer in number and easier to measure than the chemicals themselves once they have moved into production channels. Still another possibility might be to institute deposit-refund systems for chemicals. Firms would pay a deposit along with the purchase price when the chemicals were bought. They could recover that deposit, or a portion of it, by documenting a reduction of emissions, that is, of the recovery of the chemical from the normal waste stream.

One way that incentives for waste reduction have been created in recent years is through making information more widely available about the presence and release of toxic materials. One reason hazardous wastes have been hard to manage is that with the relatively small quantities often involved, and with most disposal taking place in the same location where the materials were used, it has been difficult for the public to get accurate information on the quantities and qualities of hazardous materials present in the immediate area. One objective of the Canadian Priority Substances List is to provide information on what are considered toxic substances simply by publishing the list. The Toxic Chemical Release Inventory Program of the U.S. requires firms to report emissions of a number of chemicals if they are above a specified minimum level. The information provided by these types of policies should help make the tort system a more effective deterrent to the discharge of toxic waste. However, this type of information provides no guidance on what actual damages may be coming from the hazardous materials cited, and, in some cases, real damages and public concern may not be closely connected.

Canadian Policies on the Management of Toxic Wastes

The control of airborne and waterborne toxic residuals does not address the major issue of the large quantities of hazardous materials that are left over after production (and recycling) is completed, and which must then be disposed of. Until our Priority Substances Lists are published and data collected on toxic substances, we won't know exactly how much is being generated and what must be disposed of. Hazardous waste consists of a diverse set of materials. In liquid form there are waste oils, solvents, and liquids containing metals, acids, PCBs, and so on. There are hazardous wastes in solid form, such as metals dust, polyvinyls, and polyethylene materials. There are many materials between liquid and solid, called sludges, such as sulfur sludge, heavy metal, solvent and cyanide sludges, and dye and paint sludges. Then there are a variety of mixed substances such as pesticides, explosives, lab wastes, and the like. Environment Canada in conjunction with Health and Welfare Canada and the provinces have power to define what is considered a hazardous waste. Hazardous waste generation is not spread evenly over the country. As expected, areas where the most manufacturing and resource processing occurs will produce the most waste. The industrialized provinces contribute the most to hazardous waste—Ontario and Quebec combined constitute 80 percent of the waste generated (Ontario 59 percent, Quebec 21 percent). Hazardous wastes can be disposed of in injection wells, that is, deep wells driven into underground geologic formations (salt caverns and aquifers). From an industry standpoint this method is relatively cheap and flexible. However, a substantial proportion of these wastes are no doubt discharged in wastewater, either directly into a stream or river or into a municipal waste treatment plant. Surface impoundment and landfill disposal, into both hazardous waste (lined) landfills as well as unlined landfills, accounted for most of the remaining hazardous waste. Disposal of hazardous wastes through chemical treatment is probably a relatively small proportion of the total. Most hazardous waste is probably disposed of on-site; that is, at the site of the industrial plant where it was manufactured and/or used. Environment Canada estimates that in 1986, approximately 65 percent of hazardous wastes are managed on site.[9]

The two major pathways leading to damage are through accidental releases and through releases stemming from improper handling, either at the site of use or at waste disposal facilities. A Quebec study found, for example, that approximately one-third of the hazardous wastes sent off site for processing or disposal could not be accounted for. Wastes are obviously not being controlled properly either through mismanagement or deliberate avoidance. Accidents have led to severe and obvious damages, to humans and to other parts of the ecosystem.[10] It has been less easy to document the damages coming from long-run exposure to small amounts of hazardous wastes. Ecosystems in the vicinity of industrial waste dumps are sometimes visibly affected. Human health effects have been harder to show, particularly when what is at issue is long-run exposure to small quantities of hazardous materials. Much more epidemiological and laboratory work remains to be done.

In this section, we look at two issues for regulation: the disposal of toxic wastes and the clean-up of toxic waste sites. In the next section, we compare Canada's efforts to the activities in the United States. Canada is only beginning to address the problems associated with toxic waste disposal and storage. Federal jurisdiction over toxic waste disposal and management is limited to interprovincial and international flows.

---

[9] Environment Canada, *State of the Environment 1991* (Ottawa: Ministry of Supply and Services), 14–12.

[10] In Chapter 7 we discussed current efforts to develop techniques to estimate ecosystem damages arising from hazardous waste releases.

The disposal of toxic wastes (like all waste products) is governed by provincial and municipal authorities. As usual, even when the federal government does have jurisdiction, there is the question of provincial enforcement of the acts.

The Disposal of Toxic Wastes

Federal policies are covered by three acts—The Ocean Dumping Control Act, the Transportation of Dangerous Goods Act, and the Atomic Energy Control Act which deal with radioactive wastes. The Transportation of Dangerous Goods Act came into effect in 1985 and specifies requirements for equipment, procedures, the training of personnel, and emergency preparations for accidents and spills. Another important feature of the act is that it requires all shippers of toxic materials to provide documentation that allows the shipment to be tracked at every point throughout its transport. This is analogous to U.S. regulation we discuss below requiring a manifest, that is, complete record for each product shipped. The act makes the generators of waste responsible for its proper handling at all stages.

Each province regulates how hazardous wastes are stored and specifies security measures, fire protection, labelling, container design and other aspects that relate to environmental safety. Provinces may require all waste dischargers to have a permit which specifies the quantities allowed and where disposal can occur. A fee may or may not be levied. British Columbia's Waste Management Act of 1982 illustrates this type of policy. The Waste Management Act establishes strict liability against the discharge of wastes into the environment without a permit. The B.C. Ministry of Environment, Lands and Parks issues and manages the permit system. Each permit specifies the maximum quantity of pollutants allowed for discharge. There may also be other specific provisions connected to individual permits.[11]

In designing these permits, the government had to set maximum discharge levels. These are called "pollution-control objectives" and they have been set for five industrial groups—chemicals and petroleum; mining, smelting and related activities; forest products; food processing and miscellaneous agriculture; and municipal waste. A permit is needed for each environmental medium into which wastes are discharged (air, water, land) and there is also a permit for special waste storage. By the late 1980s, 3,360 permits had been distributed. The provincial government monitors discharges and enforces the scheme.

Fees for the permits were introduced in 1987 and modified in 1992. The system in place until September 1992 had a different fee structure for industrial and municipal sources. For industrial sources, the fee was based on industry production levels rather than wastes discharged from individual sources. Municipal effluent fees were based on the volume of effluent discharged. There were separate permits for solid wastes and liquid effluent for municipalities. The system from 1987 to 1992 went part

---

[11] The permit can also require the permittee to: repair, improve or construct new works; post security; monitor the method of landing, treating, transporting, discharging and storing wastes; conduct studies and report information; use specified procedures in waste handling; recycle certain wastes to recover certain resources, e.g., energy.

way toward using an economic instrument for waste disposal. Effluent fees for municipalities could provide an incentive to reduce emissions, if set at a level that reflects
environmental costs. The industrial fees were based only on the government's costs
of administering the system, not any measure of the economic and environmental
costs of waste disposal. One B.C. government estimate was that 15 percent of the
administrative costs of the permit system were covered by the fees; the rest came out
of general revenues. Fees that are not only low, but unconnected to actual discharges
provide no incentive to reduce (or recycle) wastes. The old fee system was also based
on increasing block charges. This meant that average and marginal fees per unit volume fall as volume increases. This fee structure likewise provides no incentive on the
margin to reduce wastes.

In 1992, a new system was announced that moved the province much closer to
effluent taxes. Starting in September of that year, each permit holder paid an annual
fee that consisted of a $100 fixed fee plus a variable fee that was based on the annual
volume of each type of contaminant the ministry authorized for discharge, multiplied
by the new unit fee per tonne set by the regulation.[12] Tables 18-2 and 18-3 list the
fees that came into effect September 1, 1993, for contaminants released into air and
water. To ease adjustment to the new fee system, for the one-year period, September
1992 to September 1993, fees were one-half those shown on the tables. Fees are now
based on the government's assessment of the risks of the contaminant to the environment, as well as the administrative costs of the program. They will be adjusted as
information about environmental impacts improves. Allowed discharges are still
based on industry production characteristics, not actual discharges. The government
is contemplating changing this to base at least part of the fee on actual discharges.
For some industries, there was a substantial increase in fees. Revenues from the permits are being placed in a special fund, the Sustainable Environment Fund, rather than
deposited into general revenues. The fund is to be used to address environmental
problems and develop environmental protection projects.

One problem not yet addressed by the new fee structure is that the permits are
based on the volume of discharges, not concentrations. If the province moves to fees
based on actual discharges, they should consider changing the base to concentration.
If they don't, environmental damages may increase. Under a volume-based system,
dischargers have an incentive to increase the concentration of the waste material per
unit volume. Higher concentrations of wastes generally lead to more environmental
problems. Of course if concentration was used as the unit for the permit, monitoring
of discharges would become essential to ensure compliance. This could raise the costs
of the program substantially.

The Cleanup of Toxic Waste Sites

Canadian governments have been coming to terms with the management of toxic
waste sites slowly. There have been various cleanups of waste sites, but these tend

---

[12] The new regulation is called the Waste Management Permit Fees Regulation, Order in Council No.
1264, approved and ordered, July 30, 1992.

TABLE 18-2   CONTAMINANT FEES FOR AIR EMISSION PERMITS IN B.C., 1993

Contaminant	Fee per tonne discharged
Ammonia	$11.30
Asbestos*	11.30/unit
Carbon monoxide	0.30
Chlorine and chlorine oxides	7.60
Fluorides	453.60
Hydrocarbons	11.30
Hydrogen chloride	7.60
Metals	453.60
Nitrogen oxides	7.60
Phenols	11.30
Sulphur and sulphur oxides	8.80
Total particulate	11.30
TRS	378.00
VOCs	11.30
Other contaminants not otherwise specified	11.30

Note: *Units of asbestos are equivalent to 5 cubic metres of air emissions per minute at a concentration of 2 fibres per cubic centimetre.
Source: Waste Management Permit Fees Regulation, B.C. Order in Council No. 1264, July 30, 1992, Appendix, adapted from Schedule "B."

to be on an ad hoc basis. No government in Canada has an explicit program to deal with waste sites. There is no identified source of revenue to fund these very expensive activities, no procedures to establish priorities for which sites to clean up, and no legislation governing any of these activities. Determining where and how to dispose of ongoing toxic waste being generated is also an extremely contentious and unresolved issue in Canada. We now turn to the activities of federal and provincial governments in dealing with toxic waste sites.

Existing toxic waste sites are located primarily in urban areas. They are the result of past industrial activity, such as coal gasification in the nineteenth century. Many of these sites are known as "orphans" because the company or person responsible for the waste discharge is no longer in business. Site remediation is required by municipal laws before a piece of land can be used for redevelopment. Many sites in metropolitan Toronto have had to be cleaned before new residential and commercial development could occur. A politically contentious issue in B.C. has been the cleanup of the 1986 Expo site in Vancouver. One reason why federal and provincial action on waste sites has been minimal could be because these sites have been construed as "local" problems.

The identification of toxic sites in Canada began in the 1980s stimulated by the revelations at the Love Canal. The Atlantic and western provinces, and the territories joined the federal government in attempting to locate problem sites. Ontario and Quebec carried out their own surveys. Federal involvement in the activity was cancelled by the Mulroney government in 1984, due to budget cuts to Environment Canada. The provinces continued on their own. By 1990, 10,000 sites had been iden-

TABLE 18-3   CONTAMINANT FEES FOR EFFLUENT PERMITS IN B.C., 1993

Contaminant	Fee per tonne discharged
Acute toxicity*	$10.10/unit
Ammonia	69.30
AOX	184.00
Arsenic	184.60
BOD	13.90
Chlorine	184.00
Cyanide	184.00
Fluoride	69.30
Metals	184.00
Nitrogen and nitrates	46.20
Oil and grease	46.20
Other petroleum products	46.20
Other solids	9.20
Phenols	184.00
Phosphorous and phosphates	69.30
Sulphates	2.70
Sulphides	184.00
Surfactants	46.20
Suspended solids	9.20
Other contaminants not otherwise specified	9.20

Note: *Units of acute toxicity are determined using the following formula:
$$\text{Units of Acute Toxicity} = \frac{(\text{Average daily flow}/20) \times (100 - \text{LC50})}{100}$$
LC50 represents the "lethal concentration" at which 50 percent of fish die.
Source: Waste Management Permit Fees Regulation, B.C. Order in Council No. 1264, July 30, 1992, Appendix, adapted from Schedule "C."

tified, of which 719 were classified "Priority 1" which essentially meant that they represented a high risk to health and the environment and should be immediately assessed. The Canadian Council of Ministers of the Environment (CCME) has made a study of these sites, but has not made public any list of priorities for cleanup. In 1989, the CCME announced that $200 million of federal and provincial funds would be used to clean up 50 abandoned or orphan sites and another $50 million would be available to help develop technologies to decontaminate sites. These 50 sites were said by the CCME to represent 5 percent of the total. If cleanup costs for the others are at all comparable to these 50, the total bill would come to $4 billion. Of course, this is a very crude estimate as there is no way of knowing whether the other priority sites would be more or less expensive on average than the 50. In the fall of 1990, a program to set up guidelines for cleanup priorities and activities began, but nothing concrete has yet come of this activity. The first actual cleanup activities began in B.C. at a site in the Cariboo Mountains. Ontario announced in 1986, the creation of an Environmental Security Fund that would provide initially $10 million (changed to $20 million the next year) to support the costs of site remediation. These funds are to be drawn from general revenue.

One further set of actions regarding remediation of damaged areas involves the International Joint Commission (IJC), Canadian and U.S. governments. The IJC is a binational organization set up to deal with Canada–U.S. border issues. It has identified 42 sites around the Great Lakes which require decontamination and ongoing efforts to reduce further discharges. The IJC facilitates coordination among all the involved governments, the public and industry to accomplish what are called Remedial Action Plans (RAPs), established by these groups. Statistics Canada estimated that the total cost of implementing all the RAPs could range between $100 and $500 billion for Canada and the U.S. combined. These costs include not just remediation of sites, but, for example, construction and upgrading of sewage treatment plants to prevent further damage to health and the ecosystem. One RAP, the St. Lawrence Action Plan, has identified 50 sources of toxic emissions for which a target of 90 percent reduction in discharges by 1993 was set. Twenty of the sources are already covered by federal or Quebec regulation. Of the 30 not covered, 22 have signed agreements with the Quebec government to establish clean-up plans. Toxic cleanup is thus very costly. A benefit-cost study of toxic cleanup is needed to determine the efficient policy. There is no evidence that economic calculations of marginal benefits and costs are being made.

U.S. Federal Policy on the Management of Hazardous Wastes

U.S. federal policy on the management of hazardous waste is very different from that of Canada. They have an extensive legal and regulatory apparatus to deal with the issues we have been discussing. Federal policy in the U.S. has been directed at two types of problems: (1) developing a system to manage the storage, transportation, and disposal of current hazardous wastes, and (2) cleaning up land disposal sites where large quantities of hazardous wastes were dumped in years past. There are two major federal hazardous-waste laws that address these issues: The Resource Conservation and Recovery Act of 1976 (RCRA) and the Comprehensive Environmental Response, Compensation, and Liability Act of 1980 (CERCLA). We now look briefly at each of these.

There are four major parts to RCRA. The first is a definition of "hazardous wastes." The EPA's definition is based on physical properties that apparently are capable of causing damage, in particular corrosivity, toxicity, reactivity, and explosivity. If a substance meets the criteria under any of these headings, it is deemed to be hazardous. Politics being what it is, however, certain well-known substances were expressly excluded in the act; in particular, waste lubricating oil, wastes from oil and natural gas exploration, and radioactive wastes. The next is a "manifest" system. This is the process of recording how much of the material has been produced and how and where it moves through the system to final disposal. The 1976 act directed EPA to create a paper-trail system to track hazardous waste through the system. When material is generated, transported, stored, treated, or disposed of, it is supposed to be accompanied by a manifest stating the origin, quantities, and destination of the material. As it moves through the economic system, all waste is to be accompanied by its manifest. This would allow regulatory authorities to know the location of the waste at any point in time, which is fundamental to establishing any kind of control program.

The third part deals with standards for treatment, storage, and disposal facilities. Performance and design standards are to be enforced on operators engaged in handling and disposing of hazardous materials. For example, a performance standard on hazardous waste incinerators is that they destroy 99.99 percent of the organic wastes in the incinerator feedstock. A design standard applied to hazardous waste landfill operators is that the landfills be constructed with approved liners to reduce the risk of contaminating nearby groundwater. Finally, there is a permit system to enforce the standards. In order to stay in operation, hazardous waste transporters and disposers must obtain a permit from public authorities. The permit is supposed to be obtained only after all design and operating standards have been met.

At the present time there are about 500 licensed commercial treatment, storage, and disposal facilities in the U.S. The vast majority of hazardous waste in the U.S. is actually used and disposed of at the site where it is generated; for this material the manifest system is obviously less useful, though the permit system still applies. There are currently about 2,500 generator-owned treatment, storage, and disposal facilities and 75,000 industrial landfills in the U.S.

In 1984 Congress enacted a significant set of amendments to RCRA. The growing efforts to control hazardous emissions under air- and water-pollution laws were pushing more of these materials toward land disposal. Simultaneously there was increasing concern about the safety of groundwater resources and possible contamination from hazardous waste-disposal sites, even at sites that had supposedly been designed expressly to handle hazardous materials. The result was a law that severely restricts land disposal of hazardous wastes and directs the EPA to identify acceptable disposal means for various types of hazardous materials. It also extended control to hazardous waste sources not previously covered, such as underground storage tanks and small sources of hazardous waste (those producing between 100 and 1,000 kg of hazardous waste per month). The 1984 law continued and accelerated the trend in federal law in the direction of direct CAC-type controls: uniform technology and performance standards applied throughout the industry without regard to questions of cost-effectiveness or efficient risk reduction.

The Comprehensive Environmental Response, Compensation and Liability Act of 1980 (CERCLA) is the law directed at cleaning up past hazardous waste-disposal sites and has come to be called "Superfund," perhaps in reference to the massive sums of money involved. CERCLA was enacted in response to heightened public fears about the health impacts of past, and often forgotten, hazardous waste-disposal sites. In some cases, as in the Love Canal incident mentioned above, people were exposed directly to hazardous materials that migrated through the soil; in other cases, the fear was, and is, of groundwater contamination from these old dump sites. CERCLA has several main features:

1 A financial fund, derived from a tax on chemical and petroleum feedstocks used by industry, and from private parties held to be responsible for past dumping. This fund is to be used to carry out site investigations and cleanups.

2 A method for selecting sites for cleanup actions. This is called the National Contingency Plan (NCP) and specifies procedures for identifying and investigating sites, determining cleanup plans, and deciding on who will pay for it. Part of the procedure involves a state-federal effort to create the list of sites that are in greatest need of action; this is called the National Priorities List (NPL), and it involves a hazard-ranking system taking into account the types and quantities of hazardous materials at the site and the possibility of human exposure.

3 Authority for the EPA to clean up sites itself, or to identify responsible private parties to clean up the sites.

4 A liability provision for natural resources damage. Besides cleanup liability, CERCLA has a provision for holding responsible parties liable for damages to natural resources stemming from spilled or released toxic materials. Thus, if a chemical is accidentally released into a river, the people causing the spill can be held liable for the damages this causes. Or, if an old landfill leaks toxic compounds, responsible parties may be held liable not only for cleaning up the site but also for damages to surrounding groundwater resources.

In 1986 Congress passed the Superfund Amendments and Reauthorization Act, or SARA. This act extended the fund and broadened the tax to include, along with the feedstock tax, an "environmental tax" on all corporations of 0.12 percent of their taxable income over $2 million.

The Superfund cleanup process is very long and complicated, starting with identifying the site and the "potentially responsible parties" (PRPs) who have used the site at some time in the past, then proceeding with cleaning up the site and delisting it from the NPL. Each step involves public authorities at all levels as well as numerous private parties. It is a process full of conflict, and the costs of the legal actions on a site can sometimes rival or even exceed the actual costs of cleaning up the hazardous material.

Financing Hazardous Waste Site Cleanups

Cleaning up past hazardous waste sites is a lengthy and expensive process that involves complicated issues of liability, technical alternatives, and public risks. We have seen estimates for the Great Lakes. The EPA estimates that cleaning up the sites currently listed on the NPL will take more than $30 billion. This substantially exceeds the sums that will be raised under CERCLA through taxes on chemical feedstocks and the general corporate tax. A big question, therefore, is how to get greater resources from past or present dumpers, or their insurers, to help clean up the long list of sites currently on the NPL and new ones that may be listed. Several private insurers have suggested establishing large environmental trust funds, from mandatory or voluntary contributions, to be devoted to cleaning up hazardous waste sites. Others have suggested changing the current systems of financing and liability.

Ultimately the success in this effort may depend most critically on introducing changes that increase incentives for private firms to enter into cleanup agreements, among themselves and between themselves and government. In the U.S., the courts have ruled that in pursuing potentially responsible parties to obtain cleanup funds, the EPA may use the doctrine of strict, joint, and several liability by responsible parties. What this means is that when more than one firm has dumped hazardous wastes into the site, the EPA may nevertheless sue and recover total cleanup costs from just one of the responsible parties. So, for example, a company that has dumped only a small portion of the wastes into a site can nevertheless be held responsible for the total cleanup costs at the site. The effect of this is to provide an incentive for this one firm to identify and recover costs from other parties that were responsible for dumping at the site. But there are also strong negative aspects to this approach. The doctrine can hold individual firms responsible for total cleanup costs of a site even though they may have dumped only a small proportion of total wastes at the site. This no doubt leads firms to hold back because the admission of even partial responsibility opens them up to the risk of having to pay total cleanup costs. This and other features make the process highly litigious, with firms spending enormous amounts of money suing one another, the EPA, municipalities, states, insurance companies, and so on. It is not at all clear that Canada wants to follow the U.S. down this sort of path. Indeed, most Canadian legislation and policy attempts to avoid this sort of litigiousness. Exhibit 18-3 on page 375 illustrates why Canadian governments don't want to adopt this part of the U.S. policy. The advantage of having our neighbour to the south with a generally more advanced set of environmental policies is that we can learn what works and what doesn't. The "cost" of the Canadian conservatism on environmental regulation is that we may wait too long before acting and pay a high price for delay.

ECONOMIC INCENTIVES IN TOXIC WASTE MANAGEMENT

The policy debate on hazardous waste management is fuelled by the public fears and alarms that follow the highly publicized exposure incidents, like Love Canal, the Hagarsville, Ontario tire fire, the PCB-contaminated drinking water of the town of Smithville, Ontario, and similar events. It is not hard to understand why public authorities in the U.S. have relied on conventional CAC-type operating standards to address these issues. Canadian authorities give every indication of doing the same. CAC regulations give the impression that policymakers have established a system of positive control based on rational technical decisions. The CAC approach is certainly justified in some cases. If a landfill is to receive hazardous wastes, presumably it should be built to certain minimum technical specifications. This is especially true because of the difficulties of monitoring leaks from hazardous waste landfills. But this is a problem where economic incentive approaches can also be useful.

Waste-End Taxes

Taxes on hazardous wastes, levied at the place where they are generated or where they are disposed of, are a feasible way of providing the incentive for reducing the quantities produced, as well as directing the flow of wastes toward various channels. These have come to be called "waste-end taxes." The monitoring problem is much less a factor than with toxic emissions, since wastes are often in bulk form that lends itself to quantitative measurement. In fact, a tax of $2.13/ton of hazardous waste is currently charged at qualified disposal sites to support Superfund's Post-Closure Liability Trust Fund. Raising this tax would stimulate industry efforts at waste reduction. It would also lead to an increase in the prices of products that produce substantial quantities of waste in their manufacture. It has one unfortunate effect, however, in that it will also create an incentive to dispose of hazardous materials surreptitiously.

Deposit-Refund System

A major problem with many hazardous wastes is that they are in quantities that are difficult to monitor. This will continue to be the case even with the manifest system. Any kind of tax placed on hazardous material creates an incentive for disposers to conceal material discharged, perhaps by disposing of it on-site, into a public sewer system, or in some unapproved landfill. One way of turning these incentives around is to offer a subsidy for hazardous materials disposed of in approved ways. This, of course, would require a source of funds. A possibility would be to institute deposit-refund systems for hazardous materials. Firms would pay a deposit per unit of hazardous chemical at the time of purchase from a chemical supplier. They would then be paid a refund on materials when they were properly disposed of.[13]

SUMMARY

The coming of the chemical society has led to new sources of environmental damage and opened up new requirements for managing toxic and hazardous materials. Canadian policy is only beginning to come to terms with the problems of toxic materials. Federal regulation of toxic compounds involves the identification and regulation of dangerous contaminants once they have entered the ecosystem. While thousands of potentially dangerous compounds are in everyday use, only 13 of them have been banned or strictly regulated by the early 1990s. The cornerstone of federal policy is the creation of the Toxic Substances List which will initiate study and ultimate regulation. The pulp and paper industry was highlighted as one area that has received a good deal of regulatory effort in the last few years. The regulations have all been command and control and may require the installation of much new capital equipment. The recent regulations apply to all mills, new and old.

Management of waste sites is also just beginning in Canada. No Canadian government has an explicit and funded program to deal with the cleanup of existing sites. This is contrasted with the extensive liability and fee system for waste discharge and remediation of sites in the United States. In Canada, there are federal regulations over

---

[13] For more on this idea see Clifford S. Russell, "Economic Incentives in the Management of Hazardous Wastes," *Columbia Journal of Environmental Law* 13 (Spring 1988): 257–274.

EXHIBIT 18-3

THE REAL CLEANUP

Insurers' Superfund Focus: Hiring Lawyers.

By Michael Parrish, Times Staff Writer

Nearly 90% of the billions of dollars insurance companies have spent on Superfund toxic waste sites has been sunk into legal battles—mostly with their own policymakers, according to a RAND Corp. study released Thursday.

The money spent in court is enough, according to the study, to clean up 15 Superfund sites a year.

In contrast, the big industrial firms in the study have mostly gone ahead and paid for cleanups without fighting them in court, spending an average of just 21% of their Superfund money on legal costs.

Critics of the Superfund law, which is up for reauthorization by 1994, say the study supports their call for drastic reform.

"The only people cleaning up in Superfund are the lawyers," said Anne Ligon, assistant general counsel of the Superfund Action Coalition, a Washington lobbying group formed in January to represent companies faced with Superfund liabilities.

Insurers generally agreed.

But environmentalists, regulators and the RAND authors themselves found support for the current process in the study.

"It shows you the legal costs are not a big issue—except for the insurance companies." said Doug Wolf, an attorney with the Natural Resources Defense Council. "And I don't think we should let them dictate our policy for cleaning up abandoned waste sites."

The EPA spends about $1.5 billion a year in taxpayer dollars on Superfund cleanups. It has recovered $295 million from responsible parties since 1987 and is seeking $1 billion more.

While no one knows how much these parties have paid out for cleanups, their insurers are spending about $500 million annually in costs associated with the Superfund law.

The RAND researchers found that fully 88% of that $500 million is spent on lawsuits, with 47% of that sum being used to contest the claims of the insurance companies' own customers. Another 42% goes to defending policyholders against the EPA or other parties.

The RAND authors and others predict that some legal expenditures are bound to occur as state case law, which controls many of the legal battles, is sorted out.

And they see some evidence that the system is creating incentives for private companies to undertake cleanups before being forced to by the EPA: The study estimates that fully 10% of all cleanups costing a company more than $100,000 are being done without government involvement.

The large companies "have been willing to step forward and pay remedial costs which many had doubted at the beginning of the program," noted Lloyd S. Dixon of RAND's Institute for Civil Justice, one of the study's authors.

The insurance companies and such groups as the Superfund Action Coalition want to replace the existing system with one using taxpayer funds to finance a public works cleanup, much as billions of federal dollars have been spent in recent years to build new sewage treatment plants around the country.

"It's clear as a bell that Superfund's incredibly harsh and inequitable liability scheme has created and is going to continue to create considerable controversies," said Karl S. Lytz, an attorney at Latham & Watkins. He represents Montrose Chemical Corp. of California at one of the first Superfund sites listed in the nation—the Stringfellow acid pits in Riverside County.

Relations between companies such as Montrose and their insurers have grown "only more litigious over recent years." Lytz said, "And that level of fighting will continue."

But environmentalists, particularly, remain opposed to shifting to a public-works scheme.

"This report highlights (the insurance companies') self-interest in that proposal," said Wolf of the NRDC. "They would benefit more than anyone else."

ocean dumping, transportation of dangerous goods, and radioactive wastes. The provinces however are responsible for most waste disposal and storage. Some use permits to regulate disposal. These permits do not yet have fees attached that reflect the costs of disposal. There is substantial scope for new policies to reduce wastes, that is, changes in production systems that lead to lower quantities of hazardous waste requiring disposal. Canada is now beginning to study the issues.

QUESTIONS FOR FURTHER DISCUSSION

1 Handlers of hazardous wastes—that is, firms that accept hazardous materials and transport them for disposal—sometimes dispose of the materials illegally or in unapproved landfills. How might a deposit-refund system be designed to provide incentives to dispose of hazardous materials in approved ways?

2 What are the advantages and disadvantages of using a limited liability approach to cleaning up hazardous waste sites; that is, an approach whereby firms that dumped material in a site are held liable only for their own wastes?

3 The costs of cleaning up toxic waste sites is thought to be enormous. At present there is no dedicated funding for this task. How might Canadian governments finance remediation while simultaneously providing incentives to reduce waste generation?

4 What type of fee structure would you recommend for provincial disposal permits?

5 It has frequently been suggested that taxes be placed on toxic materials at point of production; these would be easier to administer (as compared to taxes in intermediate-use stages) and would discourage overall use of the chemicals taxed. What are the efficiency implications of this approach?

SELECTED READINGS

British Columbia Government. *Revising British Columbia's Waste Discharge Permit Fee System.* A Discussion Paper, Ministry of Environment, Lands and Parks, Environmental Protection Division, 1992.

Dorfman, Robert. "The Lessons of Pesticide Regulation," in Wesley A. Magat (ed.). *Reform of Environmental Regulation.* Cambridge, Mass.: Ballinger, 1982, chapter 2.

Harris, Christopher, William L. Want, and Morris A. Ward. *Hazardous Waste, Confronting the Challenge.* New York: Quorum Books, 1987.

Hirschhorn, Joel S., and Kirsten U. Oldenburg. *Prosperity Without Pollution: The Prevention Strategy for Industry and Consumers.* New York: Van Nostrand Reinhold, 1991.

Macauley, Molly K., Michael D. Bowes, and Karen L. Palmer. *Using Economic Incentives to Regulate Toxic Substances.* Washington, D.C.: Resources for the Future, 1993.

Mendeloff, John. *The Dilemma of Toxic Substance Regulation.* Cambridge, Mass.: MIT Press, 1988.

Sinclair, William F. "Controlling Effluent Discharges from Canadian Pulp and Paper Manufacturers." *Canadian Public Policy* 17(1) (March 1991): 86–105.

U.S. Environmental Protection Agency. *Waste Minimization—Issues and Options.* Vols. I, II, and III. (EPA/530/SW-86/041, 042, 043), Washington, D.C., 1986.

U.S. Office of Technology Assessment. *Technologies and Strategies for Hazardous Waste Control.* Washington, D.C., 1983.

19

LOCAL ENVIRONMENTAL ISSUES: SOLID WASTES, RECYCLING, WATER AND LAND USE

In Canada, local governments are responsible for many important activities that improve environmental quality. Table 19-1 shows the level of expenditures from 1984–85 to 1990–91 for federal, provincial, and local governments. It illustrates the dominant role played by local governments in solid wastes, water purification and supply, and sewage treatment. Note as well the rapid escalation in the costs of pollution control over this period. Federal expenditures grew in nominal terms by 44 percent, provincial by 55 percent, and local government expenditures by a whopping 107 percent! In this chapter we examine the issues of solid waste disposal and the potential to reduce it through recycling, reduction, and reuse. We also look at the activities of local governments in providing sewage and water treatment. Finally, we briefly consider water and land use issues.

MUNICIPAL SOLID WASTE

The disposal of solid wastes has emerged as a leading problem in many cities and towns across the country, especially in localities with large populations and/or constrained landfill space. The problem is of less immediate concern in areas with the opposite characteristics. Landfilling, for a long time the preferred disposal method for urban solid waste, has come up against a scarcity of sites willing to take wastes. Some localities have had to ship their solid wastes long distances for disposal, while others are moving into incineration. Additionally, rising fears of groundwater contamination from landfills and of air pollutants from incineration have turned what once was a disposal activity to which nobody gave a second thought into a prime environmental concern.

TABLE 19-1   GOVERNMENT EXPENDITURES ON ENVIRONMENTAL IMPROVEMENTS, 1984–1990

| | (Millions of current dollars) | | | | | | |
	1984-85	1985-86	1986-87	1987-88	1988-89	1989-90	1990-91
Federal							
Water purification and supply	—	—	—	—	—	—	—
Sewage collection	13.0	2.3	—	—	—	—	—
Pollution control	58.6	55.9	62.0	62.3	81.1	—	119.4
Garbage and waste collection	—	—	—	—	—	—	—
Other	419.7	363.9	383.7	435.7	442.9	590.0	587.7
Total	491.3	422.1	445.7	498.0	530.0	590.0	707.1
Provincial							
Water purification and supply	660.1	694.2	765.1	757.2	NA	NA	NA
Sewage collection	—	—	—	—	—	—	—
Pollution control	148.8	170.6	209.4	228.2	NA	NA	NA
Garbage and waste collection	—	—	—	—	—	—	—
Other	386.0	567.4	242.2	314.7	NA	NA	NA
Total	1195.0	1432.2	1216.8	1300.1	1702.0	1643.6	1848.0
Local							
Water purification and supply	1248.0	1353.1	1519.0	1678.2	1732.4	2198.7	2271.5
Sewage collection	965.0	992.9	1138.9	1208.6	1305.3	1701.8	1937.5
Pollution control	—	—	—	—	—	—	—
Garbage and waste collection	514.4	564.4	628.7	714.5	796.0	921.4	1065.3
Other	43.4	70.1	76.9	87.9	113.6	104.4	97.7
Total	2770.9	2980.4	3363.5	3689.2	3952.3	4948.4	5731.9
Total expenditures for all governments	4457.2	4834.7	5026.0	5487.3	6148.3	7182.0	8287.0

Source: Based on Statistics Canada, *Human Activity and the Environment*, Catalogue No. 11-509E (Ottawa: *Statistics Canada*, 1991), Table 3.2, 101–102.

The Nature of the Problem

The municipal solid waste (MSW) stream is actually a trickle at the end of a long and very large flow of materials used in the Canadian economy. From the Local Government Waste Management Practices Survey, Statistics Canada estimates that in 1990, between two and three kilograms of solid waste per dwelling per day are collected in municipalities with populations of 50,000 or greater.[1] Figure 19-1 illustrates the survey results for the different regions of the country. Household waste is com-

---

[1] Craig Gaston and Alan Goodall, "Local Government Waste Management Practices Survey," *Environmental Perspectives 1993*, Catalogue No. 11-528E Occasional (Ottawa: Statistics Canada, 1993), 69.

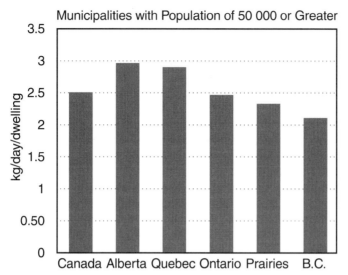

FIGURE 19-1   Garbage Collected per Dwelling, 1990.

Source: Statistics Canada, Public Institutions Division and National Accounts and Enviroment Division, as cited in Statistics Canada, *Environmental Perspectives 1993*, Cataloge No. 11-52BE Occasional, Statistics Canada, 1993, p. 69. Reproduced by authority of the Minister of Industry, 1994.

posed of a very diverse set of materials—everything from lawn clippings to moldy bread to household chemicals to used refrigerators to construction debris. The solid-waste problem is not equally acute everywhere.

Technical Options for Reducing MSW

We define the following terms: TM is total materials used, by a firm or industry or economy, in a period of time; VM is virgin materials used; and RM is recycled materials used. Then it must be true that for any time period:

$$TM = VM + RM$$

Materials-balance considerations[2] tell us that all materials inputs taken into an economic system must eventually end up back in the environment in some fashion. The form may change, as when solid materials are burned to yield energy and waste products. The time span can differ; some materials do not lend themselves to reuse and so are discarded almost immediately, while others can be recycled, perhaps many times. But recycling can never be perfect, because of conversion losses, wastage in

[2] See Chapter 2.

consumption, etc. This means we should focus on the quantity of virgin materials used. Rearranging the above expression gives:

$$VM = TM - RM, \text{ or}$$
$$= TM \, (1 - r)$$

where r is the rate of reuse, or RM/TM. There are essentially two ways to reduce the use of virgin materials: reduce the overall quantity of materials (TM), and/or increase the reuse rate r; in other words, waste reduction and recycling.

Total materials use can be reduced in two ways: by reducing the rate of economic activity or by reducing the materials intensity of that activity. By "materials intensity" we mean the quantity of materials used per unit of production or consumption. And this in turn can be done in two ways: (1) by rearranging the composition of output and consumption away from products that use relatively large amounts of materials and toward those that use less; for example, a shift away from tangible goods toward services, and (2) by decreasing the materials intensity of particular products; for example, reducing the amount of packaging material in consumer electronics or food products.

The other alternative is recycling. This means reaching into the waste stream to extract materials that may be reused. Some may be reused directly, as when consumers reuse old boxes. But most require some reprocessing. Of course, the separation, transportation, and reprocessing technologies that are available critically affect the costs of recycled materials, and thus their ability to displace virgin materials.

Current Policy

The present policy picture is very complicated, as you would expect from the nature of the physical problem, the large number of materials involved, and the thousands of municipalities, small and large, searching for solutions. Table 19-2 lists some of the measures that are being pursued in various provinces. For the most part these focus on some facet of recycling. When solid waste first became an issue, it was regarded primarily as a disposal issue—people were taking to the landfill materials and products that could be recycled. Thus, the initial response of most communities was to think about materials recovery and recycling. Voluntary recycling programs began in many municipalities during the 1980s. Statistics Canada's survey of local government waste practices (cited above), notes that 73 municipalities (which represented 88 percent of the total sampled) report having an organized recycling program. Collection and preparation for sale of recyclable materials are generally handled by private contractors. Fifty-four of the municipalities responding provided details of their recycling programs. Table 19-3 reports the type of materials recycled in these programs and where they are coming from. The amount of waste recycled as a proportion of total waste collected in 1990 was 4 percent in the Atlantic provinces, 5 percent in Quebec, 13 percent in Ontario, 6 percent in the Prairie provinces, 10 percent for B.C., and 9 percent overall for Canada.

TABLE 19-2 SOLID WASTE REDUCTION AND RECYCLING ACTIVITIES UNDERTAKEN IN PROVINCES AND MUNICIPALITIES

Returnable disposal fees: returnable deposits on beverage containers

Taxes on: tires, beverage containers, high-energy consuming motor vehicles, car batteries

Mandatory bottle deposits

Consumer fees on municipal solid wastes

Prohibitions on landfilling certain products, e.g., tires

Voluntary material separation and curbside recycling

Recycled or recyclable labels on products

Technical assistance for recycling programs

Grants and loans to municipalities for recycling programs

Public construction of waste separation and reprocessing plants

Public construction of waste-to-energy plants

Tax credits and exemptions for waste control investment by private businesses

Municipal recycling of household waste is a controversial program, as illustrated in Exhibit 19-1 by the debate over "Blue Boxes." Many municipalities thought recycling would pay for itself. They were wrong. But, one shouldn't forget that it is important to correctly price the environmental costs of disposal in landfills. We will look in more detail at the economics of recycling below. There is some recycling of mate-

TABLE 19-3 RECYCLING COLLECTION PROGRAMS AND DEPOTS, 1990

	Recycling Collection Program			
	Low-density dwellings	Medium-density dwellings	High-density dwellings	Depots
Recyclable material	(% collected)			
Newspaper	100	61	37	54
Cardboard	50	30	20	35
Fine paper	20	7	4	28
Glass	96	59	35	41
Ferrous metal	85	50	30	39
Nonferrous metal	76	48	33	37
Plastic	67	37	30	37
Compostable materials	33	17	9	13
Used motor oil	15	7	2	13

Note: Based on detailed information provided by 54 municipalities that offered details of their recycling programs.

Source: Statistics Canada, Public Institutions Division and National Accounts and Environment Division, as cited in Statistics Canada, *Environmental Perspectives, 1993*, Catalogue No. 11-528E Occasional (Ottawa: Statistics Canada, 1993), 72. Reproduced by authority of the Minister of Industry, 1994.

EXHIBIT 19-1

BLUE BOX: BOON OR BANE?

Is recycling of household waste a cost-effective way of reducing the amount of solid waste being dumped in landfills? We have yet to see a definitive study of this in Canada, but the newspapers reflect some of the differing beliefs. The article below illustrates some of the difficulties municipalities are facing.

"Blue Boxes: Why They Don't Work"

By Bob Reguly
Special Correspondent

ONTARIO mayors are singing the blues over the Blue Box recycling system. Municipal recycling programs now trap the detritus of 2.8 million households, 75% of Ontario homes. The much-admired system won the province a United Nations environmental award in 1989. Today, it is falling apart.

In spite of the system's shortcomings, the provincial NDP government has introduced legislation that would force every municipality of 5,000 or more to introduce multimaterial curbside recycling. Proving once again that ideology can trash economics, Ontario will strong-arm towns into participating even if they are a thousand miles from where they must deliver their collected glass or steel—to get back as little as one-tenth of the cost of collection.

The big beneficiaries are Coca-Cola Ltd. and Pepsi-Cola Canada Ltd., both of Toronto, which split 80% of Ontario's billion-dollar soda pop market. By persuading the previous Liberal provincial government to allow one-way pop cans and plastic bottles on the market instead of refillables, they passed disposal costs to taxpayers.

Since the two bottlers-turned-canners kick-started the Blue Box program into high gear with a one-time $20-million setup fund, 80% of the in-dependent bottlers in the province have been bought up or closed down as Coca-Cola and Pepsi-Cola centralized production in suburban Toronto. Pollution Probe estimates that the Blue Box saves the pop giants $60-million to $80-million a year by replacing the need for refillable containers. By volume, beverage containers form most of what goes into Blue Boxes.

The Blue Box program does not and cannot pay for itself. And municipal ratepayers must bear the full cost after the initial five-year provincially subsidized launch.

The gearing-up costs are also daunting. For Metro Toronto, the cost of Blue Box recycling last year—its third year of operation—was about $15-million more than if the municipality had continued its previous dumping practices, according to Bob Ferguson, Metro works commissioner.

Ferguson foresees the demise of the Blue Box in two years, when the first five-year funding agreement with the province runs out. "We can no longer afford to pay $192 a tonne for the disposal of garbage," he says. That's more than triple the cost of normal collection and dumping. Metro now subsidizes its six members municipalities' Blue Box costs from the $150-million a tonne tipping fee at its

rials from industrial and commercial sectors. For example, in 1990, 12 percent of the total amount of packaging material used by industry was recycled. There is also a "waste exchange" in Canada that facilitates exchange of recyclable material between those wishing to discard the material and those who can use it. However only about 25,000 tonnes (or less than 1 percent) of the 8 million tonnes of total industrial wastes are recycled in this manner. In the United States, about 13 percent of municipal solid waste is currently recycled.

landfill site. That brought in $105 million in 1991. It also scared away 500,000 tonnes to the U.S. dumps which charge $35. The arrangement ends in January 1994, when the municipalities put the cost on property tax bills. That's when the true costs will begin to bludgeon Ontario's average homeowners: when they see those costs added onto their tax bills.

Helen Cooper, mayor of the eastern Ontario city of Kingston and president of the 800-member Association of Municipalities of Ontario, calls recycling a "boondoggle." Except for aluminum cans and, to a lesser extent, old newspapers, markets for the other materials—glass, plastics, steel cans—are scant. Instead of growing to the point where the Blue Box system would pay for itself, as promoters had once envisaged, these markets are in decline.

Buyers have been chopping prices. Glass that brought $60 a tonne last fall now fetches about $40 delivered to the only buyer in the province, Consumers Glass, in west Toronto. Moreover, Consumers is choosy. "They reject too much colored glass," says Ferguson. So hundreds of tonnes are routinely trucked to landfill sites where the glass is used as aggregate fill for the dump roads. That allows recycling's promoters to claim with straight faces that nothing that gets collected in a Blue Box ends up as landfill.

Metro Toronto now gets $16 a tonne for newsprint, down from $30 last fall. The result: the municipality is about to dump nearly 7,000 tonnes of rotting newspapers that were collected at a cost of more than $1-million. The newsprint was Blue Boxed when the Quebec and Ontario Paper de-inking plant at Thorold, then the only one in Ontario, underwent a five-month strike and the paper was stored outside. During the strike the provincial government provided $1-million to subsidize the export of old newspapers to South Korea and Nigeria.

Since then, two other de-inking plants have opened in the province. For the long term, a market should develop for newsprint.

Steel brings $77 a tonne. That's only $115 less than the cost of collecting it. And the two-litre clear plastic PET pop bottles bring revenue of $300 a round ton if delivered to the Ontario buyer, Twinpak Inc., in Mississauga, in 15-ton loads. Twinpak pays $125 a ton for smaller loads. It takes 18,600 PET bottles to make a ton—enough to fill a large house. The plant chops up the bottles and ships them to North Carolina. The Association of Municipalities' Cooper says, "The cost of recycling PET bottles is horrendous."

The justification for the Blue Box recycling system is that it saves scarce landfill space. The figures are slippery. For Metro Toronto, about 10% of municipal garbage was diverted last year, or only 4% of the total that goes to the dump, when industrial waste is added to the equation. It's an expensive way to save a minuscule amount of land.

"Recycling is a good idea for materials which are truly recyclable," says Helen Cooper. "It sounds facetious but I'm serious. We got off on this frenzy of recycling before there were markets for the material, except for aluminum and, to a lesser extent, newsprint.

"For ratepayers to subsidize public transit and swimming pools is a proper thing. Whether ratepayers should subsidize the consumption of Coca-Cola is a totally different thing. So many municipalities are facing a financial crunch that, if it comes between reducing the staff of a fire department or abolishing the Blue Box, the answer is fairly obvious."

Source: The Financial Times, February 3–9, 1992, 1, 4 by Bob Reguly.

THE ECONOMICS OF RECYCLING

In the recycling process there are two types of exchanges of interest: that of material from producers-suppliers to consumers-demanders; and that of recycled material from consumers-suppliers to producers-demanders. As in any economic transaction, the size and composition of the two flows of materials depend on the information sent from demanders to suppliers. This information stems from the countless decisions producers and consumers make that have repercussions for materials use. Producers design products and the materials used with them; they make decisions on the total quantities of materials used and the amounts of virgin and recycled feedstocks they will use. Consumers choose products that contain different types and amounts of materials; they also decide how to dispose of the various materials that are left after the products have been "consumed."

Solid waste is a problem because of defects in the pricing systems that govern these transactions. Discarded solid waste produces a variety of environmental damages. For social efficiency these have to be reflected in disposal costs of people who make disposal decisions; namely, consumers. Solid-waste disposal by households is generally paid for by flat fees levied to cover the costs of collection and disposal. These fees can go up or down to reflect overall disposal costs (fees are going up in many areas because of increasing scarcity of landfill space), but the per-family fees do not vary according to the quantities of material discarded per family. Thus, there is no incentive for consumers to be very concerned about the amounts of solid waste they discard, nor any reason for them to be concerned about the amount of "excess" materials that accompany their purchases. Figure 19-2 illustrates inefficient versus efficient disposal of household waste. Demand for goods is shown by curve D. Implicit in the price of the goods people buy is a subsidy when they are not paying the full social cost of waste disposal. Consumption of goods is too high at Q_0 and the price too low at P_0 to have social efficiency. Now suppose a fee per bag of trash disposed is introduced. Consumers' demand curve shifts down reflecting the fee. Because goods now include a waste disposal charge, the quantity of goods demanded declines and therefore so does waste produced. Consumers pay P_0, which is the market price P_1 plus the fee per bag. Of course, in practice the situation will be more complicated than this simple diagram illustrates. Goods will have different amounts of waste associated with them. We would expect to see a reallocation of spending away from waste-intensive to less waste-intensive goods in response to the efficient pricing of waste disposal. We would also expect more recycling of wastes when disposal is efficiently priced.

Waste disposal and recycling are also decisions producers have to make. Environmental costs of input use and waste disposal have to be reflected in the prices paid by producers to achieve social efficiency. One consequence of an inefficient price system that is not incorporating environmental costs into input and output prices, is a misallocation of resource use between virgin materials and recycled inputs. Environmental costs of harvesting of virgin materials are often external to the harvesting firms, making the prices of virgin materials too low from the standpoint of social efficiency.[3] This, together with technological changes that have increased the cost of recycled materials (e.g., the advent of the large trash-compacting collection truck) have led to a substantial reduction in the proportion of materials recovered from the waste stream. Figure 19-3 shows the effect on producers of having their costs of production fully reflect environmental costs. Full social cost pricing of inputs will shift

[3] A variety of public programs also have the effect of lowering the costs of virgin materials.

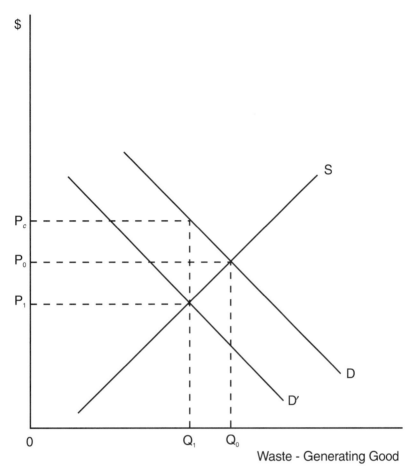

FIGURE 19-2   Waste Disposal Fees and Household Consumption.

producers' supply curve from S to S'. Quantity produced will fall, prices will rise. With less output produced, input use will decline as well. We can then combine Figures 19-2 and 19-3 to see the effect in the goods markets of efficient pricing of waste generation. Figure 19-4 illustrates a possible result. All we know for certain is that efficient waste pricing will reduce the quantity of goods produced and consumed, holding constant the waste generation per good. Because the demand curve shifts down and the supply curve shifts up, we cannot predict what will happen to market prices. However, it is clear that consumers will pay more for their garbage relative to the case without efficient pricing (P_c exceeds P_0), and producers will receive less per unit good sold (P_0 exceeds P_s). In the next two sections we will look at these producer and consumer sides of the solid waste phenomenon and take into account, using a more complicated model, decisions to recycle.

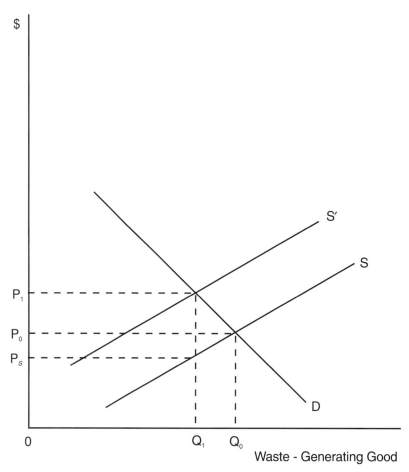

FIGURE 19-3   Efficient Input Pricing and Production.

Producer Use of Recycled Material

Figure 19-5 is an analysis of the producer side. The demand curve applies to a firm or industry; it shows the quantity demanded of a particular type of material in a given period, like a year. There are two sources of this material, virgin and recycled. We assume that this firm or industry is small relative to the total use of this material; thus, it can obtain virgin material feedstocks in whatever quantity it wishes at a constant price. This price is marked p_v and is shown as a horizontal line intersecting the demand curve at a quantity level q_0. But this material may also be obtained from recycled sources. Here, however, the procurement cost picture is more complicated. Reaching into the waste stream for recycled materials involves a number of special costs—of collection, separation, transportation, reprocessing, etc. We assume that these costs increase with the amount of recycled material used. The supply curve of

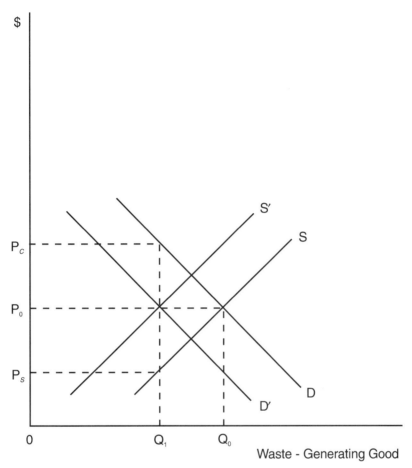

FIGURE 19-4   Efficient Consumption and Production with Wastes.

recycled material to this firm or industry is therefore an increasing function like S_1 or S_2. These two supply curves refer to situations with different recycling technology.[4] For S_1, costs go up relatively rapidly; S_2 increases much less rapidly. Consider for the moment the recycled material supply curve labelled S_1. If this is the one faced by this firm or industry, it will end up using q_1 of recycled materials. In other words, the producer will use recycled materials up to the point where its cost is equal to the price of virgin materials. Since the total materials use is q_0, the difference $(q_0 - q_1)$ consists of virgin materials.

[4] In recent decades there have been rapid changes in the technologies of collecting, sorting, sifting, and reprocessing of various types of solid waste.

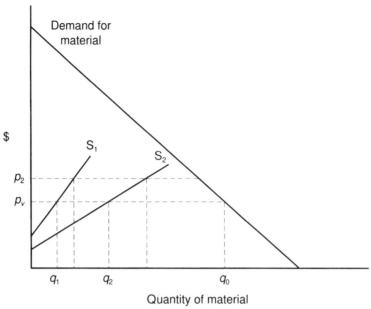

FIGURE 19-5   Use of Recycled Materials in Production.

The reuse ratio, the proportion of total materials coming from recycled feedstock, is q_1/q_0. If our analysis of the socially efficient amount of waste generations leads to the conclusion that the reuse ratio is too low, there are a variety of ways to change the relative price of recycled to virgin materials to provide incentives to producers to change the ratio. We can increase this ratio in three ways; increase q_1 while holding q_0 constant, decrease q_0 while holding q_1 constant, or both. Most community efforts at recycling are aimed at the first of these. For example, public curbside sorting and collection programs are ultimately aimed at making the supply of recycled material more abundant and, hence, less costly to producers. In terms of the model of Figure 19-5 these programs have aimed at shifting the recycled supply curve downward; say, from S_1 to S_2. If this is done, recycled materials use increases to q_2 and the recycling rate increases to q_2/q_0.

Another way of increasing the recycling ratio is to reduce the demand for materials in general, while holding constant the use of recycled materials. Diagrammatically this means shifting the whole materials demand curve back. This might be done, for example, by finding ways of producing output using fewer materials. It also might simply happen as consumers shift away from materials-intensive products to products that are less so. Finally, there is one way of simultaneously reducing total materials used and increasing recycled materials: Increase the price of virgin materials. If on Figure 19-5 we lift the virgin materials price to, say, p_2 through a tax, this will lead both to a move up the recycling supply curve and up the materials demand curve.

This means an increase in the quantity of recycled materials and a decrease in the quantity demanded of materials in total. Raising the price on virgin materials with a tax thus has a double effect on the reuse ratio, since it works at both ends of the problem.

We can use this simple model to examine recent proposals for recycled-content standards in materials-using industries. Early enthusiasm for community recycling efforts led to situations in which the amounts of collected material outstripped technical ability to turn it into useful raw material, and in the absence of demand large quantities of sorted and collected material actually ends up in landfills. This has generated quite a bit of controversy about the "success" of recycling programs. It may be the case that public policies have subsidized recycling activities more than that required to achieve social efficiency. Alternatively, it could be that externalities associated with waste generation still haven't been fully internalized, for example, if waste disposal fees are too low to achieve social efficiency.

To deal with these problems in the U.S., recent policy efforts have turned toward trying to increase the strength of demand for the recycled material. A number of states have thought to try this by introducing minimum content standards for materials-using production processes. Minimum content standards require that all materials-using products manufactured or sold within a given state contain some specified percentage of recycled material. Some Canadian jurisdictions are also contemplating standards such as these.

We have talked many times of the cost-ineffectiveness of uniform standards in the face of heterogeneous emissions withholding costs. In the case of uniform content standards for materials, the same principle applies, but here the important factor is heterogeneity across materials-using firms in terms of the costs of obtaining and using recycled materials. For a truly cost-effective approach to the problem we would want to achieve equality across industries and materials in terms of *marginal recycling costs*. What this implies is having higher rates of recycled materials use by industries whose recycling costs are relatively low and lower rates for industries with relatively high recycling costs. One way to achieve this is to apply a tax on virgin materials. As we mentioned above, a tax of, say, $p_2 - p_v$ per unit of virgin materials, charged to all firms, would lead each to increase its recycling ratio in a way that satisfied the equimarginal principle. Another way would be to initiate a tradable permit system in the recycling market. A regulatory agency or statute would set an overall recycling objective for an industry, expressed in terms of the socially efficient recycling rate. Each individual firm would then have three choices: (1) Increase its own recycling rate to the industry standard; (2) increase to a rate higher than the standard, and sell "excess" recycling permits; or (3) increase to less than the industry standard, buying however many permits are necessary to make up the difference.

In the real world, of course, things are a lot more complicated than they appear in our simple model. For example, one underlying assumption built into Figure 19-5 is that recycled material and virgin material are physically interchangeable. This is hardly ever true in practice. Although newspaper can be produced largely from recycled newspaper, some virgin newsprint is usually necessary to achieve minimum-quality levels. The same is true of many recycled metals. It is also true that the recycling market, like any economic market, is very dynamic, whereas the model displayed in Figure 19-5 is essentially static; that is, it is limited to events happening in a single time period. But producers normally look well into the future when making decisions. For example, even though current virgin materials prices are low, producers may nevertheless invest today in recycling and reprocessing works, if they *anticipate* that prices will increase in the future. But the simple model offers insight into basic recycling economics.

Consumer Recycling Decisions

It is sometimes easy to get the impression that in matters of solid waste the basic decision facing consumers is whether or not to recycle. But there are some prior decisions that are equally as important, decisions having to do with which particular goods to buy, and in what quantity. These decisions critically affect the total quantity of the solid waste stream and its composition. Figure 19-2, discussed above, illustrated efficient versus inefficient consumption of waste-generating goods. Subsequent recycling decisions determine how much of that waste stream ends up in the landfill.

To examine these choices we will use some illustrative benefit and cost numbers pertaining to two goods. Assume there are two similar products, but perhaps with different packaging, like bulk cereal and cereal in boxes, or drinks in plastic and drinks in glass containers. The data are in Table 19-4, and they apply to the situation of a single consumer. Goods A and B each sell for the same price, but one, because of handling convenience, has a higher value to this consumer. Of course for other consumers the numbers pertaining to "value to consumer" could be different. For this consumer the net value before disposal of these two goods is in favour of Good B.

Disposal Costs   We now introduce the disposal costs of materials coming with the product. We consider first the costs of disposal in the conventional way—in the community landfill. Disposal costs are in two parts, private and social. The private costs refer to the consumer's costs of handling and discarding the materials, while the social costs refer to the environmental damages caused by the material when disposed of in the community's landfill. The private disposal costs of the two containers are the same—the time it takes to bag up the trash and set it on the curb is the same no matter which product the consumer is dealing with. But the environmental costs for Good B are substantially above those of Good A, for example, because there is much more material involved, or because it uses a different type of material. We can now calculate the net benefits of the two goods for the consumer and for the community. Remember that the full social costs contain the costs borne by the individual consumer plus the other damage costs. Here we arrive at the nub of the problem, because from the individual's standpoint Good B is the preferred choice, while for the community Good A is the preferred choice. The environmental costs stemming from conventional disposal are essentially external costs; if consumers do not take

TABLE 19-4   INDIVIDUAL AND COMMUNITY BENEFITS AND COSTS IN PRODUCT CHOICE AND
RECYCLING (numbers are assumed to be in cents)

	Product A	Product B
Purchase price	100	100
Value to consumer	140	160
Net value	40	60
Conventional (landfill) disposal alternative		
Disposal costs		
Private	10	10
Social	10	40
Net benefits		
Private	30	50
Social	20	10
Recycling alternative		
Disposal costs		
Private	10	40
Community transport	(cannot be recycled)	10
Environmental damage	10	0
Value of recovered material	0	20
Net benefits		
Private	30	20
Social	20	30

them into account when making purchasing decisions, they will make choices that are best from their standpoint but not best from the perspective of the community.

Recycling   Let us now introduce recycling. The products are different in this respect. Product A cannot be recycled for technical reasons; thus, it will continue to be disposed of in the landfill. But Product B may be recycled, and the costs of doing so rest partly on consumers and partly on the community. There are private costs coming from the need to separate trash and handle the recycled goods in the home. The community also faces a transport cost, but offsetting this is the fact that the recycled material has a market value. These costs are shown in Table 19-4. With the items as indicated, we can calculate the benefits of the two goods in the presence of the recycling program. The net benefit of Product A stays the same, since it cannot be recycled. The net benefit of Product B is now substantially higher than it was before the recycling program, primarily because of the avoided environmental damage and the market value of the recycled material.

The Consumer's Choice   The consumer now has three alternatives: (a) Buy Product A, disposing of it in the community landfill; (b) buy Product B, recycling the associated material; and (c) buy Product B, but disposing of it in the landfill. We can tabulate the net benefits to individual and community as follows:

	Net benefits	
Option	Individual	Community
(a) Buy A	30	20
(b) Buy B, recycle	20	30
(c) Buy B, landfill	50	10

The individual's preferred choice is Product B without recycling, the community's preferred choice is B *with* recycling. The fundamental question is, What can we do to provide the incentive for the individual consumer to adopt the recycling alternative?

Consider one alternative that has been tried by communities in the United States: mandatory recycling. We pass a local regulation making it illegal not to recycle the material from B if that product has in fact been purchased. That is, the ordinance requires that all purchased recyclable products must in fact be recycled. What this does, if it is enforced, is to take away option (c) from the consumer. So the consumer falls back on the next best alternative: buying the nonrecyclable Product A. This simple problem illustrates an important point: The recycling process starts back at the choice of purchase made by the consumer, and we have to look at the impacts of recycling ordinances on this purchase decision as well as on recycling decisions themselves. In the present case the mandatory recycling law has the effect of causing the consumer to shift purchasing away from recyclable products to nonrecyclable ones, thus substantially undermining the intent of the law.

Disposal Charges   A basic principle in environmental economics is that emission taxes can provide the incentive for polluters to adopt socially efficient rates of emissions. In the present situation the counterpart of emission taxes is consumer disposal charges. A completely efficient set of disposal charges would involve a charge on each item at a level equal to the social costs of disposal. A unit of Good A produces damages of 10¢, so its tax would be that much. The tax on a nonrecycled unit of Good B would be 40¢. For a recycled unit of B the tax is a little more complicated. If B is recycled, there is no environmental cost, but there is a community transportation cost of 10¢. But this is more than offset by the fact that the item has a 20¢ market value. Thus, the net tax is actually 10¢ – 20¢, or –10¢. The tax is actually a 10¢ payment to the consumer. If we levy these taxes on these products at the point of disposal, the net benefits of the various options to the individual consumer would now become: (a) 20¢, (b) 30¢, (c) 10¢, which are the same as the social net benefits of the previous tabulation. Now the consumer will choose (b), the recycling option. In effect, *these taxes have changed the pattern of private net benefits so that they are the same as community net benefits.* When this is done a consumer will have the incentive to (1) choose the product and (2) make the recycling decision, in ways that are efficient from the standpoint of the community. In fact, a charge based on the social costs of disposal for each item is not going to be feasible in the real world; it would require authorities to evaluate the waste stream of each individual and charge according to the different items identified. What many communities are doing, rather, is to establish a single charge, per bag or can, of undifferentiated waste, and collecting separated and recyclable materials free. In this case the charge on non-separated trash ought to be some average of the disposal costs of the various items in the waste stream. In our example, the social costs (in terms of environmental damages) of a unit of A are 10¢, and of a unit of B if not recycled, 40¢. If the authorities took an intermediate value, setting a charge of 25¢ per container thrown away, the private net benefits of the different alternatives would be: (a) 5¢, (b) 30¢, (c) 25¢. So in this case the tax would be sufficient to lead the consumer to buy B and recycle.[5] A tax much lower than this, however, would lead the consumer to buy B and dispose of it in the landfill, owing to the relatively high private costs of recycling.

A Deposit Program   We can look also at the effect of a *deposit program* on recyclable items. If a 40¢ deposit were put on item B, reflecting the damages done if it were thrown away rather than recycled, the array of net benefits for the individual would now be: (a) 30¢, (b) 20¢, (c) 10¢. The consumer refrains from throwing out the recyclable item, but also shifts back to (a), the nonrecyclable good. This is the same effect we saw earlier with mandatory recycling; the bottle bill leads this particular consumer to choose nonrecyclable items when shopping. One way around this is to have a deposit on *all* materials, equal to their disposal costs. For Good A, the nonrecyclable item, this essentially acts as a tax, and gives a result similar to the "perfect" tax discussed above.

We need to stress that these results depend on the particular numbers shown in Table 19-4. Some of these, like environmental damage costs and purchase price, would be the same for all consumers, but others, like private disposal costs, depend on the individual's own subjective valuation of the burdens of handling different types of products. These could differ among consumers and this could obviously lead to differences in response to various solid-waste policies. It is also quite true that many people obtain a certain amount of civic satisfaction from engaging in behaviour that is efficient from the community's standpoint. But to get as much benefit as we can from recycling decisions made by consumers, we have to consider the benefits and costs of these decisions through their eyes.

WATER USE: SEWAGE AND WATER TREATMENT AND GROUNDWATER PROTECTION

Sewage and Water Treatment

As we saw in Table 19-1, municipalities are also responsible for the construction and operation of sewage and water treatment facilities. These are typically very capital-intensive operations, and continue to represent approximately 50 percent of total (all levels) government environmental expenditures. The federal and provincial govern-

---

[5] This is the essence of the "pay per bag" system that we discussed at the beginning of the book.

ments have contributed financially to construction of these plants; the federal government under the Canada Water Act of 1970, the provinces in block grants to the municipalities. Currently 75 percent of the population is served by some form of sewage *collection* system; the rest by septic tanks. As a result of the government programs, the percentage of the population served by some form of sewage *treatment* has risen from just over 50 percent in 1977 to 84 percent in 1991. However, for the remaining 16 percent of the population with a collection system, the sewage collected is released untreated into receiving waters (e.g., the city of Victoria, B.C.).

Municipal sewage thus remains an important source of water pollution either because it is untreated or inadequately treated. Beach closures in the summer due to coliform bacteria are still a frequent occurrence in many parts of the country. There is also increasing concern, as noted in previous chapters, about the composition of the effluent. Secondary treatment technologies do a reasonably good job of decomposing the BOD and suspended solids in sewage. Toxic substances and other compounds may remain. Many municipalities also discharge their treated sewage into the same water body from which they draw their drinking water. Finally, many treatment plants and their collection systems have been in place for many years and have deteriorated considerably. For all these reasons, there is increasing pressure to continue to install some form of sewage treatment for all people on a collection system and to upgrade many existing treatment plants from secondary to tertiary technologies. This is going to cost very large amounts of money. In the current fiscal climate of large federal and provincial government deficits and cutbacks in all aspects of government spending, it is not clear where the money is going to come from to make these improvements in sewage treatment. One suggestion economists have been making for years is to price the services offered per unit of water used.[6]

Many municipalities continue to charge flat rates for water consumption and sewage services. In 1991, Canada as a whole had just over 50 percent of its municipal population on water meters. When people are charged per unit of water consumed, total water consumption is substantially less than that for people who pay flat rates independent of water use. For population centres with over 20,000 people, those with meters consumed approximately 250 litres of water per capita per day. Those without meters consumed around 400 litres/capita/day, or over 60 percent more![7] Unit pricing alone won't solve the financial difficulties of providing for sewage and water treatment, but it is a step in the right direction.

Groundwater Protection

Groundwater is an important source of drinking water for many communities, especially those in rural areas. Over 6 million Canadians rely on groundwater for domes-

---

[6] It's not possible to easily price sewage treatment per unit sewage produced, as this sort of metering does not exist. However, water use is a good proxy for sewage throughput. It also helps to address the problem of supplying drinking water to people.

[7] Environment Canada, *The Urban Environment: Water Supply,* State of the Environment Reporting, Environmental Indicator Bulletin No. 93-8 (1993), 4.

tic and drinking water needs. The proportion of people in Canada consuming ground-water more than doubled since 1960 from 10 to 26 percent. All of Prince Edward Island, parts of the prairies, many rural and some urban municipalities are dependent on groundwater completely or partially.[8] Groundwater is also the source of bottled water, an increasingly important commodity for domestic consumption and export. Ironically, consumption of bottled water has increased greatly in recent years because of concerns about the quality of drinking water from surface-water supplies. The quality of groundwater resources has been increasingly threatened from a variety of sources—agricultural runoff, industrial waste disposal, landfill leakage, underground storage tanks, etc. Groundwater resources are substantially different from surface water in terms of their regenerative capacity; once contaminated, groundwater aquifers are likely to be lost to use for a long time because of the very slow rate at which they are replenished.

Most groundwater pollutants stem from nonpoint-source emissions. As we have discussed many times, this essentially rules out any type of emission-control policy that requires direct monitoring of emissions. Thus, groundwater pollution-control programs must focus on controlling the various practices and behaviours of sources that normally could be expected to threaten groundwater resources. To do this there is the full array of emission-control policies, both CAC types and economic-incentive strategies. Among the latter, for example, would be taxes on nitrogen fertilizers used by farmers, leading to lower rates of fertilizer use and therefore less nitrate runoff. Among the former are various types of technology specifications for underground waste disposal to reduce the probabilities of groundwater contamination. Because groundwater aquifers cover large areas, responsibility for their management will probably be at the provincial level, with perhaps some federal involvement. Policy initiatives include, under the Green Plan, the establishment of a federal-provincial working group on groundwater management. They are in the very preliminary stages of attempting to develop a national strategy for groundwater protection and management. An example of provincial response is in British Columbia. In the Lower Mainland, there appears to be a problem of nitrate contamination of the groundwater in the Abbotsford Aquifer. Some of these nitrates may come from manure stored on farms or used as fertilizer for fruit producers in the region. Although study of the problem is under way, the B.C. government is contemplating changing its Waste Management Act (which we discussed in Chapter 18) to include agricultural operations in its permitting system. Agriculture is currently exempt from requiring a permit if it discharges wastes from farming operations in a "reasonable manner as organic fertilizers to promote crop production."[9]

---

[8] Environment Canada, *The State of Canada's Environment* (Ottawa: Ministry of Supply and Services), 3–22.

[9] Waste Management Act (B.C. Reg. 432/82) as cited in Don Reddick, "Economic Rent and Environmental Policy: The Case of Poultry Manure Management over the Abbotsford Aquifer" (mimeo, Simon Fraser University, Department of Economics, 1992).

LAND-USE CONTROL POLICIES

Land-use issues, and the public control over land-use decisions, are also matters that historically have been left to the provinces and individual communities in Canada. As part of the Green Plan there are a variety of land-use initiatives, for example, wetlands preservation and management, the creation of "Action Plans" for the Fraser River Basin and Atlantic Coast, and study of Alberta-NWT Northern Rivers (see Chapter 15). While these projects involve all levels of government, it is felt by many that land use is primarily a local issue and therefore requires local policy responses. The environmental issues we have talked about heretofore have been about the management of flows of production and consumption residuals. We have discussed the various policy tools, standards, emission fees, TDPs, etc., to affect these residual flows. When it comes to land, the problem is somewhat different. The land surface of the earth is fixed in quantity, and human beings spread themselves around on it in accordance with varying incentive patterns and with varying impacts. The key problem, then, is how decisions are arrived at to devote particular pieces of land to particular human and nonhuman uses.

Since almost all environmental externalities have a spatial dimension, it might be tempting to think of all pollution as essentially a land-use issue. But while many of the large cases of air and water pollution are indeed spatial, they do not lend themselves to solutions through altered land-use patterns. The acid rain problem is not a land-use problem, for example. Certain local cases of environmental externalities, however, may be more closely related to decisions on land use. Local air-pollution problems may be the result of transportation patterns produced by sprawling housing development. A community faced with noise pollution from a local airport may be able to manage it through land-use controls in the vicinity of the airport.

But many contemporary land-use issues are not pollution related; rather, they are about the human use of land that substantially reduces or destroys its environmental value. Within any localized region there are usually lands that have special environmental value, because of strategic ecological linkages or aesthetic values, or both. Some cases of this are:

• Wetlands, which provide important environments for plants and animals and are linked into other components of the ground- and surface-water system.
• Coastal lands, where scenic and recreational qualities are important.
• Critical habitats, where land-use patterns affect the health or survival of plant and animal species.
• Scenic and open land, where people may find vistas and experiences that have spiritual significance and recreational value.

To examine the economic logic of public and private land-use decisions let us focus on an example involving one particular piece of land. All land parcels are essentially unique and will have varying values in different uses, but we can use illustrative numbers to demonstrate the essence of the problem. The parcel is currently in open space, with all environmental values intact, and it is owned by a single individual. Suppose there are three mutually exclusive options for the parcel: (a) It may be developed without public restraints, (b) it may be preserved in its current state, or (c) it may be developed but with certain restrictions set by the local environmental agency. The illustrative numbers in Table 19-5 show the returns and costs of these different courses of action. Naturally, when land-use decisions of this type are made, there is actually a stream of returns and costs off into the future, so the numbers in Table 19-5 in effect represent the *present* values of these streams of returns and costs.[10]

Let us first consider options (a) and (b). If the owner were to develop the land, he or she would realize a gross return of 100 and have construction costs of 80. But developing the land would have serious environmental costs; namely, the destruction of its ecological value, which we set at 50. We assume, and this is critical, that this lost ecological value is a loss to society but not a loss to the individual. The land owner and those people interested in ecological values could attempt to bargain over the use of the land. If transactions costs are low and no other market imperfections exist, the party with the highest value for the land will bid the most for it and a socially efficient use results. However, for many land-use decisions, transactions costs will be very high and this private bargaining approach to land use will not work. For example, those interested in ecological values may be dispersed across the country and not be aware of each other's existence. It is hard to imagine that information about all such land-use decisions will be available to the ecologically concerned public. If private transactions are impossible, the owner of the land will be unable to realize the ecological value of the land. The owner's decisions about using the land then will be predicated on its private development value. The private net return is 20, while the

---

[10] For a discussion of the present-value concept see Chapter 6.

TABLE 19-5   RETURNS AND COSTS OF VARIOUS LAND-USE OPTIONS

	Land use		
	Develop (a)	Preserve (b)	Develop with restrictions (c)
Returns			
Private	100	—	90
Public	—	50	—
Total	100	50	90
Costs			
Private	80	20	80
Public	50	—	10
Total	130	20	90
Net return			
Private	20	−20	10
Public	−30	30	0

full social return of developing the land is –30. In the absence of any public land-use policy the land would presumably be developed even though it represents a net loss to society.

It is instructive to look at it from the reverse perspective, the returns and costs of option (b): preservation. In this case private returns are nil, but public returns from the preserved ecological values of the land are 50. The cost in this case is the foregone net return from developing the land, or 20. Thus, the net social returns from preservation are 50 – 20 = 30. Market failure prevents the attainment of this socially efficient equilibrium.

We may now consider certain policy options. The most common local land-use tool is outright prohibition of certain land uses that are thought to have low or negative social returns, even though they may have positive private returns. This is done through the exercise of the *police power*, which is a power that communities have of prohibiting private activities that are detrimental to the wider public. The most common technique is *zoning*, in which communities rule out certain types of land uses where they would be destructive to the surrounding land values; for example, factories in residential areas. Environmental restrictions on development also come under this heading, since these contribute to the health and welfare of the community. Thus, a police power approach to our problem would be simply to develop a zoning law or environmental preservation law that rules out option (a).

A major problem with a police power approach like this is that, although it may legally prohibit certain land uses like option (a), it does not change any of the numbers in the table, so it does not change any of the underlying incentives of the situation. An owner whose land has been subject to a development restriction by public authorities has much to gain by getting the authorities to relax the restraint. In fact it would make sense for the landowner in Table 19-5 to spend some portion of the expected net returns to try to get the authorities to reverse themselves.

Instead of outright prohibition the police power may be used to place conditions on development. For example, a developer might be required to leave a certain amount of open space, to avoid certain ecologically sensitive areas, or to install a public sewer system. This approach is sometimes called "incentive zoning." Table 19-5 depicts a third alternative, called "develop with restrictions," to capture this type of option. The owner is allowed to develop, but certain constraints are placed on this process, which have the effect of avoiding some of the ecological costs. Since the restrictions lower the developed value, the private net return is now only 90 – 80 = 10. The social net return is now 90 – 90 = 0, because all but 10 of the ecological costs have been avoided by the development restrictions.

The "Taking" Issue

One of the most contested issues in using local land-use controls for environmental protection purposes is the "taking" problem. In Canada, an individual's property rights are protected in the Constitution, but governments can appropriate one's land under certain conditions. Generally, the government has to show that the appropriation or taking is reasonable, clearly enhances public welfare, and is not arbitrary or discriminatory. The problem is in knowing when these conditions are met. In the example of Table 19-5, a local restriction that ruled out option (a) but permitted option (c) would lower the net private return from 20 to 10, thus lowering the private value of the land by that amount. Is this a valid taking? A major difficulty with cases like the table illustrates is that although private revenues and costs of land-use restrictions are usually known with accuracy, the same cannot be said about environmental values. In the example of Table 19-5, we assumed we knew exactly how much the environmental attributes were worth, but usually this is not true. So there is a need to try to balance known private values with unknown public environmental values. From the standpoint of public health, there may be little difficulty barring development in sensitive wetlands, on the grounds that these are linked into the hydrological systems on which many people depend for water supply.

But when public health is not so directly involved, things can be much less clear. Suppose that you own a particular farm in a community and that over time the people of the community have come to value the scenic qualities of your land. Clearly the land has environmental (scenic) value, but may the town pass a regulation saying that you can't develop it for that reason? In doing this, the town is essentially putting on you the entire burden of providing these scenic values.

One way around the taking issue is compensation to the landowner. A straightforward way of doing this is for a public agency or a private environmental group to purchase "in fee simple" the land in question. In the case of Table 19-5 a purchase price of 20 would just compensate the landowner for the lost development opportunities. The land is then taken out of the private market and its environmental values are preserved. As we noted above, if this sort of market transaction is possible, no further regulation may be needed. These transactions may require that the community or some private group have substantial financial resources. The Nature Conservancy, for example, is a private group, funded largely through contributions, that preserves sensitive land by outright purchase. It may be difficult however to get people to contribute to land purchases because of free-rider problems, inefficient capital markets (will banks loan an individual money to preserve ecological values if that person doesn't have title to the land?), and other types of market imperfections. Thus, takings with compensation may be necessary to reach the socially efficient land use. Governments, too, face budget constraints, so compromises might be necessary. For example, governments may purchase certain partial rights in the land, not the land in its entirety. In the case of Table 19-5, for example, the community might buy from the landowner just the right to undertake option (a), but not the right to pursue option (c). The value of this one right would be 10, the difference in net returns between the two options. This purchase of just the development right would preserve some, though not all, of the land's environmental values. Social efficiency may be difficult to obtain.

In Canada, compensation for a taking is not established in the Constitution. Compensation is thus becoming an increasingly important public policy issue because of the growing public pressures for preservation of environmentally important regions of the country. While many of the areas in question are Crown lands, the rights to extract resources from these lands had frequently already been granted to private individuals or corporations by provincial governments. This is where much of the conflict lies. In British Columbia, a Commission of Inquiry into Compensation for the Taking of Resource Interests recently reported its findings, and is stimulating a lot of discussion. As yet, there is virtually no official policy established by any level of government.

SUMMARY

Local governments deal with important aspects of environmental quality—providing clean drinking water, sewage treatment, and solid-waste disposal. Provinces and localities have had the primary responsibility for land-use controls. Community efforts at recycling are a major part of the effort to address solid-waste issues. We saw how recycling decisions depend on complex incentive situations facing consumers in their buying and disposal decisions and producers whose demands for recycled materials may lead them to reach into the solid-waste stream for sources of raw materials. Municipalities in Canada face major expenditures to construct and upgrade water and sewage treatment plants. Unit pricing of water would provide an incentive for users to consume water more efficiently. The allocation of land among competing uses—some which promote environmental protection and others which do not, involves all levels of government as well as private decision makers. Here the major issue is the change in land values produced by land-use regulations and the fine line between what may be considered a legitimate exercise of the police power and what is an unconstitutional "taking" of private property.

QUESTIONS FOR FURTHER DISCUSSION

1 Many communities have been successful in collecting recyclable material, but have been unable to find buyers for the recovered materials. How do you interpret this in terms of the concepts shown in Figure 19-5?

2 Another way of increasing the use of recycled material by industry is to subsidize its purchase of materials taken from the waste stream. How would you analyze this in terms of Figure 19-5?

3 If the reuse ratio is lower than is socially efficient, what economic incentives could be used to encourage the recovery and recycling of a substantially larger proportion of the solid-waste stream?

4 Suppose there is a wetlands that can be used for ecological values or drained and houses built on it. How could the socially efficient use of the wetlands be reached?

5 Many communities are instituting a "pay as you throw" system for solid waste. Discuss the equity implications of this type of system.

SELECTED READINGS

Conservation Foundation. *Groundwater Protection.* Washington, D.C., 1987.
Fischel, William. *The Economics of Zoning Laws.* Baltimore, Md.: Johns Hopkins Press, 1985.

Jaffe, Martin, and Frank DiNovo. *Local Groundwater Protection.* Washington, D.C.: American Planning Association, 1987.

Malone, Linda A. *Environmental Regulation of Land Use.* New York: Clark Boardman, 1990.

Menell, Peter S. "Beyond the Throwaway Society: An Incentive Approach to Regulating Municipal Solid Waste." *Ecology Law Quarterly* 17(4) (1990): 655–740.

U.S. Environmental Protection Agency *Economic Incentives for Land Use Control.* (EPA-600/5-77-001). Washington, D.C.: EPA, 1977.

U.S. Office of Technology Assessment. *Facing America's Trash: What Next for Municipal Solid Waste?* Washington, D.C., 1989.

INTERNATIONAL ENVIRONMENTAL ISSUES

The prospects for the twenty-first century are for the world to continue to shrink and nations to become increasingly interconnected. These interactions will grow in environmental matters. Regional and global problems will demand greater levels of cooperation and more effective international institutions. As demonstrated by the 1992 "earth summit," problems of environmental degradation in developing countries and the relationships of growth and environmental values will become more important. As all countries struggle, to a greater or lesser extent, to manage their own environmental problems, greater value will attach to the exchange of information, technology, and policy experience. A look at this international experience can substantially deepen our perspectives on the nature of environmental issues and the way people have thought to address them.

We will first review some of the environmental policy efforts being made in other industrialized countries and in developing countries. We will then discuss several global environmental problems: stratospheric ozone depletion and the greenhouse effect. Finally, we will offer some perspective on the economics of international environmental agreements.

20

ENVIRONMENTAL POLICIES
IN OTHER INDUSTRIALIZED
COUNTRIES

We begin by looking at experience in other industrialized countries of the East and the West. In North America we have seen that there was a great burst of political energy in the early 1970s that launched many of the environmental initiatives. Much the same took place in other countries; their primary environmental policies date from around the same time.

INTERNATIONAL COMPARISONS OF ENVIRONMENTAL QUALITY

Perhaps the best place to start is to look at several comparisons among countries in terms of environmental achievements. Good comparative data are not easy to obtain because the monitoring efforts of the countries have not been established with the primary goal of facilitating international comparisons. Each country collects and publishes its own data, using whatever bases, indices, and systems it finds most useful for its purposes. Thus, comparability is a problem. Efforts are slowly under way, especially among the European countries, to achieve some degree of uniformity in monitoring and data reporting. It is also the case that within any country environmental quality varies substantially among regions. In Canada, Vancouver and the urban corridor from Windsor to Quebec City have severe air problems. In Germany there is the heavily industrial Ruhr Valley. Japan has the Tokyo-Osaka corridor. This means that international comparisons have to be made with care and confined to situations that are reasonably similar.

The most cogent comparisons are in terms of achieved levels of ambient quality. Table 20-1 shows comparative ambient SO_2 levels for six large cities around the world over the decade 1975–1985. At both the beginning and end of this period Mon-

TABLE 20-1 AMBIENT LEVELS OF SO$_2$ FOR SIX MAJOR WORLD CITIES (annual average concentration, in μg/m³)

	U.S. New York	France Paris	Germany Berlin	U.K. London	Japan Tokyo	Canada Montreal
1975	43.7	114.8	NA	118.7	60.0	40.6
1980	38.0	89.0	90.0	69.0	48.0	39.9
1981	39.5	71.2	77.4	71.8	NA	34.5
1982	39.1	67.6	81.9	57.3	42.2	24.8
1983	36.1	61.4	66.8	49.0	29.3	18.2
1984	38.4	57.0	NA	46.2	26.9	23.6
1985	NA	54.3	NA	40.7	NA	16.2

Sources: U.S. Environmental Protection Agency. *International Comparison of Air Pollution Control* (Washington, D.C., 1988) 11–12; as presented in Raymond J. Kopp, Paul R. Portney, and Diane E. DeWitt, *International Comparisons of Environment Regulation (Washington, D.C.: Resources for the Future, 1990),* 11; Environment Canada, average for Montreal monitoring stations, Sulfur Dioxide Annual Means, μg/m³.

treal had the lowest concentration. It also had the largest decrease in ambient SO$_2$ levels for the cities surveyed. New York started the period at a level close to Montreal, but had only a slight improvement over the decade. Paris and London began with much higher ambient levels of SO$_2$ than Montreal or New York, and had improvement of roughly 50 percent. Berlin appears to fall into the same pattern. Tokyo is another success story. It started somewhat higher than North American cities but ended the decade with ambient concentrations approaching those of Montreal.

Table 20-2 shows some comparative data on various environmental measures for selected OECD (Organization for Economic Cooperation and Development) countries. The first two columns pertain to water-pollution measures. Per capita expenditures on water-pollution control in the mid-1980s varied from a low of $31 in Canada to a high of $71 in West Germany. The percentage of population served by at least secondary treatment facilities varied from 37 percent in Norway to 94 percent in Sweden. These are substantial differences among countries. We defer until the next section a discussion of how to interpret these differences.

The third column of Table 20-2 shows data on fertilizer application in some of the countries. Application of fertilizer is associated with fertilizer runoff and consequent water pollution. But since this is a nonpoint-source emission, it is basically impossible to measure accurately the quantity of pollutant runoff. Thus, the next best thing is to look at the comparative rates of fertilizer application. Note the particularly high rates of use in European countries (Netherlands, U.K., and "West" Germany) and the relatively low rates in Canada and the U.S. These differences clearly relate to differences in population pressure and the amounts of cultivable land in the various countries. Finally, the last column in the table shows data on noise pollution. You can clearly see why concern about noise pollution has been much higher in Europe than in Canada.

Table 20-3 contains some revealing data on emissions in a variety of European countries. It shows emissions per $1,000 of gross domestic product for individual

TABLE 20-2   SELECTED ENVIRONMENTAL DATA, OECD COUNTRIES

Country	Per capita expenditures for water pollution control[a]	Percentage of population served by secondary or tertiary water treatment facilities[b]	Tons of fertilizer applied per square kilometre of agricultural land	Percentage of population exposed to noise greater than 65 dB from road traffic[c]
Canada	31	66	2.6	7
Denmark	66	90	—	—
France	44	—[d]	13.3	16
Germany[e]	71	88	20.6	13
Italy	—	—	7.6	18
Japan	60	—	13.7	30
Netherlands	59	82	46.7	—
Norway	48	37	—	—
Spain	—	—	5.5	—
Sweden	52	94	7.6	—
United Kingdom	39	78	20.9	11
United States	54	74	5.1	7

[a]Mid-1980s, in U.S. dollars, at 1980 prices and exchange rates.
[b]Applies to late 1980s.
[c]Average sound level over a given period, normally 6 a.m. to 10 p.m.
[d]Dashes indicate data are not available.
[e]"West" Germany only.
Source: Organization for Economic Cooperation and Development, *The State of the Environment* (Paris: OECD, 1991), 58–59, 810, 217, and 241.

countries in Eastern Europe, the former USSR, and the European Economic Community as a whole. The interest in these numbers stems from the comparison of emissions performance in Western Europe with that of the former socialist countries of Eastern Europe. The EEC performance is markedly better in SO_2 and particulate emissions and somewhat better in emissions of "gases." Its solid-waste "emissions," on the other hand, are higher than those for the GDR and Hungary, though nowhere near as high as those shown for Poland. In fact, the number for Poland is hard to believe.[1]

Interpreting Differences in Environmental Performance

We must take care in interpreting these comparative environmental data.[2] The first reaction might be to interpret different environmental indices as indicating the effort each country has put into pollution control. But a moment's reflection shows that this is not necessarily the case. Differences in ambient environmental quality between different countries can be explained in essentially two ways: (1) as differences in the

---

[1] Solid-waste data are notoriously difficult to interpret and compare because different reporting entities, even different cities within the same country, will often define the term differently.
[2] The same might be said about comparisons among different regions of the same country.

TABLE 20-3   ENVIRONMENTAL EMISSIONS IN EASTERN EUROPE, USSR, AND EEC

Country	Emissions per $1,000 of GDP				
	Sewage (km^3)	PM[a] (kg)	Gases (m^3)	Solid waste (kg)	SO$_2$ (kg)
Bulgaria	195	—	17.4[b]	—	20
Czechoslovakia	54	17.6	54.1	—	38
GDR	39	13.3	47.4	158	29
Hungary	27	17.7	65.3	93	37
Poland	86	23.3	65.0	1,251	30
Romania	—	—	30.0[b]	—	33
Former USSR	145	—	52.4[c]	—	20
EEC[f]	—	1.4[d]	25.5[a]	249[e]	7

[a]Particulate matter.
[b]1982, SO$_2$ only.
[c]1981, includes gases and particulate matter.
[d]Excluding Ireland and U.K.
[e]Excluding Ireland.
[f]European Economic Community.
Source: Zbigniew Bochniarz, Statement in "U.S. Environmental Initiatives in Eastern Europe," hearings before the Subcommittee on Transportation and Hazardous Materials of the Committee on Energy and Commerce, U.S. Congress, House of Representatives, 101st Congress, 2nd Session, April 23, 1990, 62–63.

efficient, or desired, levels of ambient quality and/or (2) as differences in the extent to which each country, through policy and its enforcement, have achieved these efficient levels.

These are depicted in Figure 20-1, which shows three familiar marginal damage/marginal abatement cost diagrams, with ambient quality indexed on the horizontal axes. Suppose that in comparing ambient quality levels in two countries, you find two points like e_1 and e_2 indicated on each diagram in the figure. Panel (a) shows that this could be the result of differences between the two countries in terms of their marginal abatement costs, given the same preferences for environmental quality in the two countries. In the short run this could be the result of different technological means for pollution control available in the two countries. But in the long run this factor would be less important, since pollution-control technology is mobile; whatever is available in one country can be made available in the other. Of course, the difference in marginal abatement cost functions could arise also because one country has adopted more cost-effective environmental-control policies than the other. Other factors may also be at work. As we have stated many times, ambient conditions are the result of emissions *and* the assimilative capacity of the environment. So a country that has achieved low emissions may still suffer relatively high ambient concentrations because of the way its environment works: Similar emissions in Mexico City and Toronto will produce much dirtier air in the former because of its prevailing meteorological patterns. By the same token, similar ambient levels do not imply that countries have made similar efforts to control emissions, because in one the assimilative

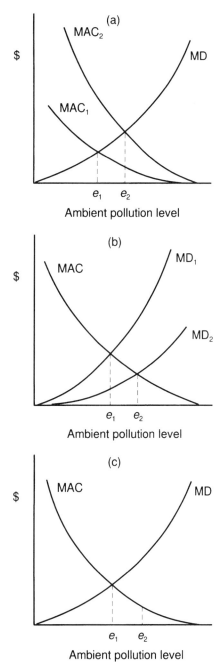

FIGURE 20-1 Interpreting International Differences in Ambient Pollution Levels.

capacity of the environment may be greater.[3] Another real possibility is that there are differences in economic circumstances of the two countries—one relatively rich and the other relatively poor—so that the opportunity cost of pollution control in terms of foregone conventional income is higher in one than in the other. Note that the country with the highest ambient concentration may actually have spent more in total on abatement costs than the country with the lower concentration. We will have more to say on this point in Chapter 21 on the relationship of environmental quality to economic development.

Panel (b) depicts the case where the difference between e_1 and e_2 is explained by differences in the damages flowing from ambient pollution loads in the two countries. This could stem, for example, from real differences in willingness to pay for pollution control by people in similar economic and social circumstances—that is, environmental quality as a matter of tastes and preferences—or from the fact that the two countries give a different priority to environmental quality. As an example of the former, consider the following case, which actually applies to the siting of an industrial plant that has some small but nonzero probability of catastrophic accident:

> Recently California and the United Kingdom have approved sites for Liquefied Energy Gas (LEG) terminals. In this, and perhaps this alone, they are the same. After a long drawn-out process in which it proved impossible to approve any of the proposed sites, California finally, with the help of a new statute passed expressly for the purpose, was able to give approval for an LEG facility at the remotest of all the sites on the list of possibles: Point Conception. Scotland has a longer coastline than California and most of the country is very sparsely populated (less than 25 persons to the square mile) and yet the approved site, at Mossmorran and Braefoot Bay on the Firth of Forth, lies within the most densely populated part of the entire country (with a population density of between 250 and 500 persons per square mile). Moreover, laden tankers will pass within a mile or so of Burntisland (an industrial town) and sometimes within four miles of Edinburgh—the capital city of Scotland! If the California siting criteria (explicit in Statute 1081) were to be applied to the Scottish case it would be quite impossible to approve the Mossmorran/Braefoot Bay site, and if the United Kingdom criteria (implicit in the Mossmorran/Braefoot Bay approval) were to be applied to the California case, any of the suggested sites could be approved, which means that the terminal would go to the first site to be suggested—Los Angeles harbor.[4]

Finally, panel (c) depicts the situation of different enforcement efforts. While both have the same desired level of ambient quality, one country has devoted more resources to enforcement and thus its actual level is lower. Throughout this book we

---

[3] For example, there has been a running dispute between Great Britain and the other members of the European Commission (EC) over the basis of water-pollution control. It stems from the fact that rivers in Great Britain tend to be short and have very substantial assimilative capacity, while those on the continent are longer, with less capacity. Thus, Great Britain has been in favour of an ambient standard approach to water quality improvement within the EC, while other member states have leaned toward emission standards.

[4] Michael Thompson, "A Cultural Basis for Comparison," in Howard Kunreuthen and Joanne Linnerooth (eds.), *Risk Analysis and Decision Process, The Siting of Liquefied Energy Facilities in Four Countries* (Berlin: Springer, 1983), 233.

have talked about the importance of enforcement. Most developed countries have significant antipollution laws on the books; most also have significant enforcement problems, as is illustrated in the following comments:

> Some people here say the problem is that there is not an adequate body of environmental law in Ireland. But that is not true. There are 55 or so laws that affect what private industry can do to the environment. They are just not enforced. You can take it for granted that every single law is not being adequately enforced. Local authorities and corporations, too, actually have a pretty good record for responding to citizen complaints about pollution, since by then it is a political matter. But what you very rarely find is a local authority playing watchdog, checking up to see if regulations are being followed.[5]

> In Spain, we have beautiful laws to protect the environment, but nobody is really complying with them. Industry knows that the chances are not very great that the government is going to suddenly crack down and begin enforcing the laws. They say they will gradually get tougher, but in my opinion it would be better to have fewer and simpler regulations and get a better record of compliance from the very beginning.[6]

Of course, when making comparisons among countries all three factors will normally come into play: abatement costs, damages, and enforcement efforts.

ENVIRONMENTAL POLICY IN OTHER COUNTRIES

Regardless of where one lives, there is much to learn through comparing one's own experience with that of others. The rest of this chapter examines some of the distinguishing environmental policy efforts of developed countries other than Canada. It is not intended to try to offer a catalogue of events in each country; this would be impossible in the space we have, and also because environmental issues and responses are changing so rapidly that a catalogue of this type would quickly be out of date. Instead, we will try to single out particularly noteworthy policies or trends that characterize environmental policy in particular countries or groups of countries.

General Considerations

It is accurate to say that all countries rely heavily on "command and control" as the primary approach to pollution control. This means administrative determinations of such things as what technologies are to be installed, what emissions are to be, where firms may locate, how buildings and equipment should be designed, what fuels and inputs may be used, how certain substances are to be handled, etc. The institutions set up to do this, and the degree of participation encouraged and allowed by other groups, vary greatly from country to country. In most countries, some concept has

---

[5] Interview with Irish water quality official, quoted in H. Jeffrey Leonard, *Pollution and the Struggle for World Product* (Cambridge, England: Cambridge University Press, 1988), 211.
[6] Interview with a private-company manager for energy conservation and environmental affairs, quoted in Ibid.

been adopted to establish the technological level(s) on which to base command-and-control decisions. In Great Britain it is "best practicable means," which refers to "reasonably practicable and technically possible to prevent the emission of gases and render these discharges harmless."[7] In Canada, Ontario's MISA program uses terms very similar to these in its BATEA technological standards. Germany relies on the basic idea that pollution-control programs must involve "state-of-the-art" technology. In Sweden the underlying decision criterion is to choose "what is technically feasible using the most effective technical devices and methods that are available in the area in question."[8] Italy has a standard calling for emissions reductions to "the lowest level possible through available technologies."[9] As we have mentioned several times in previous chapters, this approach actually allows regulators to make implicit trade-offs between damage reduction and technical and economic feasibility.

National Political Styles in Environmental Policy

From our discussion of the different policy options available in environmental policy, one might get the impression that policy matters are primarily technical exercises in picking the right approach to match the environmental problem being addressed. But a number of studies have shown that environmental policies in different countries are also a reflection of their unique political cultures and institutions. In one study of air-pollution policy in Sweden and the U.S., the author characterized the differences between the two countries as the difference between the hare and the tortoise.[10] The U.S. was the hare, with bursts of speed followed by pauses and rests, while Sweden was the tortoise, with slower but steadier progress. As we've seen in Section 5, Canada's political style is much closer to that of Sweden than to the United States. The author's comparison of U.S. and Swedish policy approaches is the following:

U.S.	Sweden
1. Statutory ambient standards.	1. Nonstatutory emission guidelines.
2. Strict timetables for compliance.	2. Compliance timetables set on basis of economic feasibility.
3. Technology-forcing emission standards.	3. Adjustments of standards to technological developments.

---

[7] Roy Gregory, *The Price of Amenity: Five Studies in Conservation and Government* (London: Macmillan, London, 1971), 12.

[8] Göran A. Persson, "Sweden," in Edward J. Kormondy (ed.), *International Handbook of Pollution Control* (Westport, Conn.: Greenwood Press, 1989), 219–232.

[9] Giancarlo Pinchera, Silvia Brini, and Mario Cirillo, "Italy," in *European Environmental Yearbook*, 4th ed. (Milan: Doc Ter, Institute for Environmental Studies, 1990), 415.

[10] Lennart J. Lundquist, *The Hare and the Tortoise: Clean Air Policies in the United States and Sweden* (Ann Arbor: University of Michigan Press, 1980).

In general, the U.S. style, at least during the 1970s covered in this study, emphasized formal and sharply defined objectives written into public laws, after much political wrangling, with later administrative compromises and delays to accommodate reality. The Swedish approach was to set policy with far less public fanfare, negotiating voluntary agreements that were based on technical and economic feasibility. Despite these differences, the changes through time in ambient air quality were quite similar between the two countries. He concludes: "At this point, the overall result seems very much to be a dead heat. Neither of the two countries seems to have been remarkably more successful than the other in relieving its citizens from the blight of air pollution."[11]

Another interesting study has been done on the introduction of vinyl-chloride (VC) standards into industrial workplaces. VC is used to make polyvinyl chloride (PVC), which in turn is shaped into thousands of products—piping, flooring, food wrapping, credit cards, baby pacifiers, shoes, medical devices, etc. High levels of VC exposure in the workplace were identified in the early 1970s as a cause of serious health conditions among workers, particularly cancer. So, around this time many countries, including Canada addressed the task of reducing VC exposure in plants producing PVC. The study was a comparison of the way the policy process worked in five countries: France, Great Britain, Japan, the U.S., and West Germany.[12] The basic contrast is between the adversarial style of the U.S. and the cooperative negotiating style of the others. Again, Canada's style is closer to the cooperative approach than the adversial one. The author characterizes the U.S. effort in the following way:

> . . . the key decisions in the adversarial case were made by agency officials and judges on the basis of virtually secret deliberations. Industry and labor did not cooperate but instead took steps to impede and discredit each other. Industry and government behaved similarly. Lawyers were active from start to finish, and no intermediaries acted as buffers among the parties. The various parties had only an indirect influence on the major decisions, and this was largely confined to public, highly publicized, courtlike hearings. Basic information was communicated through documents, and cost/benefit considerations were not an explicit part of the agency's decision process. In the end, OSHA issued its final regulations and required that industry achieve— under penalty of law—a very strict standard, one which exceeded the industry's technical capability at the time it was promulgated.[13]

By contrast, the cooperative styles of standard setting are characterized in the following way:

> . . . the parties involved directly influenced the critical decisions and actually made many of them. They achieved consensus through negotiations and discussions among middle-level officials over a period of several years. There were important intermediaries, and very few lawyers, involved in the process. Representatives of the major

---

[11] Ibid., 194.

[12] Joseph L. Badaracco, Jr., *Loading the Dice, A Five-Country Study of Vinyl Chloride Regulation* (Boston: Harvard Business School Press, 1985).

[13] Ibid., 124–125.

parties developed personal relationships in small working groups. Meetings were held in private—informally, and without rigid timetables. The working parties explicitly discussed cost and benefit. In the end, the decisions that emerged from these multi-partite discussions were less formal, they followed technology, and they included flexible open-ended recommendations that companies should seek to achieve the lowest feasible levels of VC exposure.[14]

Having established these two styles, however, the results show that the ambient workplace exposure standards arrived at in the adversarial process (the U.S.) were stricter than those established through the cooperative process.

Japan provides another interesting example. Japanese environmental policy is based on a series of ambient standards that represent objectives, together with specific emission standards to move toward those objectives. National, generic emission standards are set, but at the local, or prefecture, level, particular emission standards are worked out on a source-by-source basis. This approach involves two characteristics that are specific to the Japanese experience. One is a high degree of negotiation between local pollution-control authorities and polluting sources, the results of which are to produce emission standards that are to some extent specific to each source. The other feature is the large amount of "administrative guidance." According to the basic national water pollution-control law, any operating unit that is the source of water-based emissions must submit a detailed plan showing the location, timing, type, etc., of emissions, and the methods and technologies to be used to control these emissions. Local pollution-control authorities then become heavily involved in the administrative guidance of these plans, along with the regular plant operators. The Japanese experience includes much more discretion at the local level. Pollution-control agreements may be struck between local authorities and firms. At first,

> . . . many contracts were simply "gentlemen's agreements" (shinshi kyotei). For example, many early agreements declared that a company had an abstract duty to prevent pollution, to supply information, or to cooperate with local officials in a factory inspection. The company simply promised to take feasible and "appropriate" measures to prevent pollution. Such contracts in most cases did not contain provisions to handle violations.[15]

But more recently, local agreements have started to be

> . . . drafted more precisely, and are richer in content. For example, many agreements require companies to meet emission or effluent standards stricter than national standards; others stipulate that a factory use special low sulfur fuel; some require the use of the most advanced pollution prevention technology, contain stipulations on factory operations, or provide for inspection of the factory. In some cases these contracts also authorize drastic enforcement measures like stop-work orders, emergency enforcement by proxy, strict liability for damages, fines, cancellation of a contract (where a sale

---

[14] Ibid., 124.
[15] Julian Gresser, Koichiro Fujikura, and Aiko Morishima, *Environmental Law in Japan* (Cambridge, Mass.: MIT Press, 1981), 248.

of land between local government and a factory is involved), and as previously mentioned, interruption of the municipal water supply upon notice of violation.[16]

It needs to be stressed that these differences in style and institutions, though they may sound significant, may not have significant impacts on the levels of ambient quality actually achieved. They should not be interpreted as better or worse styles from among which a country may choose. Each national style is unique, stemming from a country's own political culture, and the effectiveness of policy has to be considered within the context of these particular styles.

Statutory Laws for Compensating Victims of Pollution

Many countries have common law systems whereby individuals who have been injured by the pollution of some other individual can sue for damages. The fact-finding and award of compensation are then worked out in courts of law. In recent years also various statutory provisions have been enacted to make hazardous waste dumpers, or oil spillers, liable for damage they cause. But in several countries explicit statutes allow for individuals who have been damaged by pollution to collect compensation.

In Japan the compensation statute enacted in 1973 is called The Law for the Compensation of Pollution-Related Health Injury. The law establishes an administrative structure and a health certification procedure, whereby victims living in designated parts of the country can be compensated for medical expenses and lost earnings from specific, officially designated, pollution-related diseases. These diseases are *minamata* (mercury poisoning), *itai-itai* (cadmium poisoning), chronic arsenic poisoning, emphysema, chronic bronchitis, asthma, and asthmatic bronchitis. The effect of this law is to replace what in many countries would be a piecemeal process of individual court cases with an overall, centrally directed system for compensating those damaged by pollution. Although it is probably much less expensive than a case-by-case court approach, it still has many of the same problems; for example, determining whether health cases are in fact pollution-related, establishing fair compensation levels, and so on.

The incentive effects of this approach may also be questioned. In a system where victims are free to sue particular companies for compensation of pollution-related disease, there is presumably a direct incentive for polluters to take steps to reduce their potential liability. But this incentive may be quite weak if a firm is just one among many that contribute to a particular case of pollution, because here the public-good nature of pollution works against individual responsibility. In the Japanese system the direct link between the behaviour of individual firms and its compensation payments is broken. The fund from which victims are compensated is derived from taxes on polluters, especially on SO_2 emissions. The tax rate varies by regions, but is the same for all sources within the same region. The tax is not set, however, at a level equal to full marginal damages from emissions, and thus does not have the emissions-

---

[16] Ibid.

reducing incentive of a tax, as we have discussed earlier. The tax is established as a revenue source to get sufficient funds to cover compensation payments. Theoretically, this would be a reasonably efficient tax if compensation covered all damages. But the law specifies that only medical costs and lost wages may be compensated, which probably understates total damages by a substantial margin. The part of the law dealing with compensation for air-pollution damages was terminated in 1988 as a result of pressure from industry and finance interests. Their view was that since ambient standards were then being met, there was no further need for compensation.[17]

A law of compensation for pollution damage also exists in the Netherlands. The compensation is paid from a special fund at whose expense "any person suffering damage which is due to air pollution occurring above the territory of the Netherlands, and which for reasons of equity shall not be borne by that person, may be granted, on application, compensation."[18]

Guiding Principles of Pollution Control

In various countries around the world authorities have sought to adopt governing principles for the design of pollution-control policies. In Japan pollution-control efforts were initially developed under the principle of "harmonization," which was essentially a requirement that pollution-control laws be "harmonized" with the requirements of economic growth. In China, new industrial construction is supposed to be pursued within the principle of "three at the same time." Each new construction plan is supposed to contain a special section on environmental protection showing how pollution-control methods will be designed, installed, and operated.[19]

Countries of the Organization for Economic Cooperation and Development (OECD) have sought to pledge their allegiance to what is called the "polluter pays principle" (PPP). This principle states that it is the polluters themselves who should bear the cost of measures to reduce pollution to levels specified by public authorities. While this may sound like a rule based on ethical considerations, it is really grounded in political economics. It is meant to rule out situations where governments subsidize pollution-control expenditures of firms or industries in order to give them an economic advantage over competitors who must pay their own compliance costs. This is regarded as especially important among the closely competing firms and industries of the countries of Europe. There are exceptions allowed to the PPP in certain cases of undue economic hardship, short-term transition periods, and cases that have no significant impacts on international trade and investment. Since most countries, in OECD as elsewhere, subsidize pollution reduction to a greater or lesser

---

[17] Ken'ichi Miyamoto, "Japan" in *European Environmental Yearbook*, 4th ed. (Milan: Doc Ter, Institute for Environmental Studies, 1990).

[18] Alfred Rest, "Responsibility and Liability for Transboundary Air Pollution Damage," in Cees Flinterman, Barbara Kwiatkowska, and Johan G. Lammers (eds.), *Transboundary Air Pollution, International Legal Aspects of the Co-operation of States* (Dordrecht, Holland: Martinus Nijhoff Publishers, 1986), 324.

[19] Rui Lin Jin and Wen Liu, "Environmental Policy and Legislation in China," in *Proceedings of the Sino-American Conference on Environmental Law* (Boulder, Colo.: Natural Resource Law Center, University of Colorado School of Law, 1989), 173.

degree, it has been necessary for political diplomats to find ways of reconciling principle and reality. In general, this has been done by defining the PPP abstractly enough that it can be held compatible with a wide number of arrangements.

Emission Charges

In some countries emission charges have been widely used for many years. This is especially the case in Europe. In recent years many governments in Europe have been moving toward a greater use of charges. Our discussion of emission taxes in Chapter 12 focussed on taxes as a means of bringing about cost-effective emission reductions. These might be called "incentive" taxes or, as they are sometimes called in Europe, "balancing" taxes. The emission taxes employed in Europe are not incentive taxes of this type. Rather, they are employed primarily to raise money that can then be used to subsidize pollution-control activities of public and private organizations.

This is depicted in Figure 20-2, which shows the marginal abatement cost of a single polluter. The initial emission level is e_1, and the authorities set a maximum target of e^* for the firm. An emission tax rate of t^* would provide the incentive needed to bring about a reduction of emissions to e^*. But this would entail a substantial tax obligation for the firm. Instead, the authorities establish a charge at a rather low level; for example, t_1. This has very modest incentive effects; it leads the firm to reduce emissions from e_1 to e_2. But it provides a tax revenue to the regional agency equal to the crosshatched area. This amount, together with the sums from other water polluters who are taxed in the same fashion, is used to subsidize the installation of water pollution-control efforts among these and other sources. The tax is justified because it is a good source of funds needed for the subsidy program, not because it provides incentives for polluters to reduce their emissions.[20]

Although this is a tax program, the real incentive effects, if there are any, are in the subsidies. We saw earlier that subsidies, if they were given out at a common rate per unit of emissions reduced, would meet the criterion of cost-effectiveness. There is no evidence that this is actually the way the European programs work, however. Rather, regional pollution-control authorities, such as the Agences Financieres de Bassin in France and the Genossenschaften in Germany, establish budgets each year that include the various projects and programs to be supported, then set the tax at whatever level is needed to raise enough money to cover these plans.

It appears that many European countries have moved even more strongly in the direction of revenue-raising emission taxes. Germany is planning a tax on hazardous wastes. France has recently enacted a tax on SO_2 and NO_x from power plants and other industrial firms. Italy has a plastic bag tax, 90 percent of which is waived if the bags are biodegradable. Denmark has instituted a tax on building materials (e.g., sand and gravel) to encourage recycling. Spain is planning taxes on waterborne emis-

---

[20] The emphasis on revenue raising is so primary that emissions to be taxed are often estimated rather than measured exactly. But this is not as controversial as it might be because the tax rates are low and because the tax revenues are recycled back into the industry or region from which the taxes were collected.

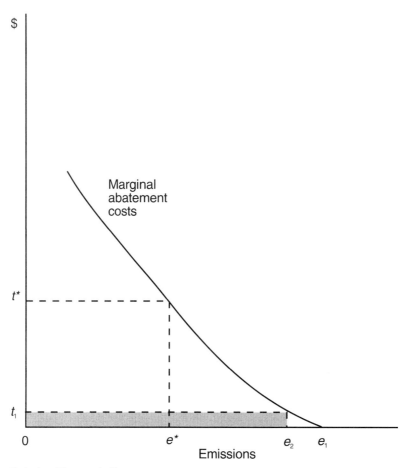

FIGURE 20-2   Emission Charges in Europe.

sions. However, in very recent years, there is some indication that a few European countries are introducing taxes designed to have incentive effects as well as to raise revenue. [21]

For example, Finland has had a tax on the lead content of gasoline since 1986. In 1993, it added to this tax charges for other pollutants. Greece has had a tax since 1990 on cars that do not meet the 1983 U.S. emission standards. This tax has provided an incentive to scrap old cars more quickly. But perhaps the most important new source of revenue or to provide incentives to change behaviour will be carbon, or CO_2, taxes, which many European countries are contemplating or have introduced. These are jus-

---

[21] For information on recent tax iniatives in OECD countries, see Organization for Economic Cooperation and Development, *Taxation and the Environment, Complementary Policies* (Paris: OECD, 1993).

tified on the basis of the global-warming problem. Some of these taxes are designed to raise revenue. An example is in the Netherlands where motor fuel taxes have been raised a small amount. The proceeds of the new tax are to fund government environmental investments. Sweden introduced a carbon tax in 1991 on motor and other fossil fuels, but reduced other energy taxes by 50 percent at the same time. Thus, it would not seem that it's "carbon" tax was designed solely to raise revenue. Finland increased a tax on leaded gasoline by 50 percent from 1991 to 1992. It's stated objectives are both to raise revenue and to reduce fuel consumption and therefore emissions. Time will tell whether other countries will follow suit and introduce carbon taxes and whether or not their objective will be revenue based.

Environmental Benefit Analysis

European countries are following the lead of the United States and are attempting to measure the social benefits of environmental improvement. The control of air and water pollution there is complicated by the presence of many international boundaries in a relatively small geographical area. Efforts at harmonizing environmental laws, spearheaded by the European Economic Commission, can be helped along by the accumulation of results of benefit-measurement studies.

German scholars have sought to measure losses in agricultural and forest outputs resulting from decreased yields caused by air pollution. Air-pollution damages have also been measured through increased expenditures for maintenance, replacement, and cleaning of buildings and windows in high-emissions areas.[22] European environmental economists have been interested in measuring the damages of noise pollution. A study in Switzerland sought to measure these damages by looking at the negative effects of traffic noise on house prices. A study in the Netherlands looked at rent levels. In that country renters of houses and apartments may sometimes obtain reductions in their monthly rent payments if they are exposed to high noise levels. The value of these rent reductions indicates the extent of damages. Travel cost methods have also been used to estimate the recreational value of environmental resources. In France, for example, this approach was used to estimate damages caused by the grounding of the tanker Amoco *Cadiz* in 1978.[23] European environmental economists are turning increasingly to contingent valuation (CV) methods to assess the benefits of improvements in environmental quality, although these results are not as widely accepted among policy administrators as they are beginning to be in the U.S.[24]

Residents of Berlin were asked how much they would be willing to pay for better air quality, as specified in several alternative possibilities—for example, the avoidance of more severe air pollution, or an improvement that would make air quality on

---

[22] O. J. Kuik, F. H. Oosterhuis, H. M. A. Jansen, K. Holm, and H.-J. Ewers, *Assessment of Benefits of Environmental Measures* (London: Graham and Trotman for the Commission of the European Communities, 1992), 37–88.

[23] F. Bonnieux and P. Rainelli, *Catastrophe écologique et dommages économiques* (Paris: Institut national de la recherche agronomique, 1991).

[24] O. J. Kuik et al., *Assessment of Benefits of Environmental Measures*, 29.

normal days as good as it currently was on holidays. In Norway, researchers have used CV methods to investigate the benefits produced when the level of acidity was reduced in certain lakes heavily used for fishing.[25]

In Sweden, a CV study was done to estimate the visual benefits people get from a scenic agricultural landscape.[26]

ENVIRONMENTAL POLICY IN SOCIALIST COUNTRIES

It may be tempting to think that socialist economic systems would be better than market economies in managing environmental quality issues because they involve pervasive central direction over all economic decisions. Administrative agencies, apparently with control over all the important variables, could make sure that all "externalities" were properly accounted for in production planning, and plant managers would be directed to pursue courses of action that ensured efficient levels of emissions and ambient environmental quality.

It has not worked out this way, however. Not only have centrally planned economies failed miserably in environmental matters, but their failures even in basic economic planning and administration have led their citizens to move toward market systems. With the opening up of the former Soviet Union and the countries of Eastern Europe, it has become apparent that the state systems have produced extreme environmental damages in many regions. Large environmental assets have been seriously degraded, and in many places ambient air and water quality was allowed to get bad enough to have severe repercussions on human health.

To some extent this is because of the basic philosophy of the political leaders, coupled with a closed political system, and to some extent it relates to the perverse incentives built into the concept of planning. Central economic planning requires that economic power and political power be merged in the same institutions and authorities. Thus, economic decisions—how and where resources are to be used—are made by reference to what their implications are for the continuation and consolidation of political power. Economic production is needed to buttress political power. Efforts to regulate that production have the potential to reduce that power. Thus, in the choice between economy and environment, the winner will normally be production.

One aspect of this power relationship has been the lack of avenues for local groups to protest environmental damages and bring about changes in production plans. This hinged importantly on the lack of public information on environmental matters. Communist regimes were reluctant to collect, tabulate, and publish data on the state of environmental problems in their countries. Thus, it was impossible for groups to mon-

---

[25] S. Navrud, "Estimating Social Benefits of Environmental Improvements from Reduced Acid Deposition: A Contingent Valuation Survey," in H. Folmer and E. van Ierland (eds.), *Valuation Methods and Policy Making in Environmental Economics* (Amsterdam: Elsevier, 1989), 69–102.

[26] L. Drake, *The Nonmarket Value of the Swedish Agricultural Landscape* (Uppsala: Swedish University of Agricultural Sciences, Department of Economics, 1987).

itor environmental damages and "lobby" for change.[27] Instead, environmental issues were "buried under mountains of paper and streams of declarations and statements."[28]

Incentive problems also are important. In a centrally planned economy, each enterprise and industry is programmed into the plan and is assigned certain output and input targets. Once the plan is adopted, it imparts great inflexibility to the economic system. For pollution-control equipment to be installed in a firm, for example, the entire plan had to be reworked, with new input and output targets. In a market economy, the market would adjust to the new pollution-control costs; prices would adjust in related markets, and inputs and outputs would be adjusted in response. This flexibility simply was not possible in centrally planned economies. Only if the environmental problem constitutes a dire emergency is there likely to be any response. In the former USSR, for example, the environmental oversight units created within the various enterprises had little authority to interfere with the smooth running of production. This rigidity and inability to enforce regulations that might upset the grand production plan has been commented on also in China.[29]

The other element is the incentive structure at the industry and factory levels. Plant managers were supposed to meet the planned output and input targets for their enterprises. In the USSR, plan fulfillment led to the managers receiving a bonus. But this has perverse incentives because plant managers are led to do all they can to reduce plan targets as much as possible, so that they will be easy to fulfill. In 1978 a law:

> . . . required that bonuses and rewards for workers and managements be made contingent upon a plant's fulfillment of all sections of its plan, including the environmental section, not just the production norms. The resolutions assign the individual enterprise a large number of environment "rights." These include the right to plan its environmental targets, to create environmental sections, to improve its environmental technology, to undertake capital construction in the area of environmental protection, to design a bonus and reward system to stimulate the observance of environmental norms, to provide environmental education, and to account to the responsible ministry for the fulfillment of its environmental norms.[30]

But what happens to production targets can easily happen to environmental targets. If a firm is given the power to develop its own environmental targets, then rewarded for meeting them, it is certain that the targets will be extremely modest.

In this there is an important lesson for pollution-control policy in market economies. Tying environmental target fulfillment to the bonus system ensures that the targets will be set as low as managers can get them, and that firms will do the min-

---

[27] Cynthia B. Schultz and Tamara Raye Crockett, "Economic Development, Democratization, and Environmental Protection in Eastern Europe," *Environmental Affairs* 18(1) (Fall 1990): 53–84.

[28] Ibid., 63.

[29] Yan Liu, "The General Policy of Controlling the Environment Comprehensively to Make the Chinese Economy and Environment Gradually Develop in Harmony," in *Proceedings of the Sino-American Conference on Environmental Law* (Boulder, Colo.: Natural Resources Law Center, University of Colorado School of Law, 1989), 195–201.

[30] Barbara Jancar, *Environmental Management in the Soviet Union and Yugoslavia* (Durham, N.C.: Duke University Press, 1987), 131.

imum necessary to achieve them. The same can be said of standard setting in market economies. If firms are required to meet certain standards, they have the incentive to try to get them set as low as possible and to do no more than is necessary to meet the standard. There is no incentive to look for better ways of pollution control and to reduce emissions even beyond the standard if that is efficient. It is only through incorporating economic incentives into the pollution-control policy that these stronger incentives can be brought into play.

Another public policy failing pointed up especially clearly by the experience in socialist countries is the environmental damages resulting from what might be called the "grandiose project" syndrome. With all economic planning and policy strictly centralized, authorities often begin to devote their efforts to large-scale projects meant to have very substantial impacts on economic growth in various sectors and regions. The possible local environmental impacts of such projects can often be overlooked because the decision process does not permit effective representation by people who will experience these damages. Exhibit 20-1 recounts a particularly egregious case, the destruction of the Aral Sea in the former Soviet Union by a grandiose scheme to produce irrigated cotton.

This discussion should not be taken to imply that nothing was ever done in socialist countries to protect the environment. It would be just as false to give the impression that market economies always automatically adjust to give the efficient levels of ambient environmental quality. Any economic system, if it is intent on putting its entire emphasis on material development, will downplay the impacts of this on the natural environment. Exhibit 20-2 shows a case of this in a market economy. Lack of regulatory oversight in the markets of a developing Chilean economy have led to environmental chaos. The story points up another vital factor: To get the necessary regulatory intervention it is vital to have open, responsive political systems where those who suffer environmental damage can seek redress.

DEVELOPMENTS IN ENVIRONMENTAL ACCOUNTING[31]

A number of countries have begun to take steps to either alter or augment their national income accounts to take into account the effects of economic growth on natural resource and environmental assets. Canada is a leader in these efforts. Statistics Canada has an Environmental Accounts Division working on a variety of measures to include the environment in our system of national accounts. National income accounting was developed around 50 years ago by governments who felt the need for a way of knowing how the overall economy was doing from year to year. Familiar measures like gross domestic product, net domestic product, and the rate of unemployment are meant to give us a summary of the total amount of economic activity in a year's time and of the status of certain aggregate variables that affect overall economic welfare. But in recent years conventional national income accounting has been

---

[31] For a discussion of issues in this section, see Henry M. Peskin and Ernst Lutz, *A Survey of Resource and Environmental Accounting in Industrialized Countries*, Working Paper No. 37 (Washington, D.C.: World Bank Environment Department, August 1990).

EXHIBIT 20-1

THE ARAL SEA: LESSONS FROM AN ECOLOGICAL DISASTER

The Aral Sea is dying. Because of he huge diversions of water that have taken place during the past thirty years, particularly for irrigation, the volume of the sea has been reduced by two-thirds. The sea's surface has been sharply diminished, the water in the sea and in surrounding aquifers has become increasingly saline, and the water supplies and health of almost 50 million people in the Aral Sea basin are threatened. Vast areas of salty flatlands have been exposed as the sea has receded, and salt from these areas is being blown across the plains onto neighboring cropland and pastures, causing ecological damage. The frost-free period in the delta of the Amu Darya River, which feeds the Aral Sea, has fallen to less than 180 days—below the minimum required for growing cotton, the region's main cash crop. The changes in the sea have effectively killed a substantial fishing industry, and the variety of fauna in the region has declined drastically. If current trends continued unchecked, the sea would eventually shrink to a saline lake one-sixth of its 1960 size.

This ecological disaster is the consequence of excessive abstraction of water for irrigation purposes from the Amu Darya and Syr Darya rivers, which feed the Aral Sea. Total river runoff into the sea fell from an average 55 cubic kilometers a year in the 1950s to zero in the early 1980s. The irrigation schemes have been a mixed blessing for the populations of the Central Asian republics—Kazakhstan, Kyrghyzstan, Tajikistan, Turkmenistan, and Uzbekistan—which they serve. The diversion of water has provided livelihoods for the region's farmers, but at considerable environmental cost. Soils have been poisoned with salt, overwatering has turned pastureland into bags, water supplies have become polluted by pesticide and fertilizer residues, and the deteriorating quality of drinking water and sanitation is taking a heavy toll on human health. While it is easy to see how the problem of the Aral Sea might have been avoided, solutions are difficult. A combination of better technical management and appropriate incentives is clearly essential: charging for water or allocating it to the most valuable uses could prompt shifts in cropping patterns and make more water available to industry and households.

But the changes needed are vast, and there is little room for maneuver. The Central Asian republics (excluding Kazakhstan) are poor; their incomes are 54 percent of the average in the former U.S.S.R. In the past, transfers from the central government exceeded 20 percent of national income in Kyrghyzstan and Tajikistan and 12 percent in Uzbekistan. These transfers are no longer available. The regional population of 35 million is growing rapidly, at 2.7 percent a year, and infant mortality is high. The states have become dependent on a specialized but unsustainable pattern of agriculture. Irrigated production of cotton, grapes, fruit, and vegetables accounts for the bulk of export earnings. Any rapid reduction in the use of irrigation water will reduce living standards still further unless these economies receive assistance to help them diversify away from irrigated agriculture. Meanwhile, salinization and dust storms erode the existing land under irrigation. This is one of the starkest examples of the need to combine development with sound environmental policy.

Source: World Bank, *World Development Report 1992. Development and the Environment.* (Washington, D.C., 1992), 38. Reprinted by permission.

criticized because it does not adequately deal with the resource and environmental implications of economic growth. Consider the standard production possibilities curve in Figure 20-3, showing marketed economic output on the vertical axis and environmental quality on the horizontal axis. Aggregate economic activity as reported in the conventional accounts consists only of measured marketed output. Thus, for example, a move from m_1 to m_2 would be regarded as an improvement in economic welfare. But this improvement has been accompanied by a reduction in environmental

EXHIBIT 20-2

THE GREENING OF SANTIAGO

Chile Tries to Clean Up Pinochet's Polluted Legacy

Brook Larmer *in Santiago*

Remember when the fall of dictators in Eastern Europe unveiled an environmental nightmare? Commentators called it the natural fruit of the Communist system. But take a look at Chile, Latin America's shining example of pure free-market economics. Two years after the exist of Gen. Augusto Pinochet, Chileans are starting to see the dark side of unregulated capitalist growth. Loggers have plundered the country's native forests. Fishermen have depleted the stocks of mollusks and fish. And the vital mining industry has destroyed entire valleys and river basins. The most palpable sign of trouble, however, is the blanket of noxious haze that suffocates Santiago, making it one of the world's smoggiest cities. Says Patricio Rodrigo, who helped draft a new environmental-protection law: "Chile is 15 to 20 years behind the rest of the world on this issue."

Make that 17 years. From 1973 to 1990, Pinochet ruled with absolute authority, routing the leftist opposition and rousing a dormant economy with privatization and deregulation. Growth has averaged 6 percent per year since 1985 with low inflation, Latin America's best record. But to regain Chile's edge in the global marketplace, Pinochet let industries pollute and exploit natural resources with virtually no limits. Environmentalists were seen as antigrowth troublemakers: "Scratch a green, find a red," went the motto. Finance Minister Hernan Büchi lured investors by lauding the lack of restrictions as part of Chile's "low production costs." Some 700 laws and 2,000 regulations were on the books, but only one official had the job of enforcing them. "There was an excess of faith in the market as a regulator," says Juan Escudero, general secretary of Santiago's Decontamination Commission, "It was chaos."

Both blessed and cursed by Chile's growth, President Patricio Aylwin now faces a daunting task: protect the environment without sacrificing the economy. Nowhere can the challenge be seen more clearly than in Santiago—if anything can be seen clearly these days. A thick layer of contaminants settles almost daily over the city, trapped by cold air and mountains on all sides. The causes of the filth: haphazard development and an out-of-control bus system that Pinochet began de-regulating in 1975. Two thirds of the smog's harmful elements come from the 11,000 privately owned buses that spew diesel fumes through the city. The government bought out 2,600 of the worst offenders. But pollution still reached lethal levels for two days in July, forcing the government to shut schools and factories and to warn parents to keep their children indoors. The government now hopes to put the brakes on the bus mess by selling routes, favoring operators with newer buses and lower fares.

The smog not only obscures the view of the majestic snowcapped Andes, it threatens to fog up Chile's economic future. A recent U.S. government report warned that Chile's lack of environmental standards and regulations could hurt its long-desired free-trade agreement with the United States. Partly in response, Aylwin's government has gone green: proposing new measures requiring all new vehicles to use catalytic converters, charging cars for driving downtown, creating a "pollution bourse" in which companies buy and sell the right to pollute. A broad environmental-protection bill is moving through the legislature, albeit as slow as sludge. But after 17 years of neglect, it signals a change in the atmosphere.

quality from e_1 to e_2. To get a complete picture of changes in social welfare we need to take into account both the increase in marketed output and the reduction in environmental quality.

Researchers and public authorities in different countries are approaching this problem in several ways. The basic question is how to measure and treat the "quantity" $e_1 - e_2$ in Figure 20-3. A number of countries have sought simply to measure annual total costs of pollution-control expenditures. The next logical step is perhaps to deduct these costs from measured output, on the grounds that they do not represent a true increase in economic welfare but expenditures necessary to protect ourselves from pollution. This procedure has been undertaken in the United States, France, and Japan.

But the method of deducting pollution-control expenditures does not get directly at measuring the values of environmental quality change as represented by the distance $e_1 - e_2$ in the figure. The first step in doing this is to measure the *physical* quantities of environmental resources and changes in these quantities over time. Attempts to measure physical changes in the total resource endowments of a nation are being undertaken in several countries, including Canada, France, and Norway. In Canada, two pilot projects for crude oil and natural gas reserves in Alberta and forests in Ontario have been undertaken by Statistics Canada.[32]

[32] For a discussion of the preliminary estimates of the value of crude oil and natural gas reserves, see Alice Born, "Preliminary Estimates of the Value of Crude Oil and Natural Gas Reserves in Alberta" in Statistics Canada, *Environmental Perspectives 1993*, Catalogue No. 11-528E (Ottawa: Statistics Canada, 1993).

FIGURE 20-3   National Income Accounting and the Neglect of Environmental Quality.

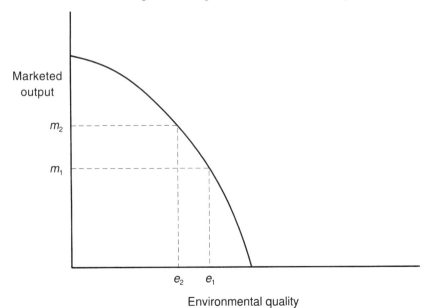

The objective is to compile a system of physical and monetary accounts for these natural resource stocks. Once made, the natural resource accounts can be combined with our National Balance Sheet accounts so that the value of Canada's resource base is included. At present, there is no systematic accounting for natural resource and environmental depletion (or accumulation). The ultimate goal is to develop a complete environmental accounting system which can be used to measure physical changes in natural and environmental resources resulting from economic production and consumption, and to value these quantities. Work on physical measures is also under way in France. The Netherlands and the United Nations as well are trying to put monetary values on the various dimensions of environmental degradation, including the reduced value of resources and the damages from pollution.

We are just at the beginning of efforts to incorporate environmental values into national income accounts. The conceptual and measurement problems are very difficult, and it will be some time before acceptable procedures can be developed and believable numbers estimated. But if it is successful this work could have a profound impact on public policy decisions.

SUMMARY

In many other industrialized countries major pollution-control efforts started in the decade of the 1970s, as they did in Canada. Policy in different countries is pursued through means that are congenial to the political culture and institutional history of each one. For the most part, pollution-control efforts have relied on various command-and-control approaches involving standards of various types. In many European countries, emission taxes have been widely used, but historically these have been primarily to raise revenues, which can then be used to subsidize pollution-control efforts. In the future, these could perhaps easily be transformed into incentive taxes with a primary pollution-control objective.

Environmental standards may be set at the national level (as in, e.g., the U.S., Germany, and Italy), at the local level (as in France and England), or at both the national and subnational levels as in Canada. But their *enforcement* tends to be very local, involving "bargaining" between emitters and local officials—not bargaining in the formal sense, but give-and-take between these parties as to what courses of action are to be undertaken by different sources to control emissions.

The large-scale environmental degradation of the ex-socialist countries bears an instructive lesson for pollution control in all countries. The initial reaction to environmental pollution is to think that it comes about because authorities lack the necessary means of control to bring about emission reductions. But in the ex-socialist countries, authorities presumably had total control and environmental damages have still been massive. This points up the importance of having open political systems, readily available information on what the state of the environment really is, and incentive systems that lead polluters to internalize the damages their emissions produce.

QUESTIONS FOR FURTHER DISCUSSION

1 How would the "polluter pays principle" apply to the case of mobile-source air pollution?
2 Suppose a law is enacted in which everyone is compensated fully for whatever environmental damage he or she suffers. What would the incentive effects of such a law be?
3 Consider the "European" approach to emission taxes. For a single source, is it possible that a low emissions tax could produce enough revenues to pay for all of the abatement costs required to reduce this source's emissions to an efficient level? What factors affect this? (Hint: You will want to explore this with the help of our standard emission-control model.)
4 What factors determine whether it would be more effective to proceed against polluters by hammering them in court or by sitting down with them to try to work things out on a "reasonable" basis?
5 Canada spends less per capita on environmental quality programs than many other OECD countries. Does this mean that we aren't devoting enough of our national income to the environment?

SELECTED READINGS

Barde, Jean-Philippe, and David W. Pearce (eds.). *Valuing the Environment, Six Case Studies.* London: Earthscan Publications, 1991.

Bower, Blair T., Rémi Barré, Jochen Kühner, and Clifford S. Russell. *Incentives in Water Quality Management, France and the Ruhr Area.* Washington, D.C.: Resources for the Future, 1981.

Brown, Gardner M., Jr., and Ralph W. Johnson. "Pollution Control by Effluent Charges: It Works in the Federal Republic of Germany: Why Not in the U.S.?" *Natural Resources Journal* 24 (4), (October 1984): 929–966.

Downing, Paul B., and Kenneth Hanf (eds.). *International Comparisons in Implementing Pollution Laws.* Boston: Kluwer Nijhoff Publishing, 1983.

Folmer, Henk, and Charles Howe. "Environmental Problems and Policy in the Single European Market." *Environmental and Resource Economics* 1(1) (1991): 22–45.

Gresser, Julian, Koichiro Fujikura, and Akio Morishima. *Environmental Law in Japan.* Cambridge, Mass.: MIT Press, 1981.

Huppes, Gjalt, and Robert A. Kagan. "Market-Oriented Regulation of Environmental Problems in the Netherlands." *Law and Policy* 11(2) (April 1989): 215–239.

Johnson, Ralph W., and Gardner M. Brown, Jr. *Cleaning Up Europe's Waters* New York: Praeger, 1976.

Johnson, Stanley P., and Guy Corcelle. *The Environmental Policy of the European Community.* London: Graham and Trotman, 1989.

Kormondy, Edward J. *International Handbook of Pollution Control.* Westport, Conn.: Greenwood Press, 1989.

Lutz, Ernst, ed. *Toward Improved Accounting for the Environment.* Washington, D.C.: The World Bank, 1993.

Park, Chris P. (ed.). *Environmental Policies: An International Review.* London: Croom Helm, 1986.

Peskin, Henry M., and Ernst Lutz. "A Survey of Resource and Environmental Accounting in Industrialized Countries." Environment Department Working Paper No. 37.
Washington, D.C.: World Bank, August 1990.

Reese, Craig E. *Deregulation and Environmental Quality.* Westport, Conn.: Quorum
Books, 1983.

Russell, Clifford S.: "Monitoring and Enforcement of Pollution Control Laws in Europe
and the United States," in Rüdiger Pethig (ed.). *Conflicts and Cooperation in Managing Environmental Resources.* Berlin: Springer-Verlag, 1992, 195–213.

Wilczynski, Piotr. *Environmental Management in Centrally-Planned Non-Market
Economies of Eastern Europe.* Environment Working Paper No. 35. Washington,
D.C.: World Bank, July 1990.

21

ECONOMIC DEVELOPMENT, SUSTAINABILITY, AND THE ENVIRONMENT

There was a time, several decades ago, when problems of environmental quality were widely regarded as being unique to developed, industrial economies. Industrial development was associated with air and water pollution, overreliance on chemicals, visual blight, etc. Developing countries, on the other hand, were thought to have fewer environmental problems because their preindustrial technology was more environmentally benign, and because they had not yet committed themselves to a materialistic style of life, with the negative trade-offs many feel that this implies.

Ideas have changed in recent years, however. For one thing, it has become clear that massive environmental degradation has in fact occurred in the developing world. Rural areas have seen large-scale soil erosion and water quality deterioration, deforestation, and declining soil productivity. Urban areas have experienced seriously diminished air and water quality. Furthermore, this environmental deterioration in developing countries was not just a matter of aesthetics or quality of life, but rather a more serious issue involving the diminishment of economic productivity and the acceleration of social dislocation. Out of this realization grew the idea of "sustainability" as a guide to decisions affecting the natural resource system.

In this chapter we will explore the interrelationship of economic development and the environment among the nonindustrialized countries of the world. In keeping with the distinction made back in Chapter 2, we will approach it on two levels: the positive and the normative. From the positive standpoint we want to understand how development and environmental degradation are related, and what factors account for this interrelationship. From a normative standpoint we will take up questions about the types of public policies that are best in these circumstances.

GENERAL CONSIDERATIONS

It is common to distinguish between economic *growth* and economic *development*. There is a simple, as well as a more complicated, way of distinguishing between these concepts. In simple terms, growth refers to increases in the aggregate level of output, while development means increases in per capita output. Thus, a country could grow, but not develop, if its population growth exceeded its rate of economic growth. The more complicated way is to say that economic growth refers to increases in economic activity without any underlying change in the fundamental economic structure and institutions of a country, while development also includes a wider set of technological, institutional, and social transformations. Changes in such things as education, health, population, transportation infrastructure, and legal institutions are all part of the development process. This should alert us to the fact that when talking about environmental issues in developing countries we will usually be talking about situations where the social and technological milieu can be very different from those in industrialized countries. At the same time it implies that, in environmental policy matters, a wider set of choices may be available because of the more thoroughgoing institutional transformations taking place in many developing countries.

In speaking of these issues, there is the tendency to divide the world into just two parts: developed and developing. Of course, any brief classification like this is an enormous oversimplification of the real world. At the very least we should think not of a simple categorization like this but of a continuum, running from the poorest to the richest, or along any other dimension of interest. The countries of the world are spread along that continuum, though not necessarily evenly. It's also true that national aggregates can tend to obscure some important development problems *within* particular countries. Many countries that look reasonably good on the basis of national macrodata have pockets of poverty and underdevelopment that would be sufficient to put these regions in the less developed ranks if national political boundaries were located differently.

ENVIRONMENTAL DEGRADATION IN DEVELOPING ECONOMIES

Many people in the developed world have been brought to a realization of the existence of environmental problems in the developing world through recent global concerns, such as global warming and the rapid pace of species extinction. A disproportionately high proportion of the world's endangered species are residents of developing countries, so efforts to preserve the habitats of these species have brought people to focus on the development-environment linkages in nonindustrialized countries. Similarly, the developed world's concern about global warming has heightened concern about deforestation, because forests act to absorb atmospheric CO_2. In many developing countries the harvesting of fuel wood and timber, and the conversion of forested lands to agricultural uses, have led to high rates of deforestation. Thus, large-scale deforestation has the potential to worsen the global greenhouse effect.

But from the standpoint of the developing countries themselves, their worst environmental problems are probably the water and air pollution they suffer, especially in their expanding urban areas. In the developed world, the chemical treatment of water supplies, together with the treatment of wastewater, have largely neutralized the water system as a source of human disease; continued water-pollution control is justified on recreational and aesthetic grounds. This is not the case in many developing countries where water pollution is still responsible for vast amounts of disease and death. Lack of treatment facilities leads to widespread exposure to disease-bearing human wastes. In places where there has been an expansion of industry, mining, and the use of agricultural chemicals, rivers have become contaminated with toxic chemicals and with heavy metals. Seepage of hazardous materials from industrial sites and waste dumps is increasingly threatening the groundwater resources toward which many countries have been turning as surface waters have become more heavily contaminated.

In a recent review of studies by the U.S. Agency for International Development (USAID) and the World Health Organization (WHO), the World Bank concluded that providing access to safer water and adequate sanitation to those who currently lack it would have the following impacts:

- 2 million fewer deaths from diarrhea each year among children under five years of age
- 200 million fewer episodes of diarrheal illness annually
- 300 million fewer people with roundworm infection
- 150 million fewer people with schistosomiasis
- 2 million fewer people infected with guinea worm.[1]

Air pollution is also a significant problem in developing countries. Data from the United Nations Global Environment Monitoring System (GEMS) indicates that in the mid-1980s about 1.3 billion people around the world were exposed to levels of particulate matter that exceeded WHO standards; most of these were in developing countries. In many countries gasoline is still virtually all leaded, leading to serious damages from airborne lead pollution. Indoor air pollution is also a more serious problem than in developed countries, owing to the continued heavy reliance on biomass fuels for cooking and heating.

ECONOMY AND ENVIRONMENT

While the concern about environmental problems has been of more recent origin, issues related to economic growth in the less developed world have been uppermost for many years; indeed, they have been historically the defining focus of this group of countries. This emphasis on economic development will continue, as they strive to

---

[1] World Bank, *World Development Report 1992*, Development and the Environment (New York: Oxford University Press for the World Bank, 1992), 49.

close the economic gap with the developed economies. What we need to look at, therefore, is the relationship between economic development and environmental quality.

A Static View

Probably the most frequently mentioned viewpoint on these matters is that developing countries simply cannot afford high levels of environmental quality. According to this view, the situation of these countries, in comparison to developed economies, can be pictured by the production possibilities curves of Figure 21-1. "Marketed output" refers to the conventional types of goods and services produced and distributed through economic markets. The PPC labelled A is for a typical developed country, while B refers to a developing nation. Because of past resource exploitation, or population pressures, or less sophisticated technology, B lies entirely within A. Thus, to achieve higher levels of marketed income, which it must if it is to develop, it must be willing to put up with lower levels of environmental quality. For example, for the developing country to reach a level of marketed output of c_1 it must trade off environmental quality back to the level e_2. The developed country, because of the factors mentioned above, can have c_1 of marketed output with a much higher level of environmental quality e_1 instead of only e_2. As one economist has put it:

> . . . the poorer countries of the world confront tragic choices. They cannot afford drinking water standards as high as those the industrial countries are accustomed to. They cannot afford to close their pristine areas to polluting industries that would introduce technical know how and productive capital and that would earn urgently needed for-

FIGURE 21-1   Production Possibilities Curves of Developed and Developing Countries.

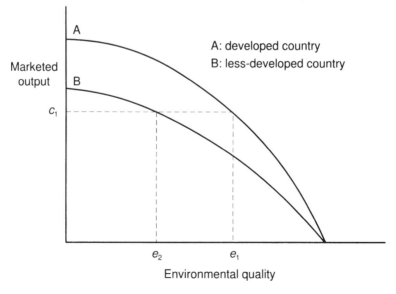

eign exchange. They cannot afford to bar mining companies from their unexploited regions. Nor can they afford to impose antipollution requirements on these companies that are as strict and expensive as those in richer industrial countries. They should always realize that environmental protection measures are financed out of the stomachs of their own people; the multinationals cannot be made to pay for them.[2]

Developing countries, according to this view, cannot afford the high levels of environmental quality sought in the developed world because this would mean lower monetary incomes and a lessened capacity to support their populations.

There is another side to this argument, however. The production possibilities curve approach sees marketed output and environmental quality as substitutes; more effort devoted to reducing environmental impacts must necessarily lead to lower monetary incomes. But in the developing world there are clear cases where environmental quality and measured GDP are complementary. Most developing countries depend proportionately more on primary industries than do developed ones. For example, they usually have a greater proportion of their population involved in agriculture. Thus, degradation of environmental resources has the potential for being more highly destructive of productive assets in developing countries. In industrial countries, environmental quality issues hinge primarily on matters of human health and the aesthetic quality of the environment. Furthermore, technological developments have decoupled, to a considerable extent, the resource-using sector from the rest of the economy. In developing countries, on the other hand, environmental issues are related to human health and productivity and also to the degradation of the future productivity of the natural resource base on which many people are directly dependent. According to this argument, the environment and the economy are not so much substitutes as they are complements.

Sustainability

But these are essentially static arguments, and the essence of economic development is long-run change. So the relevant question is: How is long-run economic development likely to affect environmental quality? The normal expectation is that development would shift the production possibility curve of Figure 21-1 outward. As economies change, becoming less tied to natural resources, and as less polluting technologies are adopted, this outward shift would improve the potential trade-offs between marketed output and environmental quality. Developing countries could then devote more resources to improving environmental quality.

There have been instances where the opposite has happened, however; cases where the short-run effort to increase or maintain marketed incomes have, in effect, tended to shift the PPC curve to the left and worsen the available choices. This has occurred when the search for short-run economic growth has led to irreversible reductions in the productivity of some part of a country's environmental assets. Here we consider

---

[2] Robert Dorfman, "An Economist's View of Natural Resources and Environmental Problems," in Robert Repetto (ed.), *The Global Possible* (New Haven, Conn.: Yale University Press, 1985), 67–76.

"environmental assets" very broadly, to include such things as soil fertility and forestry resources along with urban air and water pollution. The concept that has become widely used to talk of this phenomena is *sustainability*. A practice is sustainable if it does not reduce the long-run productivity of the natural resource assets on which a country's income and development depend.[3]

Sustainability is fundamentally a matter of renewable resources. When nonrenewable resources are used, they automatically become unavailable to future generations. The rule to follow here is to use them at the correct rate neither too fast nor too slow and to see to it that the natural wealth that they represent is converted into long-lived human-made wealth as they are used. Thus, for example, the petroleum resources of many developing countries must be converted to long-term productive capital, both private and public, if it is to contribute to the long-run economic development of the extracting country. By productive capital we mean not only physical capital (roads, factories, etc.), but also human capital (education, skills) and what we might call "institutional capital" (an efficient legal system, effective public agencies, etc.).

Long-Run Relationships

It is widely anticipated that, over the next few decades, developing countries will experience relatively rapid rates of economic growth. The World Bank, for example, estimates that collectively they will grow at a rate of 4–5 percent a year.[4] With long-run growth rates of this type, what impacts can we expect on environmental quality in these countries? If all technological factors were to stay the same over this period, environmental impacts and damages would increase along with this economic growth. But these factors are unlikely to remain constant. Economic development brings with it many changes. The most obvious is an increase in per capita incomes and, as people's income goes up, so does their willingness to sacrifice for improved environmental quality. Developing economies usually also experience a variety of structural changes, often in the direction of replacing relatively high-polluting industries with those that pollute less.

Studies have been done to investigate the relationship between various environmental quality indices and the income levels attained in different countries. The objective is to see if, as income levels change, there are systematic changes also in environmental quality variables. Several of the leading results are shown in Figure 21-2. These are based on "cross-section" analyses of income levels and environmental quality. This involves looking at the environmental characteristics of a large number of countries, with widely varying income levels, and then using statistical methods to

---

[3] The concept of "sustainability" received its major impetus in the influential report put out by the World Commission on Environment and Development: *Our Common Future* (Oxford, U.K.: Oxford University Press, 1987). This report is popularly called "The Brundtland Report" because the commission, created by the United Nations in 1983, was headed by Mrs. Gro Harlem Brundtland, Prime Minister of Norway.

[4] World Bank, *World Development Report 1992*, 9.

discover the underlying relationships, if indeed there are any. In fact, studies show clear relationships between income levels and a variety of environmental quality indices. In Figure 22-2, note that there are essentially three types of relationships:

1 Those showing steady declines as incomes increase. This applies to access to safe water and sanitation facilities, which countries can presumably more easily afford as incomes rise, but which also are normal goods in the sense that as incomes increase people are willing to pay larger amounts for them.

2 Those that first increase but then decrease with income, which applies to ambient amounts of particulates and SO_2. This pattern is probably due to the fact that in early stages of development industrial development leads to greater air pollution, while with continued development there is a shift in industry-type more towards cleaner industries, as well as a rising public demand in more well-to-do countries for pollution control.

3 Those showing a steady increase with income gains; this applies to municipal solid wastes and CO_2 emissions per capita. The first is a reflection of the growth in

FIGURE 21-2   Environmental Indicators in Relation to Country Income Levels.

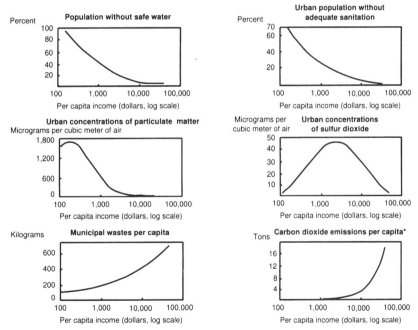

*Emissions are from fossil fuels.
Note: Estimates are based on cross-country analysis of data from the 1980s.

Sources: World Bank, World Development Report 1992, Development and the Environment (Oxford University Press for the World Bank, New York), 1992, 11, based on a paper by Nemat Shafik and Sushenjit Bandyopadhyay, "Economic Growth and Environmental Quality: Time Series and Cross-Section Evidence"; Gene Grossman and Alan B. Kreuger, "Environmental Impacts of a North American Free Trade Agreement," Discussion Paper No. 158 (Woodrow Wilson School, Princeton University), 1991.

material standards of living as incomes increase, while the second results from the increasing demand for fossil-based energy that normally accompanies development.

These relationships as pictured are not inevitable. They can be taken as general tendencies, which may be different in particular countries, depending on technology choices adopted as well as the preferences of their citizens. It points out that for many environmental problems the situation will likely get better as development occurs, indeed economic development may be seen as a way of combating these problems. Which is all the reason why continued efforts need to be directed at encouraging equitable growth and open political processes in the developing world.

THE POLLUTION-HAVEN HYPOTHESIS

In recent years we have heard much of the idea of developing countries being "pollution havens," places where firms can move and operate without the strict environmental controls of the developed countries. The idea has essentially two parts:

• That stringent environmental standards in industrialized countries are causing a flight of some firms, especially "pollution-intensive" ones, to countries with less stringent standards,

• That some developing countries have tried, with some success, to attract pollution-intensive firms with the promise of lower pollution-control standards, in the hopes of bolstering their rates of economic growth.

Sometimes these ideas are wrapped into the issue of the "multinationals," that is, firms owned in one country but operating establishments in others.

It is surprisingly difficult to get conclusive data on this matter.[5] Most opinions are formed on the basis of anecdotal, or episodic, events like the Bhopal disaster in India. But these are not good sources from which to draw conclusions about general trends. Nor is it possible to approach this question by looking at different environmental regulations in the various countries. Almost all countries, developing and developed, have regulations on the books that appear to place emissions under reasonably strict controls, but that is not usually achieved in practice because of weak enforcement. Ideally, we would like to have data on the emissions performance of firms, or groups of firms, before and after they have moved from developed to developing countries. But data like these are not available. Thus, the way we have to proceed is to identify "dirty" industries and look at how they have grown or declined in different countries, developed and developing. "Dirty" industries are simply those industries that normally emit relatively large amounts of pollutants, while "clean" industries are all the rest.

---

[5] For a discussion of the pollution haven hypothesis as it applies to Canada, see N. Olewiler, "Environmental Quality and Policy in a Global Economy," in D. Purvis and T. Courchene, eds., *Bell Papers in Economic Policy* (Kingston: John Deutsch Institute for Economic Policy, 1993); and N. Olewiler, *The Impact of Environmental Regulation on Investment Decisions* (Ottawa: Investment Canada Working Paper, 1993).

The problem with this approach, of course, is that there are many factors besides environmental regulations that could cause dirty industries to migrate among countries, for example, labour costs, raw materials availability, infrastructure availability, and especially the state of the product cycle. By the last we mean the fact that during the process of growth of any economy certain industries will tend to expand and decline at different times. Certain basic manufacturing industries, which may be "dirty," will often expand early in a country's development and decline later as incomes increase. So these industries might be moving around from one country to another (not literally moving, but rather expanding in some countries and declining in others) in response to where those countries are in the product cycle, rather than because of environmental regulations.

To date a number of studies have been done on this issue, mostly for the United States. Figure 21-3 shows some data like that used in this work. It shows the capital investments made in developing countries by affiliates of U.S. corporations, between 1971 and 1992. For "all manufacturing," the trend is very modestly increasing over this time. Two "dirty" sectors are identified, metals and chemicals. The data for chemicals also show a modest increase in the 1970s, but the 1980s show a modest decline. The data for the metals industry are very volatile, with large spikes in 1976–1977 and 1982–1973; overall, however, the trend seems to be modestly increasing. On the basis of results like this, the conclusion seems warranted that there has been no large-scale

FIGURE 21-3   Capital Expenditures in Developing Countries Made by Affiliates of U.S. Corporations, 1971–1986.

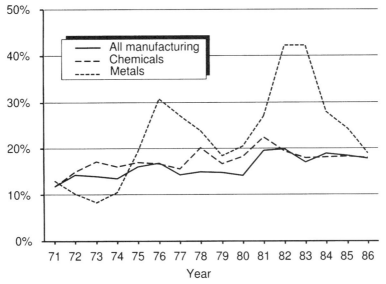

Source: Survey of Current Business, 52–60 (10), October 1972–October 1982; 63–66 (3), March 1983–March 1986.

flight of industrial corporations to pollution havens in developing countries. As one of them concluded:

> Most individual industries have responded to environmental regulations with techno-logical innovations, changes in production processes or raw materials, more efficient process controls, and other adaptations that in the United States have proved more eco-nomical and less drastic than flight abroad. Even when these adaptations have not reduced regulatory burdens, the environmental problems have generally not been sub-stantial enough to offset more traditional factors market considerations, transportation, availability of raw materials, labor costs, political stability that determine how most firms select overseas locations for branch-plant construction.[6]

Several more recent studies are less clear, however. One group of researchers took a look at the relative rates of growth of toxic-intensive industries in developed and developing countries. A toxic-intensive industry is one that releases relatively large amounts of toxic chemicals per unit of output produced. They conclude that the poor-est economies have the highest rate of growth in toxic-intensive industries, a result that is consistent with the pollution-haven hypothesis.[7] Other researchers have also obtained results that are consistent with the hypothesis.[8] But at this point in time it is impossible to rule out other competing explanations, as mentioned above. Further studies are needed.

ENVIRONMENTAL POLICY CHOICES IN DEVELOPING COUNTRIES

While it may be true that development can help to alleviate some environmental prob-lems, there is nothing automatic about this; appropriate public policies are still called for. This is especially true for those factors, like CO_2 emissions and solid waste, that get worse with development. Most discussions of the strengths and weaknesses of alternative policies have been directed toward developed countries. There is an impor-tant question about how much the lessons learned in this context apply also to devel-oping countries. While the environmental problems are in principle the same, involv-ing externalities, common-property resources, public goods, etc., the sociopolitical situations are markedly different from those in most developed countries.

---

[6] H. Jeffrey Leonard, *Pollution and the Struggle for the World Product* (Cambridge, U.K.: Cambridge University Press, 1988), 113. Other studies include: Charles Pearson, *Multinational Corporations, Envi-ronment and the Third World* (Durham, NC: Duke University Press, 1987); C. Duerksen and C. J. Leonard, "Environmental Regulations and the Location of Industries: An International Perspective," *Columbia Journal of World Business* 15 (Summer 1980): 52–68.

[7] Robert F. B. Lucas, David Wheeler, and Hemamala Hettige, "Economic Development, Environ-mental Regulation and the International Migration of Toxic Industrial Pollution, 1960–1988," in Patrick Low (ed.), *International Trade and the Environment*, World Bank Discussion Paper No. 159 (Wash-ington, D.C.: World Bank, 1992), 67–86.

[8] Patrick Low and Alexander Yeats, "Do 'Dirty' Industries Migrate?", in Ibid., 89–104.

Benefit-Cost Analysis

The basis of effective policy is in the analysis of the benefits and costs of different courses of action. Much more than in developed countries, damages in developing countries affect economic productivity through impacts on human health, soil fertility, resource depletion, and the like. Thus, there is a critical need for estimates of environmental damages in developing countries. In recent years, a number of international agencies have sponsored a series of "country environmental studies" (CES) in various developing countries. But so far these have been aimed primarily at taking inventories of the physical dimensions of environmental problems. They have not dealt with policy issues to any great extent, nor have they gotten to the point of trying to value the damages caused by environmental deterioration.[9] These studies would be especially important to pursue in those countries because they would show more clearly the extent of pollution-related damages and provide support for more active public policies.

There are several important issues regarding the use of standard benefit-cost approaches in developing countries. One is the emphasis on willingness to pay as a measure of the benefits of pollution reduction. Willingness to pay reflects not only tastes and preferences, but also ability to pay. In many developing economies poverty is widespread, so a standard willingness-to-pay approach to valuing environmental damages may yield only modest estimates of these damages. In the face of enormous poverty, willingness-to-pay estimates may be quite small despite what looks to be high rates of environmental degradation. Thus, if willingness-to-pay approaches are used, it must be done with frank recognition that the distribution of income is heavily skewed, and value judgments are called for in making decisions on environmental quality programs. This argues also for putting more emphasis on lost productivity, particularly in the long run, in assessing the damages of environmental degradation.

Another special difficulty in applying benefit-cost analysis of environmental programs to developing countries is discounting. In developed economies, discounting is a relatively benign procedure that helps make choices among programs with different time profiles of benefits and costs. But in developing countries the focus is more on long-run development, and here the role of discounting is less clear. It's often asserted that people in developing countries, especially those with lower incomes, discount the future very highly, preferring to emphasize actions that will pay off in the short run because of their immediate need for income. Thus, environmental improvement programs, if they deliver the bulk of their benefits only in the long run, may take lower priority to economic development projects that pay off more quickly. High rates of discount can also lead people to overlook negative environmental impacts that occur far off into the future. The present value of even severe long-run environmen-

---

[9] Walter Arensberg, "Country Environmental Studies, A Framework for Action," in Denizhan Eröcal (ed.), Environmental Management in Developing Countries, Organization for Economic Cooperation and Development, Paris, 1991, 279–295.

tal damage can be quite low when it is evaluated with a positive discount rate.[10] For some people these arguments imply using a very low, perhaps even zero, discount rate in evaluating environmental and developmental projects in developing countries. But this would make it impossible to coordinate public policies and development projects with decisions being made in the private sector, and would treat a dollar of net benefits ten years from now as equivalent to a dollar of net benefits today. It is perhaps better to utilize a normal discount rate in evaluating programs, but to augment the typical benefit-cost study in developing countries with an analysis of the impacts of the program on long-run sustainability.[11]

Reducing Environmental Disincentives of Current Policies

We normally view environmental policy as requiring activist intervention to remedy the problems of uncontrolled externalities, the undersupply of public environmental goods, etc. But there are many cases where environmental improvements can be had by altering current policies that have negative environmental impacts. In many cases these policies have been put in place in the belief that they will spur economic growth. But their impact is to create distortions in local economies that lead both to lower growth rates and environmental degradation.

A good example of this is the practice many governments have of subsidizing pesticide use by farmers. In many cases these subsidies were undertaken in the belief that they would spur farmers to adopt new crop varieties and intensive methods of cultivation. But the subsidies continue in many cases well after their usefulness in this regard has ceased. Table 21-1 shows the estimated annual rate of pesticide subsidies offered to farmers in eight developing countries. The range is from 19 percent to 89 percent of the retail cost of the pesticide. The result of these subsidies is predictable: the overuse of agricultural chemicals and the damages that result. These include heavy pesticide exposure of farm workers, contamination of nearby surface and groundwater resources, and the rapid development of immunity by target pests. Throughout the developing world, the subsidies involve hundreds of millions of dollars that could better be spent in other ways, or simply left in the private sector.

Other agricultural subsidies, for example on irrigation water and fertilizer, have similar effects. In recent years much attention has focussed on overly rapid rates of deforestation in developing countries. In many cases this happens because of government policies. Policies that underprice the value of timber concessions offered to logging companies increase the incentive to harvest timber at a high rate. Uncontrolled private access to communal forest resources reduces the incentive to conserve

[10] We are not talking here about unpredictable consequences, rather those that are predictable but far into the future. When CFCs were introduced as refrigerants in the early twentieth century, nobody predicted the impacts they would have on the global atmosphere. Likewise, nobody foresaw the negative effects of DDT. At the time these substances were introduced, science was not well enough advanced to have predicted these outcomes. There is a difference, however, between consequences that are not predictable and those that are predictable but far enough in the future that they are neglected in today's decision making.

[11] David Pearce, Edward Barbier, and Anil Markandya, *Sustainable Development, Economics and Environment in the Third World* (Aldershot, England: Edward Elgar Publishing, 1990).

TABLE 21-1 ESTIMATED AVERAGE RATE AND VALUE OF PESTICIDE SUBSIDIES IN EIGHT DEVELOPING COUNTRIES

Country	Percentage of full retail costs	Total value ($ million)
China	19	285
Colombia	44	69
Ecuador	41	14
Egypt	83	207
Ghana	67	20
Honduras	29	12
Indonesia	82	128
Senegal	89	4

Source: Robert Repetto, "Economic Incentives for Sustainable Production," in Gunter Schramm and Jeremy J. Warford (eds.). *Environmental Management and Economic Development* (Baltimore, Md.: Johns Hopkins Press for the World Bank, 1989), 72.

timber stocks. Misguided public road building can open up large areas to timber harvesting. In some cases land grants to individuals cannot become permanent unless and until the land is cleared and put into agricultural production, which obviously creates the incentive to get rid of the trees as soon as possible. The result of these policies is timber harvest that is higher than it should be, pursued in places it should not be, with the resulting impacts in soil loss, polluted water, reduction in the global CO_2 sink, and so on.

We should not think, however, that distorting public policies with negative environmental impacts are features solely of the developing world. In fact, the developed world also has plenty. Canada engages in many of the policies discussed in the previous paragraph, such as subsidized irrigation water and underpricing forest resources. We have also until recently giving substantial tax concessions to our mining industry which may have influenced rates of extraction.

Institutional Policy: Property Rights

Economic development usually implies wide-ranging economic and political transformations. An important part of this is developing modern economic institutions which can provide the appropriate incentive structures to shape the decisions that will lead toward development. Inappropriate property-rights institutions have often been singled out for having environmentally destructive consequences. Thus, one major avenue for policy to protect environmental resources is to alter property-rights institutions.

In a recent study of resource depletion in Ethiopia, the author lists a series of stages through which a portion of the rural economy had evolved.[12]

---

[12] Kenneth J. Newcombe, "An Economic Justification for Rural Afforestation: The Case of Ethiopia," in Gunter Schramm and Jeremy J. Warford (eds.), *Environmental Management and Economic Development* (Baltimore, MD: Johns Hopkins Press for the World Bank, 1989), 117–138.

Stage 1 Because of population pressure the average harvest of fuel wood begins to exceed the average rate of wood production.

Stage 2 Peasants begin to use straw and dung for fuel, thus less of these are available for maintaining soil fertility.

Stage 3 Almost all tree cover is removed, all dung is sold for cash, and wheat yields begin a serious decline.

Stage 4 Soil erosion becomes dramatic because of reduced tree cover and declining fertility.

Stage 5 There is a total collapse of fertility; peasants abandon their land, swelling urban populations.

The basic question is: Why did this sequence of stages take place? It might be more instructive to ask this the opposite way: Why didn't something like the following scenario happen? Fuel wood harvest increases because of increasing demand, this increases the price of fuel wood because of increased scarcity. Peasants see the increasing incomes to be made by growing and selling fuel wood, so they devote portions of their land to growing fuel wood and act to conserve the remaining supplies in the face of its increasing value. Finally, a substantial fuel wood harvest and market appear, with a considerable proportion of the land devoted to fuel wood production. Why, in other words, did the rising market price of fuel wood lead to wiping out the forest? Why did not the peasants act to make themselves better off by conserving and even increasing the production of an increasingly valuable resource?

One part of the answer is property rights. Most of the forested land was not owned by individuals or small groups, but was essentially an open-access resource. Anyone who wanted to harvest wood from these lands had the right to do so. In Chapter 4 we examined a simple model of an open-access resource showing that individuals making decisions on the basis of benefits and costs to themselves will overlook open-access externalities they inflict on others. Thus, a resource of this type often will be overexploited. Viewed from another angle, when there is open access to a resource, the incentive that any individual might have to reduce their rate of use and conserve the resource is totally undermined. If they should reduce their harvest, others will simply take what has been left. Open-access resources promote a "use it or lose it" situation.

Thus, one of the root causes of the deforestation, which began the whole unravelling process in the example, was an institutional one, a property-right system that created incentives for wiping out the resource even though rising scarcity was making it socially desirable to conserve it. This problem has occurred with great regularity in developing countries, especially with land and forest resources. The most straightforward response would seem to be to change the property-rights system so that the normal incentives for conservation can operate. This means instituting a system of individual or small-group property rights.

We have to keep in mind that, like any single policy recommendation, this one is no panacea for all of the environmental problems of developing countries. It will work in some situations and not in others. Overuse of resources, such as the deforestation mentioned above, can occur on "private" lands if the owner(s) cannot effectively defend their boundaries and keep out would-be encroachers. This means, among other things, that there has to be effective and equitable legal institutions to settle land-use conflicts. Establishing private-property rights in developing countries also has to face the demographic realities. In places with great population pressure, private-property rights would hardly be feasible if that would cut off a substantial proportion of the population from resources they need in order to subsist. Even in places without noticeable population pressure, essentially the same problem could occur if the property rights are distributed inequitably in the first place.

There are many other dimensions of the property-rights issue which there is not space enough here to go into. It is a topic of great controversy, and the debate is often carried out in overly simplistic terms. It is clear, however, that there is a wide range of resource and environmental problems in developing countries that have been made much worse by ill-defined property rights and the open-access externalities to which these give rise. In those situations, innovations in property-rights institutions can be extremely effective.

Population Policy as Environmental Policy

There are many people who feel that the only effective way to control environmental destruction in developing countries is to control the number of people in those countries. In the simplest possible terms, the total impact of a group of people on their environmental resources can be expressed in the following way:

$$\text{Total Environmental Impact} = \frac{\text{Environmental Impact}}{\text{Per Person}} \times \frac{\text{Number of}}{\text{People.}}$$

It is clear that total environmental impact can increase as a result of increases in either or both of these factors. The contrary is also true: Decreases in total impact can result from decreases in either or both of the factors. More complicated scenarios are possible: Changes in technology, economic structure, etc., that lower the per capita environmental impacts in a country can be more than offset by population increases. But there are two factors involved. Population declines, or declines in the rate of population increase, may be very helpful but are not sufficient in themselves to ensure a reduction in aggregate environmental degradation.

The world population is generally expected to increase from the current 5 billion to perhaps 15 to 20 billion over the next century, with two-thirds of this increase occurring in the developing world. Whether the increase is at the high end of this range, or perhaps substantially lower, depends in large part on the long-run behaviour of fertility rates in these development countries.[13] While fertility rates in developing countries are sometimes very high, many have started to decline in recent years. To some extent this is a reflection of rising incomes, because increasing incomes are

---

[13] The fertility rate is the average number of children born per woman over her lifetime; a rate of 2.0 implies zero population growth. Some developed countries have fertility rates of less than 2.0. In the developing world, fertility rates currently average about 3.8.

almost always associated with lowered fertility rates. Other important causal factors are a reduction in infant mortality, increased availability of family planning services, and (especially) increases in educational opportunities for women. Continued emphasis on these factors is in the best interests of people in the developing world, not solely for environmental reasons, but also to reduce poverty directly and to make it easier to institute developmental changes.

However, while reductions in population growth rates can certainly help to reduce the overall impacts any group of people has on its environmental resources, it is no substitute for undertaking environmental policies in their own right. For one thing, diminished population growth rates do not necessarily imply, automatically, diminished environmental damages. Even with comparatively lower populations, for example, it is anticipated that developing countries will experience marked increases in urbanization in the next half century, and probably beyond. Unless confronted directly, this will lead to more severe air and water pollution in these burgeoning urban areas. As another example, decreases in agricultural populations may not be accompanied by reduced resource damages if, simultaneously, a shift to chemical agriculture occurs without proper safeguards against water pollution and increased pest resistance. In other words, although population policies may be facilitative of reduced environmental damages, they are no substitute for direct environmental policy itself.

Command-and-Control or Market Incentives?

We come, therefore, to the important question of the types of environmental policies that are most appropriate for developing economies. We have stated several times, in the context of developed economies, that no single policy approach will be the best for all environmental problems; certain problems call for one approach, others call for something else. The same is true of developing countries. But beyond this, we must ask if there is anything characterizing the developing world that might cause us to lean more heavily in one direction or another. In particular, should policymakers in these countries rely relatively more on command-and-control, through standards of various types, or would it be better to emphasize economic incentive types of policies?

One especially relevant factor is that developing countries can ill afford, given the resource requirements of economic development, to devote more resources to environmental quality improvement than is necessary. This is an argument for making sure that the pollution-control policies adopted are cost-effective, and this in turn is an argument in favour of incentive policies. We have seen repeatedly throughout this book that incentive-type policies, in situations where monitoring emissions is possible and where materials-balance problems are addressed, can be expected to be substantially more cost-effective than command-and-control strategies. They make it possible to take advantage of different abatement costs across sources, and also provide long-run incentives for firms to search for cheaper ways of reducing emissions.

Tradition is strong, however, and to date developing countries have been following in the early footsteps of the developed economies, that is, they have relied primarily on command-and-control policies. There are some exceptions. Singapore has instituted a program to charge drivers for using urban roads in heavily congested peak-use times of the day. The primary element of the program is the requirement that drivers using the central city at peak hours purchase daily or monthly licenses. Substantial improvements in air quality have resulted.[14]

Nevertheless, command-and-control is still the dominant trend in environmental policy in most developing countries. This may be the result of relatively weak policy institutions. It is a common observation that the capacities and performance of public regulatory agencies are relatively weak in many third-world countries. This is not, of course, a problem unique to them; administrative deficiencies in developed countries account for part of the large gap between the laws and their enforcement. But most observers agree that this is a particularly thorny problem for developing countries. It is not solely a matter of professionalism and lack of political clout. It is also a fact that centralized public bureaucracies in many developed countries have grown so large that they have become not only unproductive but actually predatory.

For some observers, this institutional weakness implies that developing countries ought to move away from command-and-control measures toward economic incentive policies. For others, who perhaps are impressed that developed countries themselves are only beginning to place greater reliance on incentive measures, these institutional shortcomings imply that environmental regulations in developing countries are best kept relatively simple and direct. In other words, simple command-and-control strategies through uniform standards. The Brundtland Commission itself concluded that in developing countries, "regulations imposing uniform performance standards are essential to ensure that industry makes the investments necessary to reduce pollution."[15]

The resolution of this question rests on recognizing that the category "developing countries" actually includes a wide range of experience. At one end of the spectrum are countries that are still almost totally agricultural, substantially uniform technologically, and with only the beginnings of a modern economic sector. At the other end of the spectrum are countries that have developed relatively large industrial, financial, and transportation sectors, important economic links to the rest of the world, and, most importantly, comparatively sophisticated political institutions. In the former countries, simple command-and-control approaches are likely to be best: a prohibition on a certain pesticide for example, or limits on a certain irrigation practice. These may be enforced without sophisticated monitoring, and technical uniformity among producers means that these steps will be reasonably cost-effective. But in more advanced developing countries, incentive-based policies have much more to recommend them. Here the necessary political institutions may have been put in place, technological complexity makes it much more difficult to achieve acceptable levels

[14] Theodore Panayotou, "Economic Incentives in Environmental Management and Their Relevance to Developing Countries," in Denizhan Eröcal (ed.), *Environmental Management in Developing Countries* (Paris: Organization for Economic Cooperation and Development, 1991), 83–132.

[15] World Commission on Environment and Development, *Our Common Future* 220.

of cost-effectiveness with command-and-control approaches, and strong long-run incentives for continued technical innovation in pollution control are of paramount importance.

THE ROLE OF THE DEVELOPED COUNTRIES

Developing countries are struggling with a wide array of economic, political, and social problems that stand in the way of lasting economic modernization. To graft environmental concerns into the process puts an added burden on everyone in these countries, whatever their position. The developed countries have an important role to play in helping the third world make this transition, not just for humanitarian reasons but also because many environmental problems are becoming increasingly international in scope. As these countries catch up to the developed economies, their technical choices and emission-control efforts will have a direct bearing on important global problems, such as CO_2 emissions and the global greenhouse effect, toxic chemical releases, nuclear radiation emissions, and so on.

Technology Transfer

By "technology transfer" we refer to the transfer, from developed to developing countries, of technologies and skills that can provide the impetus for economic development with lower environmental impacts than could be attained without the transfer. The focus is not on direct investment,[16] per se, but on the transfer of knowledge that citizens of developing countries themselves can adapt to their own needs and styles of operation. Technology transfer has been an important concept in economic development efforts for decades. But it has taken on new urgency in the context of recent environmental problems. It has become evident that if the rest of the world goes through the same high-pollution course of development as the developed countries have done, the draft on world resources will be enormous and the impact on the global environment potentially disastrous. Thus, technology transfer is essential to convert developing countries more quickly to environment-friendly techniques without having to go through intermediate developmental stages.

Concrete provisions for the transfer of technology has been written into some recent international environmental treaties. The 1989 Basel Convention on hazardous waste obligates the signatories to provide technical assistance to developing countries in the implementation of the treaty. The 1990 amendments to the Montreal Protocol on protection of the ozone layer has a requirement that developed countries make available to developing countries, on reasonable terms, new reduced-CFC tech-

---

[16] "Direct investment" occurs when a foreign company, usually a "multinational," builds and operates an enterprise in a developing country. "Indirect" or "portfolio" investment occurs when a foreign firm invests money in a domestic enterprise. For example, if Laidlaw (a big Canadian company in waste management and pollution control) starts its own company in, say, South Korea, this is direct investment. If it chooses instead to get into that market by investing in an existing South Korean waste management firm, this is indirect investment.

nology; it also establishes a fund to help developing countries meet the requirements for reduced emissions.[17] In 1990 the five Nordic countries formed the Nordic Environment Finance Corporation to provide help for environmentally sound investment in Eastern and Central Europe.

Technology transfer has two important parts. The first is the initial development of new technologies and procedures. These are a product of innovation in industries searching for ways of reducing emissions and in the pollution-control industry itself. Thus, one element in technology transfer is the provision of incentives for a brisk level of innovation in the originating countries. This implies pollution-control policies that provide these incentives, about which we have said a lot in earlier chapters. In particular, we have discussed the positive incentives for innovation provided by economic-incentive types of policies, and the negative effects provided by technology-based standards.

The second element of environmental technology transfer is getting the ideas, technical means, and necessary training effectively into the receiving countries. The word "effectively" is important because history is full of cases where transferred techniques have failed to work as anticipated. It is much more than just moving a machine from one location to another, there is a tremendous array of problems that must be worked out to bridge the informational, cultural, commercial, and political gaps that separate people in different countries. At the end of the process, which normally will involve many different business, trade, political, and environmental groups, the objective is to transfer technology that is compatible with local skills and labour availabilities.

Just as the policy environment in the originating countries has much to do with rates of innovation there, so does the policy environment in receiving countries play a strong role in providing the incentives for local firms to search for, and be receptive to, new pollution-control technologies. Exhibit 21-1 contains a story about the leather industry in Kenya. It illustrates several things, for example, the role of a research institute funded by foreign donors, and a local policy environment that will provide leather tanning companies with a sufficient "regulatory push" to improve their environmental performance.

Debt-for-Nature Swaps

Suppose A and B are neighbours and that A owes B $100 on a past loan. Suppose further that A keeps a very untidy yard, never mowing the grass and keeping several junk cars next to the garage. B offers to wipe out the $100 debt if A will agree to clean up the yard. That is a debt-for-nature swap. Many developing countries owe large sums to lenders in developed countries, particularly commercial banks. These loans have been made for a variety of purposes, primarily to support investment and consumption in the developing countries. In many cases the debtor nations have found it difficult to pay back the loans. Debt-for-nature swaps are where environmental

---

[17] Chapter 23 contains a discussion of international environmental treaties in general, while Chapter 22 discusses the specific provisions of the Montreal Protocol.

EXHIBIT 21-1

ISSUES IN THE TRANSFER OF ENVIRONMENTAL TECHNOLOGY TO DEVELOPING COUNTRIES

Making leather has traditionally been a dirty and often unsociable exercise. Tanneries have been located outside towns, downwind and downstream to carry away noxious smells and wastes. Today, leather production still involves considerable use of water and generation of wastes. On average, one metric ton of raw hide yields only 200 kilograms of leather. The by-products include 50 cubic meters of wastewater, containing a range of chemicals, and half a metric ton each of wet sludge and solid wastes.

Increasingly, however, industrialists and researchers are finding ways both to reduce the generation of pollution and waste and to upgrade the efficiency of the production process. A wide range of techniques and approaches can be applied, from simple low-cost housekeeping improvements through the substitution of less damaging chemicals to the introduction of intrinsically cleaner production technologies. Innovative ways of using tanning wastes as raw materials for glue, fertilizer, and animal fodder are also being developed.

The challenge of diffusing "best practice" has been increased by the relocation of leathermaking during the last 30 years from the industrial to the developing world, where pollution control regimes are often weaker and where resources for environmental protection are scarce. In many developing countries, the leather industry has played a central role during industrialization; it is agro-based, labor-intensive, and adaptable to small-scale, low-technology production.

There is no such thing as a standard tannery; processes differ widely depending on location, sophistication, and the market for the final product. International best practice has to be translated into the local context; pilot projects are often needed to demonstrate the feasibility of change. Research institutes and trade associations together play a vital role in this process. In Kenya, the lead agency for the tanning industry is the Leather Development Centre (LDC) at the Kenya Industrial Research and Development Institute (KIRDI).

A weak institutional and legislative framework has meant that Kenyan industry has to date not received a sufficient regulatory push for improved environmental performance. In addition, lack of information and financial resources has limited the ability of local companies to assess and install cleaner technologies from abroad. An expert working at the Leather Development Centre sums up the challenge thus: "It is common among Kenyan tanneries to rely on traditional methods of processing leather, resulting in heavy production and discharge of pollution in the wastewater."

Collective efforts led by research institutes and/or industry associations can help spread the costs of improvement while minimizing the inherent risks of innovation. This is the role that the Leather Development Centre plays. It has been developed in phases over 10 years with technical and financial assistance from the United Nations Industrial Development Organization (UNIDO) and the Federal Republic of Germany. The center's aim is to provide advice and support to local companies on two interconnected issues: identifying and developing enhanced process and product technologies, which will boost the industry's domestic and export potential, and developing and diffusing better ways of reducing the environmental hazards from leather production. The LDC has established a pilot tannery plant, a leather design and production unit, a quality control laboratory, and a wastewater demonstration unit at its facilities in Nairobi. Although most of its funding comes from domestic and external government sources, a nominal fee is charged for the centre's services.

The first step toward sustainable development for the leather industry is the creation of awareness among industrialists of the need for change. Once awareness has been raised, the center can provide tools to help companies overcome pollution problems. It uses its pilot production and treatment plants as models for training and demonstration purposes during seminars and workshops. This is coupled with regular visits to the tanneries themselves by LDC experts, and targeted assistance programs.

groups in the developed world buy portions of this debt and retire it in return for environmental preservation efforts by the developing country that owes the debt.

The first debt-for-nature swap was in 1987. Conservation International, a private group, bought $650,000 of Bolivia's commercial debt from the Citicorp Investment Bank for $100,000. In return for retiring this debt, the government of Bolivia agreed to place a four million acre piece of tropical rain forest in protected status, and create a fund for the management of the area. Debt-for-nature swaps have since been concluded with numerous other countries, including Ecuador, Costa Rica, the Philippines, Madagascar, and the Dominican Republic.[18]

How effective debt-for-nature swaps can be is a difficult question. As a debt-retiring device, the approach can have little impact because of the vast amount of debt outstanding. As an environmental tool, it can be more effective, even though the scope of the overall problem is huge in comparison to the means. Perhaps their primary use will be to target very specific instances where critical environmental links are threatened, or where they can be used to get a larger program started. Even in these cases, however, significant problems remain. One of the most difficult is something we have talked about throughout this book: enforcement. Once a private group has bought and retired a certain amount of debt, it may be hard to ensure that the country with which they have made the agreement will continue to abide by the deal.

Environmental Values in International Aid Institutions

Some of the most egregious cases of environmental damage in developing countries have actually stemmed from projects initiated and funded by international aid organizations, whose objectives are primarily to help these countries develop economically. A well-publicized example is the project funded partly by the World Bank to build roads and encourage colonization in the northwestern part of Brazil. The building of the roads attracted many more migrants into the area than was anticipated, "making already underfunded public agencies even less capable of controlling large-scale deforestation."[19] Many international donors have often leaned toward the big project: dams, power stations, infrastructure, etc. These have often been pursued in ways that were not sensitive to environmental impacts because the donors, together with governments in recipient countries, have been so focussed on spurring economic growth.

What this calls for is a more complete adoption of the general benefit-cost approach, interpreted broadly to mean the accounting for, and comparison of, all benefits and costs, whether or not they can be monetized in a formal framework. In particular, more attention must be given to working out the environmental impacts of these development projects. In recent years many international lending organizations have begun to take environmental issues of developing countries more seriously. For

---

[18] Catherine A. O'Neill and Cass R. Sunstein, "Economics and the Environment: Trading Debt and Technology for Nature," *Columbia Journal of Environmental Law* 17 (Winter 1992): 93–151.

[19] World Bank, *World Development Report 1992, Development and Environment* (New York: Oxford University Press, 1992), 80.

example, the World Bank has created a new Environmental Department and changed its procedures so that the environmental implications of proposed projects will be accounted for and taken into account in making lending decisions. Bank policy now requires that environmental assessments be completed for all projects that have significant impacts on the environment.

SUMMARY

Environmental problems in developing countries have become increasingly critical in the last few decades. While the appearance of global issues has helped people see that all countries are inextricably linked in the global environment, more attention has also been directed at traditional air- and water-pollution problems of developing countries. The issue of long-run sustainability of the natural resource and environmental assets of these countries has become a policy focus point.

Analysis of past trends show that development tends to make some environmental problems worse and others better. Some phenomena, such as SO_2 pollution, seem to get worse as countries initially begin to develop rapidly and then improve as development leads to higher per capita incomes. There is some evidence, though it is not particularly strong, that "dirty" industries in developed countries have been migrating to developing ones, but the reasons for this are still not clear. The "pollution-haven" hypothesis does not receive strong support in the data.

Policy institutions in developing countries have historically been relatively weak, but this is changing. Most environmental policy in these countries has followed the lead of the developed world, in terms of being based on command-and-control principles. Some have suggested that developing countries should emphasize incentive-based policies so as to achieve higher levels of cost-effectiveness. Population control, as a means of lessening environmental impacts, has frequently been recommended. While lower rates of population growth may facilitate environmental improvements, they are not sufficient for attaining improvements in environmental quality.

Finally, the developed world can play a substantial role in helping third-world countries develop without large-scale environmental destruction. The primary mechanism for this is through technology transfer, understood broadly to include the transfer of skills and technological capabilities that are culturally sound, not solely the transfer of Western capital goods.

QUESTIONS FOR FURTHER DISCUSSION

1 How does the notion of "sustainability" square with the fact that developing countries must usually draw heavily on their natural resource base if they are to develop economically?
2 Do the imperatives of "sustainability" imply that benefit-cost analysis applied to programs in developing countries should be different from benefit-cost analysis as it is applied in developed countries?

3 When a multinational business firm from the developed world opens operations in a developing nation, should it be held to the environmental standards of its country of origin, or to those of the country in which it is operating?

4 Suppose we introduce a new criterion, "administrative feasibility" for evaluating environmental policies in developing countries. How might this affect choices among different types of policies?

5 We have spent a great deal of time in this book discussing the importance of having strong incentives for firms to engage in R&D to find improved means of pollution control. Apply this idea to the notion of "technology transfer."

SELECTED READINGS

Baker, Doug S., and Daniel B. Tunstall (eds.). 1990 *Directory of Country Environmental Studies: An Annotated Bibliography of Environmental and Natural Resource Profiles and Assessments.* Washington, D.C.: World Resources Institute, 1990.

Binswanger, Hans P. "Brazilian Policies that Encourage Deforestation in the Amazon." *World Development* 19 (7) (July 1991): 821–829.

Bojo, Jan, Karl-Goran Maler, and Lena Unemo (eds.). *Environment and Development: An Economic Approach.* Boston: Kluwer Academic Publishers, 1992.

Eröcal, Denizhan (ed.). *Environmental Management in Developing Countries.* Paris: Organization for Economic Cooperation and Development, August 1991.

Eskeland, Gunnar, and Emmanuel Jimenez. *Choosing Among Policy Instruments in Pollution Control: A Review.* Washington, D.C.: Country Economics Department, World Bank, June 20, 1990.

_____. "Curbing Pollution in Developing Countries." *Finance and Development* 28 (1) (March 1991): 15–18.

Logan, Bernard I. "An Assessment of the Environmental and Economic Implications of Toxic-Waste Disposal in Sub-Saharan Africa." *Journal of World Trade* 25 (1) (February 1991): 61–76.

Lyon, Randolph M. "Transferable Discharge Permit Systems and Environmental Management in Developing Countries." *World Development* 17 (8) (August 1989): 1299–1312.

Mayda, Jaro. "Environmental Legislation in Developing Countries: Some Parameters and Constraints." *Ecology Law Quarterly* 12 (4) (1985): 997–1023.

Pearce, David, Edward Barbier, and Anil Markandya. *Sustainable Development, Economics and Environment in the Third World.* London: Earthscan Publications, 1990.

Pearce, David, Edward Barbier, Anil Markandya, Scott Barrett, R. Kerry Turner, and Timothy Swanson. *Blueprint 2: Greening the World Economy.* London: Earthscan Publications, 1991.

Ramakrishna, Kilaparti. "The Emergence of Environmental Law in the Developing Countries: A Case Study of India." *Ecology Law Quarterly* 12 (4) (1985): 907–935.

Ross, Lester. *Environmental Policy in China.* Bloomington, Ind.: Indiana University Press, 1988.

Walter, Ingo. "Environmentally Induced Industrial Relocation to Developing Countries" in Seymour Rubin and Thomas Graham (eds.). *Environment and Trade.* Totowa, N.J.: Osmon Allanheld, 1982, 67–101.

The World Bank. *World Development Report 1992, Development and the Environment.* Oxford: Oxford University Press, 1992.

22

THE GLOBAL ENVIRONMENT

People all around the world are struggling to come to grips with local environmental problems and improve their immediate surroundings. But over the last few decades, we have had to broaden our outlook, for we have started to become aware of problems in which the "environment" is that of the entire world. For all of history, one of the ways humans have reacted to local environmental destruction is migration. But at the planetary level this option is not available. There is no escape if we inadvertently make the planet less habitable.

Complementing the daunting physical facts are the sobering political/economic facts that have made it virtually impossible for the world's nations to act collectively. We seem to be in a race between the accumulating scientific data that scientists, still with great uncertainty, are straining to interpret, and the growing efforts to develop international institutions and perspectives that will make concerted action possible.

In this chapter we will look at several of these global environmental problems. We will consider first the problems of the global atmosphere and its degradation—specifically stratospheric ozone depletion and the global greenhouse effect. We will then look at the issue of diminishing biological diversity which, though it is occurring at different rates in various parts of the world, nevertheless has truly global significance. Each of these issues is very complicated scientifically and politically, and we can only touch on their most important elements. We will focus on their economic aspects.

OZONE DEPLETION

The Physical Problem

At sea level ozone is a pollutant produced when emissions of hydrocarbons and nitrogen oxides interact in the presence of sunlight. A variety of health problems and agricultural crop damages have been traced to elevated levels of surface ozone. But most of the ozone in the earth's atmosphere is located in the stratosphere, a zone extending from about 10 km to about 50 km in altitude. This stratospheric ozone is critical in maintaining the earth's radiation balance. The atmosphere surrounding the earth essentially acts as a filter for incoming electromagnetic radiation. The atmospheric gas responsible for this is ozone, which blocks a large percentage of incoming low-wavelength, or ultraviolet, radiation.

Several decades ago scientific evidence began to appear that the ozone content of the atmosphere was showing signs of diminishing. In the late 1970s a large hole appeared in the ozone layer over Antarctica. More recently, significant ozone reduction has been found throughout the entire stratosphere, including those areas over the more populated parts of the world. In the 1970s scientists discovered the cause of this phenomenon. It had been known for some time that the chemical content of the atmosphere has been changing at a rapid rate and on a global scale. Atmospheric concentrations of CO_2, CH_4, N_2O, and various chlorinated gases are estimated to be increasing at a rate of 0.2 percent to 5.0 percent per year.[1] Ozone disappearance was linked to the accumulation of chlorine in the stratosphere. Chlorine was found to insert itself into what was normally a balanced process of ozone production and destruction, vastly increasing the rate of destruction. And the source of the chlorine turned out to be a variety of manufactured chemicals which, released at ground level, slowly migrated up to higher altitudes. The culprits are substances called halocarbons, chemicals composed of carbon atoms in combination with atoms of chlorine, fluorine, iodine, and bromine. The primary halocarbons are called chlorofluorocarbons (CFCs), which have molecules consisting of combinations of carbon, fluorine, and chlorine atoms. Another subgroup is the halons, composed of these elements plus bromine atoms; bromine, in fact, acts similarly to chlorine in breaking down ozone molecules. Carbon tetrachloride and methyl chloroform are also implicated in ozone destruction.

CFCs were developed in the 1930s as a replacement for the refrigerants in use at the time. Unlike those they replaced, CFCs are extremely stable, nontoxic, and inert relative to the electrical and mechanical machinery in which they are used. Thus their use spread quickly as refrigerants and also as propellants for aerosols (hair sprays, deodorants, insecticides), industrial agents for making polyurethane and polystyrene foams, and industrial cleaning agents and solvents. Halons are widely used as fire suppressors. When these substances were introduced attention was exclusively on their benefits; there was no evidence that they could have long-run impacts on the atmosphere. The very stable nature of these gases allows them to migrate very slowly in the atmosphere. After surface release, they drift up through the troposphere into the stratosphere, where they begin a long process of ozone destruction.

---

[1] Robert T. Watson, "Atmospheric Ozone," in James G. Titus (ed.), *Effects of Changes in Stratospheric Ozone and Global Climate, Volume 1, Overview* (Washington, D.C.: U.S. Environmental Protection Agency, 1986), 69.

Damages from Ultraviolet Radiation

Several years ago it was thought that ozone depletion might confine itself to small parts of the stratosphere, in which case damages from the increasing surface flux of ultraviolet radiation would be limited. But recently strong evidence has appeared that significant ozone depletion is occurring over large portions of the world's highly populated regions. Thus, damages are likely to be much more widespread. It is generally believed that each 1 percent drop in stratospheric ozone will produce a 2 to 3 percent increase in ultraviolet radiation at the earth's surface.[2] On this basis, radiation increases over the next century are expected to be at least 3–4 percent at the tropics and 10–12 percent at the higher latitudes.

Current research indicates that there are two main sources of damage to humans: health impacts and agricultural crop losses. Health damages are related to the increased incidence of skin cancers and eye disease. The dose-response relationships developed by the EPA indicate that for each 1 percent increase in UV_B radiation, basal-cell and squamous-cell cancer cases would increase by 1 percent and 2 percent, respectively, while melanoma skin cancers would increase by less than 1 percent, and cataracts by about 0.2 percent.[3] Increased UV_B radiation can also be expected to increase food production costs because of the physical damages it produces in growing plants. Damages are also expected in other parts of the earth's physical ecosystem.

Policy Responses[4]

The potential seriousness of the ozone-depletion problem has concentrated peoples' minds and led to some relatively vigorous policy responses. Initially several countries took unilateral actions. In 1978 Canada, the U.S., Sweden, Norway, and Denmark banned CFCs in aerosol cans, but not as a refrigerant. In the 1980s the continued scientific evidence of ozone depletion led to international action. Under the auspices of the United Nations, 24 nations signed in 1987 the *Montreal Protocol on Substances That Deplete the Ozone Layer*. It committed the high CFC-using signatories to a phasedown of CFCs and halons to 50 percent of their 1986 levels, to be achieved by 1998. Signatory countries currently using low levels of CFCs were given a 10-year grace period: Starting in 1999 they were to cut back to 1995–1997 levels, as shown in Table 22-1.

Soon after the Montreal agreement it became clear that this reduction was not enough, partly because continuing research showed that the problem was getting worse, and partly because some large CFC-producing countries had not signed the

---

[2] Alphonse Forziati, "The Chlorofluorocarbon Problem," in John H. Cumberland, James R. Hibbs, and Irving Hoch (eds.), *The Economics of Managing Chlorofluorocarbons* (Washington, D.C.: Resources for the Future, 1982), 54.

[3] U.S. Environmental Protection Agency, *Regulatory Impact Analysis: Protection of Stratospheric Ozone*, Vol. II, Appendix E (D.C.: Washington, 1987), E3–E4.

[4] For a good discussion of the issues in this section see Peter M. Morrisette, "The Evolution of Policy Responses to Stratospheric Ozone Depletion," *Natural Resources Journal* 29 (3) (Summer 1989): 793–820.

TABLE 22-1   SUMMARY OF THE TERMS OF THE MONTREAL PROTOCOL FOR OZONE-DESTROYING
CHEMICALS

Original 1987 Agreement

Substances controlled: CFCs-11, -12, -113, -114, -115, halons 1211, 1301, 2402.

High-CFC-using countries:
   Reduce production and consumption to 50% of 186 levels by 1998.
   As of 1992, halon production to be held at or below 1986 levels.

Low-CFC-using countries:
   As of 1999, cut back to 50% of 1995–1997 levels over the next 10 years.

1990 Agreement

Regulates 10 additional substances, including CCl_4.

High-using countries (consumption greater than 0.3 kg/person):
   20% reduction in production and consumption from 1986 levels by 1993.
   50% reduction in production and consumption from 1986 levels by 1997.
   100% reduction in production and consumption from 186 levels by 2000.

Halons frozen at 1986 levels by 1992, then phased out by 2000, except for certain "essential" uses.

CH_4 to be phased out by 2005.

Low-CFC-using countries: 10-year grace period on phaseout schedules, no export of CFCs.

Multilateral fund to aid developing countries with phaseout problems and to foster technology transfer.

No imports or exports of controlled substances with nonparties after 1990.

1992 Agreement

For all signatories:
   Eliminate all consumption and production of CFCs, carbon tetrachloride and methyl
      chloroform by January 1, 1996.
   Eliminate all consumption and production of halons by January 1, 1994.
   Freeze production of methyl bromide at its 1991 levels by 1995.
   Phase out HCPCs by 2030.

Source: Office of Technology Assessment, *Changing by Degrees: Steps to Reduce Greenhouse Gases* (Washington, D.C., 1991), 67–68; Environment Canada, *Stratospheric Ozone Depletion* (Ottawa: State of the Environment, SOE Bulletin 93-2, November, 1993).

original agreement. Follow-up meetings for the Montreal Protocol countries have occurred since the initial agreement was signed. In 1990 they agreed to phase out the production of CFCs completely by the year 2000, to add carbon tetrachloride and methyl chloroform to the list, and to introduce a longer-run schedule for phasing out HCFCs. It also instituted a fund, created from contributions of developed countries, to be used to help finance CFC-reducing technological changes in developing countries. Additional countries signed the agreement in subsequent years. In the 1991 meeting, China finally agreed to sign the protocol, leaving only India as the major

CFC-using nation still outside the agreement. In November 1992 phaseout of ozone-depleting compounds was accelerated once again. By December 31, 1995, production, importation and exportation of CFCs, carbon tetrachloride, and methyl chloroform is supposed to cease. All halon consumption was to end on January 1, 1994. It is felt that substitution of hydrochlorofluorocarbons (HCFCs) for CFCs will result in limiting equivalent CFC use to 5 percent of its 1989 level. HCFCs are then supposed to be phased out by 2030. Another ozone-depleting substance, methyl bromide, used as a pesticide and soil fumigant is to be frozen at 1991 production levels by the year 1995.

The Montreal Protocol has been a success in many ways. It has found wide agreement among nations of the world. It very effectively focussed attention on the burgeoning body of scientific evidence of ozone depletion, using it to motivate political agreement. And it created conditions where both developed and developing countries could find agreement. It remains to be seen whether it will provide a model for future international agreements. What is unique in the CFC agreement is that we are dealing essentially with a restricted set of substances. In all producing countries, the CFC-producing industry is composed of a few large chemical companies. So international policy has been driven not only by scientific results, but also by international competition in this industry. Large multinational firms such as DuPont have been leaders in developing substitutes for CFCs, and they, therefore, have led the charge for a CFC phaseout. Other international environmental agreements in the future may not have the same kind of economic realities behind them.

It is too early to tell whether the phaseout schedule specified in the Montreal Protocol will be achieved by the signatory states. There are no direct enforcement steps that may be undertaken by international authorities, in this or in any other agreement. Each country must, therefore, enforce its own cutbacks as it sees fit. If they do not do so with sufficient vigour, the available sanctions are international embarrassment or trade sanctions, with uncertain results.[5]

The Economics of CFC Controls

In economic terms we have a problem here similar to the phasing out of leaded gasoline. The objective is reasonably clear and widely shared; the basic problem is how to bring it about in different countries. In advanced economies the main focus has been put on developing substitute chemicals that will perform the same tasks as CFCs—as refrigerants, cleaning agents, etc.—but have little or no ozone-depleting impact. Table 22-2 shows the major CFCs and some of the substances chemists are looking at as substitutes. CFC-11, -12, and -113 are the most common substances in use, but these have very long atmospheric lifetimes and rather high ozone-depletion potentials (ODPs). The halons have even higher ODPs. Research has emphasized the

---

[5] In the meeting at which the protocol was adopted, the parties voted to postpone taking up enforcement issues until their next meeting. At the next meeting, enforcement issues were again postponed. There are provisions within the protocol for imposition of trade sanctions, but there are many difficulties with using them, not the least of which is incompatibility with GATT agreements.

TABLE 22-2   MAJOR OZONE-DEPLETING CHEMICALS

		Atmospheric lifetime (years)	Estimated ozone-depletion potential*
Chlorofluorocarbons			
CFC-11	CCl_3F	40–80	1.0
CFC-12	CCl_2F_2	80–150	1.0
CFC-113	$C_2F_3Cl_3$	100	0.8
CFC-114	$C_2F_4Cl_2$	270	1.0
CFC-115	C_2F_5Cl	600	0.6
Halons			
H-1211	CF_2B_RCl	15	3.0
H-1301	CF_3B_R	110	10.0
H-2402	$C_2F_4B_{r2}$		6.0
Carbon tetrachloride	CCl_4	60	1.06
Methyl chloroform	$C_2H_3Cl_3$	6	0.1
Hydrochlorofluorocarbons			
HCFC-22	$CHClF_2$	20	0.05
HCFC-123	CF_3CHCl_2	2	0.02
HCFC-124	$CHClFCF_3$	4	0.02
HCFC-141b	CCl_2FCH_3	10	0.1
HCFC-142b	CH_3CClF_2	22	0.06
Hydrofluorocarbons			
HFC-125	CHF_2CF_3	15	0.0
HFC-134a	CH_2FCF_3	5	0.0
HFC-143a	CH_3CF_3	40	0.0
HFC-152a	CH_3CHF_2	2	0.0

*The ozone-depletion potential (ODP) of a compound is defined as the estimated ozone depletion of a unit mass of the compound divided by the ozone depletion of a unit mass of CFC-11.
    Source: U.S. Congress, House Committee on Energy and Commerce, Subcommittee on Oversight and Investigations, *Ozone Layer Depletion*, Hearings, 101st Congress, 1st Session, May 15, 1989.

development of a variety of HCFCs, mentioned above, and hydrofluorocarbons (HFCs) that have both shorter atmospheric lifetimes and much lower, or zero, ODPs. So what is essentially driving the rate of CFC phaseout in advanced economies is the cost of developing these substitutes, together with the costs of changeover from the old to the new chemicals. Some substances may be simply "drop-in" substitutes, while others will require getting rid of old capital equipment (refrigerators, air conditioners, etc.) and installing new equipment.

To meet the phaseout timetables agreed upon under the Montreal Protocol each country has had to adopt some explicit control policy on production, imports, and exports of the targeted substances. In Canada, manufacture of CFCs ceased early in 1993. New supplies of CFCs can be imported until the end of 1995 when all consumption is banned. Environment Canada has used a type of quota system to phase out the chemicals. The quota limited total supply (production and importation) of

CFCs and halons to their 1986 levels, beginning in 1989.[6] There are no restrictions on the supply of *specific* CFCs or halons. The quota is in terms of ODP. This allows for flexibility in meeting the target. For example, a company can increase its production of a CFC compound with a low ODP as long as it cuts production of another CFC compound enough that the total ODP is not exceeded. Greater efficiency in use and in the phase-down of production and importation is expected under this policy than with the usual performance standard that requires each producer to meet a pollutant-specific target. But, as noted above, ozone-depleting compounds are somewhat unique in that it is the total stock of these chemicals that matters, not how much of each type. This would not be the case for many pollution problems. As well, the producers had substitutes for CFCs. Although the quota was not marketable, it is possible that private agreements were struck among the Canadian producers to redistribute production of the different CFC compounds in a cost-effective way. Total costs of the phase out were likely lower than they would have been if producers had to meet specific quotas for each chemical. As well, the market system will work with regard to consumption. Given the quota on ODP, we would expect to see price variability among the types of CFCs in response to production costs, degree of substitutability in use, and so on. The key point is that efficiency is enhanced by putting the quota on ODP as opposed to each compound. However, as pointed out below, producers of CFCs could still have earned high profits due to the restriction in aggregate suppy.

In the U.S., the approach has been for their Environmental Protection Agency to allocate transferable production quotas among the five domestic CFC producers. Each of these firms is required to reduce its CFC production in stages to meet the mandated phaseout schedule. A major problem with setting production ceilings in this way is that it can lead to unwarranted increases in profits for current manufacturers of CFCs. In effect it gives firms in the industry, who may have been operating as rivals, a way of acting like monopolists. Figure 22-1 illustrates this with a simple market model. It shows a typical downward-sloping demand curve for CFCs, together with a flat marginal cost curve. Left to itself, competitive forces would lead to a production level of q_1 and a price that equals marginal production costs. But if public authorities limit production to q_2, the price will now increase to p_2, which is substantially above production costs. Thus, an amount equal to area a becomes potential excess profits earned in the industry because of the output restrictions.

When tighter CFC controls and faster phaseouts of CFCs were being discussed by the U.S. Congress in the late 1980s, there was widespread feeling that at least some of these excess profits should accrue to the public. Several means were discussed. One was to auction off CFC production rights to the various chemical-producing companies. The bidding process, if it worked well, would transfer some portion of the excess profits to the public. The other approach, which was finally adopted, was to tax the production of CFCs. In theory, a tax equal to $(p_2 - p_1)$ would transfer all of the excess

---

[6] Information on the Canadian CFC policy is taken from Douglas A. Smith, "The Implementation of Canadian Policies to Protect the Ozone Layer," in G. Bruce Doern, *Getting it Green* (Toronto: C. D. Howe Institute), 1990.

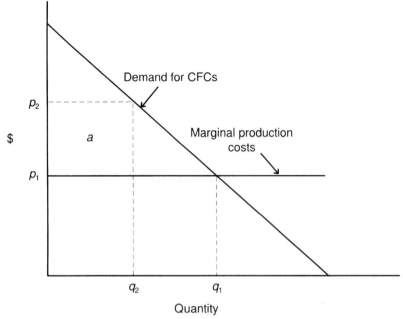

FIGURE 22-1   Government-Imposed Production Limitations Lead to Monopoly Profits.

profits to the public. It could then be used for any number of purposes, perhaps put into general revenues or used specifically to help the CFC conversion process. The system adopted establishes a base tax rate, then sets different taxes on the various ozone-depleting chemicals according to the expression:

$$\text{Tax rate} = \text{Base rate} \times \text{Ozone-depleting potential.}$$

The base rate was initially $1.37 per pound, to increase to $1.67 in 1992, to $2.65 in 1993, and finally to $3.10 in 1995. Thus, the initial tax on, for example, CFC-113 was $1.096 ($1.37 × 0.8).[7]

Canada did not experiment with any taxes on ozone-depleting chemicals. One of the difficulties seen with using a tax in Canada is that we import products containing ozone-depleting chemicals. The U.S. deals with this problem by levying a tax on the amount of these chemicals in the products. Canadian officials were unwilling to implement this complex tax. To deal with the problem of these compounds still in use in refrigerators, air conditioners, and other products, all provinces were to begin implementing CFC recycling and recovery initiatives by the end of 1992. A variety of proposals have been suggested; most are in the form of regulations on the disposal

---

[7] Because of the insistence of halon makers and users, the tax on halons was set at $0.25 per pound.

of products containing ozone-depleting compounds, rather than any economic incentive-based strategies.

The Montreal Protocol also contains a type of pollution-trading arrangement which could reduce the overall cost of meeting its targets. This is the trading of emission-reduction credits among countries. Thus, if a country fails to meet its required production cutback because of the needs of "industrial rationalization," it is supposed to offset the excess emissions by getting comparable reductions in other countries.

GLOBAL WARMING

The Physical Problem

Another major global problem is the threat of a long-run increase in the surface temperature of the earth. This goes under the name of "global warming," or sometimes the "greenhouse effect." The principle of a greenhouse is that the enclosing glass (or nowadays plastic) allows the passage of incoming sunlight, but traps a portion of the reflected infrared radiation, which warms the interior of the greenhouse above the outside temperature. Greenhouse gases in the earth's atmosphere play a similar role; they serve to raise the temperature of the earth's surface and make it habitable. With no greenhouse gases at all, the surface of the earth would be about 30°C cooler than it is today, making human life impossible.

Under "normal" (i.e., preindustrial) conditions, trace amounts of greenhouse gases were in global balance. They were given off by decaying plant and animal materials and absorbed by forests and oceans. Into this rough balance came human beings and one of their greatest cultural accomplishments: the industrial revolution. That event was basically a revolution in energy use, involving a vast increase in the extraction of energy from fossil fuels—first coal, and later petroleum and natural gas. Combustion of fossil fuels, together with deforestation and a few other activities, has led to an increase in the CO_2 content of the atmosphere by about 20 percent from the beginning of the industrial revolution. In the last three decades alone it has increased 8 percent, and many scientists predict an approximate doubling by the middle of the next century. The main greenhouse gases, their approximate proportionate contribution to global warming, and their major sources are shown in Table 22-3.

If the global climate changes as many have predicted, we will be moving into a world very different from the one we now know. Widespread scientific opinion today suggests that the accumulation of greenhouse gases will lead sometime in the next century to a rise in surface temperature of 1.5–4.5°C.[8] The rate of heating is put at about 0.3°C per decade. This may not sound like a very rapid change, but historical studies have shown that in past episodes of warming and cooling, during which agri-

---

[8] James G. Titus and Stephen R. Seidel, "Overview of the Effects of Changing the Atmosphere," in James G. Titus (ed.), *Effects of Changes in Stratospheric Ozone and Global Climate, Volume 1, Overview* (U.S. Environmental Protection Agency, 1986), 3–19.

TABLE 22-3   MAJOR GREENHOUSE GASES AND THEIR PRIMARY SOURCES

Gas	Proportionate effect (%)	Major source
CO_2	49	Fossil fuel combustion, deforestation, cement production
CH_4 (methane)	18	Landfills, agriculture, termites
N_2O (nitrous oxide)	6	Fertilizers, land clearing, biomass burning, fossil fuel combustion
Other (CO, NO_x...)	13	Various

cultural societies of the time suffered major dislocations, climate change occurred at a rate of only about 0.05°C per decade. Today's rate of change, in other words, is expected to be very much faster than those faced by humans in the past.

Global warming is expected to bring about a general rise in sea level because of the expansion of sea water, the melting of glaciers, and perhaps eventually the breaking up of polar ice sheets. Although this will be a general rise, it will have different local impacts on tidal and current patterns. Changes in meteorological patterns will also vary widely among regions. In the northern hemisphere, polar regions will warm faster than equatorial zones; on the continental landmasses the centres will become drier than the peripheries, etc. Our ability to predict these changes will improve as the global climate models of atmospheric scientists are better developed.

Human and Ecosystem Impacts

Although this is a problem of the global environment, its impacts on humans and ecosystem will vary greatly from one country and region to another. A sea-level rise would have devastating impacts in certain societies, like those of the Pacific islands, or those concentrated in low river deltas. Impacts will be relatively less in countries where development may be redirected toward interior regions. The drowning of coastal wetlands throughout the world could have important impacts on fisheries and, thus, on societies that rely heavily on marine resources. There will be very substantial impacts on ecosystems and individual species of plants and animals, not just because of the amount of change but also because the rate of change will be fast by evolutionary standards. In ice ages of the past, weather changes have happened slowly enough to allow many species of plants and animals to migrate and survive. The rapid pace of change expected in the greenhouse phenomenon may be too quick for many organisms to adjust to changing habitats. It will also put a severe strain on species that occupy narrow ecological niches because relatively small changes in weather patterns can destroy the habitats on which they depend.

Perhaps the biggest impacts on humans will be through the effects of changed climate patterns on agriculture and forestry. Here the story gets very complicated, not only because weather patterns will be differently affected throughout the world, but also because crops, and the systems of cultivation adopted by farmers, vary a lot in terms of their ability to withstand changes in temperature and water availability. A recent study commissioned by the U.S. Environmental Protection Agency concludes that the agricultural impacts of atmospheric warming will hit developing nations harder than developed countries. As the news clip in Exhibit 22-1 indicates, it is expected that African nations will be impacted the most. Previous studies had tended to conclude that agriculture could be adapted to future climate changes through crop development and technical changes. The new study casts some doubt on the ability of many developing countries to do this, because many of their crops are already closer to the limits of tolerance for warmer temperatures. Research on the impacts of the greenhouse effect will challenge scientists for many years to come.

Scientific Uncertainties and Human Choice

The discussion in the last few paragraphs may represent widespread thinking among scientists, but we must recognize that the predictions about global warming remain uncertain. The results come from highly complex models of the earth's atmosphere, which require enormous amounts of meteorological and socioeconomic data and incorporate large numbers of interrelationships and feedbacks. Small changes in the models can greatly change the conclusions. Unforeseen events can upset the phenomenon, as the recent eruption of Mount Pinatubo in the Phillipines seems to have done. Other person-made factors can intervene; for example, it now appears that accumulated SO_2 in the lower atmosphere reflects sunlight, thus working against the greenhouse phenomenon. The same may be true of CFCs in the upper atmosphere. Small wonder, then, that there are still differences among scientists about the seriousness of the problem. The news clip shown in Exhibit 22-1 depicts some of these differences.

What are we to do in the face of these uncertainties? Some have argued that we should do little until clear evidence of greenhouse warming actually occurs, then adapt to it if and when it does. The problem with this is that the results could be devastating for countries that cannot easily adapt. Equity considerations suggest that we ought to take action now rather than wait. But even without the equity issue, action is still called for. In Chapter 6 we introduced a few concepts to help in analyzing situations involving risk. We talked in particular about risk aversion in cases involving small probabilities of very large losses. There is scientific uncertainty about the extent of global warming in the future, but the potential negative consequences are so great that it behooves us to be risk averse. In plain terms: better to be safe than sorry. All of which suggests strongly that we undertake steps today to reduce the probability of serious global warming in the future. We have to recognize, however, that we are still in a trade-off situation. We are trading off the cost of measures taken today against benefits in terms of reduced future risk. This means we need to pay close attention to the cost-effectiveness of different policies.

EXHIBIT 22-1

THE DIFFERENTIAL IMPACT OF THE GREENHOUSE EFFECT

Warming Will Hurt Poor Nations Most

The name implies a place where plants thrive, but don't let words fool you. The expected greenhouse warming will likely harm agriculture in many countries, particularly the poorer ones, warns the first international study on this topic.

"Our main conclusion is that the developing countries are most vulnerable to climate change in terms of agriculture," says Cynthia Rosenzweig, an agronomist at Columbia University and NASA's Goddard Institute for Space Studies in New York City. Rosenzweig led the agriculture study with Martin Parry of the University of Oxford in England.

Conducted by scientists in 25 countries, the study indicates that the global warning from greenhouse gas pollution will enhance agricultural disparity between rich and poor nations. In temperate zones, where developed nations reside, global warming may increase crop yields; but a warming will probably diminish yields in tropical areas, where many developing nations are located.

Agriculture in mid-latitude and high-latitude countries may benefit from global warming because it will help plants currently limited by the colder temperatures of these regions. Conversely, countries nearer the equator will suffer because conditions there already lie close to the limit of temperature tolerance for many crops. Warmer temperatures will stress these plants even more, Rosenzweig says.

According to the study, decreased crop yields and increased food prices could significantly swell the ranks of people suffering from hunger. By the year 2060, the number of people at risk of hunger could rise 10 to 50 percent above the level projected with no climate change, a number estimated at 640 million people for that year. The hunger threat will hit African nations hardest, the study finds.

In the real world, farmers continually alter their methods to suit the weather, so Rosenzweig and Parry tested the impact of modest adaptation strategies, such as altering planting dates, changing the crop varieties, or stepping up irrigation efforts in areas where it is already practiced. Such methods could offset most negative aspects of climate change in developed countries, but the developing world would benefit little from these minimal strategies, the researchers report.

Even extreme adaptations—such as installing irrigation systems or developing new crop varieties—would not erase the negative impacts of climate change in the developing world, the study suggests. However, slowing population growth could offset the increase in hunger caused by even severe climate change.

To make the agricultural projections, Rosenzweig and her colleagues started with three different climate forecasts provided by separate general-circulation models, which simulated how a doubling of greenhouse gases will alter climate. The scientists plugged the climate forecasts into models that estimate crop growth, taking into account how increasing carbon dioxide will fertilize plants. The crop-growth results then went into a model that simulates world food trade.

In the past, scientists lacked a clear view of how climate change might affect tropical regions—in part, says Rosenzweig, because projections suggest that temperatures would increase less dramatically in tropical areas than in mid-latitude and polar zones. Prior to the new study, researchers could argue that enhanced crop growth from higher carbon dioxide levels would balance the relatively small temperature rise expected in the tropics, she says.

The agriculture study, commissioned by the U.S. Environmental Protection Agency, is the first to take a detailed global look at the agricultural impacts of climate change. In doing so, it offers a bleaker picture than previous reports.

Gary Evans, head of the Agriculture Department's global change office, says the study's disturbing conclusions don't square with observations about agricultural trends in the United States.

"Technological capabilities in agriculture have proven for the last 50 to 75 years to be able to keep up with any shifts and changes that have taken place," he says, suggesting that similar developments around the world may be able to cut the losses from climate change in developing nations. Pointing to the current famine in Somalia, Evans speculates that war and other problems will cause greater food shortages than will climate change.

Source: Science News, 142 (8) (August 1992): 142. Reprinted by permission from Science News, the weekly Newsmagazine of Science, copyright 1992 by Science Service, Inc.

Technical Responses to the Greenhouse Effect

The greenhouse effect results from an increase in the production of greenhouse gases relative to the ability of the earth's ecosystems to absorb them. So the primary means of reducing the warming lies in reducing the output of greenhouse gases and/or augmenting the CO_2-absorbing capacity of the natural world. Since CO_2 is the main greenhouse gas, we will focus on the issue of reducing global CO_2 emissions.

To get an overall view of the current world production rate of CO_2 and how it may be altered, consider the following equation:

$$\frac{\text{Total } CO_2}{\text{production}} = \text{Population} \times \frac{\text{GDP}^{10}}{\text{Person}} \times \frac{\text{Energy}}{\text{GDP}} \times \frac{CO_2}{\text{Energy}}$$

			Rates of change		
Global	1.7	1.7	1.0	−0.6	−0.4
India	4.5	2.0	1.2	1.2	0.1
U.S.	3.7	0.9	3.8	−1.0	0.0

The quantity of CO_2 emissions depends on the interaction of four factors. The first is population. Other things remaining equal, larger populations will use more energy and therefore emit larger amounts of CO_2. The second term is GDP per capita, a measure of the domestic output of goods and services per capita. We normally associate increases in this factor with economic growth. Neither of these first two factors can be considered likely candidates for reducing CO_2 emissions in the short run. Deliberate population control measures are unlikely to be effective, and no country is likely to be willing to reduce its rate of economic development. In the long run, however, the interaction of these two factors will be important, as history seems to show that lower population growth rates can be achieved by substantial improvements in economic welfare.

This means that significant near-term CO_2 reductions will have to come from the last two terms in the expression. The third is what we mean by "energy efficiency," the amount of energy used per dollar (or per franc or rupee or cedi) of output. The key here is to move toward technologies of production, distribution, and consumption that require relatively smaller quantities of energy. The last term is CO_2 produced per unit of energy used. Since different energy forms have markedly different CO_2 outputs per unit, reductions in CO_2 can be achieved by switching to less CO_2-intensive fuels.

The table under the equation shows how these four factors have been changing in recent years. The first row shows the annual growth rate in global CO_2 output, which is the sum of the global growth rates of the factors comprising the formula. Note that, worldwide, although energy use per unit GDP and CO_2 intensity are declining, these are being more than offset by high growth rates in population and GDP per capita. But growth rates in the underlying factors differ a great deal among countries. In the table we compare those of India and the U.S. for illustrative purposes. In India, increases in all factors, especially population, have contributed to a very rapid rate of growth in CO_2 emissions. In the U.S., lower population growth rates, together with increases in energy efficiency (decreases in energy per GDP) have moderated the growth rate of CO_2 emissions. It is differences among countries in these contributing factors that complicate the adoption of effective worldwide agreements to limit CO_2 emissions. We will come back to this point below.

In the short run, that is, over the next few decades, we will have to fight the greenhouse effect chiefly with increases in energy conservation and efficiency, a switch to low-carbon fuels, and a reduction in the use of chemicals with high greenhouse impacts. Table 22-4 lists the major types of changes that could be made in different economic sectors. There is no single source that we could call on to get drastic reductions in CO_2 production. Instead, significant changes could be made in hundreds of different places—transportation, industry, households, and agriculture. These changes

TABLE 22-4   MEANS OF REDUCING GREENHOUSE GASES

Energy production
Reduce demand for electricity (see Households).
Switch to nonfossil fuels (solar, biomass, nuclear, hydroelectric).
Switch from high-carbon (coal) to low-carbon (gas) fossil fuels.
Reduce energy transmission losses.
Remove carbon from fuel and emissions.

Households
Reduce demand for energy (less heating, air conditioning, ...).
Switch to less energy-intensive products.
Switch to more energy-efficient technologies (solar heaters, insulation,...).
Switch out of CFCs in car air conditioners...

Industry
Increase energy efficiency of production processes.
Switch to low- or no-carbon fuels.
Increase energy efficiency in buildings, lighting,...
Switch out of CFCs and other greenhouse gases.

Transportation
Reduce miles driven and travel speeds.
Increase fuel efficiency of vehicles.
Switch to mass transit systems.

Agriculture and food system
Reduce methane production from livestock production and rice paddies.
Improve energy efficiency in farming.
Reduce CFC use in refrigeration.
Reduce energy use in transportation.
Increase land uses that lead to greater carbon storage.

Forestry
Reduce rates of deforestation.
Increase rates of reforestation.

Source: From material in U.S. Office of Technology Assessment, *Changing by Degrees, Steps to Reduce Greenhouse Gases* (Washington, D.C., 1991).

are both technical—as, for example, the switch to more energy-efficient equipment and low-CO_2 fuels—and behavioural—for example, changing driving habits and adopting less energy-intensive lifestyles. Two primary questions have to be asked about these changes: First, what are they likely to cost and, second, how can we best bring them about?

Costs of CO_2 Emission Reductions

How costly would it be for different countries to reduce substantially their emissions of greenhouse gases over the next several decades? We can be sure that the marginal costs of CO_2 reduction are increasing; the greater the reduction, the more it will cost. But how steeply they increase is a matter of great complexity. Any meaningful CO_2 reduction is going to take many years, probably decades, to bring about, because it means shifting the major technological and fossil fuel biases that have been built into contemporary economies over a long period. Thus, to cost out any control program, it's necessary to predict technological and economic changes well into the future. In a world that is as technically and politically dynamic as the one we live in today, this is very hard to do.

One way to estimate costs, called a "bottoms-up" analysis, is to put together technical information from specific economic sectors to construct a generalized picture of CO_2 reduction costs for the entire economy. One result of an analysis like this is estimates of CO_2 control costs for different technological options. Table 22-5 shows some cost-effectiveness results obtained in a large study by the U.S. Office of Technology Assessment (OTA). They show the estimated costs per ton of reducing CO_2 emissions in the U.S. by adopting different technical alternatives. The estimates are relatively short run, in the sense that the OTA was looking at things that could be accomplished over the next 25 years. Several options have negative CO_2 reduction costs. These are approaches that would pay for themselves without even considering CO_2 removal, primarily through savings in energy. Several things stand out in these numbers. Many are in the general range of $100–$300 per ton of CO_2 removed. Considering that the total quantity of CO_2 emissions in the U.S. today is about 5 billion tons per year, one can get a rough idea of the costs of decreasing these emissions by a substantial fraction. These are also marginal costs; that is, they are costs of reducing CO_2 emissions starting with where we are today. If we ever succeed in moving to a much more energy-efficient economy, the costs of making further reductions in CO_2 emissions will no doubt increase, probably a lot.

Some cost figures that stand out are the low estimates for afforestation, as essentially an add-on to the current conservation reserve program, and the high costs of CO_2 removal through shifting to mass transit. Afforestation looks like a good buy for CO_2 removal, but the other side of the coin is that because of the relatively small numbers of acres involved, the total amount of CO_2 that could be removed through this means in the U.S. is relatively modest.

A study by van Kooten, Arthur, and Wilson looks at the cost-effectiveness of sequestering carbon in Canadian forests and also finds that increasing the forests is

TABLE 22-5   COST-EFFECTIVENESS OF ALTERNATIVE MEANS OF REDUCING CO_2 U.S.

Means	Costs per ton of CO_2 ($)
Cofiring boilers with natural gas	510
Early retirement of coal plants, replaced with nonfossil fuels	280
Increased energy efficiency in homes	175 to 300
Increased energy efficiency in commercial buildings	−190 to 75
Cogeneration—commercial	85 to 210
Increased fuel efficiency in cars	−220 to −110
Increased fuel efficiency in light trucks	−510 to −410
Mass transit	1,150 to 2,300
Cogeneration—industry	55 to 120
Urban tree planting	180
Afforestation with CRP*	35
Increased CO_2-absorbing capacity through management of existing forests	150 to 200

*CRP stands for Conservation Reserve Program, a program to help farmers reduce production on marginal lands. The program would emphasize tree planting on these acreages.
Source: U.S. Office of Technology Assessment, *Changing by Degrees, Steps to Reduce Greenhouse Gases* (Washington, D.C. 1991), Appendix A.

a low-cost method of reducing carbon. However, even in Canada, with it's large land potential for forestation, the reductions in CO_2 generated would also be quite small.[9] They find that the amount of carbon that could be sequestered by reforestation and afforestation is at most 19.4 tonnes per year, or less than 0.7 percent of the world's total carbon accumulation. The carbon sequestered would reduce Canada's contribution to atmospheric CO_2 by 15.1 percent. While this is not a large amount of carbon reduction, the costs per tonne are quite low compared to the U.S. figures cited above. Their estimates of sequestering costs are between $6 and $23 per tonne of carbon (Canadian dollars). They also looked at two other alternatives: scrapping all cars made before 1983 and replacing them with newer, more energy-efficient models, and converting all passenger cars in Canada to natural gas. The first alternative would reduce Canadian carbon emissions by 4.54 tonnes per year and this actually yields a net benefit to society over the lifetime of the new cars. This result is analogous to that shown in Table 22-5 for increased fuel efficiency in cars and trucks, and happens for the same reasons. Switching all cars to natural gas is alternatively a very expensive way to reduce carbon emissions. Their estimate is that it would cost approximately $322 per tonne, or close to the top end of the estimates done for the United States. The amount of carbon reduced per year would also be less than that for scrapping vehicles (3.8 tonnes per year).

The high cost estimates for rapid transit in Table 22-5 show the effects of the long-run growth patterns in the economy. The trends in population dispersion and trans-

[9] G. C. van Kooten, Louise M. Arthur, and W. R. Wilson, "Potential to Sequester Carbon in Canadian Forests: Some Economic Considerations," *Canadian Public Policy* 18:2 (June 1992).

portation technology over the last century have left the U.S. and Canada with a situation that is not amenable to mass transit to reduce transportation energy requirements. This is a strong reminder, if one is needed, of how decisions taken at one point in time can have consequences much later, when conditions have totally changed.

The other approach to estimating the cost of CO_2 control is a "top-down" analysis, where one studies national economies as single units, factoring in assumed rates of technical change and measuring other critical parameters like how the use of different fuels has responded to changes in their relative prices. A common approach is to measure the effects of CO_2 emission reductions on rates of economic growth. One way of summarizing the results is to estimate the extent to which GDP, at the end of the study period, would be reduced from the level it would have attained if there had been no program of CO_2 reduction. Table 22-6 summarizes some of the results of these studies, expressed as "end-year GDP as percentage of baseline." The first column shows the percent reduction from the baseline (–20%, –36%, and so on), as well as the end year for the study. Note that the estimates vary a lot; they range from a low of –0.2 percent to –15.0 percent. To a large extent this is because of different research approaches—different assumptions, data, and the like. But it also reflects the inherent difficulty and uncertainty of doing studies that try to extrapolate well into the future. This is especially true when we make assumptions about rates of techno-

TABLE 22-6   RESULTS OF STUDIES ON THE COST OF CO_2 REDUCTIONS

Study	Emission reduction from baseline (end year)	End-year GDP as percentage of baseline
Mann-Richels		
U.S.	–20 (2030)	–3.3
Other OECD	–20 (2030)	–1.2
Russia, Eastern Europe	–20 (2030)	–4.5
China	–20 (2030)	–5.0
Rest of world	–20 (2030)	–1.0
Department of Finance (Canada)	–30 (2000)	–2.3
Congressional Budget Office (U.S.)	–36 (2000)	–0.6
Jorgenson/Wilcoxen (U.S.)	–36 (2060)	–1.1
Blitzer et al. (Egypt)	–35 (2002)	–15.0
Glomered et al. (Norway)	–26 (2010)	–2.7
NEPP (Netherlands)	–25 (2010)	–4.2
Bergman (Sweden)	–51 (2000)	–5.6
Dixon et al. (Australia)	–47 (2005)	–0.2

Sources: The studies were summarized in P. Hoeller, A. Dean, and J. Nicolaisen, *A Survey of Studies of the Cost of Reducing Greenhouse Gas Emissions*, Working Paper No. 89 (Paris: Organization for Economic Cooperation and Development, Department of Economics and Statistics, 1990); and Joel Darmstadter, *The Economic Cost of CO_2 Mitigation: A Review of Estimates for Selected World Regions*, Discussion Paper ENR91-06 (Washington, D.C.: Resources for the Future, 1991); Beauséjour, L., G. Lenjosek, and M. Smart, *An Environmental CGE Model of Canada and the United States*, Fiscal Policy and Economic Analysis Branch, Working Paper No. 92-04 (Ottawa: Department of Finance).

logical change that are likely to occur in the future, in situations with and without the constraints on CO_2 emissions.

A study by Canada's Deparatment of Finance looked at the cost effectiveness of different regulatory policies in reaching CO_2 targets in terms of impact on real income.[10] Their model assumed that the target was stabilization by the year 2000 of CO_2 emissions at their 1990 level. They also investigated how real income would decline with different CO_2 target reductions. The most cost-effective policy to reach the 1990 target was a tax on the carbon content. It led to a reduction in real income of just slightly over 0.2 percent. Corresponding estimates for emisssion standards and a tax not directly targeted on carbon content were approximately 0.4 percent and 0.5 percent respectively. The Department of Finance also found, not surprisingly, that as the target level of reduction of CO_2 rose, real incomes declined by an increasing proportion. For example, the target of 1990 levels implies about a 15 reduction in CO_2 emissions. If the reduction in emissions is 30 percent, real income decreases by close to 2 percent, rather than about a half of a percent. At 45 percent reduction in CO_2, real incomes could fall by over 3 percent. Recall that these cost estimates would have to be compared to the value of the benefits of mitigating global warming to determine the efficient target. Studies of this sort are potentially useful in determining both the mix of policy instruments and the targets chosen.

Policy Responses

Identifying possible CO_2-reducing technical and behavioural changes is one thing; adopting policies that can motivate their widespread adoption is another. Possible policy approaches for greenhouse gases fall into the same two categories we have discussed before: (1) standards, either emission or technology standards, and (2) incentive-based strategies. In thinking about policies on global warming, there are two levels to consider, the international and the domestic. At the international level, steps must be undertaken to obtain reductions in the aggregate CO_2 emissions from each country. At the national level, total emission reductions must be obtained through domestic policies. Policies at the two levels could be a complex mix of command-and-control (CAC) and incentive-based strategies.

We have no international agreement for CO_2 reduction as of yet (1993). But the precedent for one may have been established in other agreements, especially the CFC treaty. The Montreal Protocol divided the world's countries into two groups, then prescribed essentially equiproportionate reductions for the countries in each group. Similarly, the various SO_2- and NO_x-reducing provisions in present transboundary air-pollution agreements call for equiproportionate reductions in emissions. These are, therefore, essentially CAC types of approaches, and they have the same built-in per-

---

[10] Department of Finance Canada, "An Environmental CGE Model of Canada and the United States," Working Paper forthcoming, as cited in Environment Canada, *Economic Instruments for Environmental Protection*, Catalogue No. En21-119/1992E (Ottawa: Environment Canada, 1992).

verse incentives we have talked about earlier: They reward those who have been prof-ligate in the past and penalize those who have been frugal. Countries like Canada, where relatively little emphasis has been placed on fuel efficiency, will have an eas-ier time meeting such standards for CO_2 reduction than countries like France, where carbon output per dollar of GDP are substantially below those of Canada.

We can be sure that the assignment of CO_2 limits to the many countries of the world will be especially controversial. What formula might be followed in setting these allocations? Consider the following possibilities:

- Equiproportionate reduction in emissions.
- Ability to pay. Base emission reductions/transfer payments on current per capita income levels.
- "Polluter pays" principle. Base emission reductions/transfer payments on cur-rent or past contributions to the problem.
- Equal per capita consumption. Base emission reductions on the idea that all per-capita consumption levels should be the same.

These rules would have substantially different implications for different countries of the world. The data in Table 22-7 show population, income, and CO_2 emissions data for a selected group of countries. The countries were selected to illustrate the differ-ential impacts of the rules, not because they are in any way more significant than oth-ers. If the cutback were based on total emissions, the largest reduction would be allo-cated to the U.S., followed by China, then India, and France. But if it were based on emissions per capita, the order would be U.S., France, China, and India. If emissions reductions were based on energy efficiency, the largest cutbacks would actually be allocated to China and India because, although their emissions per capita are low, incomes are even lower, giving them relatively high numbers for emissions per dol-lar of GDP. Finally, if we were to allocate emission reductions on the basis of pro-

TABLE 22-7   ECONOMIC AND CARBON EMISSIONS DATA FOR SELECTED COUNTRIES, 1987

Country	Population (millions)	GDP per capita ($)	Total emissions (mil tons)	Emissions per capita (tons)	Emissions per dollar GDP (grams)	Emissions (% of total)
China	1,031.9	320*	578	0.56	2,024	9.6
France	54.3	16,234	92	1.70	133	1.5
India	685.2	371	130	0.19	655	2.2
U.S.	226.5	18,506	1,139	5.03	276	18.9
World (average or total)			6,030	1.08	327	—

*1989.
Source: Emissions per capita and total emissions taken from John Walley, "The Interface Between Envi-ronmental and Trade Policies." *The Economic Journal* 101(405) (March 1991): 103. Population and income data are from United Nations, *1987 Demographic Yearbook* (New York, 1989): 173–175.

portionate share of total CO_2 emissions, the U.S. would have the largest cutback, followed by China, India, and France.

One important item these data do not include is the costs to the various countries of doing nothing; that is, simply adapting to global warming. These costs are likely to place limits on the extent to which any particular country will readily accept CO_2 emission-reduction requirements, since it is unlikely to be interested in spending more in control costs than the cost of accommodating to the change. For cooler countries in higher latitudes, with relatively little critical shoreline, adaptation costs may be fairly "modest." Countries in the opposite situation will have very high costs of adapting to higher temperatures and rising sea levels. Countries differ also in terms of agricultural adaptability, the ability to shift crops, varieties, cultivation methods, and so on, to maintain production in the face of climate changes. So countries are likely to have very different perceptions about how they will be affected by global warming. The obstacles to an effective international agreement on CO_2 reduction are many, and the need for creative treaty diplomacy is great.

We have talked many times in this book about the cost-ineffectiveness of proportionate cutbacks in emissions from different sources. The same principles are at work here, where by "sources" we mean countries. To have a CO_2 program that is *globally* cost-effective, some economists have suggested that we institute a system of transferable discharge permits at the international level. Countries would be allocated CO_2 emission permits equal to their permitted base-level emissions, as determined by some formula such as one of those discussed above. These permits would then be tradable among countries. The marginal costs of CO_2 reduction could be expected to differ substantially among countries, on the basis of such factors as wealth and economic growth rates, fossil fuel availabilities, and energy technologies. Thus trading opportunities exist that could substantially reduce the overall global costs of reducing CO_2 emissions. Another salutary feature of global carbon TDPs is that they could easily be used to address questions of international equity. The current belief is that it will cost developing countries more, relative to their current wealth, to reduce CO_2 emissions than developed economies. Thus the direction of transfers would in general go from less to more developed countries. On top of this, developing countries might be given proportionately larger numbers of permits in the initial distribution. In buying these extra permits developed nations would be transferring extra amounts of wealth to the developing countries, which they could use to switch to low-carbon development paths. However, the political practicability of this approach is open to serious question.

But a CO_2 treaty might be reached in which countries committed themselves to cutbacks of various amounts. To achieve such a cutback a country would have numerous policy options. Technology and emission standards are possibilities. In some cases governments may be able effectively to dictate certain economywide technology choices; for example, the widespread adoption of nuclear power in France. Or a country might adopt performance or emission standards. An example is Canada's and the U.S.'s fuel efficiency standards for motor vehicles. These require that car manufacturers meet minimum average fuel-use standards among all models made in a given year. But the enormous number and variety of different fuel-using technologies would work against using technology or performance standards as the primary policy approach to CO_2 reduction.

This kind of situation would lend itself well to the use of carbon taxes to provide the incentive to reduce fuel consumption and to shift to lower carbon forms of energy. These would be charges on the carbon content of fuels consumed. In a recent study of carbon taxes for Canada, the Department of Finance estimated that a carbon tax of $27.70 per tonne of CO_2 on final demand (combined with emission reductions of 19 percent achieved by regulation in iron and steel, electric power, transportation and service industries) would achieve the 1990 emission levels by the year 2000. This target represents approximately a 15 percent reduction in emissions below what they would have been by 2000.[11] Naturally the coal industry and heavy energy-using industries would be the hardest hit by such a tax. The tax might also be regressive if low-income people spend a higher proportion of their incomes on energy and energy-using products.[12] In recent years many other countries have considered the adoption of carbon taxes.[13]

Suggestions have been made for a worldwide CO_2 emissions tax, a single tax that would apply to all sources in all countries. This would achieve cost-effectiveness at both the intercountry level and intersource level within each country, provided governments did nothing to thwart the uniform application of the tax domestically. Economic studies of this approach have been neatly summarized by Nordhaus. Figure 22-2 shows the relationship between different levels of carbon tax and the percentage of reduction in CO_2 emissions. The points shown in the graph are the results of the different studies reviewed by Nordhaus. The studies differed in terms of the countries and exact circumstances to which they applied, but they do seem to tell a reasonably consistent story. The curved line drawn through the points represents what the author feels is the best summary of the studies. In effect the curve shows the marginal costs of reducing CO_2 emissions. To get a worldwide reduction of 20 percent in CO_2 emissions would require a tax of about $45/ton of carbon. A 50 percent CO_2 reduction would need a $140 tax, and the curvature of the graph shows that deeper CO_2 cutbacks would require progressively larger taxes.

Whether any significant international effort can be mounted to establish a worldwide carbon tax is highly problematic. A tax high enough to produce significant CO_2 reductions would be especially burdensome in developing countries. Support might be encouraged if the proceeds of the tax could be shared out among countries so as

---

[11] L. Beauséjour, G. Lenjosek, and M. Smart, *An Environmental CGE Model of Canada and the United States*, Fiscal Policy and Economic Analysis Branch Working Paper No. 92-04 (Ottawa: Department of Finance, 1992).

[12] A study by Kirk Hamilton, "The Distributional Effects of a Hypothetical Canadian Carbon Tax," *Canadian Public Policy* (December 1994), finds that the lowest income group (the lowest quintile) would find their disposable income fall by between 2.9 percent and 3.4 percent compared to a decline of 2.3 percent to 2.7 percent for households on average, for a hypothetical tax of $101.56 per tonne of carbon.

[13] These countries are Australia, Austria, Denmark, France, Germany, Japan, The Netherlands, New Zealand, Norway, Sweden, the United Kingdom, and the United States. See Peter M. Morrisette and Andrew J. Plantinga, "The Global Warming Issue. Viewpoints of Different Countries," *Resources* 103 (Spring 1991): 3.

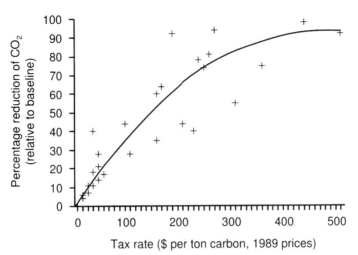

FIGURE 22-2   Estimates of the Reductions of CO_2 Emissions Produced at Different Tax Rates.

Source: Based on William D. Nordhaus, "A Survey of Estimates of the Cost of Reduction of Greenhouse Gas Emissions," paper prepared for the National Academy of Science, Committee on Science, Engineering, and Public Policy, February 1990.

to reduce the overall impact on poorer nations. Along with these equity matters, real questions exist about the difficulties of monitoring and enforcing the tax. Self-monitoring by the individual countries is likely to be the only practical solution to this issue, since it is unlikely that countries would willingly permit international monitoring efforts. Sanctioning countries that exceed their TDP quotas or fail to pay taxes would be difficult. The United Nations lacks executive power to enforce international environmental agreements. The International Court of Justice (ICJ) acts chiefly as a place for discussing disputes and lacks mechanisms to enforce rulings. This leaves enforcement up to a combination of moral pressure and whatever unilateral actions states might take, like trade sanctions.

Prime Minister Mulroney signed the United Nations Framework Convention on Climate Change which was ratified in December 1992. The convention commits Canada to work toward the establishment of specific targets and schedules for the reduction of CO_2 and other greenhouse gases. Thus far, no specific Canadian targets have been set. The U.S. has not committed itself to specific CO_2 emission reductions. For many years the U.S. has opted for what is called a "no-regrets" policy. This means that it will adopt policies with desirable greenhouse effects only if they also have more immediate environmental impacts (including CFC reduction and energy consumption), so that if the greenhouse problem later turns out not to be serious, there will be "no regrets" for having adopted the policy.[14]

[14] C. Boyden Gray and David B. Rivkin, Jr., "A No-Regrets Environmental Policy," *Foreign Policy* 83 (Summer 1991): 47–65.

BIOLOGICAL DIVERSITY

Another problem that we have begun to appreciate in recent years is the worldwide reduction in diversity among the elements of the biological system. This can be discussed at several levels: diversity in the stock of genetic material, species diversity, or diversity among ecosystems. But the long-run health of the whole system requires that there be diversity among its parts. Biological uniformity produces inflexibility and weakened ability to respond to new circumstances; diversity gives a system the means to adapt to change.

The human population cannot maintain itself without cultivating certain species of animals and plants. But the continued vigour of this relationship actually depends also on the stock of wild species. About 25 percent of the prescription drugs in the developed societies are derived from plants.[15] Diseases are not static; they evolve in response to efforts made to eradicate them. Thus, wild species of plants constitute a vital source of raw material needed for future medicines. Wild species are also critical for agriculture. Through traditional plant and animal breeding, and even more through modern methods of biotechnology, genetic material and the qualities they entail may be transferred from wild species into cultivated ones. In 1979 a species of wild maize resistant to an important crop virus was discovered in a remote corner of Mexico. When transferred to species of domestic corn, this characteristic substantially enhanced the agricultural value of that crop.

The stock of species at any particular time is a result of two processes: the random mutations that create new species of organisms and the forces that determine rates of extinction among existing species. Scientists currently estimate the number of extant species at between 5 and 10 million, of which about 1.4 million have been described. When a species goes extinct, we lose forever whatever valuable qualities that organism may have had. The normal, long-run rate of species extinction has been estimated at about 9 percent per million years, or 0.000009 percent per year.[16] Thus, this is the normal rate at which the information contained in the species stock vanishes. At several times in the geological past, the rate of extinctions has been very much higher. One of these times was the period, millions of years ago, during which the dinosaurs died off. Another is today. But while the earlier period was the result of natural causes, today's rapid destruction of the stock of species is due primarily to the actions of human beings.

Some species go extinct because they are overexploited. But the vast majority are under pressure because of habitat destruction. This comes primarily from commercial pressures to exploit other features of the land—logging off the trees for timber or wood, converting the land to agricultural uses, clearing the land for urban expansion, etc. This has been a particular problem in many developing countries, which contain a disproportionately large share of the world's wild species, but which are also under great pressure to pursue modern economic development. But we should

[15] U.S. Office of Technology Assessment, *Technologies to Sustain Tropical Forest Resources and Biological Diversity* (Washington, D.C., May 1992), 60.
[16] Edward O. Wilson (ed.), *Biodiversity* (Washington, D.C.: National Academy Press, 1986.

not forget that developed countries have already had massive changes in habitats and have seen extinction of species and reductions in biological diversity.

The information contained in the global stock of genetic capital has consistently been undervalued. This is partly because we do not know what is there or what portions of it may turn out to be important in the future. It is also because, almost by definition, it is impossible to know the value of the genes in a species that has gone extinct; we cannot miss something we never realized we had. But primarily the undervaluation of the stock of wild germ plasm is a function of the institutional structures governing the management of wild species. Whereas the market values of conventional products ensure that their production will be pursued with vigour, there are normally no comparable market values for the information contained in the wild gene pool.

Canada's efforts with regard to biological diversity are varied, but involve little in the way of specific regulation. Canada has no endangered species legislation. We are monitoring certain at-risk species, particularly migratory birds. The federal government contributes to the Endangered Species Recovery Fund which involves the World Wildlife Fund Canada, the Natural Sciences and Engineering Research Council and Environment Canada. The fund's objective is to support universities and the private sector in undertaking projects that benefit endangered species and their habitat. We are also a signatory of the U.N. Convention on Biological Diversity. As part of the Green Plan, the federal government is committed to setting aside 12 percent of the country as protected space. Whether these iniatives will promote and preserve diversity remains to be seen.

The effective maintenance of biodiversity depends on the maintenance of habitats in amounts big enough that species may preserve themselves in complex biological equilibria. This involves first identifying valuable habitats and then protecting them from development pressures that are incompatible with preserving the resident species. Canada has a network of reserved lands which have been preserved in the public domain, in national and provincial parks, wilderness areas, wildlife refuges, and the like. The fact of the matter is, however, that the world's primary areas of genetic and species abundance and diversity are in developing countries in Central and South America, Africa, and Southeast Asia.[17]

Efforts have been made in some of these countries, sometimes vigorously and sometimes not, to protect areas of high biological value by putting them into some sort of protected status—sanctuaries, reserves, parks, etc. But here the situation is usually much more complicated by high-population pressures. People who are struggling to get enough resources to achieve some degree of economic security may feel that something called "biological diversity" is not particularly relevant. Land reservation for species preservation is essentially a zoning approach, and it suffers the same fundamental flaw of that policy: It does not reshape the underlying incentives that are leading to population pressure on the habitats.

[17] The countries especially recognized for biological diversity are Mexico, Columbia, Brazil, Zaire, Madagascar, and Indonesia.

One suggestion that has been made to change this is to create a more complete system of property rights over genetic resources. At the present time, property rights are recognized for special breeder stock, genetically engineered organisms, and newly developed medicines. This provides a strong incentive for research on new drugs and the development of improved crops. But this incentive does not extend backward to the protection of wild gene plasm, especially in developing countries. Thus, the suggestion is to clarify property rights in wild species and let countries themselves exercise these property rights in world markets for genetic information.[18] By allowing them to sell the rights to parts of the genetic stock, countries would have a way of realizing the values inherent in these stocks and so would be motivated to devote more effort and resources to their protection. Countries would also have stronger incentives to inventory and describe species that are still unknown.

In fact, events may be moving in this direction already. A contract was recently signed between Merck and Company, a U.S. pharmaceutical firm, and the Instituto Nacional de Biodiversidad of Costa Rica. The contract calls for an up-front payment of $1 million, plus royalties on discoveries of commercial value, while the Costa Rican agency will undertake steps to catalogue and preserve biological resources in that country. The American Cancer Institute has negotiated contracts with Zimbabwe, Madagascar, and the Philippines for access to genetic resources in these countries. A British firm named Biotics is functioning as a broker between potential suppliers and buyers of genetic resources.[19]

Especially important is how this type of approach would filter down to affect individuals who are actually using the land. It is highly doubtful if substantial amounts of land could be put off limits to any type of development if population pressure continues high. So attention needs to be directed also at developing modes of commercial agriculture that are compatible with genetic and species preservation.[20] Production based on retaining natural habitat requires two things: that cultivators have secure property rights and that there be strong markets for the types of "crops" produced in this kind of system.

SUMMARY

In recent years we have seen the rise of truly global environmental problems, especially those dealing with the disruption of the global atmosphere. In these cases it is as if all the nations of the world were homeowners living around a small lake, each one dependent on the lake for water supply, but each one also using the lake for waste disposal.

---

[18] See the discussion in Roger A. Sedjo, "Property Rights for Plants," *Resources* 97 (Fall 1989): 1–4.

[19] R. David Simpson and Roger A. Sedjo, "Contracts for Transferring Rights to Indigenous Genetic Resources," *Resources* 109 (Fall 1992): 1–5.

[20] Tim Swanson, "Conserving Biological Diversity," in David Pearce (ed.), *Blueprint 2: Greening the World Economy* (London: Earthscan Press, 1991), 181–208.

Depletion of the earth's protective ozone layer has been a result of the widespread use of chlorofluorocarbons for refrigerants, solvents, and other uses. What once were regarded as miracle chemicals now have turned out to be life-threatening. The increased ultraviolet radiation this will produce at the earth's surface is expected to increase skin cancers and eye cataracts, and have a substantial impact on agricultural production. In recent years chemical companies have had success in developing substitutes for CFCs. This greatly facilitated the signing of the Montreal Protocol, an international agreement among most of the nations of the world that will lead to a phaseout of the production and consumption of CFCs over the next few decades.

The global greenhouse effect will be more difficult to deal with. Burning fossil fuels has increased the CO_2 content of the atmosphere, affecting the earth's radiation balance and leading to an increase in mean global temperatures. Substantial impacts are expected on weather patterns around the globe. These are expected to disrupt agricultural operations in significant ways. A rise in the sea level will have profound impacts on coastal communities. A substantial attack on the phenomenon will require cutting back on the use of fossil fuels. Virtually all countries are dependent to a greater or lesser extent on fossil fuels to power their economies. Thus, we must emphasize cost-effective policies to improve energy efficiency and to switch to fuels that emit less CO_2. It is likely to be many years before a meaningful international agreement can be reached on this problem.

The destruction of biological diversity is a subtler global problem, but it may be just as costly in the long run. Dealing with this problem will require greater efforts to preserve habitat and develop agriculture that is compatible with species preservation. Effective action will mean doing something about the incentives that currently lead to species destruction.

QUESTIONS FOR FURTHER DISCUSSION

1 Many countries are adopting a "wait and see" strategy on CO_2 emissions and atmospheric warming. What would a rational "wait and see" strategy look like?

2 When CFCs were first introduced 50 years ago, their benefits were obvious, and nobody appreciated the long-run impacts they might have. How do we guard ourselves against unforeseen long-run effects like this?

3 In the absence of a worldwide agreement to reduce CO_2 through a carbon tax, how effective might it be if just one, or a small number, of countries instituted a tax unilaterally?

4 Rather than placing a tax on fuels or the carbon content of fuels, taxes might be put on fuel-using items, such as "gas-guzzling" cars, less efficient appliances, or houses with poor insulation. Which type of tax would be more efficient?

5 Global warming is predicted to affect countries differently, which is one reason it is difficult to get all countries to agree on a global CO_2 treaty. Do you think it will be easier to get agreement *after* the results start showing up in different countries?

6 How many different formulas can you think of for allocating a reduction in global CO_2 among the nations of the world? Compare and contrast these in terms of efficiency and equity.

SELECTED READINGS

Benedick, Richard. *Ozone Diplomacy*. Cambridge, Mass.: Harvard University Press, 1991.

Binswanger, Hans. "Brazilian Policies that Encourage Deforestation in the Amazon." *World Development* 19 (7) (1991): 821–829.

Broome, John. *Counting the Cost of Global Warming*. Isle of Harris, U.K.: White Horse Press, 1992.

Chandler, William U. (ed.). *Carbon Emission Strategies: Case Studies in International Cooperation*. Washington, D.C.: World Wildlife Fund and the Conservation Foundation, 1990.

Chapman, Duane, and Thomas Drennen. "Equity and Effectiveness of Possible CO_2 Treaty Proposals." *Contemporary Policy Issues* 8 (3) (July 1990): 16–25.

Cline, William R. *Global Warming: Estimating the Economic Benefits of Abatement*. Paris: Organization for Economic Cooperation and Development, 1992.

Dixon, John A., and Paul B. Sherman. *Economics of Protected Areas: A New Look at Benefits and Costs*, Washington, D.C.: Island Press, 1990.

Donaldson, D. M., and G. F. Betteridge. "The Relative Cost Effectiveness of Various Measures to Ameliorate Global Warming." *Energy Policy* 18 (6) (July/August 1990): 563–571.

Dudek, Daniel J., and Alice LeBlanc. "Offsetting New CO_2 Emissions: A Rational First Greenhouse Policy Step." *Contemporary Policy Issues* 8 (3) (July 1990): 29–42.

Firor, John. "The Straight Story About the Greenhouse Effect." *Contemporary Policy Issues* 8 (3) (July 1990): 3–15.

Lashof, Daniel A., and Dennis A. Tirpak. *Policy Options for Stabilizing Global Climate*. New York: Hemisphere Publishing Company, 1990.

Manne, Alan S., and Richard G. Richels. *Buying Greenhouse Insurance, The Economic Cost of CO_2 Emission Limits*. Cambridge, Mass.: MIT Press, 1992.

Marchant, Gary E. "Freezing Carbon Dioxide Emissions: An Offset Policy for Slowing Global Warming." *Environmental Law* 22 (2) (1992): 623–683.

McNeely, Jeffrey. *Economic and Biological Diversity, Developing and Using Economic Incentives to Conserve Biological Resources*. New York: Columbia University Press, 1989.

Nordhaus, William D. "The Costs of Slowing Climate Change: A Survey." *The Energy Journal* 12 (1) (1991): 37–65.

Victor, David G. "Limits of Market-Based Strategies for Slowing Global Warming: The Case of Tradable Permits." *Policy Science* 24 (2) (May 1991): 199–222.

Smith, Douglas A. and Keith Vodden. "Global Environmental Policy: The Case of Ozone Depletion." *Canadian Public Policy* (16 December 1989): 413–423.

23

INTERNATIONAL
ENVIRONMENTAL
AGREEMENTS

In the last chapter we discussed several global environmental issues. In one of these—stratospheric ozone depletion—nations of the world have signed an international agreement to reduce emissions of the main chemicals causing the problem. Today many nations are urging a treaty on global warming. As countries continue to grow, more and more environmental problems will spill beyond national borders—not just these global cases, but also a rising number of environmental externalities inflicted by people in one country on those of another. So while environmental policies continue to evolve within individual countries, there will be a growing need to develop multicountry attacks on environmental problems.[1] In the final chapter of this book, therefore, we will take a look at some of the economic issues involved in the creation of international environmental agreements.

International environmental policy has a distinctly different character from national policies. The most salient difference is that on the international level there are no effective enforcement institutions. Within any country authoritative regulatory authorities can be called upon to enforce whatever laws are passed, though this does not imply by any means that all environmental laws will be adequately enforced. But on the international level enforcement authorities do not exist. Thus, environmental policy at this level consists essentially of international agreements among sovereign states, where each country pledges to follow certain specified courses of action as regards emissions reductions or other steps for environmental protection. Enforce-

[1] The international scope of many environmental problems was first highlighted by the 1972 United Nations Conference on the Human Environment (the "Stockholm Conference" or first "earth summit"), which led to the United Nations Environment Program (UNEP) and the 1992 global environmental conference in Brazil.

ment then has to be carried out either through voluntary means like moral suasion, or else through retaliation by whatever pressure a country or group of countries may be able to exert on recalcitrant countries.

In this chapter we review some of the main features of international environmental agreements, focussing especially on the incentive situations facing countries that are considering an agreement. We begin with a brief descriptive section that will show the great variety of international environmental agreements that have been concluded to date. We then discuss cases that involve just two countries, followed by the case of multiple-country agreements. We will end with a discussion of an issue that will become increasingly important as national economies continue to grow: the environmental quality implications of international trade.

GENERAL ISSUES

The history of international agreements on natural resource matters goes back many centuries, to the time when countries sought to agree on navigation rules to cover ocean passages. In the twentieth century, international treaties have proliferated as a result of the rapidly expanding list of environmental problems involving multiple countries. Table 23-1 shows a partial list of current multilateral agreements pertaining to natural and environmental resources. Numerous treaties have been concluded on marine pollution, beginning with oil-pollution agreements and later extending to more general pollution-control measures. Although much attention has been given recently to the issue of protecting the resources of biological diversity, the first international treaties on flora and fauna were actually made decades ago. By now there are many such treaties, including the important 1973 convention on international trade in endangered species.[2]

The agreements listed in Table 23-1 are all multilateral treaties, involving anywhere between 3 and 161 countries. Note the difference in almost all cases between the year of adoption and the year of entry into force. An agreement once "adopted" does not come into force, that is, does not become binding, until it has been signed by the appropriate political authorities of a certain proportion of the participating countries. Thus, some agreements, including the comprehensive convention on the "Law of the Sea," have never come into force. A standard international agreement will contain provisions specifying the actions to be undertaken by each signatory country, as well as numerous institutional and logistical matters, such as what kind of governing agency is to be established, how its work is to be funded, what information is to be shared, and so on.

Many of the multilateral treaties are actually regional in scope. This includes, for example, the water and air pollution-control treaties among the countries of Europe.

---

[2] A "treaty" is an agreement in which all the details have presumably been worked out and expressed in the document to which each signing country agrees. A "convention" is an agreement in which parties agree on a general framework that is expected to be supplemented in the future by one or more "protocols" that work out the details.

TABLE 23-1   SELECTED INTERNATIONAL ENVIRONMENTAL AGREEMENTS

Name of agreement	Date of adoption	Date of entry into force	Number of signatories
Marine Pollution			
International Convention for the Prevention of Pollution of the Sea by Oil (as amended 11/4/62 and 11/21/69)	1954	1958	71*
Agreement for Cooperation in Dealing with Pollution of the North Sea by Oil	1969	1969	8
International Convention on Civil Liability for Oil Pollution Damage (as amended)	1969	1975	63
International Convention Relating to Intervention on the High Seas in Cases of Oil Pollution Casualties	1969	1975	54
Convention on the Prevention of Marine Pollution by Dumping of Wastes and Other Matter ("London Dumping")	1972	1975	
International Convention for the Prevention of Pollution from Ships, 1973	1973	—	19
Convention on the Prevention of Marine Pollution from Land-Based Sources	1974	1978	13
Convention for the Protection of the Mediterranean Sea Against Pollution	1976	1978	18
International Rivers			
Protocol Concerning the Constitution of an International Commission for the Protection of the Moselle Against Pollution	1961	1962	3
Agreement Concerning the International Commission for the Protection of the Rhine Against Pollution	1963	1965	6
Convention on the Protection of the Rhine Against Chemical Pollution	1976	1979	6
Convention Creating the Niger Basin Authority and Protocol Relating to the Development Fund of the Niger Basin	1980	1982	8
Flora and Fauna			
European Treaty on the Conservation of Birds Useful to Agriculture	1902	1902	11
Convention Relative to the Preservation of Fauna and Flora in Their Natural State	1933	1936	54
Convention of Nature Protection and Wildlife Preservation in the Western Hemisphere	1940	1942	19

*Four countries have renounced the Convention.

TABLE 23-1   SELECTED INTERNATIONAL ENVIRONMENTAL AGREEMENT (*Continued*)

Name of agreement	Date of adoption	Date of entry into force	Number of signatories
Flora and Fauna			
International Convention for the Regulation of Whaling (as amended)	1946	1948	43[1]
International Convention for the Protection of Birds	1950	1963	10
International Plant Protection Convention	1951	1952	92
International Convention for the High Seas Fisheries of the North Pacific Ocean (as amended)	1952	1953	3
Convention on Fishing and Conservation of the Living Resources of the High Seas	1958	1966	35
International Convention for the Protection of New Varieties of Plants (as amended)	1961	1968	17
Convention on the African Migratory Locust	1962	1963	16
African Convention on the Conservation of Nature and Natural Resources	1968	1969	29
European Convention for the Protection of Animals During International Transport	1968	1971	20
Benelux Convention on the Hunting and Protection of Birds (as amended)	1970	1972	3
Convention on Wetlands of International Importance Especially as Waterfowl Habitat	1971	1975	50
Convention for Conservation of Antarctic Seals	1972	1978	12
Convention on International Trade in Endangered Species of Wild Fauna and Flora	1973	1975	96
Agreement on Conservation of Polar Bears	1973	1976	5
Convention on Conservation of Nature in the South Pacific	1976	—	3
Nuclear			
Convention on Third Party Liability in the Field of Nuclear Energy (as amended)	1960	1968	14
Vienna Convention of Civil Liability for Nuclear Damage	1963	1977	10
Treaty Banning Nuclear Weapon Tests in the Atmosphere, in Outer Space and Under Water	1963	1963	117
Treaty on the Prohibition of the Emplacement of Nuclear Weapons and Other Weapons of Mass Destruction on the Sea-Bed and the Ocean Floor and in the Subsoil Thereof	1971	1972	79
Convention on Early Notification of a Nuclear Accident	1986	1986	31

[1]Three withdrawals

TABLE 23-1   SELECTED INTERNATIONAL ENVIRONMENTAL AGREEMENT (*Continued*)

Name of agreement	Date of adoption	Date of entry into force	Number of signatories
Air Pollution			
Convention on Long-Range Transboundary Air Pollution	1979	1983	30
Protocol to the 1979 Convention on Long-Range Transboundary Air Pollution on Long-Term Financing of the Co-operative Programme for Monitoring and Evaluation of theLong-Range Transmission of Air Pollutants in Europe (EMEP)	1984	1988	27
Protocol to the 1979 Convention on Long-Range Transboundary Air Pollution on the Reduction of Sulphur Emissions or Their Transboundary Fluxes by at Least 30 Percent	1985	1987	18
Protocol to the 1979 Convention on Long-Range Transboundary Air Pollution Concerning the Control of Emissions of Nitrogen Oxides or Their Transboundary Fluxes	1988	—	24
Vienna Convention for the Protection of the Ozone Layer	1985	1988	36
Montreal Protocol on Substances that Deplete the Ozone Layer	1987	1989	43
Miscellaneous			
The Antarctic Treaty	1959	1961	32
European Convention on the Protection of the Archaeological Heritage	1969	1970	17
Convention on the Prohibition of the Development, Production and Stockpiling or Bacteriological (Biological) and Toxin Weapons, and on Their Destruction	1972	1975	101
Convention Concerning the Protection of the World Cultural and Natural Heritage	1972	1975	98
Treaty for Amazonian Co-operation	1978	1980	8
Convention on the Conservation of Antarctic Marine Living Resources	1980	1982	21
Convention Concerning Occupational Safety and Health and the Working Environment	1981	1983	9
United Nations Convention on the Law of the Sea	1982	—	161
Convention on the Regulation of Antarctic Mineral Resource Activities	1988	—	6
Basel Convention on the Control of the Transboundary Movements of Hazardous Wastes and Their Disposal	1989	—	116

Source: Scott Barrett, "Economic Analysis of International Environmental Agreements: Lessons for a Global-Warming Treaty," in Organization for Economic Cooperation and Development, *Responding to Climate Change, Selected Economic Issues* (Paris: OECD, 1991).

The United Nations has sponsored a number of regional agreements involving countries bordering particular seas (Mediterranean, Red Sea, southeastern Pacific, western African coastal waters, Caribbean, etc.). Besides the multilateral treaties there are
hundreds of bilateral treaties, addressing the environmental problems of just two
countries. Canada and the U.S. have concluded a number of bilateral agreements,
including those dealing with acid rain and with the management of the Great Lakes.
NAFTA, a trilateral trade agreement with Canada, the U.S., and Mexico has a number of specific provisions regarding environmental policies in the three countries. The
passage of NAFTA in the U.S. Congress was dependent in part on reaching side
agreements about enforcement of environmental regulations in each country.

THE ECONOMICS OF INTERNATIONAL AGREEMENTS

When international agreements are being negotiated, the focus is usually on political issues. This is natural, since what is going on are complex negotiations among
sovereign states. But underlying the political interactions—national sovereignty,
political assertiveness, creative diplomacy, etc.—lie many bedrock economic factors
that affect the perceived benefits and costs accruing to the different participants and
the incentives they have for entering into environmental agreements. In the next few
sections we will discuss some of these issues.

Bilateral Agreements

Let us first consider the case of just two countries—call them Country A and Country B. B is downwind from A, so SO_2 emissions from A contribute to acid rain both
at home and in B. In B, SO_2 emissions contribute to acid rain only in that country;
because of prevailing wind patterns, there is no reciprocal acid rain externality
inflicted by B upon A. This situation is pictured in Figure 23-1. It shows the marginal
abatement costs in A (MAC) and the marginal damage functions associated with the
emissions of that country. Marginal damages arising in A itself are shown as MD_A,
while MD_T are aggregate marginal damages for both A and B. The marginal damages
in B from A's emissions, in other words, are $MD_T - MD_A$. If A were managing its
emissions without regard to the externalities produced in B, it would regard point e_1
as the efficient level of emissions.

But for emissions in A to be internationally efficient, it is necessary to take into
account the effects on B. The "globally efficient" level of emissions is e_2. The added
attainment costs in A to achieve this further reduction in emissions is an amount equal
to the area $(d + f)$. But this is more than offset by a reduction in damages totalling
$(c + d + f)$, of which f represents damage reduction in A, while $(d + c)$ is damage
reduction in B.

We saw in Chapter 10 that negotiations between polluters and those damaged can
result in efficient emission levels, given that property rights are clearly defined and
that transactions costs are minimal. On the international level, direct negotiations
between private parties involved are essentially ruled out, because under international

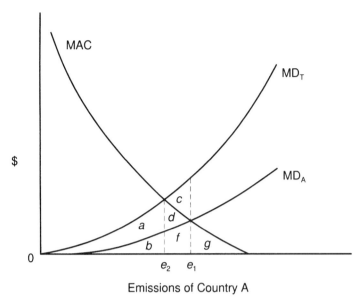

Emissions of Country A

FIGURE 23-1   Bilateral Transboundary Pollution and the Economics of Reaching an Agreement.

law private citizens of one country do not have the right to sue private citizens in another country. Instead, negotiations must be carried out among political authorities of the two countries. This is where diplomacy comes in because, in the example above, the reduction in A's emissions from e_1 to e_2 involves negative net benefits *in that country*—added costs of $(d + f)$ and reduced damages of only f. So, in effect, authorities would be asking people in Country A to make a sacrifice to benefit people in another country. This kind of thing happens all the time within individual countries. But across countries the institutions of policy are weaker, depending essentially on diplomatic skills and whatever international sanctioning can be carried out through moral, economic, or political means.

According to the precedents in international law, cases like this are supposed to be covered by a polluter pays principle (PPP). The Trail Smelter case of 1935 is an important source of that precedent. Trail Smelter was a metal refinery in British Columbia whose SO_2 discharges damaged farm crops across the border in the U.S. The tribunal finding in favour of the farmers stated that under the principles of international law "no State has the right to use or permit the use of its territory in such a manner as to cause injury by fumes in or to the territory of another."[3] This declaration was embodied in the Declaration of the 1972 United Nations Conference on the Human Environment (the first "earth summit"), which covered all types of trans-

---

[3] Quoted in William A. Nitze, "Acid-Rain: A United States Perspective," in Daniel Barstow Magraw (ed.), *International Law and Pollution* (Philadelphia: University of Pennsylvania Press, 1991), 346.

boundary pollution. Most international agreements seek to incorporate the polluter pays principle.

But since international agreements are voluntary, we may suppose that individual countries will never sign any agreement that makes them worse off. In other words, each prospective signatory must regard the agreement as leaving them at least as well off as they would be without it. In our example, this means that we may have to shift partially to a "victim pays principle" (VPP). The net loss to A in going from e_1 to e_2 would have to be compensated by Country B. A has added abatement costs of ($d + f$) in going from e_1 to e_2, but it also experiences added benefits (reduced damages) of f, so its extra costs are equal to d. Since B's damage reduction totals ($c + d$), it could compensate A for these costs and still be ahead by an amount equal to c.

There are many issues that come up in international bargaining about environmental externalities of this type. Bargaining depends critically on the perceptions by each country of its own marginal damages and marginal abatement costs, as well as on how convincing it can be in expressing these views to other countries. In the case of Figure 23-1, for example, A has an interest in convincing B that the added abatement costs of going from e_1 to e_2 are very high, while its own domestic benefits from this move are quite low. B, on the other hand, has an interest in convincing A that it would experience real reductions in damages from a reduction in emissions, but not so high that it could afford very large compensation payments. Countries engaged in negotiations of this type will usually be involved at the same time in negotiations on other problems, as well as with negotiations with other countries. Thus, they will be concerned with the net outcome of all these negotiations, and this could dictate a position on this one issue quite different from what one would expect solely on the basis of the merits of this particular case. John Krutilla's study of the agreement between Canada and the U.S. over use of the Columbia River, for example, indicates that the distribution of costs in the treaty was primarily related to the desire of the U.S. to stimulate economic development in Canada.[4]

Multilateral Agreements

Let us now consider a situation where a number of countries all contribute to an environmental problem that affects all of them. Examples are acid rain pollution stemming from SO_2 emissions, pollution of a regional sea by riparian countries, stratospheric ozone depletion through emissions of CFCs, and the greenhouse effect stemming from CO_2 emissions. In these cases the damages suffered by each country are related to the level of total emissions, present and probably past, of all the countries. From an economic standpoint there are both efficiency and equity issues in these types of international agreements. There is the basic efficiency question of balancing overall benefits and costs. For most international agreements, especially the truly global ones, there are enormous difficulties in the way of estimating total global ben-

---

[4] John V. Krutilla, *The Columbia River Treaty: A Study of the Economics of International River Basin Development* (Baltimore, Md.: Johns Hopkins Press, 1968).

efits with any accuracy. The impacts are too massive, and there are extraordinarily difficult problems of trying to compare benefits across countries that are in very different economic circumstances. So on the benefit side we usually settle for an enumeration of the physical impacts of various environmental changes and some idea of how these impacts might be distributed among countries. This means that most of the emphasis is likely to be placed on abatement costs and their distribution.

There are two major issues related to cost: (1) what methods to adopt in various countries to meet the performance required by the agreements, and (2) how to share the overall costs among the participating countries. Of course, the questions are related because cost-effective measures undertaken by signatory countries can substantially reduce the costs of the overall program that must be shared. The importance of cost distribution arises because these global emission control agreements supply global public goods. The benefits accruing to any particular country from, say, a 20 percent cut in CO_2 will be the same no matter where, and by whom, the CO_2 is reduced.[5] Thus, each country has some incentive to get other countries to bear as much of the total global abatement costs as they can. The costs accruing to each country can be affected in two ways:

• Through the choice of the rule by which overall emission reductions will be distributed among countries, and

• By payments going from some countries to others to help offset control costs among the recipients. These are transfer payments, sometimes called, in the jargon of economics, "side payments."

We will analyze this situation with a simple application of "game theory." Game theory is not specifically about games, like baseball or poker, although it can be applied to them. It is about making decisions when the outcomes of the decisions depend in part on the actions undertaken by intelligent opponents. More generally, game theory is about making choices in situations where the payoffs from the choices depend on the choices made by other people. A farmer trying to decide when to harvest a crop is not facing a game situation. Nature is not on the other side trying to make decisions that will improve its position relative to the farmer; nature just is. But a farmer trying to decide when to sell her or his crop is involved in a game because many other farmers are trying to make the same decision, and the outcome of one of them, in terms of, say, the price received, will depend in part on the decisions made by the other farmers as well as her or his own decision. The reason it is applicable here is that when one country acts, its impact on the regional or global environment will depend on how other nations also act.

Suppose several countries are contributing to acid deposition in a particular region. Acid deposition comes largely from emissions of sulfur dioxides, which in the atmosphere are oxidized into sulfates, and which then are removed, sometimes

---

[5] This does not mean that the benefits will be the same for all countries (we know this is not true because of the way the global meteorological system works); only that the effects on any particular country are invariant to the source of the reduction.

well downwind, by rainfall in the form of acid rain, or by dry deposition on plants or the land surface. To keep things extremely simple so we can get to the essence of the problem, suppose there are just two countries emitting SO_2 in this region.[6] Each is damaged by the resulting acid deposition, and each would benefit from a cutback in SO_2 emissions. But the benefits obtained by each country depend not only on their own SO_2 reductions but also on those made by the other country.

Let us assume, for purposes of simplicity, that each country has two available strategies: (1) to emit at current levels and (2) to reduce emissions by some substantial amount. The top panel of Figure 23-2 shows the (gross) benefits that would accrue to each country from these two options. Since each country has two alternatives, there are four possible outcomes, so the results can be depicted in a 2×2 matrix as shown. On the axes of the matrix appear the two strategies available to each country, while in the interior of the matrix appear the benefits accruing to each, expressed, say, in millions of dollars per year. The first number in each cell represents the benefit accruing to Country A, while the second is the benefit to B, of the combination of strategies chosen. Thus, for example, if A chooses to emit at the uncontrolled level, while B chooses to reduce emissions, benefits to A and B will be, respectively, 2 and 1. If they were both emitted in an uncontrolled fashion (i.e., high emissions for both), "benefits" would be –1 to each country.

If we consider only these gross benefits, the best strategy for each is to reduce its emissions; the payoff would be 4 to A and 8 to B, and neither could improve its position by doing otherwise. But this reckons without control costs. Suppose that to reduce emissions it costs A \$3 million per year and B \$6 million per year. We must now deduct these control costs from the gross benefit figures. Doing so gives the results shown in panel (b) of Figure 23-2. We have now a set of net payoffs that have a very interesting pattern, characteristic of many international environmental problems. They show a situation where individual countries, each choosing strategies that are best for themselves, can bring about a situation that is worse for everybody.

Suppose Country A is trying to decide whether to devote the resources to reducing emissions. It must do this without knowing with certainty what Country B will choose to do. But in this case it will not make any difference. Suppose B were to choose to control its emissions. In this case A would get the highest net benefits by choosing not to control its emissions (net benefits of \$2 million rather than \$1 million). On the other hand, suppose B did not control its emissions. Here again, A is better off choosing the no-control option (losses of –\$1 million rather than –\$2 million). Thus, regardless of B's choice, A's best choice is not to control emissions. You can examine B's choices in the same way, with the same result: Regardless of A's choice, B will be better off by choosing to continue with high emissions. Thus, neither country will reduce emissions, which will result in both of them realizing lower net benefits than if they were both to reduce their emissions.

---

[6] It may seem odd to analyze a case of multinational agreements using a two-country example, but since the discussion has to do with the incentives a country faces in trying to decide whether or not to conclude an agreement, this is in fact not a drawback. One good way to think of it is for A to represent a single country and for B to represent all other countries as a whole.

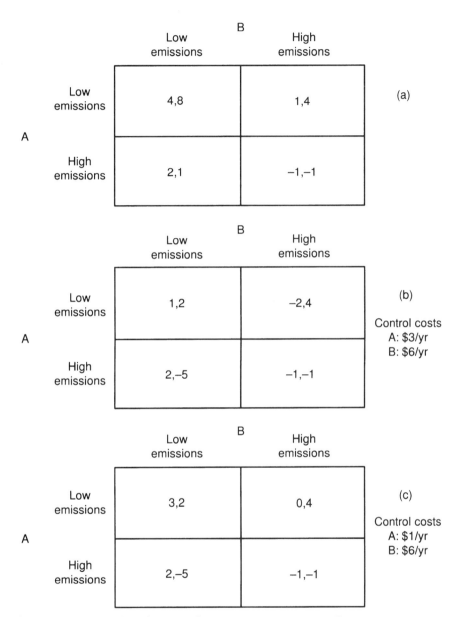

FIGURE 23-2   Payoffs Received by Two Countries Considering an International Environmental Agreement.

   This is a paradoxical result. Both countries, acting individually, choose strategies leading to a situation having total benefits of –$2 million, whereas if both had controlled emissions, total global net benefits would have been $3 million. The reason for the paradox is the following: Although both countries would be better off if they both reduced emissions, compared to both emitting at the high level, each would be

still better off if they could be in a situation where the other country controls emissions while they do not. You can see this most clearly by starting from a position of
low emissions for each country. Under these circumstances B would be getting benefits of $2 million per year. But if A is reducing its emissions, B could do even bet-
ter by *not* reducing emissions. Although total emissions would go up, savings in control costs would allow it to reap net benefits of $4 million per year. What it is doing
is essentially taking a free ride on A's emission-control efforts. But, of course, with
each country trying to free ride on the other's control efforts, neither country will end
up reducing emissions, so we end up in the lower right of the figure, with everybody
worse off.

The main job of any environmental agreement is to get countries to agree to reduce
their emissions and to resist the temptation to try to garner even larger net benefits
by free riding on the control efforts of others.[7]

Of course things can change over time, making it easier or harder to bring about
agreement. Suppose that technological change in Country A results in a lowering of
control costs there from $3 per year to only $1 per year. Now the payoff matrix
changes to the one shown in panel (c) of Figure 23-2. And here we have a substantial change in incentives. Because of the reduced control costs, it now is rational for
Country A to reduce emissions, regardless of what B does. If B controls emissions,
A's net benefits would go from $2 to $3, while if B does not control emissions, A's
net benefits go from –$1 to $0. This is a situation where it is efficient for one country to engage in emission reduction on its own even if other countries do not follow
suit. Note that in panel (c) it is still individually rational for B not to control emissions, implying that the two countries, in the absence of any agreement, would end
up in the northeastern corner of the payoff matrix, with A at the lower emission level
and B with uncontrolled emissions.

The two countries may try to develop an agreement whereby B also commits to
reducing emissions. This would certainly be of benefit to A, but it nevertheless
remains that B will be individually better off by refusing to reduce emissions. This,
of course, is where international diplomacy comes in—convincing Country B that it
should reduce emissions even though it may see its interests lying elsewhere. One
approach that may be useful is moral suasion; Country B could be branded an oppor-
tunist in taking advantage of others' efforts to clean up the global commons. Other
possibilities suggest themselves. With A already committed to reducing emissions,
B's net benefits are $2 higher when it persists with high emissions rather than reduces
emissions. Country A may have a way of otherwise retaliating on B, perhaps by placing restrictions on exports from B to A, in order to drive up the cost to B of continuing at the high emission level. If the total benefits of this option can be brought
below $2 through trade sanctions, Country B would find it in its interest to reduce
its emissions.

---

[7] Back in Chapter 4 we introduced the notions of public goods and open-access resources, and indicated how the temptation to free ride would lead to market failure in these kinds of situations. Here we
are simply applying the same ideas to international environmental agreements.

Another approach might be for Country A to offer financial incentives, or some other side payments, to B to get it to reduce emissions. If B reduces emissions, A would gain by $3 per year, while B would have a reduction in net benefits of $2. A payment of, say, $2.5 from A to B to reduce emissions would make both countries better off. Exhibit 23-1 shows a news clip that is relevant to this situation. It is not a negotiation between two countries but between two groups of countries, the third-world nations (the "group of 77") and the developed countries. The negotiations at the 1992 Rio conference focussed on aid that the developed nations (the "north") would give to third-world countries (the "south") to finance environmentally sound economic development. The comments of one negotiator are comments that Country B might make to Country A in the example: The north (Country A) cannot achieve the full set of environmental goals by itself, and if it wishes to have greater participation by the south (Country B) it must treat the south "more generously."

Another possibility might be technology transfer. Suppose that by transferring pollution-control technology from A to B, the emission-abatement costs of the latter could be reduced from $6 to $2. Recalculating the payoffs in the game matrix shows that if A reduces its emissions, it is now efficient for B also to reduce emissions. Of course, in actuality, international environmental agreements normally involve more than two countries. The reason for limiting the analysis to just two was to be able to show in simple fashion the nature of the underlying incentive situation. When multiple countries are involved, the same incentives are involved but it becomes more complicated to analyze them clearly. In this case, each country is in a game with all the other countries, and what is usually involved is trying to get a big enough subset of them to agree on a common course of action.[8] Thus, each country must assess its net gains from joining an agreement along with some number of other countries and compare them with their net gains if they stay out of the agreement. With each country facing different benefits and abatement costs, the overall results may be hard to discern. It's also true that when multiple countries are involved, the patterns of negotiating technology transfers, bribes, sanctions, etc., that will motivate individual countries to join an agreement become much more complicated than with just two countries.

International Agreements in Practice

The game theory matrices and payoff structures discussed in the last section are useful to depict the incentives facing individual countries that might be considering an international environmental agreement. But it's impossible to use them to predict the results of such agreements because international negotiations on environmental treaties are only one dimension of the full set of international interactions among countries. How an individual country behaves in bargaining over, for example, a

---

[8] When negotiations are taking place among a large number of countries, it often happens that subsets will form agreements among themselves to act jointly with respect to the others. For example, in working up to the Montreal Protocol, a group of four countries formed the "Toronto Group" (that's where they had their first meeting) which developed a unified position and encouraged the rest to act.

EXHIBIT 23-1

NEGOTIATORS IN RIO AGREE TO INCREASE AID TO THIRD WORLD—VITAL TO GLOBAL CLEANUP

Non-Industrialized Lands Drop Demand for Vow to Double the Funds by Year 2000.

By Paul Lewis
Special to The New York Times

RIO DE JANEIRO, June 13—Less than 24 hours before the end of the Earth Summit, North and South finally compromised today on principles that encourage richer countries to increase aid to the third world, clearing the way for approval of the global cleanup plan that is the centerpiece of the conference.

After 13 days of negotiations, third-world countries finally abandoned an attempt to obtain a specific commitment from the industrialized world to nearly double aid to poorer countries by the year 2000. The money would pay for the plan to guarantee that the third world's development is environmentally sound.

Instead, the third-world countries accepted that the United States is unwilling to be bound by a longstanding United Nations goal of raising aid levels to 0.7 percent of its economic output and that Britain, Japan, Germany and several other big aid donors refused to commit themselves to achieve that target by any particular date.

Third-World Leverage

But in this unusual North-South exchange, in which the third world almost for the first time enjoys genuine leverage, the industrialized Northern countries have committed themselves to reach that target "as soon as possible" and pledged themselves to see the environmental goals set forth in the plan, known as Agenda 21, are fully met. That implies they must find more money for the third world.

In addition, the North agreed to highlight in a statement adopted today that a new international body created to monitor compliance with environmental targets accepted at the talks will also enforce the promises they have made to give the third world more assistance.

On Sunday, during the summit talks' concluding session, Pakistan, the current chairman of the Group of 77, as the third-world countries are known at United Nations meetings, will express those nations' disappointment at the financial offers the North has made so far.

And Pakistan will implicitly remind the North that it cannot significantly improve the environment without Southern cooperation. Their statement will warn that without the additional assistance it has been promised, the developing South will be unable to develop in an environmentally sound manner.

"We are saying we cannot generate the new resources needed to start up Agenda 21 without new help, so if the North wants us to meet those goals they must treat us more generously," Pakistan's United Nations representative, Jamsheed A. Marker, commented after the meeting.

Third-world countries say they think that they are owed that assistance because the developed northern nations are responsible for most of the damage industrialization has inflicted on ecological systems so far. Third-world countries say the North should be willing to pay for the limits it has put on the development of poorer countries.

The compromise on financing Agenda 21 was finally hammered out by a small group of developed and developing countries today and awaits approval by a wider plenary meeting of all the 178 nations attending.

According to the compromise declaration, industrial countries that have not met the 0.7 percent aid target "agree to augment their aid programs in order to reach that target as soon as possible and to endure a prompt and effective implementation of Agenda 21."

treaty reducing CO_2 emissions depends not only on the merits of that particular problem but on the whole gamut of international relationships in which it is involved. If it is involved simultaneously in negotiations on other matters, it may be more concerned with the total outcome and be willing to compromise in some areas in return for concessions in others. In addition, when countries are involved in many negotiations they may be concerned particularly with shoring up their reputations as hard bargainers, which may lead them to behave in certain cases in ways that look to be inconsistent with their self-interest. The outcomes of treaty negotiations depend on context and the strategic possibilities that the times have made available, which is another reason we use the simple models of the previous section for depicting the underlying economic logic of international agreements, and not for actually predicting events.

Cost-Effectiveness in Multinational Agreements

The discussion above was couched in terms of an international agreement to secure certain emission reductions from each of the participating countries. This is the way most international agreements are shaped; there is a strong bias toward treating each country in the same way by applying the same reduction goals to each. Only in the recent CFC-reduction treaty (the Montreal Protocol) has there been a differentiation among countries, and here it was a simple distinction between developed countries as a group and developing ones as another group. Within each broad group the CFC-reducing targets are the same for each country.

We have discussed the efficiency aspects of this approach many times throughout the preceding chapters. The main problem is that it does not take advantage of differences in marginal abatement costs among sources, meaning countries in this case. To accomplish this would require larger cutbacks from nations with relatively low marginal abatement costs and less reduction from those with higher costs. But these nonuniform reductions appear to run counter to the principle of treating everybody alike. Suppose each of two countries would benefit the same amount from cutbacks in emissions, but have different marginal abatement cost functions. These are pictured in Figure 23-3. The marginal abatement costs of Country A rise much more steeply than those of Country B. Current emissions are 100 from A and 80 from Country B. An agreement requiring a uniform 50 percent reduction would put A at 40 and B at 50. But the costs of achieving this would be much higher for A ($a + b + c$) than for B ($d + e$). Country A might very well fail to agree with uniform reductions when there would be such a large discrepancy in total abatement costs. If it were desired nonetheless to specify a treaty in terms of specific cutbacks from each, they could perhaps be set so that the total abatement costs of each country were the same (assuming each country had reliable information about the other country's abatement costs), but this would violate the uniform emission reduction principle; nor would it be cost-effective.

When abatement costs differ among countries, in other words, it will be difficult to achieve cost-effectiveness if there is strong allegiance to the same type of equipro-

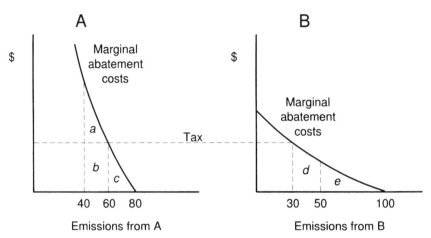

FIGURE 23-3   Cost-Efffectiveness in International Agreements.

portionate rule. One possible way of doing this would be to institute a global transferable discharge permit system (TDP), whereby the number of permits given out in the initial distribution met some equiproportionate reduction principle, with trading then moving the distribution of permits toward one that more nearly satisfied the equimarginal rule. Whether this is even remotely feasible in today's international political climate is highly doubtful.

INTERNATIONAL TRADE AND THE ENVIRONMENT

Another connection between international affairs and the environment is through patterns of international trade. Profound changes are occurring in the world economy and in the economic interactions among the 200 or so countries that make it up. It once appeared simple: Industrialized countries produced manufactured goods, some of which they traded among themselves, and some of which they exported to developing countries in return for primary products. But in the latter part of the twentieth century things are changing dramatically through the rise of the multinational company, owing allegiance to customers and suppliers, not to particular countries; the development of a truly global, integrated, financial market; the appearance of briskly expanding industrial countries from among the previously less developed group; the development of huge new regional trading blocs, southeast Asia, North America, the European Community; and the massive change in the old socialist bloc and its reintegration into the world economy.

The full range of environmental implications of these changes will be hard to sort out. We can summarize the general issues as follows:

• The reciprocal interaction of trade flows and environmental protection. How will increased trade affect environmental damages in trading countries, and how will national efforts to protect the environment impact on international trade? These issues can be looked at from the standpoint of just two trading countries, or from that of more comprehensive trading networks.

• The question of whether, and under what conditions, an individual country may legitimately put restrictions on its trade, by restricting either imports or exports, in the name of preserving environmental quality.

• The circumstances under which the world community as a whole can effectively improve the world environment by placing restrictions on international trade.

Free Trade vs. Environmental Trade Restrictions

Over the last four decades or so the countries of the world have made special efforts to foster free and unhindered trade. This has been done in the name of improved economic welfare. Free trade allows countries to prosper by giving them expanded markets for things on which they have a comparative advantage in production, and gives them greater opportunities to procure goods for which they have a comparative disadvantage. The prosperity of many countries, both developed and developing, depends critically on international trade. The problem is whether the emphasis on moving toward free trade may make it more difficult for countries to protect the environmental resources that they value.

The main international institution governing trade is the General Agreement on Tariffs and Trade (GATT), which came into being in the late 1940s. Its purpose is to set out a list of rules and procedures to be followed by nations in their international trade relationships. It is especially aimed at reducing the barriers to trade, to get nations to refrain from putting tariffs and quotas on imports or subsidies on exports, and in general to move toward conditions of free trade among the world's nations, almost all of whom are GATT signatories. One section of the GATT agreement also outlaws what are called nontariff barriers such as excessive inspection requirements, excessive product specifications, and the like. But there is a very broad list of conditions that are exceptions to GATT rules; for example, governments are allowed to set restrictions in order to achieve the "protection of human, animal or plant life or health," and the "conserving of natural resources."

Consider the analysis of Figure 23-4. It shows the behaviour of producers and consumers of a product in a particular country that also relies upon imports for a large part of its supply. The demand curve (D) is domestic demand for the product, while S is the domestic supply curve; that is, the supply curve of domestic producers. Without imports, price and quantity would settle at the intersection of these two curves. But let us introduce an import supply curve, labelled I. This supply curve is actually horizontal because we assume that a relatively large amount of this item is produced in the world, so this importing country could import larger or smaller quantities without affecting the world price. With the addition of imports, this country now ends up with a total consumption at q_0. Domestic production, meanwhile, is q_1. The difference, $(q_0 - q_1)$, is imported. The domestic price is also equal to the world price.

The GATT rules allow governments to set import restrictions on products that have direct health implications, as long as it is done in a nondiscriminatory way. Suppose the good in question is automobiles, the use of which causes air pollution. Setting

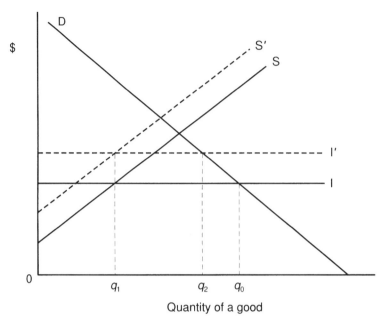

FIGURE 23-4   Effects of Environmental Regulations on Domestic Production and Imports.

tight emission standards increases the production costs for automobiles and therefore their prices. The importing country may require imported cars to meet strict emission standards, which would have the effect of lifting the import supply curve to I'. This is nondiscriminatory as long as domestic producers are held to the same standards, in effect shifting the domestic supply curve up to S'. The result of this is first to lower the total quantity of cars purchased by people in this country, from q_0 to q_2. Second, assuming that the emission standards increase the costs of domestic supply as much as they do imports, the pollution control applied to both domestically produced cars and imports will leave domestic production unchanged but reduce imports, from $(q_0 - q_1)$ to $(q_2 - q_1)$.

In this case the purpose of the strict emission standards was to protect human health. When it is not a matter of human health but, say, one of environmental aesthetics, the case may be less clear. In recent years Denmark placed a ban on the use of nonrefillable drink containers. This was presumably done in the name of reducing litter. It also proceeded to ban the importation of nonrefillable containers from neighbouring European countries. These countries objected, saying that the ban was really just a way of protecting Danish drink producers from competition. But in this case the European court ruled in favour of Denmark.

Things become decidedly less clear when it is not the consumption of a good that causes pollution but its production. Suppose that a country produces a product, in the process also causing a certain amount of air pollution. Suppose further that it adopts an air-pollution program to curb emissions from this industry. Suppose even further that the item is produced in other countries and imported, but that the countries from which it is imported do not undertake any type of pollution-control efforts. The producers of the importing country are now at somewhat of a cost disadvantage because they have to operate under environmental constraints and their competitors don't. Can this country legally (i.e., within the GATT rules) put a tariff on the importation of this item to equalize the cost burden? One might argue that this would tend to protect people in other producing countries who are exposed to air pollution from the firms making this item, but GATT rules allow countries to take action only to protect their own citizens, not those in other countries. And a tariff against the good may have no impact on lessening air pollution in other countries; the only way that could be done would be through explicit pollution-control programs in those countries, and there is certainly no way for the first country to enforce such programs.

The interrelationship of environmental issues and trade problems has recently raised the possibility that environmental standards will be co-opted by those whose interest is primarily to protect themselves against international competition. It is a familiar sight to see representatives of some industry that feels threatened by producers in other countries appealing to political authorities for a tariff or some other barrier against imports. Environmental factors may now give them added ammunition. If they can plausibly argue that the foreign competitors are causing damage to environmental resources, they may be better able to justify the trade barrier. The key is whether the environmental impacts of foreign producers are legitimately a concern of the importing country. In a recent case, the U.S. barred imports of tuna from Mexico that had been caught using methods that cause excessive mortality among dolphins. The question that needs to be sorted out is whether Americans really do have a substantial willingness to pay for protecting dolphins, wherever they may be, or whether this was just being used as an excuse by U.S. tuna companies to shield themselves from foreign competition.[9]

Trade Restrictions to Advance International Environmental Goals

In some cases international environmental agreements involve trade agreements.

Montreal Protocol   As part of the international effort to reduce ozone-depleting chemicals, the Montreal Protocol prohibits exports of controlled substances (basically CFCs) from any signatory nation to any state not a party to the protocol. Furthermore, signatory countries may not import any controlled substance from any nonsignatory state. The purpose of these trade regulations is to ensure that production of CFCs and other ozone-depleting chemicals does not simply migrate to nonsigning countries.

---

[9] In the tuna/dolphin case, the U.S. was held to be in violation of the General Agreement on Tariffs and Trade (GATT) because the U.S. was not allowed to extend its jurisdiction over resources which reside outside its boundaries. Countries are allowed to protect their domestic natural and environmental resources for conservation purposed under article XX of GATT.

London Guidelines on Chemicals   As we have discussed many times throughout this book, one major obstacle to controlling environmental pollutants is lack of information—information on pollutant emissions, damages, control costs, etc. On the international level the problem is even more severe than it is domestically because of the different ways countries have approached pollution-control problems and the vastly different information requirements and availabilities among them. In 1989, 74 countries agreed to adopt the "London Guidelines for the Exchange of Information on Chemicals in International Trade," under the auspices of the United Nations Environment Program (UNEP). The guidelines require that any country banning or severely restricting a particular chemical notify all other countries of its actions, so that the latter can assess the risks and take whatever action they deem appropriate. The guidelines also encourage "technology transfer," stating that states with more advanced chemical testing and management technology should share their experience with countries in need of approved systems.

Basel Convention on Transboundary Movements of Hazardous Wastes   This 1989 agreement is aimed at the issue of international trade in hazardous wastes. It does not prohibit this trade but does put requirements on it, especially information requirements. It puts an obligation on countries to prohibit any export of hazardous wastes unless appropriate authorities in the receiving country have consented in writing to the import and unless it has assurances that the waste will be properly disposed of. It also has provisions on notification, cooperation on liability matters, transmission of essential information, and so on.

Convention on International Trade in Endangered Species of Wild Fauna and Flora (CITES)   There is currently a large international trade in flora and fauna, dead and alive: roughly 500,000 live parrots, 10 million reptile skins, 10 million cactus plants, 350 million ornamental fish, 50 million furs, etc., each year.[10] CITES came into force in 1975. Under it, each country is supposed to establish its own permit system to control the movement of wildlife exports and imports. It is also supposed to designate a management body to handle the permit system and a scientific body to determine whether trade is likely to be detrimental to the survival of the species. Species are separated into three classes: I—species threatened with extinction, in which commercial trade is banned and noncommercial trade regulated; II—species that may become threatened if trade is not held to levels consistent with biological processes, for which commercial trade is allowed with conditions; and III—species that are not currently threatened but for which international cooperation is appropriate, for which trade requires permits.

The endangered species trade is considered by many to be a qualified success, though much more remains to be done, especially in improving national permit

---

[10] Laura H. Kosloff and Mark C. Trexler, "The Convention on International Trade in Endangered Species: Enforcement Theory and Practice in the United States," *Boston University International Law Journal* 5 (Fall 1987): 327–361.

processes. There are some simple lessons to be derived from considering this type of trade restriction, which we will pursue by looking at an international supply-and-demand model of an endangered species. The same conclusions can apply to other cases; for example, export restrictions on logs to protect rain forests. Consider the market model of Figure 23-5. This shows the world, or aggregate, supply and export-demand conditions for a species of wildlife. The supply function is based on the costs of hunting, transporting, processing, recordkeeping, etc., necessary to bring the wildlife to the point of export. It is an aggregate supply function made up of the supply function of the various countries in which that species grows. The demand function shows the quantities that the export market will take at alternative prices. The intersection of the two functions shows the market price and quantity of this type of wildlife that will be traded in a year's time.

Two types of trade constraints could be used to reduce the quantity of this species moving in international trade: export controls and import controls. Each will reduce the quantity traded, but they will have very different impacts on price. Export controls work by essentially making exporting more costly, which has the effect in Figure 23-5 of shifting the supply function upward from supply curve S_0 to supply curve S_1. The result of this is a reduction in quantity traded, in this case to q_1. The amount that quantity falls depends on the extent to which the supply curve shifts up and also on the slope of the demand function; the steeper this slope the less will quantity contract. But this approach to trade reduction also leads to an increase in price, from the original price p_0 to p_1. This price increase could have several impacts, depending essentially on property rights. Imagine a case where the endangered species is subject to private ownership, either by individuals or by small, well-defined groups. Perhaps the habitat of the species is under private ownership, for example. The higher price for the species now becomes a signal for its owners to be more concerned about its safety and welfare because, in this circumstance, efforts at conservation will have a direct market payoff.

The added price will have the opposite effect, however, when property rights in the endangered species are ill-defined or completely absent, which is the usual case. Most of the habitats for the world's endangered species are open access, in the sense that either everybody has the right to enter and harvest the animal or plant, or that, as in public parks, authorities are unable to keep people from taking the species "illegally." We saw, in Chapter 4, the problem to which open-access resources are prone: Since other users cannot be kept out, nobody has an incentive to conserve the resource. It's either use it or lose it to some other harvester. The increased price for the endangered species in this case will work against conservation. It will encourage higher rates of extraction, higher rates of poaching on open-access habitats, and thus higher pressure on the endangered species.

Controlling imports, on the other hand, drives the price downward. Import controls have the effect of reducing the demand for the imported species. In Figure 23-5 this leads to a backward shift in demand, from D_0 to D_1. This has been drawn so as to give the same quantity reduction as before. But in this case the price drops to p_2. The effect of this price decrease is to decrease the incentives discussed in the previ-

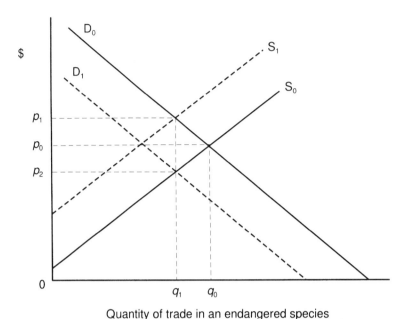

FIGURE 23-5   Effects of Trade Policy on the International Market in an Endangered Species.

ous paragraphs. In particular, where endangered species are subject to open-access exploitation, the lower price would lead to reduced pressure to harvest and less rapid population decline. Something of this sort has happened recently as a result of an international ban on ivory imports. The ban has led to a substantial drop in the world price of ivory, which has reduced the pressure of poachers on the elephant in many parts of Africa.

SUMMARY

With environmental issues becoming more international in scope and significance, there will be increasing interest among countries to address these issues with international agreements. International agreements are much more problematic than domestic policies because enforcement is much weaker on the international level. International externalities are essentially of two types. In the first, one country's pollution causes damage in another country. Here the problem of who pays (polluter or victim) when agreements are negotiated is of primary relevance. In the second, each country's emissions affect all countries, including itself. Here the basic problem is how to get individual countries to forego attempts to free ride on the control efforts of others. The strength of the incentive to free ride depends on a country's perceived benefits and costs of an international agreement, together with whatever "side payments," money subsidies, technology transfers, etc., are part of the agreement.

In recent years serious issues have arisen over the relationship of environmental damage and international trade. Some people see free international trade as being environmentally destructive and are in favour of placing restrictions on trade in the name of environmental values. In these cases there is a problem in sorting out legitimate and justified concern for elements of the environment, especially in another country, from purely commercial interests that are seeking shelter from international competition.

QUESTIONS FOR FURTHER DISCUSSION

1 The game theory presentation in Figure 23-2 shows each country with only two options: high emissions or low emissions. How different does the game become when what is at issue is not whether to cut back or not, but how much to cut back?

2 In panel (b) of Figure 23-2 each country has an incentive to free ride on the other's emission reductions. Suppose we institute a deposit-refund system to enforce emission reductions. At the beginning of the year they both pay a deposit, which they get back at the end of the year if their emissions are still low. If there can be only one deposit amount for both countries, what should it be?

3 We talked about "side payments" in the form of technology transfers, given to developing countries to lower the costs to them of joining international environmental agreements. What other types of side payments might be effective in this regard?

4 Suppose Country A imports a product from Country B, and that Country B lacks environmental laws governing the production of the item. Under what conditions might Country A be justified in putting a tariff on the imported item?

5 If all countries adopted the same emission standards in similar industries, would this tend to equalize production costs and put each country on the same footing with respect to environmental matters?

6 "International environmental agreements are very much shaped by the fact that enforcement on the international level is difficult, if not impossible." Discuss.

7 In a recent case, the U.S. attempted to put restrictions on the importation of tuna from Mexico because Mexican fishers used methods that destroyed relatively large numbers of dolphin when catching the tuna. These fishing methods are illegal for U.S. tuna fishers. Is this trade restriction efficient? Is it equitable?

SELECTED READINGS

Anderson, K. and R. Blackhurst (eds.). *The Greening of World Trade Issues.* Ann Arbor: The University of Michigan Press, 1992.

Andresen, Steinar, and Willy Ostreng. *International Resource Management, The Role of Science and Politics.* London: Belhaven Press, 1989.

Barrett, Scott. "Economic Analysis of International Environmental Agreements: Lessons for a Global Warming Treaty," in Organization for Economic Cooperation and Development. *Responding to Climate Change: Selected Economic Issues.* Paris: OECD, 1991, Chapter 3.

_____. "The Problem of Global Environmental Protection." *Oxford Review of Economic Policy* 6 (1) (Spring 1990): 68–79.

Charnovitz, Steve. "Trade Negotiations and the Environment," in *International Environment Reporter*. Washington, D.C.: Bureau of National Affairs, March 11, 1992, 144–148.

d'Arge, Ralph C., and Allen V. Kneese: "State Liability for International Environmental Degradation: An Economic Perspective." *Natural Resource Journal* 20 (3) (July 1980): 427–450.

Flinterman, Cees, Barbara Kwiatkowska, and Johan G. Lammers. *Transboundary Air Pollution, International Legal Aspects of the Co-operation of States.* Dordrecht, Holland: Martinus Nijhoff Publishers, 1986.

Low, Patrick (ed.). *International Trade and the Environment.* Discussion Paper No. 159. Washington, D.C.: World Bank, 1992.

Mäler, Karl-Göran. "International Environmental Problems," in Dieter Helm (ed.). *Economic Policy Toward the Environment.* Oxford, England: Blackwells, 1991, 156–201.

Organization for Economic Cooperation and Development: *Economics of Transfrontier Pollution*, Paris: OECD, 1976.

Rubin, Seymour J., and Thomas R. Graham (eds.). *Environment and Trade, The Relation of International Trade and Environmental Policy.* Totowa, N.J.: Allanheld, Osmun Publishers, 1982.

INDEX OF NAMES

INDEX OF SUBJECTS

— — — — — — — — — cut here — — — — — — — — —

STUDENT REPLY CARD

In order to improve future editions, we are seeking your comments on
Environmental Economics, First Canadian Edition, by Barry C. Field and
Nancy D. Olewiler
Please answer the following questions and return this form via Business Reply
Mail. Your opinions matter. Thank you in advance for sharing them with us!

Name of your college or university: _____

Major program of study: _____

Course title: _____

Were you required to buy this book? _____ yes _____ no

Did you buy this book new or used? _____ new _____ used ($_____)

Do you plan to keep or sell this book? _____ keep _____ sell

Is the order of topic coverage consistent with what was taught in your course?

— — — — — — — — — — fold here — — — — — — — — — —

Are there chapters or sections of this text that were not assigned for your course?
Please specify:

Were there topics covered in your course that are not included in the text?
Please specify:

What did you like most about this text?

What did you like least?

If you would like to say more, we would appreciate hearing from you. Please write
to us at the address shown on the reverse of this page.

- - - - - - - - - - - - - - - *cut here* - - - - - - - - - - - - - - - -

- - - - - - - - - - - - *fold here* - - - - - - - - - -

Postage will be paid by

MAIL ⇒ POSTE

Canada Post Corporation / Société canadienne des postes

Postage paid
If mailed in Canada

Port payé
si posté au Canada

Business Reply

Réponse d'affaires

0183560299　　01

0183560299-L1N9B6-BR01

Attn.: Sponsoring Editor
College Division

MCGRAW-HILL RYERSON LIMITED
300 WATER ST
WHITBY ON　L1N 9Z9

tape shut

cut here